BY ALISON WEIR

NONFICTION
ENGLAND'S MEDIEVAL QUEENS
Queens of the Conquest
Queens of the Crusades

The Lost Tudor Princess: The Life of Lady Margaret Douglas
Elizabeth of York: A Tudor Queen and Her World
Mary Boleyn: The Mistress of Kings
The Lady in the Tower: The Fall of Anne Boleyn
The Mistress of the Monarchy: The Life of Katherine Swynford, Duchess of Lancaster
Queen Isabella: Treachery, Adultery, and Murder in Medieval England
Mary, Queen of Scots, and the Murder of Lord Darnley
Henry VIII: The King and His Court
Eleanor of Aquitaine: A Life
The Life of Elizabeth I
The Children of Henry VIII
The Wars of the Roses
The Princes in the Tower
The Six Wives of Henry VIII

FICTION
SIX TUDOR QUEENS
Katharine Parr: The Sixth Wife
Katheryn Howard, The Scandalous Queen
Anna of Kleve, The Princess in the Portrait
Jane Seymour, The Haunted Queen
Anne Boleyn, A King's Obsession
Katherine of Aragon, The True Queen

The Marriage Game
A Dangerous Inheritance
Captive Queen
The Lady Elizabeth
Innocent Traitor

Queens of the Crusades

Queens
of the
Crusades

England's Medieval Queens

BOOK TWO

1154–1291

ALISON WEIR

Ballantine Books | New York

Published in the United States by Ballantine Books,
an imprint of Random House,
a division of Penguin Random House LLC, New York.

BALLANTINE and the HOUSE colophon are registered trademarks
of Penguin Random House LLC.

Originally published in hardcover in Great Britain by Jonathan Cape,
a division of Penguin Random House London, in 2020.

LIBRARY OF CONGRESS CATALOGING-IN-PUBLICATION DATA

Names: Weir, Alison, author. | Weir, Alison, Queens of the conquest.
Title: Queens of the Crusades: England's medieval queens, 1154–1291 /
Alison Weir.
Other titles: England's medieval queens
Description: New York: Ballantine Books, 2021. | Series: England's medieval
queens; Book two | Book one titled Queens of the conquest. | Includes
bibliographical references and index.
Identifiers: LCCN 2020034731 (print) | LCCN 2020034732 (ebook) | ISBN
9781101966693 (hardcover) | ISBN 9781101966709 (ebook)
Subjects: LCSH: Eleanor, of Aquitaine, Queen, consort of Henry II, King of
England, 1122?-1204. | Berengaria, Queen, consort of Richard I, King of
England, approximately 1163–approximately 1230. | Isabella, Queen, consort
of John, King of England, -1246. | Eleanor, of Provence, Queen, consort of
Henry III, King of England, 1223 or 1224–1291. | Eleanor, Queen, consort of
Edward I, King of England, -1290. | Queens—Great Britain—Biography. |
Monarchy—Great Britain—History—To 1500. | Monarchy—France—
History—To 1500. | Great Britain—History—Plantagenets, 1154–1399—
Biography. | Plantagenet, House of.
Classification: LCC DA28.2 .W453 2020 (print) | LCC DA28.2 (ebook) |
DDC 942.03092/52—dc23
LC record available at https://lccn.loc.gov/2020034731
LC ebook record available at https://lccn.loc.gov/2020034732

Printed in the United States of America on acid-free paper

randomhousebooks.com

2 4 6 8 9 7 5 3 1

First US Edition

Book design by Virginia Norey

This book is dedicated to
my incomparable goddaughter, Eleanor Borman,
who is named for the incomparable Eleanor of Aquitaine.

Contents

Contents

England and Wales in the
twelfth century

SCOTLAND

North Sea

Irish Sea

E N G L A N D

WALES

Berwick

Carlisle
Durham

York

Tickhill
Chesterfield • Lincoln
Clipstone
Newark
Nottingham • Grantham
Harby
Rockingham
Oakham • Stamford
Geddington
Kenilworth Northampton • Hardingstone
Worcester Stony Stratford
Evesham
Woodstock • Woburn
Gloucester Oxford • Dunstable
Godstow Ashridge • St Albans
Quenington Berkhamsted Langley • Waltham
Wallingford LONDON • Havering
Westminster
Bristol Marlborough Runnymede • Bermondsey
Devizes Rochester
Wells Ludgershall • Guildford Leeds Canterbury
Old Sarum • Amesbury
Glastonbury Salisbury • Clarendon
Sherborne • Tarrant New Southampton Portsmouth
Forest Chichester • Lewes
Beaulieu
Exeter Corfe Carisbrooke Castle
Isle of Wight

Rhuddlan
Conwy
Caernarfon • Chester

Carmarthen

Walsingham
Bishop's Lynn Norwich

Ely
St Edmundsbury
Cambridge

Tutbury

Sandwich

Dover

N

0   50   100 miles

0   50   100   150 km

France in the twelfth century

N

Wissant
Boulogne
Abbeville
Cherbourg
Barfleur
Bonneville-
sur-Touques
Les Baux
Rouen
Norman Vexin
Bec-Hellouin
Gisors
Bayeux · Caen
Château Gaillard
Coutances
NORMANDY
Rheims
PARIS
Falaise
Montreuil
Avranches · Argentan
Nonancourt
Domfront
Bures
BRITTANY
Chartres
Rennes
MAINE
Sens
CHAMPAGNE
Le Mans
Fréteval
Vendôm
Beaugency
Auxerre
Beaufort-
en-Vallée
Blois
Vézelay
Angers
ANJOU
Tours
Nantes
Saumur
Chinon
Fontevraud
Mirabeau
POITOU
Poitiers
Niort
Lusignan
Mâcon
La Rochelle
Île d'Oléron
AQUITAINE
Saintes
Limoges
Châlus
Cognac
Montferrand
Talmont
Angoulême
AUVERGNE
Bay of
Biscay
Périgueux
Bordeaux
Rocamadour
Uzeste
Bazas
Cahors
Agen
Najac
Avignon
Tarascon
Grandmont
Arles
Dax
GASCONY
Aigues-Mortes
PROVENCE
Bayonne
Toulouse
Marseilles
Asasp-Arros
HOLY ROMAN EMPIRE
SPAIN
Mediterranean
Sea

0   50   100   150 miles
0 50 100 150   200 km

Illustrations

✠

The window in Poitiers Cathedral donated by Eleanor of Aquitaine in commemoration of her wedding to Henry II in 1152. (Alamy)

The Hall of Lost Footsteps in Eleanor of Aquitaine's palace at Poitiers. (WikiCommons)

The tomb effigy of Henry II in Fontevraud Abbey. (Getty)

The tomb effigy of Henry, the Young King, in Rouen Cathedral. (Alamy)

Archbishop Thomas Becket, window in Canterbury Cathedral. (WikiCommons)

Fair Rosamund by John William Waterhouse, 1916, National Museum of Wales. (Alamy)

Chinon Castle, one of the great strongholds of the Plantagenets. (Shutterstock)

The mound on which once stood the city, cathedral and castle of Old Sarum. (Getty)

The tomb effigy of Eleanor of Aquitaine in Fontevraud Abbey. (Shutterstock)

The tomb effigy of Richard I in Fontevraud Abbey. (Alamy)

The kitchen Eleanor of Aquitaine built at Fontevraud. (© BrokenSphere / WikiCommons)

A mural in the church of Sainte-Radegonde at Chinon, which may depict the Plantagenets, with Eleanor of Aquitaine, crowned, in the center. (WikiCommons)

The tomb of "the beautiful Navarroise," Berengaria of Navarre, in the abbey of l'Epau, Le Mans. (WikiCommons)

The Pedlar by Charles Allston Collins, 1850, Manchester Art Gallery. (WikiCommons)

The tomb effigy of William the Marshal, "the best knight who ever lived," in the Temple Church, London. (Alamy)

The tomb effigy of King John in Worcester Cathedral. "He was a very bad man." (Alamy)

The tomb effigy of Isabella of Angoulême in Fontevraud Abbey. (Getty)

The seal of Hugh de Lusignan X, Isabella of Angoulême's second husband. (WikiCommons)

The tomb effigy of Henry III in Westminster Abbey. (Alamy)

The abbey of l'Epau, founded by Queen Berengaria in 1229. (WikiCommons)

The marriage of Henry III and Alienor of Provence. Historia Anglorum, Chronica Majora of Matthew Paris, Royal MS 14 C VII f. 124v, British Library. (Getty)

A thirteenth-century Corbel head of Alienor of Provence, in Westminster Abbey. (Used by kind permission of the Dean and Chapter of Westminster)

A thirteenth-century head of Alienor of Provence in Bridlington Priory. (Author's own)

Peter of Savoy, above the entrance to the Savoy Hotel, which stands on the site of his palace. (Alamy)

Statues of Richard, Earl of Cornwall, King of Almayne, and his wife, Sanchia, in Meissen Cathedral. (Alamy)

Edward I and his wife, Eleanor of Castile. Chronica Roffense [Flores Historiarum made at Roch], British Library. (Alamy)

The abbey of Las Huelgas at Burgos, Castile. (Alamy)

Eleanor of Castile, window in St. Mary Magdalene's Church, Himbleton, Worcestershire. (Alamy)

Edward I, painting above the sedilia in Westminster Abbey. (Alamy)

Leeds Castle, a dower palace of the queens of England. (Alamy)

An illustration in the Alphonso Psalter, Additional MS 24686, British Library. (Author's own)

The tomb effigy of Eleanor of Castile in Westminster Abbey. (Getty)

Eleanor's statue on the Eleanor Cross at Hardingstone. (Alamy)

The Eleanor Cross at Geddington. (Alamy)

The Eleanor Cross at Hardingstone. (Alamy)

The Eleanor Cross at Waltham. (Alamy)

Introduction

✠

THIS BOOK TELLS THE STORIES OF THE LIVES OF ENGLAND'S queen consorts during the early Plantagenet period, 1154–1291. It covers five queens. Eleanor of Aquitaine needs no introduction, for she was one of the towering female figures of the Middle Ages, and the subject of a biography I published in 1999. Much scholarship has been undertaken since then, and I have revised certain aspects of her story, focusing chiefly on her career as queen of England. Her daughters-in-law, Berengaria of Navarre and Isabella of Angoulême, deserve to be better known, especially for their careers after the deaths of their husbands, Richard I and King John. The thirteenth-century queens Alienor of Provence and Eleanor of Castile dominated the English establishment for nearly seven decades. Both were controversial, and I hope I have presented a fair view of them.

In regard to the title, *Queens of the Crusades*, I am aware that only three of these queens actually went on crusade, but they lived in an age dominated by the crusading movement, which touched all their lives.

This is the story of the history of England through the perspective of its queens, but much of the action takes place on a wider stage, for England was just a part of the Angevin Empire founded by Henry II and Eleanor of Aquitaine. The book does not comprise a series of biographies, but tells the stories of the queens in a continuous, chronological narrative.

It is also important to understand how power was devolved in a feudal age. In the twelfth century, Europe was a hierarchical society, a patchwork of realms and principalities. There was no concept of nationhood or patriotism: all subjects owed fealty to their immediate overlord and to the King, who was the ultimate secular authority and answered only to God. Fealty was enshrined in the ceremony of homage, in which a kneeling vassal would place his hands between those of his king or overlord and swear to render him service and obedience. In return, an overlord was bound to offer protection and aid. A breach of fealty was held to be highly dishonorable, but feudal oaths were readily broken. English kings, in particular, resented paying homage to French kings for the continental lands they held of them.

Feudal vassals owed military service to their lords, supplying knights and men on demand for a certain number of days each year. This was how feudal levies were raised. There were no standing armies, although the levies might be supplemented by paid mercenaries.

Feudal custom and the developing code of chivalry demanded certain courtesies, even between enemies. Captive kings and lords were often on good terms with their captors; they met socially, exchanged gifts and even feasted together. This laid the foundation for future amicable relations once the captives had been ransomed.

As this book is intended for a general readership, I have kept references to a minimum and restricted them to original sources. Limitations on the word count do not permit me to list secondary sources in the references, so I wish warmly to acknowledge my indebtedness to the modern historians of the period and the recent biographers of these queens, especially (in alphabetical order) Darren Baker, Rachel Bard, Helen Castor, Sara Cockerill, Nancy Goldstone, Lisa Hilton, Margaret Howell, Elizabeth Norton, John Carmi Parsons, Ffiona Swabey, Anne Trindade, Ralph Turner, Nicholas Vincent and Kelsey Wilson-Lee. Their research, wisdom and insights have helped to inform this book.

It is difficult to calculate the modern equivalents of monetary values before 1270. Figures in parentheses after monetary amounts are rough, rounded estimates of their worth today. A *livre tournois* equated on average to about a quarter of an English pound and ⅘ of a *livre* of Paris.

I am truly grateful for the tremendous support and creative input of my editor, Anthony Whittome. Warm thanks are due also to the publishing teams at Penguin Random House in New York and London. Special thanks go to my agent, Julian Alexander, and my husband, Rankin, for their unfailing kindness and understanding, especially when I was panicking about my deadline!

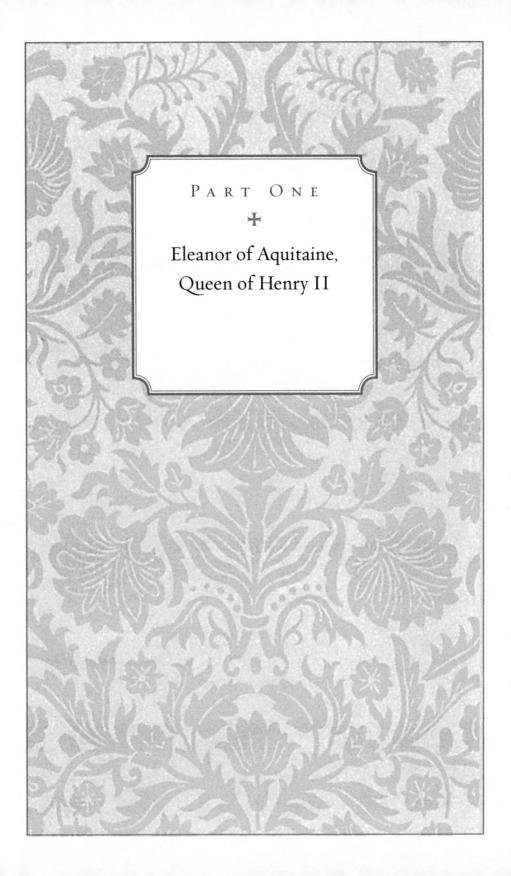

PART ONE

✠

Eleanor of Aquitaine,
Queen of Henry II

I

"An Exceedingly Shrewd and Clever Woman"

✠

ON SUNDAY, DECEMBER 19, 1154, HENRY II, THE FIRST PLAN-
tagenet King of England, was crowned in Westminster Abbey,
along with his Queen, Eleanor of Aquitaine, amid great splendor and
rejoicing. Monarchs had about them an aura of spiritual sovereignty,
conferred on them at their anointing with holy oil. The coronation of a
queen sanctified her and set her apart from lesser women. It enhanced
the dignity of her husband the King—especially so in this case because,
through his marriage to Eleanor, Henry II had become master of a great
continental domain.

The royal dynasty established on that day was to rule England for 331
years.

There are many perceptions of Eleanor of Aquitaine. Debate rages over
the extent of her political activity and her influence on culture. As a
stateswoman, her influence was felt for over six decades—she was both
notorious and respected. It is possible to regard her as a romantic heroine in the widest sense, even though the wilder myths about her have now
been dispelled. She inspires the imagination today, just as she did in her
own time. But the sources form an incomplete record, so there will always be room to ask the question: who was the real Eleanor?

She was undoubtedly a forceful character. She was heiress to one of the richest domains in medieval Europe. In the twelfth century, Europe was divided into feudal domains, and what is now France then comprised the kingdom of France itself and several vassal domains, or demesnes. The county of Poitou and the duchies of Aquitaine and Gascony covered a vast region in the southwest, about one-third of modern France. By comparison, the kingdom of France was small, centered mainly upon Paris and the surrounding area. As descendants of the Frankish Emperor Charlemagne, whose empire had encompassed much of western Europe, French kings were overlords of all the fiefdoms, including Aquitaine, in the region roughly corresponding to modern France. This often led to power struggles between the kings and their vassals.

Aquitaine—named "land of waters" after its great rivers—had been established as a duchy by the middle of the tenth century, and it was now very prosperous. In 1058, the southern wine-producing duchy of Gascony, with its bustling port of Bordeaux, had been absorbed into Aquitaine. Poitou lay to the north, where its northern border marched with those of Brittany, Anjou and Touraine, and its chief city was Poitiers. Eleanor's was a rich inheritance.

"Opulent Aquitaine [was] sweet as nectar thanks to its vineyards dotted about with forests, overflowing with fruit of every kind, and endowed with a superabundance of pasture."[1] Aquitanians spoke the *langue d'oc* (Provençal), or Occitan, a Romance language derived from the dialect spoken by Roman invaders centuries before. North of the Loire, and in Poitou, they spoke Poitevin, or the *langue d'oeil*.

The Aquitanian lordships and castles were controlled by hostile, feuding vassals who resented interference from their ducal overlords and were notorious for their propensity to rebel and create disorder. They enjoyed a luxurious standard of living compared with their unwashed counterparts in northern France, and were regarded by northerners as soft and idle, yet they could be fierce and violent when provoked. Successive dukes had consistently failed to subdue their vassals or establish cohesion within their own domains, and their authority still did not reach far beyond the vicinities of Poitiers and Bordeaux. They did not have the wealth or resources to extend their power into the feudal wilderness and forests beyond these areas.

Nevertheless, the duchy was wealthy, thanks to its lucrative trade in wine and salt, and its religious life flourished. Successive dukes built and endowed many fine churches and monasteries, notably the Romanesque cathedrals in Poitiers and Angoulême. The twelfth century witnessed a great monastic revival, with the founding of several new orders: the Cistercians; the Augustinian canons, whose double houses admitted both men and women; the Carthusians, who lived under an austere rule requiring them to embrace a life of solitude and silence; and the Order of Fontevraud, especially dear to Eleanor of Aquitaine and her family. The nuns' necrology records that Eleanor "was from her earliest life a patron of the church of Fontevraud."

Eleanor "sprang from a noble race"[2] of dukes who had been blessed with pious, feisty wives. Her grandfather, William IX, married Philippa, heiress to Toulouse, which bordered Gascony in the south. It was an important fiefdom, for through it wound the major trade routes that linked Aquitaine with the Mediterranean. But Philippa's uncle, Raymond, Count of Saint-Gilles, had usurped her inheritance and she saw in William IX a ruler with the power and resources to recover it.

This was an age of great religious fervor that witnessed thousands undertaking long, sometimes dangerous, pilgrimages to holy shrines, notably St. James's at Compostela, St. Peter's in Rome and Christ's burial place, the Church of the Holy Sepulchre at Jerusalem. Since AD 640, Palestine had been under Arab rule. In 1095, Pope Urban II had exhorted Christians to take part in the First Crusade, in the hope of liberating Jerusalem. William IX, who did not don the cross that was symbolic of a vow to go on crusade, seized Toulouse in the absence of the usurping Raymond, who had led a crusading army to the East, having renounced his claim to Toulouse in favor of his son, Bertrand. William incurred the anger of the Church by violating the Truce of God, which required all Christians to refrain from invading the lands of a crusader during his absence.

In 1099, news of the taking of Jerusalem prompted William belatedly to take the cross. In 1101, at Heraclea, his army was cut to pieces by the Muslims (or Saracens, as Christians called them) and he had to return home. Back in Poitiers, inspired by the culture of the East and the erotic works of Ovid, he began writing sensual poems celebrating female beauty and the pleasures of love, for which he is called the first of the troubadours.

Feudal Europe was essentially a military society. Warfare was the business of kings and noblemen, increasingly conducted by the evolving rules of chivalry, a knightly code enshrining ideals of courage, loyalty, honesty, courtesy and charity. In this martial, male-dominated world, women had little place. The Church taught that the descendants of Eve were the weaker vessel and the source of all lechery. They were seen as feeble, irrational creatures who needed to be governed by men, and were expected to be chaste, humble, modest, sober, silent, charitable and well behaved.

Kings and noblemen married for political advantage, and women rarely had any say in how they or their wealth were to be disposed in marriage. Heiresses and rich widows were sold off to the highest bidder, for political or territorial advantage. The betrothal of infants was not uncommon, although the Church laid down the minimum ages for cohabitation as twelve for girls and fourteen for boys. Personal choice and love were not paramount considerations.

The early *chansons de geste* (songs of deeds) had celebrated military ideals of courage in battle, loyalty, honor and endurance, but the troubadours of the south popularized the concept of courtly love, revolutionary in its day. William IX's court at Poitiers quickly became renowned for this new literary trend, and by 1100 it had become the foremost cultural center in France. With this impetus, romantic literature flourished in the twelfth and thirteenth centuries, particularly in Aquitaine and Provence.

Drawing on Plato and Arab writers and influenced by the growing popularity of the cult of the Virgin Mary, the troubadours composed lyric poetry and songs. They deified women, according them superiority over men, and laid down codes of courtesy, chivalry and gentlemanly conduct. Thus were born ideals of honor and courtship that, in the centuries to come, would permeate European literature and culture to such a degree that their influence is still with us today.

The rules of courtly love gave a mistress mastery over her humble, worshipping suitor, who had to prove his devotion before his love was even acknowledged. The mistress (the word was the female equivalent of "master") was an idealized figure, often high-born and frequently married, who was supposedly unattainable. In this aristocratic game—for such it was—the woman always enjoyed supremacy and the man was her servant. Her wishes and decrees were absolute, and any suitor who did not comply was deemed unworthy of the honor of her love. The ultimate favor was rarely to be granted, yet ideals of chastity permitted courtly lovers to sleep naked together so long as they did not have sex. The tenets of courtly love had little to do with contemporary notions of courtship and marriage, but, in the relaxed cultural atmosphere of the south, they flourished as an absorbing intellectual pastime of the upper classes; in the more sober north, courtly love was regarded as an excuse for adultery. There, a noblewoman who betrayed her spouse could be banished or imprisoned; for the man who cuckolded his overlord, the penalty was castration. Aquitanians, however, took a relaxed view of such matters.

The age of the troubadours came to a brutal end in the thirteenth century with the vicious persecution of the Cathar heresy in what became known as the Albigensian Crusade. This movement was led by Pope Innocent III and the kings of France, who were determined to eradicate the heretics, and it culminated in 1244 with the holocaust at Montségur, where 220 Cathars who had held out to the end were burned to death. The crusade left southern France so devastated that its native culture was effectively suppressed and, in many respects, irrevocably lost.

William IX's contemporaries were outraged by his amoral behavior, and his wife turned increasingly to religion for solace. She had heard of Robert d'Arbrissel, an inspired teacher who wandered the roads of northwestern France with his growing band of followers. His reputation was spreading, yet there were those who resented his assertion that women were in some respects the superior sex and made better administrators and managers of property than men. To some, this sounded like heresy. But many women were attracted by his enlightened and sympathetic views and his compassion for the outcasts of society, such as prostitutes and lepers.

Philippa persuaded William IX to grant Robert land in northern Poitou, where he could establish a religious community dedicated to the Virgin Mary. In 1101, by a fountain at Fontevraud, near the River Vienne, Robert founded a double monastery for priests, canons regular, lay brethren and 300 segregated nuns, all under the rule of an abbess—a revolutionary innovation for its time. In other respects, the abbey followed the rule of St. Benedict. The men did the manual work and the women spent their lives in prayer. In 1104, building commenced on a new stone church, consecrated in 1119.

Robert stipulated that the abbess of Fontevraud must be nobly born and a widow, in order to confer prestige on the order and ensure that it was administered by someone familiar with running a large household. The office was to be filled by several royal and noble ladies. By the time of Robert's death in 1117, Fontevraud had become extremely popular with aristocratic women wishing to retire or temporarily retreat from the world. They were accommodated in their own apartments and could enjoy worldly comforts while living in seclusion. Most of the nuns came from noble families and had lay sisters as maids, but no one, however humble, was turned away. Thanks to the endowments of wealthy bene-factors, Robert was able to establish daughter houses and cells elsewhere. The order quickly came to enjoy a towering reputation for piety and con-templative prayer, and thus fulfilled its founder's aims of enhancing the prestige of women in general.

In 1115, William IX conceived a violent passion for Amauberge de l'Isle Bouchard, aptly nicknamed "Dangerosa." She was the wife of his vassal Aimery de Rochefoucauld, Viscount of Châtellerault, and had five chil-dren: Hugh, Raoul (who would marry the heiress of Faye and become one of Eleanor of Aquitaine's chief advisers), Aenor, Amable and Aois. Wil-liam abducted Dangerosa and bore her off to his palace at Poitiers, where he installed her in the newly built Maubergeonne Tower, which lent her another nickname, "La Maubergeonne."

When the Duchess returned from a visit to Toulouse, she was shocked to find her husband living in open adultery and begged the Papal legate to remonstrate with him. But it was useless; even excommunication had no effect. Philippa retired in grief to Fontevraud, where she died in 1118. Eleanor of Aquitaine was damned even before she was born by her grand-father's "detestable adultery," which was said to taint her blood with li-centiousness.[3]

In 1121, William IX's son and heir married Dangerosa's daughter Aenor. The future Duke William X was tall, broad and robust, with a quarrelsome nature. Little is known about Aenor. Her first child, the daughter who became known to history as Eleanor of Aquitaine, was probably born in 1123–4. A genealogy of the dukes of Aquitaine, made in Limoges in the late thirteenth century, stated: "In 1136 [sic], on the fifth ides of April, William [X], Count of Poitou and Duke of Aquitaine, died at St. James in Galicia, leaving his only [*sic*] daughter, named Eleanor, aged thirteen years." This is a late source,[4] and William IX actually died in 1137, but the genealogy is based on the contemporary chronicle of the knowledgeable Geoffrey de Vigeois. Eleanor's place of birth is not recorded.

Her name was a pun on the Latin *alia*-Aenor, "the other Aenor," to differentiate her from her mother. It would later be said that it was "an amalgam of 'pure' [*ali*] and 'gold' [*or*],"[5] but that was written with the benefit of hindsight.

Aenor bore William X two other children: Aelith, who later called herself Petronilla, and William Aigret.

William X's brief reign was marred by strife with his vassals and quarrels with the Church, but the court at Poitiers remained an important cultural center. The new Duke patronized the troubadours Marcabru and Cercamon and perhaps the Welshman Bleddri, who may have told the courtiers some very early tales of King Arthur. William also patronized Fontevraud and other religious houses, displaying an innate piety that probably influenced the upbringing of his children, for it is clear that Eleanor's faith was the guiding principle of her life.

Her name first appears in contemporary records in July 1129, when she, her parents and her brother witnessed a charter granting privileges to the abbey of Montierneuf. Each inscribed a cross by their name, while the infant William Aigret made a print with a finger dipped in ink. In March 1130, the Duchess and her children took up residence at William X's hunting lodge at Talmont on the coast of Poitou. Aenor and William Aigret died there soon afterward, leaving Eleanor as her father's heiress presumptive. At the age of six, she was old enough to realize that she was a very important little girl—the most important in Christendom.

Eleanor enjoyed a privileged girlhood, "brought up in delicacy and reared with abundance of all delights, living in the bosom of wealth," according to the chronicler Richard le Poitevin. She grew up speaking Poitevin, and also knew French and some Latin. Later, she would master the Norman French that was spoken at her second husband's court, but she would never learn English.

Like all feudal courts, William X's was itinerant, and Eleanor traveled with him. His chief seat—and, later, hers—was the ancient palace at Poitiers, dating from the ninth century. Sited on the banks of the River Clain, it was surrounded by beautiful gardens and a moat. In the tenth century, William V had erected a great hall, which survives today, much altered, and is known colloquially as "the Hall of Lost Footsteps." The ducal apartments were in the imposing Maubergeonne Tower. Eleanor also spent time at the Ombrière Palace at Bordeaux, a tall keep known as "the Crossbowman," which was set in courtyards with tiled fountains and beautiful semi-tropical gardens. Bordeaux was surrounded by a Roman wall, beyond which stood another residence used by the ducal family, the Tutelle Palace.

The education of women was generally considered unimportant. Unusually, Eleanor received a formal education in history, arithmetic, Latin and literacy skills. The troubadour Bertran de Born, who addressed chansons to her, commented, "They were not unknown to her, for she can read." A contemporary poet, Benoît de Sainte-Maure, called her "one in whom all knowledge abounds." It is possible that Eleanor received some education at Fontevraud, as two of her children later did.

That she shared her grandfather's enjoyment of literature and poetry can be inferred from her later patronage of troubadours such as Bernard de Ventadour, Arnaut Guilhem de Marsan and Rigaud de Barbezieux. Yet there is little evidence to connect her to any others, which suggests that the extent of her patronage has been overstated.

Eleanor had wit and a welcoming manner. Like her female ancestors, she was strong-willed, independent-minded, intelligent, sophisticated and impetuous. She was blessed with great energy, vitality and robust health. She enjoyed hunting and hawking, riding astride as women usually did before the late fourteenth century, and kept royal gerfalcons at her hunting lodge at Talmont. Growing up in a sophisticated and highly civilized court, she developed a "taste for luxury and refinement."[6] Above all, she conceived a great love for her ancestral domains: throughout her life, they would always be her first priority.

All contemporary sources agree that she was beautiful. In an age in which chroniclers invariably described royal and noble ladies as fair, their praise of her sounds genuinely enthusiastic. Even when she was old, the chronicler Richard of Devizes described her as "beautiful." No one, however, left an actual description of her. Her tomb effigy shows a tall, large-boned woman, but may not be an accurate representation. The contemporary ideal of beauty was the blue-eyed blonde, and several historians have suggested that the chroniclers would not have praised Eleanor so highly if she had not conformed to it. Yet she perhaps had auburn hair, if the crowned lady in a mural in the church of Sainte-Radegonde in Chinon depicts her.

She enjoyed dressing elegantly in fine clothes, often of silk embroidered in gold thread—the famous *Opus Anglicanum* (English work). She loved jewelry, amassing many pieces during her life, including jeweled circlets to hold in place the veils that married women wore in the twelfth and thirteenth centuries.

In a martial world, it was not considered practicable or fitting for a woman to rule a feudal state or wield dominion over men. It was imperative that a strong and powerful husband be found for Eleanor, to rule in her name.

2

"Mutual Anger"

✠

IN 1137, WILLIAM X DIED WHILE ON PILGRIMAGE TO THE SHRINE of St. James at Compostela, leaving Eleanor, at thirteen, countess of Poitou and duchess of Aquitaine in her own right, and the richest and most desirable heiress in Europe. Suger, Abbot of Saint-Denis and chief adviser of William X's overlord, Louis VI of France, claimed that the dying Duke had requested that Louis take Eleanor under his protection and marry her to his son, another Louis. William had also insisted that her domains should not be incorporated into the French royal demesne, but should remain independent and be inherited by her heirs alone.

France was then immersed in a struggle for supremacy with its feudal vassals, who had extended their territories and become more powerful than the Crown, whose authority held little weight beyond the royal domains. Louis VI was ecstatic at the prospect of marrying his son to Eleanor. The annexation of her rich domains was greatly to his advantage, for it would give him equality with his richest, most powerful vassals and provide him with twice the amount of land and resources he had at present. Furthermore, if Eleanor bore an heir to France, her lands would be absorbed into the royal demesne in perpetuity.

The King wasted no time in dispatching his son to Aquitaine to claim his bride. The younger Louis was then about fifteen and, in 1131, according to Frankish custom, had been crowned king during his father's lifetime. A simple, sweet-tempered, unworldly and pious youth, he had lived as a "child monk" at the abbey of Saint-Denis near Paris and was reluctant to abandon the religious life. But he knew his duty. In July 1137, he and Eleanor were married in Bordeaux Cathedral. As they rode toward Paris, they learned that Louis VI had died and that they were now king and queen of France.

They were unalike in temperament. Louis VII loved Eleanor "almost beyond reason," but his conjugal visits were infrequent and resulted only in the birth of a daughter, Marie, in 1145, which was a disappointment, as the Salic law forbade the succession of females to the French throne. Virtually nothing is recorded of Marie's childhood, though the course of events suggests that Eleanor was a distant mother.

Bernard of Clairvaux later wrote that Eleanor took "a determined political stance," yet, unlike previous French queen consorts, she rarely appeared in royal charters, even those Louis issued for Aquitaine. When she did, she either consented to his acts or confirmed them. She was, of course, just thirteen when she became queen, but the situation did not change with time. During her time as consort, there was a definite shift in the Queen's role, which broke with tradition and set a precedent for future French consorts, who mostly found themselves without political influence. Like their Norman counterparts in England, French queens had, until now, been active politically, having been consulted by their husbands on matters of policy and allowed to share in decision-making. But Eleanor played no more than a ceremonial role in public life and there is barely a mention of her in contemporary sources, especially in official documents. The almost total absence of criticism of her on the part of the chroniclers during these early years suggests that she accepted the redefined role expected of her.

William IX had mortgaged Toulouse to Bertrand, but when Bertrand died in 1122, leaving it to his brother, Alfonso Jordan, he had lost the heart to reclaim it. Eleanor inherited his claim and, in 1141, Louis attempted to take Toulouse, but failed. In 1142, Eleanor's sister Petronilla's adulterous affair with the King's cousin, Raoul, Count of Vermandois, who was married to the sister of Theobald II of Champagne, led to a war between Louis and Theobald, in which the town of Vitry-sur-Marne was burned with hundreds of its inhabitants. This left Louis weighed down by guilt, fearing that his soul was forever damned. Spiritual relief was at hand, however.

The First Crusade to capture the Holy Land from the Saracens, in 1096–9, had resulted in the establishment of four crusader states dominated by the Latin kingdom of Jerusalem. These states, ruled mainly by Normans and Frenchmen, were collectively known to Europeans as Outremer ("beyond the sea"). The need to maintain a military presence to guard the holy places in Palestine against the Saracens and protect pilgrims had brought into being two crusading orders of knights under monastic vows: the Knights Hospitaller, founded in 1099, and their rivals, the Knights Templar, founded in 1118. Both guarded and protected pilgrims to the Holy Land, but the powerful and wealthy Templars also acted as bankers to the kings of Europe.

In 1144, the security of the Christian kingdoms was threatened when the city of Edessa in Outremer was occupied by Saracens. The way now lay clear for the Infidel to occupy the neighboring principality of Antioch and the Latin kingdom of Jerusalem itself. The catastrophic news provoked widespread alarm throughout Christendom. The Pope proclaimed a second crusade, and Eleanor's uncle, Raymond of Poitiers, Prince of Antioch, appealed to Louis for aid.

In June 1147, Louis and Eleanor departed for the Holy Land. The crusade was a failure, for many reasons, and what happened in Antioch ruined Eleanor's reputation, for "the attentions paid by the Prince to the Queen and his constant, indeed almost continuous conversation with her aroused the King's suspicions."[1] Attraction there may have been, but Raymond's ambition was to extend his territory, and "he counted greatly on the interest of the Queen with the Lord King."[2] He wanted the crusading army to help him defend Antioch, although Louis refused, being bent on recovering Jerusalem. A furious Raymond resolved to deprive the King of his wife. Eleanor "readily assented, for she was a foolish woman. Contrary to the King's dignity, she mocked the laws of marriage and did not respect the marriage bed."[3]

The Poitevin troubadour Cercamon, in a song thought to have been composed during the crusade, deplored the conduct of a woman who lay with more than one man—probably a veiled reference to Eleanor—and wrote: "Better for her never to have been born than to have committed the fault that will be talked about from here to Poitou."[4] English chroniclers were more reticent, although by the time they were writing, the matter was notorious. Gervase of Canterbury thought it prudent to remain silent about matters best left unspoken. Giraldus Cambrensis wrote, "It is enough to note how Eleanor, Queen of France, conducted herself at first beyond the sea in the parts of Palestine." Richard of Devizes commented cryptically in a margin, "Many know what I wish none of us knew. This very Queen was at Jerusalem in the time of her first husband—let none speak more thereof, though I know it well. Keep silent."

Later writers would tell wilder stories. Around 1260, the anonymous Minstrel of Rheims claimed that Eleanor was "a very evil woman" who carried on a love affair by letter with the Muslim Sultan, Saladin, and tried to elope with him on a galley at Tyre, only to be seized by Louis at the jetty. "You are not worth a rotten pear!" she is said to have screamed at him. The Minstrel omitted to say that Saladin was just thirteen at the time. His tale is typical of the legends circulating about Eleanor after her death.

In reality, Eleanor warned Louis that, if he did not support Raymond, she would stay in Antioch with her vassals. "When the King made haste to tear her away, she mentioned their kinship, saying it was not lawful for them to remain together as man and wife, since they were related in the fourth and fifth degrees."[5]

Louis was "deeply moved." He loved Eleanor and did not wish to lose her, or her domains, but "he consented to divorce her if his counsellors and the French nobility would allow it." Acting on the advice of his advisers, he forced her to depart for Jerusalem with him, which caused a bitter rift between them. "Their mutual anger growing greater, the wound remained, hide it as best they might."[6]

In Rome, on the way home, they confided their marital problems to Pope Eugenius III, who would not hear of an annulment, but "made them sleep in the same bed, which he had decked with priceless hangings of his own; and daily he strove to restore love between them."[7] But there was still discord between the couple, and Eleanor complained "that she had married a monk, not a king."[8]

The birth of a second daughter, Alix, in 1150, was the final straw for Louis, who took it for a sign that God frowned on his marriage. His barons of France urged him to set Eleanor aside and marry someone less controversial who could give him sons.

Suger urged caution. If the marriage was dissolved, Louis would lose Eleanor's inheritance, which would then pass to whoever else she married—and she might choose someone hostile to French interests. Suger now devoted his energies to restoring amicable relations between the King and Queen. But then Henry FitzEmpress, the future Henry II of England, arrived in Paris, and everything changed.

3

"My Very Noble Lord Henry"

✠

BY 1150, WHEN HE WAS ONLY SEVENTEEN, THE REPUTATION OF Henry FitzEmpress was formidable.

His father, Geoffrey, Count of Anjou, was a vassal of the King of France and had been nicknamed "Plantagenet" after the sprig of broom—*Planta genista*—that he wore in his hat (the name was not adopted as a royal surname until the fifteenth century). Henry II and his sons founded the Angevin royal dynasty, but the county of Anjou was lost to England in the thirteenth century, so modern historians have come to use the surname Plantagenet for them and their descendants, who ruled England until 1485.

The Angevins—as the ruling dynasty of Anjou were known—had a poor reputation. "From the Devil they came and to the Devil they will return,"[1] observed St. Bernard of Clairvaux, the great twelfth-century mystic and reformer. He was referring to the notorious legend of an ancestress of the House of Anjou, a tale often fondly repeated by her supposed descendants. One of the early counts was said to have returned from a journey with a new wife, a beautiful woman called Melusine. She bore him four children and was satisfactory in every way, except that she would not remain in church for the sacrament of the Mass. This troubled the Count, who secretly arranged for four knights to stand upon her cloak and prevent her from leaving the service. As the priest prepared to elevate the host, Melusine tore free and flew shrieking out of a window. She was never seen again, for—it was concluded—she had been the Devil's daughter and could not bear to look upon the body of Christ.

Anjou was a rich and fertile territory on the River Loire. Emerging in the ninth century from an obscure past, its rulers were first styled counts in the tenth century and steadily increased in fortune, territory and power by virtue of brilliant diplomacy and a series of advantageous marriages with the heiresses of neighboring domains. Anjou's location ensured that it was of great strategic importance in western Europe. To the west was the duchy of Brittany, to the north that of Normandy, to the east the counties of Blois and Champagne and the kingdom of France, and, to the south, Poitou and Aquitaine. There had been little love lost between the Normans and Angevins since 1066, when the Normans had gained ascendancy in northern Europe through William the Conqueror's acquisition of the kingdom of England.

The counts of Anjou were famously "ferocious and combative."[2] Henry of Huntingdon, writing in 1154, observed, "It is well-known that the Angevin race has flourished under high-spirited and warlike rulers, and that they have dominated the people surrounding them with terror." The Angevin greed for land and power was notorious. The counts were renowned for their hot temper, voracious energy, military genius, political acumen, engaging charm and robust constitution; the spectacular Angevin temper, violent behavior and a tendency to go to extremes were all attributed to their demonic ancestry. No one was surprised that the counts of Anjou were often at loggerheads with the Church. Some were intelligent, cultivated men; most were known for their cruelties, their debaucheries and their feuds.

The Angevins were a good-looking race. Many were tall, with a strong physique and red-gold hair, and their physical presence commanded respect from their peers and vassals. They were, in the main, dynamic and capable rulers.

Geoffrey Plantagenet had married Maud, daughter of the Conqueror's son, Henry I, King of England, and widow of the German "Roman" Emperor, Henry V. She had become her father's heir when her brother William drowned in 1120. There was no precedent for a female sovereign, either in England or Normandy, yet the Norman queen consorts of England had proved that a woman could rule firmly and efficiently when serving as regent for an absent husband.

Geoffrey's shield, which appears on his tomb, is the earliest known example of what was probably a hereditary blazon—three golden lions, given to him by Henry I, who may have used the symbol of a lion as his personal badge. This shield was probably one of the devices on which the heraldic trio of lions adopted by the Plantagenets was based.

The Empress Maud was "a woman who had nothing of the woman in her."[3] She despised Geoffrey for being merely the son of a count and unworthy of her. Yet they produced three sons to continue their line; the eldest was Henry FitzEmpress, born on March 5, 1133, at Le Mans.

When Henry I died in 1135, Maud's cousin, Stephen of Blois (son of the Conqueror's daughter Adela), usurped the throne. Stephen, who proved a weak and ineffectual ruler, also inherited Normandy, but Geoffrey immediately claimed it in right of his wife and proceeded to take it by force.

Maud focused on wresting England from Stephen. She launched a civil war and, in 1141, emerged victorious and was recognized as Lady of England and Normandy. In triumph, she went to London to be crowned, "but she was swollen with insufferable pride by her success in war and alienated the affections of nearly everyone. She was driven out of London."[4] After that, it became apparent that her cause was hopeless. England descended into anarchy as unscrupulous barons took advantage of the weakness of Stephen's rule to devastate the land, building unlicensed castles and engaging in private feuds and wars. Men said that, for nineteen winters, "Christ and His saints slept."[5]

In 1145, Louis VII of France acknowledged Geoffrey as duke of Normandy. In 1147, Maud relinquished her cause and her claim to England to her son, Henry FitzEmpress, and settled in Rouen. In 1150, Geoffrey invested Henry as duke of Normandy. The English barons were now heartily sick of civil war and anarchy, and were eager to have the succession settled. They, and the oppressed English people, wanted a ruler who would govern firmly and wisely and maintain the peace, as Henry I had, and they looked to his grandson as their hope for the future.

Henry FitzEmpress was to play a role of immense importance in the history of Europe. He had leonine features and cropped red hair, and was "of middle height, reddish, freckled complexion, with grey eyes that glowed fiercely and grew bloodshot in anger, a fiery countenance and a harsh, cracked voice. His chest was broad and square, his arms strong and powerful." His stocky frame had "a pronounced tendency to corpulence, which he tempered by exercise; in agility of limb he was second to none."[6] He was immensely hardworking and possessed of prodigious energy, "liberal in public, frugal in private"[7] and abstemious when eating and drinking.

Henry had a formidable and forceful personality, being self-assured, articulate, intelligent and, unusually for a twelfth-century ruler, "remarkably polished in letters."[8] As a child, he had been taught by several renowned scholars, including Geoffrey of Monmouth, whose *History of the Kings of Britain* inspired in him a lifelong fascination with the Arthurian legends. As an adult, "he had a ready knowledge of nearly the whole of history and a great store of practical wisdom."[9] He knew "all the languages from the French sea to the Jordan," but spoke only Latin and French.[10]

Henry was complex, unpredictable and wary. He kept his own counsel and preferred to do things himself rather than delegate. He had a will of iron and "was never one to procrastinate."[11] Hugh of Avalon, the saintly Bishop of Lincoln, thought him volatile, crafty and unfathomable. Walter Map, who wrote *De Nugis Curialum*, a gossipy "little book I have jotted down by snatches at court," stated that no one compared with Henry in "good temper and affability." Yet, when he erupted in wrath, his face became empurpled with fury and he would throw himself raging on the ground, roll around yelling, or grind his teeth on the rushes. When angry, he could be vindictive. "He readily broke his word"[12] and would be described by Thomas Becket as a Proteus in slipperiness. Caustic and cynical at times, he "answered roughly on every occasion,"[13] freely using his favorite oath, "by the eyes of God,"[14] which was considered blasphemous. He was eloquent in argument, had a sharp wit and particularly enjoyed a joke at someone else's expense.

Although he was a competent general, he despised violence and hated war, which he would avoid if he could reach a settlement by diplomatic means. He was not, by nature, a cruel man, unlike his Norman predecessors, but a restless and impatient soul who could not bear to stay still for long. "Except when riding a horse or eating a meal, he never sits."[15] He transacted business pacing back and forth and was forever fidgeting, even at Mass.

Henry was "addicted to hunting beyond measure"[16] and would happily spend all day in the saddle. He chased women with the same kind of fervor. His vigorous sexual appetite was notorious. He had numerous casual encounters and several bastard children.

Henry was determined to unite Normandy, Anjou and England into one vast domain. Given the aggressive and increasingly threatening power of the House of Anjou, it was hardly surprising that, when he pointedly failed to pay homage to King Louis for Normandy, Louis refused to confirm him as its duke; the prospect of Henry building up such a formidable power bloc was alarming in the extreme.

Suger's death in January 1151 removed the last obstacle to the annulment of the marriage of Louis and Eleanor, who seized her moment and pushed for a divorce. By the summer, Louis was reconciled to an annulment.

First, however, the problem of Henry FitzEmpress had to be resolved. He and his father were summoned to Paris, where Geoffrey astonished everyone by advising Henry to offer Louis the Norman Vexin, a strip of land on the Norman–French border, in return for Louis recognizing Henry as duke. In the tenth century the Vexin had been partitioned: the north was absorbed into Normandy, and the south became part of France. Since then, the Norman Vexin had been a bone of contention between the kings of France and the dukes of Normandy.

A satisfactory treaty was concluded. Henry paid homage to Louis for Normandy, was formally invested with the duchy and received the kiss of peace.

Writing in the 1180s, the knowledgeable Walter Map, who was later a trusted member of Henry's household, and in his confidence, stated that it was in Paris that his future master first cast lustful eyes on Eleanor— who, at twenty-nine, was eleven years his senior and still very beautiful— and that she, in response, "cast her unchaste eyes" at him. He added that it was "secretly reputed that [Eleanor] had shared Louis's bed with Geoffrey," Henry's father. Giraldus Cambrensis also asserted that "Count Geoffrey of Anjou had carnally known Queen Eleanor. The Count later confessed this to his son" and "frequently forewarned him, forbidding

him in any wise to touch her, both because she was the wife of his lord
and because he had known her himself." In twelfth-century society, sleeping with your lord's lady was considered treachery of the worst sort, while
adultery in a queen was a particularly serious offense, since it jeopardized
the succession.

Giraldus claimed he had heard about Eleanor's adultery with Geoffrey
from the saintly Bishop Hugh of Lincoln, who had learned of it from
Henry FitzEmpress himself. At that time, Henry was trying to divorce
Eleanor, so it would have been to his advantage to declare her an adulterous wife who had had carnal relations with his father, which would have
rendered their marriage incestuous and provided grounds for its dissolution. The grounds on which Henry sought an annulment were shrouded
in secrecy, but the fact that it was not granted is significant; incest of this
kind would not have been overlooked.

Giraldus Cambrensis (also known as Gerald of Wales) was one of the
foremost prolific and popular writers of his time. He was personally ac-
quainted with most of the important contemporary public figures of the
age and was an eyewitness to many great events. An ambitious man, he
was appointed archdeacon of Brecon in 1172, and four years later was
elected bishop of St. David's by the cathedral chapter, although Henry II
refused to confirm the appointment because he was suspicious of Gerald's royal Welsh blood. An embittered Giraldus became very antagonis-
tic toward the King and wrote of him from a hostile point of view. He
disapproved of Eleanor of Aquitaine and, in regard to her supposed adultery with Geoffrey, may have been tempted to exaggerate or massage the
facts.

According to Giraldus, Henry ignored his father's warning. "It is related that [he] presumed to sleep adulterously with the Queen of France.
How could a fortunate generation spring from these copulations?" Walter Map also believed that the offspring of Henry and Eleanor were
"tainted at the source."

Lust was only a part of the attraction fizzing between Henry and Eleanor. He was "tempted by the quality of this woman's blood, but even
more by her lands."[17] The acquisition of such a bride would make him
the greatest prince in Europe, greater than his overlord, King Louis. Eleanor was just as determined. "She aspired to marriage with the Norman
Duke, whose manner of life suited better with her own, and for this rea-

son she desired and procured a divorce."[18] Henry left Paris full of joy, probably because he and Eleanor had reached a secret understanding that they would marry as soon as her marriage was dissolved.

On September 7, Count Geoffrey died of a fever after swimming in the river at Château-du-Loir. Henry took possession of Anjou, Touraine and Maine and set about securing the allegiance of his father's vassals.

On March 21, at Beaugency on the Loire, Louis and Eleanor were granted an annulment on a plea of consanguinity within the fourth degree. It was agreed that Eleanor's domains would be returned to her. "She now had the power to marry whomever she wished,"[19] provided she preserved her allegiance to Louis as her overlord. According to Gervase of Canterbury, "people said that it was she who had cleverly brought about that contrived repudiation."

When the proceedings were over, Louis and Eleanor took their leave of each other. They would never meet again. The previous September, when she had left Paris for the last time, Eleanor had probably said farewell to her two daughters, who were aged just seven and two. She must have known that losing them was the price she would pay for her freedom.

That freedom was threatened when Theobald of Blois and Geoffrey of Anjou, Henry's younger brother, with greedy eyes on her vast domains, each tried to abduct her on her way south, and she only narrowly evaded capture. It was now imperative that her marriage to Henry FitzEmpress be arranged without delay, or it might never take place at all. As soon as she arrived in her capital, she "sent secretly to the Duke and announced that she was free."[20]

Vassals and heiresses could not wed without the consent of their overlords. By all the laws of feudalism, protocol and courtesy, Eleanor and Henry should have sought King Louis's permission before marrying. Yet it was certain that Louis would refuse it. The prospect of Henry acquiring his former wife's domains would have horrified him. Marrying without his consent was an act of the greatest provocation, not to mention discourtesy, but the couple had decided to risk the consequences and keep their plans secret. Robert of Torigni, Abbot of Mont-Saint-Michel, was not sure whether Henry had married Eleanor "on impulse, or by premeditated design." Giraldus believed that the marriage was Henry's idea, and that he was guilty of "taking her from his own lord and marrying her himself."

Eleanor summoned her chief vassals to renew their allegiance to her as duchess of Aquitaine. She granted honors and privileges to those she favored, among them Saldebreuil de Sanzay, Constable of Aquitaine, whom she made her seneschal, and her maternal uncle, Raoul de Faye. She underlined her autonomy by annulling all acts and decrees made by Louis in her domains, issuing charters in her own name and renewing grants and privileges to religious houses. Her industry suggests that she had been stifled by the constraints placed upon her as queen of France.

In March, a delegation from England had visited Henry in Normandy and begged him to delay no longer, as his supporters were losing patience. On April 6, the day he received Eleanor's message, he met his Norman barons at Lisieux. His priority now was his marriage, and he wished to obtain their approval for the match before hurrying south to Poitiers. "The Duke, allured by the nobility of that woman and by desire for the great honours belonging to her, impatient of all delay, took with him a few companions, hastened quickly over the long routes and, in little time, obtained his long-desired union."[21]

On Whitsunday, May 18, 1152, Henry and Eleanor were married in Poitiers Cathedral without pomp or ceremony. There is no record of a dispensation being sought, even though there existed between them the same degree of affinity as there had been between Eleanor and Louis.

Eleanor was now duchess of Aquitaine and Normandy and countess of Poitou and Anjou, and Henry had acquired a third of what is now modern France, more than doubling his continental possessions and gaining vastly in status, power, wealth and resources, as well as acquiring cities and castles of great strategic importance. He was now master of a domain that was ten times larger than the royal demesne of France. In marrying Eleanor, he founded an Angevin Empire; when he inherited England, that empire would extend "from the further boundary of Scotland to the Pyrenean mountains."[22] At nineteen, he had become the most powerful ruler in Christendom; and, by divorcing one husband and wedding another, Eleanor had managed to shift the balance of power in Europe.

She had a seal struck with her new titles; she continued to issue charters in her own right and made generous gifts to religious houses. On May 26, eight days after her wedding, she visited Montierneuf Abbey, where, styling herself "Eleanor, by the grace of God, Duchess of Aquitaine and Normandy, united with the Duke of Normandy, Henry of Anjou," she confirmed the privileges granted by her forebears. The next day, she was at the abbey of Saint-Maixent to restore the forest of La Sèvre, which had been granted by Louis but taken back by Eleanor after her return to Poitiers. "This gift I have renewed with a glad heart, now that I am joined in wedlock to Henry, Duke of Normandy and Count of Anjou," she declared in her charter.[23]

Early in June 1152, Eleanor made a pilgrimage to Fontevraud, where she was received by the Abbess Isabella, Henry's aunt. Eleanor's affection and reverence for Fontevraud comes across in the wording of the new charter she granted at this time to the abbey:

> After being joined to my very noble lord Henry, most noble Count of the Angevins, by the bond of matrimony, divine inspiration led me to want to visit the sacred congregation of the virgins of Fontevraud and, by the grace of God, I have been able to realise this intention. Thus, have I come to Fontevraud, guided by God. I have crossed the threshold where the sisters are gathered, and here, with heart-felt emotion, I have approved, conceded and affirmed all that my father and forebears have given to God and to the church of Fontevraud.

The charter is interesting because it also refers to Henry "governing the empire of the Poitevins and Angevins," an early indication that the couple regarded their domains as an imperial entity.

The buoyant tone of her charters suggests that Eleanor was happy in her new marriage. Like most aristocratic marriages of the period, it was primarily a business arrangement between feudal magnates, with both partners committed to safeguarding their interests. Although little is known of relations between the couple before 1173, much may be inferred from circumstantial evidence. Henry and Eleanor had a great deal in common, being strong, dynamic characters with forceful personalities and boundless energy. Gervase of Canterbury implies that, at least to begin with, there was a strong mutual attraction between them; there was certainly a high degree of shared ambition and self-interest. Eleanor now had no cause to complain of a lack of husbandly attention, for the births of nine children are evidence that, for the first fifteen years of their marriage, Henry was a regular visitor to her bed. Naturally, he was the dominant partner, but he allowed Eleanor a certain degree of autonomy in regard to her own lands.

William of Newburgh claimed that Henry did not commit adultery until Eleanor was past childbearing age, but Giraldus stated that, before then, Henry was "an adulterer in secret." He took his sexual pleasure wherever he found it, with noble ladies and the "creatures of the night" who regularly infiltrated his court.[24] In fact, he was unfaithful to Eleanor almost immediately. Of all Henry's bastards, the most famous was Geoffrey. According to Giraldus, Geoffrey had just turned twenty in April 1173 when he was elected bishop of Lincoln, so he was born probably in the spring of 1153, suggesting a date of conception just weeks after Henry's marriage.

Between 1158 and 1166, probably in commemoration of her marriage to Henry, Eleanor herself commissioned the stained-glass east window in Poitiers Cathedral, which was then being rebuilt in the Gothic style. Her role as donor is suggested by her position below the right hands of Christ, who is shown both crucified and risen in majesty. She kneels with Henry and their four eldest sons, two at either side; their presence determines the date of the window. This is perhaps the earliest surviving representation of Eleanor, although several biographers have suggested that one or more pairs of the statues of the kings and queens of Judah on the west porch and façade of Chartres Cathedral, completed around 1150, are likenesses of Eleanor and Louis. As Eleanor was queen of France at the time they were sculpted, she may have been the personification of queenship that inspired them.

There was little concept of portraiture in the early Middle Ages, so the few surviving representations of Eleanor are purely images of a queen. For example, two identical heads from the church of Notre-Dame-du-Bourg at Langon near Bordeaux (now in the Metropolitan Museum of Art, New York) are thought to represent Henry and Eleanor and to date from 1152, the time of the couple's nuptial progress through Aquitaine.

Other heads said to be Eleanor can be seen in Bordeaux Cathedral, the churches at Chaniers near Saintes, Sharnford, Lincolnshire, Barfreston, Kent, and Bradwell Abbey, Northamptonshire, and at Oakham Castle, Rutland. Two heads at Fontevraud, one of a young crowned queen, the other of an old woman in a wimple and barbette, may be images of her.

An illustration of a queen in the *Codex Manesse* (*c.*1304–40) in the university library at Heidelberg has often been assumed to be Eleanor, but there is no evidence for it. In the so-called "Psalter of Eleanor of Aquitaine," executed probably in Paris in the late twelfth century (now in the National Library of the Netherlands), the donor portrait shows a lady at prayer wearing a cream cloak, a belted blue gown and embroidered shoes. Her hair is worn loose under a thin circlet and short veil. But Eleanor was a widow when the manuscript was produced, and widows, even queens, did not wear their hair loose. Moreover, a lordly figure portrayed in the manuscript is shown wearing a cloak lined with ermine, denoting his high status; the woman's cloak lacks ermine, showing her to be of lower rank. So this is almost certainly not Eleanor.

4

"Behold, the Lord the Ruler Cometh"

THE MARRIAGE OF HENRY AND ELEANOR "WAS THE CAUSE AND promoter of great hatred and discord between the King of France and the Duke."[1] Louis was "greatly incensed" when he heard of it. He "had no wish that [Eleanor] should have sons by another, for thus his own daughters by her would be disinherited."[2] Convening a council of outraged barons, he complained that Henry had breached feudal law by having "basely stolen his wife"[3] and summoned the guilty pair to his court to account for their conduct. Receiving no response, he felt fully justified in going to war. In June, he invaded Normandy.

Henry, who had left Eleanor in Poitiers and was preparing to sail from Barfleur, Normandy, to England with an invasion force, was forced to abandon his plans. In six weeks, he laid waste the Vexin and the domain of Robert of Dreux, Louis's brother. Louis gave up his cause as lost and returned to Paris.

Late in August, Henry and Eleanor made a four-month tour through her domains to introduce the new Duke of Aquitaine to his vassals. Their reception of him was cool. Always fiercely independent, they had resented French interference in the duchy, but Henry represented a more potent threat to their autonomy. They were deeply suspicious of his aspiration to be king of England and feared he would milk Aquitaine dry to achieve this. Some lords, although loyal to their Duchess, firmly informed her that they owed Henry no allegiance, save as her husband.

Henry and Eleanor were well received at Limoges, making camp outside the city walls, but, having been served a sparse dinner in their tent on the first night, Henry demanded to know why the burghers of Limoges had failed to provide the royal kitchens with the customary supplies. The Abbot of Saint-Martial explained that these were delivered only when the Duchess lodged within the city walls. Full of "black bile," Henry gave orders for the walls of Limoges, so recently rebuilt, to be razed to the ground. In future, he declared, no abbot would be able to use them as an excuse to withhold from their Duke his just and reasonable dues.

After that, the sullen vassals of the south held their peace and the progress proceeded without further incident. In Gascony, Henry was able to recruit men for his invasion force, gather supplies and charter ships from the ports.

On January 6, 1153, he sailed from Barfleur, determined to win England. He left Normandy in the care of the Empress Maud, and Anjou and Aquitaine in the custody of Eleanor, who seems to have taken up residence at Angers, while Raoul de Faye acted as her deputy in Aquitaine. The massive castle of Angers was "worthy to be called a palace for, not long ago, vast chambers were constructed, laid out and adorned in a luxurious manner, entirely worthy of a king. On the one side it looks out over the river [Maine] flowing past, and on the other towards the vine-clad hills."[4]

It has often been stated that one of the troubadours Eleanor welcomed to her court at this time was the celebrated Bernard de Ventadour. Our only source for this is a short biography of him written by Uc de Saint-Circ in the thirteenth century.[5] Bernard, who was blessed with good looks and a fine singing voice, was the son of a kitchen maid in the household of Eble III, Viscount of Ventadour in the Limousin. Eble, whose family had a tradition of patronizing troubadours, realized that the boy had talent and tutored him in the arts of poetry and composition. But, when Bernard repaid his noble patron by attempting to seduce his wife, he was ejected from the household and made to leave the district, while his hapless paramour was locked up by her enraged husband.

"Bernard left and went to the Duchess of Normandy, who was young and of great worth, and she had understanding of matters of valour, honour and fine flattery, and liked songs in praise of her. Bernard's voice and songs pleased her greatly, and she received him warmly as her guest.

He was at her court for a long time and fell in love with her, and she with him, and he composed many excellent songs for her. And all that I have told you about him [wrote Uc] was told to me by Viscount Eble of Ventadour, who was the son of the Viscountess Bernard loved so much."

There are errors in this account, and some historians believe Uc fabricated parts of it, but the man from whom he got his information, Eble IV of Ventadour, was married to Eleanor's cousin, Sybille, daughter of Raoul de Faye, so there is probably some truth in it.

If Eleanor did encourage Bernard, and gave the impression that she returned his feelings, it was probably in the spirit of courtly love. It is difficult to identify the "many excellent songs" he wrote for her. In some, he referred to "the beautiful woman" who "draws me to her like a magnet," describing her as "noble and sweet, faithful and loyal, gracious, lovely, the embodiment of charm, one meet to crown the state of any king," which suggests that he was referring to Eleanor.

When, after a stormy crossing, Henry arrived on the south coast of England in January 1154, "the earth quivered with sudden rumours like reeds shaken in the wind."[6] When he went into a church to hear mass, he heard the priest declare, "Behold, the Lord the ruler cometh, and the kingdom is in His hand." Interpreting this as a good omen, Henry pressed on in a buoyant mood, bent on relieving his chief supporters, who were under siege at Wallingford Castle.

"God Himself appeared to fight for the Duke." In July, after months of skirmishing, during which he took many towns and castles and earned an impressive reputation for bravery and military skill, Henry at last confronted Stephen's forces before Wallingford. "The noble youth was at the head of his army, his physical beauty betokening that of the soul, and marked out by arms that did not so much become him as he his arms."[7] The English barons and bishops, prominent among them Archbishop Theobald of Canterbury, urged the two leaders to negotiate, many feeling that Stephen should acknowledge Henry as his heir. The sudden death of Stephen's son, Eustace, Count of Boulogne, on August 17, probably from food poisoning, made things much simpler.

On that very day, in far-off Angers, Eleanor bore a son whom she baptized William, "the distinctive attribute of the counts of Poitou and dukes of Aquitaine."[8] She clearly intended to make him her heir, as he was styled count of Poitiers. Soon after giving birth, she granted a petition of the Abbot of La Trinité de Vendôme "for the safe rearing of my son William." God, it seemed, had manifested His approval of Henry's marriage and his cause.

Exhausted and demoralized, Stephen, now in his late fifties, lost the will to fight on and, in November, a peace was quickly brokered. He acknowledged Henry as his heir and, in turn, Henry "generously conceded that the King should hold the kingdom for the rest of his life."[9] Their agreement was enshrined in a treaty ratified at Westminster at Christmas 1153. "So God granted a happy issue and peace shone forth," wrote Henry of Huntingdon. "What boundless joy! What a happy day!"

When Henry entered London with Stephen, "he was received with joy by enormous crowds and splendid processions. Thus, by God's mercy, peace dawned on the ruined realm of England, putting an end to its troubled night."[10]

That winter, Henry, who was also Bernard de Ventadour's patron, summoned him to England, but Bernard sent a messenger to tell the King "that my magnet holds me, and so I do not go to him." In keeping with the secrecy implicit in courtly love, this told Henry only that Bernard had a mistress whom he was loath to leave. But Henry insisted he come and, reluctantly, Bernard had to obey. Before he left, he urged one Huguet, "my courtly messenger, sing my song eagerly to the Queen of the Normans." He hoped, "if the English King and the Norman Duke allows, that I will see her before winter overtakes us. Were it not for my magnet, I would stay until Christmas is over."

Miserable in his exile, he begged in vain for leave to return to Eleanor's court, once more to mingle with "ladies and chevaliers, fair and courteous." Eventually, he did go back, apparently without first obtaining Henry's permission, and lost the Duke's patronage as a result.

In March 1154, Henry "returned triumphantly" to Rouen. Eleanor came north to celebrate Easter with him, bringing with her eight-month-old William. They lodged in Maud's chief residence, the palace built by

Henry I beside the church of Notre-Dame des Prés, just outside the city walls. This was the first recorded occasion on which Eleanor met her formidable mother-in-law. Maud cannot but have been delighted that Henry had acquired a bride who brought him so much territory and so many political advantages, yet little is known about relations between the two women. The slender evidence that survives suggests that they cooperated with each other.

That summer, Louis VII married Constance, the daughter of Alfonso VII, King of Castile. After the wedding, he relinquished the title "duke of Aquitaine" and, at a meeting in August, was finally reconciled to Henry.

When Henry rode to crush a rebellion in the Norman Vexin, Eleanor remained with Maud in Rouen, where, on October 26, they received a messenger with important news from Archbishop Theobald in England. On October 25, the "nineteen long winters"[11] of Stephen's reign had ended with the King's death. News of his passing reached Henry early in November, as he was besieging a rebel stronghold. He destroyed the castle, then set about putting his affairs in order before joining Eleanor in a flurry of preparations for their departure. Among the items packed in her baggage were forty-two gowns of silk, linen and wool, many richly embroidered, fourteen pairs of shoes (six of them embroidered with gold thread), five mantles furred with ermine, many veils and ten warm undershirts. It took Henry just two weeks to assemble an escort sufficiently imposing to impress his new subjects. Eleanor took a train of three dozen servants. Bernard de Ventadour was not among them. Left behind, "sad and ailing," he sought the patronage of the Count of Toulouse.

Heavy storms, gales and sleet delayed the royal couple's departure from Barfleur until December 7, when they sailed for England in the royal galley, which was known as an *esnecca* (snake). They braved a tempest and a violent sea, but despite the risks, and Eleanor being seven months pregnant, Henry would delay no longer. England had been without a King for six weeks. Fortunately, with Archbishop Theobald in charge, the realm had remained at peace "for love of the king to come."[12] Such was Henry's reputation that "no man dared do other than good, for he was held in great awe."[13]

On December 8, after a storm-tossed voyage lasting twenty-four hours, the royal party landed safely in a harbor south of the New Forest and made straight for Winchester, so that Henry could take possession of the royal treasury and receive the homage of the English barons. Then it was on to London, where the people received their sovereign "with transports of joy,"[14] acclaiming him as "Henry the Peacemaker."[15]

Since the Palace of Westminster had been vandalized by Stephen's supporters, Henry and Eleanor lodged in the old Saxon palace at Bermondsey on the Surrey shore of the Thames opposite the Tower of London.

On Sunday, December 19, they were "crowned and consecrated with becoming pomp and splendour"[16] in Westminster Abbey by Archbishop Theobald. At Eleanor's insistence, the officiating clergy wore splendid vestments of silk embroidered in gold, such as had never been seen in England, while the royal couple and their lords were attired in robes of silk, brocade and gauze. Eleanor shimmered in a tight-fitting robe in many shades of gold brought from Constantinople, over which she wore a mantle of royal purple richly embroidered with gold fleurs-de-lis and lions and lined with ermine. On her head, she had a circlet of wrought gold set with great pearls, rubies and emeralds and a veil of silver tissue.

Henry received the heavy gold crown commissioned by William the Conqueror in imitation of the imperial crown of Charlemagne and was "blessed as king with great joy and many crying for happiness, and splendidly enthroned."[17] Gervase of Canterbury states that Eleanor was crowned with him. Afterward, as the new King and Queen rode in procession along the Strand, the citizens ran alongside crying, "*Waes hael!*" and "*Vivat Rex!*"[18] Thus Henry "took possession of his hereditary kingdom to the acclaim of all. The people hoped for better things from the new monarch, especially when they saw he possessed remarkable prudence, constancy and zeal for justice, and at the very outset already manifested the likeness of a great prince."[19]

The long rule of the Plantagenets had begun.

5

"High-Born Lady, Excellent and Valiant"

✣

THE NORMAN KINGS HAD GOVERNED BOTH ENGLAND AND
Normandy, which had necessitated their being absent from one territory or another at times. During these absences, their very able queens had ruled as regents, notably William I's wife, Matilda of Flanders, in Normandy, and Henry I's wife, Matilda of Scotland, in England. In 1068, William the Conqueror had amended the coronation rite to make his Queen an equal sharer in the royal authority, but that passage was removed in the twelfth century. By 1200, it was made clear that the coronation of a queen did not confer regal authority; all it did was confirm her as the King's lawful wife, raised by God to be the mother of his heirs. At her coronation, she was obliged to pause as she entered Westminster Abbey, while prayers were offered up that she might overcome female frailty. Her crown was an emblem of honor, the ring she received represented faith, and she was allowed a silver-gilt scepter, an empty symbol of regal power. She would now sit enthroned on the King's left, on a lower chair.

When royal power had centered upon the King's court, wherever it was, the Norman queens had participated in government, exercised control over the royal household and had access to the King's treasure. But their power had gradually decreased as government became more centralized. After Henry II facilitated efficient rule by establishing the royal administration at Westminster and Rouen, the early Plantagenet queens—

with the exception of Eleanor of Aquitaine—did not enjoy the same authority and independence as their predecessors.

English queens of the early Plantagenet period were expected to bear heirs to continue the dynasty, be charitable helpmeets to their husbands and grace ceremonial occasions. They had no formal authority, but might wield great influence through patronage, and they could still be a dynamic force in politics, as the careers of Eleanor of Aquitaine and Alienor of Provence illustrate.

The English Crown held territory in southern France and, throughout this period, royal marriages were made to protect those domains. Five queens in this period would come from southern Europe—from France, Navarre and Spain. They brought with them the sophisticated culture of those regions, trading opportunities, Byzantine and Moorish influences and a more civilized style of living.

A queen's life was one of prescribed ritual: coronation, childbirth, religious observance, public ceremonial and intercession with the King on behalf of others. Her role as a wife and mother was exalted, but it was subordinate to that of the King, and her submissiveness—in theory—absolute. If she exerted her influence unduly, it was frowned upon. Her power was meant to be limited. She might appear in majesty with the King, but this was merely an illusion.

Medieval queens were expected to mirror the virtues of the Virgin Mary, as the coronation rite made clear. To the King's subjects, the Queen was the gracious, charitable and merciful image of the Virgin Mother. Married women had to cover their hair, but queens could wear it loose in token of their symbolic virginity.

In the coronation rubric, queens were exhorted to emulate the biblical Queen Esther, who was humble, self-effacing, passive, obedient and modest, yet gifted with the inner strength to save her people, the Jews, from the wrath of her husband. She was wise, just, compassionate and thoughtful, filled with inner beauty, all character traits expected of the ideal medieval queen. Those who failed to live up to expectations might be branded with the epithet "Jezebel," likening them to the most notorious queen in the Bible.

A queen could enhance her husband's reputation through her public demonstrations of piety and charity and strengthen her own standing as an intercessor. Her wealth enabled her to succor the less fortunate of the

King's subjects. Her intercessions on behalf of others enabled the sovereign to show the kinder face of monarchy without losing authority. Both king and queen would then be seen as agents of mercy. It was also important for a queen to be visibly associated with the clergy, attending episcopal enthronements and the consecrations of cathedrals, visiting shrines and endowing religious houses. These activities conferred on her an aura of sanctity and special privilege. Of course, some queens exceeded their remit and interfered in the appointing of clergy.

As the King's bed was a symbol of majesty where the monarch held meetings, so the Queen's stood for the basis of her influence. Her bedchamber was not just her private domain, but also the seat of her power, the place where she had sex with the King and where heirs to the throne were born, so it is not surprising to find her receiving petitioners before her bed. It was through patronage that she could wield influence and might built up an affinity of support.

Queens had their own courts on their dower estates and officers to hear pleas and dispense justice in their name. By law, the Queen of England could control her own property. Medieval queens received an income from the dower lands settled on them by their husbands upon marriage, and from wardships and other privileges granted them, including queen-gold, an additional tenth payable to the consort on any voluntary fine over the value of 10 marks (£4,900) paid to the King in exchange for a license or pardon from the Crown, and on taxes on Jews.

The dower was supposed to fund the Queen in the event of her widowhood, but it is clear that queens were allowed the use of their dower lands, and the money they yielded through rents and other payments, in their lifetimes. However, most early Plantagenet queens did not control their dower lands while their husbands lived. The Queen paid for her own clothes, jewels and presents, but her daily expenses—her food, the alms she customarily distributed to the poor, and the wages and liveries of her servants—were covered by the King.

At Christmas 1154, Henry and Eleanor presided over a great court at Westminster, which was attended by the chief barons and prelates of England. Henry knew it was essential to restore public confidence in the monarchy, establishing a strong grip on affairs and controlling his magnates, and immediately set to work to tackle the evils and decay that beset his kingdom and establish good government. He began by ordering the destruction of 1,100 unlicensed castles, and so "earned the praise and thanksgiving of peace-loving men."[1]

Henry "was at great pains to revive the vigour of the laws of England. Throughout the realm he appointed judges and legal officials to curb the audacity of wicked men and dispense justice to litigants."[2] He deferred frequently to the laws and customs of his hero, Henry I, which he was determined to restore and enforce. He instituted legal circuits, whereby his justices would visit each region to ensure that the King's Peace was being kept and administer justice through assize courts. He gradually replaced trial by ordeal with trial by jury. It was during his reign that the foundations of English common law were laid down.

Henry reorganized the royal finances, which were in chaos. He levied new taxes, minted a purer coinage and ensured that all royal revenues were collected by the Exchequer. This policy led to a boom in trade and prosperity, and royal income, which amounted to £22,000 (£16,000,000) in 1154, increased to £48,000 (£35,000,000) by the end of the reign.

There was no aspect of government that escaped his attention. Soon after his accession, it was said that a virgin could walk from one end of the realm to the other with her bosom full of gold and suffer no harm, and that evil barons had vanished like phantoms.[3] By the summer of 1155, order had been re-established in England, and with such thoroughness that it would remain at peace for nearly two decades. Small wonder that Henry's contemporaries accounted him "the greatest of earthly princes."[4]

His benefactions to the Church were lavish. He gave generously to the abbeys of Fontevraud, Reading (where Henry I lay buried) and Grandmont in the Limousin, to which he had a great attachment. He and Eleanor endowed many leper hospitals, including those at Caen, Angers and Le Mans, and Eleanor patronized that at St. Giles in the Fields near London, founded by Matilda, queen of Henry I.

The chroniclers, however, were scandalized by the King's anticlericalism. Giraldus deplored his ridiculing the clergy, and his frequent blasphemies. Louis VII, he wrote, did not—unlike some princes he could mention—swear by the eyes, the feet, the teeth or the throat of God, and his device was not bears or lions, but the simple lily. This reference to lions alludes to the royal arms: Henry probably used his father's device of three lions, derived from Henry I, while Eleanor's device was a golden lion on a red background. In 1172, she would become the first recorded member of the royal house to sport the heraldic device of three lions.

Henry worked hard to establish his authority in England, but his chief interests lay on the Continent. He found his continental domains more difficult to govern than his kingdom, especially Aquitaine, which remained in a state of almost constant revolt against him. Ruling such far-flung territories presented many practical difficulties in an age of poor communications, but, with his tremendous energy, Henry strove to overcome them. Henceforth, he would be constantly on the move, as he enforced his authority in his various lands. King Louis was astonished at the pace of Henry's travels: "Now in Ireland, now in England, now in Normandy, he must fly rather than travel by horse or ship!"[5]

By the time she became queen of England, at the age of thirty, Eleanor was already something of a legend. In Germany, her beauty was lauded in the contemporary collection of anonymous student songs known as the *Carmina Burana*:

> *If all the world were mine*
> *From the seashore to the Rhine,*
> *That price were not too high*
> *To have England's Queen lie*
> *Close in my arms.*[6]

In England and France, Eleanor's praises were sung in a more conventional manner, as in this tribute by Benoît de Sainte-Maure in his *Roman de Troie*:

> *High-born lady, excellent and valiant,*
> *True, understanding, noble,*
> *Ruled by right and justice,*
> *Queen of beauty and largesse,*
> *By whose example many ladies*
> *Are upheld in emulous right-doing;*

In whom all learning lodges,
Whose equal in no peer is found.
Rich lady of the wealthy King,
No ill, no ire, no sadness
Mars your goodly reign.
May all your days be joy.

In the introduction to his *Li Bestiaire* (*Bestiary*), formerly dedicated to Adeliza of Louvain, second queen of Henry I, and re-dedicated to Eleanor in the hope of acquiring a new patroness, the writer Philip de Thaon took a similar laudatory approach:

God save Lady Eleanor, Queen, who is the arbiter
Of honour, wit and beauty,
Of largesse and loyalty.
Lady, born were you in a happy hour
And wed to Henry, King.

For all her later fame, the chroniclers of Henry's reign rarely mention Eleanor, unless it is to record her presence by his side, the births of her children and her shortcomings. Some biographers have therefore concluded that she enjoyed little political power. Yet, although queens had no formal political role, there is evidence in official documents and the writings of John of Salisbury, secretary to Archbishop Theobald, that Henry allowed Eleanor an almost equal autonomy in decision-making and administrative matters, especially during his frequent absences abroad. Until 1163, even when he was in England, she issued numerous official documents or writs under her own name and seal. In short, she assisted effectively in the rule of the Plantagenet domains, especially Aquitaine.

But most chroniclers are strangely silent on all this, possibly because of prejudice against her sex and her role being overshadowed by Henry's achievements. The few observations the chroniclers did make about Eleanor are perceptive. Thomas Agnell, Archdeacon of Wells, called her "a woman of great discernment," and Gervase of Canterbury described her as "an exceedingly shrewd woman, sprung from noble stock, but unstable."

In 1156 and 1158, when Henry was away on the Continent, Eleanor acted as regent of England. At other times, up to 1163, she was co-regent with the Justiciar, the King's chief minister, and acted in association with him, sometimes overruling his decisions. Assisted by Henry's trusted advisers and "the faithful care of the Archbishop of Canterbury,"[7] she was entrusted with the power to defend the realm and take military action, should it be deemed necessary. She dealt with routine business, implemented orders sent by the King from abroad, approved the acts of his ministers, arbitrated in legal disputes and supervised accounts. Occasionally, she presided over courts and dispensed justice at Westminster, Cherbourg, Falaise, Bayeux and Bordeaux. According to John of Salisbury, she appointed bishops and fully dispensed royal power. Her rulings were drawn up by her clerk, Master Matthew, and her letters, dictated to her clerks and written in Latin, were signed "Eleanor, by the grace of God, Queen of England," although not in her own hand; the earliest extant signature of an English queen is that of Joanna of Navarre in the fifteenth century.

When the Bishop of Worcester resisted Eleanor's attempts to advance her clerk, Solomon, "a learned and honourable man" to the archdeaconry of Worcester, Archbishop Theobald intervened. It was the wish of the King and Queen, he told the Bishop, "but perhaps you will say that Master Solomon does not deserve such a favour, since he has stirred up the Queen's mind against your innocence. What else is this, but to accuse the Queen of lying? For she has excused him in your hearing?" The Bishop still refused to confer the post on Solomon.[8]

Eleanor was zealous in dealing with injustices. This is clear from letters recording her intervention in disputes. One was to John FitzRalph, a baron of London:

> I have received a complaint from the monks of Reading to the effect that they have been unjustly dispossessed of certain lands in London. I command you to look into this without delay and, should it be true, to ensure that these lands are returned to the monks without delay, so that, in future, I shall hear no more complaints about deficiencies in law and justice. I will not tolerate their being unjustly deprived of anything that belongs to them. Greetings.

Another letter was sent to the knights and tenants of Abingdon Abbey:

> I command that in all equity, and without delay, you provide Vau-
> quelin, Abbot of Abingdon, with those same services which your an-
> cestors provided in the days of King Henry, grandfather of our
> sovereign lord; and if you do not do so, then the King's justice and my
> own will make you do so.

This is not the tone of a woman conscious of the narrow parameters of
her authority, but of a ruler confident in her power to enforce her decrees, working in concert with her husband.

In a letter to the Sheriff of Suffolk, Eleanor castigated him for not
obeying Henry's order, "which much displeased my lord the King and
me. If you do not wish to [comply], the King's justice will be made to be
done."[9] To one of the sheriffs of London, she barked, "Until you enforce
the King's justice for London, I do not wish to hear more complaints
about default of justice."[10]

Yet Eleanor also had an innate kindness. Once, finding a child abandoned in the road near Abingdon, she arranged for him to be reared by
the monks at the abbey. And it will be seen how she took pity on those
suffering under an interdict.

6

"Rich Lady of
the Wealthy King"

✠

AS QUEEN, ELEANOR WAS RICH—HER INCOME HAS BEEN ESTI-
mated at £400 (£292,000) a year, twice the average of that of a
baron. On his accession, Henry provided her with an annual income in
cash, and endowed her with castles, towns, estates and manors. The earliest extant charter for an English queen's dower is that of Isabella of
Angoulême, wife of King John, which states that Isabella's assignment
was identical to Eleanor's. Eleanor held the lands that had been assigned to the queens of Henry I and Stephen, which were already regarded as the Queen's dower, with some assignments dating back to
Saxon times.

Her dower manors should have provided her with substantial revenues
in the form of annual rents, taxes and yields, and houses in which to
lodge while on her travels. Yet she did not gain control of her dower until
Henry's death; during his lifetime, all her revenues went to the Exchequer, which paid the running costs of her household and the salaries of
her servants and the officials who administered her estates. If she needed
money for private expenditure, the Keeper of the Royal Wardrobe provided it. Not until the thirteenth century were queens of England allowed to administer their own estates and income.

But Eleanor had income from other sources. By "custom of the kingdom,"[1] she had the right to claim queen-gold, which represented a considerable portion of her income. It was paid direct to a clerk of the

Exchequer she herself appointed, who had a thankless task collecting it, for it was very unpopular.

The Queen had her own household and officers: her treasurer, chancellor, attorneys and clerks, who administered her estates (which were run by her stewards and bailiffs), and her personal servants, including her chamberlain, butler, knights, esquires, chaplains, ladies, damsels and master of the horse—about forty people in all, including English servants and many Poitevin knights and clerks.

Eleanor was a pious woman and a great benefactress of religious institutions, especially in Poitou and Aquitaine, where she bestowed rich gifts and privileges on many abbeys and churches. She is said, without foundation, to have built the tiny church of Saint-Pierre de Mons, near Belin, where local annalists claimed she buried her "numerous bastards." Considering that her life was lived on so public a stage, it is hardly likely that she could have produced one bastard, let alone several, without the gossipy chroniclers of the age recording the fact.

The abbey of Fontevraud benefited especially from the Queen's patronage. She granted lands to the order, with the right to take timber and firewood from her forests. Around 1195, she built a great octagonal kitchen for the nuns, which boasted five fireplaces and twenty chimneys, and which still stands today. She also erected a wall around the cloister. Thanks to her patronage, Fontevraud's prestige increased, and it became an aristocratic institution fashionable with the daughters of kings and nobles.

In 1177, Henry II, a generous patron of Fontevraud, co-founded with Audeburge of Hautes-Bruyères, Abbess of Fontevraud, a cell of the order, the priory of Amesbury, Wiltshire, of which Eleanor was a benefactress. However, she fell out with the prioress, who threw a clerk out of Canterbury Cathedral "with violence and without any process of law, a wrong done to the Holy Roman Church and an affront to the King's Majesty," according to Archbishop Theobald. It was not the prioress's only offense. She refused to obey a command from Eleanor to arrange restoration works ordered by the King in the priory church. "If our lady the Queen corrects your breach of the King's proclamation by condign punishment, we shall ratify it!" Theobald thundered.[2]

Eleanor and Henry befriended the future saint, Gilbert of Sempringham, founder of the Gilbertine order. In the 1160s, when his lay brothers, irked by their poverty, accused the nuns and canons of fornication, the King and Queen rallied to Gilbert's side and five bishops declared the charges unfounded.

Henry II was said to have had more learning than any other European monarch of the age. When at leisure, "he occupies himself with private reading or takes great pains in working out some knotty question among his clerks."[3] He patronized poets and men of letters, especially those who glorified him and his dynasty.

Eleanor certainly wielded some intellectual influence over the cultural life of the court. However, her role as a literary patron was, until recently, overstated by historians. There is no record of her commissioning any works, although several writers and poets dedicated theirs to her, among them the Norman Robert Wace, a native of Jersey, who, around 1155, presented his *Le Roman de Brut* (a translation into French of Geoffrey of Monmouth's *History of the Kings of Britain*) to "the noble Eleanor, high King Henry's Queen, generous, gracious, wise and of great virtue." Henry II, whose patronage extended more widely than Eleanor's, also liked Wace's works and made him official court reader, with responsibility for giving lectures and readings; in 1160, he asked Wace to write a metrical history of the dukes of Normandy, *Le Roman de Rou* (Rou being Rollo, first Duke of Normandy and direct ancestor of William the Conqueror), such tales of ancestral heroic deeds being part of the literary traditions in which Henry and Eleanor had been raised.

Other works dedicated to Queen Eleanor included romances of Oedipus and Aeneas. A letter written by Peter of Blois reveals that she enjoyed performances of mystery and miracle plays, and he congratulated his brother, Abbot William of Blois, on his tragedy "Flora and Marcus," which had been played before the Queen, either at Westminster or Winchester. A life of "St. Edward the Confessor, King of England," by an anonymous nun of Barking, was dedicated jointly to Henry and Eleanor between 1163 and 1170.

Since the appearance of Geoffrey of Monmouth's *History of the Kings of Britain* around 1135, the Arthurian legends had rapidly won popularity in England. Henry had been taught them in childhood, while Eleanor may have been familiar with a poem in which Bernard de Ventadour compared his love for his lady with that of the doomed lovers, Tristan and Yseult. It has been suggested by more than one historian that Eleanor was the inspiration behind Wace's dark heroine, Guinevere. When the poet Layamon wrote his version of the *Brut* around 1300, basing it on Wace's original, he portrayed Guinevere as an evil woman; that too may have been inspired by Eleanor. As the Queen's reputation suffered after her death, so did that of her fictional counterpart.

Prior to 1173, the poet Thomas wrote a romance of Tristan and Yseult, which was probably dedicated to the King and Queen. A manuscript illumination in the Bibliothèque Nationale in Paris shows Henry and Eleanor listening to a poet reciting the story of Lancelot du Lac.

In the 1170s, Eleanor's court at Poitiers may have attracted Arthurian scholars, although there is little evidence for it, but the daughters she bore Henry carried the legends with them when they married into the courts of Germany, Castile and Sicily. The poet Marie de France, who spent much of her life at the English court, wrote five narrative poems, or lays, of King Arthur and Tristan and Yseult. Eleanor's daughter by Louis, Marie, Countess of Champagne, was the patron of Chrétien de Troyes, who wrote at least five poems based on the Arthurian legends and was the first to set them at Camelot and to recount the doomed romance of Lancelot and Guinevere.

Within decades, King Arthur had come to embody every contemporary ideal of knighthood and kingship. The stories told of him were widely accepted as historical fact and avidly embellished by writers and poets. By the 1170s, largely as a result of royal interest, the Arthurian legends had become enormously popular throughout Christendom. Their chivalric ethic reflected the aristocratic values of the age. There was so much speculation that Arthur still lived and was waiting on the Isle of Avalon to reclaim his kingdom that Henry II instituted a search for the hero-king's grave at Glastonbury Abbey, which many believed was Avalon, where Arthur was carried, mortally wounded. In 1191, the supposed bones of Arthur and Guinevere were discovered there at a depth of sixteen feet, along with a leaden cross inscribed "Here lies Arthur, the famous King, in the Island of Avalon." It was probably a clever fraud. The abbey had been gutted by fire in 1184 and, with pilgrimages having ceased, revenues had dried up. The miraculous discovery of the remains was timely indeed. The bones, genuine or not, were reburied with great ceremony in the Lady Chapel, which had survived the fire, as those of Arthur and Guinevere.

Walter Map grumbled that, although Henry II loved learning and was a friend to scholars, the Muses flourished less at his court than at any other. Cultivated the court may have been, but it was no haven for those with a taste for luxurious living, being a hive of frenetic activity encircling the ever-restless person of the King. Like all medieval courts, it rarely remained in one place for long. Its frequent moves were made in order to serve the interests of the state, facilitate the King's hunting expeditions or enable a residence to be cleaned, for twelfth-century sanitation comprised only primitive garderobes or chamber pots. When 250 people had been staying in a house for any length of time, the stink became intolerable, especially in summer.

Henry was "forever on his travels, covering distances in unbearably long stages, and in this respect merciless beyond measure to his household."[4] The court on the move was a straggling procession of horses, wagons, baggage carts and pack animals, including oxen, laden with luggage. The Queen and her ladies rode either on horseback or in brightly painted unsprung, barrel-shaped wagons with leather roofs.

Only on the great religious festivals did the court become a theater of ceremony. Henry was aware of the political value of royal display and, although fine clothes, luxury and personal comforts meant little to him, he purchased rich furs, silken robes, plate and jewels for great ceremonial occasions.

John of Salisbury, who compared Henry's court to ancient Babylon, particularly condemned the effeminate garments of the fashion-conscious nobles and gallants, and the newfangled polyphonic music Eleanor had introduced into England, which he believed kindled all kinds of licentiousness. He was scathing about the hangers-on who thought they could fawn their way to favor and advancement.

The food served at court was appalling, as was the wine. Peter of Blois recorded: "I have seen wine set before persons of eminent rank which was so thick that to get it down a man had to close his eyes, clench his teeth and sift it rather than drink it, grimacing with horror. On account of the great demand, cattle are sold to the court whether they are healthy or diseased, meat is sold whether it be fresh or not, and fish—four days old—is no cheaper for being putrid or foul-smelling." Nothing was ever done to improve matters because food was not important to the King. When the monks of St. Swithun at Winchester complained, weeping, that their bishop allowed them only ten courses at meals, Henry snapped, "In my court, I am satisfied with three. Perish your bishop if he doesn't cut your dishes down to the same."[5]

Eleanor played a prominent ceremonial role. She was often with the King when he received important visitors or envoys, and at royal banquets, religious ceremonies and state occasions. She was attended by the wives and daughters of the nobility; the records of payments and gifts to them contain the first references to ladies-in-waiting in England.

She had little success in imposing sophistication on Henry's court, but, in her own chambers, she enjoyed a higher standard of living than the King did, which she achieved through importing luxury items from abroad, including gold plates and goblets, and incense or musk for her chapel or to disguise the smell of the London fog. Payments for regular shipments of spices such as pepper, cumin and cinnamon show that she liked spicy food. In 1159, Henry sent her chestnuts, which cost him 3s. (£110). Her favorite wines came from La Rochelle or the Rhine.

Eleanor's rooms boasted tiled floors, glazed windows, silken hangings, and carpets imported from the Orient, and she always took tapestries and cushions with her on her travels. The Pipe Rolls of government expenditure record purchases of "oil for her lamps," linen for tablecloths, brass bowls, and sweet-scented rushes for the floor. Some of her servants gave her ivory dice each year instead of paying a monetary rent for lands they held of her. Large sums were spent on rich gowns and mantles with decorative embroidery in gold and silver, and linings or trimmings of fur. One robe alone cost £20 (nearly £15,000).

Eleanor was deeply devout, retaining many chaplains and clerks in her household, and would have spent a significant part of each day at her devotions. When not attending to her state and administrative duties, she may have read books and poetry and indulged her love of music, or perhaps undertaken some sewing and embroidery, those age-old pastimes of queens.

* * *

During Henry II's reign, the Crown owned perhaps sixty castles and several hunting lodges. Of the chief royal residences, three are still in use today: the Palace of Westminster, the Tower of London and Windsor Castle. Other important castles, such as those at Winchester, Nottingham, Ludgershall, Gloucester and Marlborough, are now lost or ruinous. In each residence, the royal apartments comprised a hall, chamber, bedchamber, wardrobe and chapel.

King Edward the Confessor's Thames-side palace at Westminster had been rebuilt by William II, who also erected the vast Westminster Hall, completed around 1099–1100, although its hammerbeam roof is fourteenth century. From Henry II's reign, the King's judges sat here to dispense justice. Nothing else survives of the Norman Palace of Westminster, although William FitzStephen described how it rose high above the river and was "an incomparable building ringed by an outwork and bastions." In 1153, King Stephen had built a new range of royal apartments, surrounded by orchards and woodlands extending down to the river. The older palace lay to the south and accommodated the various departments of state.

One of William the Conqueror's priorities had been to strengthen the defenses of London. Around 1078, in a corner of the ancient Roman wall on the north shore of the Thames, he began building a mighty keep. It was completed in 1097 and remained unchanged until 1190, when the building of two curtain walls, bisected by towers, began. The keep stood ninety feet high, with walls eleven feet thick. The Tower dominated London. It was not only a fortress and palace, but also a state prison, garrison, arsenal, armory, mint, wardrobe and treasure house—the crown jewels have always been kept there. On the upper floors of the Tower were a galleried hall, the royal apartments and a Norman chapel dedicated to St. John the Evangelist.

In 1070–80, completing his ring of fortresses around London, the Conqueror had erected a defensive wooden castle at Windsor. It commanded far-reaching views across a wide area and was surrounded by forests offering excellent hunting. William's tower had been built in Norman fashion on the summit of a steep earthwork, with courtyards known as the Lower Ward and Upper Ward on either side of it, forming a figure of eight, and it was surrounded by a wooden palisade and a ditch. The entrance was via a drawbridge and gate in the Lower Ward. The later Norman kings had added a range of royal apartments, a great hall, a kitchen and a chapel.

Around 1166–70, Henry II ordered that Windsor Castle be rebuilt in stone. The palisade was replaced by half a mile of massive stone walls, and other buildings including the tower (rebuilt in 1180 and thereafter known as the Round Tower) and the private royal apartments in the Upper Ward were also reconstructed in stone. Henry II's buildings have long disappeared. The earliest surviving room at Windsor is a thirteenth-century dungeon.

7

"All Things
Were Entrusted to Thomas"

✛

IT WAS PROBABLY DURING THE CHRISTMAS COURT OF 1154 THAT Archbishop Theobald recommended his most promising clerk, Thomas Becket, to the King as an excellent candidate for the office of chancellor. Becket, who was of Norman parentage, had been born in London *c.* 1118 and attended the schools of Paris. In 1143, influential friends, recognizing his talent as an administrator, secured him an appointment as a clerk in Theobald's household. The Archbishop soon recognized Becket's ability and earmarked him for promotion. Before long, he was being sent on diplomatic missions to Rome and elsewhere. By the time of Henry's accession, Theobald was convinced that his protégé would make a good chancellor and be a loyal champion of the Church.

Henry took an instant liking to Becket and agreed to the appointment without hesitation. Thus began one of the most famous friendships in history.

Becket was tall and slim, with dark hair, chiseled features and elegant, tapering hands. Like Henry, he was a man of vigor and versatile talent. His chief pleasures were hunting, hawking and chess, although he avoided women, having taken a vow of chastity in youth. He was elegant, witty, generous, vain and ambitious, and thrived on the public role that went with his promotion to chancellor, indulging his love of display in magnificent clothes and an extravagant standard of living. He took things to extremes, being self-willed and uncompromising.

"The King and Becket played together like little boys of the same age, at the court, in church, in assemblies, in riding."[1] Henry, who was fifteen years younger, recognized Becket's worth, and Becket served him faithfully and efficiently as chancellor. "All things were entrusted to Thomas. While the King gave himself up to youthful pursuits, Thomas governed the whole realm according to his will."[2] "Throughout the kingdom there was none his equal save the King alone."[3]

History does not record what Eleanor thought of this friendship, although it almost certainly undermined her influence with the King. When Henry was abroad, it was now Becket, rather than the Queen, who dispensed patronage on his behalf and received important visitors to England. He sometimes assisted Eleanor during her regencies, but her political influence was being relentlessly eroded and, after 1163, she issued no more writs. It is possible that Becket deliberately sidelined her. There is no evidence that she resented him when he was chancellor, although her mother-in-law, the Empress Maud, disapproved of him and made no bones about saying so. Yet this was one issue on which Henry ignored his mother's otherwise welcome advice.

Eleanor was still at Bermondsey when on Monday, February 28, she gave birth to a second son, who—to underline royal continuity—was baptized Henry, after her husband's hero, Henry I. Giraldus states that Henry's sons were "brought up by their mother, Queen Eleanor," who was assisted by nurses, servants and tutors. Queens and noblewomen did not nurse their infants, but handed them over at birth into the care of wet nurses, freeing themselves to become pregnant again.

In 1156, young Henry was provided with a governor called Mainard, who stayed until 1159, when the boy's military training began under the guidance of one of the King's marshals. Governors were appointed for all Henry and Eleanor's sons during their infancy. They provided for the princes' material needs and were in charge of their servants.

The records show that Eleanor kept her children with her as often as possible, took them on her travels and showed great interest in them, concerning herself particularly with their education and marriages, as was expected of a queen. High-born ladies were not expected to be hands-on mothers involved in the daily care of their children. Their duty was to appoint suitable nurses and attendants who would look after them. While her children were young, Eleanor's official commitments seem to have taken up much of her time, but that is not to say that she was not close to them—her love for them is manifest in her later actions, when they were adults. Accusations that she was a bad mother, measured against what was expected of a royal mother in her day, do not stand up.

In April 1155, at a council at Wallingford, Henry and Eleanor presented their sons to the barons and clergy, whom Henry commanded to swear allegiance to two-year-old William as the heir to England; in case William died young, they were also required to swear fealty to young Henry.

At Easter, Henry ordered Becket to oversee restoration works at the Palace of Westminster. Becket undertook his task with such energy and enthusiasm that the palace was ready for occupation by Whitsun, when Eleanor took up residence there. Around this time, she commissioned the building of her own dock in Thames Street, known as Queenhithe. Here, ships from Aquitaine would, in future, find moorings.

Soon afterward, Eleanor accompanied the King on a tour through his realm, visiting Worcester, Salisbury and other important towns, after which Henry spent some weeks hunting with Becket in the New Forest. In September, Eleanor rejoined him at Winchester for a great council, accompanied by the Empress Maud, who was making her only visit to England during her son's reign. William the Conqueror had built the King's Castle at Winchester, although nothing remained of his works after its demolition by Oliver Cromwell's men in the seventeenth century, and the surviving great hall dates only from 1235. From 1155, Henry II rebuilt the castle in stone along with "the King's houses" within its precincts. The castle boasted a painted chamber in Eleanor's time.

The King and Queen spent the autumn on progress, visiting Salisbury, Cirencester, Worcester, Northampton, Woodstock, Newbury and Windsor, and celebrated Christmas at Winchester.

In January 1156, Henry returned to Normandy to attend to the affairs of his continental fiefs, leaving the Justiciar, Richard de Lucy, as regent and placing Eleanor and their sons under the guardianship of Archbishop Theobald and John of Salisbury. On February 5, he met King Louis on the Norman border and finally, as its duke, paid him homage for Aquitaine, making it clear who was now in control. This marked the end of Eleanor's political authority in her domains; she issued no more charters for the next ten years, although she retained her seal and continued to patronize religious establishments. Henceforth, Henry would hold sway in Aquitaine and Poitou.

That spring, Eleanor spent time in London and traveled through the southern shires, running up a high expenditure of £350 (£256,000). Although she was not officially associated with Richard de Lucy in the regency, the numerous writs issued in her name at this time attest to the fact that she was actively involved in government.

In April, she was at Wallingford when her eldest son, William, who was not quite three years old, died there of a seizure. Henry was still abroad. It may have been at his wish that Eleanor, who was in the last months of pregnancy, arranged the child's burial at the feet of his great-grandfather, Henry I, in Reading Abbey. It was probably Eleanor's benefactions, made for the soul of her son, that prompted the monks to admit her to the confraternity of Reading Abbey, a rare privilege that conferred on her the patronal status of charitable sisterhood. At her request, Henry gave a gift to Hurley Priory, Berkshire, for William's soul.

The grief Henry and Eleanor felt at losing their firstborn may have been assuaged a little by the birth of a daughter in June, in London. She was baptized by Archbishop Theobald in the church of the Holy Trinity at Aldgate and named Matilda in honor of the Empress, Maud being a variant of that name. The Pipe Rolls list the purchase of a baby carriage for the child, one of the first ever recorded.

Late in July, Eleanor crossed the Channel with Matilda and the Lord Henry. By August 29, she had been reunited with the King in Anjou. In October, they undertook a great progress through Aquitaine, with Henry receiving homage from Eleanor's vassals and taking hostages to ensure that they did not break their oaths. At Limoges, to underline his authority, he installed Norman officials. One baron who had caused trouble for Eleanor in the past was Geoffroy IV, Viscount of Thouars. Henry expelled him from his lands in Poitou and razed all his castles.

Archbishop Geoffrey of Loroux invited Henry and Eleanor to keep their Christmas court at Bordeaux, where more of Eleanor's lieges came to swear fealty to the Duke and he proclaimed his peace over Eleanor's domains. She may have felt resentful that they did not pay homage to her too, as their sovereign duchess.

By the end of February 1157, she was back in London with her children. In April, Henry rejoined her in England, and at Whitsun they were at St. Edmundsbury (the town was not called Bury St. Edmunds until the fifteenth century) for a ceremonial crown-wearing and a meeting of the Great Council.

When, at the end of July, Henry set out at the head of his army on a campaign against Owain Gwynedd, Prince of North Wales, who was threatening to take Chester, Eleanor acted as regent and Archbishop Theobald and John of Salisbury were again entrusted with "the safe custody of the illustrious Queen of the English and the King's sons."[4]

Henry was unused to the guerrilla tactics employed by his Welsh opponents, who paid no heed to the normal rules of warfare and routinely decapitated their enemies. During an early skirmish, he barely escaped with his life, leaving many of his men dead in the field. Defeated, he negotiated a truce, then embarked on a progress that would take him the length and breadth of England, enabling him to see his kingdom and be seen by his subjects. Becket was among those summoned north to join the King, but Eleanor, who was pregnant, remained at Westminster.

In early August, she joined Henry at Oxford and took up residence in the King's House, later known as Beaumont Palace, which stood near the north gate of the city. Built around 1130 by Henry I, it was a massive complex of wooden and stone buildings, surrounded by a defensive wall. It had a great chamber, a great hall adorned with murals, two chapels, a cloister and private quarters for the use of the Queen. It was in the King's House, on September 8, 1157, that Eleanor gave birth to a third son, named Richard, probably after the early dukes of Normandy.

The infant was given into the care of a nurse, Hodierna of St. Albans, whose own son, Alexander Nequam, had been born the same night. Alexander grew up to be one of the greatest scientists of the age, the author of a treatise on natural history and the first European to study magnetism. Richard grew fond of Hodierna and, years later, when he became king, he rewarded her with a large pension.

It seems likely that Richard was designated the heir to Poitou and Aquitaine, while his older brother Henry was to inherit England and Normandy. Ralph of Diceto recalled one of the ancient prophecies of Merlin, which were widely believed to apply to Henry II and his family:

"The eagle of the broken covenant shall rejoice in her third nesting."[5] Eleanor was the eagle, the broken covenant the dissolution of her marriage to Louis, and the third nesting was the birth of her third son, Richard.

The Queen seems to have gone to nearby Woodstock to rest after her confinement. The royal hunting lodge there had also been built by Henry I, and was surrounded by forest and a well-stocked deer park. Here, Henry I had founded the first royal menagerie in order to house the animals sent to him as gifts by foreign rulers. They included lions, leopards, lynxes, camels, a porcupine and, later, Richard I's crocodile.

From Woodstock, Eleanor joined Henry on his progress. Over the next year, he traveled a staggering 3,500 miles and, for much of that time, she was with him. The Christmas court of 1157 was held at Lincoln, where the King and Queen wore their crowns. They had revived a tradition established by the Conqueror to underline the sacred nature of his kingship, ceremonially wearing their crowns at courts held at Christmas, Easter and Whitsun.

In the middle of January, as Henry rode north, Eleanor went to Winchester, then to London. At Easter, they were together at Worcester. After the Easter mass and crown-wearing in the cathedral, "they took off their crowns and offered them up on the altar, vowing to God that never in their lives would they be crowned with any others."[6] Then they laid them upon the tomb of the saintly Bishop Wulfstan.

After visiting Shropshire, they traveled to London via Gloucestershire, Wiltshire, Somerset, Devon, Dorset and Kent. Then they journeyed through the eastern counties to Northamptonshire and Rutland, continuing north to Carlisle, which they reached in June.

During this arduous progress, Eleanor realized she was pregnant again. Still mourning her son William and fearing that she might lose another child in infancy, she asked Robert of Cricklade, Prior of St. Frideswide's, Oxford, who was going to Rome, if he could obtain for her a book on infant and child care. Her request found its way to Constantinople, whereupon the Emperor Manuel Comnenos sent an envoy to England with a Byzantine text, the *Gynaecia Cleopatrae*, a manual that also gave advice on bearing and rearing children and was believed to have been written by Cleopatra herself.

* * *

Early in 1158, Constance of Castile had borne Louis VII a daughter, Marguerite, prompting him to complain about "the frightening superfluity of his daughters."[7] Henry was keen to marry Marguerite to the Lord Henry. Should Louis die without a male heir, she would be his co-heiress with her half-sisters. The Salic law forbade succession to the French throne by or through a woman, but Henry was apparently confident of his ability to overcome this difficulty and annex the kingdom of France to his empire. Even if Louis did have a son, the marriage would bring peace between the two kingdoms and a settlement advantageous to Henry.

In the summer of 1158, Henry sent Becket to France to negotiate with Louis. Becket traveled with a magnificent escort, his purpose being to overwhelm Louis with this display of England's wealth and persuade him to agree to the marriage. To sweeten the French, he brought with him rich gifts, including chests full of gold. The ploy worked: Louis received Becket like a visiting prince and agreed to the betrothal.

At the end of July, the long progress came to an end when the King and Queen reached Winchester. On August 14, having received news of the death of his brother Geoffrey, Count of Nantes, Henry crossed to France, leaving Eleanor, nearly eight months pregnant, at Winchester with their children, acting as co-regent with Richard de Lucy.

Henry met Louis near Gisors, where the final terms of the marriage alliance were agreed upon. Louis ceded his claim to the Norman Vexin and the castle of Gisors. He also agreed to recognize Henry as his brother's successor in Brittany, to the detriment of the rival heirs of the late Count Conan III. As a pledge of Louis's good intentions, Marguerite was to be handed over to Henry immediately. After the meeting, Henry rode straight to Brittany and took possession of Nantes, its capital. His plan was to conquer the whole of Brittany, but, having other claims on his resources at present, he was obliged to content himself with leaving his new vassal, Conan IV, grandson of Conan III, in charge.

In September, Henry was warmly welcomed by Louis in Paris, where Queen Constance relinquished her six-month-old daughter Marguerite into his custody. Louis had stipulated that under no circumstances was Marguerite to be brought up by Queen Eleanor, which speaks volumes about his opinion of her; Henry therefore placed the child in the care of the trustworthy Robert of Neubourg, chief justice of Normandy, whose castle stood near the French border.

On September 23, Eleanor presented Henry with a fourth son, who was named Geoffrey after the King's late brother. After her churching—the religious ceremony of purification after childbirth—she heard a great many cases in her own assize court, traveling through ten counties and dispensing justice "by writ of the King from over seas." Toward the end of the year, leaving Geoffrey in England, she joined Henry at Cherbourg for Christmas. Early in 1159, they set out on another tour of Aquitaine.

By then, Henry had resolved to reassert Eleanor's ancestral rights to the county of Toulouse. She must have been keen for him to do so, although Henry would have realized for himself, as Louis had eighteen years earlier, that there were considerable advantages to be gained from the acquisition of a wealthy domain that encompassed the key trade routes to the Mediterranean. When Louis heard of Henry's intentions, he begged him to desist, for the sake of their alliance, since Raymond V, Count of Toulouse, was married to his sister Constance, whose son was the heir to Toulouse, and Louis did not want to see his nephew dispossessed. But Henry would not be deterred, demanding that Raymond relinquish Toulouse to Eleanor. Raymond refused.

Eleanor was probably in Poitiers when, early in July, Henry's forces laid siege to Toulouse. When Louis arrived and took charge of the city's defenses, Henry found himself in a difficult position, for he was reluctant to break his oath of allegiance and make war on his overlord, as it would set a dangerous precedent for his own vassals. He withdrew from Toulouse and deployed his men in harrying the surrounding area, in the hope of forcing Raymond to surrender. He also sent a force north to raid the royal demesne, hoping to lure Louis away. But Louis stayed entrenched in the city. By the autumn, Henry's army had been decimated by dysentery and, at the end of September, he was obliged to abandon the campaign. He and Eleanor were reunited in time for Christmas, which they celebrated at Falaise in Normandy.

Henry had now been out of England for seventeen months, but his presence was still needed on the Continent, so he arranged for Eleanor to cross the Channel to look to the affairs of his kingdom and arrange the transfer of urgently needed funds from his treasury. On December 29,

1159, in a violent storm, the Queen sailed from Normandy with young Henry and Matilda in the royal *esnecca*. Having docked safely at Southampton, she rode to Winchester to collect the gold, escorted it back to Southampton and herself accompanied it on its voyage to Barfleur. After entrusting it there to Henry's officials, she immediately returned to England.

For the next nine months, she was busy with her duties as regent, since Becket had remained in France with Henry. Despite the severe weather, she embarked on an extensive tour through ten counties, wishing to see for herself that the kingdom was being administered properly. During this period many writs were issued in her name. Thirteen were for Exchequer payments amounting to £226 (£164,940) for her own expenditure and £56 (£40,870) for that of the Lord Henry. At Winchester, she paid £22 13s. 2d. (£16,537) "for the repair of the chapel, the houses, the walls and the garden of the Queen, and for the transport of the Queen's robes, her wine, her incense and the chests of her chapel, and for the boys' shields."[8]

8

"The King Has
Wrought a Miracle"

✠

I N THE SUMMER OF 1160, ARCHBISHOP THEOBALD PLEADED
with the King to return to England, reminding him that it was a long
time since he had seen his children. "Even the most hard-hearted father
could hardly bear to have them out of his sight for long," he wrote. But
Henry had his hands full on the Continent and when, in September, he
commanded Eleanor to join him in Rouen, bringing with her Henry and
Matilda, his motive was political. The Queen of France was about to bear
a child; if it was a boy, Henry hoped to arrange his betrothal to Matilda.
He took his son to the border to present him to Louis as the heir to Normandy. The child knelt before the French King and did homage for the
duchy.

On October 4, Queen Constance bore another daughter, Alys, "and
passed from this world."[1] Desperate for a male heir, Louis, now forty, immediately negotiated a marriage with Adela of Champagne, the sister of
Henry of Champagne and Theobald of Blois, both of whom were hostile
to Henry II. News of the betrothal dashed Henry's hopes of absorbing
France into his empire. Even if Adela failed to bear Louis a son, the powerful House of Blois would conspire to subvert Henry's schemes. It was
imperative that the marriage of the Lord Henry and Marguerite take
place without delay. Louis's consent was implicit in the marriage contract, so there was no need to consult him. All the King needed was a
dispensation. It so happened that, following a schism in 1159, rival popes

had laid claim to the triple crown of St. Peter and, at that very moment, two cardinal legates, emissaries from Pope Alexander III, were at Henry's court, seeking his support for their master. It was therefore easy for Henry to procure what he needed.

Marguerite and the Lord Henry were married at Rouen. The bridegroom was five, the bride not yet three—"as yet little children crying in the cradles."[2] Henry took Marguerite into his own household as a hostage against any reprisals by her father, but by 1164, she was in Eleanor's establishment, against Louis's express wish.

On November 13, Louis married Adela of Champagne. When he found out how Henry had tricked him, he was furious. He protested that, since his daughter's wedding had taken place earlier than he had intended, he was not obliged to surrender her dowry, and he encouraged Theobald of Blois to take up arms against Henry. Fearing that Touraine was under threat, Henry hastened south and took Theobald's castle of Chaumont on the Loire as a warning.

The arrival of winter put an end to the fighting season. In December, Henry rode to Le Mans, where he and Eleanor kept court in great state throughout Advent and Christmas.

On April 18, 1161, Archbishop Theobald died. Eleanor may have been present at his burial in Canterbury Cathedral. His death left the King with the problem of finding another such to him. Immediately, Henry thought of Becket, but Eleanor, the Empress and the respected Gilbert Foliot, Bishop of Hereford, tried to dissuade him, warning him that Becket was too worldly a man for high ecclesiastical office.

There the matter rested, for, in the spring of 1161, Henry was busy preparing for war against Louis. Trouble in Aquitaine, however, took him south in the summer. "Amongst other vigorous deeds, he laid siege to Castillon-sur-Agen, and took it within a week, to the wonder and terror of the Gascons."[3] He was apparently installing Norman administrators in the duchy to enforce centralized government on its unruly barons. Unlike Eleanor, he did not repose much confidence in the ability of her uncle, Raoul de Faye, to act as her deputy.

His interference was widely resented. "The Poitevins withdrew from their allegiance to the King of the English because of his pruning of their liberties."[4] They even tried to have his marriage to their Duchess dissolved, sending a deputation to the Papal legates with a genealogical table showing that Henry and Eleanor were related within the forbidden degrees of consanguinity. But the legates were in no position to offend Henry by even suggesting such a thing; they were still busy ingratiating themselves on Pope Alexander's behalf. Henry was able that year to secure the canonization of the Saxon King, Edward the Confessor, and thereby enhance the prestige of the English monarchy.

Eleanor was back in Normandy by September 1161, when she gave birth to another daughter at Domfront Castle. The child was named after her; to distinguish her from her mother, she will here be called Leonor, the Castilian name she adopted on marriage. She was baptized by the legate, Cardinal Henry of Pisa, and Robert of Torigni and the Bishop of Avranches were her godfathers. Three years had elapsed since the birth of Geoffrey, and historians have conjectured why, after Eleanor had borne four children in as many years, there was such a gap. Ralph of Diceto states that she had six sons with Henry, two of whom died in boyhood. One was William; the other may have been born during this gap, or between the births of Leonor in 1161 and the Queen's third daughter in 1165. John Speed, whose *History of Great Britain* was published in 1611, stated that Henry and Eleanor had a son named Philip, who was born between 1158 and 1162, but died young. Speed did not cite his source. The name Philip was favored by the French monarchy, but had never been used by the forebears of Henry and Eleanor, although the name John, which they bestowed on their sixth son, hadn't either.

Louis had realized that warring with Henry over Marguerite's marriage was futile and, in October, the two kings met at Fréteval and made peace. Henry and Eleanor kept Christmas at Bayeux. In March 1162, they were at Fécamp for the reburial of Henry's ancestors, dukes Richard I and Richard II of Normandy. The King was still considering who should fill the vacant archbishopric of Canterbury and, by the time he and Eleanor held their Easter court at Falaise, he had made up his mind to appoint Becket. Becket was loyal and would, he felt sure, support the radical plans he was formulating for reforming abuses within the Church.

In 1161, concern had been expressed in several quarters that the Lord

Henry, now seven years old, was still living with his mother and had not begun his formal education. Hugh, Archbishop of Rouen, had written to the King: "All your bishops unanimously agree that Henry, your son and heir, should apply himself to letters, so that he whom we regard as your heir may be the successor to your wisdom as well as your kingdom."[5] Henry took the point. It was customary for princes and the sons of the nobility to be sent to aristocratic households to be nurtured and educated. Becket already had charge of a number of noble boys and, that Easter, at Falaise, the King and Queen entrusted to him the Lord Henry "to bring up and instruct in courtly ways."[6] Henceforth, Becket would refer to the boy as his adopted son. The King commanded him to take his charge to England and have the barons swear fealty to him as their future monarch. When Becket brought Henry to say farewell to his parents, the King took him aside.

"You do not yet fully comprehend your mission," he said. "It is my intention that you should become Archbishop of Canterbury."[7]

Becket was horrified. He was aware of Henry's planned reforms and realized that, as archbishop, he would be honor-bound to oppose them. He begged the King to reconsider, warning him that, if he forced this appointment, their friendship would turn to bitter hatred. Besides, he was not even a priest, and had never celebrated mass.

Henry ignored his protests. His mind was made up. With a heavy heart, Becket departed for England. His last act as chancellor was to arrange the ceremony at which the barons paid homage to the Lord Henry, which took place at Whitsun in Winchester. He also paid £38 6s. (£27,950) "for gold for preparing a crown and regalia for the King's son,"[8] for Henry intended to have his heir crowned in his lifetime, as French kings did.

On June 3, 1162, Becket was consecrated archbishop in Canterbury Cathedral, with tears of emotion streaming down his face. It seemed to contemporaries that a miraculous transformation took place that day. "As he put on those robes, reserved at God's command to the highest of His clergy, he changed not only his apparel, but the cast of his mind."[9]

Overnight, the proud and worldly Becket had become an ascetic priest committed to his spiritual duties. He had changed, he declared, "from a patron of play actors and a follower of hounds to a shepherd of souls."[10] Beneath his monk's habit, to mortify his flesh, he wore "a hair shirt of the roughest kind, which reached to his knees and swarmed with vermin." He ate "the sparest diet"[11] and performed extravagant acts of charity and humility, washing the feet of thirteen beggars every day, and exposing his bare back to the discipline of flagellation by his monks. "The King has wrought a miracle," observed the sceptical Bishop Foliot. "Out of a soldier and a courtier he has made an archbishop."

After his consecration, Becket shocked Henry by returning the great seal of England and resigning the chancellorship, making plain his intention to devote his life to the Church. Yet, to begin with, he would still play a prominent political role, for medieval archbishops, however saintly, were powerful politicians and landowners, and acted as the King's counselors.

The King and Queen had intended to return to England in December, but were prevented by storms in the Channel and were obliged to hold their Christmas court at Cherbourg. On January 25, 1163, they sailed from Barfleur to Southampton. It was the first time Henry had set foot in his kingdom since August 1158.

The royal couple were received by a large deputation of nobles and clergy, headed by Archbishop Becket. They hastened to him as he came forward holding the hand of the Lord Henry, who greeted his parents with fond embraces as onlookers cried, "*Vivat rex!*"[12] Henry and Becket embraced warmly and exchanged kisses of peace. The following day, they rode side by side to Westminster, deep in amicable conversation.

In February 1163, the Pipe Rolls record Eleanor's purchases of pork and sheep for the festivities arranged for the Lord Henry's eighth birthday, which he apparently celebrated with her and his siblings at Winchester.

The King would spend the next three years in England, implementing his plans for enforcing law and order in his realm. His return marked the end of Eleanor's intermittent spells as regent. He had not lost confidence in her ability to rule in his absence, for he would in future delegate authority to her on the Continent, but it was the all-powerful Becket who now undertook the administrative duties she had carried out in England.

* * *

One of Henry's chief concerns at this time was the recent increase in crimes committed by the clergy. Lay felons were dealt with in the King's courts, where they were punished with due severity, but anyone in holy orders—even the lowliest clerk—could claim benefit of clergy and be tried in the church courts, which were not allowed to shed the blood of offenders and imposed only light penalties. The King thought this situation scandalous and unfair, and he was determined to ensure that all offenders were tried in the royal courts. He was aware that the enforcement of such a measure would be seen by many as an attack on the Church and would meet with resistance, yet he was determined to have his way.

In July, Eleanor was present at Woodstock when Henry's lieges swore fealty to young Henry as his successor. The royal family then moved to Windsor for August.

On October 1, at a meeting of the Great Council at Westminster, the King proposed that the Church should hand over "criminous clerks" to the royal courts "for corporal punishment."[13] Becket refused to sanction any infringement of the authority and liberties of the Church, and Henry stormed out of the hall. The following day, before he left Westminster at dawn, he removed the Lord Henry from Becket's household and gave him an establishment and servants of his own. Thus began one of the most famous rifts in history.

On October 13, both king and archbishop were present in Westminster Abbey when the body of St. Edward the Confessor was translated to a new shrine. Probably Eleanor and her children were there too. Outwardly, relations were amicable. But it soon seemed to Henry that Becket was deliberately trying to provoke him, going out of his way to ensure that crimes committed by clerks—including theft, manslaughter, rape and murder—went unpunished or earned only the lightest sentences.

Counseled by the Empress, who always gave him sensible advice on how to deal with Becket, Henry had Becket's enemy, Gilbert Foliot, transferred to the see of London to lead the opposition to him. Other bishops, perturbed by the Archbishop's aggressive stance, began to distance themselves from him, and Pope Alexander III, who had reason to be grateful to Henry, urged Becket to submit to his master. In December, Becket acknowledged defeat and swore to uphold the King's laws.

* * *

The year 1164 saw the marriages of Eleanor's daughters by Louis: Marie married Henry, Count of Champagne, and Alix married his brother, Theobald, Count of Blois. Eleanor did not attend. There is no record of her having any contact with her daughters in the years following her divorce from Louis. It may be significant that neither Marie nor Alix named any of their daughters after their mother.

At Clarendon, near Salisbury, stood a hunting lodge much favored by Henry II. At a council held there on January 25, 1164, Henry demanded that the clergy endorse a new code of laws, which became known as the Constitutions of Clarendon, and which he claimed enshrined the customs of his ancestors. The third article, which did not, laid down that criminous clerks should be handed over to the royal courts for sentencing. Becket protested hotly against it, and was backed by the Pope, who condemned nearly every clause of the Constitutions. Becket tried twice to escape to France, but was frustrated by adverse winds, the King's officers and Queen Eleanor. When John of Salisbury approached her for a sealed writ permitting him to travel to Normandy, she guessed that he was going there to seek a refuge for Becket and refused it.

Eleanor may have been present with the King on April 19, when Becket consecrated Reading Abbey, founded by Henry I. During the summer, the Archbishop was briefly entertained by the royal couple at Woodstock; it must have been a strained visit, for Henry was now determined to oust Becket from his see, a move that was supported by the bishops. In October, he had Becket arraigned at a council at Northampton on a charge of contempt of court. When Henry called him to account for the disposition of moneys that had passed through his hands as chancellor, it became clear to Becket that the King was out to ruin him.

At Henry's behest, the bishops agreed to inform the Pope that Becket had breached the oath he had sworn upholding the Constitutions of Clarendon, and to request his deposition. The King called for sentence to be passed on him, but Becket stalked out of the room to shouts of "Traitor!" That night, disguised as a monk, he fled to Flanders.

On the Continent, he continued to make trouble for the King. He portrayed himself to the Pope so convincingly as a victim of the King's deliberate attempt to limit the Church's power that he won Alexander's sympathy, and thereafter it would require the deployment of all Henry's skills in diplomacy to avoid an open breach with the Holy See. Becket also wrote numerous letters trying to enlist the sympathy of other European rulers, several of whom attempted to exploit the quarrel to their own advantage. Louis VII took the exiled Archbishop under his protection and offered him refuge in France. Between 1165 and 1170, he arranged no fewer than twelve interviews between Henry and Becket; all ended in failure, for neither king nor archbishop would agree to compromise. What had begun as a dispute over a legal principle had turned into a battle of wills over whose was the greater authority.

On Christmas Eve 1164, Henry was appalled to hear that the Pope had threatened him with excommunication. "The King, burning with his customary fury, threw the cap from his head, undid his belt, threw far from him the cloak and robes in which he was dressed, with his own hands tore the silken coverlet off the bed, and, sitting down as though on a dung-heap, began to chew the straw of the mattress."[14] He remained in a foul mood throughout Christmas Day and, "giving way to unbridled passion, he took an unbecoming kind of revenge by banishing all the Archbishop's relatives out of England."[15]

In February 1165, Henry crossed to Normandy. At Rouen, as a means of putting pressure on the Pope to abandon Becket, he opened negotiations for an alliance with the Holy Roman Emperor, Frederick Barbarossa, who had been supporting Alexander's rivals for the papacy. The alliance was to be cemented by the marriages of Henry's daughters: Matilda to Henry the Lion, Duke of Saxony and Bavaria, the Emperor's cousin and foremost vassal; and Leonor to the Emperor's infant son, Frederick.

The Queen had remained at Winchester. Around this time, she and her children visited Sherborne Castle in Dorset and the Isle of Wight before moving to Westminster, where, on Henry's orders, she summoned a council to confirm the German alliance. After the marriage treaty was concluded, Reinald of Dassel, Archbishop of Cologne, crossed the Channel to pay his respects to the Queen and be introduced to her daughters.

On 1 May, Eleanor left her other children in England and took Richard and Matilda to join Henry in Normandy before he left to undertake a campaign against the Welsh. After his departure, she based herself at Angers, having been entrusted with the government of Anjou and Maine in his absence.

Becket contemplated asking Eleanor to intervene on his behalf in his quarrel with the King. In August 1165, Jean de Bellesmains, Bishop of Poitiers, informed him that Theodoric, Count of Flanders, "working for your peace, at the request of the Empress and the Queen, has sent a distinguished party of men to the King." He also warned Becket that he could "hope for neither aid nor counsel from the Queen, for she puts all her trust in Raoul de Faye, who is no less hostile toward you than usual." Eleanor appears to have been influenced more by her uncle than by her husband, which is perhaps the first indication that she and Henry were growing apart. Bellesmains observed that her relationship with Raoul was subject to "conjectures which grow day by day, which make it possible to believe that there is truth in the dishonourable tales we remember mentioning elsewhere."[16] The implication was that Raoul de Faye was not just an undesirable political influence, but that there was a degree of attraction between uncle and niece. Eleanor, however, was four months pregnant with her ninth child at this time, and we hear no more rumors about her and Raoul.

9

"The Wench Rosamund"

✠

ELEANOR WAS AT ANGERS AT THE END OF AUGUST WHEN NEWS arrived from France that Queen Adela had borne King Louis a healthy son, who was baptized Philip and nicknamed "Dieudonné" (God-given) and "Augustus," after the month of his birth. There were joyous celebrations in Paris, but the birth of this prince would have fatal consequences for the Angevin Empire.

Eleanor was hearing lawsuits "in the court of our lady the Queen" and having trouble enforcing her authority over Henry's vassals in Maine and on the Breton border, who were plotting rebellion against him. At her command, the Constable of Normandy raised a force, but was unable to overcome them, largely, it appears, because her orders were treated with contempt by his men. Nor could the King come to her aid because he was heavily beset in Wales.

In September 1165, Henry returned to England, having failed to subdue the Welsh. In savage retribution, he ordered the mutilation of the hostages he had taken, then took himself off to Woodstock. The Pipe Rolls and other records show that he was chiefly based there until March 1166, leaving only for brief trips to Winchester and Clarendon. It was unheard of for him to stay in one place for six months. When, in October 1165, Eleanor gave birth to another daughter, Joanna, at Angers, he did not join her, nor, for the first time since their marriage, did he keep Christmas with her, at Angers, but held court alone at Oxford.

It is not known when Henry began his notorious affair with the beautiful Rosamund de Clifford, but the attraction may have flowered at this time and been sufficiently strong to keep him rooted in one place. During the Welsh campaign, Rosamund's father, Sir Walter de Clifford, a knight of Norman extraction with six daughters, had performed his feudal service for the King, and it is possible that Henry received hospitality at Sir Walter's border stronghold at Bredelais and there made Rosamund's acquaintance.

According to Giraldus, Rosamund was very young when the affair began, and it had lasted some years before it was publicly acknowledged in 1174. In 1166, probably during his long stay at Woodstock, Henry constructed a water garden by the spring at Everswell, west of the palace, with pools and baths surrounded by a cloister. The remains of it were described by John Aubrey in the seventeenth century. From his drawings, it appears that Everswell was modeled on the water gardens of Moorish Spain. In the early thirteenth century, when there was a small range of royal apartments at Everswell, there is a reference to "Rosamund's chamber, unroofed by the wind," which was probably built for her by Henry II. But it was only from the sixteenth century that Everswell was known as "Rosamund's well." The ruins of Everswell are now under the lake at Blenheim Palace, but the well can still be seen. There was a "Rosamund's chamber" at the royal hunting lodge Henry built at Clipstone in Sherwood Forest, and one at Winchester too.

Rosamund is barely mentioned in contemporary sources. It is through later legends, which have evolved over eight centuries, that she has become famous. No other mistress of an English king has ever inspired so many romantic myths.

Early in the fourteenth century, the chronicler Ranulf Higden asserted in his *Polychronicon* that Henry II "was privily a spouse breaker" and was not ashamed "to misuse the wench Rosamund. To this fair wench the King made at Woodstock a chamber of wonder craft, wonderfully made by Daedalus' work [i.e. a labyrinth], lest the Queen should find and take Rosamund." This is the first reference to Henry building a bower and labyrinth for Rosamund at Woodstock.

By 1458, the legend had been embroidered:

> One day, Queen Eleanor saw the King walking in the pleasance of Woodstock with the end of a ball of floss-silk attached to his spur. Coming near him, unperceived, she took up the ball and, the King

walking onward, the silk unwound, and thus the Queen traced him to a thicket in the labyrinth of the park, where he disappeared. Soon after, the King left Woodstock for a distant journey, then Queen Eleanor searched the thicket in the park and found a low door cunningly concealed; this door she had forced, and found it was the entrance to a winding subterranean path, which led out at a distance to a sylvan lodge in the most lonely part of the adjoining forest.

There, of course, she found Rosamund.[1]

In the late fifteenth century, the London chronicler Robert Fabyan, drawing on Higden, described "the house of wonder working or Daedalus' work, which is a house wrought like unto a knot in a garden called a maze." By Elizabethan times, the Rosamund legends had evolved into a literary tradition. When Michael Drayton wrote of the tower and labyrinth at Woodstock, the bower had become a strong building of stone and timber, with 150 doors and a maze "so cunningly contrived with turnings round about, that none but with a clue of thread could enter in or out." During the centuries that followed, many famous writers—among them Joseph Addison, Agnes Strickland, Algernon Swinburne, Alfred, Lord Tennyson, in his play, *Becket*, and even Winston Churchill—wrote of the legends as fact. Yet there is no evidence that a labyrinth ever existed at Woodstock.

At the beginning of March 1166, Henry prepared to sail to Normandy, but changed his mind and returned to Woodstock with the intention, some writers suggest, of saying farewell to Rosamund. On March 16, he was at Southampton, whence he crossed to Falaise; he would not return to his kingdom for another four years. He marched immediately on Maine to teach the barons who had rebelled and slighted Eleanor a lesson they would not forget, destroying their castles and crushing their resistance.

In late March, he joined Eleanor for the Easter court at Angers. All their children except Henry were present. Around this time, Eleanor conceived her last child. Late in May, she and Henry moved to Le Mans and Chinon, an imposing fortress above the River Vienne in Anjou, which was one of the King's favorite residences. There he was laid low by illness.

At Pentecost, in exile at Pontigny Abbey, Becket excommunicated all the authors of the Constitutions of Clarendon except the King. Henry wept tears of rage when the news reached Chinon and, at his urgent request, the Pope agreed to annul the sentences and forbade Becket to molest Henry further.

In July, Henry was well enough to depose his vassal, Conan IV, secure control of Brittany and betroth his son Geoffrey, aged eight, to Constance, Conan's five-year-old heiress. At Rennes, in Geoffrey's name, he formally took possession of what he was now pleased to call the duchy of Brittany.

By October, he was at Caen, preparing to deal with the Aquitanian rebels. Summoning them to meet him at Chinon on November 20, he declared his intention of honoring them by holding his Christmas court at Poitiers, where he would present to them their future overlord, the Lord Henry. The Poitevins were unimpressed and went home to resume their plotting.

Eleanor was still in Angers. That winter, Henry sent her and Matilda back to England. She did not join him in Poitiers, as she was in the last stages of pregnancy. He may not have wanted her there, knowing that she would oppose his choice of the Lord Henry, rather than the Lord Richard, as the heir to her domains. Henry was already destined to inherit England, Anjou and Normandy, while Geoffrey had Brittany. If Henry received Aquitaine as well, Richard would have no inheritance at all. Eleanor might have protested strongly against that.

At the end of the year, having arranged for the Lord Henry to cross the Channel and join his father, Eleanor was in Oxfordshire. Some writers have suggested that, during her travels, she visited Woodstock with the intention of having her child there, only to find Rosamund de Clifford installed, which prompted her to withdraw in anger to Oxford, but there is nothing to support this.

The earliest evidence that the future King John was born in the King's House in Oxford is a prose amendment to the late-thirteenth-century chronicle of Robert of Gloucester; since other amendments were drawn from the writings of Robert of Torigni, it would appear that John was indeed born at Oxford. One of Robert of Torigni's unchronological insertions places his birth on Christmas Eve 1167. The year must be incorrect: in 1167 Henry was on the Continent and Eleanor in England at the time when she would have conceived, and both spent Christmas in Normandy. Ralph of Diceto gives the year of John's birth as 1166, stating that he was "barely seven" in February 1173.

He was probably baptized John because he was born on December 27, the feast day of St. John the Evangelist, one of Fontevraud's patron saints. Given that he would go to Fontevraud as an oblate, his parents might already have decided to dedicate him to the Church, a not unusual practice in a devout age when families were large and it was difficult to make adequate provision for every child.

John was Eleanor's last child. The Pipe Rolls record no expenses for him before 1176. He probably spent his early years in his mother's household, being looked after by Hodierna of St. Albans, who had cared for Richard in his infancy; as an adult, John too would reward her with a pension.

Henry presided over his Christmas court at Poitiers and presented the Lord Henry to the Poitevins as their future duke. Eleanor remained in England, mostly at Winchester, probably simmering in rage. The Pipe Rolls record visits with her children to Carisbrooke Castle and payments to their nurse, or governess, Agatha; she was long held in affection by the Queen, who would reward her with two estates in 1198 and 1200.

Preparations were in train for eleven-year-old Matilda's wedding to Henry of Saxony. In July, the Emperor's envoys arrived in England to escort the princess to Germany. Henry had provided her with a magnificent trousseau, in which Eleanor may have had a hand. It included clothing worth £63 (£46,000), "two large silken cloths and two tapestries, one cloth of samite and twelve sable skins." The total cost amounted to £4,500 (£3,284,000), which was equal to almost a quarter of England's entire annual revenue and was raised by taxation.

Henry had just suppressed an insurrection in Brittany when he received news that his mother was seriously ill in Rouen. She died on September 10, before he could reach her. That month, Eleanor, attended by a large retinue, accompanied Matilda to Dover, whence she departed for her new life in Germany. Young Henry later thanked the prior of Dover for his hospitality toward his mother and sister. Gervase of Canterbury wrote that Eleanor sailed with Matilda to Normandy; she may have attended the Empress's funeral at the abbey of Bec-Hellouin. She must have returned to England immediately because, for the next few weeks, she was resident at Winchester.

On February 1, 1168, Matilda was married to the Duke of Saxony at Brunswick. Twenty-four years her senior, Henry the Lion was a brave, cultivated and enlightened man who was a notable patron of the arts and the Church. The marriage proved happy and fruitful and led to the expansion of trade between England and the Empire. A manuscript in the Herzog August Library in Wolfenbüttel shows the hands of God placing ducal crowns on the couple's heads; the deceased Empress Maud is shown standing beside Henry II, with Eleanor of Aquitaine relegated to a position behind her, which may have mirrored their roles in life.

10

"A Whirlwind of Clouds"

✠

ELEANOR WAS DETERMINED TO PLAY A MORE ACTIVE ROLE IN the governance of her duchy. In Angers, she had learned of the extent of the unrest in Aquitaine and that Raoul de Faye and other lords were contemplating withdrawing their allegiance to Henry, who they resented for depriving them of their liberties; it was evident that her presence was needed there. It must have rankled that, for the past eleven years, her name had been absent from all the royal charters issued in Aquitaine. Her subjects would welcome the prospect of having their hereditary ruler back among them, and many problems would be solved by her return.

During the autumn of 1167, Eleanor decided to separate from Henry and remain permanently in her domains, a decision that "troubled" the King "like that of Oedipus,"[1] although he realized that her presence in the south, and the reassertion of her authority as duchess, would calm the opposition to his rule, which he had struggled to enforce. He agreed that Eleanor should be based in Poitiers as his deputy for the foreseeable future. Needing her support, he conceded that ten-year-old Richard should be her heir after all and accompany her.

That it was Eleanor who initiated the separation is evident from a letter written by Rotrou of Warwick, Archbishop of Rouen, in 1173 (cited on p. 98). Throughout their marriage, for political reasons, she and Henry had spent long periods apart, so another prolonged separation was not unusual, but it seems that the arrangement was to be permanent. Eleanor would continue to work in partnership with Henry, taking an interest in events in his domains and appearing in public with him on occasions. This, outwardly at least, was an amicable, pragmatic separation.

That there were personal as well as political issues involved is likely. Eleanor was forty-three, an aging woman by medieval standards, while Henry, at thirty-four, was a vigorous man in his prime. Her childbearing days were over, and he had tired of her sexually, according to William of Newburgh. Giraldus wrote that, "in domestic matters, [the King] was hard to deal with." Eleanor may have found marriage to an overbearing husband exhausting. According to William FitzStephen, Henry was not above venting his wrath on her and, out of fear and respect, she would resort to subterfuge and massage truths in order to avoid the lash of his harsh tongue. Sometime before 1170, she engaged in a correspondence with the visionary nun, Hildegarde of Bingen, who wrote to her: "Your mind is similar to a whirlwind of clouds. You look all around, but find no rest. Flee that, and remain firm and stable, with God as with men, and God will then help you in all your tribulations. May He give you His blessing and His aid in all your undertakings."

Eleanor may have decided that living in her native land with a relative degree of autonomy as its Duchess was preferable to her life in a subordinate role as Henry's Queen. His chaotic existence contrasted unfavorably with the relaxed, civilized lifestyle she could enjoy in Aquitaine. It may be that she found in the love of her son Richard the emotional fulfilment that was lacking in her relationship with Henry. The evidence suggests that mother and son had a special bond.

It is unlikely that Henry's love for Rosamund de Clifford was a factor. No contemporary chronicler asserts that Eleanor was jealous of Rosamund, but the King's seduction of Alice de Porhoët, sister of Conan IV of Brittany, might have been too outrageous for Eleanor to overlook. His conduct had been doubly reprehensible, for he had taken Alice hostage for her family's good behavior and she was supposed to be under his protection. She bore a bastard child, probably his, in 1168, and may have been the mother of two more of his illegitimate children.

In December, Eleanor commandeered seven ships to transport her possessions to Normandy, so that they could be taken south. Richard, Leonor, Joanna and John accompanied her across the Channel. At Christmas, she and Henry held their court at Argentan.

Before Eleanor could be established in Poitiers, resentment in Aquitaine erupted into serious revolt. The powerful Lusignan family were a great but unruly power in Poitou. Robert of Torigni stated that they "yielded to no yoke or ever kept faith with any overlord." They had joined William VI, Count of Angoulême, and other lords in another rebellion against Angevin rule, threatening to switch their allegiance to King Louis. In January 1168, Henry hurried south to deal with them, taking Eleanor, Richard, John, Leonor and Joanna with him; Eleanor's presence would remind her vassals to whom they owed allegiance.

It was almost certainly on the way south that Henry and Eleanor left one-year-old John at Fontevraud. When the nuns recorded John's obituary in 1216, they recalled that "he was given to us and to our church as an oblate by his most illustrious father, King Henry and, for a period of five years, was cared for by us." Since John was back with his father in 1173, he must have been placed at Fontevraud in 1168.

An oblate was a child dedicated by his parents to God, to be raised in the religious life. In time, when he was old enough to make the choice for himself, he would enter the novitiate with a view to taking vows as a monk. A child had to be at least ten years old before he could be accepted as an oblate; until he reached that age, John was to be reared by the nuns under the auspices of the abbess, Audeburge of Hautes-Bruyères, a model of piety and good government. The choice of Fontevraud was probably dictated by its accessibility to both parents. Eleanor has been criticized by historians for depositing her youngest child in a convent at such a tender age, but the decision to send him there was Henry's. To contemporary eyes, the boy was being afforded an excellent upbringing. Joanna may have been left at Fontevraud too, while Leonor seems to have resided with her mother in Poitiers. Neither was destined for the Church, being valuable marriage pawns for extending Henry's political reach through foreign alliances.

Henry left Eleanor and Richard in Poitiers with Patrick, Earl of Salisbury, whom he had appointed as Eleanor's military adviser. Marching on the reputedly impregnable castle of Lusignan, he razed it to the ground and ravaged the surrounding lands. By Easter, the rising had been crushed, and Henry had ridden north to meet Louis for a peace conference on the Norman border.

But the Lusignans were out for revenge. On March 27, Eleanor, accompanied by Earl Patrick and a small escort, was out hawking near Lusignan. Without warning, they were ambushed by an armed force led by Guy de Lusignan and his brother Geoffrey, bent on taking the Queen hostage and ransoming her for generous concessions from Henry. Hastily, Earl Patrick bade Eleanor mount his fastest horse and seek safety in a nearby castle while he dealt with their attackers. During the ensuing skirmish, he was fatally stabbed in the back, and it was left to his courageous nephew, Sir William, son of John the Marshal, to hold off the enemy before being wounded and captured.

William's later surname, "the Marshal," derived from the office of marshal of England, which he would inherit from his brother in 1199, but, for the purposes of clarity, it will be used throughout this book. Now aged about twenty-two, he was a tall, brown-haired man of dignified bearing. As a fourth son, he had no inheritance to look forward to; he had made a living as a soldier of fortune and gained a reputation as a champion at tournaments, winning many rich prizes and attracting the admiration of Henry and Eleanor by his impressive exploits.

William was devoted to the Angevins, who would come to recognize the loyalty, integrity and courage for which Eleanor now had cause to be grateful. "The Queen gave hostages for the Marshal, who had suffered torment and pain in the cruel prison," and secured his release. "Valiant and courteous lady that she was, she bestowed upon him horses, arms, gold and rich garments, and opened her palace gates and fostered his ambition, who had fought like a wild boar against dogs, for she was very worthy and courteous."[2] She also gave money to the church of Sainte-Hilaire in Poitiers for masses for Earl Patrick's soul; in her charter, she referred to Henry as "my lord the King" rather than "my dearest husband," as in her earlier charters—another sign of a growing breach between them.

William spent two years as one of Eleanor's household knights until the King, probably on her recommendation, appointed him guardian, tutor and master in chivalry to the Lord Henry, to whom he became an inseparable companion. Thus was William the Marshal—to whom Stephen Langton, Archbishop of Canterbury, would later refer as "the best knight who ever lived"—launched on a spectacular career that would see him loyally serving five English kings.

Eleanor set up her court at Poitiers, where the recently refurbished private apartments in the Maubergeonne Tower were spacious and luxurious. She continued to wear rich clothes and jewelry, as her grants to Poitevin merchants in the early 1170s confirm. Henry allowed her to keep their children with her and let them visit her, and she would also receive into her household—which is said to have included sixty ladies—her daughter-in-law Marguerite of France and the affianced wives of her younger sons. Eleanor's advisers were mostly Poitevins, chief of whom was Raoul de Faye.

Throughout 1168, she seems to have remained in Poitiers, where she kept Christmas. For the next five years, Henry trusted her to rule her domains autonomously, as is clear from the fact that, while she issued many charters in her own name, he did not confirm them, or issue a single one relating to Aquitaine and Poitou. It was Richard, her heir, with whom Eleanor associated herself in her acts, not Henry. Some of her fifteen known charters to "the King's faithful followers and heirs" in Aquitaine were issued in the names of "I and Richard, my son," under her own seal.

The return of "the venerable Eleanor" to her domains and the reestablishment of a ducal court did much to heal the wounds caused by thirty years of alien rule. She did everything in her power to recover the loyalty of her vassals. Wishing to show eleven-year-old Richard to the people, she took him on a progress throughout Poitou and Aquitaine and received the homage of local lords. She dismissed some of Henry's unpopular seneschals, replaced them with her countrymen, encouraged exiled barons to return home and be restored to their lands, revived old fairs and customs, ensured that taxes and customs on wheat, wine and salt were fairly levied, and granted or renewed the ancient privileges of towns and abbeys.

Two of her letters survive from this time, one showing her trying (successfully) to obtain the restoration of a kinsman, Pierre Raymond, to the abbacy of Saint-Maixent. The other was to Pope Alexander III:

> The devotion of [your] humble daughter does not cease to exult and praise God, and abounding in the fervour of filial love, often breaks out in paternal praise. Whenever there is talk about factions in my presence, I am not afraid to do battle against the attempts of the enemy power, but subdue them with my arguments, confidently defending your side. I had, in any case, most justly rejoiced in, and embraced, your success before, but the glorious condescension of your writing and the greeting of great commendation were enough to obtain all the favour of my smallness.[3]

Eleanor was probably referring to the deaths of Alexander's rivals, the antipopes Victor IV in 1164 and Paschal III in 1168. Henry II had allied himself to the Emperor Frederick Barbarossa, who had supported them. Effectively, in championing the Pope, Eleanor was aligning herself against her husband, which was a new departure and points to a growing estrangement between them.

Eleanor's court at Poitiers was modeled on that of her Aquitanian forebears and imbued with the chivalric culture and the traditions of the south. In a poem written to her a few years later, Richard le Poitevin recalled: "Tender and delicate, you enjoyed a royal freedom, you abounded with riches." She indulged her love of music, delighting in "the melodies of the flute and rejoicing in the harmonies of the musicians. Young girls surrounded you and sang their sweet songs to the accompaniment of the tabor [tambourine] and cithara [lyre]. You enjoyed the sound of the organ and you leaped to the beating of drums."

It appears that Eleanor welcomed troubadours to her court. Arnaut Guilhem de Marsan is known to have visited. Rigaud de Barbezieux praised the Queen as being "more than a lady," while the notorious Bertran de Born, a robber baron who would become a close friend of the Lord Henry, dedicated many of his chansons to "noble Eleanora."

Until the twentieth century, historians believed that, in association with her daughter, Marie, Countess of Champagne, Eleanor presided at Poitiers over the now legendary Courts of Love, but they were no more than a literary conceit invented between 1174 and 1196 by Andrew the

Chaplain for his treatise on love, entitled *De Amore*. He has long been described as a chaplain at the court of Marie of Champagne at Troyes, but there is no contemporary evidence to support this, and barely anything is known of him.

His work was inspired by Ovid and written some years after Eleanor's court at Poitiers had been dismantled. He imagined her, Marie and other noble ladies including Ermengarde, Viscountess of Narbonne (a far more notable patroness of troubadours than Eleanor), presiding over a tribunal at which young gallants sought judgment in intellectual disputes about courtly love. Those who had acted properly toward their ladies were awarded the palm of amorous courtesy. One gets the impression that Andrew was mocking courtly love as well as celebrating it.

Eleanor's appearance in *De Amore* owes far more to her reputation than her actual deeds. She is recorded as giving six judgments, while Marie is alleged to have pronounced in 1174 (the only date given in the book) that true love cannot exist between husband and wife—a sentiment Eleanor would perhaps have echoed.

II

"We Are from the Devil"

✝

WHILE ELEANOR HELD A MAGNIFICENT COURT AT POITIERS, Henry spent the Christmas of 1168 at Argentan. On January 6, 1169, he and Louis concluded the Treaty of Montmirail, which provided that, after Henry's death, his dominions were to be divided between his three eldest sons: Henry was to receive England, Normandy and Anjou; Richard was to have Aquitaine, and hold it—as his mother did—as a vassal of the French Crown; and Geoffrey was to retain Brittany, holding it as a vassal of his oldest brother. John, who was destined for the Church, would get nothing. Richard was to marry Louis's daughter Alys. After the betrothal, Alys was formally handed over to Henry.

Most chroniclers were puzzled at Henry's decision to partition his empire, but he had learned through experience how difficult it was to govern such an unwieldy collection of territories. In negotiating the treaty, he took into account Eleanor's opinions, ensuring that Richard was acknowledged by Louis as the heir to Aquitaine.

Henry was now eager to see Becket restored to the see of Canterbury, for he wanted him to crown young Henry. He offered to recall him if he would retract his denunciation of the Constitutions of Clarendon. At the plea of King Louis, a reluctant Becket agreed and, coming face to face with Henry for the first time in over four years, prostrated himself and begged for mercy. Then he ruined the moment, offering to submit to the King's pleasure in all things "saving the honour of God." Henry exploded in abuse, leaving the meeting to break up in uproar, with everyone, including Louis, castigating the Archbishop for his obduracy.

* * *

In May 1169, ten-year-old Geoffrey was enthroned in Rennes Cathedral and invested with the ducal crown of Brittany. Around August, Henry opened negotiations for the marriage of Joanna to William II, King of Sicily, which he hoped would further cement the ancient ties of friendship between the dukes of Normandy and the Norman kingdom of Sicily. At Christmas, he held court with Geoffrey and Constance at Nantes. There is no record of Eleanor being present.

Henry was set in his resolve to have the Lord Henry crowned, a decision supported "by the counsel of the Queen."[1] Traditionally, it was the prerogative of the Archbishop of Canterbury to crown the monarch, but Becket was *persona non grata*, so Henry appointed Roger de Pont-l'Evêque, Archbishop of York, to officiate—a gross insult to Becket, who forbade both the King and Roger to proceed with the coronation, on pain of excommunication. The Pope also prohibited the ceremony.

Henry was determined to have his son crowned, regardless of any opposition. In March 1170, braving violent storms, he sailed to Portsmouth, leaving Eleanor at Caen, in charge of Normandy. With the assistance of Richard du Hommet, the Seneschal, she ensured that the Channel ports remained closed, to prevent Becket from crossing the sea. Bishop Roger of Worcester, on his way to England with the Papal prohibition, was, to his chagrin, forcibly detained in Dieppe by the Seneschal, on Eleanor's orders.

On the Lord Henry's arrival in England, his father knighted him in the presence of a great assembly of lords and prelates. Splendid coronation robes costing £26 (£19,000) had already been made in London for Marguerite and her household, but she was obliged to remain behind with Eleanor at Caen because Henry had decided that having her crowned with her husband in the face of Papal prohibition might offend Louis more than if she were not crowned at all.

On Sunday, June 14, the Lord Henry was crowned king in Westminster Abbey by Archbishop Roger of York, with six bishops assisting. Henceforth, he would be distinguished from his father by the title "the Young King," although Henry had no intention of relinquishing any degree of sovereign power, "retaining for himself all land pertaining to the kingdom, with all its fruits and revenues,"[2] and with good reason. The Young King was already exhibiting an alarming contempt for his father, which became apparent at the coronation banquet in Westminster Hall. The thirteenth-century chronicler Matthew Paris related how, preceded by trumpets, Henry carried a boar's head on a platter to the high table where his son sat with the Archbishop of York, and jested, "It is surely unusual to see a king wait upon table!"

The Young King retorted, "Certainly, it can be no condescension for the son of a count to serve the son of a king."

The Archbishop rounded on him. "Be glad, my good son, there is not another prince in the world that has such a sewer [server] at his table."

"Why do you marvel at that?" the youth retorted. "My father thinks it not more than becomes him, that he, being born of princely blood only on the mother's side, serves me that am born having both a king to my father and a queen to my mother." One might suspect where young Henry had got this view of himself.

Becket condemned the coronation ceremony as "this last outrage." King Louis was mortally offended that his daughter had not been crowned and began making threats. Henry placated him by promising to arrange another coronation for the young couple at a future date.

The Young King was assigned his own household in England, under the control of William the Marshal. Now fifteen, young Henry was described as "the most handsome prince in all the world."[3] He was "tall, but well proportioned, broad-shouldered with a long and elegant neck, pale, freckled skin, bright and wide blue eyes and a thick mop of reddish-gold hair." Walter Map described him as "lovable, eloquent, handsome, gallant, in every way attractive, a little lower than the angels, beautiful above all others in both form and face." Medieval chroniclers habitually described royalty in glowing terms, but Map was no sycophant and these concurring accounts do suggest that young Henry was indeed good-looking.

His popularity was due not only to his charm, but also to his reputation as a "fountain of largesse,"[4] which encouraged a great following of young aristocrats, eager for advancement. He kept a splendid court, dispensed lavish hospitality and enjoyed an extravagant lifestyle, living well beyond his means. Thanks to the training of the Marshal, he displayed "unprecedented skill in arms."[5] Jousting was his passion. He was brave, energetic when he chose, and hailed by many as a chivalrous knight.

Yet, in the years to come, this boy who had been so blessed would "turn all these gifts to the wrong side"[6] and become "a prodigy of un-faith."[7] He grew to be "a restless youth"[8] and "inconstant as wax."[9] At the root of this was his deep dissatisfaction with his father's refusal to allow him any political power. Despite his repeated requests to be permitted to govern England or, failing that, Normandy or Anjou, Henry would not permit him to take possession of any part of his inheritance. Nor would he allow him to rule England as regent during his absences abroad, del-egating this responsibility to the Justiciar.

Fueling the Young King's resentment, Henry assigned him a shame-fully meager allowance and insisted on choosing the members of his household. He also banned the tournaments his son loved, on the grounds that too many young knights were being killed.

Henry and Eleanor had high hopes of all their children and Henry was still confident that he could mold the Young King, his favorite, into an-other ruler such as himself. The boy had had the best tutors and had mastered the skills of reading and writing. Since childhood, he had at-tended the ceremonial court gatherings at Christmas, Whitsun and Eas-ter, had sat with his father in the assize courts, accompanied him on progress, inspected garrisons and been taught about the English legal and taxation systems. None of it seems to have made much impression on him.

Henry was a fond parent: "on his legitimate children, he lavished in their childhood more than a father's affection."[10] Often absent, he took it for granted that his love was returned. He found it hard to find fault with his sons and forgave them all too readily, even after they had caused him almost irreparable injury and pain. The Young King could usually allay his father's wrath simply by bursting into tears. It did not help that both parents apparently competed for their children's affection. By all accounts, Eleanor was an indulgent mother. Her sons grew up spoiled and headstrong, determined to get their own way. They had little affec-tion or respect for their father, an attitude she may have encouraged, since, as they grew older, she seems to have been more in touch with their developing minds than Henry was (she was certainly more sympathetic) and consequently exerted greater influence over them.

Henry was aware of the growing alienation of his sons and, as they matured, "he looked askance at them, after the manner of a stepfather."[11] It was probably Eleanor who had told him about a curse laid by a hermit on William IX of Aquitaine, that his descendants would never know happiness in their children, a tale Henry was fond of repeating, and which was sadly apposite, for he would soon be violently at odds with his sons.

On his way to Falaise in late June, Henry met the Bishop of Worcester. Unaware that Eleanor had prevented the Bishop from going to England, or that he had acted as a courier from the Pope, he angrily denounced him as a traitor for boycotting the coronation.

"The Queen is in the castle of Falaise and Richard du Hommet is probably there also," he raged. "Are you naming them as the instigators of this? You cannot mean that either of them intercepted you in contravention of my summons!"

Bishop Roger replied, "I do not cite the Queen, for either her respect or fear of you will make her conceal the truth, so that your anger at me will be increased; or, if she confessed the truth, your indignation will fall upon that noble lady. Better that I should lose a leg than that she should hear one harsh word from you."[12] The Bishop evidently knew how volatile the King's temper could be, and that it could rebound on Eleanor.

The Pope was now insisting that Becket and Henry make up their quarrel. Henry declared that he was ready to make peace, and, through the good offices of King Louis and Archbishop Rotrou of Rouen, the two men met at Fréteval on July 22. Throwing his arms around Becket, Henry admitted he had wronged the Church over the matter of the coronation. When he asked him to return in peace to Canterbury and crown the Young King and Marguerite, Becket agreed. King and primate retired in a spirit of reconciliation, although Henry had still not given Becket the kiss of peace. That, he promised, would be bestowed on him after he returned to England.

Around August 10, Henry fell seriously ill at Domfront with a tertian fever and dictated a will confirming the dispositions made under the Treaty of Montmirail and appointing the Young King John's guardian, "that he might advance and maintain him."[13] At the end of September, after Henry had recovered, he went with Eleanor on a pilgrimage of thanksgiving to Rocamadour, to visit the oldest shrine to the Virgin in France. Returning through Aquitaine, he attended to administrative business that had fallen into abeyance during Eleanor's absence and dealt with local disputes, making it plain that he was still in overall control of the duchy.

During 1170, relations between Henry and Frederick Barbarossa cooled, and a match between ten-year-old Leonor and the Emperor's son no longer seemed desirable. Instead, Henry sought to extend his influence across the Pyrenees and prevent a Franco-Castilian alliance by betrothing Leonor to twelve-year-old King Alfonso VIII of Castile. In September, accompanied by the Archbishop of Bordeaux and a great retinue, Eleanor conducted her daughter to Bordeaux. There, she received the Castilian envoys and concluded the arrangements for the marriage, which would be solemnized when Leonor was twelve. She bade farewell to her daughter and entrusted her to the care of the envoys, who took her south to complete her upbringing at the Castilian court. Later, Alfonso would claim that he had been promised Gascony as Leonor's dowry on the death of her mother, but there is no contemporary evidence to support this, and it is highly unlikely that Henry would have given Castile such an important part of his empire, especially since he and Eleanor meant Richard to have it.

On December 1, Becket was warmly welcomed at Canterbury by the clergy and the people. But the Young King, whom he had once called his adopted son, refused to receive him. On Christmas Day, from his pulpit in Canterbury Cathedral, the Archbishop excommunicated the bishops who had participated in the coronation, precipitating an atrocity that shook Christian Europe to its very foundations.

Eleanor spent Christmas with Henry at his hunting lodge at Bures in Normandy. Richard, Geoffrey, Joanna and John were present. On Christmas Day, three of the excommunicated bishops arrived at Bures and complained to Henry of Becket's high-handed conduct.

"My lord, while Thomas lives, you will not have peace or quiet or see good days," warned one lord.[14] The King "waxed furious and indignant beyond measure and, keeping too little restraint upon his fiery and ungovernable temper, poured forth wild words from a distracted mind."[15]

"Who will rid me of this turbulent priest?" he is supposed to have cried, although no contemporary source quoted these words. What he did say was something like: "A curse on all the false varlets and traitors I have nursed and promoted in my household, who let their lord be mocked with such shameful contempt by a low-born priest!"[16]

Without confiding their intentions to anyone, four knights of the King's household slipped away from Bures and made haste to England. When Henry discovered they had gone, he guessed what they had in mind and sent messengers to summon them back, but it was too late.

On the evening of December 29, when Becket entered Canterbury Cathedral, the four knights approached "with swords sacrilegiously drawn" and demanded that he lift the ban on the excommunicated bishops. When he refused, they brutally murdered him, leaving the top of his head severed, "so that the blood white with brain and the brain red with blood dyed the surface of the Virgin Mother Church."[17]

Henry suffered two days of unbearable tension at Bures, dreading to hear news of the knights. Abandoning the Christmas festivities, he dismissed his vassals and retired to Argentan. There, he was informed of Becket's murder. "The King burst into loud lamentations and exchanged his royal robes for sackcloth and ashes. For three whole days he remained shut up in his chamber and would neither take food nor admit anyone to comfort him, until it seemed, from the excess of his grief, that he had determined to contrive his own death."[18]

News of Becket's murder sent Christendom into shock. Some declared it was the worst atrocity since the crucifixion of Christ. The Archbishop of Sens asserted that it surpassed the wickedness of Nero, the cruelty of Herod and even the sacrilegious treachery of Judas, while King Louis wrote to the Pope: "Such unprecedented cruelty demands unprecedented retribution. Let the sword of St. Peter be unleashed to avenge the martyr of Canterbury."[19] "Almost everyone laid the death of the blessed martyr at the King's door,"[20] and Henry was reviled throughout Christendom.

For six weeks, he remained in seclusion, calling upon God to witness, "for the sake of his soul, that the evil deed had not been committed by his will, nor with his knowledge, nor by his plan. He directly submitted himself to the judgement of the Church and, with humility, promised to undertake whatever it should decide."[21] For many months, the Pope deliberated as to whether he should excommunicate Henry, as most people expected him to do. In the meantime, he forbade him to venture onto consecrated ground until he had been absolved of his guilt.

It had become apparent that Becket dead was infinitely more powerful than Becket living. No sooner had he fallen than he was being revered as a martyr, and the cult of "God's doughty champion"[22] spread with remarkable speed throughout Christendom. By Easter 1171, miracles were said to be taking place at his tomb.

12

"Beware of Your Wife and Sons"

✠

D ID THE MURDER OF BECKET PLAY A PART IN ALIENATING
Eleanor from Henry? It inspired extreme revulsion throughout
Europe, and certainly aroused the anger of the Young King against his
father, to the extent that his friends were saying that, in instigating the
atrocity, Henry had forfeited his right to kingship. There is no record of
the Queen consoling her husband in his anguish, or of her being at Argentan; she had probably set out for Poitiers after the Christmas festivities were abandoned.

Other factors could account for an escalating rift, especially Eleanor's
likely resentment at Henry limiting her authority in her own domains
and keeping her short on funds, which restricted her power to take up
arms. When, in the spring of 1171, the Abbot of Saint-Martial had to
deal with an uprising, he appealed to Henry for aid, not his Duchess. But
the chief reason for Eleanor's alienation was probably Henry's refusal to
devolve power upon their sons.

In 1171, being desirous of gaining a powerful ally, Humbert, the Count
of Maurienne, an Alpine domain in Savoy, offered King Henry the hand
of his only child, Alice, for John, who was coming up to five. If the marriage took place, John would in time inherit the Count's domains and
the Angevins would gain the strategic advantage of controlling the western Alpine passes, which was enough to change Henry's mind about ded-

icating his youngest son to the religious life, although he left him at
Fontevraud while negotiations for the marriage dragged on.

Richard was present at the great Christmas court Eleanor kept at Limoges that year. By April, Hugh de Saint-Maur and Raoul de Faye had
stirred up Eleanor's anger against Henry[1] and now, on her advice, "so it
is said, began to turn away from his father the mind of the Young King,
suggesting that it seemed incongruous to be a king and not exercise the
rule of a kingdom."[2] According to William of Newburgh, "certain persons had whispered in his ear that he ought now by rights to reign alone,
for, at his coronation, his father's reign had, as it were, ceased." It was at
this time, Giraldus wrote, that "the conspiracy of nobles against their
prince, and of the sons against the father" took root.

On May 12, 1172, in Avranches Cathedral, Henry declared on oath
that he had neither wished for nor ordered Becket's death, but that he
had, unwittingly and in anger, uttered words that had prompted the four
knights "to avenge him,"[3] and was formally absolved by the Archbishop
of Rouen of any complicity in the murder and reconciled with the
Church. Afterward, clad in a hair shirt, the King knelt on the pavement
outside the cathedral and was flogged by monks. He was required to do
further penance at some future date and renounce any laws he had introduced that were detrimental to the Church. It seemed that Becket, in the
end, had won the moral victory, yet Henry did reserve to the Crown the
right to protect its interests if threatened by the processes of the Church,
and this liberty eventually became enshrined in English law.

In 1173, Becket was canonized by Pope Alexander III. Many miracles
were attributed to the new saint and numerous churches were dedicated
to him. The shrine erected to him at Canterbury grew rich and remained
the most popular place of pilgrimage in Christendom until the Reformation, when Henry VIII had it dismantled, appropriated its jewels for the
royal treasury and had Becket's bones exhumed and burned for having
dared to oppose his king.

Richard was made of sterner stuff than the Young King. "Henry was a
shield, but Richard was a hammer," observed Giraldus. He was very tall—
about six feet five inches—and "graceful in figure, his hair between red
and auburn; his limbs were straight and flexible, his arms long and not

to be matched for wielding the sword, while his appearance was commanding."[4] He had inherited his father's piercing blue eyes.

Richard was essentially a child of Poitou. He had spent most of his formative years in his mother's domains. He had received a good education, not only in knightly and military skills, but also in the schoolroom, where he learned to read and write and mastered Latin. He had inherited his mother's love of music, composed competent verses and songs and would sing with, and conduct, the choir in his private chapel. He was also a patron of artists and poets such as Bertran de Born. It was Bertran who bestowed on his patron the nickname "Oc e No" ("Yea and Nay"), which reflected Richard's duplicity. The name "Coeur de Lion," or "Lionheart," is not recorded until a decade after his death, although Richard of Devizes had called Richard "that fearful lion" during his lifetime.

Richard may have been his mother's favorite child. She referred to him as "the great one," while he, she knew, "reposed all his trust in her, next to God."[5] Ralph of Diceto stated that Richard "strove in all things to bring glory to his mother's name."

He was a man of consummate ability, immense courage and daring. A natural leader, he would become renowned as one of the best generals and strategists of the age, greatly feared and respected by his enemies. "Why need we expend labour extolling so great a man?" asked one chronicler. "He was superior to all others."[6] Like all the Angevins, Richard was of a volatile disposition and had a savage temper. He was more violent and cruel than his father, ruthless, unscrupulous, predatory, "bad to all, worse to his friends, and worst of all to himself."[7]

As he grew older, he gained a reputation for promiscuity. He "carried off the wives, daughters and kinswomen of his freemen by force, and made them his concubines, and when he had sated his lust on them, he handed them over to his knights for whoring." He was once accused by a preacher of begetting three shameless daughters: Pride, Avarice and Sensuality—to which he cynically retorted, "I give my daughter Pride to the Knights Templar, my daughter Avarice to the Cistercians, and my daughter Sensuality to the princes of the Church."[8]

Richard "cared not an egg"[9] for England: all his ambition was focused on Poitou and Aquitaine, where he was well known and popular. Now that he was nearing fifteen, Henry and Eleanor met in Normandy to discuss his future and Henry "transferred to Richard, by the will of his mother, the duchy of Aquitaine."[10] Eleanor did not intend to relinquish her power, but wished to formalize her son's position as her heir and rule her domains in association with him. Two lavish ceremonies were planned.

She took Richard to Poitiers for his investiture as count of Poitou. On May 31, 1172, wearing the comital coronet of Poitou, a silk mantle and a scarlet cloak emblazoned with the lions of England, Anjou and Aquitaine, and carrying the golden staff of Aquitaine and the golden scepter she had received at her English coronation, she escorted her son into the abbey of Saint-Hilaire, where they knelt before the high altar. Bishop Jean de Bellesmains removed the coronet from Eleanor's head and set it on Richard's, then immediately replaced it with a silver circlet and returned the coronet to Eleanor, demonstrating that the son's authority was subordinate to the mother's. Then the holy lance and standard of St. Hilaire, the city's patron saint, were presented to Richard, who swore an oath to rule well, to loud acclaim. Celebratory banquets and jousts were held to mark the occasion. Afterward, at Niort, he was presented to the lords of Poitou as their future overlord.

On June 11, in the abbey of Saint-Martial at Limoges, wearing a silk tunic and gold coronet, Richard was invested with the ring of St. Valerie, the city's patron saint, and proclaimed duke of Aquitaine. After the investiture, there was a banquet such as had not been seen in the city for many years. While in Limoges, Eleanor received envoys from the kings of Navarre and Aragon. Both feared the expansionist policies of the Count of Toulouse and were probably seeking her support or mediation, or asking her to appeal to Henry II on their behalf; for Eleanor, the imperative was to protect her dominions from invasion.

Between June and December of that year, Eleanor and Richard resumed their travels through her lands, visiting many religious houses and issuing joint charters. Those she issued in her own name were now addressed to "her own faithful followers," rather than to "the King's faithful followers and hers," as previously. Dissociating from Henry was apiece with her policy of regaining the support of her subjects, though, given the events to come, it may have been part of a broader plan. Yet she lacked the resources to rule independently, for most of her revenues were diverted to the King, who was still legally the ultimate authority in the region.

Determined to keep Young Henry under supervision, Henry dragged him to a meeting with Humbert of Maurienne, who had come to the Auvergne to finalize his daughter's betrothal to John. Henry told Humbert that, on his death, John would receive three castles—Chinon, Loudun and Mirebeau—and some estates in the English Midlands, all of which had been assigned to the Young King. Despite his fury, Young Henry was forced to witness the marriage treaty.

On August 27, he was crowned a second time, at Winchester, this time with Marguerite, in Eleanor's presence. In no way did Marguerite displace Eleanor as queen; she remained a cipher, subordinate to her mother-in-law.

In November, Louis invited young Henry and Marguerite to Paris. On the way, they visited Henry in Normandy and the Young King again demanded his inheritance. When Henry refused, "a deadly hatred sprang up" between them.[11] In Paris, Louis listened sympathetically to the Young King's grievances and urged him to persist in demanding a share of his father's dominions. But Henry, suspecting that Louis was up to no good, summoned his son back to Normandy for Christmas. Burning with resentment, the Young King refused to join his parents. On a whim, he ordered his heralds to summon all the knights in Normandy called William to feast with him: 110 of them turned up.

Henry and Eleanor spent Christmas at Chinon with Richard and Geoffrey. It is likely that, during the festive season, Eleanor took the Young King's part, which was one of the chief reasons for the final falling-out between her and Henry. It must have seemed that Henry was pursuing his "successors with a hatred which perhaps they deserved, but which nonetheless impaired his own happiness. Whether by some breach of the marriage tie, or as a punishment for some crime of the parent, it befell that there was never true affection felt by the father towards his sons, nor by the sons towards their father, nor harmony between the brothers themselves."[12] By 1173, Eleanor's sympathies lay wholeheartedly with her sons. Like a lioness fighting to protect her cubs, she was determined to ensure that they received their rights. She may also have been intent on regaining complete control of her domains.

In February, Eleanor was present at a court convened by Henry at Montferrand. Among those attending were the kings of Aragon and Navarre,

Humbert of Maurienne and Raoul de Faye. During this assembly, the betrothal of John to Alice of Maurienne was concluded. Four-year-old Alice was committed to the care of Henry, who placed her in Eleanor's household.

Henry and Eleanor then hosted a week of lavish banquets and festivities at Limoges in honor of their guests, who had been joined by Raymond V, Count of Toulouse. Raymond had never conceded Eleanor's ancestral claim to Toulouse, but Henry preferred to have him as an ally rather than an enemy and had summoned him to Limoges to pay homage to himself, the Young King and Richard, acknowledging them as his overlords. It amounted to a tacit recognition by Henry of Raymond's claim to Toulouse.

Some Poitevin nobles were angry that Raymond had paid homage to Henry and the Young King before swearing fealty to Richard, whose right to Toulouse had just been acknowledged by King Louis. Eleanor must have been incandescent, not only on Richard's behalf, but also because Raymond had paid no homage to her at all, ignoring her own claim to Toulouse and thereby undermining the independent standing of Aquitaine. And Henry had blithely failed to consult her before recognizing Raymond as the lawful lord of Toulouse. It was an unforgivable betrayal. She and Richard had been slighted. Her anger must have strengthened her resolve to fight for her sons' rights, especially Richard's, and her own autonomy within her domains. Her estrangement from Henry was now virtually complete and she began "corrupting the minds of her sons with folly and sedition."[13]

The stage was now set for the most dangerous rebellion ever to confront Henry II. The King's heavy-handed imposition of his authority and his loss of international prestige following the murder of Becket had already led to the disaffection of a large number of his vassals, particularly in Poitou and Aquitaine. Eleanor and her three eldest sons were now ready to exploit this enmity. She wanted just treatment for her boys and autonomous power for them and herself. Henry's vassals wanted an end to his dictatorial government. Eleanor must have known that these aims could only be achieved through the removal of her husband, and this she was now prepared to countenance.

The chroniclers are vague as to her exact role in the rebellion that followed, but almost all imply that she was a prime mover. Gervase of Canterbury and William of Newburgh claimed that the whole uprising had been devised and executed by her, while Richard FitzNigel asserted that, while the King's sons "were yet young and easily swayed by any emotion, certain little foxes corrupted them with bad advice, so that at last his own bowels [i.e. his wife, the bowels being considered a seat of violent passions] turned against him and told her sons to persecute their father." Roger of Howden and the anonymous author of the *Gesta Henrici Secundi* stated that the authors of this "heinous treachery" were King Louis and, "as some say," Eleanor and Raoul de Faye. If all this is true, then the rift between Eleanor and Henry went so deep that she was prepared to resort to treason to have her revenge.

The seer Merlin had foretold: "The cubs shall awake and shall roar loud, and, leaving the woods, shall seek their prey within the walls of the cities. Among those who shall be in their way they shall make great carnage."[14] The cubs were widely believed to be the sons of Henry II, who were now ready to rise against their father.

During the week at Limoges, the Young King spoke out publicly against his father's refusal to delegate power to him and his brothers, and against Henry's decision to assign to his brother John castles and lands that were rightly his. When Henry refused to accede to his demands, the Young King pointed out that it was King Louis's wish, and that of the barons of England and Normandy, that he do so. Roger of Howden wrote that he had been put up to making trouble by Henry's enemies. Eleanor, backed by Raoul de Faye and Hugh de Saint-Maur, now incited the Young King to rise against his father, saying, "It is not fitting that a king should be seen to be unable to exercise in his kingdom the power he has a right to."[15]

According to Geoffrey de Vigeois, Raymond of Toulouse warned Henry, "I advise you, King, to beware of your wife and sons." Henry apparently gave little credence to this, but he did summarily banish many of the knights of the Young King's household, believing it was they who were sowing the seeds of sedition. Naturally, this further fueled his son's hatred.

That there was contact at some point between Eleanor and Louis is certain—he was her overlord and she had the right to ask him for aid against her enemies. He was ready to seize any chance to undermine the might of the Angevins, even to the extent of allying himself with his estranged former wife.

Henry soon realized there were forces at work against him and suspected that Louis and others were actively working to drive a wedge between him and his heir. It does not seem to have occurred to him that his wife might be foremost among them. Early in March, he hastened north with the Young King, leaving Eleanor at Poitiers with Richard and Geoffrey, which he surely would not have done had he suspected them of plotting treason. He was convinced that the Young King was causing all the trouble and, determined not to let him out of his sight, he pressed on toward Normandy, dragging his son with him and placing his garrisons on war alert. But, on the night of March 5, the Young King escaped from Chinon, crossed the Loire and headed north. Henry gave chase, but his son had swung east and fled to Paris. His escape had clearly been planned, since fresh horses had awaited him along the route, and it was said "that he did this by the advice of his mother."[16] It has been suggested that Eleanor had devised his escape with Louis's assistance.

In Paris, the Young King and Louis pledged to aid each other against their common enemy. When Henry sent a deputation of bishops to ask the King to return his son, Louis asked, "Who sends this message to me?"

"The King of England," was the bishops' reply.

"That is not so," retorted Louis. "The King of England is here. But if you still call king his father, who was formerly king of England, know that he is no longer king. All the world knows that he resigned his kingdom to his son."[17]

Henry correctly interpreted Louis's words as an open declaration of war. His bishops warned him, "Look to the safety of your castles and the security of your person."[18] Soon afterward, many of his vassals on both sides of the Channel, including William the Marshal, openly declared their support for the Young King.

"Devising evil against his father from every side by the advice of the French King, the Young King went secretly into Aquitaine where his two youthful brothers, Richard and Geoffrey, were living with their mother, and, with her connivance, so it is said, he incited them to join him."[19] They "chose to follow their brother rather than their father, in this, they say, following the advice of their mother, Eleanor."[20] Richard FitzNigel stated that she influenced Richard and Geoffrey against the King, Roger of Howden that she actually sent her younger sons to France "to join with [young Henry] against their father."

When Geoffrey was later asked why he could not be at peace with his family, he replied, "Do you not know that it is our proper nature, planted in us by inheritance from our ancestors, that none of us should love the other, but that always, brother against brother and son against father, we try our utmost to injure one another?"[21]

Eleanor's younger sons "took up arms against their father at just the time when, everywhere, Christians were laying down their arms in reverence for Easter."[22] They made for Paris, where King Louis knighted Richard and urged him to rise against King Henry. The conflict that now broke out was "a war without love" and a "deplorable betrayal." William of Newburgh called the Young King an "ungrateful son" whose rebellion against his father was "a violation of nature."

By late spring, the rebel coalition included the formidable might of the counts of Flanders, Boulogne, Champagne and Blois, and several lords of Anjou, Maine, Poitou, Brittany and England. Of Henry's legitimate sons, "John alone, who was a little boy, remained with his father,"[23] having been withdrawn from Fontevraud; it was too near Poitou for Henry's comfort.

Hostilities broke out in May when the King's sons "laid waste their father's lands on every side, with fire, sword and rapine. Everywhere, there was plotting, plundering and burning."[24] Some of Henry's vassals openly renounced their loyalty to him. Throughout the summer of 1173, he fought valiantly to suppress the rebels, but he was hard pressed to vanquish all his enemies.

Ruthless in her resolve, Eleanor followed her sons into rebellion. She and her commander, Raoul de Faye, summoned the lords of the south to rise against Henry. There is evidence to suggest the King had spies at her court, and he soon learned—too late—of the extent of her treachery. It

was the greatest and most shocking betrayal of all. He commanded the
Archbishop of Rouen to send her a stern letter:

> Pious Queen, most illustrious Queen, we all of us deplore, and are
> united in our sorrow, that you, a prudent wife if ever there was one,
> should have parted from your husband. Those whom God has joined
> man must not put asunder. That woman who is not subject to her hus-
> band violates the condition of nature, the command of the Apostles
> and the law of the Gospel. For man is the head of woman. Once sepa-
> rated from the head, the body no longer serves it. The wife is guilty
> when she parts from her husband, when she does not faithfully respect
> the marriage contract. Still more terrible is the fact that you should
> have made the fruits of your union with our lord King rise up against
> their father. With your woman's way and childish counsel, you provoke
> offence against the lord King, to whom even the strongest kings' necks
> bow. You alone are the guilty one. Unless you return to your husband,
> you will be the cause of ruin for all in the kingdom. So, before events
> carry us to a dire conclusion, O illustrious Queen, return with your
> sons to the husband whom you must obey and with whom it is your
> duty to live. Return, lest he mistrust you or your sons. Most surely, we
> know that he will, in every way possible, show you his love and grant
> you the assurance of perfect safety. Exhort your sons, we beg you, to be
> obedient and devoted to their father, who, for their sakes, has under-
> gone so many difficulties, run so many dangers, undertaken so many
> labours. You are one of our flock, as is your husband, but we cannot
> ignore the demands of justice. Either you will return to your husband,
> or we will constrain you by canon law, and will be bound to enforce the
> censure of the Church to bear on you. We say this with great reluc-
> tance, and shall do it with grief and tears, unless you return to your
> senses.[25]

Eleanor had no intention of returning to Henry or abandoning her sons'
cause, and there is no record of her replying to the Archbishop's letter. In
September, her vassals expelled Henry's officials. There was jubilation at
the prospect of an end to the rule of the autocratic Angevin, which the
troubadour Richard le Poitevin echoed in a verse composed around this
time:

Rejoice, O Aquitaine! Be jubilant, O Poitou!
For the sceptre of the King of the North Wind
Be removed from you.

Henry responded by invading Poitou with a large army of mercenaries, who destroyed or seized castles, burned vineyards and uprooted crops. He was beset on all sides. To the east, a rebellion in Brittany was speedily put down. England was invaded from the north by the opportunist William the Lyon, King of Scots. A simultaneous invasion of East Anglia was launched from Flanders on Michaelmas Day. Both attacks were repelled, leaving a few pockets of rebellion in the North and the Midlands. Only by skill, swiftness and wise strategies did the King retain control, and soon his enemies began suing for peace. On September 25, in Louis's presence, he met his sons for a parley at Gisors and offered them castles and allowances—Richard was promised half the revenues of Aquitaine— but made no offer to delegate any authority to them. On Louis's advice, they rejected his terms.

In the autumn, when Henry again marched south into Poitou, Eleanor was at Raoul de Faye's castle at Faye-la-Vineuse near Poitiers, although Raoul had already left to join her sons in Paris. As Henry advanced, she realized that she would be safer at Louis's court and took the road north toward Chartres and Paris, accompanied by a small escort. Soon afterward, Henry captured the castle at Faye-la-Vineuse.

Discovering that she was being pursued, Eleanor "changed from her woman's clothes" and continued her journey disguised as a nobleman or knight, riding astride her mount like a man. Late in November, "along some road in the north of Poitou, the Queen's little band was accosted" and she was "apprehended" by Henry's soldiers. "Her capture was accomplished swiftly and silently." She was "detained in strict custody"[26] and taken to the King in Rouen.

Gervase of Canterbury is the only chronicler to mention Eleanor's arrest, and her wearing male attire, which was then considered heresy, for the Bible condemned it as an abomination. Gervase placed the arrest of the Queen between his accounts of her sons' departure for Paris and the outbreak of hostilities in May; however, it is more likely that it happened in the autumn, perhaps in November. It seems that Eleanor was followed and arrested by spies working for Henry, since four Poitevins, three of whom were close to her, received grants of land from him soon afterward.

Henry had her confined in one of his fortresses, although no chronicler specifies which one; Rouen was the most obvious choice, since it was in territory friendly to him. He may have had her moved several times; her whereabouts in the next few months are unknown, as he probably intended. Her domains were taken into the King's custody and she was fortunate to escape with her life, for her supporters were "condemned to a foul death." Some were blinded, exiled or obliged to "flee to scattered places."[27]

The world was appalled by her conduct. "It was said that all these happenings were prepared through her scheming and advice."[28] People found it shocking that a queen had betrayed her husband. The chroniclers were unanimous in condemning such treachery, which violated every contemporary ideal of wifely fidelity and duty. Ralph of Diceto stated that Eleanor's conduct was "something great, new and unheard-of"; he could cite more than thirty examples of a son rising against his father, but none of a queen raising revolt against her husband. Richard FitzNigel claimed that, without cause, Eleanor was angry with her husband, and her sons with their father. Giraldus believed that her conduct was inspired by God to punish the King for having made an incestuous marriage. The impact of her treachery was such that, for more than forty years afterward, English queen consorts would be allowed to exercise no power at all.

13

"The Eagle of
the Broken Covenant"

✠

THE ONSET OF WINTER FORCED BOTH SIDES TO NEGOTIATE A
truce, but, in the spring of 1174, the fighting broke out again,
forcing Henry to subdue his rebels in Anjou and Poitou. On May 12,
Whitsunday, he visited Poitiers, where he dismissed Eleanor's servants
and dismantled her court. When he left, he took with him Joanna, Marguerite and Alys of France, Constance of Brittany, Alice of Maurienne
and his bastard sister, Emma of Anjou.

In June, he learned that the King of Scots had crossed the border again
and was laying siege to Carlisle; the North and the Midlands were seething with revolt, and the Young King was planning another invasion of
England. The Justiciar and other royal officials began once more to bom-
bard the King with appeals for help. Ever superstitious, Henry saw these
new misfortunes as divine punishment for his failure to do proper penance for the murder of Becket and decided that this must be his priority
before he attempted to deal with the insurgents. On July 8, 1174, he
sailed to England from Barfleur. With him were John, Joanna, Marguerite, Alys, Constance, Emma, Alice—and Eleanor: this is the first reference
to the Queen by the chroniclers for over a year.

"A considerable number of ships had been assembled against the
King's arrival,"[1] and it required forty of them to transport his family, his
household and his army of mercenaries to England. When told that the

wind was against them and steadily getting worse, Henry lifted his eyes to the sky and said, "If the Lord of the Heavens has ordained that peace will be restored when I arrive, then in His mercy may He grant me a safe landing."[2] The weather held and they disembarked at dusk that same day at Southampton.

Henry meant to keep Eleanor a prisoner, recognizing that she would always pose a threat to the stability of his domains. Immediately after they had "eaten a simple meal of bread and water,"[3] she was taken away under guard. Ralph of Diceto, Gervase of Canterbury and the *Gesta Henrici Secundi* all stated that she was held in custody at Winchester Castle; only Geoffrey de Vigeois asserted that she was first confined at Sarum Castle in Wiltshire. Her imprisonment, Giraldus wrote, was "a punishment for the destruction of [her] marriage," revealing that Henry's anger and sense of injury were emotional as well as political. His retaliation extended to confiscating her dower lands and revenues, depriving her of the means to plot against him.

Marguerite, her sister Alys and Constance of Brittany were sent to the castle of Devizes and there kept securely until the King's sons could be brought to heel. Alice of Maurienne may have been with them, but died soon after arriving in England.

Having disposed of his womenfolk, Henry rode on to Canterbury. On June 12, he prostrated himself before Becket's tomb and received three to five lashes "from every one" of the seventy monks who are estimated to have flogged him.[4] Back in London, sore and exhausted, he received news that an army led by Geoffrey, his bastard son, had achieved a decisive victory at Alnwick and captured the King of Scots. Henry was so jubilant that he ordered all the bells in London to be rung. Many saw the hand of a forgiving God at work on his behalf and believed the victory had come about through the intercession of the martyred Becket.

Henry's enemies had lost their confidence and knew they were fighting a losing cause. By the end of July, England was finally at peace. On August 8, Henry returned to Barfleur with a formidable force and advanced on Rouen. Louis and the Angevin princes now had to concede defeat.

Henry's masterful victory against such overwhelming odds restored his reputation. He now seemed more invincible than ever. Louis was jumping "to heal the breach between the King of England and his sons." The Young King and Geoffrey had no choice but to sue for peace. Henry was willing to negotiate, "foreseeing the possibility of recalling his sons, whom he loved so much."[5]

Furious at the imprisonment of his mother, Richard went on campaigning against his father until the bitter end. Forced to accept that he could not win, he came face to face with Henry at Montlouis, near Tours, on September 23, threw himself weeping at his feet and begged his forgiveness. The King gave him the kiss of peace. On September 30, a settlement was reached. Henry was more than generous, thanks to his "inordinate love" for his sons,[6] but he did not delegate one iota of his power and forced the Young King to accept the settlement of his former estates and castles on John. "Thus, the mighty learned that it was no easy task to wrest Hercules' club from his hand," commented Richard FitzNigel.

Henry, Richard and Geoffrey promised that they would never again abandon their father. Henry generously excused their treason on the grounds of their "tender age," choosing to believe that they had been led astray by their mother and the King of France,[7] yet his relationship with his three eldest sons would never recover from their devastating disloyalty. From now on, he would look to his other sons for true affection, making it clear that John was his favorite. But John was not yet eight, and it was with his bastard Geoffrey that Henry enjoyed the most satisfying fatherly bond. "Baseborn indeed have my other children shown themselves," he said of Geoffrey. "This alone is my true son."[8]

Henry proclaimed a general amnesty for all who had risen against him—save his wife. Eleanor's reputation was now in the dust. For the rest of Henry's life, she was to remain under restraint or supervision, a hostage for the good behavior of her sons. For the best part of a decade, "on guard against her reverting to her machinations,"[9] the King kept her in strict custody. Never again would he trust her.

Because she effectively disappeared, the chroniclers have very little to say about her during this period, and details of her imprisonment—which most of them found "mysterious"—are fragmentary. According to the Pipe Rolls, she was confined mainly at Winchester and Sarum, although she did occasionally stay elsewhere, since an allowance for her keep was also sent to Ludgershall Castle in Wiltshire and to houses in

Berkshire and Nottinghamshire, but she was always held in "well guarded, strong places."[10] From 1175 to 1180, when she was mostly at Sarum, the Sheriff of Wiltshire outlaid substantial sums for her maintenance, and she regularly received clothing from London. Her custodians were men the King could trust: Robert Mauduit, constable of Sarum, and Ralph FitzStephen, a royal chamberlain.

Eleanor's was a gilded cage. Roger of Howden recorded that her prison was no worse than her palace at Winchester. She was well provided for, yet completely cut off from the outside world and deprived of any means of plotting her escape, conspiring against her husband or contacting her sons. Henry knew how dangerous she could be and was taking no chances.

At Winchester, Eleanor was confined in the royal apartments, but Sarum was less comfortable. The twelfth-century city occupied a wind-swept hilltop site, now known as Old Sarum. It was abandoned after the nearby city of Salisbury was founded in 1217. In Eleanor's day, Sarum was dominated by its Norman keep and cathedral and surrounded by walls and a deep ditch. Water was scarce, the city was overcrowded and the severe gales so terrible that the cathedral suffered repeated damage. On the north side of the castle's inner bailey stood the two-story Court-yard House, built after 1130 and linked by a door to the Great Tower. It afforded the best domestic quarters in the castle, having four ranges sur-rounding a quadrangle, with a hall, chamber, chapel and service wing. Eleanor was probably held here, where she would have had some protec-tion from the severity of the weather.

Her allowance during these early years was a generous £161 (£117,500) annually, although thereafter it might have been as paltry as £30 (£22,000). Her household was small, and she was permitted only one damsel, her foster daughter Amaria, daughter of Ivo Pantulf, Lord of Wem. After 1180, she seems to have lived in greater state, with a chamber-lain presiding over her household and more damsels in attendance. Henry was then outlaying up to £180 (about £131,500) a year on her keep.

In Poitou and Aquitaine, the imprisonment of the Duchess provoked grief and anger. A Poitevin scribe, Guernes de Pont-Saint-Maxence, pro-tested: "There was no need for the King to fear this eagle any more. She will never make her nest somewhere else, since she has lost her feathers and will never hatch anything again." His prayer was that the King, the Queen and their children would be reconciled.

We have no insights into Eleanor's feelings at this time, but she cannot but have felt stifled and desperate. Deprived of everything that mattered to her, and of her children, she must have gone through a dark night of the soul. Richard le Poitevin wrote a poignant lament in which he envisaged her suffering and weeping in her prison:

> Daughter of Aquitaine, fair, fruitful vine! Tell me, Eagle with two heads, where were you when your eaglets, flying from their nest, dared to raise their talons against the King of the North Wind? It was you, we learned, who stirred them to bring sore affliction upon their father. For this reason, you have been ravished from your own country and carried away to a strange land. Your harp has changed into the voice of mourning, your flute sounds the note of affliction, and your songs are turned into sounds of lamentation.
>
> Reared with abundance of all delights, you had a taste for luxury and refinement and enjoyed a royal liberty. You lived richly in your own inheritance; you abounded in riches of every kind. Now, Queen with two crowns, you consume yourself with sorrow, you ravage your heart with tears.
>
> I beg of you, put an end to your continual self-affliction. Why consume yourself with sorrow, why ravage your heart with tears each day? Return, O captive, return to your own lands if you can, poor prisoner.
>
> Where is your court, where are your guards, your royal escort? where are the members of your family? Where are your handmaidens? Where are the young men of your household? Where are your councillors of state? Some, dragged far from their own soil, have suffered a shameful death, others have been deprived of their sight, and still others are banished and are counted fugitives.
>
> O Eagle of the Broken Alliance, you cry out unanswered because the King of the North Wind holds you in captivity. But cry out and cease not to cry; raise your voice like a trumpet, so that it may reach the ears of your sons. For the day is approaching when they shall deliver you and then shall you come again to dwell in your native land.

Like other commentators of the period, Richard le Poitevin saw Eleanor as the queen "described by Merlin as the Eagle of the Broken Covenant" and Henry as Merlin's King of the North Wind. His hopes were highly unrealistic. Eleanor had no means of returning to her native land; nor were her sons, sympathetic though they were to her plight, in any position to rise in her favor.

"After the great wrong committed against their father by his sons, under their mother's influence, the King openly broke his marriage vows, returning incorrigibly to his usual abyss of vice." Ralph Niger thought that Henry had imprisoned Eleanor "in order that he might more freely indulge his debaucheries." When he began living openly with Rosamund de Clifford, Giraldus was scandalized, although not enough to resist some satirical punning: "The King, who had long been a secret adulterer, now blatantly flaunted his paramour for all to see, not a rose of the world [rosa mundi], as some vain and foolish people called her, but a rose of unchastity [rosa immundi]." In 1174, Henry granted Sir Walter de Clifford a manor "for love of Rosamund."[11]

There is no evidence that Rosamund presided over the court in Eleanor's place; despite Giraldus's claim that Henry blatantly flaunted her, other chroniclers hardly mention her, and it was possibly the young Queen Marguerite who, on ceremonial occasions, stood in for her mother-in-law; her allowance was increased at this time to a level far exceeding Eleanor's.

In the summer of 1175, the King took steps to have his marriage annulled. Alys of France, eighteen-year-old Richard's affianced bride, was now fifteen, and Henry had decided to marry her himself. Giraldus stated that he intended to disinherit his sons by Eleanor and raise with Alys a new progeny, who would inherit his empire. It was also said that he intended naming John his heir, John being the only one of Eleanor's sons who had not had his mind poisoned by her.

Henry's friend Hugh of Avalon, a devout Carthusian, had always held that the King's marriage was adulterous and invalid and warned that no good issue would come of it. But an annulment could have had disastrous consequences, for the King risked losing Eleanor's vast inheritance. Her lands would revert to her and, on her death, pass to her sons, giving them the wherewithal to make war on their father. Furthermore, since she would no longer be Henry's subject, he had no grounds for keeping her a prisoner, but would have to send her back to Aquitaine, where she would be free to make mischief. She might remarry and install a hostile neighbor on his borders. He had to find a way of setting her aside without any loss to himself.

He asked Pope Alexander to send a legate to England to hear his case. The matter had to be handled with absolute discretion because his sons would certainly have opposed it. Therefore, when the legate, Cardinal Uguccione Pierlone of Sant'Angelo, arrived that autumn, it was on the pretext of resolving a quarrel between the sees of York and Canterbury. Most chroniclers guessed, however, what was really on the agenda.

The Cardinal was royally lodged in the Palace of Westminster and magnificently entertained. On November 1, Henry met him at Winchester, where an annulment was almost certainly discussed. Gervase of Canterbury learned that the King, who was not noted for his generosity, had bribed the legate with a large amount of silver—in vain. The Cardinal refused even to listen to his pleas for a hearing, and, having warned him of the risks involved in repudiating Eleanor, left England soon afterward.

At Easter 1176, Richard and Geoffrey joined their father and the Young King at Winchester. Eleanor was allowed to be present—it was the first time she had seen her sons since the outbreak of the rebellion—and Henry allocated the sum of 56s. (£2,000) for her expenses. There was an ulterior motive for his leniency. Giraldus recalled that, at that Easter court, the King had "striven eagerly with such great desire and such earnest endeavours to confine Queen Eleanor in a nun's habit," for an annulment could easily be obtained if she entered religion. He offered to set her at liberty if she promised to take the veil at Fontevraud, where she would be in Angevin territory and could be kept under supervision. He even offered her the revenues from her domains as an inducement. But Eleanor had no intention of retiring from the world or giving up her crown or her inheritance. When she appealed to the Archbishop of Rouen, he refused to consent to her being committed to Fontevraud against her will.

Back she went to her prison. The Young King continued to chafe against being denied his independence, but she was powerless to help him. In May 1176, Henry may have permitted her to be present when ambassadors of William II, King of Sicily, came to England to arrange William's marriage to Joanna. They were feasted at Winchester, where Joanna remained until August 27, when she bade her mother farewell and departed with a great train to Sicily, taking with her a costly wedding dress that may have been made to Eleanor's instructions.

Eleanor was still at Winchester at Michaelmas, when the Pipe Rolls record a payment of £28 13s. 7d. (£21,000) "by the King's writ" for "two cloaks of scarlet, two capes of scarlet, two grey furs and one embroidered coverlet for the use of the Queen and her servant girl." Joanna, seeing her mother a prisoner, may have pleaded with her father to treat her more kindly. Significantly, the damsel Amaria got the same high-status clothes as the Queen, while the provision of one coverlet suggests that they shared a bed. Later, Eleanor received a leather garment, probably for riding, for she was provided with a gilt saddle covered with scarlet, indicating that she was now allowed outdoors, accompanied by Amaria, who received a saddle of lesser worth.

On September 28, 1176, John was betrothed to his three-year-old cousin, Isabel of Gloucester, the heiress of William, Earl of Gloucester. The marriage would bring John vast estates in England. As great-grandchildren of Henry I, the couple were within the forbidden degrees of consanguinity, which raised concerns among the clergy, but the King made no efforts to obtain a dispensation.

Rosamund de Clifford died in 1176, having retired to the priory of Godstow, near Oxford. Henry, who had been generous with gifts to Godstow for her sake, had a beautiful tomb erected to her memory before the altar.

Her death would give rise to many legends. The fourteenth-century *French Chronicle of London* was the first source to assert that Eleanor brutally murdered her. However, the queen's name is given as Alienor of Provence, wife of Henry III, and the date of the murder as 1262. The fourteenth-century chronicler Ranulf Higden claimed that Rosamund was "poisoned by Queen Eleanor," who discovered her hiding place at Woodstock when she found "a clue of thread or silk" from Rosamund's sewing casket, learned the secret of the labyrinth "and so dealt with her that she lived not long after."

Over the centuries, the legends were further embroidered in popular ballads and became accepted as fact. Only in the nineteenth century was their veracity questioned. Of course, Eleanor could not have murdered Rosamund, being in custody at the time and cut off from the outside world.

In 1191, Bishop Hugh of Lincoln visited Godstow and noticed Rosamund's tomb. He ordered that she be reburied outside the church, "for she was a harlot."[12] Her body was re-interred in the nuns' chapter house in a tomb inscribed: "Here lies the rose of the world, not a clean rose; She no longer smells rosy, so hold your nose."[13]

According to Giraldus, after Rosamund retired to Godstow, the King consorted openly and shamelessly with Alys of France, his son's betrothed. That Alys was Henry's mistress is attested to by several chroniclers, although their allusions are discreet, for this new liaison was far more scandalous than that with Rosamund, since Alys was a royal princess and her precontract with her lover's son rendered it incestuous. By Christmas 1176, the affair was notorious. King Louis, hearing gossip, demanded that his daughter's marriage to Richard be celebrated without delay.

In June 1177, Henry received the "unwelcome tidings"[14] that Marguerite's newborn son, William, had lived for only three days. Soon afterward, he learned that the Papal curia had rejected his plea for an annulment and that a Papal legate was on his way to England to lay an interdict on all the King's lands if he did not at once marry Alys to his son. Henry managed to placate Louis with a promise that Alys would be married as soon as the legal formalities concerning the transfer of her dowry were completed.

In her gilded prisons, Eleanor was excluded from events, and the eternal quarrels between her husband and sons. In September 1177, her elegant and gracious daughter Leonor was sent to Castile for her marriage to King Alfonso VIII. In 1179, Henry required the Queen formally to relinquish her rights in Poitou to Richard, who took control there and was received in England with great honor by his father.[15] There is no record of his seeing his mother.

In August 1179, Louis suffered a major stroke, which effectively ended his reign; he died in September 1180. By then, his fourteen-year-old son Philip had been crowned. Philip's fiercest desire was to break up the Angevin Empire and incorporate Henry's continental domains into the kingdom of France. This imperative was to govern all his policies and make him a very dangerous adversary. He had real ability as a ruler, being tough, clever, calculating and far more astute than his father. His triumphs were to earn him a reputation as one of France's greatest kings.

Early in 1180, in place of Robert Mauduit, Henry appointed as Eleanor's custodian Ranulf Glanville, who had captured William the Lyon and succeeded Richard de Lucy as justiciar. Glanville appears largely to have delegated custodianship to Ralph FitzStephen, and Eleanor seems henceforth to have resided mainly at Winchester. References in the Pipe Rolls show that she also lodged in Somerset, Dorset and Berkshire, and enjoyed greater freedom of choice as to where she went. Sometimes Henry was at Winchester when she was there.

In 1181, Geoffrey was at last married to Constance of Brittany. After the wedding, Henry returned to England and appointed his bastard Geoffrey chancellor. Late that year, Matilda and her husband, Henry the Lion, Duke of Saxony, sought refuge at Henry's court at Rouen after the Duke had quarreled with the Emperor Frederick Barbarossa and been exiled. The King welcomed them with "sumptuous hospitality"[16] and proceeded, through diplomatic channels, to negotiate with the Emperor for their peaceful return to Germany. He also took a special interest in his grandchildren and treated them as Angevin princes, especially Otto, who was to spend most of his youth at the English court.

Henry kept the Christmas of 1182 at Caen. "Anxious to make peace between his sons," who were fighting for supremacy in Aquitaine, he attempted to bring about a reconciliation, but Richard stalked out, "uttering nothing but threats and defiance."[17] After that, the war between the eaglets resumed, and Henry marched south to subdue it. When he appeared before Limoges, the Young King's soldiers shot at him twice, and nearly killed him. His son apologized, but it was obvious that he secretly lusted for his father's death.[18] When Henry stopped his allowance, the Young King began plundering monasteries and shrines and terrorizing rural communities. After looting the holy treasures of Rocamadour, he fell violently ill with dysentery at Martel, in Quercy. As his condition worsened, the King was sent for, but his advisers suspected a trap. Instead of hastening to his son's bedside, he sent his physician and, as a token of his forgiveness, a sapphire ring that had belonged to Henry I. He also sent a message expressing his hope that, when his son had recovered, they would be reconciled.

On Saturday, June 11, the Young King, realizing that he was dying, asked to be clothed in a hair shirt and a crusader's cloak and laid on a bed of ashes on the floor, with a noose around his neck and bare stones at his head and feet, as befitted a penitent. When Henry's ring was brought to him, he begged that his father would show grace and mercy to the Queen his mother, and that all his companions would plead with Henry to set her at liberty. He died late that evening, aged only twenty-eight.

When Henry heard the news, he "threw himself upon the ground and greatly bewailed his son."[19] He was so distraught that Peter of Blois was moved to reprove him for his "excess of grief."

The King sent Thomas Agnell, Archdeacon of Wells, to break the news to Eleanor at Sarum. Agnell found her calm and unsurprised. She had had a dream that foretold her loss. She had seen her son lying on a couch with his hands together as if in prayer, and it had struck her that he looked like a tomb effigy. On his finger could be seen a great sapphire ring—the one his father, unknown to Eleanor, had sent him—and, above his white face, there hovered two crowns. The first was the one he had worn at his coronation, but the second was a circlet of pure dazzling light that shone with the incomparable brightness of the Holy Grail.

"What other meaning than eternal bliss can be ascribed to a crown with no beginning and no end?" the Queen asked Agnell. "And what can such brightness signify, so pure and so resplendent, if not the wonder of everlasting joy? This second crown was more beautiful than anything which can manifest itself to our senses here on Earth. As the Gospel says, 'Eye hath not seen, nor ear heard, neither have entered into the heart of Man, the things which God hath prepared for them that love Him.'"

Agnell praised her composure and the way in which she had "fathomed the mystery of the dream and had, in consequence, borne the news of her son's death with great discernment, strength and equanimity."[20] Yet her grief went very deep: a decade later, she told Pope Celestine III that she was tortured by the memory of the Young King.

The prince's death removed one of the most dangerous threats to Henry's security and left Richard the undisputed heir to England, Normandy, Anjou, Poitou and Aquitaine.

14

"Freed from Prison"

✝

I N 1183, HENRY II WAS FIFTY. GRAY-HAIRED, CORPULENT, BOW-legged from years of sitting in a saddle and, thanks to a kick from a horse, lame in one leg, he was in deteriorating health, often troubled by chronic illnesses. The death of the Young King, and his dying request, together with the pleas of Matilda, may have prompted a change in Henry's attitude toward Eleanor, but it was for political reasons that he freed her and summoned her to Normandy.

King Philip was insisting that certain properties in the duchy belonged to the Young Queen in right of her late husband, but Henry was adamant that they had belonged to Eleanor and that she had assigned them to her son for his lifetime, after which they would revert to her. To reinforce his point, he wanted her to visit those domains. This marked the beginning of a period in which she would be allowed greater freedom, albeit under supervision.

Geoffrey de Vigeois says that Eleanor stayed in Normandy for six months. After ten years of estrangement, she and Henry apparently achieved a working, mutually beneficial relationship designed to preempt their sons resenting him for his treatment of her. There may have been some vestiges of affection between them, for, according to Giraldus, those "whom [Henry] had once loved, he rarely regarded with hatred." Nevertheless, as events would show, he remained suspicious of Eleanor.

At this time, he was keeping Alys under guard at Winchester and still stalling in the face of Philip's demands that he marry her to Richard without delay, fearing that Philip would try to turn Richard against him.

He wanted peace between his sons and was seeking to make a fairer division of his empire between Richard and John, who was so much the poorer in lands that Henry nicknamed him "Lackland."

John was now sixteen. He had curly auburn hair and a strongly built body, which, as he grew older, became portly as a result of "an excessive voracity by which his belly was always insatiable."[1] He had been well educated in the household of Eleanor's custodian, the Justiciar, Ranulf Glanville, who may have allowed him to visit his mother.

John was intelligent, with a sharp, inquiring mind. In later life, he acquired many theological manuscripts and works by Pliny and French historians, which would form the nucleus of the future royal library. Yet he was "light minded,"[2] self-indulgent and greedy. He had a relaxed approach to life, and loved hunting, hawking, carousing and gambling. His wit, conversational skills and accessibility made him popular. Aware of the need to dress as befitted his status, he spent extravagantly on fine clothes and accumulated a large collection of jewelry. His accounts list cloaks and girdles encrusted with diamonds and sapphires and white gloves studded with a ruby and a sapphire.

When he bestirred himself, John could exert as much energy and vigor as his father and brother. He disliked war, but occasionally displayed brilliance as a military commander, yet he was often fatally dilatory, a failing that earned him the nickname "John Softsword." He was ruthless, vindictive, cruel, restless, cynical and impatient, and temperamentally incapable of keeping faith with anyone. Having inherited the notorious Angevin temper, he would, in a rage, bite and gnaw his fingers, and once set fire to the house of someone who had offended him.

John was notoriously promiscuous and fathered up to twelve bastards. The names of some of his mistresses appear in the records, but few seem to have enjoyed his attentions for long, although he could be generous while they were in favor. John's critics would claim that his immorality led him astray from the teachings of the Church. He "led such a dissipated life that he ceased to believe in the resurrection of the dead and other articles of the Christian faith [and] made blasphemous and ribald remarks,"[3] his favorite oaths being "By God's teeth!" and "By God's feet!"[4] He took gleeful pleasure in shocking churchmen, never attending mass and rarely observing feast or fast days. Once, seeing a slaughtered buck, he remarked, "You happy beast, never forced to patter prayers nor dragged to Holy Mass."[5]

Eleanor had been a prisoner for much of John's childhood. He was spoiled because his charm blinded his indulgent father to his faults. Now, Henry made a great blunder. He demanded that his sons make peace with each other and that Richard cede Poitou and Aquitaine to John. Burning with resentment, Richard declared that under no circumstances would he yield a furrow of his land to anyone.

Richard soon had further cause for grievance. The repeated postponement of his marriage to Alys had led Philip to believe that Henry still intended to repudiate Eleanor and dispossess his sons so that he could marry Alys himself. Richard himself was suspicious of Henry's intentions, and aware that his own marriage to Alys was now politically to his advantage, for it would gain him a powerful ally in the French King.

When Henry and Philip met in December 1183 at Gisors, Henry again protested that he could not assign the Young King's lands in Normandy and Anjou to Marguerite because they belonged to Eleanor. He did promise that, if Alys were not immediately married to Richard, she would be married to John. This alarmed Philip and Richard, for it seemed to confirm their suspicions that Henry meant to make John his heir. When Henry did homage to Philip, he ominously revoked into his own hands all the territories he had assigned to his sons, thus making them once more completely dependent on him. He had desired to be at peace with them, but it was clear that this would be on his own terms. Their resentment would cause such discord during the remaining years of his life that "he could find no abiding state of happiness or enjoyment of security."[6]

Eleanor returned to England late in 1183 to "make a progress about her dower lands."[7] She kept Easter at Berkhamsted, where, in June 1184, she was joined by her daughter Matilda, who was to remain with her for a year.

She was now allowed more freedom of movement. After Easter, she moved to Woodstock, where she seems to have remained until June, when Henry returned to England. She was present at Winchester when Matilda bore a son, William. Her name begins to appear more frequently in the Pipe Rolls, which record Henry's gifts of a scarlet gown lined with gray miniver, a saddle worked with gold and trimmed with fur, embroidered cushions, and items for Amaria. Together, they cost over £28 (£20,500).

It is likely that Henry's secret affair with Alys was still ongoing, unknown to Richard, although an entry in the Pipe Rolls might suggest that he had another mistress at this time. There is an intriguing payment of £55 17s. (£40,800) "for clothes and hoods and cloaks, and for the trimming for two capes of samite and for the clothes of the Queen and of Bellebelle, for the King's use." Historians have often assumed that Bellebelle was Henry's mistress, or one of Eleanor's damsels. It has been more convincingly suggested that the entry actually refers to a *"belle baubel,"* a pretty trinket.

In July, Eleanor returned with Henry the Lion, Matilda and their children to Berkhamsted for the rest of the summer. Her sons were still warring over the assignment of Aquitaine to Sona, but, in November, Henry summoned them to England. Eleanor and Matilda traveled to London from Windsor—evidently in great state, for £104 (£76,000) was outlaid on their expenses—to join him at a court convened at Westminster to bring about a concord between the princes. There, on November 30, St. Andrew's Day, Eleanor was reunited with her sons.

Henry needed her support for his plans regarding their inheritances. Wearing samite trimmed with fur, she sat in the place of honor in the council chamber and watched as Richard, Geoffrey and John were called forward to make peace with one another. The King then asked her to approve the assignment of Poitou and Aquitaine to John, on the grounds that it constituted a fairer distribution of his empire, but the Queen, supported by an angry Richard, alongside Baldwin of Forde, the newly elected Archbishop of Canterbury, and some councilors, refused. Realizing that Philip, as her overlord, would also support her, if only to drive a wedge through the Angevin family, Henry backed down.

At Archbishop Baldwin's behest, the King agreed to permit Eleanor to remain "freed from prison."[8] She spent Christmas with her family at Windsor. Afterward, Richard returned to Poitiers. Early in 1185, Eleanor was at Winchester in the company of Matilda and her family. Later that year, Matilda and her husband were able to return in safety to Germany, leaving three of their children—Otto, William and Matilda—to be brought up in Henry's household.

On April 16, Henry sailed to Normandy, determined to bring Richard to heel. In late April, he summoned Eleanor, Henry the Lion and Matilda to join him for a family summit. When they arrived at Alençon in May, Henry commanded Richard to surrender the whole of Aquitaine to his mother because it was her heritage; if he did not, she would make it her business to ravage the land with a great host.

How far Eleanor concurred in this is not known. She had herself ceded her lands to Richard and had not been afraid to speak out against Henry giving them to John. She would surely have protested against this new demand if it had not found favor with her, yet perhaps her newfound liberty was too precarious for her to risk defying Henry again. It is unlikely that she had any real intention of laying waste to Poitou; it was Henry who was determined to assert her right to it, to teach Richard a lesson.

Richard "heeded the wise advice of his friends" (and perhaps Eleanor) and surrendered "the whole of Aquitaine to his mother."[9] He returned to Henry's court in Normandy "and remained with his father like a tamed son."[10] Eleanor stayed with them; she was to travel around the Continent with Henry until April 1186.

From now on, although Henry was in overall control of the government of Aquitaine, he would at various times share it with Eleanor and Richard, and some charters would be issued by all three; Eleanor's were submissively granted "with the assent and will of my lord, Henry, King of England, and of my sons, Richard, Geoffrey and John." She was reinvested with the ducal coronet of Aquitaine, and Roger of Howden asserts that, for a time, she was exercising sovereign power in Bordeaux; yet, within the next two years, she would resign her authority to Richard.

In the early spring of 1186, Henry and Eleanor held court together in Normandy. On April 27, they crossed from Barfleur to Southampton.[11] Eleanor stayed at Winchester while Henry went on a summer progress; Alys may have been there too. A second custodian for the Queen, Henry of Berneval, was appointed around this time, prompting some historians to infer that she had once again begun plotting rebellion, although there is no evidence for this. In fact, payments of queen-gold were resumed after her return and, the following year, the Waverley annalist was of the opinion that "King Henry and Queen Eleanor" were reconciled. By then, Eleanor was receiving a generous allowance of £20 (£14,500) a month. She now had several damsels waiting on her, and she and they were well provided with clothes.

In August 1186, Geoffrey, Duke of Brittany, was trampled to death in a tournament at Paris. He was buried in the choir of Notre-Dame "with but few regrets from his father, to whom he had been an unfaithful son, but with sore grief to the French."[12] Eleanor later wrote that she was "tortured with the memory of [her] dead" sons. Henry visited her at Winchester in October, but there is no mention of her being present when he kept Christmas with John at Guildford, nor did she accompany him to Normandy in February 1187. She seems to have resided mainly at Winchester and Sarum that year.

On March 29, at Nantes, Constance bore Geoffrey a posthumous son. Henry wanted him named after himself, but "the Bretons called their new duke Arthur,"[13] in memory of the legendary king who had once, it was believed, ruled Brittany; it was a defiant gesture of independence against Angevin rule. Eleanor protested, but Constance, who hated her husband's relations, ignored her.

Philip was growing increasingly angry and frustrated about Henry's repeated deferment of Alys's marriage to Richard and demanded that both she and her dowry be immediately returned to him. When Henry tried to put him off, Philip seized Châteauroux, the first engagement in a war that would drag on intermittently for many years. When Henry and Richard joined forces to resist him, Philip requested a parley, and on June 23, 1187, the two kings concluded a truce.

15

"His Heart's Desire"

✠

S OMETIME IN THE 1180S, ACCORDING TO BERTRAN DE BORN,
Richard freed himself from his obligation to marry Alys and obtained
from Sancho VI, King of Navarre, the promise of the hand of his eldest
daughter, Berengaria. This was probably in April 1185, when Richard
met with Alfonso II of Aragon at Najac, Gascony, and offered to mediate
in a dispute with Sancho. In 1185, Sancho granted Berengaria the fief of
Monreale, which conferred on her the status of an independent magnate
and may have been intended to enhance her appeal for Richard.

Navarre was a small kingdom that straddled the Pyrenees and the pilgrim route to Compostela. An alliance with Sancho would have helped to
protect Aquitaine from the ambitions of the counts of Toulouse, while
Navarre would gain a mighty ally against the hostile neighboring kingdoms of Castile and Aragon. When meeting with Sancho, Richard may
have seen Berengaria. According to the later account of Richard de Templo, the probable compiler of the *Itinerarium Perigrinorum et Gesta Regis
Ricardi* (*The Itinerary of King Richard I*), "a long time previous, while yet
count of Poitou, he had been charmed by the graces of the damsel and
her high birth, and felt a passion for her." The chronicler Ambrose stated
that Richard "had loved her very much from the time when he was count
of Poitou and she had been his heart's desire." Another contemporary
asserted that he "was attracted by her graceful manner and high birth"
and "had desired her for a very long time."[1] Richard of Devizes wrote that
Richard so greatly admired the accomplishments of Berengaria's mind
and the attractions of her person that he addressed verses to her. There

is no evidence to support the romantic tale that he had visited the Navarrese court at Pamplona in 1177 and seen her at a tournament.

King Sancho VI, known as "El Sabio" ("the Wise"), was the great-grandson of the famous hero warrior El Cid, who fought to free Spain from Moorish rule. He was a liberal monarch who founded religious houses, made beneficial laws, looked to the prosperity of his people and protected his realm from encroachments by his enemies. In 1140, the kings of Castile and Aragon had made a pact to overrun and partition Navarre between them, and they had since made inroads upon its border, which Sancho had tried to reclaim—unsuccessfully until 1168, when the King of Aragon allied with him against Castile.

Sancho and his wife, Sancha of Castile, were a handsome couple. Berengaria, whose name meant "bear spear," was one of seven children. Her eldest brother, Sancho, born around 1157, was heir to the Navarrese throne. She was close to her younger, sole surviving sister, Blanche. In 1960, an analysis of remains thought to be Berengaria's suggested that she had been born around 1165–70, while a chronicle written by Rodrigo Jiminez de Rada, Archbishop of Toledo, around 1240, placed her birth in the mid 1170s. As will be seen, she was probably born a decade earlier.

Berengaria spent her formative years in the palaces of her father: the colonnaded Romanesque Palacio de los Reyes in Estella; the rather stark Palacio Real de San Pedro in Pamplona; the Olite Palace in Pamplona, of which only the outer walls remain from Berengaria's time, and the monastery of Leyre, where her ancestors were buried. The Navarrese court divided its time between Pamplona, Estella, Tudela and Najera, and the princesses would have been cared for by an *aya*, or governess.

Berengaria was taught literacy skills and must have been imbued with some of the learning so prized by her father, a cultivated man who enjoyed the works of Virgil and Ovid, patronized scholars, founded libraries and amassed a large collection of illuminated manuscripts. His court had its own school of polyphony; it was frequented by troubadours and welcomed musicians from Barcelona, all of whom may have inspired in Berengaria a love of poetry and music, interests she could share with Richard.

Apart from Bertran's account, there is no other record of negotiations for a marriage alliance with Navarre at this time. Bertran wrote of the shame Philip must have felt on hearing of Richard's new betrothal with

Berengaria, and claimed that Henry II vetoed the match. In fact, Richard was never free to pursue it. He remained betrothed to Alys, which must have rankled, even though his father continued to ensure that his own affair with her was kept private. During the next few years, Alys would secretly bear Henry a son and a daughter, "who did not survive."[2]

Richard's resentment against his father had long festered, and he now deserted him and rode to Paris to ally himself with Philip, who "so honoured him that every day they ate at the same table, shared the same dish, and at night the bed did not separate them. And the King of France loved him as his own soul and their mutual affection was so strong that, because of its vehemence, the Lord King of England was dumbfounded."[3]

Some modern writers have inferred from this passage that Richard and Philip had a homosexual relationship. Yet Roger of Howden, who wrote this account, expressed no moral outrage. It was not unusual for people of rank to share beds; it was customary for men to take each other by the hand, or exchange kisses, both signs of peace and political amity. The friendship between Richard and Philip was political and their sharing a bed a sign of royal brotherhood, and a great honor. They may have gone out of their way to demonstrate their affection, if only to provoke Henry, who was justified in feeling alarmed, for Philip convinced Richard that his father meant to marry Alys to John and make John duke of Aquitaine. Stung at such perfidy, Richard offered to assist Philip in his war against Henry.

In 1180, Guy de Lusignan, a scion of the turbulent Lusignan family of Poitou, had married Sybilla of Jerusalem and, six years later, in her right, had become king of Jerusalem. On July 4, 1188, his army was annihilated by Muslim forces led by their brilliant commander, Saladin. After that, the Muslims swept all before them and, on October 2, to the horror of Christendom, occupied Jerusalem—that most holy of cities and the destination of vast numbers of pilgrims. All that now remained of the great crusader kingdom was three seaports.

The duty of the leaders of the West was clear: they must unite to free the holy city from the Infidel. The Pope proclaimed a new crusade and, on the day after receiving news of the fall of Jerusalem, Richard took the cross, vowing that he would dedicate his life to liberating the Holy Sepulchre. But he told his father he would not depart until Henry assured him that his position as heir to the Angevin Empire was secure. Henry refused, which left Richard all the more certain that he meant to leave everything to John.

In spring 1189, Henry and Philip again began quarreling over Alys and, in June, hostilities erupted again. On July 10, Henry left England for the last time, having visited Sarum, probably to make arrangements for Eleanor to be held more securely. That she had again been deprived of her liberty can be inferred from Gervase of Canterbury's statement that she was released from prison on Henry's death, and from that of Ralph of Diceto, who wrote that she had then been "for many years under close guard." Henry had good reason to fear that she would take Richard's part against him.

At Easter 1189, Philip and Richard invaded Henry's domains, taking castle after castle. The King's barons in Maine, Touraine and Anjou, tired of his autocratic and oppressive rule, deserted him. When Philip's army appeared before the walls of Le Mans, Henry's birthplace, the King ordered that a suburb be fired as a defensive tactic, but the wind fanned the flames and the city itself began to burn, enabling the French to breach its defenses, forcing Henry to flee. Suffering from an anal fistula and the effects of blood poisoning, he retreated to Chinon, worrying about John, who had mysteriously disappeared.

On July 4, the day after Tours fell to the French, Henry dragged himself from his sickbed and rode to a meeting with Philip at Colombières, complaining, "My whole body is on fire."[4] Philip offered to have a cloak spread on the ground for him to sit on, but Henry retorted stiffly that he had not come to sit, but to learn the price he must pay for peace. He had no choice but to agree to leave all his territories to Richard, surrender Alys into Philip's custody and arrange, without delay or excuse, for Richard to marry her after returning from Jerusalem; finally, he was to pay Philip an indemnity of 20,000 marks (£980,000) in token of his good faith. Defeated, Henry accepted these humiliating terms without demur. Philip insisted that he give Richard the kiss of peace, which he reluctantly did, saying, "God grant that I may not die until I have had a fitting revenge on you."[5]

He was carried back to Chinon in a litter, cursing his sons. On July 5, as he lay sick, he was shown a list of those vassals who had treacherously supported Richard and were to be spared punishment. The first name on the list was John's.

For Henry, this was the worst blow of all. But he had known in his heart that John was untrustworthy. Some years earlier, he had commissioned murals for the painted chamber in Winchester Castle. "There was an eagle painted, and four young ones perched upon it, one on each wing and a third upon its back, tearing at the parent with talons and beaks, and the fourth sitting upon its neck, awaiting the moment to peck out its parent's eyes. When the King's close friends asked him the meaning of the picture, he said, 'The four eaglets are my four sons, who cease not to persecute me even unto death. And the youngest, whom I now embrace with such tender affection, will some day afflict me more grievously and perilously than all the others.'"[6]

John's betrayal deprived Henry of the will to live. Delirious, he cried, "Shame, shame on a conquered king!"[7] On July 6, 1189, he died at Chinon. His bastard Geoffrey, faithful to the end, was the only one of his sons present at his deathbed.

16

"Her Third Nesting"

✠

WHEN RICHARD WAS INFORMED BY WILLIAM THE MARSHAL of Henry's death, he hastened to Chinon. As he looked upon the body on the bier, "one could not tell from his expression whether he felt joy or sorrow, grief, anger or satisfaction,"[1] and it was noted with disapproval that he knelt to pray for "scarcely longer than the space of a paternoster."[2] Everyone watched, horrified, as blood flowed from the nostrils of the dead King and did not cease for as long as his son remained there, as if his spirit was angered at Richard's presence.

Weeping, Richard accompanied the body of his father to Fontevraud. Henry had asked to be buried at Grandmont, but the weather remained hot, the body would not keep, and Fontevraud was near Chinon. Giraldus thought it fitting that he was buried in that "obscure and unsuitable" abbey where he had wanted to immure Eleanor as a nun.

The burial took place on July 10. Around 1200, a tomb was built, probably commissioned by Eleanor, with an effigy that mirrors contemporary descriptions of Henry and is the earliest surviving effigy of an English king. Ralph of Diceto transcribed the epitaph: "I am Henry the King. To me divers realms were subject. Eight feet of ground doth now suffice for whom the Earth was not enough."

The judgments passed on Henry II by his contemporaries were harsh. Clerics such as Giraldus, Gervase of Canterbury and Ralph Niger viciously condemned what they described as his oppression, injustice, immorality and perfidy. Only Ralph of Diceto wrote of Henry's good qualities. Later, the King's critics had cause to revise their opinions. "The evils that we are now suffering have revived the memory of his good deeds, and the man who in his own time was hated by many is now declared everywhere to have been an excellent and beneficial ruler."[3]

In opposing his father, Richard had "earned the disapproval of good and wise men. Now he sought to make up for all his past excesses by doing all he could to show honour to his mother," hoping to atone "for his offences."[4] Immediately, he sent William the Marshal to England with orders for the release of Queen Eleanor from "her husband's prison"[5] and letters authorizing her to act as ruler of England until he was ready to take possession of his royal inheritance.

When he arrived at Winchester, William found Eleanor "already at liberty and happier than she was accustomed to be."[6] News of Henry's death had preceded him, and her custodians, bearing in mind the love King Richard had for his mother, and his fearsome reputation, had not demurred when she demanded to be set free. The Marshal found the Queen "more the great lady than ever,"[7] presiding over a hastily assembled court, with people rushing to pay their respects.

He informed Eleanor that she had been "entrusted with the power of acting as regent by her son" and "ordaining what she wished in the kingdom." The King had "issued mandates to the princes of the realm," almost in the style of a general edict, that the Queen's word should be law in all matters.[8]

Eleanor now came into her own. At sixty-five—then a great age—she still had boundless energy, and her new authority sat easily upon her. Invested with more power than she had ever enjoyed, she was eager to grasp the reins of government and aid her son. Such was the respect she commanded that she would remain the second power in the realm during the first half of Richard's reign.

Effortlessly, she took command, devoting her energies to winning support for Richard in England; having spent most of his life in Aquitaine, he was a stranger to his new subjects. Gathering her retinue, which included the Justiciar, Ranulf Glanville, Eleanor rode to Westminster, where she decreed "that every freeman in the whole realm must swear that he would bear fealty to the Lord Richard, lord of England."[9] Barons and prelates flocked to her and, on behalf of the King, she received their oaths of allegiance in the presence of the Archbishop of Canterbury.

She ordered a new seal, not that of a queen mother, but of a queen regnant of England, "by the grace of God," a new style adopted by Henry II in 1172; it shows her holding a scepter with an orb surmounted by a dove.

After a few days in London, Eleanor set off on a progress through the southern shires, "moving her queenly court from city to city and from castle to castle, just as she thought proper."[10] "She arranged matters in the kingdom according to her own pleasure, and the nobles were instructed to obey her in every respect."[11] Wherever she went, she received oaths of homage on Richard's behalf and dispensed justice in his name. She also sent forth "a body of trustworthy men, both clergy and laity, throughout all the counties of England" to extract oaths of loyalty to the new King and to herself, and to stamp out local abuses. She transacted the business of court and chancery, using her own seal on deeds and official documents, while writs were given by the Justiciar "by the Queen's precept." She issued edicts decreeing that uniform weights and measures were to be used, and that a new standard coinage was to be issued. In Surrey, she founded a hospital for the poor, the sick and the infirm.

As Richard had directed, Eleanor sent messengers to every shire relaying his wishes that, "for the good of King Henry's soul," exiles were to be recalled to the King's peace and all those who had been unjustly imprisoned were to be released, on condition that they promised to preserve the peace of the realm.[12] Although William of Newburgh spoke for many when he complained that, "through the King's clemency, these pests who came forth from the prisons would perhaps become bolder thieves in the future," this amnesty held much personal appeal for the Queen, who had found, "by her own experience, that confinement was distasteful to men, and that to be released therefrom was a most delightful refreshment to the spirits."[13]

It was generally a popular measure, one of several designed to win the people's love for their new monarch. Eleanor also ordered a relaxation of the harsh forest laws, pardoned felons who had been outlawed for trespassing or poaching in the royal forests, and "contained the depredations of those sheriffs who were charged with the care of the forests, intimidating them with the threat of severe penalties."[14] She married off wealthy heiresses formerly in Henry's wardship to powerful men known to be loyal to Richard, or to those whose loyalty needed to be courted. "Learning that King Henry II's horses had been kept in the stables of the abbeys," at great expense she "distributed them as gifts with pious liberality,"[15] a move that was thankfully welcomed, especially by the poorer monasteries. She intervened out of "urgent necessity" in a dispute between Archbishop Baldwin and his clergy over his plan to establish a collegiate church dedicated to St. Thomas Becket at Hackington, Kent, which the monks felt would rival Canterbury Cathedral. Eleanor supported the Archbishop and had the monks digging ditches and building walls at Hackington.

Her measures were implemented on a tide of approval because she stood for legitimacy. Her authority and mandate extended across the whole of the Angevin Empire. She had the experience, the personal qualities and the sheer force of personality to operate effectively in the political milieu that was her natural habitat. In her every act, she displayed "remarkable sagacity,"[16] showing herself to be a wise, benevolent and statesmanlike ruler. Surviving documents show how closely she was bound up with government and administrative matters. In the years to come, she would issue more than ninety charters.

Many now found it hard to credit the scandalous rumors about her conduct in her younger days. Her contemporaries saw her as a venerable elder stateswoman. Her rule made her "exceedingly respected and beloved."[17] It is on her performance in these later years that her modern reputation chiefly rests. Already, chroniclers such as Roger of Howden were hurriedly censoring their earlier accounts of her.

In the midst of all this activity, Eleanor made time to ensure the salvation of Henry's soul. She gave alms from the revenues of Winchester in his memory, and gifts to Amesbury Priory, which he had founded, in return for prayers to speed him through purgatory. Her mercy did not, however, extend to Alys of France, of whom she now had custody. On her orders, the princess remained confined at Winchester.

On July 29, 1189, Richard was invested as duke of Normandy in Rouen Cathedral. Two days later, at Gisors, he assured Philip that he intended to marry Alys after returning from the Holy Land and agreed to depart on crusade with him the following spring. On August 13, he sailed from Barfleur to Portsmouth, where he was welcomed with enthusiasm. Two days later, he was reunited with his mother just outside Winchester and "was received with stately ceremony."[18]

Thus was fulfilled the prophecy, that the Eagle of the Broken Alliance should rejoice in her third nesting. "They called the Queen the eagle because she stretched out her wings, as it were, over two kingdoms, France and England. She had been separated from her French relatives by divorce, while the King had separated her from her marriage bed by confining her to prison. Richard, her third son, was her third nestling, and the one who would raise his mother's name to great glory."[19]

Richard formally pardoned Ranulf Glanville for releasing the Queen from captivity in contravention of the late King's orders, but imposed a heavy fine on him. He granted Eleanor powers to punish those who had been her jailers, but she declined to do so. On September 17, Richard dismissed Glanville and appointed William de Mandeville, Earl of Essex, a loyal servant of his father, and Hugh de Puiset, Bishop of Durham, as co-justiciars in his place. Hugh, a nephew of King Stephen, was a cultivated man with vast experience of politics and diplomacy.

Shortly after Richard arrived in Winchester, John joined the court and accompanied the King and Eleanor to Windsor, where they were greeted by Geoffrey, the Chancellor. Richard seems to have suspected Geoffrey— with little cause—of having designs on the throne. Yet he could not afford to alienate him, since he dared not risk leaving an enemy to make mischief in his kingdom while he was away on crusade. He therefore honored his father's dying wish and appointed Geoffrey archbishop-elect of York. Eleanor, who also distrusted the late King's bastard, was against the appointment. Despite Geoffrey's talents and abilities, he was hotheaded, difficult and quarrelsome, and had no love for the half-brothers who had betrayed their father—but the King overrode her protests.

As chancellor, the King appointed in Geoffrey's place a Norman, William Longchamp, Bishop of Ely, who had been his chancellor in Aquitaine. Of short stature, with a limp and a stammer (Giraldus likened him to a deformed, hairy ape), Longchamp was regarded by the barons as an upstart. Overambitious and overconfident, he used his newly won power to advance his own interests. He made no secret of his loathing for all things English and alienated many by his arrogance and blundering tactlessness, yet, for all his faults, he was unswervingly loyal to the King.

John was eager to marry Isabel of Gloucester and gain control of her vast estates. Archbishop Baldwin had forbidden them to wed because they were second cousins, and many churchmen denounced the marriage as uncanonical, but Richard gave permission for it to take place. John did not wait for Pope Clement III to reply to his request for the necessary Papal dispensation. On August 29, he married Isabel at Marlborough, and was thereafter styled earl of Gloucester. An outraged Archbishop Baldwin summoned him to explain why he had gone ahead with the marriage and, when John did not appear, pronounced it null and void and laid both parties' estates under an interdict. John appealed to the Papal legate in England, who revoked the ban and applied to Pope Clement, who is said to have granted a dispensation but forbidden the couple to have sexual relations. There is no record of John and Isabel having any children. They toured Normandy together more than once, but seem to have separated by 1193.

When John married, Richard gave him the county of Mortain in Normandy and six English counties, making him the wealthiest and most powerful English magnate. Many believed this advancement betokened Richard's intention of naming John as his heir, even though Arthur of Brittany had a prior claim. It could also have been a strategy designed to keep him content while Richard was away on crusade.

Eleanor had been preparing for Richard's coronation and advising which earls, barons and sheriffs were to be invited. On September 1, she and the King rode in state through London streets hung with tapestries and garlands to St. Paul's Cathedral, whence they were escorted by "a ceremonious procession" of nobles and prelates to Westminster. Two days afterward, on September 3, Richard proceeded to Westminster Abbey for the most magnificent coronation England had ever witnessed. There "were present his brother John and his mother Eleanor, counts and barons, and an immense crowd of men and soldiers."[20] Women were barred from Richard's coronation because the King was as yet unmarried, but Queen Eleanor was invited at the request of the nobility and sheriffs. Richard had authorized her to spend lavishly on robes for them both;

those she ordered for herself and her attendants cost £7 0s. 6d. (about £5,000) and included a cape made of silk trimmed with squirrel and sable, luxurious scarlet cloth, two sables, a piece of miniver and linen.

Richard "celebrated the occasion by a festival of three days, manifesting his liberality and great excellence."[21] Women, even Eleanor, were excluded from the coronation banquet in Westminster Hall, where guests "feasted so splendidly that the wine flowed along the pavement and walls of the palace."[22]

Then "the leaders of the Jews arrived, against the express decree of the King."[23] The Jews were deeply unpopular. They were blamed for sending Jesus Christ to his death and rumored to have sacrificed or crucified Christian children. They were envied for their wealth and resented because of the profits they made from moneylending. Universally, they were seen as usurers, making money by charging interest on loans. Usury was banned by the Church, which regarded it as a sin, yet many Christians were not averse to borrowing large sums from the Jews.

At Richard's coronation feast, "the courtiers laid hands on the Jews and stripped and flogged them and threw them out of the King's court. Some they killed, others they left half dead. The people of London, following the courtiers' example, began killing and robbing and burning the Jews."[24] Despite measures taken by the King to halt it—the Jews were officially under his protection—this flaring of anti-Semitism spread throughout his realm. There were attacks on the Jews in Bishop's (now King's) Lynn, Norwich, Lincoln, Stamford and York.

For all his lion-hearted reputation, Richard I was to prove a failure as king of England. He would spend only ten months of his reign in his realm. He spoke no English and was in every respect a Poitevin. He lacked his father's skills as an administrator. Yet, despite his ferocity and severity, he captured the imagination of his subjects, who admired his chivalrous exploits and applauded his dedication to freeing the Holy Land from the Infidel.

As soon as he was crowned, he threw himself with superhuman energy into preparing for the crusade. He milked England dry, imposing crippling taxes. "Everything was for sale: powers, lordships, earldoms, shrievalties, castles, towns, manors and suchlike."[25] "The King most obligingly unburdened all those whose money was a burden to them," observed Richard of Devizes.

"If I could have found a buyer, I would have sold London itself," Richard declared.[26] He regarded his kingdom as no more than a bank from which to draw funds. When he forced Abbot Samson of St. Edmundsbury to buy the royal manor of Mildenhall for twice its assessed value, Eleanor was due her ten percent in queen-gold. The Abbot offered her a gold cup worth 100 marks (£49,000) in lieu, but she generously returned it to him "on behalf of the soul of her lord, King Henry."[27]

On November 25, 1189, Eleanor was present in council at Canterbury when Richard made peace between the Archbishop and his monks. In December, he restored her dower, augmenting the dower rights enjoyed by the consorts of Henry I and King Stephen. She was also assigned lands in Normandy, Touraine, Maine and Poitou. Richard allowed her to resume collecting queen-gold and to draw freely on the revenues of her southern domains. For three years, three clerks were busy at the Exchequer sorting out a backlog of payments due to her.

Richard now made arrangements for the government of his kingdom during his absence on crusade. Eleanor was to be effectively regent, assisted and advised by Hugh de Puiset and William Longchamp. The two men were rivals, and Longchamp's prime objective was to oust de Puiset from power and rule alone, but both deferred to Eleanor's authority, as the King expected them to do, hoping that she would keep the peace between them. Richard temporarily resigned to her his powers as count of Poitou and duke of Aquitaine, which she delegated to her grandson, Otto of Saxony. John was not given any share in the regency.

On December 12, Richard left England to settle affairs in his continental domains before setting out on crusade. As his fleet of more than a hundred ships was assembling on the English coast, he accumulated provisions and drew up strict rules of conduct for his crusading forces. Knowing how the presence of Eleanor and her ladies had hampered the progress of the Second Crusade, he decreed that no women were to accompany the army, a decision endorsed by a Papal bull.

On February 2, 1190, while holding a Candlemas court at La Réole by the Garonne river, Richard summoned Eleanor, John, Alys and the archbishops of Canterbury and York to attend him. They joined him at Bures. Alys was then sent, under guard, to Rouen, where she remained a prisoner.

In March, Richard convened a family conclave at Nonancourt, attended by Eleanor, John, the two archbishops and a host of prelates. He made John swear on oath that he would not set foot in England for three years. Eleanor protested that this was unjust and persuaded Richard to release John from his promise on condition that he would faithfully serve his brother, and that Longchamp agreed to his coming. It was a decision both Richard and Eleanor would have cause to regret. Archbishop Geoffrey was also required to undertake to stay out of England for three years.

Concerns about the succession were probably expressed at the conference, since the King had no direct heir to succeed him in the event of his dying on crusade. It is likely too that Richard's marriage was discussed. The King needed an heir, and Alys's anomalous position had to be resolved. Her affair with Henry II would forever lie as an impediment between her and Richard, compromising the legitimacy of any children they might have. Marriage with her was therefore out of the question, and the eminent clergy present were probably consulted on the canonical implications of breaking the betrothal.

Eleanor was implacably opposed to Richard marrying Alys. It was at her insistence that he pursued the marriage alliance with Navarre because her hatred of Louis VII would not, at any price, allow her to permit her son to marry Louis's daughter.[28] A late-thirteenth-century Castilian chronicle of the Third Crusade, *La Gran Conquista de Ultramar*—the earliest Spanish source to refer to Berengaria of Navarre—stated that Eleanor "could not endure that Richard should espouse Alys," but, above all, "she wanted to provide her son with a worthy wife who would give him an incontestable heir."[29] "She enquired as to where she could find such a worthy wife, and learned that the daughters of Sancho VI, King of Navarre, were still unwed and that she could probably get one of these for her son." Richard asked her to write to King Sancho and open negotiations.[30]

The King had recently renewed an alliance with Aragon; it made sense to make a treaty with Aragon's ally, Navarre. Sancho VI was friendly and could be relied upon during Richard's absence to protect his southern borders from the French and the ambitions of Raymond of Toulouse. An alliance with Sancho would promote trade between England and Navarre and afford easier travel between England and the Iberian peninsula, and it would cement good relations with Aragon, which was allied with Navarre against the pretensions of Alfonso VIII of Castile in Gascony.

Another advantage was that Berengaria had a substantial dowry. Her reputation was unbesmirched. She had had experience of the duties of queenship: after the death of her mother, Sancha of Castile, in 1179, she had effectively acted as consort to her grief-stricken father, whose love for his wife "prompted the King to remain a widower for the rest of his life."[31] To have been mature enough for that, Berengaria must have been born sooner than 1170–75, perhaps around 1165, at the latest.

King Sancho "was happy when he heard this news [of Richard's proposal] and he prepared the elder [daughter], Berengaria, as was fitting for this princess."[32] For Berengaria, Richard was a splendid match. But Richard had yet to disentangle himself from Alys. It is likely that, at Nonancourt, he and Eleanor discussed "how it might be possible to rescind this marriage."[33] Eleanor must have stressed to Sancho that, until that was accomplished, negotiations with Navarre would have to be conducted with discretion.

In the spring, Eleanor accompanied Richard to Anjou to help him set his affairs in order. While he was away on a progress through Poitou and Aquitaine, she was issuing charters at Chinon. One was to the abbey of Fontevraud, "for the repose of Henry's soul"; the others conferred endowments on other religious institutions, in return for prayers for a successful outcome to the crusade and Richard's safe return.

During his southern progress, which took him to Bayonne, not far from the Navarrese border, Richard came to an understanding with Sancho. Their meeting, and their negotiations, had to be kept secret for fear of offending Philip, who still expected Richard to marry Alys, who was now thirty-one, after the crusade. It was arranged that Eleanor would travel south to collect Berengaria and escort her to wherever Richard was at the time, so that the nuptials could take place.

On June 24, Richard said a final farewell to Eleanor at Chinon before departing on his great venture. He then joined Philip at Vézelay, where the crusader hosts were gathering. On July 4, with banners flying, the vast army set off for the Holy Land. It was an awe-inspiring sight. "Had ye but seen the host when forth it came! The Earth trembled with its coming."[34]

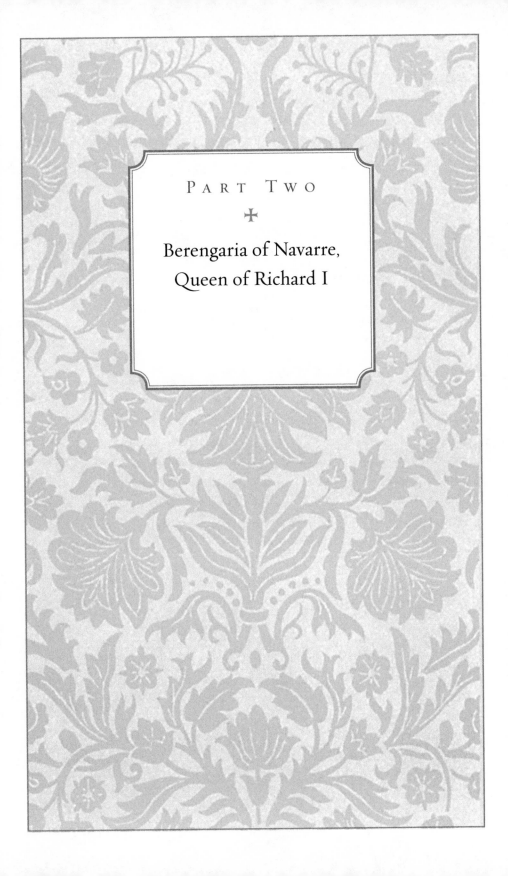

PART TWO

✦

Berengaria of Navarre,
Queen of Richard I

I

"The Beautiful Navarroise"

✠

A FTER A BRISK COUP IN WHICH HE HAD HUGH DE PUISET imprisoned, Longchamp took sole charge of the government as both chancellor and acting justiciar. From June 1190, he was Papal legate too, at Richard's behest. "The laity found him more than a king, the clergy more than a pope, and both an intolerable tyrant."[1] Eleanor dispatched John to England to keep an eye on Longchamp, then left Chinon on the first stage of her journey to collect Berengaria.

She reached Bordeaux in the autumn. Some writers suggest that the princess was brought to her there, but there are contemporary accounts of Eleanor and her Poitevin retinue setting out in September and crossing the Pyrenees to Navarre, "with no thought for her age"[2] or the dangers of traveling through the Alps in winter. Richard of Devizes describes her as "still indefatigable for every undertaking, although sufficiently advanced in years [she was sixty-six]. Her power was the admiration of her age." How far her reputation had been rehabilitated may be perceived from his description of her as "an incomparable woman, beautiful yet virtuous, powerful yet modest, meek and eloquent, strong-willed yet kind, humble yet sagacious, qualities which are rarely to be met with in a woman." She was "unwearied by any task, and provoked wonder by her stamina."

Sancho VI received Eleanor with great honor and presented his daughter to her. Berengaria was then about twenty-five. The historian Ambrose, who saw her in 1191, described her as "a prudent maid, of gentle womanhood, wise, gentle, valiant and fair, neither false nor a slanderer. She was the wisest lady in all truth that might anywhere be found." According to the *Gesta Regis Richardi*, she was of good character and had "accomplished manners."[3] William of Newburgh described her as "a damsel famed for her beauty and wisdom," while Roger of Howden called her "the beautiful Navarroise." Others praised her good sense and probity. Richard of Devizes thought her "more wise than beautiful." The fine effigy on her tomb in the abbey of l'Epau at Le Mans was sculpted decades after her death, so cannot be considered a faithful representation.

Berengaria was "learned"[4] and could probably read. She spoke Castilian, her mother's native tongue and that of the Navarrese upper classes. Her sister Blanche could not speak Latin, so it is unlikely that Berengaria learned it. She may have been able to converse with Eleanor in the *langue d'oc*.

King Sancho "handed over" his daughter to Eleanor, "who was longing for her to be brought to [Richard], for the King loved her very much."[5] In sending his daughter to Richard with no formal betrothal in place, Sancho was taking a leap of faith.

In November or December, not wishing to delay, Eleanor and Berengaria left Navarre, escorted by Sancho's envoys and a large retinue. Eleanor "declined the perils of the sea"[6] and chose to travel overland via Toulouse and Montpellier, crossing the Rhône at Avignon and trekking eastward over the Alps. In the depths of winter, they made the hazardous journey over Mount Janus via Montgenèvre and the St. Bernard Pass. By Advent, Richard had received news that they had safely traversed the mountains and were on their way south to meet up with him in Sicily.

Richard and Philip had gone their separate ways to the Mediterranean. Philip, who was in a bad humor with his ally after Richard had refused to be pinned down over Alys, took the overland route, while Richard rode south to Marseilles, bound for Sicily to succor his sister Joanna. In 1189, Tancred of Lecce had usurped the throne on the death of her husband, William II. By rights, the crown should have passed to William's aunt, Constance of Hauteville, wife of the Emperor Henry VI, but anti-German feeling was rife in Sicily, and Tancred was the obvious choice of the people. Needing money, he had seized Queen Joanna's dowry, stolen her treasures and placed her under house arrest in a fortress in Palermo.

When Richard arrived in Messina at the end of September, he found her a prisoner and King Philip installed in Tancred's palace. He demanded her release, whereupon Tancred sent her to him with her treasure, but refused to surrender her dower. Wrangles over this kept Richard in Sicily until the spring of 1191.

When the married Philip saw twenty-six-year-old Joanna, his face "glowed with a joyful expectation."[7] Hastily, Richard appropriated the priory at La Bagnara on the coast of mainland Calabria and settled her there, out of Philip's reach.

In February 1191, Richard made an act of penitence outside a church in Messina. "Gathering together all the archbishops and bishops who were present, [he] prostrated himself naked at their feet and did not shrink from confessing to them all the foulness of his sins against nature, with great humility and contrition," assuring them that "the thorns of lust had departed from his head."[8] A bishop granted him absolution and thrashed his bared back as a penance, while pious hopes were expressed that the King would return to his iniquity no more.

Eleanor and Berengaria had been crossing the plains of Lombardy. Food was scarce because Philip's army had recently passed through and stripped the region of its crops and provender, leaving very little sustenance for the inhabitants. Danger lurked, for the Queen and her party were without safe-conducts and at risk from the predatory freebooters who roamed the ravaged land, waiting to ambush and rob unwary travelers.

Having emerged unscathed and rested in Milan, the royal ladies arrived at Lodi by January 20. Here, Eleanor had a meeting with the Emperor, Henry VI, who was on his way to Rome to be crowned by the Pope, and witnessed one of his charters. She would have been concerned about the political stability of Sicily and for her daughter Joanna's future, while the Emperor may have sought the meeting to express the hope that Richard would not undermine his wife's claim to Sicily.

At Messina, "couriers informed Richard that his mother Eleanor was hastening after him and was close at hand, bringing with her the noble damsel, daughter of the King of Navarre. All rejoiced at their coming."[9]

At Pisa, having failed to obtain a sea passage to Sicily, the Queen waited for instructions from Richard. He ordered her to proceed to Naples, where his galleys and a large escort would be waiting to take her to Messina. Late in February, Eleanor and Berengaria arrived in Naples, whence they were to be escorted by ship by Count Philip of Flanders, who was on his way to join the crusading host.

It had not escaped King Philip's notice that Eleanor was on her way south with a bride for Richard. Determined to prevent anything from blocking the marriage of Richard and Alys, he persuaded Tancred to forbid the ladies to land. Tancred's officials in Naples refused to let Eleanor and Berengaria leave in the galleys, saying they had too great a retinue to be accommodated in Messina, and forced them to travel 215 miles overland to Brindisi. It took them a month.

On March 3, a furious Richard met Tancred at Catania and demanded to know why his mother and his bride had been so rudely treated. Tancred showed him letters in which Philip had written that Eleanor had formed a league with the Emperor, with a view to setting Richard up as king in Tancred's place. Richard assured Tancred that his fears were groundless and recognized him as king of Sicily, whereupon Tancred handed over Joanna's dower. Richard confronted Philip with the letters, but Philip dismissed them as forgeries and accused Richard of fabricating excuses for not marrying Alys. Angrily, he demanded that the marriage take place without further delay.

Richard now divulged the real reason for his failure to go through with the marriage, revealing that "the King of England, his own father, had been intimate with [Alys] and had a son by her."[10] Philip reacted violently, seeing this as an insulting excuse, but, when Richard offered to produce dozens of witnesses to testify to the truth, he grudgingly released him from his betrothal, on payment of a quit-claim of 10,000 marks (£4,900,000) as compensation for Richard's breach of promise. Richard promised to send Alys to Philip when they returned from the Holy Land and to return her dowry. The two kings then signed a treaty of friendship, but it did little to allay Philip's bitterness. He would not stay to receive the bride who would supplant his sister. On March 30, barely on speaking terms with Richard, he left Messina for the Holy Land, mere hours before Eleanor and Berengaria's arrival.

Richard had sent a large ship to convey Eleanor and Berengaria south from Brindisi, "for the news had been brought to him that his mother had arrived there, bringing the King his beloved."[11] He sailed to Reggio when "he heard that the Queen his mother and Berengaria" had arrived there.[12] On March 30, 1191, he welcomed them with great honor and ceremony and took them on board his own ship, then sailed with them up the coast to La Bagnara, where Joanna was waiting to greet them.

There is no eyewitness account of the meeting between Richard and his future bride, but, according to William of Newburgh, he was pleased with her. Berengaria must have been relieved to learn that there was now no impediment to her marriage and that she was not to be sent ignominiously home. Nor is there any reference to the reunion between Eleanor and Joanna, who had not seen each other for fourteen years, in which time Joanna had grown into her mother's mirror image, "a woman whose masculine spirit overcame the weakness of her sex."[13]

Leaving Berengaria under the chaperonage of Joanna at La Bagnara, Richard escorted Eleanor across the Straits of Messina to join the crusading host in Sicily. She told him that, during her journey through Italy, she had received disturbing news from England of William Longchamp's abuse of power. On her advice, Richard issued a mandate to Walter of Coutances, Archbishop of Rouen, to go to England and take charge. Coutances was no friend to Longchamp and had secretly counseled John to raise baronial support against him. Richard asked Eleanor to return immediately to Normandy, where she would be able to monitor events. Because of the critical situation in England, she spent only four days in Sicily.

Berengaria and Joanna joined the King and his mother in his luxurious quarters just outside the walls of Messina. There had sprung up a warm friendship between the young women, who were about the same age: "Queen Joanna held [Berengaria] dear; they lived as doves in cage."[14] The Church did not solemnize marriages during Lent, so the King's nuptials could not immediately take place. Eleanor ordered wedding garments for him, and helped to finalize the arrangements for Berengaria's dower, ceding certain interests in Poitou to the princess for her lifetime. Richard had agreed that Berengaria would receive the full dower of the queens of England on Eleanor's death.

"The Queen could not tarry." Before she left, she entrusted Berengaria to Joanna, saying, "Fair daughter, take this damsel to the King your brother and tell him I command him to espouse her speedily."[15] On

April 2, Richard bade farewell to Eleanor as she began her journey back to Normandy, escorted by Walter of Coutances and several great lords. With her, she carried various royal mandates and letters patent issued by the King, enabling her to "look after his land that he had left."[16]

On April 21, Easter Sunday, Eleanor arrived in Rome in time for the consecration of the new Pope, Celestine III. At Richard's request, she had an audience with the octogenarian pontiff at the Castello Radulphi, during which she secured the appointment of Walter of Coutances as super-legate, with powers overriding those of Longchamp. She then set off, via Acquapendente, for the long trek across the Alps.

In Holy Week, Richard's fleet of 219 ships sailed for Outremer. In accordance with the ruling that no women accompany the crusading army, Berengaria and Joanna traveled separately in the *Buza di Luna*, a large, fast galley, or dromond, escorted by Stephen de Turnham, the royal admiral. The King's flagship, the *Trenc-de-Mer*, sailed ahead, its lanterns a beacon to the fleet. On Good Friday, April 19, the ships were divided by severe storms in the Gulf of Adalia, and Richard's was carried to Crete and Rhodes. Twenty-five vessels were feared lost, among them the ladies' ship.

On May 3, Berengaria and Joanna were blown to Cyprus and barely escaped being shipwrecked. Three accompanying vessels were broken up on the rocks near Limassol and plundered by soldiers of the ruler of Cyprus, the Greek usurper Isaac Comnenus, who styled himself "Emperor of the Orient." Some of those on board drowned; others were taken prisoner or slain when they swam to shore. Berengaria's ship took shelter "in the harbour of Limassol."[17] She and Joanna were "burning with gnawing anxiety"[18] and did not dare "to go on shore because they did not know the state of the country and were afraid of the cruelty and treachery of the Emperor."[19]

Presently, the usurper Isaac approached with a great force, intent upon seizing their ship. Berengaria and Joanna were cursing "the day that had brought them to shores so hostile that they dare not land there." As "the chevaliers who guarded the royal ladies got the galley ready to be rowed out of the harbour at the first indication of hostility," Isaac saw Berengaria on board and demanded to know "what damsel that was with them. They declared she was the sister [*sic*] of the King of Navarre, whom the King of England's mother had brought for him to espouse." Isaac "sent two boats and demanded if the Queen would land,"[20] but Berengaria declined, saying all she wanted was to know whether the King of England's ship had passed. No one knew. Isaac assured her that she could disembark in safety and sent her gifts of food and wine, which she refused.

She and Joanna were "anxious that, if they submitted to the Emperor's persuasions, they would be taken captive," which would greatly hamper Richard's plans. "On the other hand, they were afraid that [Isaac] would attack them in their refusals,"[21] for he was fortifying the beach. On April 28, praying that Richard and his fleet would arrive and hoping "to hold the Emperor off for a while, they gave a non-committal reply." This angered Isaac and, when Joanna asked if some of the sailors could go ashore to buy provisions and get fresh water, he refused. The situation looked so perilous "that Stephen de Turnham gave signal to heave up the anchor, and the Queen's galley rode off with all speed into the offing."[22]

Providence came to her rescue. On May 6, as her ship was tossing in the Bay of Famagusta and she and Joanna, both very seasick, were "gloomily discussing and bewailing their situation to each other and gazing out across the sea, two ships appeared in the distance."[23] It was the King's fleet.

Landing at Limassol in a rowing boat, grasping an axe, Richard was informed of the ladies' plight and the capture of the shipwrecked crusaders, and angrily demanded that the latter be freed, and that compensation be given for his losses and the treatment of his womenfolk—only to receive a rude response. He leapt on this as a pretext for challenging Isaac to arms. That same day, he took Limassol.

His advisers, and Joanna, insisted that he marry Berengaria in Cyprus, as her reputation would suffer if they traveled to the Holy Land unwed. He knew that, if he put off the wedding until he arrived in Acre, it would be overshadowed by the presence of King Philip, who might make trouble; more importantly, since women were barred from the crusade, it would be inappropriate to marry in the Holy Land. He therefore agreed that the wedding should now take place.

* * *

After Cyprus had been subdued, and Isaac had fled to the mountains, Stephen de Turnham was signaled to sail into harbor. As Berengaria was conveyed into the city, Richard "his [wedding] feast did cry." On Sunday, May 12, 1191, he donned his wedding clothes, a belted tunic of rose samite, a mantle of striped silk tissue threaded with gold crescents and silver suns, a scarlet bonnet embroidered with gold beasts and birds, buskins of cloth of gold with gilded spurs, and a scabbard of gold and silver. "Now was the King in all his glory over his marriage with her whom he held so dearly."[24] Mounted on his Spanish charger, decked out in caparisons studded with gold and silver, he rode to the chapel of St. George. "There, in the joyous month of May, in the flourishing isle of Cyprus, formerly the very abode of love [Cyprus was said to have been the home of the goddess Aphrodite], did Richard take to wife his beloved Lady Berengaria,"[25] with his chaplain, Nicholas (later bishop of Le Mans), officiating, assisted by the archbishops of Auch and Apamea. According to Richard de Templo, Berengaria was "the fairest bride that could be found" and the nuptials "were solemnly celebrated in a royal manner." The King was "in a genial mood, overjoyed at his victory and because he has married the one to whom he had pledged himself."[26] He was "glorious on this happy occasion and cheerful to all, and showed himself very jocose and affable."[27]

On their wedding day, Richard issued a charter assigning Berengaria her dower, which comprised lands in England and all his possessions south of the Garonne, which she was to hold while Queen Eleanor lived; on Eleanor's death, she would receive in addition the old Queen's revenues and dower lands in England, Normandy, Touraine, Maine and Poitou. No mention was made of queen-gold and, as Eleanor retained the right to it, it is unlikely that Berengaria was ever permitted to claim it.

She was to play a passive role, not only with her husband, but also with her mother-in-law. She might be queen, but Eleanor was too powerful to be displaced, and it was Berengaria who became the subordinate, signing herself as "the humble Queen of England" and remaining very much in the background.

Richard of Devizes wondered if Berengaria was "perhaps still a virgin," implying that Richard had anticipated his wedding night, but the consummation of the marriage was probably deferred until they reached

Acre, for the crusaders had vowed that they would abstain from sex until they arrived in the Holy Land.

Three days were given over to wedding celebrations; it was "the richest spousing that ever maked any king" and "there was joy and love enough." On the third day of the feast, Berengaria was crowned queen of England. Then she and Richard were crowned emperor and empress of Cyprus.[28] The King was "happy and splendid, laughing and pleasing everyone."[29] The chapel may still be visited today, along with various other sites connected with Richard and Berengaria in Cyprus, among them the ruined Berengaria Tower (of which the royal couple laid the foundations) on the outskirts of Kolossi, and Little Berengaria Village near Pannicon, north of Limassol.

Ambrose believed that Berengaria was "beloved" by Richard: "most dear did the King love and revere her." According to Geoffrey de Vinsauf, she returned that love. Ambrose, William of Newburgh, and the late-thirteenth-century chronicler Walter of Guisborough claimed that Richard had married her "as a salubrious remedy against the great perils of fornication," yet, almost immediately, he courted scandal.

2

"The Disturber of Your Kingdom"

✝

ISAAC COMNENUS HAD FLED TO THE MOUNTAINS, BUT, ON MAY 31, Richard took him captive. The next day, after Isaac had learned that his daughter, the "Damsel of Cyprus" (whose name is not recorded), had been taken hostage, he surrendered Cyprus. Having given his word not to put Isaac in irons, Richard had him fettered in silver chains.

The Damsel of Cyprus was brought before Richard at the castle of Limassol and fell to her knees "tenderly weeping." He took pity on this "young and appealing girl"[1] and "caused the maiden to be sent in gentle manner to his wife, to cherish and instruct."[2] She would remain with Berengaria for the duration of the crusade. According to Geoffrey de Vinsauf, an eyewitness, she was a mere child, but several chroniclers allege that the King spent long hours in her company and hint that his interest in her was less than honorable. It was sufficient to arouse disapproval among the clergy who attended him, especially in view of his recent penance and marriage.

On June 5, the fleet sailed east from Famagusta to the Holy Land. The queens' ship arrived at Acre a week ahead of Richard's and had a rough landing, in which Berengaria "lost her little shoes" and her cloak snagged on the rigging. King Philip was there to greet them, still aggrieved "that Richard was married to any other than his sister; yet he received Berengaria with great courtesy, taking her in his arms and lifting her onshore himself from the boat to the beach."[3]

The ladies were probably accommodated in tents. For two years now, Acre had been under siege by the forces of King Guy. Acre was the major port for Jerusalem and its recapture was the primary objective of the crusaders. The arrival of Richard's army boosted the confidence of the exhausted, famished and demoralized besiegers. He took command at once and reorganized operations with his usual energy and efficiency, despite having contracted malarial fever. Saladin himself was so impressed by his fortitude that he sent him gifts of fruit and food. Richard chivalrously responded with a present of a black slave. Although the two leaders never met and were bitter foes, they had a high regard for each other.

On July 12, Acre fell to Richard. Afterward, he was annoyed to find the standard of his ally, Duke Leopold of Austria, flying alongside his own from the gate, for Leopold had played little part in the taking of the city. Richard ordered it to be torn down and flung into the filthy moat, and made disparaging remarks, insults Leopold never forgot. That night, he withdrew from the crusade, swearing vengeance.

On July 21, Richard moved with Berengaria, Joanna and the Damsel of Cyprus to the royal palace, known as the Knights' Halls, north of Acre. It had been built by the Knights Hospitallers after the city was taken by the Christians in 1104, and the King now made it his headquarters. It was a strong fortress, occupying an area of 8,300 square meters. Built around a courtyard, it boasted the massive vaulted "Hall of Pillars." Berengaria and Joanna were safe here, even if they did have to be confined to the palace complex, but they had minstrels in their household and enjoyed embroidery and each other's company. With Richard absent for long periods, there was little opportunity for Berengaria to exercise any queenly influence, even if he had allowed it, but it is clear that she was excluded from his political life.

Richard's victory had aroused jealousy in his other ally, Philip, who, pleading that he was too ill with malaria to continue with the crusade, returned to France on August 8, plotting to undermine the stability of Richard's continental domains during his absence.

The victory at Acre was followed by a stalemate. Saladin would not come to terms and did his best to demoralize the crusaders. There was talk that the Muslims had poisoned 600 Christian captives. Richard threatened that, unless an agreement was reached within a week, every

Saracen prisoner would be put to death. Saladin refused to comply. On the afternoon of August 20, Richard rode out of Acre and ordered the massacre of more than 3,000 captives. It was an act that forever sullied his reputation, although some said it was a reprisal for Saladin's slaughter of Templars and Hospitallers in 1187. The story that Berengaria was so shocked when she heard of the massacre that she miscarried is a modern myth.

By June 24, Eleanor had returned to Normandy and taken up residence at Bonneville-sur-Touques. Walter of Coutances had traveled on to England, where, to his dismay, he found political chaos. At the end of March, John had taken his advice and incited a revolt against the chancellor, Longchamp, seizing the royal castles of Tickhill and Nottingham. There was an insurrection on the Welsh border. Longchamp dealt with that, then besieged Lincoln, which John had occupied. John's anger knew no bounds when he heard that Longchamp supported Richard's decision to name his nephew Arthur as his heir, and he was now consumed with a deadly determination to bring down the chancellor.

Walter of Coutances donned the mantle of conciliator. It became clear that, while Longchamp was acting in what he thought to be the King's best interests, John was intent only upon serving his own. Yet it was possible that John might soon be king. Many believed—and John deliberately fostered this belief—that Richard would never return from the Holy Land, and it seemed unlikely that the English barons would accept Arthur of Brittany as their ruler. John, whose popularity had benefited from his self-appointed role as leader of the opposition to the hated Longchamp, would almost certainly be their preferred choice.

By the end of July, thanks to Coutances's careful negotiations, John had surrendered the castles he had taken. Longchamp, realizing that his power had been cleverly limited, and eager to make concessions, now sought to ally himself to John by agreeing to support his claim to the succession over that of Arthur. But John continued intriguing against the chancellor, who warned Walter of Coutances that he was plotting to seize the crown itself.

* * *

On August 21, Richard began his march toward Jerusalem, which lay 103 miles to the south. He left Berengaria and Joanna at Acre in the care of two knights, Longchamp's brother Stephen and Bertram de Verdun, the trusty castellan of the Knights' Hall. On September 7, Richard won a brilliant victory on the plains of Arsuf, fighting with terrifying ferocity. Two days later, the crusaders took Jaffa. So far, the crusade had been a resounding success, but Richard now succumbed to malaria and dysentery, and was seriously ill for several weeks. Yet he was determined to press on with the great enterprise.

On August 18, Geoffrey had been consecrated archbishop of York at Tours. Ignoring his undertaking to remain out of England for three years, he crossed the Channel to take up his episcopal duties. No sooner had he landed at Dover than Longchamp had him imprisoned in a dungeon in the castle, provoking outrage. Recalling the fate of Becket, the people hailed Geoffrey as another champion of the liberties of the Church. Longchamp hastened to order his release and Geoffrey was brought in triumphal procession through London.

John now pressed home his advantage, setting himself up as the champion of the righteous and oppressed. Longchamp barricaded himself into the Tower of London and Walter of Coutances called for his deposition, to which everyone agreed. On the authority of the Papal mandate obtained by Queen Eleanor, he himself was appointed head of a council of regency. In this capacity, "he acted well and wisely, by the advice of the Marshal and the barons, and also by the advice of the Queen."[4]

Longchamp was taken to Dover Castle, but escaped, disguised as a woman, aiming to flee the realm. John was much amused to hear that he had been arrested after his disguise had been discovered by an amorous fisherman, and agreed that he be allowed to go into exile in France.

John now devoted all his energy, charm and talent to consolidating his position as the future king. He bestowed upon the citizens of London the right to self-government under an elected mayor, a privilege they had long coveted. He traveled throughout England, courting the favor of the people and showing himself affable, magnificent and lavishly hospitable. He also spread rumors that Richard had named him his heir and that the King would never return from the crusade. "It lacked nothing but that he should be hailed as king," observed Richard of Devizes. But the English barons had no intention of replacing Richard with his untrustworthy brother while there was a chance that the King might return to reproach them for it. Even so, John might soon be king, so most magnates showed themselves friendly, fearful of his future vengeance if they did not.

Longchamp made his way to Rouen, demanding to lay his grievances before the Queen. Eleanor would not see him, so he went to Paris, where he met two cardinals who had been sent by the Pope to heal the rift between Longchamp and Walter of Coutances and were willing to lay Longchamp's grievances before Eleanor. She refused to see them too, declaring she was satisfied that justice had been done. Secretly, she feared that the cardinals had come on Philip's behalf, since Alys was still a prisoner at Rouen and Eleanor had received no instructions from Richard for her release. When the cardinals tried to cross the Norman border at Gisors, the Seneschal of Normandy informed them that they could not pass without the Queen's safe-conduct. Eleanor refused to be intimidated by their threats of excommunication and, in the end, they were obliged to depart. As a parting shot, they excommunicated the Seneschal and placed Normandy under an interdict, although Eleanor was specifically excluded.

It was the season of anathemas. Longchamp excommunicated every member of the regency council except John and, in retaliation, the bishops excommunicated Longchamp and placed his diocese of Ely under an interdict.

In the autumn of 1191, more than one chronicler noted that Richard had been divided from the company of his Queen by accidents of war; he had also been ill. In August, on Richard's orders, Berengaria and Joanna traveled south to the city of Arsuf, perched on a cliff overlooking the Mediterranean Sea.

In October, unwell as he was, the King rejoined them and escorted them to Jaffa. There they remained after he had dragged himself from his sickbed and pressed on toward Jerusalem, unaware that his allies had concluded a truce with Saladin's brother, Malik al-Adil, Sultan of Egypt, and left him to take the Holy City alone. When he found out, his rage was terrible indeed. He tried to make his own peace with Saladin, offering Joanna to Malik as a bride, with a view to their jointly ruling the Holy Land as king and queen of Jerusalem, on condition that Christians be granted access to the holy places, but this plan was scuppered by Malik, who had no intention of converting to Christianity, and by an enraged Joanna, who stoutly refused to marry a Muslim.

In November, Richard traveled southeast to Ramleh with Berengaria and Joanna. In December, they reached Beit-Nuba, just twelve miles from Jerusalem, but severe rain precluded any assault on the Holy City. They spent Christmas at the hilltop castle at Latrun, west of Jerusalem, in the company of King Guy, in whose honor Richard hosted a feast. There were rumors that the King and Queen had quarreled. Early in 1192, Berengaria and Joanna returned to Jaffa.

The see of Canterbury had been vacant for a year since the death of Archbishop Baldwin in November 1190. In a letter to Eleanor, the chapter asked her to uphold their right to elect his successor. Unfortunately, their candidate died a month later and the see remained vacant.

Eleanor spent Christmas 1191 at Bonneville-sur-Touques. Receiving the alarming intelligence that Philip was planning to invade Normandy, she commanded the seneschals of castles guarding the Angevin borders to repair and strengthen their fortifications and ensure that their garrisons were fully manned. When, in the third week of January, Philip launched an assault on Gisors, it failed. That same month, he demanded the return of Alys, but Eleanor, who had no mandate for this, refused.

Early in 1192, Philip offered John all Richard's continental domains in return for his undertaking to marry Alys. Although he already had a wife, John eagerly agreed and prepared to cross the Channel with an army of mercenaries to pay homage to Philip for the promised lands and lay Normandy wide open to him. He also undertook not to make peace with Richard without Philip's consent.

Word of this reached Eleanor. It may not have surprised her, for she knew her youngest son had "the shallow mind of an adolescent."[5] "Fearing that the light-minded youth might be going to attempt something, by the counsels of the French, against his lord and brother, his mother grew anxious and tried every possible means of stopping him from going abroad. Remembering the fate of her two elder sons, how both had died young before their time because of their many sins, her heart was sad and wounded. She was therefore determined, with all her strength, to ensure that faith would be kept between her younger sons, so that their mother might die more happily than had their father."[6]

Immediately, she made haste to England. On February 11 she arrived in Portsmouth, just in time to prevent John from sailing from Southampton. She arrested his Flemish mercenaries and closed the Channel ports, blocking his means of escape. She "tried in every way" to make him abandon his treasonous schemes. Backed by the barons and Walter of Coutances, she threatened to confiscate all John's castles and estates if he defied her and went to Paris. Eventually, "through her own tears and the prayers of the nobles, she was with difficulty able to obtain a promise that John would not cross over for the time being."[7] John retired sulking to Wallingford, another royal castle he had appropriated.

That effectively put paid, for the present, to Philip's plans to invade Normandy. The French barons refused to violate the Truce of God by attacking the lands of an absent crusader, so his hands were effectively tied. Nevertheless, the Queen and the regency council were taking no chances. Eleanor resolved to remind the lords of England of their vows of allegiance to the King, because some were on the verge of going over to John. She summoned meetings of the Great Council at Windsor, Oxford, London and Winchester. At each, she proclaimed her loyalty to the absent Richard and made every English magnate swear a new oath of fealty to him. She also ordered that castles and towns be manned against an invasion.

While in England, Eleanor claimed her share of queen-gold on the aid levied on the tenants-in-chief of the Crown for the King's marriage. She granted her damsel, Amaria, the manor of Winterslow, near Salisbury, as a reward for faithful service, whereupon Amaria donated half the estate to the nuns of Amesbury Priory "for the weal of her lady, Eleanor, Queen of England."[8]

While making a tour of her properties, "that worthy matron, Queen Eleanor, was visiting some cottages that were part of her dower" in Longchamp's diocese of Ely, which still lay under an interdict. There, she saw for herself how badly the people's lives had been affected by the Church's ban. "There came before her, from all the villages and hamlets, wherever she passed, men, women and children, a people weeping and pitiful, their feet bare, their clothes unwashed, their hair unshorn. There was no need for an interpreter: they spoke by their tears, for their grief was so great that they could not speak."

Eleanor listened as they told her of the miseries they were enduring through being deprived of the sacraments. She was appalled to see that "human bodies lay unburied here and there in the fields because their Bishop had deprived them of burial." She "took pity on the misery of the living because of the dead, for she was very merciful. Immediately dropping her own affairs and looking after the concerns of others, she went to London," where she "compelled" Walter of Coutances to revoke the interdict and allow Longchamp to return to England and resume his pastoral duties.[9]

In March, Longchamp landed at Dover, armed with a renewed legateship. His arrival was announced to the Queen in council by two Papal nuncios who had accompanied him, provoking deep concern among the magnates, and it was made clear to Longchamp that he was only welcome in his capacity as bishop of Ely, and not as chancellor. In March, he turned up at a council meeting, but the magnates shunned him. Only Eleanor spoke up for him; although there was gossip that he had bribed her to do so, her prime concern was that he attend to the suffering souls in his diocese.

In London, she asked Hugh de Puiset to go to France to persuade the Roman cardinals to lift their interdict on Normandy. But he refused to leave England until Archbishop Geoffrey, who had excommunicated him for failing to attend his consecration, lifted the ban. Eleanor summoned the warring prelates to appear before her on March 15 in the Templars' church in London, to account for their conduct and submit to her mediation. They obeyed, but Geoffrey foolishly attempted to overawe her by having himself preceded into the church by a solemn procession of clergy, with his archiepiscopal cross borne ceremonially before him, which was only permitted him in his own diocese. He also flatly refused to cooperate with her in resolving his differences with Hugh. When she angrily threatened the sequestration of the estates of the see of York, he made a pretense of patching up the quarrel, but to little effect, since it dragged on for years.

At Walter of Coutances's insistence, Hugh went to France on the Queen's behalf and asked the cardinals to remove their interdict on Normandy. They proved stubborn, and it was only lifted after Eleanor made a personal appeal to the Pope.

Still determined to be rid of Longchamp, the councilors turned to John for support. He agreed to help in return for a hefty consideration. "I am in need of money," he told them shamelessly. "To the wise, a word is sufficient."[10] The lords agreed that it was "expedient" to pay up, for they dared not antagonize John. He had gone off again on his perambulations of the realm, exacting oaths of loyalty to himself from various barons and appropriating funds from the Exchequer. In April, an alarmed Eleanor sent John of Alençon, Archdeacon of Lisieux, to Richard, warning him of Philip's attempt to lead John into treachery and John's subversive activities, and imploring him to come home.

Eleanor now realized that Longchamp's presence in England would only cause further problems. She, John and the barons "admonished him to cross the Channel without delay—unless he has a mind to take his meals under the custody of an armed guard."[11] On April 3, Longchamp went abroad. His departure brought Eleanor some peace of mind. John remained on his estates. Philip had succeeded in undermining the loyalty of some of Richard's southern vassals, but the Seneschal of Gascony, aided by Berengaria's brother Sancho, held firm and crushed the rebels.

Richard had now been in the Holy Land for a year and was still no nearer to launching an assault on Jerusalem than he had been the previous December. He knew now that he had to relinquish his dream of reconquering the Holy City; he could not do it alone. In July, ascending the heights above Emmaus, he glimpsed Jerusalem in the distance and shielded his eyes, that he might not behold the city God had not permitted him to deliver.

He sailed north, just in time to relieve Jaffa from an assault by Saladin— and perhaps rescue his wife and sister-in-law, although they may already have gone back to Acre. It was the last engagement of the crusade. In August, Richard fell ill again, and, at his request, Saladin sent him fruit packed in snow. Worn out by his ceaseless exertions, illness and the extremes of the eastern climate, which alone had killed thousands of crusaders, he decided to go home. His mother's letters and other disturbing news from England had convinced him that he should return, and he began negotiating a long truce that would enable him to do so.

He returned to Acre, where he arranged for Berengaria, Joanna, the Damsel of Cyprus and Bourguigne de Lusignan, the niece of King Guy, to leave the Holy Land ahead of him, planning to catch up with them in Rome. On September 29, they boarded a ship commanded by Stephen de Turnham and bound for Sicily. Richard said an emotional farewell, but his tears and lamentations were for the Holy Land, not for his Queen.

In November, Berengaria and her companions landed at Brindisi, where they were hospitably entertained by Tancred. By Christmas, they would reach Rome, where Pope Celestine welcomed them with much honor.

Having concluded a truce that secured for Christians the right to make pilgrimages to Jerusalem unmolested by the Muslims, Richard left Acre on October 9 in the company of his chaplain, a clerk, two noblemen and a party of Knights Templar, intending to be back in England for Christmas. There were reports that his ship, the *Franche-Nef*, had been sighted near Brindisi or had stopped briefly at Cyprus and Corfu before sailing on toward Marseilles. In Normandy, expecting his imminent return, his subjects gathered to welcome him.

Bewilderingly, there was no further news of him. As autumn turned into winter, the crusaders began arriving home, boasting of the brave deeds of King Richard, but no one knew where he was. Fears were voiced that some calamity had befallen him on his journey, and throughout England his subjects lit candles and offered up prayers for his safety. It was whispered that Philip and John had colluded in a plot to assassinate him. The situation in Normandy was so tense that Eleanor again gave orders for the strengthening of defenses on the border. She kept her Christmas court at Westminster, anxiously wondering what had happened to her son.

3

"The Devil Is Loosed!"

✠

RICHARD'S SHIP HAD BEEN WRECKED ON THE COAST OF ISTRIA, south of Trieste. With just three remaining attendants, he decided to make his way homeward overland. Having struck north through Hungary, he had to cross into the territory of the hostile Duke Leopold, whom he had deeply offended after the fall of Acre. He disguised himself first as a merchant, then as a pilgrim, but was recognized and captured "in a humble house in a village in the vicinity of Vienna."[1] Imprisoned in solitary confinement in the secure fortress of Durnstein, high above the River Danube, he was guarded day and night by soldiers with drawn swords.

Leopold hastened to inform his overlord, the Emperor Henry VI, of Richard's capture. Henry had already earned a notorious reputation for cruelty, and was no friend to Richard, who had recognized his rival Tancred as king of Sicily. In his letter announcing the news to King Philip, he wrote that he knew it would "afford most abundant joy to your own feelings." While he insisted that Richard was being held as a punishment for "the treason, treachery and mischief of which he was guilty in the Promised Land,"[2] both he and Philip were aware of just how valuable a prisoner he was, and each planned to gain the greatest advantage to himself from the situation. Anxious that Richard should not escape, Philip urged the Emperor to ensure that he was kept in close confinement.

Fortunately, Walter of Coutances had spies in France. Early in January 1193, Eleanor received from him a copy of the letter sent by the Emperor on December 28 to the King of France, informing him that, a week earlier, "the enemy of our empire and the disturber of your kingdom, Richard, King of England" had been taken prisoner by "our dearly-beloved cousin, Duke Leopold of Austria."[3] In a covering note of his own, Coutances exhorted Eleanor, with many scriptural precepts, to bear the news with fortitude.

Knowing what it was to be a prisoner, her sorrow was great. Her first thought was that she must go to Austria herself to see Richard and negotiate his release, but she dared not leave the realm at such a time. Tormented by the conviction that her son's imprisonment was a punishment from God for her sins, and wasting away with anxiety, the Queen twice solicited the prayers of the nuns of Fontevraud, sending them gifts from Winchester and Westminster.

There was general consternation in England when the King's fate was made public. No one knew where he was being held, so Eleanor sent the abbots of Boxley and Robertsbridge to Austria to find him. A popular tale, first recounted by the Minstrel of Rheims around 1260, told how Richard's minstrel, Blondel de Nesle, went searching for him, loudly singing familiar songs outside castle after castle, hoping for a response. At Durnstein, when a familiar voice issued from an arrow-slit high above, Blondel knew he had found the King. By then, it was no secret that Richard was at Durnstein, so the tale is probably fictitious. In real life, Blondel was probably Jehan II de Nesle, a French *trouvère* from Picardy who went on the Third Crusade and wrote songs under the name "Blondel de Nesle." The legend portrays him as Berengaria's rival; in a nineteenth-century version, he is Berengaria in disguise.

Provençal tradition had it that Berengaria and Joanna saw a jewel-studded belt for sale in Rome and recognized it as Richard's, which first aroused their suspicions that something was amiss. Roger of Howden says they heard reports of his being shipwrecked while still in Rome, and decided to remain there under the protection of the Pope and Stephen de Turnham, fearing, correctly, that the Emperor would try to take them hostage if they began journeying north; indeed, he would hint to the English council that he was planning to seize them. They were to stay in Rome for six months, being honorably entertained by the Pope and Roman nobles. It is possible that Berengaria pleaded with the Pope to help secure Richard's release, for Celestine, shocked to learn that Leopold had violated the Truce of God by imprisoning a crusader, excommunicated him, and threatened Philip with an interdict if he trespassed on Richard's lands.

In Rome, on April 9, 1193, the two queens issued a joint charter in favor of traders at the fair of Troyes, who were owed money by two returning crusaders. This was the only charter Berengaria issued as queen.

Eleanor's priority was to keep England secure until Richard's return. She was concerned about John's intentions, for "he was enticed by a great hope of becoming king. He won over many people all over the kingdom, promising much, and he quickly strengthened his castles," then sped across the Channel to Normandy and proclaimed himself Richard's heir. Receiving a lukewarm response from the Norman lords, he moved on to Paris, where "he made a pact with the King of France that his nephew Arthur, Duke of Brittany, should be excluded from the hopes the Bretons nourished for him."[4] He and Philip agreed to do everything in their power to keep Richard in captivity. John did homage to Philip for all his brother's lands on the Continent, as if he were in possession of them— and, it was rumored, for England as well, over which Philip had no feudal jurisdiction. John's sights were chiefly set on England and, with money given him by Philip, he raised an army of Flemish mercenaries. Philip, meanwhile, gathered a fleet at Wissant.

Realizing that the unity of the kingdom was essential at this time of crisis, Eleanor exacted new oaths of allegiance to Richard from the lords and clergy to counteract John's treachery. She, Walter of Coutances "and other barons did their utmost to conserve the peace of the kingdom, seeking to join together hearts which were permanently at loggerheads."[5] "By the mandate of Queen Eleanor, who ruled England at that time,"[6] England's southern coastal defenses were strengthened against the threat of invasion from France.

In February 1193, in return for part of the ransom Henry VI intended to demand, Leopold handed Richard over to the Emperor, who had him moved to the castle of Trifels on the Swabian border. On March 23, Richard was brought before the imperial council, or Diet, at Speyer to answer certain charges. He spoke up so well for himself that the Emperor was moved to give him the kiss of peace.

Present at this ceremony was Hubert Walter, who had traveled to Germany on the advice of the Pope. Richard had a high opinion of Hubert, who was an expert lawyer and administrator and had served the Angevins well. When Hubert arrived at Speyer, the King decided that he was the obvious candidate to fill the vacant see of Canterbury and sent him back to England with a letter authorizing his "dearest" and "sweetest mother" to secure his election as primate and work with him, and wishing her "all the happiness that a devoted son can desire for his mother." He also wrote to the chapter at Canterbury instructing them to seek the Queen's advice when electing their new archbishop.

In March, Eleanor learned that the Emperor was likely to demand a large ransom in return for Richard's release. It was probably this that prompted her to write the first of three extraordinary letters to Pope Celestine, who had promised thrice to send a legate to intercede with Richard's captors, but had failed to do so. Eleanor felt he should be doing a lot more to alleviate the situation.

Copies of these letters were preserved among the papers of the brilliant scholar Peter of Blois, Eleanor's chancellor and Latin secretary. His style is evident in parts of them. Some historians believe that Peter composed the letters himself as an exercise in Latin rhetoric. There is no record of their dispatch, nor of their receipt in Rome. This does not mean that the Pope never received them, since many letters of the period are lost. The letters were not attributed to Eleanor until the seventeenth century; why the connection was not made earlier remains a mystery, given the contents. Moreover, there is some evidence of a Papal response to the second letter, and Eleanor referred to her complaints in a later letter to Celestine. It is likely, therefore, that they are genuine.

The first (much abridged here) affords a graphic and intimate view of the anguish and anger Eleanor felt at this time, and her fears for her son—rare in a medieval royal letter:

> To the reverend Father and Lord Celestine, by the grace of God, the
> Supreme Pontiff, Eleanor, the miserable and—would I could add—the
> commiserated Queen of England, Duchess of Normandy, Countess of

Anjou, entreats him to show himself to be a father of mercy to a pitiful mother.

I must give vent to my grief a little. I am all anxiety, whence my very words are full of suffering. I cannot take one breath free from the grief caused by my afflictions. I am all defiled with torment, my flesh is wasted away, and my bones cleave to my skin. My years pass away full of groans, and I wish they were altogether passed away. I have lost the staff of my old age, the light of my eyes. Mother of mercy, look upon a mother so wretched. If your Son requires from my son the sins of the mother, then let Him exact complete vengeance on me, for I am the only one to offend.

Why have I, the lady of two kingdoms, the mother of two kings, reached the ignominy of this abominable old age? My bowels are torn away, my very race is destroyed and passing away from me. The Young King and the [Duke] of Brittany sleep in the dust, and their most unhappy mother is compelled to live that, without cure, she may be ever tortured with the memory of the dead.

Two sons yet survive to my comfort, who now live only to distress me. King Richard is detained in bonds, and his brother John depopulates the captive's kingdom with the sword and lays it waste with fire. In all things the Lord has become cruel towards me, turning His heavy hand against me. His anger is so against me that even my sons fight against each other, if indeed it can be called a fight in which one languishes in bonds and the other, adding grief upon grief, tries by cruel tyranny to usurp the exile's kingdom.

O impious, cruel, and dreadful tyrant [the Emperor], who has not feared to lay sacrilegious hands on the Lord's Anointed! Yet the Prince of the Apostles still reigns in the Apostolic See. It rests with you, Father, to draw the sword of Peter against these evildoers. The Cross of Christ excels the eagles of Caesar, the sword of Peter is a higher authority than the sword of Constantine, and the Apostolic See higher than the Imperial power.

Why then do you so long negligently, nay cruelly, delay to free my son? Alas, alas for us, when the chief shepherd has become a mercenary, when he flies from the face of the wolf. My son is tormented in bonds, yet you do not send anyone. Three times you have promised us to send legates, yet they have not been sent. If my son were in prosperity, we should have seen them run in answer to his lightest call, expecting plentiful rewards from his munificent generosity. But what profit could they consider more glorious than the freeing of a captive king and the restoring of peace to the people?

Where is my refuge now? You, O Lord my God. O King of kings, save the son of Your handmaiden. Do not visit upon him the crimes of his father or the wickedness of his mother.[7]

It appears that the Queen received no response. Celestine was of too timid a disposition to risk incurring the enmity of the Emperor, whose armies were even now invading Papal territory and whose men had recently cut the throats of Papal emissaries. For decades, the Papacy had been in conflict with the Empire, and Celestine needed to preserve the peace.

In Lent, John returned to England ahead of his mercenary force, intent upon establishing himself as king. In London, he demanded that the regency council surrender its powers to him. When the magnates refused, he did his best to convince them and his mother that the King would never return; he even announced that Richard was dead, although no one believed him. The council's firm stand was boosted by Eleanor's refusal to be intimidated by her son.

John began stirring up rebellion. He garrisoned Windsor Castle, to which, on Eleanor's orders, Walter of Coutances and other lords immediately laid siege, while Hugh de Puiset invested John's castle at Tickhill. Windsor surrendered, thanks in part to William the Marshal arriving with a contingent of Welsh troops, earning himself "a joyous welcome" from the barons, while "Queen Eleanor, who was entirely loyal to him, welcomed the Marshal warmly."[8] John rejoined his mercenaries in France.

Philip invaded Normandy, as Eleanor had feared. On April 12, he took Gisors, then overran the Norman Vexin, laying open the rest of the duchy to conquest. Expecting John's army to arrive in England at any time, the Queen and council took urgent measures for the defense of the realm. "By order of Queen Eleanor, at Passiontide and Easter and thereafter, nobles and common people, knights and peasants, flew to arms and guarded the sea coast that looks towards Flanders,"[9] while fresh oaths of fealty to Richard were again exacted from the magnates. When the first mercenaries arrived, they were either killed or imprisoned in chains. Those following prudently turned their ships about and sailed back to Flanders.

This was the situation when Hubert Walter returned to England. Not optimistic about Richard's chances of an early release, he urged the Queen and the council to adopt a conciliatory policy toward John, who, as one of the King's foremost vassals, had a duty to help raise the ransom money, and whose cooperation might be needed. Eleanor and the magnates took Hubert's advice, and a truce was agreed. John was allowed to retain the castles of Nottingham and Tickhill, while those of Windsor, Wallingford and the Peak (Peveril) "were transferred into the hand of Queen Eleanor,"[10] who would hold them for Richard.

Not having heard from the Pope, Eleanor wrote to him again, signing herself as "Eleanor, by the wrath of God, Queen of England":

> I had decided to remain quiet in case I was accused of insolence and arrogance. Certainly, grief is not that different from insanity while it is inflamed with its own force. It does not recognise a master, it has no regard for anyone, and it does not spare them—not even you.
>
> Please listen to the cry of the afflicted, for our troubles have multiplied beyond number. You [are] the father of orphans, the judge of widows, the comforter of those who mourn and those who grieve, a city of refuge for everyone; and, because of this, in a time of so much misery, you are expected to provide the sole relief for everyone from the authority of your power.

After another blistering castigation of Celestine's failure to act on Richard's behalf, she concluded:

> God will look upon the prayers of the humble and He will not despise them. O Lord, in Your virtue will the King be exalted, and the Roman Church, which must now take too much of the blame for delaying his release, will feel ashamed, since it did not recognise how much difficulty so great a son as mine was in.[11]

On April 19, Richard wrote to "his dearest mother, Eleanor, Queen of England," and his councilors, thanking them for taking good care of his realm and informing them that he had just concluded with the Emperor "a mutual and indissoluble treaty of love." Philip had offered Henry VI a large bribe to keep Richard in prison, but Henry, a megalomaniac who cherished dreams of reigning supreme over the princes of Europe, had no intention of furthering Philip's territorial ambitions. Instead, he resolved to obtain every last advantage to himself from Richard's release, and had agreed to grant him his freedom upon payment of the extortionate sum of 100,000 silver marks (twice England's annual revenue and worth about £49,000,000 today) and the delivery of a number of noble hostages, to be chosen from the sons of the King's barons. Richard was also to promise to help the Emperor overthrow Tancred of Sicily. He had had no choice but reluctantly to agree.

He urged his subjects to do everything in their power to raise the ransom and commanded that the money "be delivered to our mother and such persons as she shall think proper." He asked Eleanor to inform him of the sums donated by each of his barons, that he might know how much gratitude he owed them. He informed the council that William Longchamp, hearing of his plight, had come winging his way from Paris and used his diplomatic skills to help negotiate the treaty and have him moved to Hagenau, "where we were received with honour by the Emperor and his court."[12]

Richard was now being treated not so much as a prisoner as an honored guest. He was permitted to hold court at Speyer or Worms and attend to the business of his kingdom, which was facilitated by his being in constant correspondence with his "much beloved mother"[13] and his councilors. When informed of the treachery of John, the King appeared unconcerned. "My brother John is not the man to conquer a country if there is anyone to offer the feeblest resistance," he observed.[14] "Always cheerful," he was confident that he would soon be returning home to deal with his enemies.[15]

With her customary vigor, Eleanor set to work to raise the King's ransom from a land that had already been bled dry to finance the crusade. At her urging, the justiciars imposed a harsh levy throughout the land. "No subject, rich or poor, was overlooked."[16] Churches and abbeys would be stripped of their gold and silver plate, on the King's promise that they would be recompensed in kind.

In May, despite the canons of Canterbury pleading with Eleanor to hold a free election, she and Walter of Coutances insisted that the chapter obey Richard's orders and secure the speedy election of Hubert Walter as archbishop, with the Queen managing to preserve the "concord" of the clergy.[17]

On June 1, at a council held at St. Albans, she appointed Hubert Walter and four other officers to oversee the raising of the ransom. As the money came in, it was stored in large chests in the crypt of St. Paul's Cathedral, under the seals of the Queen and Walter of Coutances. Eleanor sent her officers into Anjou and Aquitaine to collect ransom money, and herself commanded 100 marks (£49,000) from the abbey of Saint-Martial at Limoges, where Richard had been invested as duke of Aquitaine.

At last, the Pope bestirred himself, threatening the King's captors with excommunication and England with an interdict if Richard's subjects failed to raise his ransom. Eleanor responded with humility: "I beseech you, O Father, let your benignity bear with that which is the effusion of grief rather than of deliberation. I have sinned and used the words of Job; I have said that which I would I had not said. But henceforth I place my finger on my lips and say no more. Farewell."

Because of the King's great reputation, many of his subjects gave willingly. John, however, who had agreed to assist in raising the ransom, ruthlessly milked his tenants, then forged the great seal in order to appropriate for himself the money collected to fund his treasonable activities.

In council at Ely, the Queen set about choosing which noble boys should go to Germany as hostages, an obligation that would bring great grief to many families. Richard had directed that those selected be taken there by Longchamp, but several barons, alarmed by rumors of Longchamp's homosexuality, declared they would rather entrust their daughters to him than their sons, which enabled Eleanor to veto a suggestion that her grandsons of Saxony be among the chosen. At her request, Richard summoned Longchamp to rejoin him in Germany, whereupon she was the more easily able to arrange the transfer of the hostages.

Late that spring, learning of Berengaria's distress at her husband's imprisonment, Pope Celestine appointed Cardinal Meliore to escort her and her companions north through Italy. In June, Berengaria, Joanna, the Damsel of Cyprus and Bourguigne de Lusignan traveled overland via Pisa to Genoa and there took ship for Marseilles. At Celestine's request, Count Raymond of Toulouse sent his heir, Raymond, Count of Saint-Gilles, to receive them there and escort them to Poitou. Berengaria's kinsman, Alfonso II of Aragon, was also waiting for them and gave them safe conduct through his Provençal domains, sending them on under the escort of the Count of Saint-Gilles to Poitou. The journey was not uneventful. The Count took one look at Bourguigne and announced that he was dispatching his wife to a nunnery. Not bothering to obtain an annulment, he married the enchanting Bourguigne bigamously.

Berengaria did not go to England, where she was unknown and where her mother-in-law was firmly entrenched. There was no opportunity for her to play a formal role as queen, and no one seems to have encouraged her to assert her position. She settled in the castle of Beaufort-en-Vallée, just north of Saumur, and helped to raise Richard's ransom. Sometimes she stayed at the chateau of Saumur or at Chinon. Joanna remained with her and the Damsel of Cyprus stayed with them for a short while.

From Richard, Berengaria apparently received no word, although he wrote often to his mother while he was in captivity. In these letters, there is no mention of his wife. It was obvious which queen held his heart and his trust.

At Worms, in June, Richard and the Emperor agreed that, instead of aiding Henry VI against Tancred, the King would increase his ransom by 50,000 marks (£24,500,000) and the number of hostages to 200. Richard also agreed to the betrothal of his niece, Eleanor of Brittany, Arthur's older sister, to the son of Leopold of Austria, and to the surrender of Isaac Comnenus and his daughter to the Emperor.

Anticipating that Richard would soon be free, Philip sent John a warning: "Look to yourself. The Devil is loosed!" John abandoned his plans to usurp the throne and fled to Paris, where he agreed to surrender parts of Normandy and Touraine to Philip in return for the latter's promise to help him take possession of the rest of Richard's continental domains. When John wrote to England, canvassing the support of the barons, Eleanor persuaded the council to confiscate all his estates, including his wife's lands. The lords of Normandy also resisted John's ambitions, and the Pope carried out his threat and pronounced both him and Philip excommunicate.

In England, the government struggled to meet the increased ransom demand. Despite the stringent measures taken, not nearly enough money had been raised. The council was forced to impose a second, then a third levy, while those who had rebelled with John were heavily fined.

Richard was experiencing the frustration common to many captives and had taken to composing songs to express his feelings, the most famous of which is *"J'a nuns hons pris"* ("No prisoner can tell his honest thought"), in which he complained that everyone had forsaken him. This song, one of only two of his compositions to survive, was written in Provençal with a musical score, and was dedicated to his half-sister, Marie, Countess of Champagne.

In October, envoys from the Emperor arrived in London to see how the collection of the ransom was progressing and were royally entertained. When they left, they took with them 100,000 marks (£49,000,000). The balance was to be delivered as soon as it could be collected. Richard commanded Eleanor and Walter of Coutances to bring it to Speyer in person with the hostages, his royal regalia and an impressive retinue. It had been agreed by the Emperor that, subject to the receipt of both money and hostages, he would be released on January 17, 1194.

As soon as the ransom had been raised, Eleanor assembled a fleet at the east-coast ports of Dunwich, Ipswich and Orford. In December 1193, with the King's approval, she appointed Hubert Walter justiciar and, leaving him in charge in England, departed for Germany. With her she took Walter of Coutances and an impressive train, which included some of her southern vassals, notably the aging Saldebreuil de Sanzay, Aimery, Viscount of Thouars, and Hugh IX de Lusignan, nephew of Guy, King of Jerusalem, as well as her ten-year-old granddaughter, Eleanor of Brittany, and the Damsel of Cyprus. Accompanying them was a strongly armed force to guard the great chests containing the ransom money.

The Queen's ships had a smooth crossing over the North Sea. She and her entourage made their way overland to the Rhine and took a boat toward Speyer. On January 6, 1194, they arrived in Cologne in time to celebrate the Feast of Epiphany and were welcomed and entertained by

Archbishop Adolf. By January 17, the date set for Richard's release, the Queen had arrived in Speyer, eager to free her beloved son, only to learn, to her utter dismay, that the release date had been postponed because Philip and John had offered the Emperor a sum greatly exceeding the English ransom if he would either deliver Richard to them or keep him in custody until Michaelmas, by which time they hoped to have overrun his territories. Henry was making a pretense of considering their offer in order to wring new concessions from Richard.

At Candlemas, February 2, Eleanor was received by the Emperor at Mainz in the presence of King Richard and a host of German princes. The Queen was overjoyed to be reunited with Richard after a separation of nearly three years. Backed by the archbishops of Cologne and Mainz, she and Walter of Coutances made strong representations to Henry VI, while the German princes protested violently against his failure to honor his word. After two days of fraught negotiations, Henry agreed to release Richard in return for his acknowledgment of the Emperor as his overlord for England and the surrender of Walter of Coutances as a hostage for the King's good faith. It was Eleanor who, "with great difficulty," helped to negotiate this mitigated settlement[18]—Henry had originally demanded that Richard recognize him as the suzerain of all his lands. Nevertheless, these were humiliating terms, and the Queen, Walter of Coutances and many lords approached the King in person, telling him the unhappy news. On Eleanor's advice, he reluctantly accepted the Emperor's conditions and delivered up his kingdom. After paying homage to Henry, he received it back as a fief of the Empire.

At nine o'clock on the morning of February 4, after the ransom and hostages had been handed over, the archbishops of Mainz and Cologne delivered the King "into the hands of his mother"[19] and he was restored to freedom. Eleanor broke down in tears, as did many of those looking on. That day, she and Richard set off for England, traveling north up the Rhine. On the way, they spent three days being feasted at Cologne, and attended a Mass of thanksgiving in the cathedral, where the Archbishop took as his introit the text "Now I know truly that the Lord has sent His angel and has rescued me from the hand of Herod"[20]—a gracious compliment to Eleanor. The royal travelers received similar welcomes in Louvain, Brussels and Antwerp. Wherever he went, Richard had Eleanor seated in the place of honor at his right hand. He seems to have given little thought to his Queen, who was still at Saumur. He made no move to summon her or send her to England.

On March 4, the King and Eleanor boarded an English ship, the *Trenchemer*, in the Scheldt estuary. The voyage took several days because of the need to evade French ships in the North Sea and the Channel. On the morning of March 12, 1194, the little convoy docked at Sandwich, and the King set foot in his realm for the first time since December 1189. The sun shone exceptionally brightly, and many later claimed they had seen it as an omen of the crusader's arrival.

4

"An Incurable Wound"

✠

R ICHARD AND ELEANOR GAVE THANKS AT THE SHRINE OF Becket for the King's safe return, then pressed on to Rochester, where Hubert Walter and a vast throng were waiting to greet them. "The news of the coming of the King, so long and so desperately awaited, flew faster than the north wind,"[1] extinguishing the last vestiges of support for John. One of his adherents dropped dead with fright on learning that the King had returned.

On March 23, with Eleanor riding by his side, Richard made a state entry into London, where, to tremendous acclaim, he went in procession to St. Paul's Cathedral to give thanks for his restoration. Afterward, as he and Eleanor rode to the Palace of Westminster, they were hailed with joy along the Strand. A few days later, the King and Queen visited St. Albans Abbey and St. Edmund's shrine in Suffolk, where they again gave thanks for Richard's safe return.

The King interrupted the celebrations to root out John's few remaining supporters from Nottingham Castle and other strongholds; Eleanor went with him. Nottingham surrendered at his approach and, on March 30, Richard presided over a meeting of the Great Council in the castle. Eleanor was present, first among the magnates who attended, and for four days they discussed the affairs of the kingdom.

High on the agenda was the question of what to do with John; the barons wanted to auction off his confiscated possessions, but the Queen pointed out that this might drive him further into the arms of Philip. In the end, the council summoned John to appear within forty days to ac-

count for his conduct or suffer banishment and permanent forfeiture of
all his honors, titles and estates. In gratitude for Longchamp's loyal service, Richard restored him to full authority as chancellor. He also ransomed Walter of Coutances, who returned to England in May.

On April 2, Richard and Eleanor stayed at the royal hunting lodge at
Clipstone in Sherwood Forest. The King had never visited Sherwood before, and it "pleased him greatly."[2] This is the context in which the later
legends of Robin Hood were set, but the evidence for his identity is sparse
and confusing: if he existed at all, he probably lived in the thirteenth or
fourteenth century. It was not until 1521, when *The History of Greater
Britain* was written by the Scots writer John Major, that the Robin Hood
legends were set in the reign of Richard I.

The King and his mother celebrated Easter at Northampton. It was
possibly to mark his restoration that Richard added the third lion to his
coat of arms; the three lions of England first appeared on his seal, and
that of Eleanor, in 1194.

The royal party journeyed south to Winchester. There, on April 17, in
the cathedral, in order to purge himself of the dishonor of imprisonment, Richard "received the crown of the kingdom from Hubert Walter,
Archbishop of Canterbury."[3] The wording of this passage suggests that
the ceremony was a second coronation rather than a formal crown-
wearing; the triennial ceremony of crown-wearing had fallen into disuse
over the past forty years. Eleanor proudly watched the proceedings from
a dais in the chancel, surrounded by her ladies. Berengaria was notable by
her absence, being still in Poitou.

Richard was impatient to recover the lands Philip had seized in Normandy. In May, having raised a large army, he and Eleanor set sail with a
hundred ships. Neither would ever set foot in England again.

Having been received in Normandy with great rejoicing, they made a
triumphal progress via Bayeux and Caen to Lisieux, where they were welcomed by the Archdeacon, John of Alençon, and lodged in his house.
While they were at supper one night, John arrived "in a state of abject
penitence," and begged to speak to his mother, beseeching her to intercede for him with the King. Richard could have had him tried for treason, but, "through the mediation of Queen Eleanor," he agreed to see

John and be reconciled with him.[4] "Falling at his feet" and bursting into tears, John "sought and obtained his clemency."[5] John was now twenty-six, but Richard had never taken his brother seriously. He gave him the kiss of peace, saying, "Think no more of it, John. You are but a child and were left to evil counsellors. Your advisers shall pay for this. Now come and have something to eat." So saying, he commanded that a gift of fresh salmon, meant for his own table, be cooked and served to John.[6]

For the next five years, John served his brother loyally, attending to the affairs of his estates, which Richard restored to him in 1195, and staying out of mischief. This left Richard free to focus his attention on expelling Philip from Normandy. Walter of Coutances and William Longchamp joined him there, leaving England in the capable hands of Hubert Walter. Until his death in 1197, Longchamp served Richard faithfully, while Coutances helped him rule Normandy for the rest of the reign.

Richard quickly drove off Philip and recovered lands in Touraine that John had ceded to the French. Berengaria, who was then in Aquitaine, had persuaded her older brother Sancho to march up to Normandy with 200 knights, who helped Richard wrest back fortresses seized by the French. However, on receiving news that his father, Sancho VI, had died on June 27 at Pamplona, Sancho had to return south to claim his kingdom. Sancho VII would become known as Sancho *"El Fuerte"* ("the Strong"), for he was a man of martial character and a firm ruler.

Eleanor, meanwhile, had withdrawn to the abbey of Fontevraud, where she apparently intended to live out her days. At seventy, after ruling England for five turbulent years, she doubtless felt entitled to a rest. She did not take the veil, but lived at the abbey as a guest in her own apartments, making generous donations and bestowing gifts on the community—vessels of gold and silver, silks, jewelry and a processional cross studded with gems.

She was honored and served as a queen. She had her own household, staffed by knights, sergeants, ladies, clerks and servants. She was attended by her chaplains, her secretary, Guy Diva, and "her dear maid, Aliza, Prioress of Fontevraud."[7] For company, she had high-born boarders, and she is said to have loved every nun at Fontevraud like a daughter. Abbess Matilda had long been a good friend, and Eleanor's granddaughter, Alix

of Blois, who would become abbess in 1228, entered Fontevraud as a nun
while she was in residence. Joanna visited soon after Eleanor came to the
abbey.

After 1194, references to Eleanor in contemporary sources are few and
mainly connected with the payment of queen-gold and matters arising
from her dower rights, or the dozen or more grants she made to Fontevraud, but there is enough evidence to show that, although she had ostensibly retired from public life, she was still in touch with worldly affairs
and active politically. Powerful men continued to defer to her wisdom.
Fontevraud was centrally placed between Anjou and Poitou, enabling her
to keep an eye on her own lands and her son's. Richard sometimes stayed
at nearby Chinon, and doubtless rode over to see her, while she herself
made forays to Chinon, Saumur and various other places.

At Christmas 1194, Richard held court at Rouen. There is no record of
Eleanor's presence. From now on, it appears, she made a habit of keeping
Christmas at Fontevraud. She was perhaps looking to the salvation of
her soul and preparing for death. By contemporary standards, she had
been granted an extraordinarily long span, and could not expect to live
much longer. But Eleanor was no ordinary woman, and her public life
was by no means over.

Berengaria was not present at Richard's Christmas court. Since his lib-
eration, she had stayed mainly at Beaufort-en-Vallée. After arriving in
Normandy, he had made no attempt to see or summon her, although, in
November, he had settled her household accounts and Joanna's, and the
expenses of the two knights whose duty it was to protect them. It was
common knowledge that Richard had long neglected Berengaria. Their
marriage had begun well, but circumstances had kept them apart and,
when he could have been reunited with her, he had not chosen to. As
king, it was incumbent upon him to sire an heir, but it is recorded that
he did not expect to have children with Berengaria. His later actions show
that he regarded himself as the guilty party in their estrangement.

Since the eighteenth century, when it was first hinted that he was ho-
mosexual, scholars have wondered what foul "sins against nature" the
King had confessed to in 1191. In 1948, in his book *The Plantagenets*, John
Harvey stated that he was breaking the conspiracy of silence that sur-

rounded the heroic Lionheart, who was in fact bisexual. Nowadays, many accept that theory as fact. But the evidence is conflicting.

In 1195, "a certain hermit came to King Richard and said, 'Remember the destruction of Sodom; refrain from what is forbidden, for the Lord shall exact just revenge.' But the King, intent on earthly things, rather than the things of God, was not able to turn his mind so quickly from unlawful conduct, without seeing some sign from above."[8]

The hermit's reference to the destruction of Sodom, and Richard's sharing a bed with King Philip in 1188, are the chief grounds for speculation by modern historians that the King was bisexual. It has already been argued here that the flaunting of a close relationship between Richard and Philip was political rather than sexual. It is clear from references to Sodom in scripture that the cities of the plain were guilty of many sins, which included homosexuality and sexual practices forbidden by the Church, but, by the first century AD, early Christian writers were defining the sin of Sodom as intercourse with a member of the same sex. By the twelfth century, that interpretation was widespread; in 1300, sodomy was referred to in England as an "unkindly sin that is not twix woman and man."[9]

This is not conclusive evidence that Richard was bisexual. The hermit could have been alluding to the King's notorious promiscuity. His reputation in his lifetime was that of a womanizer and a rapist. This had been established early on, when he was castigated for forcibly abducting "the wives, daughters and kinswomen of his freemen," raping them, then passing them on to his knights "for whoring." William of Newburgh and later sources testify to his pursuit of women, while the thirteenth-century chronicler Walter of Guisborough asserted that Richard's need for them was so great that he even summoned them to his deathbed, against his doctor's advice. He had one known bastard, Philip, whose mother may have been an Austrian woman called Elezebet; Richard married Philip to his ward, Amélie, the heiress of Cognac, in a move to check the territorial ambitions of the counts of Angoulême. There may have been another bastard called Fulk.

Just before Easter 1195, Richard fell seriously ill. Believing this to be a sign from God, he recalled the hermit's warning and heeded the command of Pope Celestine, who had ordered him to return to Berengaria and be faithful to her. "Summoning to his side holy men, the King did not flinch from confessing the foulness of his life and, having accepted penance, received his wife, whom he had not known for a long time, and, renouncing unlawful intercourse, was united with his wife and the two became one flesh, and the Lord gave him health of body and soul."[10] Contemporaries would have seen his Queen as his redemption, through whom he had been restored to grace.

It is not known how soon after Easter 1195 Richard was reunited with Berengaria. They were described as living conjugally at Poitiers later that year, yet there are few mentions of their being together thereafter. In April 1196, they jointly purchased land at Thorée-les-Pins in the Loire Valley, and had a house built there with a mill, a fishpond, woodland, vineyards and meadows, yet there is no evidence that they ever stayed there. They never had any children, and it was rumored that Richard was so certain he would never have a legitimate heir that he resolved to name Arthur of Brittany as his successor.

In August, when Richard finally delivered up Alys, Philip married her off to his vassal William III, Count of Ponthieu. She spent the rest of her life in obscurity and died around 1220.

At Christmas 1195, Richard and Berengaria held court together at Poitiers. Seeing the people suffering greatly as a result of a severe famine, she persuaded him to distribute all his surplus funds to them, which saved many from starvation.

In the spring of 1196, fearing that Philip would launch another assault on Normandy, Richard began building one of the greatest and strongest of all medieval castles, Château Gaillard, on the rock of Les Andelys, where it was strategically placed for defending Rouen. It became one of his favorite residences; he even referred to it as his daughter.

In 1196, he granted Berengaria, in augmentation of her dower, the city of Le Mans, the county of Bigorre (a small feudatory of Gascony) and 1,000 marks (£490,000) annually from the flourishing tin mines of Devon and Cornwall. That year, King Sancho became engrossed in a war with Castile and could no longer be an active ally. A Navarrese document of March 1196 speaks of Richard as a likely enemy of Navarre, suggesting that the King was unhappy about the weakening of an alliance on which he had relied. Given that, and her barrenness, Berengaria was no longer of any use to him, and it is not surprising that there is no further record of the couple being in each other's company. Later evidence suggests that this would have been a great grief to Berengaria. She had no role to play in her husband's dominions, no political presence and nothing to tie him to her.

During the spring of 1196, Richard demanded that the Bretons surrender Arthur, now nine, into his custody as his ward. But Arthur was spirited away to the French court to be brought up with Philip's son Louis. Eleanor had no wish to designate him or the unreliable John as her successor in Poitou and Aquitaine. With Richard's consent, she named her grandson, Otto of Saxony, as her heir.

In October 1196, Richard finally renounced his maternal claim to Toulouse and married his sister Joanna to Count Raymond VI, the son of Raymond V, whom Eleanor had regarded as a usurper. Raymond VI had quickly tired of Bourguigne de Lusignan and shut her up in a nunnery, as he had disposed of his first wife. His wedding to Joanna took place at Rouen in the presence of Queen Berengaria, the bride's close friend, who had lately returned from a visit to Gascony and was "filled with joy to see Joanna happily united with Count Raymond."[11] The marriage ended the ancient feud between the counts of Toulouse and the ducal house of Aquitaine, with Raymond acknowledging Richard as his overlord. Eleanor's grandson, Raymond VII, born in 1197, would one day inherit Toulouse.

In the summer of 1964, a mural was uncovered in the chapel of Sainte-Radegonde at Chinon. Somewhat damaged, it depicts a hunting party on horseback. Their leader, a bearded man wearing a crown, is followed by two women, one young with long auburn hair, the other crowned and gesturing to the first of two smaller men bringing up the rear of the procession, who leans toward her; behind him is the smallest figure, a youth in a white cap.

There are many theories as to whom these figures are meant to be. Some scholars argue that the mural depicts a scene from the life of St. Radegonde, a sixth-century queen of the Franks. Yet there are good grounds for believing that these are the Plantagenets, or figures inspired by them: the location of the mural, in the heartland of the Angevin Em-

pire; the fact that two figures are wearing crowns; and the similarity between the design on the cloak linings of the crowned figures and that on
the tomb enamel of Geoffrey of Anjou at Le Mans.

Given that the mural has been dated to the last decade of the twelfth
century, it might reflect the events of 1196. The king who leads the procession is almost certainly Richard I. The crowned woman is probably
Eleanor, who is gesturing at a young man who may be Otto of Brunswick, whom she designated her heir that year. The youth behind him
may be Arthur of Brittany, whom Richard had named as his own heir.
The young woman riding with Eleanor is uncrowned, and is likely to be
Joanna, whose marriage brought to an end the decades-old dispute over
Toulouse.

In 1197, on his deathbed, the Emperor released Richard from his feudal
oath. The German princes favored Otto of Saxony, Eleanor's grandson,
as his successor, and Otto, now twenty-two, was elected king of the Romans that year, relinquishing his right to succeed her in Aquitaine. In
1209, he would become the Emperor Otto IV.

Around this time, Bishop Hugh of Lincoln was moved to reprove Richard for his sins, especially his neglect of his wife: "Concerning you, and I
speak in sorrow, it is generally reported that you are not faithful in your
marriage bed." He asked about the state of the King's conscience, but
Richard said it was "very easy."

"How can that be, my son, when you live apart from your virtuous
Queen and are faithless to her?" Hugh asked. "Are these light transgres-
sions, my son?"[12] Richard apparently ignored the reproof.

In a charter issued that year, John referred to the likelihood of the
King dying "without heir by his wife, which God forbid." He was probably praying that Berengaria would prove barren. Richard was not living
with her, let alone sleeping with her, although it is possible that he kept
the Easter of 1198 with her at Le Mans. That year, he appealed to Pope
Innocent III to force Sancho VII to hand over the castles of Rocabruna
and Saint-Jean Pied-de-Port, which he should have received as part of
Berengaria's dowry. On May 21, Innocent wrote to Sancho, sternly threatening him with "the direst penalties" if he did not surrender the castles,
but Sancho ignored his exhortations, Innocent did not deliver on his

threat and Richard never got the castles. This was another hiatus in relations between England and Navarre, which has given rise to speculation that Richard was considering repudiating Berengaria at this time.

Roger of Howden states that, between 1198 and 1200, Berengaria passed on to the English council important diplomatic information from her brother, who was then in Morocco fighting for the Almohad Caliphate in return for aid against the encroachments of Castile. In passing on this intelligence, Sancho and Berengaria may have intended to demonstrate that they could still be useful to Richard.

Around this time, Eleanor's two daughters by Louis died. The date of Alix's death is given as 1197 or 1198, but Marie, whom Rigaud de Barbezieux called "the joyous and gay Countess, the light of Champagne," passed away on March 11, 1198, having taken the veil at the priory of Fontaines-les-Nonnes, a cell of Fontevraud near Meaux; it was said that she had died of sorrow on learning that her eldest son, Henry, King of Jerusalem, had fallen to his death from a window of his palace in Acre.

In September 1198, Richard overran the Vexin, reclaiming Gisors with such ferocity that Philip was nearly drowned in the frantic retreat of the French. Richard had imprisoned the French King's cousin, Philip of Dreux, Bishop of Beauvais, in a dungeon at Château Gaillard, which many regarded as an outrage, although, during Richard's own captivity, the Bishop had gone to Germany and urged that the King be kept a prisoner.

The formidable Pope Innocent III, who would emerge as one of the greatest pontiffs of the Middle Ages, sent a legate, Cardinal Peter of Capua, to order Richard to release him. The King heaped abuse on the legate, shouting that the Holy See had never intervened on his behalf when he was being held captive.

Eleanor was disturbed when she learned of this, having heard of Pope Innocent's ruthlessness. She counseled Richard to release the Bishop, but he would not listen, so she asked the Bishop's guardian if she might speak to him, intending to offer him asylum in her own domains. As he was being escorted to their meeting in Rouen, however, he made an abortive attempt to escape. After that, he remained a prisoner until after Richard's death.

* * *

In March 1199, Richard may have visited Eleanor at Fontevraud while marching south with his redoubtable mercenary captain, Mercadier, ostensibly to seize some treasure that had been discovered at Châlus in the Limousin. The treasure—a pot of Roman coins, it was at first said—had supposedly been unearthed in a field by a ploughman, who took it to Achard, Lord of Châlus. It was then demanded of Achard by his overlord, Aymer, Count of Limoges, an ally of King Philip.

As word of the find spread, so the description of the treasure became embroidered. Richard was told that it was a golden statue resembling an emperor and his family seated at a table. Immediately, he laid claim to it as supreme overlord of Châlus. He may have known that such a treasure did not exist; his true intention was not to get his hands on it, but to prevent Aymer and his vassals from supporting Philip and to seize all the Count's strongholds. On March 4, he laid siege to the castle of Châlus.

On the evening of March 26, "a certain arbalister, Bertram de Gourdon, aimed a crossbow from the castle and struck the King on the arm, inflicting an incurable wound. After this, the King gave himself into the hands of Mercadier, who, after attempting to extract the iron head [of the arrow], extracted the wood only, while the iron remained in the flesh. But, after this butcher had carelessly mangled the King's arm in every part, he at last extracted the arrow."[13]

The wound "being badly tended, a kind of blackness mingled with the swelling; this began to give the King intense pain."[14] Richard was apparently suffering from the effects of blood poisoning and possibly gangrene. Realizing he was dying, he sent a messenger to Fontevraud, summoning Eleanor to come without delay. He sent no messenger to summon his wife, offering the unconvincing explanation that he wished to avoid alerting the French to what was happening and giving them any chance of capitalizing on the situation. He forgave his assassin and ordered him to be released, although Mercadier later had him flayed alive and hanged.

On receiving the King's summons, Eleanor dispatched messengers to urge John to hasten to Chinon to secure Richard's treasure. Then she hurried "faster than the wind,"[15] escorted by Abbot Luke of Turpenay, across the 125 miles that separated Fontevraud from Châlus, arriving on April 6. She found Richard lying in a cubicle, with only four lords at his side and his attendants being kept at bay. Geoffrey de Vinsauf states that

Berengaria was at Richard's deathbed, but this does not chime with more reliable evidence.

Richard asked to be buried at Fontevraud, at his father's feet, in contrition for having rebelled against him. He ordered that messengers be sent to the constable of Château Gaillard, William the Marshal and the Archbishop of Canterbury, with instructions, given under his seal and Eleanor's, for the peaceful transfer of power to John, as his successor. He had changed his mind about bequeathing his kingdom and his continental possessions to Arthur. This change of heart may have been down to Eleanor, who had no time for her Breton grandson and his mother, and must have realized that, with Arthur in thrall to Philip, the future of the Angevin Empire would be in jeopardy.

That evening, around the time of Vespers, Richard "ended his earthly day"[16] at the age of forty-one, with Eleanor at his side.

5

"Motherly Solicitude"

✝

A CHARTER GRANTED BY ELEANOR TO THE ABBEY OF NOTRE-
Dame de Turpenay recorded "that we were present at the death of
our very dear son, who reposed all his trust in us, next to God, that we
would make provision for the weal of his soul, and we intend that his
wishes shall be carried out. We will attend to those wishes with motherly
solicitude."

As the Queen's messengers were racing north to find John, Bishop
Hugh of Lincoln learned of the King's death while he was riding toward
Angers, and decided to go to Fontevraud for the funeral. On the way,
hearing that Berengaria was at Beaufort-en-Vallée, he "left the high road
and journeyed through a wild forest in order to comfort her for the death
of her husband. His words went straight to the soul of the sorrowing and
almost heartbroken widow and calmed her grief in a wonderful way. He
spoke to her most beautifully on the need for fortitude in misfortune
and for prudence in happier times, and, after celebrating [mass] and giving the Queen and those with her his solemn blessing most devoutly, he
departed."[1] He asked her if she would accompany him to the funeral, but
she declined. Perhaps she could not face the ordeal. Her deep grief suggests that she had long nursed an unrequited love.

For five days, Eleanor had accompanied Richard's funeral cortège on
its long journey north to Fontevraud. On April 11, Palm Sunday, the
King "was most honourably buried with royal pomp,"[2] with Hugh of Lincoln officiating. Eleanor, as chief mourner, led a congregation that included the bishops of Poitiers and Angers and the abbots of Turpenay

and Le Pin. The Pope sent Cardinal Peter of Capua to represent him, charging him to convey his Apostolic condolences to the King's widow.

As he had instructed, Richard's entrails were interred in the chapel of Châlus Castle, his brain in the abbey of Charroux in Poitou and his heart in Rouen Cathedral in a full-size tomb surmounted by an effigy plated in silver. At Fontevraud, a fine tomb and effigy were raised to his memory, made by the same craftsmen who had worked on his father's tomb, from the same block of limestone. It was probably Eleanor who commissioned both tombs at this time. They were fashioned to represent the kings lying in state, with eyes closed in death.

"On the day of her dearest son Richard's burial," Eleanor issued a charter granting the community of Fontevraud her "town of Jaunay-Clan for their kitchen, for the weal of the soul of my very dear lord, King Richard, that he may sooner obtain the mercy of God." This was the first of several grants she made for the salvation of "our son of blessed memory; may his soul be at peace for ever."

The verdict even of Richard's enemies was that he was "the most remarkable ruler of his times." "Nature knew not how to add any perfection," wrote Geoffrey de Vinsauf. "He was the utmost she could achieve. How brief is the laughter of Earth, how long are its tears." Eleanor had lost her beloved son, the man she had called "the staff of my old age, the light of my eyes." It had been a terrible blow, but there was little leisure for grieving. She had to come out of retirement to help secure her youngest son's inheritance.

Eleanor made a foray from Fontevraud to persuade the Seneschal of Anjou to deliver up the castle of Chinon and its treasury to the new King. Members of Richard's court joined John there and offered him their allegiance. Among them were Aimery, Viscount of Thouars, one of Eleanor's most powerful vassals, his brother Guy and William des Roches. Giraldus Cambrensis arrived, bent on urging the new King to make him bishop of St. David's. Eleanor was present when he made his plea, as was Berengaria, at the late King's behest. Richard may have intended that she be better treated by his relations and accorded her due place as dowager queen of England.

Later that day, John went to Fontevraud to pay his respects at his brother's tomb, only to find that Abbess Matilda was away and had forbidden visitors to enter the crypt or enclosures during her absence. John insisted on being admitted, hammering on the abbey door until Bishop Hugh rode off and obtained Abbess Matilda's permission to escort the new King to the tombs of his father and brother. Hugh had his doubts about John's right to rule, for he regarded the marriage of John's parents as adulterous.

John and Hugh then joined Berengaria at Beaufort-en-Vallée, where the Bishop celebrated the Easter mass. John returned to Fontevraud that same day and Berengaria followed three days later. There, she witnessed one of Eleanor's charters.

On hearing of Richard's death, Philip immediately proclaimed twelve-year-old Arthur the rightful heir to the Angevin Empire. Soon after Easter, Arthur and his leading supporter, William des Roches, marched on Angers, which fell without a blow. This was the signal for the barons of Anjou, Maine and Touraine to declare for Arthur.

Eleanor was outraged. The anonymous author of the poem *Aliscans*, written around this time, may have been inspired by her to have his heroine declare, "Though my hair is grey and white, my heart is bold and thirsts for war!" The Queen ordered that Anjou be laid waste as punishment for its support of Arthur. Summoning Aimery of Thouars and Mercadier and his mercenaries, she rode at the head of her army as it ravaged the countryside around Angers, then bore down on the city itself, where Arthur was staying. At her approach, he fled, aiming to join forces with Philip near Le Mans, whereupon Mercadier and his men sacked Angers, which now fell to Eleanor.

Warned that the armies of Arthur and Philip were approaching, John fled north to Normandy, enabling the pair to make a triumphal entry into Le Mans, where Arthur swore fealty to Philip for Anjou, Maine and Touraine. Le Mans was Berengaria's city, but she was still at Fontevraud. On April 21, Eleanor joined her there and, in gratitude to Abbot Luke for his support during the last terrible weeks, made a gift to his abbey "for the weal of the soul of her dearest son Richard."

Richard's death had left Berengaria almost destitute. Having borne no children, she had no role as regent or investment in the political future of the Angevin Empire, and it seems that her in-laws lost interest in her, sidelining her as they did Constance of Brittany. To them, she was an unnecessary burden, expensive to maintain. In the first year of her widowhood, Eleanor appropriated some of Berengaria's properties in the south and John withheld most of the estates Richard had left her. Eleanor now referred to her daughter-in-law simply as "Queen Berengaria," omitting the prefix "most loved" or "dearest" that she accorded her daughters. Perhaps she thought her a failure as a queen. Berengaria, in turn, may have been intimidated by Eleanor or disliked her. She would not extend her patronage to Fontevraud, her husband's burial place,.until long after Eleanor's death, possibly because it was too closely associated with her mother-in-law.

England and Normandy had accepted John's accession without protest. On April 25, 1199, he was invested as duke of Normandy in Rouen Cathedral, then marched into Anjou aiming to wrest his troublesome nephew from Philip's clutches, only to find that Arthur had again fled. In fury, he sacked Le Mans, then returned to Normandy to guard the duchy against invasion from France.

Late in April, Eleanor rode south to her own domains, attended by a vast train of lords and prelates. Given the hostility of Philip and Arthur, she thought it politic to make a comprehensive tour through Poitou and Aquitaine to secure oaths of loyalty to herself and assurances of military aid from her vassals, towns and clergy for John. In the first year of his reign, she issued over forty charters to secure support for him.

One granted on May 4 at Poitiers states that she had returned to her capital "within a month of the death of her dearest son King Richard."[3] She granted Poitiers two charters conferring the right to self-government, a privilege commemorated in a nineteenth-century stained-glass window in the palace.

The next day, she rode southwest to Niort, where she was joined by Joanna, who was pregnant with her third child and in a desperate state. Count Raymond had treated her badly, but that was the least of her problems. While he was at war in the Languedoc in the spring, some lords of Toulouse had rebelled against him and Joanna had raised an army against them. When she laid siege to the rebel stronghold at Cassée, some of her knights turned traitor, sending provisions into the castle and setting fire to their own camp. Joanna suffered burns, but managed to escape. She had ridden north to seek help from Richard, but, at Niort, she learned from Eleanor that he was dead.

Eleanor sent her to Fontevraud, then continued her progress. She attended to business, heard petitions, dispensed justice, mediated in disputes, distributed largesse, made grants of lands and castles and conferred or confirmed privileges. Throughout her reign as duchess, and thanks in part to her enlightened policy and patronage, Aquitaine and Poitou had witnessed the extraordinary growth and increased prosperity of many towns and cities. In return for the assurance that they would look to their own defenses, Eleanor granted charters conferring independence from feudal jurisdiction to La Rochelle, Saintes and the Île d'Oléron, creating communes and putting an end to the irksome disputes that overshadowed relations between the lords and an increasingly vocal bourgeoisie. In return for the right to elect a mayor, approved by Eleanor, and independently manage their own affairs, these towns were bound to supply her with feudal levies in time of conflict. The arrangement benefited both sides.

As she had foreseen, the new communes helped to impose law and order in her unruly domains. King Philip was so impressed by her farsighted policy that he adopted it himself in France. Through these wise measures, which brought the people flocking to her, and by granting privileges to her great lords, Eleanor bought the loyalty of her vassals for John, even such troublesome lords as the Lusignans, who, with many others, now renewed their oaths of allegiance. Her long progress had borne fruit. She had secured her domains for John and tipped the scales against Arthur.

On May 25, 1199, confident that his continental possessions were secure for the moment, John crossed to England to claim his kingdom, which had been held safely for him by Hubert Walter and William the Marshal. Two days later, on Ascension Day, he was crowned in Westminster Abbey. Wisely, he appointed Hubert Walter chancellor and named William Earl Marshal of England.

As king of England, John has received a bad press, although recent studies of the official documents of his reign have shown that he was a gifted administrator who ruled "energetically enough."[4] Unlike Richard, he showed real concern for his kingdom, and traveled more widely in it than any of his Norman and Angevin predecessors, dispensing justice, overseeing public spending and the efficiency of his officials and taking an interest in the welfare of his common subjects. He built up England's navy and its maritime defenses. Thanks to his personal intervention, the Exchequer, Chancery and law courts began to function more effectively. The future looked promising.

Isabel of Gloucester had not been crowned queen. Before August 30, 1199, John had his childless marriage annulled in Normandy on a plea of consanguinity. Ralph of Diceto believed that he had "acted on wicked counsel and rejected his wife" because he was "seized by hope of a more elevated marriage." Isabel did not contest the action, which was probably why Innocent III withdrew his objection. John kept her in wardship at Winchester Castle to prevent her taking a second husband who might claim her estates, of which John had retained possession. It does not seem to have been an onerous captivity, for he maintained a great household for her and continued to send her presents of wine and fabrics.

On July 1, Berengaria was present when her sister Blanche married Theobald III, Count of Champagne, at Chartres, an alliance that had been arranged by King Richard. That same day, Eleanor arrived in Bordeaux, where she granted a charter conferring commune status on the city. Redressing complaints of unjust impositions by Richard, she made it clear that she expected from her people "the fidelity and devotion that we and our predecessors and our dearest son, John, King of England, have always had."[5] Sometime after the end of May, when she went to Fontevraud to collect Joanna, she granted the community an annuity "for the weal of her soul and of her worshipful husband of sacred memory, King Henry, of her son [the Young] King Henry, of goodly memory, and of that mighty man King Richard, and of her other sons and daughters, with the consent of her dearest son John."[6]

Having completed her grand progress, during which she is estimated to have traveled over a thousand miles, Eleanor moved north to Rouen with Joanna. On her way, she may have visited Berengaria and expressed her concern about the election of Giraldus to the see of St. David's in June, for they would join John in ruling against it.

On July 29, Eleanor met with Philip at Tours and, for the first time ever, paid homage for Poitou and Aquitaine, an extraordinary act on her part, for women rarely swore fealty for lands they held: a male relative usually did so on their behalf. But this was a politic move to ensure the legitimate succession of her heirs to her domains and to counter Arthur's claims. It underlined the independence of her fiefs from the Angevin Empire and shrewdly preempted any schemes Philip might have had for setting up Arthur as their ruler. The chroniclers record few details of the meeting, stating chiefly that Philip gave Eleanor the kiss of peace.

The next day, she met up with John at Rouen. Thanks to her efforts, his footing on the Continent was more secure, and she now formally recognized "her very dear son John as her right heir."[7] He paid homage to her, and she commanded her vassals to render him allegiance. He acknowledged his debt to her, and his trust in her, in a decree proclaiming that she was to retain Poitou and Aquitaine for the rest of her life and "be lady not only of all those territories which are ours, but also of ourself and of all our lands and possessions."[8]

Joanna was now near term and unwell. Knowing that she was dying, she begged to be veiled as a nun of Fontevraud, that she might set aside the vanities of her rank and end her life in poverty and humility. The veiling of a pregnant married woman was forbidden by canon law, but Joanna would not be dissuaded, even by her mother. Matilda of Bohemia, Abbess of Fontevraud, had the power to commute the rules and was duly sent for, but Eleanor, fearing that Joanna might not live until she arrived, asked Hubert Walter to do the veiling. He counseled her to be patient and await the coming of the Abbess, but Joanna was adamant in her resolve. Impressed by her fervor, and taking pity on her and her anguished mother, he convened the nuns and clergy, who all agreed that Joanna's vocation must be inspired by heaven. On their advice, Hubert admitted her to the Order of Fontevraud in the presence of Eleanor, Berengaria and many witnesses. Joanna was so weak that she could not stand to make her vows and died shortly afterward, having expressed a wish to be buried with Richard at Fontevraud. Her infant was born minutes later, by

Caesarean section; he survived just long enough to be baptized and named after the late King.

Late that September, Joanna was buried "among the veiled ones" at Fontevraud, Eleanor and John having followed the funeral cortège south from Rouen. When her eldest son, Raymond VII, died in 1249, he was interred next to her, and effigies were placed on both tombs.

Eleanor remained at Fontevraud. She had established her own lavish chapel, dedicated to St. Lawrence, in the abbey, where she sought solace in her grief. Yet, at seventy-five, she still remained active in the government of her domains, retaining twelve clerks to deal with her affairs. Her chaplain Roger acted as her secretary. Among the dozen or so charters she granted in her final years was one conferring new privileges on Bordeaux. She visited her lands on occasion and ordered the refurbishment of the vast "Hall of Lost Footsteps" in her palace at Poitiers; three walls still display Romanesque arcading dating from her time.

Arthur, fearing Philip's ambitions, now abandoned him, at which point Philip concluded a five-year truce with John, in which Eleanor was influential. In return for the Vexin, Evreux and 30,000 marks (£14,700,000), Philip recognized John as Richard's heir. The meeting ended with the two kings "rushing into each other's arms."[9] The truce also provided for the marriage of Philip's twelve-year-old heir, Louis, to one of John's Castilian nieces. It was decided that Eleanor would travel to Castile to select one of them and escort her to John in Normandy, a strenuous task for an old lady. But Eleanor was "tireless in all labours, at whose ability her age might marvel."[10]

Early in January 1200, she set off from Poitiers, accompanied by Archbishop Hélie of Bordeaux and the trusty Mercadier. Just south of Poitiers, she was ambushed and taken prisoner by her turbulent vassal, Hugh de Lusignan, who threatened to hold her captive until she had ceded to him the rich county of La Marche. It had long ago been sold by his forebears to Henry II, but was also claimed (through an ancestral marriage) by Count Aymer of Angoulême, a powerful, independent-spirited and untrustworthy baron who had allied himself to Philip against Richard and, in 1199, obtained Philip's pledge that he would adjudicate favorably on Aymer's right to La Marche.

Realizing that the Castilian marriage was of greater importance than a disputed fief, and believing that Hugh—who had been one of Richard's friends and had distinguished himself during the crusade—was a worthier claimant to La Marche, Eleanor ceded it to him and was set free to continue her journey south toward Bordeaux.

In January 1200, John confirmed Hugh as count of La Marche. Soon afterward, Hugh was betrothed to Aymer's heiress, Isabella, who would, in time, bring him the county of Angoulême (or the Angoumois, as it was also called). The union of two powerful and volatile vassals, and the creation of a large and powerful Lusignan fief comprising Lusignan itself, La Marche and ultimately Angoulême, posed a serious threat to the cohesion and stability of Eleanor's domains, for these combined territories would cut a swathe through most of Poitou, cleaving her demesne virtually in half. Aymer and the Lusignans would wield control of the Roman roads between Poitiers and Bordeaux, and their lands would straddle the valley of the Charente, which flowed through Angoulême to the strategically important port of La Rochelle. John would never have let Hugh have La Marche had he known of the planned betrothal. All he could do now to counter the threat was buy the loyalty of his Poitevin barons.

Before departing on her journey, Eleanor had informed her vassals in an open letter that she "has gone to Gascony, taking with her the original of the testament of her dearest daughter, Queen Joanna, that the Count of St. Gilles [sic] may see it." She begged her bishops "to carry out its provisions, according to the transcript of it she sends them, as they love God and her."[11] After what must have been a frosty meeting with Raymond in Toulouse, Eleanor once more crossed the Pyrenees, braving the hazards of winter, then traveled through Navarre to Castile, where she was reunited with the daughter she had not seen for thirty years.

Of their twelve children, King Alfonso VIII and Queen Leonor had two remaining unmarried daughters, Urraca and Blanche, who were both beautiful and dignified. Eleanor rejected Urraca on the grounds that the French would never accept a queen with such an outlandish name, and chose twelve-year-old Blanche to be "the guarantee of peace." It was a wise choice, for Blanche of Castile would prove as formidable a queen as her grandmother. Probably Eleanor perceived that she possessed extraordinary qualities; when Blanche was only sixteen, it would be said that she was "a woman in sex, but a man in counsels."[12] In choosing her, Eleanor laid the foundation for France's greatness in the decades to come.

Marriages were not solemnized during Lent, so she lingered for nearly two months at the Castilian court, which, thanks to the influence of her daughter, had embraced the culture and architecture of the south, yet offered Moorish luxuries reminiscent of the courts of the East. Late in March, Eleanor and Blanche journeyed through the pass of Roncesvalles into Gascony, reaching Bordeaux by April 9. There, they kept Easter, after which Mercadier was to escort them north through Poitou. But, in Easter week, "he was slain in a brawl in the city." The tragedy grieved Eleanor, who was already "fatigued with old age and the labour of the length of her journey." She accompanied Blanche in easy stages to the Loire Valley, where, unable to continue farther, she entrusted her to the Archbishop of Bordeaux, who took her to King John. Her duty discharged, an exhausted Eleanor "betook herself to the abbey of Fontevraud and there remained."[13] But the world kept intruding upon the peace of the abbey.

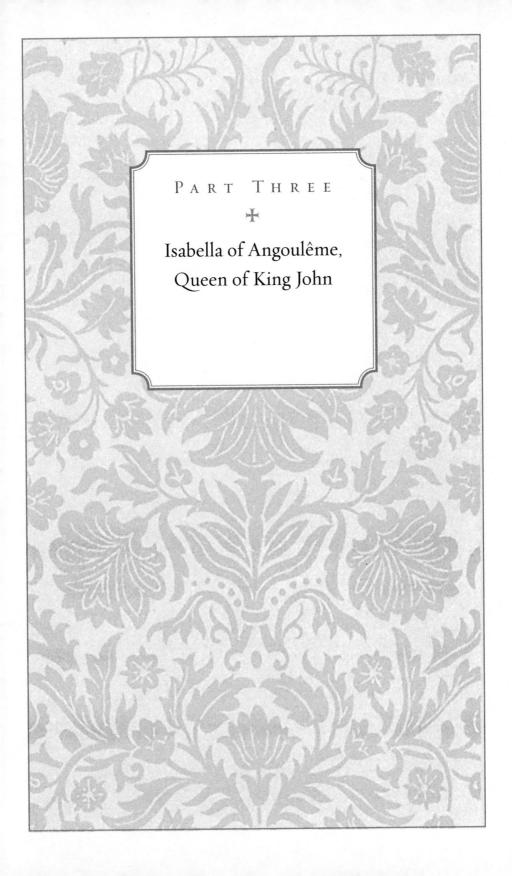

PART THREE

✠

Isabella of Angoulême,
Queen of King John

I

"A Splendid Animal"

✛

EARLY IN 1200, KING SANCHO I OF PORTUGAL HAD SENT EN-voys offering John one of his daughters and, in February, John sent an embassy to Portugal to open negotiations for a marriage. On May 22, John and Philip concluded the Treaty of Le Goulet, in which Philip formally recognized John as Richard's heir, and John paid homage to him for his continental territories. The following day, Blanche and Louis were married.

In the early summer, Eleanor fell ill, and John visited her at Fontevraud. She too was concerned about the recent alliance between Angoulême and the Lusignans and advised John to visit his Poitevin domains and, for the sake of peace, form a friendly alliance with Hugh de Lusignan. He took her advice and rode south, summoning the counts of Angoulême and Limoges, who had rebelled against King Richard, to Lusignan for a ceremony of reconciliation, during which they and Hugh de Lusignan were to pay homage to John.

On, or shortly before, July 5, the King arrived at Lusignan, one of the largest strongholds ever built in France. The tenth-century fortress was strategically sited on a narrow ridge overlooking steep valleys on either side, but it had been partially dismantled during the recent wars and was not fully rebuilt until later in the thirteenth century. Here, John joined a gathering of southern lords hosted by Raoul de Lusignan, Seigneur of Exoudun, the brother of Hugh IX de Lusignan, the new Count of La Marche.

Aymer, Count of Angoulême, now nearing forty, came from a long line of rulers who had adopted the surname Taillefer (hewer of iron), in honor of an ancestor who had crushed Viking invaders in the ninth century. Being a fourth son, Aymer had not expected to become count of Angoulême, but his older brothers had all predeceased him. While paying lip service to the rulers of Aquitaine, Angoulême was a virtually independent fiefdom that lay between Poitou and Gascony. Not long ago, Aymer had been willing to offer his allegiance to the King of France. John was determined not to let that happen again.

Some chroniclers believed that Philip had urged John to ask Aymer for the hand of his daughter and heiress, Isabella, but it is hard to see why, unless it was to foment trouble in Poitou. Most likely, the marriage was John's idea. The prospect of acquiring Angoulême and scuppering the ambitions of the Lusignans was irresistible, as was securing the friendship and loyalty of the powerful, yet fickle, Count Aymer and the wealthy fief of Angoulême on his death. John may even have envisaged seizing La Marche, and Lusignan too, with Aymer's help.

In marrying Isabella, John would be acquiring a beautiful bride—she would be called the Helen of her age—with impressive connections. She had royal blood, for her mother, Alice de Courtenay, was a granddaughter of Louis VI of France and first cousin to King Philip. Isabella's uncle, Pierre de Courtenay II, was the Latin Emperor of Constantinople. The Courtenays were related to many of the royal and noble houses of Europe and the aristocratic Courtenays of England. Alice had married Count Aymer, her third husband, before 1191, possibly around 1186. Isabella, their only child, had perhaps been born in 1188/9: several sources state that she was twelve in 1200, or looked about that age, although she was probably younger.

Her betrothed, Hugh IX—nicknamed "*le Brun*" ("the Brown")—had been born around 1163-4 and inherited Lusignan in 1172. By his first wife, whom he had repudiated in 1189, he had a seventeen-year-old son, the future Hugh X, who might have been a more fitting husband for Isabella, given the closeness in their ages; but Hugh IX evidently fancied her himself. They had promised themselves to each other *per verba de praesenti* (by words in the present tense), which sufficed to establish a valid, indissoluble union. Isabella would have been deemed old enough to consent to the betrothal, being above seven years of age. Thus, she was bound to Hugh, and her union with John could not be valid without a special dispensation. "Because she had not yet reached nubile years, Hugh did not wish to espouse her in the face of the Church" and had agreed to defer the wedding until she was old enough.[1] His mother being dead, it was not thought proper that Isabella reside with him at Lusignan, so it appears that she was sent to live in the household of his uncle, Raoul de Lusignan.

Aymer was eager to see his daughter married to John. Aside from the prestige and glory to be gained from her elevation to a throne, he still wanted La Marche and saw an opportunity to press his advantage. An agreement was reached on July 5, almost as soon as the King arrived at Lusignan, and a marriage contract secretly concluded.

John kept up the pretense that his Portuguese marriage was going ahead. On July 10, he sent another embassy to Sancho I, with instructions to bring him his bride. The envoys believed they were on a *bona fide* mission, and John appears not to have cared that his jilted bride might be publicly humiliated or that there could be reprisals from her angry father.

He must have known that marrying Isabella would make enemies of the Lusignans, who would be furious at being deprived of Angoulême. Speed and secrecy were therefore essential. He dared not risk the Lusignans getting wind of the plan and preempting it.

John returned to Chinon on July 30. Soon afterward, Count Aymer "snatched his daughter from the custody of Hugh le Brun."[2] Some chroniclers assert that she was abducted screaming in terror. She was brought back to the fortified city of Angoulême, her father's capital, which stood on a high plateau surrounded by ramparts. Having no idea why she had been summoned home, she was reunited with her parents in the great Châtelet in the center of the city.

Hugh was at Chinon when news of Isabella's capture arrived, and hastened south immediately, suspecting some conspiracy. "The Count of La Marche and his men left with anger in their hearts. They did not feel it was right that the girl had been abducted."[3]

On August 23, King John and the Archbishop of Bordeaux arrived at Bordeaux for the wedding. Count Aymer's party was already there and Isabella was informed by her father that she was to be married to John the next day. Some said she was delighted at the prospect of becoming a queen; others that she wept bitterly and protested loudly, to no avail. Four years later, she is said to have told John that she had lost the best knight in the world for him.[4]

Thirty-three-year-old John took one look at Isabella and was clearly smitten. It has often been asserted that the marriage was based on physical attraction. The chroniclers, aware that John was in thrall to Isabella's charms, deplored his headlong rush into a marriage based, as they believed, on lust. Yet it had been a purely political arrangement—until John saw his bride, by which time it was a done deal.

Canon law provided that a betrothal *per verba de praesenti* could be broken if one of the parties sought its annulment before reaching puberty, which was deemed the age of twelve for girls and fourteen for boys. Before the wedding could take place, Isabella was required to renounce her betrothal to Hugh de Lusignan, on the grounds that it had not been consummated because she had not attained the age for marriage. Thus, she must still have been under twelve. The Archbishop of Bordeaux convened a synod at which she repudiated her betrothal and it was established that there was no canonical impediment to the wedding.

John and Isabella were married on August 24, 1200, in Bordeaux Cathedral, with the Archbishop officiating. John's envoys were still on their way to Portugal, unaware that the King had abandoned the marriage negotiations "without having warned them, taking much less care for their safety than was worthy of the royal majesty."[5]

According to the chronicler Roger of Wendover, who was deeply censorious of John, the King was "madly enamoured" of his bride. He seemed chained to his bed, so hotly did he lust after her, "finding all kinds of delights in his Queen,"[6] who was "a splendid animal rather than a stateswoman."[7]

Marital delights probably stopped short of complete intercourse, for Isabella was perhaps not ready to bear children. A recent examination of nearly a thousand adolescent English skeletons showed that medieval girls began having periods later than girls today. The average age at which menarche occurred was fifteen. It was known then that a girl in her early teens was more at risk of dying in childbirth, bearing a premature child or complications in labor than an older mother, and that, the more mature a girl was, the better her chances of giving birth to a living, healthy infant. An early death in childbed could jeopardize a valuable political alliance, so princes often put pragmatic considerations before physical pleasure.

There is no surviving image of Isabella that could be said to be an accurate likeness. Her tomb effigy was sculpted at least eight years after her death. A crudely fashioned stone head in the thirteenth-century south door of Wotton Church in Surrey may represent her. Wooden busts thought to be of her and John, bearing their initials and originally in the eleventh-century "King John's Palace" at Downton, Wiltshire, were removed at the building's demolition in the early eighteenth century and placed in niches in the front brick wall of the White Horse Inn, where they remain today.

Immediately after their wedding, John rode north with his bride via Poitiers to Chinon. He may have taken her to Fontevraud to meet his mother. Eleanor was probably impressed: the beautiful Isabella was a southerner, like herself, the daughter of one of her own vassals, and she had spirit. But John, like Richard before him, had no intention of letting his wife take his mother's place. He would always give precedence to Eleanor.

On August 30, at Chinon, John settled a dower on his new Queen. But he had still not paid Berengaria hers. By 1200, according to Pope Innocent III, she was in such dire straits that poverty had forced her, "like a mendicant, to seek help from her sister Blanche," Countess of Champagne, who offered her a refuge in her palace at Troyes. Berengaria disliked living on charity and had appealed to the Pope, who had written twice to John, urging him to do justice by her. John now offered—and Berengaria accepted—an annuity of 2,000 marks (£980,000) in exchange for her dower rights in England, which he settled on Isabella.

In addition to this settlement, and with the agreement of Queen Eleanor, Isabella was assigned Niort and Saintes, the wealthiest lordships in Poitou, which must have infuriated Hugh de Lusignan, for possession of these fiefs would have made her a greater feudal magnate than he was had John allowed her to have them. In fact, they remained under Eleanor's control. Isabella also received lands in Anjou. Her continental fiefs were not far from Angoulême, enabling her to retire there with good financial support in the event of John's death. However, her dower did not make her as wealthy as the queens who had gone before her.

Leaving Chinon in September, John took Isabella on a progress through Normandy, where they lodged in opulent state at Rouen. Early in October, he crossed with her to England. The English barons had been astonished at the speed with which the King had concluded his marriage. Most believed that Philip had pushed him into it. Yet, at a council of lords and clergy at Westminster, where John introduced Isabella to the English political establishment, she was acknowledged as queen and accorded the honor due to her rank.

For her coronation, John gave her "three mantles of fine linen, one of scarlet cloth and a grey pelisse." The couple were crowned together on Sunday, October 8, 1200, in Westminster Abbey with great solemnity by Hubert Walter. Standing under a concealing canopy before the high altar, Isabella stripped to the waist, as kings did, and was anointed on the head, hands and heart with holy oil, sanctifying her queenship. As John himself announced in his letters, she was, "by God's grace, crowned queen of England with the common assent and agreement of the archbishops, bishops, counts, barons, clergy and people of the whole of the realm." He ordered that 25s. (£913) be paid from his treasure to "Eustace the Chaplain and Ambrose the songster, who sang the '*Christus Victus*' at our second coronation and at the unction and crowning of the lady Queen Isabella, our wife." After the coronation, there was a banquet in Westminster Hall.

In the Queen's coronation rite, emphasis had been laid on the nature of royal dominion; it was almost as if her crown and the holy oil were conferring regal authority on her. But John was to allow Isabella no political power at all. She is mentioned in just one of his charters, that granted to Chichester in 1204, and issued none under her own seal. Not one letter of hers survives from the time of her marriage to John. Even when she grew to maturity, she never exercised any of the power Eleanor enjoyed, and she was never permitted full access to her revenues or to claim her queen-gold. Financially, she was heavily dependent on John for everything. He ensured that her household was filled with knights, servants and attendants of his own choosing; she was not allowed anyone from the Angoumois, since he did not want her to be influenced by her countrymen. From what we know of Isabella's feisty character and her capabilities from later sources, she must sometimes have resented these restrictions.

John was generous with gifts and necessities, such as items for her chapel and payments to the keepers of her greyhounds. He outlaid lavishly on clothing for her. The Wardrobe Rolls show that, in November 1200, he bought her another gray cloth pelisse guarded by nine bars of fur, cloth for two robes (one green lined with sandal or sarcanet, the other brown), four white wimples, purple cloth for a pair of sandals, and four pairs of boots. On various other occasions, he gave her costly robes, hoods of lawn and ermine, scarlet cloth, linen, towels, a small brass bowl, and gifts of wine and her favorite fish.

He settled her at Marlborough Castle while he went north to Lincoln, where, in November, he and William the Lyon acted as pallbearers at the funeral of the saintly Bishop Hugh, who, on his deathbed, had prophesied the ruin of the Angevin dynasty: "The descendants of King Henry must bear the curse pronounced in Holy Scripture: 'The multiplied brood of the wicked shall not thrive; and bastard slips shall not take deep root nor any fast foundation. The children of adulterers shall be rooted out. The present King of France will avenge the memory of his virtuous father, King Louis, upon the children of the faithless wife who left him to unite with his enemy. And, as the ox eats down the grass to the very roots, so shall Philip of France entirely destroy this race.'"[8] His predictions were chillingly accurate.

John and Isabella were reunited for Christmas, which they kept at Guildford. News that the Pope had expressed disapproval of their marriage because of the breaking of Isabella's earlier betrothal does not appear to have troubled them. At Easter 1201, they made a pilgrimage to the shrine of Becket at Canterbury. There, John revived the ancient custom of crown-wearing. Archbishop Hubert Walter placed crowns on the royal couple's heads and hosted a lavish feast in their honor. April saw John and Isabella in Exeter and Wells. It was Isabella's first visit to the West Country, where she was to spend much of her time.

2

"An Incomparable Woman"

✠

J OHN'S MARRIAGE "DID NOT HAVE A FAVOURABLE OUTCOME."[1] When the Lusignans learned how Hugh had been robbed of his bride, they initially did nothing, yet both insult and injury rankled and festered and would soon help to fuel a deadly conflict with far-reaching repercussions. Hugh was scandalized at John having married the underage Isabella when he himself had agreed to wait until she was twelve, but he accepted the hand of John's ward Matilda, daughter of Vulgrin III of Angoulême, evidently reasoning that he could one day claim Angoulême, since she was the daughter of Aymer's older brother and arguably had a better right to it than Isabella.

Early in 1201, when Hugh finally bestirred himself to make a formal protest to John about the theft of Isabella, the King ignored him, whereupon Hugh and his kinsmen rose in rebellion. In failing to address Hugh's grievances, John undermined any advantages he had gained in marrying Isabella.

Eleanor was then unwell, but it did not prevent her from continuing to work in the interests of peace in Poitou, which was being threatened by the Lusignans. She knew there was one vassal on whom she could count in this situation. In February, she informed John:

> Know, dear son, that we summoned our well-beloved cousin, Aimery of Thouars, to come to visit me in my sickness at Fontevraud, and he came; and, because of this, thanks be to God, we are recovering better than we were. Moreover, please know that I and your faithful

Guy Diva questioned him, and he has shown us that he is completely bound in service to you, that he has wrought us no injury, nor seized unjustly any of your lands, as your other barons of Poitou are doing. And, because we spoke justly and reasonably to him, he freely conceded to us with an open heart that he and his lands and castles were from this time forth under your will and command, whatever he had done previously. As for his friends and others, who had seized your land and castles without your permission or will, unless they are willing to do your will and pleasure and peaceably restore what they have unjustly seized, he will set himself against them with all his might, for everything that belongs to you. And since he agreed wholeheartedly to the things we asked, namely that he will serve you faithfully and truly against all men, I, your mother, together with your faithful Guy Diva, urge that you treat him as a lord should his liege man; and we give pledges that he will do whatever we ask on your behalf, as noted in the letters that he sends you. I was much comforted by his presence, and through God's grace, am convalescent.[2]

She urged John to meet with Aimery in Normandy or invite him to England, which John did. She also wrote to Aimery, counseling him to protest his loyalty in writing to John. Both King and Count heeded her advice. Aimery informed John that

Queen Eleanor, my mistress and your mother, struck down by sickness at Fontevraud, summoned me to hurry and visit her while she was gravely ill. With a devoted heart, I rushed to her presence. While I was in attendance, she greatly recovered her spirits, and, in our conversation concerning you, I agreed with her on all points. Please be assured that everything she has written to you in her letters is absolutely true.

Aimery would prove a valuable ally. John was to need many more such. When he ordered the seizure of Driencourt, a castle owned by Hugh de Lusignan's brother, Raoul, the Lusignans angrily revoked their oaths of allegiance to the King and appealed to Philip II for justice.

Fearing armed French intervention, Eleanor summoned Arthur to visit her at Fontevraud and wrung from him a promise that he would do everything in his power to preserve the peace in Poitou and Aquitaine.

Pending his judgment, Philip asked the Lusignans to cease harrying John, while Eleanor and Aimery urged John to return from England to deal with them. Count Aymer also offered his support. John ordered his officials to do the Lusignans all "the harm they could."[3] Every castle belonging to them was either besieged or seized. In March 1201, he confiscated La Marche. Soon afterward, he bestowed it on Count Aymer.

On the evening of May 13, John and Isabella sailed from Portsmouth to France in separate ships. On May 31, they took up residence at Château Gaillard, where King Philip stayed with them. They then visited Rouen, where Isabella watched a mosaic pavement being laid in the palace. On July 1, they visited Philip in Paris and were "honourably entertained" and given gifts and champagne. Already, Philip had begun to devise how he might use John's quarrel with the Lusignans to break the power of the Angevins on the Continent. He offered to act as mediator, and John agreed that the Lusignans' grievances could be aired in a court presided over by Philip and the peers of France. Isabella, meanwhile, was loving Paris, dancing late into the night and sleeping until noon.

The royal couple spent the rest of the summer of 1201 enjoying fêtes and entertaining vassals at Chinon, whilst the rumbles of discontent echoed from Poitou. Eager to gain credit with Berengaria's brother, with whom he wished to forge a new treaty, John invited her to join them, entertained her munificently and, in the early autumn, promised to enlarge her dower, settling on her a reduced annuity of 1,000 marks (£490,000), the city of Bayeux and two castles in Anjou—a promise he would fail to keep. At the time of her visit, Berengaria must have been concerned for her sister, the Countess Blanche, who had been widowed in May and was now ruling a debt-ridden Champagne as regent for her young son, Theobald IV.

It has been claimed by many writers that Berengaria was the only English Queen never to set foot in England. Certainly, she did not do so in her husband's lifetime, but, in 1201, a safe-conduct was issued for her first visit, and John ordered that she be welcomed with great honor as his dearest sister. However, it is not recorded that she actually went to England at this time. In March 1206, John again invited her to visit England and sent her a safe-conduct, but she did not go. In November that year, he sent her another, reproving her for being unwilling to cross the English Channel to visit him. Again, there is no record of her accepting his invitation.

Thanks to Aymer of Angoulême and Aimery of Thouars, Aquitaine lay peaceful. Eleanor remained untroubled at Fontevraud. On February 8, 1202, she would visit Poitiers for the last time.

But John's arbitrary measures had alienated many who might have supported him. By the autumn, several southern barons had defected from their allegiance and joined forces with the Lusignans. Fearing that Philip would support this formidable coalition, John now wished to avoid having his dispute with Hugh settled by the court of France. In October, he accused the Lusignans of treason and challenged them to a trial by combat, in which both sides would be represented by champions. The Lusignans refused and again appealed to King Philip for justice. Philip summoned them and John to appear before the French court in Paris, A date for the hearing was agreed, but John spent the winter canceling or postponing it. By the end of 1201, Arthur had allied himself with Philip and the Lusignans against John, who spent Christmas at Caen with Isabella, feasting and dallying late in bed, apparently oblivious to the mounting threats from his enemies.

On February 4, 1202, he negotiated a new alliance with Sancho VII, Berengaria's brother, which Count Aymer helped to broker. On April 28, Philip issued a final summons ordering John to present himself at the French court and submit to judgment by the peers of France. John failed yet again to appear, which gave Philip the legal pretext he needed to declare him a contumacious traitor, and "the assembled barons of France adjudged the King of England to be deprived of his lands, which he and his forefathers had hitherto held of the King of France."[4] These now included Angoulême, to which John had succeeded on June 16 on the death of "his very dear father," Count Aymer, in right of Isabella, who was now countess of Angoulême. The loss of Aymer, his most powerful supporter in Poitou, left the King dangerously exposed to his enemies.

That summer, John took Isabella to Angoulême to secure her inheritance, which Hugh de Lusignan was now claiming in right of his wife Matilda. In the presence of the Seneschal of Poitou, the barons and knights of Angoulême swore fealty to Isabella, and it was arranged that her mother, the Dowager Countess Alice, would rule the city in her name, supported by John's officials, while the Seneschal was to act as John's deputy in the rest of the Angoumois. There was no question of thirteen-year-old Isabella ruling Angoulême herself.

Later, in March 1203, John would summon his mother-in-law to his court, grant her a monthly pension in return for her dower rights, relieve her of her regency and take up the reins of government himself. In 1204, he granted the city of Angoulême commune status. Thereafter, he placed the Angoumois under the rule of a seneschal or mayor, a Poitevin land-owner called Bartholomew de Le Puy. Alice remained a presence in An-goulême, occasionally issuing charters.

Meanwhile, Philip had declared the truce broken and launched an armed onslaught on Normandy's frontier defenses, determined to conquer the duchy for France and have Arthur seize John's other continental territo-ries. In July, Arthur, now fifteen, did homage to Philip for all the conti-nental Angevin domains and "marched forth with pompous noise"[5] toward Poitou. John now faced a war on two fronts, and he was by no means prepared for it.

Eleanor was outraged at Arthur's temerity in attempting to wrest Poitou from its rightful ruler. She declared her support for John and, in the last week of July, still active at seventy-eight, set out from Fontevraud with a small military escort, intending to entrench herself in her capital, Poitiers, and deter Arthur from taking possession. Twenty miles north-east of Poitiers, she lodged at the decaying castle of Mirebeau.

Unfortunately, Arthur learned of her whereabouts and set out with Hugh de Lusignan, Hugh's uncle Geoffrey and 250 soldiers "to besiege the castle of Mirebeau," intending to take his grandmother hostage and barter her for Queen Isabella, which would enable him to wrest huge concessions from John. The castle was neither adequately provisioned for a siege, nor were its defenses strong, but Eleanor, "fearing capture," instructed her men-at-arms and the garrison to defend it. She smuggled out two messengers, one urging John "to bring her aid as soon as possi-ble,"[6] the other to summon William des Roches from Chinon.

"Arthur contrived to parley with his grandmother, demanding that she surrender the castle and make over all her possessions to him. She could then go peaceably wherever she wished, for he wanted to show nothing but honour to her person. The Queen replied that she would not leave, but, if he behaved as a courtly gentleman, he would quit this place, for he would find plenty of castles to attack other than the one she was in. She was, moreover, amazed that he and the Poitevins, who should be her liegemen, would besiege a castle knowing her to be in it."[7] Arthur demanded that, in return for her freedom, she submit to Philip's disposition of her domains. When she adamantly refused, he promptly laid siege to Mirebeau.

John was on the road to Chinon when he heard of Eleanor's plight. "The King immediately set out with part of his army"[8] and marched day and night to Mirebeau, covering more than eighty miles in two days. On the way he was joined by William des Roches. On approaching Mirebeau in the early hours of August 1, he was informed that his mother had been forced to lock herself into the keep, since the walls and outer defenses of the castle had been breached by Arthur's men. Soon after dawn, as an unsuspecting Arthur and Hugh de Lusignan were breakfasting on roast pigeons, William des Roches and his troops entered the gate and launched an assault, "the armed upon the unarmed," throwing them into disarray. "After heavy fighting, the King entered the city"[9] and the besiegers were easily overcome. The siege was raised and Eleanor, unharmed, led her people out to safety.

Nearly every member of Arthur's company was captured or killed. His sister, Eleanor, "the pearl of Brittany," was also taken, and would remain a royal captive for the rest of her life. But the greatest triumph for John lay in taking prisoner Arthur, Hugh and Geoffrey de Lusignan.

On August 10, Arthur was shut up in a dungeon in Falaise Castle in Normandy. More than 250 knights, irrespective of their rank, were ignominiously chained together, bundled into ox carts and paraded as trophies along the roads leading to the Loire crossing, before being incarcerated in dungeons in England and Normandy. Hugh de Lusignan was imprisoned in irons at Caen. It was a brilliant victory, the most significant in John's career, and it left him in a very strong position, prompting Philip to withdraw his forces from the Norman border.

The Lusignans were quickly ransomed and released, after swearing fealty to John and surrendering their strongholds, but most of the knights—who could also have been ransomed to John's advantage—were kept manacled in irons. At Corfe Castle, twenty-two of them starved to death. John's treatment of his captives provoked an outcry, and many of his supporters deserted him. Even Aimery of Thouars and William des Roches transferred their allegiance to King Philip.

Before parting from John, Eleanor charged him, on her malediction, not to harm Arthur. She was now ready for the peace of the cloister. The annals of Fontevraud confirm that, on her return there, she took the veil and entered the community. Peter of Blois stated that she was received at Fontevraud for penance and put on the monastic habit. The nuns were delighted that she had chosen their abbey above all others. After her profession, Eleanor maintained contact with her officers in her domains, and remained supportive of John.

In the autumn of 1202, Aimery of Thouars and William des Roches seized Angers and the surrounding territory. In November, the Lusignans joined the rebel coalition. Despite this, John spent Christmas at Caen, "feasting with his queen and lying in bed until dinner time,"[10] to the scandal of the court. By then, rumors were circulating that Arthur was dead.

In January 1203, John had Arthur brought before him at Falaise. "The King addressed him kindly and promised him many honours, asking him to separate himself from the French King and to adhere to the side of his lord and uncle."[11] Arthur responded angrily, demanding that John give up to him his kingdom and all his territories. If he did not, Arthur vowed never to give him a moment's peace for the rest of his life. The King, much troubled, sent him back to his dungeon and rode south to deal with his rebels.

Isabella was then at Chinon, where she found herself besieged by Aimery of Thouars, who was bent on ransoming her for advantageous terms. She sent desperate messages to John, pleading to be rescued, whereupon he summoned his knights and a large force of mercenaries and raced south from Argentan, only to be informed that the roads were impassable. Fearful of being captured himself if he chose another route, he sent a mercenary force led by Peter de Preaux to rescue the Queen.

On January 23, Peter brought Isabella safely to John at Le Mans. Much relieved, "the King was extremely pleased with Peter."[12] Isabella, recalling John's mad dash to rescue his mother the year before, unheeding of his own safety, may not have been so pleased with him. When they met up, he told her, "My lady, do not worry. I know a safe place where you can have protection from the King of France and all his power." To which Isabella replied, "Sire, I really think you want to be a king checkmated in a corner square."[13]

Still fearing capture, John took Isabella back to Argentan by devious ways; after that, he would not leave her side and lost interest in conquering his enemies. Roger of Wendover described him as the most uxorious of men and claimed that his obsession with his wife made him soft and incompetent. Other chroniclers attest to his lethargy and suspicious frame of mind. But John was also preoccupied with the problem of his nephew. In February or March, he "gave orders that Arthur should be sent to Rouen to be imprisoned in the new tower there and kept closely guarded. Not long after that, Arthur suddenly vanished."[14]

What happened to him is not known for certain, but a plausible account exists in the "Annals of Margam," Glamorganshire, an abbey of which the aristocratic de Braose family were patrons. The information may have come directly from William de Braose, Arthur's custodian. The Annals state that, at Rouen, "on the Thursday before Easter," April 3, 1203, "when he was drunk with wine and possessed of the Devil, [John] slew [Arthur] with his own hand and, tying a heavy stone to the body, cast it into the Seine. It was brought up by the nets of fishermen and, dragged to the bank, it was identified and secretly buried, for fear of the tyrant."

On April 16, John wrote an open letter to "the Lady Queen his mother" and eight of her vassals, including the Archbishop of Bordeaux and the seneschals of Poitou and Gascony:

> We send to you Brother John of Valerant, who has seen what is going forward with us, and who will be able to apprise you of our situation. Put faith in him respecting these things whereof he will inform

you. Nevertheless, the grace of God is even more with us than he can tell you and, concerning the mission which we have made to you, rely upon what the same John shall tell you thereof.

It is possible, as many historians assert, that the letter refers to Arthur's death, and that the important news Brother John was to impart to the Queen at Fontevraud and her chief vassals in Poitou was too sensitive to be written down. It is obvious, from the tone of the letter, that the news would be pleasing to Eleanor, yet she would probably have had mixed feelings about the murder of her grandson, and might not have seen it as a sign of divine grace. The previous year, she had made John promise to spare Arthur. She had suffered, by her own admission, mental torture at the memory of the fate of Arthur's father Geoffrey, so she surely cannot have condoned the murder of his son—unless John led her to believe that Arthur had died of natural causes and pointed out the very real advantages of his passing.

In the spring of 1203, "opinion about the death of Arthur gained ground, by which it seemed that John was suspected by all of having slain him with his own hand; for which reason many turned their affections from the King and entertained the deepest enmity for him."[15] The lords of Maine deserted to Philip. In Brittany, Arthur's subjects rose in revolt. Their defection cut Normandy off from Poitou, which had remained loyal, and left it vulnerable to Philip's aggression.

Many Norman magnates held property on both sides of the Channel and had good reason to support John. The duchy was well fortified along its frontiers and guarded by a ring of castles, chief of which was Château Gaillard. Had John bestirred himself at this time, he could have held on to Normandy, but he seemed to be in the grip of a strange inertia.

That spring, Philip took the great fortress of Saumur on the Loire. Chinon held out against him, so he swung north and marched unopposed into Normandy, taking town after town: Domfront, Coutances, Falaise, Bayeux, Lisieux, Caen and Avranches, all former bastions of Angevin power. John asked for a truce, but Philip offered impossible terms, being determined only on conquest. When messengers came urgently beseeching John to rise up and give the French King the trouncing he deserved, he shrugged and said, "Let him alone. Some day I will recover all I have lost."[16] By then, many of his disgusted Norman vassals were transferring their allegiance to Philip. By August, most of the eastern reaches of Normandy were in French hands. In September, Philip laid siege to Château Gaillard. "In the meantime, King John was staying inactive with his queen at Rouen, so that it was said that he was infatuated by sorcery, for, in the midst of all his losses and disgrace, he showed a cheerful countenance to all, as though he had lost nothing."[17]

Little is known of Eleanor's life during these terrible months. She granted a charter granting commune status to the city of Niort, perhaps with a view to securing its support against the French; it was one of her last public acts. Philip's advance through Maine and Anjou had left her isolated at Fontevraud, and John had to deploy his forces in Anjou to prevent her from being cut off.

John finally roused himself late in September and attempted to relieve Château Gaillard, but was forced to withdraw after suffering heavy casualties. In desperation, he made inept attempts to recoup his losses in Normandy, whereupon many barons decided that they would be better off under French rule. By now, Philip had made such inroads into Normandy that it was clear that John would never recover what had been lost. Belatedly, he saw the desperate reality of his situation, but, when William the Marshal counseled him to abandon the struggle, he retorted, "Whoso is afraid, let him flee. I myself will not flee."[18] Tragically, it was months too late for such bullish heroism.

As winter drew on, John announced his intention of going to England "to seek the aid and counsel of his barons there, asserting that he would return shortly. But many, seeing that he took the Queen with him, feared that he would be away for too long." By the beginning of December, the only parts of Normandy remaining in John's hands were Rouen, Château Gaillard, the Cotentin peninsula, Mortain and the Channel coastline, but, deprived of firm leadership, these regions were degenerating into anarchy.

On December 6, the King and Queen sailed to Portsmouth. They spent a miserable Christmas at Canterbury, for John was in despair at the perilous situation across the Channel. He had not yet returned to Normandy when, on March 6, 1204, after holding out valiantly for six months, Château Gaillard, which King Richard had claimed was impregnable, fell to the French, blocking access to Rouen. It was a bitter blow that signaled the beginning of the end of the struggle for Normandy, and news of it is said to have hastened Eleanor's death. That is unlikely to have been true, for the annals of Fontevraud state that she now existed as one already dead to the world.

On April 1, 1204, Eleanor passed away "as a candle in the sconce goeth out when the wind striketh it."[19] At eighty, she was the longest-lived English medieval queen. For all her colorful career and mighty reputation, her death went virtually unremarked in the chaos surrounding the collapse of the Angevin Empire.

As she had requested in her will of 1202, her body was buried in the crypt of the abbey of Fontevraud and a fine tomb was erected beside those of Henry II, Richard I and Joanna. Unlike theirs, Eleanor's painted polychrome effigy shows her in life, with her eyes open and a hint of a smile on her lips. She holds a book, reflecting her devotional interests. She wears a chemise beneath a white *bliaut* with a diagonally crisscrossed pattern in gold, with bands of embroidery at the neck and wrists and a gold clasp at the throat, a jeweled belt, a blue mantle powdered with gold crescents, lined with rose fabric and fastened by gold cords, a white chin-barbe, a veil and a crown. The rendering of the folds of her clothing, outlining a realistic human form beneath, is particularly fine. The effigy was sculpted from the same block of limestone that had been used for those of Henry and Richard, again suggesting that Eleanor commissioned them all. The left hand and the book are nineteenth-century replacements, based on drawings made in 1638.

Such effigies were rare, and Eleanor's is one of the finest of the few that survive from this period; it is the first tomb effigy of an English queen. Completed by *c.*1210, it was not by the same sculptor who worked on the effigies of Henry and Richard, which date from around 1200, and it has been suggested that it was made by a craftsman who helped build the transepts in Chartres Cathedral.

The nuns of Fontevraud recorded in their necrology a glowing tribute to their late sister, describing her as a paragon among women, who had "illuminated the world with the brilliance of her royal progeny. She graced the nobility of her birth with the honesty of her life, enriched it with her moral excellence, and adorned it with the flowers of her virtues; and, by her renown for unmatched goodness, she surpassed almost all the queens of the world."[20] It was how Eleanor had come to be seen in her venerable old age. The chronicler of Saint-Maixent wrote, "If that lady offended the Lord in many things, she did much to please him."

After Eleanor's death, it was the scandals surrounding her that were remembered, not her wise rule during the latter years of her life. "By reason of her excessive beauty, she destroyed or injured nations," asserted Matthew Paris, although he did pay tribute to her as "an admirable lady of beauty and cleverness." Elsewhere, he alleged that even King John called his mother an "unhappy and shameless woman." Yet the evidence strongly suggests that Eleanor's memory was revered by John and her other descendants. In the cathedrals of Canterbury and Rouen, and in many other holy places, her obit—the memorial service to commemorate a soul's entry into Heaven—was celebrated annually.

Eleanor's fame rests on her later deeds and the role she played during a long career on the political stage. Denied for so long the exercise of power, for which she had a natural aptitude, she came into her own at an advanced age, standing for dynastic legitimacy and held in high respect as the wise and far-seeing mother of the royal domains. Remarkable in a period when females were invariably relegated to a servile role, she was, as Richard of Devizes so astutely claimed, "an incomparable woman."

3

"I Have Lost the Best Knight in the World for You"

✠

ELEANOR DID NOT LIVE TO SEE THE DESTRUCTION OF THE empire she and Henry had built. Her death deprived John of a wise adviser and champion who might have helped him avert the disasters that were looming ahead. It removed a legal obstacle to Philip's ambitions, for many of her subjects immediately transferred their allegiance to him. John was said by one Angevin annalist to have been "most violently saddened" by his mother's passing, so that "he feared greatly for himself" and lost the will to fight for Normandy.[1] "For the salvation of the soul of our dearest mother," and in emulation of her own order on being released from captivity, he freed all his prisoners.

Rouen fell to the French on June 24, 1204. The whole of Normandy, apart from the Channel Islands, was now in Philip's possession—lost by John, according to Roger of Wendover, under the quilts of the marriage bed. In fact, John had faced the near-impossible task of holding together an unwieldy empire in the face of unprecedented French aggression. Nevertheless, he had alienated many of those who could have aided him by his duplicity, suspicion and arbitrary acts, and few of his vassals now trusted him. Some barons were openly hostile.

The author of *L'Histoire de Guillaume le Maréchal* believed that John's marriage to Isabella "was the cause of the ignominy and war that led to the King losing his land." It had certainly been a contributory factor, for it had fueled the anger of the Lusignans and given Philip a pretext to move against John. But John's inertia, and perhaps his lust for Isabella, had been disastrous in the face of Philip's ruthless ambition.

In August, Philip took Poitiers, much of Poitou and Anjou. The sleepers at Fontevraud, architects of an empire—Henry II, Eleanor and Richard I—now lay in French territory.

With Eleanor dead, John was able to settle the dower of the queens of England on Isabella. On May 5, 1204, he assigned her the county of Rutland, the cities of Exeter and Chichester, the honors and castles of Rockingham and Berkhamsted, manors in Devon, Wiltshire and Essex, Queenhithe Dock, and the tin mines of Devon and Cornwall, which were rightly Berengaria's. She was also granted the right to collect queen-gold. She did not receive the extra properties that Richard I had granted Eleanor in 1189, and even those she did get were depleted in value, since Eleanor had granted many properties to religious houses and individuals she favored, sometimes in return only for quit rents of pepper or incense. Furthermore, Isabella's dower lands in Anjou were now lost to her, and it would be years before she was compensated with equivalent lands in England.

Again, Isabella saw little of her revenues because John appropriated most of them. He also gave away some of her properties. She was perhaps nearly sixteen now, yet he did not appoint a household for her, but sent her to reside in his ex-wife's establishment at Winchester, providing for them both at the cost of £80 (£58,400) annually. During the next two years, they would jointly be supplied with wine and money. One is tempted to wonder how the ex-wife and the current wife rubbed along.

Isabella was not at Winchester all the time. She also lodged at Marlborough Castle in the charge of its custodian, Hugh de Neville, the King's chief forester and close adviser. An entry in the Chancery records for Christmas 1204 reveals that John asked Hugh's wife, Joan de Cornhill, what it would be worth to her to return to her husband's bed, to which she jokingly replied, "Two hundred chickens." Some historians have inferred that Joan was the King's mistress, which is possible, for Hugh de Neville later sided with John's enemies, perhaps because he had a personal grievance against him.

* * *

John may have provided for his Queen, but he had still done nothing for his brother's widow. In 1203, Berengaria had again appealed to the Pope about the King's neglect, and Innocent once more took her under his protection. In January 1204, he complained to John about her being forced to live on charity and commanded him to pay what was due. He wrote a second letter to the Archbishop of Canterbury and the bishops of Ely and Winchester, ordering them to keep him informed about John's compliance. That month, Berengaria was in Paris, where, in a charter she issued as "Berengaria, humble queen of England," she ceded Loches to King Philip.

Following Eleanor's death, Berengaria had demanded that John give her the continental lands assigned to her on her marriage. After the fall of Normandy, Philip was reluctant to pay her dower revenues from Falaise, Bonneville-sur-Touques and Domfront. He had also taken her city of Le Mans. Berengaria had no choice but to recognize her husband's great enemy as her overlord and appeal to him for protection. In August, in exchange for her renunciation of her dower rights in Normandy, he issued a charter granting her the war-scarred city of Le Mans for her lifetime and an annuity of 1,000 marks (£490,000), and Berengaria paid him homage. Philip probably reasoned that John would not try to recapture Le Mans while Berengaria was in residence there, and that the French Crown could reclaim it on her death.

For Berengaria, this settlement, especially the annuity, was a godsend, since she was still vainly trying to obtain the payment of her allowance from John and had again petitioned the Pope for help. This time, Innocent threatened John with excommunication if he did not honor his obligations. Berengaria's defection to the French may have been one reason why John proved so tardy in paying her allowance.

She was now able to leave Troyes and take up permanent residence at Le Mans as its feudal lady. The medieval city, cramped within its old Gallo-Roman walls, stood on the left bank of the Sarthe. Dominating it was the Romanesque cathedral established by St. Julien, with its high tower and beautifully sculptured twelfth-century portal. The old city beside the cathedral still occupies the same footprint that it did in Berengaria's day, but the houses are of later date. That called "La Maison de la Reine Bérengère" dates only from 1460. Berengaria actually resided in the heart of the city, in the palace of the counts of Maine (the remains of which are now incorporated into the Hôtel de Ville and known as the Royal Plantagenet Palace), which was built between 970 and 1015 next to the Roman wall. Henry II had been born here in 1133. The palace had suffered from John's recent attacks and had to be repaired for Berengaria. It comprised the great hall, which served as her administrative center and was used for feasts and social functions, and "the Queen's chamber," as her private apartments were known. A Norman window survives from her time.

"She lived on as a most praiseworthy widow and stayed for the most part in the city of Le Mans, devoting herself to almsgiving, prayer and good works, witnessing as an example to all women of chastity and religion."[2] She never remarried, perhaps emulating her father's example, believing that she should remain true to Richard unto death.

She was no mere figurehead; the governance of the city was in her hands, and she was energetic in defending her rights. King Philip granted her the right to appoint a seneschal, Sir Herbert de Tucé, who rendered her faithful service until his retirement in 1214. She was assiduous in checking her accounts and the expenses of her representatives in Rome, London, Paris and Troyes. She shared her family's devotion to the Cistercian order and enjoyed the continuing friendship and support of her chaplain, King Richard's former confessor, Adam, the Cistercian Abbot of Perseigne, who witnessed some of her official documents.

Known as *"la Dame Douairière"* ("the Lady Dowager"), Berengaria devoted her life to ruling her city and to charitable and pious works, caring for beggars and abandoned children and winning the hearts of the citizens—except, perhaps, the Jews.

She had been reared in a kingdom where monarchs took an enlightened view of the Jews, and had availed herself of the latter's services as moneylenders, yet she did not scruple, on two occasions, to seize Jewish property, knowing that she could do so with impunity; in France, as in England, the law did not require her to pay recompense. In 1208, she appropriated a house and vineyard from two Jews and gave them to a servant. She also acquired a Jewish schoolhouse, *"La Juiverie,"* and donated it to the church of Saint-Pierre.

Adam of Perseigne, who witnessed one of these transfers, had great compassion for the Jews. This was the age of St. Francis of Assisi and

St. Dominic, whose new orders of friars went out into the world preaching to the people. In 1209, the year their order was founded, the first Franciscan gray-robed friars arrived in Le Mans. Berengaria was swept up in the general enthusiasm for these mendicant orders. In 1215, she donated land for a new Franciscan convent. In 1223, when some of the brothers left to establish another friary at Vendôme, she set up a fund to finance them. She and Adam of Perseigne also supported the Dominican order of black-robed friars, which was founded in 1216 and became zealous in preaching to the laity and converting Jews to Christianity. She gave them land and an old chapel by the city wall, next to the Jewish quarter, probably to encourage conversions.

Adjacent to Berengaria's palace stood the tenth-century collegiate church of Saint-Pierre-la-Cour, which served as her domestic chapel. She attended Mass there daily and worshipped in the cathedral on the feast of St. Julien. Compared to the cathedral, Saint-Pierre was small, but the canons were determined to enlarge it. They were constantly at odds with the powerful bishops of Le Mans over privileges they claimed as a royal foundation, insisting that they were answerable only to the Pope, which the Bishop disputed. Berengaria, who clearly felt that the cathedral chapter exercised too great a power in levying taxes and dispensing justice, would become embroiled in this rivalry.

Her relations with the cathedral chapter were soon severely tested. Not long after her arrival in Le Mans, two of her bailiffs extracted a payment of tax from a man called André, who was selling livestock in a part of Le Mans that lay between the jurisdictions of the Queen and the cathedral. André protested that he owed the tax to the cathedral. The chapter backed him and demanded that Berengaria's bailiffs hand over the money. When they refused, the Bishop excommunicated them and insisted that Berengaria make them comply. She refused, asserting that the livestock had been sold in her sector and ordering that André's beasts be confiscated.

According to the testimony of a canon called Clavel, given in 1245, "it was said that the Queen seized and incarcerated in the tower of Le Mans the same André and Fulk Benedict, men owing allegiance to the cathedral chapter, and (as he thought) that the Queen and her bailiff were warned concerning these men and, as I heard tell, because they refused to release them, the chapter put an interdict on the city."[3] The canons of

Saint-Pierre defiantly continued with services, rang out their bells and appealed to the Papal legate, who ordered them to obey the interdict. They petitioned the Pope himself, who, in 1206, permitted them to celebrate mass quietly with the church door closed and no ringing of bells.

Berengaria probably felt she was being persecuted and made a scapegoat for the rivalry between her chapel and the cathedral. The Pope was sympathetic and extended to her his personal protection, permitting her to exercise her devotions in private. But the people of Le Mans were not so lucky; they had to suffer spiritual deprivation.

Berengaria's relations with the cathedral chapter, at this time and later, reveal an aspect of her character at variance with the devoted Queen who had accompanied her husband on crusade and remained uncomplainingly at a distance afterward, or the wronged widow who had appealed to the Pope for support in recovering her dower. The pious Queen was clearly capable of standing up for her rights, of taking vengeance on those who opposed her, regardless of the consequences, and of maintaining her resolve when it might have been better to take a pragmatic, conciliatory approach in the disputes. It seems that she had gained confidence in her newfound role as lady of Le Mans.

John and Isabella kept the Christmas of 1204 at Holme Castle, southwest of Tewkesbury. It belonged to John's ex-wife, although he had retained the use of it. For the festive season, he ordered 4,000 plates and 500 cups, all of Staffordshire pottery, and 400 yards of linen for table napkins.

John's realization that his lust for Isabella had been a factor in losing Normandy may have quenched it. He was aware that people were saying that he had failed to return to the duchy because "he was enjoying all the pleasures of life with his Queen, in whose company he believed he possessed everything he could desire."[4] The criticism must have rankled, and he needed someone to blame. In 1205, he told Isabella that she had cost him Normandy, provoking an angry quarrel.

"You hear, my lady, all that I have lost for you," he flung at her.

"And I, my lord, have lost the best knight in the world for you!" she hit back.[5]

These words may have been uttered in the heat of the moment—or they may have marked a watershed in the royal marriage, as resentment set in on John's side and, it appears, Isabella's. Her comparison of John with Hugh, whose loss she evidently still regretted, shows that she held her husband in some contempt, which cannot but have fueled John's anger against Hugh.

Aside from grants to Chichester and Malmesbury, John gave no gifts for the weal of Isabella's soul or mentioned her in any charters, although he frequently remembered his parents and his brother Richard in such documents. He may have ceased sleeping with her until she was old enough to bear him children. Given the twenty or more years—and possibly the resentment—between them, they could not have had a lot in common.

John was certainly unfaithful to Isabella. "He deflowered the wives and daughters of his nobles. Not a woman was spared if he was seized by the desire to defile her in the heat of his lust."[6] He was "envious of many of his barons and kinsfolk and seduced their more attractive daughters and sisters."[7] "There were many nobles whose wives and daughters the King had violated to the indignation of their husbands and fathers."[8] He was even determined to seduce Matilda, the bastard daughter of William the Lyon, King of Scots. But her husband, Eustace, Lord de Vesci, cunningly smuggled "a common woman, instead of his wife, in the royal bed." When John bragged about how satisfying sex had been with Lady de Vesci, Eustace confessed to the deception, arousing such ire in John that he had to flee for his life.

In 1205, Philip confiscated Anjou, Maine, Touraine and Brittany, leaving John in possession only of part of Poitou and the duchy of Aquitaine. In less than twelve months, Philip had quadrupled his territories and laid the basis for France's future greatness. That same year, Alfonso VIII of Castile tried to press his claim to Gascony, but was unsuccessful, due in part to Sancho VII of Navarre holding Bayonne for John.

On June 1, 1206, the King crossed to France with Isabella, bent on recovering French-held Poitou. He failed to take Poitiers, but succeeded in recovering most of Poitou itself. Angoulême had stayed staunchly loyal, helping to protect English-held Poitou and Aquitaine from the French. Early in November, John wrote to the barons and knights of Angoulême, enjoining them to keep their oaths of allegiance to their "lady queen."[9] Soon afterward, Isabella visited Angoulême.

On December 12, John and Isabella returned to Portsmouth. Around Christmas, which was spent at Winchester, Isabella conceived her first child. Shortly before March 25, 1207, Hugh de Neville escorted her to Clarendon. She was attended by a great household, as is evident from the amount spent on oats for the horses, and was served Lenten fare: bread, ale, wine, oysters, herrings, mackerel and salmon. She kept Easter there on April 22. At this time, John provided her with a gilded saddle and harness, three hoods of different colors, 100 yards of fine linen, two tablecloths, four towels, half an otter skin and a belt.

It was the custom for boys of good birth to be raised in royal and aristocratic households as pages and squires, so that they could learn manners and knightly skills, but the loss of Normandy had led to mounting resentment and unrest in England, and John forced barons he distrusted to send their sons to wait on the Queen as pages, as hostages for their fathers' good behavior. They were appointed to wait on her at Winchester and Windsor, serving her at table and walking behind her when she went in procession.

Isabella had spent a lot of time at Winchester with the Countess Isabel. Sometime after March 1207, Isabel was sent to Sherborne Castle, where John maintained her at the reduced cost of £50 (£37,000) a year, and Isabella was at last given her own household, as mother of the expected heir. John was solicitous toward her during her pregnancy. In May, he urged her half-brother, Pierre de Joigny, to visit England, "since the Queen, your sister, greatly desires to see you."[10] Pierre was the son of the Countess Alice's second marriage and was at least a decade older than Isabella. It is not known if he visited her at this time, but he sent envoys to John in 1209 and he did come to England in 1215–16.

Six weeks before Isabella's baby was due, she was provided with rich fabrics for herself and her maids. In July and August, John's usual hunting season, he visited her at Winchester four times, and came again in late September when the birth of their child was imminent. On October 1, she presented him with a son and heir. The infant was named Henry, after his grandfather.

In 1208, John sent Isabella to Corfe Castle, which seems to have become one of her favorite residences. There, in the inner ward, he built a magnificent first-floor hall, or gloriette, with a three-story porch. Gervase of Canterbury, who did his best to portray John in the least favorable light, stated that Isabella was placed in custody there. Historians have made much of this, inferring that she had somehow offended John and been put under house arrest; the King's order of November 1207, that queen-gold be paid to him, and not to Isabella, has been seen as further evidence that she had displeased him. However, the word "custody" (from *custos*: guardian) then meant guarding or having in safekeeping for protection or defense; the meaning "restraint of liberty" did not come into use until the 1580s. Moreover, Isabella had just given the King an heir, which would have conferred greater status on her and won his favor and esteem.

It is clear that she enjoyed freedom of movement; she would spend almost the next decade traveling around England with John, or by herself, accompanied by a train of twelve horses carrying her escort, her valets and her damsels. While apart, the royal couple sent frequent messages to each other. They continued to sleep together and Isabella would bear several more children. This does not constitute a scenario in which the couple were estranged on account of her having committed some offense.

By now, at the age of twenty, Isabella seems to have resigned herself dutifully to her marriage. On the evidence of her later deeds and letters, she was maturing into a haughty, tempestuous, willful and unscrupulous woman whose chief character traits were greed, arrogance and selfishness. This volatility may have been the real reason why John did not permit her to take control of her revenues or exercise political influence.

4

"Clouds That Have Overcast Our Serenity"

✠

I T WAS NOW MORE THAN SEVEN YEARS SINCE JOHN HAD AGREED to pay Berengaria an annuity of 2,000 marks (£980,000), and still she had not received a penny of it. In desperation, she appealed a third time to Pope Innocent, who, on August 27, ordered the bishops of Ely and Worcester to censure their King for the delay. In September, Innocent was again moved to write to John, demanding that he pay what was due to Berengaria, and awarding her half the movable goods of King Richard, which John was to hand over. He also summoned John to appear before him to answer Berengaria's complaints. John ignored him—in fact, he ignored eight summonses to Rome—and Berengaria received little or nothing because the English bishops were too afraid of the King to confront him on the matter.

John's failure to pay Berengaria's dower was one of the reasons for the Pope laying England under an interdict on March 23, 1208. The chief reason was that John had refused to accept the Pope's candidate, Stephen Langton, as archbishop of Canterbury. The interdict meant that all the churches were closed, for no services could take place. Church bells were stilled. No one could be baptized, get married or be buried with the rites of religion. The Pope gave England to the King of France and invited him to take it.

Isabella stayed aloof from the quarrel. Late in 1208, she was described as being confined at Devizes Castle. She was awaiting her second child, and it was customary for a queen to go into confinement before a royal birth. Again, historians have suggested that she was under house arrest, but she left to join John at Bristol Castle for Christmas, having perhaps miscalculated her due date. On January 5, 1209, she gave birth to her second son at Winchester Castle and persuaded Peter des Roches, Bishop of Winchester, a kinsman of William des Roches, to baptize him, despite the interdict. The child was christened Richard, after his uncle. For the first seven years of his life, he stayed with his mother, in the care of his nurse, Eva.

In October 1209, an exasperated Pope Innocent excommunicated John. In May 2010, he complained to the bishops of Rochester and Salisbury about the King's intransigence over Berengaria's dower, describing how she had beseeched him for help "with floods of tears streaming down her cheeks and with audible cries." Her envoy was now waiting in Rome for a resolution to the problem.

In June 1210, John went to Ireland, intending to capture William de Braose, whose loyalty he had long suspected. De Braose had fled there two years earlier, having refused to surrender his wife and children to the King as hostages for his good behavior. Now he eluded John again, escaping to France. John demanded of his wife, the unfortunate Maud de Saint-Valéry, Lady de Braose, that she send her eldest son to attend the Queen as a hostage. But Lady de Braose boldly declared that she would not surrender her children to a king who had murdered his own nephew. A wrathful John had mother and son imprisoned in Windsor Castle. In vain did Maud seek the intercession of Queen Isabella, offering her a herd of 400 white cows and a white bull. She and her son were moved to Corfe Castle and starved to death.

On July 22, 1210, Isabella gave birth to a daughter, Joan, at Gloucester. Joan would be sent to the King's hunting box at Romsey to be brought up by a nurse or governess called Christiana. She is always listed as the first daughter of John and Isabella, but, in 1208–9, Peter des Roches had paid for the conveyance of songbirds to "the daughter of the King" at Witney. There is no record of the Queen bearing any children before Henry in 1207, and Richard had arrived less than sixteen months later, so this unnamed daughter is unlikely to have been Isabella's child; she must have been one of John's bastards.

In 1212, the King made reference to his son John.[1] This could have been the bastard son who was perhaps a clerk at Lincoln, but it is possible that there was a legitimate short-lived son called John, born during the three-and-a-half-year gap between the first two daughters of John and Isabella, although no John appears in royal genealogies. Possibly he did not live long enough to be noticed by the chroniclers.

Early in 1212, Llywelyn ap Iorwerth, Prince of Gwynedd, who was married to John's bastard daughter Joan, rose against the King, who marched into Wales, leaving Isabella at Marlborough with her sons. Soon he received news that his barons had been conspiring to kill him, and that Isabella had been raped and Richard murdered. Racing, distraught and vengeful, to Marlborough, he discovered that there was no basis to the tale; suspecting certain lords of trying to divert him from his purpose, he attacked their castles.

For safety, five-year-old Henry, the King's heir, was now removed from Isabella's care and placed in the household of Peter des Roches. Relations between Peter and Isabella were amicable; in 1210, he had arranged for a cheese and a bacon-pig to be delivered to the royal palace at Downton, Wiltshire, when she was staying. He also bought her songbirds that year, where she was in residence in the Bishop of Winchester's stone-built manor house at Witney, Oxfordshire.

In September 1212, John and Isabella were at Durham. Richard de Umfraville, a baron of Northumberland, had recently come under suspicion of treachery, having refused to pay the King's extortionate taxes, and was forced to surrender his castle of Prudhoe and his sons, Odinel and Robert, who were appointed pages to Isabella at Durham to serve her daily at dinner. They were sent with their tutor, but he was not allowed to appear before her because she deemed him too low-born.

By then, John was heading for a crisis. His aggressive exploitation of his barons and his subjects, and the long-standing interdict, had provoked much anger. In May 1213, in the face of fierce opposition to his rule, he made his submission to the Holy See and surrendered his kingdom to Rome, agreeing to hold England as the Pope's vassal. He promised justice and the continuance of the laws of Henry I, but was secretly determined to have revenge on those he considered his enemies.

That year, Berengaria sent two envoys to England to ask, yet again, that the revenues from her dower properties be transferred to her. John informed her that he was still negotiating a settlement. After some prevarication and the Pope again intervening, the King promised to pay the arrears due to her. She would wait in vain for them. Early in 1214, John wrote to "his dear sister, the illustrious Berengaria, praying that the Pope's nuncio might arbitrate what was due to her," because he couldn't pay what he had promised.

In January 1214, needing money to reconquer the rest of Poitou, John returned Isabel of Gloucester's lands to her, then promptly sold her to the highest bidder. Geoffrey de Mandeville, Earl of Essex, was ready to pay 20,000 marks (£9,800,000), the greatest sum ever outlaid in England for the marriage of a medieval heiress. He and Isabel were married that January. When Mandeville defaulted on the first installment of the settlement, John confiscated the Gloucester estates.

Sometime before the summer of 1214, Isabella bore a second daughter, named after herself. Margaret Bisset, who came from a family that had long served the Crown, was appointed nurse.

In the winter of 1213–14, fearing both the Lusignans and the French, Isabella's mother, the Dowager Countess Alice, had come to England seeking the King's protection. John was now determined to make peace with the Lusignans, settle their claim to Angoulême and recover more of the territories he had lost to France. At Candlemas, February 2, 1214, he took ship at Portsmouth, taking with him Isabella, her mother, Richard, Joan, Eleanor of Brittany, the royal household and an army.

John's quarrel with the Lusignans was resolved on May 25, 1214, when he and Hugh IX made peace at Parthenay. Isabella was prominent in the negotiations, the only sphere in which John allowed her any power. Now that Angoulême had no resident ruler, he and Isabella were counting on the Lusignans to guard Poitou and look to its defenses. In 1212, John had discussed a marriage between Joan and Alexander II, King of Scots, but he now abandoned that plan because Isabella needed to cement the alliance with Hugh de Lusignan. Four-year-old Joan was offered as a bride for Hugh's son, the future Hugh X, who was twenty-nine. Her dowry was to comprise Saintes and the Île d'Oléron. Hugh IX, for his part, was to guard the borders of English-held Poitou against French invaders and relinquish his claim to Angoulême. Joan was handed over immediately to the Lusignans to be brought up by her future husband's family. Evidently the peace rankled with Matilda of Angoulême, for she would not cede her claim to Angoulême to Isabella until 1233.

On June 17, John and Isabella entered French-held Angers in triumph. But their confidence was misplaced. At the Battle of Bouvines on July 27, John's nephew, the Emperor Otto IV, and his ally, Ferrand, Count of Flanders, were soundly defeated by the French, thanks largely to the lords of Poitou, who had not forgiven Isabella for jilting Hugh IX and had refused to take up arms against Philip. The defeat at Bouvines was a crushing blow for John and put paid to his hopes of regaining his lost territories.

John's barons were furious about the debacle at Bouvines, and the King, who was running out of money, began garrisoning his castles against the likelihood of civil war. In September, needing Papal support, he informed Pope Innocent that he would be settling Berengaria's dower.

Once more, John took Isabella south to Angoulême, then returned north, leaving her to spend time in Angoulême with her mother and five-year-old Richard. While they were apart, he sent her tongues and chines of venison killed by his huntsmen.

On October 15, 1214, John and Isabella sailed home from Poitou and landed at Dartmouth. Isabella went to stay at Exeter Castle, her dower property, while John rode to London and took up residence in the Tower. That month, the barons tried to force him to sign a charter protecting their rights, but he refused. Craftily, he vowed to go on crusade, which won him the support and protection of the Pope.

On October 30, as tensions mounted, he wrote from the Tower to Thierry the Teuton, Isabella's constable at Berkhamsted, who had been given charge of the Queen's household:

> Know that, by God's grace, we are in good health and unharmed. We shall shortly be coming to your part of the country, and we shall be thinking of you like a hawk; and, though it might be ten years since we

last saw you, at our coming it shall seem to us no less than three days. Take good care of the custody that we have entrusted to you, letting us know regularly of the condition of this custody.[2]

Among the veiled references in the letter, the final sentence referred to Isabella, who had recently discovered that she was pregnant again. It has been credibly suggested that John intended Thierry to tell Isabella that he was well and coming to see her, and to keep him updated on her health. His refusal to name her was probably motivated by fear that the letter could get into the wrong hands, betraying her whereabouts to his enemies.

On November 3, Thierry was commanded to ensure safe passage for the Queen, accompanied by an armed mounted escort of twelve supplied by Peter des Roches, who was now justiciar of England. Isabella was to travel via Reading to Berkhamsted. The armed escort would have been there for the pregnant Queen's protection, given the uncertain political situation.

In November 1214, a group of barons gathered before the high altar of St. Edmundsbury Abbey armed with Henry I's coronation charter setting forth the laws of St. Edward the Confessor and other English liberties. In that holy place, they swore that if the King should refuse to uphold these laws and liberties, they would make war on him and repudiate their fealty, until such time as he confirmed to them by charter all the things they sought. John's situation was now perilous. On December 3, concerned for Isabella's safety, he ordered Thierry "to go to Gloucester with our Lady Queen and there keep her in the chamber where the Princess Joan had been nursed, till you hear further from us."[3]

John may have sent Isabella to Gloucester because he was himself in the West Country. That December, he was in the city and probably visited her. Yet many writers have assumed that Isabella was imprisoned there for adultery. Now aged about twenty-seven, she was imperious, hot-tempered, demanding and determined—but was she unfaithful too? Around this time, a knight called Robert of London wrote a fanciful and largely invented account of his embassy to Morocco (in which he claimed, preposterously, that John was willing to surrender his realm to Islam), and stated that the Queen was "hateful to [John] and hates him too. She has often been found guilty of incest, sorcery and adultery, so that the King, her husband, has ordered those of her lovers who have been apprehended to be strangled with a rope in her own bed." Matthew Paris, writing after 1240, embroidered this account: "His Queen hates him, and is hated by him, she being an evil-minded, incestuous and depraved woman, so notoriously guilty of crimes that King John seized her paramours and had them strangled with a rope on her bed."

It has been claimed that, because of her immorality, Isabella was deprived of the company of her children while she was held at Gloucester, yet they were there with her. And, while she was at Marlborough in 1215, John ordered that roach (a kind of carp) and "little pike" be caught for her to eat,[4] which was hardly the act of an aggrieved, cuckolded husband. There are no other references in contemporary sources to Isabella taking lovers or dabbling in witchcraft, or of John wreaking revenge.

Yet what of the allegation of incest? In 1233, when a man called Piers the Fair was killed in a skirmish in County Cavan, Ireland, an Irish chronicler recorded that he was "the son of the English Queen."[5] The only English Queen alive in 1233 was Isabella. Given the similarity in names, it has been conjectured that Piers was the bastard offspring of an incestuous affair between Isabella and her half-brother, Pierre de Joigny. Clearly, Pierre was not strangled with a rope on John's orders because he remained a loyal supporter of the King, who granted him a pension in reward, and died in April 1222, leaving a wife and children. He had been in Poitou with John in 1214 and would be in England in 1215–16, when he visited Isabella.

Adultery in a queen was a serious, scandalous matter with grave implications for the succession, but medieval queens led highly visible, public lives; it would have been hard to conceal an illicit pregnancy, still less the hanging of her partners in crime. Isabella's supposed immorality therefore rests on one isolated, unsubstantiated report from an unreliable source.

Matthew Paris asserted that the Queen was confined at Gloucester from the time the King began an affair with Matilda, the daughter of a baron, Robert FitzWalter. There was already bad blood between John and FitzWalter, who was soon to emerge as one of the foremost leaders of the baronial opposition to the King. In 1212, he had claimed that John had

tried to rape or seduce his daughter, but that was just one of several pre-
texts for his committing treason. A thirteenth-century chronicle written
at Dunmow claimed that the King sent a messenger to Matilda to press
his suit, "whereunto, [when] she would not consent, she was poisoned."[6]
The truth is that her very existence is surrounded by uncertainty, and it
is unlikely, given the weakness of the historical evidence, that Isabella's
sojourn at Gloucester had anything to do with her.

John spent Christmas 1214 at Worcester, while Isabella remained at
Gloucester. Before April 1215, she bore a daughter, Eleanor, who may
have been named for Leonor, the late Queen of Castile, or for Eleanor of
Aquitaine; her date of birth is not recorded, but she was nine in April
1224.

Letters between Berengaria, King John and the Pope reveal that, in March
1215, they were corresponding in secret. These letters are lost. Afterward,
John promised Berengaria never to reveal anything of what had passed
between himself and her messengers, who had also sworn oaths never to
divulge it, and she too promised to maintain secrecy. It is hard to see why
any discussion of her unpaid dower merited that. Possibly she confided
to John truths about her marriage to Richard, hoping to win his sympathy. If so, it did her no good. On September 25, at Le Mans, she issued a
charter giving details of an agreement she and John had reached, whereby
she would receive 2,000 marks (£980,000) immediately in respect of her
annual allowance and some of the arrears due, and an extra 1,000 marks
(£490,000) yearly in lieu of the rest of the arrears. In an empty gesture,
the King confirmed to her the city of Le Mans and two Poitevin castles,
in the event of their being recovered from the French. He solemnly ratified the agreement, swearing on his soul to abide by its terms and asking
the Pope to confirm it. He also promised Berengaria another safe-conduct
whenever she wished to visit England. Again she received nothing of
what had been promised.

In 1215, the English barons came out in open rebellion against King
John in what became known as the First Barons' War. In May, the rebel
lords took London, and John had to bring in Poitevin mercenaries to

counter the threat they posed. On his orders, Thierry the Teuton escorted the Queen to Winchester, where the Lord Henry was staying with Peter des Roches. John joined them there. Later that month, when Isabella was at Marlborough, he again visited her, and they spent several days hunting in Savernake Forest.

When the barons took Southampton and Lincoln, John had no choice but to agree to their terms. On June 15, 1215, at Runnymede, he signed the great charter known as Magna Carta, which promised justice and good government, and was intended to curb the arbitrary rule of tyrants. Long regarded as the foundation of English liberties, Magna Carta bound even kings to abide by the law. But John had no intention of honoring it. In a fury, he withdrew to Windsor, where, swearing in rage, he gnashed his teeth, rolled his eyes and gnawed sticks and straw. He later sent for more mercenary troops from France and again appealed to the Pope, who declared Magna Carta invalid and threatened anyone who tried to enforce it with excommunication. The magnates were furious, and the conflict escalated.

In August 1215, while Isabella was still at Marlborough, John sent her gifts of fabric and furs, then dispatched her and Henry to the greater security of Corfe Castle while he gathered an army to face his barons. Isabella and her son were guarded by the castle's new custodian, a Poitevin called Peter de Maulay, who had just been named Richard's guardian. The other royal children were still at Gloucester, and Isabella soon took Henry there. John placed one of the signatories of Magna Carta in her custody, evidence of his trust in her.

He had sworn to be revenged on his rebellious subjects. In January 1216, he was at Berwick, having marched almost the length of his realm, wreaking the worst destruction since William the Conqueror's harrying of the north in 1069–70. When he returned south, he left another trail of devastation in his wake. The barons' patience had now run out. At a council convened early that year, they offered the throne to Louis, King Philip's son and heir.

John reached Dover at the end of April, poised to repel the French, but, on May 20, Louis and his army landed unopposed on the Isle of Thanet. By then, England was in chaos. Louis seized Rochester, then, meeting little resistance, he entered London. Before a crowd of cheering citizens, he was proclaimed king at St. Paul's Cathedral with great pomp.

Many barons, and the King of Scots, rendered him homage. On June 14, he captured Winchester. Other towns and castles fell to him. In the months that followed, John was constantly campaigning to recover his ascendancy as king and ensure that Isabella and their children were safe.

But the war raged on. In July 1216, John made a brief visit to his family, who were then at Corfe. After he left for the West Midlands, he sent for them to follow him. That summer, they stayed for a time at Bristol, still under the protection of Thierry the Teuton. John's desire for Isabella's company, and his visits to her, suggest that he still held her in affection. But he had put in place a contingency plan for her and the children to escape abroad if they were in any danger of being taken as hostages.

By the autumn, Louis was in control of much of the south of England. At the beginning of September, John said farewell to Isabella and Henry in the Cotswolds, then rode eastward. He was now nearing fifty and his hair was "quite hoary."[7]

On October 9, he left Lincolnshire for Bishop's Lynn and led his entourage across the hazardous estuary of the Wash. As they approached the opposite shore, the tide changed. John managed to reach land safely, but part of the convoy was engulfed by the sea, "carriages, horses, treasures and men being swallowed up in a whirlpool."[8] "The greatest distress troubled him, because he had lost his chapel with its relics and some of his packhorses, and many members of his household were submerged in the waters of the sea and sucked into the quicksand there."[9] It is often stated that he lost the crown jewels as well, but the chroniclers made no mention of these.

At Bishop's Lynn, John "gorged himself to the point of intoxication, by which his greedy belly flowed with dysentery."[10] Notwithstanding, he pressed on to Swineshead Abbey, near Boston. There, "he fell into such despondency on account of his possessions having been swallowed up by the waves that, being seized by a sharp fever, he became seriously ill. But he aggravated this discomfort by disgusting gluttony, for, that night, by indulging too freely in peaches and copious draughts of new cider, he greatly increased his feverishness"[11] and took a turn for the worse. He may have suffered a perforated ulcer when he tried to mount his horse the next morning; he had a high temperature and was gripped with burning pain. Nevertheless, he insisted on being carried in a litter to Newark Castle. There, he dictated a brief will, in which he made no mention of Isabella or his children; Isabella, of course, was already provided for through her dower.

On October 19, 1216, John died "panting and groaning," having commanded the lords with him to swear allegiance to his son Henry as the heir to the throne and named William the Marshal, who had remained consistently loyal, as guardian of the realm during the boy's minority. A priest who went to Newark to say a mass for the King's soul told the Abbot of Coggeshall that he had seen men leaving the town laden with loot, which possibly included the crown jewels.

5

"Cease to Molest Your Son!"

✝

WHEN JOHN DIED, ISABELLA, A WIDOW OF TWENTY-EIGHT, was at Devizes with her children and the royal treasure, under the protection of Peter de Maulay. Knowing that Louis would try to seize the crown, she acted quickly, taking nine-year-old Henry to Gloucester, where she and William the Marshal had the "pretty little knight" proclaimed Henry III. There were fears that the country would turn to Louis but, in the event, many barons preferred to acknowledge John's son as their King. The Papal legate, Gualo Bicchieri, urged that the coronation take place without delay, and, on October 28, the boy was crowned in Gloucester Abbey with "a sort of chaplet" provided by his mother. Peter des Roches, Bishop of Winchester, officiated, as the Archbishop of Canterbury was in Rome. Matthew Paris called Henry "the glory and the hope of England."

No one suggested that Isabella should rule as regent for her son; later chroniclers asserted that this was because of her immorality. More likely, the barons were aware that she had played no role in politics and had no experience or political following. Given her later high-handed conduct and self-interest, they may have had good reason to exclude her. On the day after the coronation, William the Marshal, now over seventy, was prevailed upon to serve as regent and guardian of the young King, according to the late King's wish. He was to act in concert with the Papal legate and Peter des Roches, in whose household the young King was living. Late that year, Isabella's younger daughters were sent to join him there.

As soon as he learned of the death of John, Geoffrey de Marisco, the

Justiciar of Ireland, urged that either the Queen or the Lord Richard take up residence there as viceroy, to safeguard the succession. Isabella heeded his counsel. A letter issued in the King's name at the time of his coronation stated: "The Lady Queen, our mother, has, upon advice, and having our assent to it, sent our brother Richard to Ireland." Peter de Maulay, Richard's guardian, went with him.

At his own request, King John was buried in Worcester Cathedral, near the shrine of his favorite saint, Wulfstan, who had been canonized in 1203. The stone figure of the King—the earliest surviving royal effigy in England—was probably sculpted in 1232 when the tomb was rebuilt, and cannot be a likeness. The sepulchre was opened sixty years after John's death so that his heart could be sent for burial at Fontevraud. It was again opened in 1529, when the King's body was found wrapped in gold and silver, and wearing a crown, jeweled gloves and a ring, and holding a rod and scepter. In 1797, when the tomb was opened a third time, the crown was nowhere to be seen and the skull was clad in what was described as a monk's cowl, fastened with a buckle under the chin; this could have been a coif that had been worn under the crown. The corpse was covered in a robe of crimson damask embroidered with the arms of England and the King's skeletal hand was grasping a sword. The body turned to dust as soon as it was exposed to the air.

"Foul as it is, Hell itself is defiled by the presence of John," thundered Matthew Paris, who regarded the late monarch as "a tyrant, not a king, a destroyer instead of a governor, crushing his own people and favouring aliens, a lion to his subjects, but a lamb to foreigners and rebels. He was an insatiable extorter of money; he invaded and destroyed his subjects' property. As for Christianity, he was unstable and unfaithful." Roger of Wendover called John a cruel tyrant who had failed as a king. Bertran de Born wrote: "No man may ever trust him, for his heart is soft and cowardly." To William of Newburgh, he was "Nature's enemy."

John was by no means a good man, yet later monastic chroniclers, looking back on his reign, would paint a much darker picture of him than those writing in his youth or his early years as king. Some embellished and exaggerated the scandalous tales and rumors that abounded during his reign and after his death. His "bad press" in the monastic chronicles may be attributed not just to his failures as a king, but to his cynical contempt for religion, the long interdict on England and his rumored murder of his nephew, Arthur. It is not unlikely that his nasty reputation extended to his Queen and that, by association, hers suffered.

Modern historians mostly agree that John's infamy was fully deserved. He was cowardly; when it came to military confrontations where the odds were against him, he usually fled. He was cruel, killing or starving his enemies, which shocked his contemporaries. He imposed upon his subjects the worst extortions in English medieval history. Clerical chroniclers and laymen alike blamed him for the disasters of his reign. "He was a very bad man," wrote a lay chronicler of Béthune. "He was greatly hated. He was brim-full of evil qualities."[1]

Some of John's troubles arose from sheer bad luck, but the worst failures of his reign were the result of his own indolence and stubbornness. His son inherited a kingdom at war, with the loyalties of the barons divided between himself and Louis of France. Louis had not given up hope of overthrowing Henry and seizing the English crown. Late in 2016, he was in possession of the Queen's castle at Berkhamsted, showing that John's concern for her security there had been well founded.

The Marshal had called for the barons to "defend our land" against the French. On May 20, 1217, he soundly defeated Louis's army at the Battle of Lincoln; four days later, Louis's naval forces were routed at the Battle of Sandwich, after which the Marshal demanded that he renounce his claim to the English throne.

After John died, Isabella continued to use her royal title and her seal as queen of England. On November 1, 1216, the English council awarded her possession of her dower properties. For the weal of her husband's soul, she issued just three charters; thereafter, she is not known to have referred to him in any document. This strongly suggests that, having paid lip service to his memory, she was glad to be free of a marriage she had never wanted in the first place.

Louis's teeth had been drawn, but he was still in England. In August 1217, Isabella, who was staying with the young King at Windsor, met with a French nobleman, Hervé, Count of Nevers, for a peace conference. This led to another conference on September 18 at Staines, where the

Queen, William the Marshal and the Papal legate, Gualo Bicchieri, stood on one side of the River Thames, with Louis and his advisers on the other, shouting across the water. The English had the advantage and, on August 24, Louis was obliged to make peace on their terms. In September 1217, the Treaty of Lambeth enshrined the agreement made at Staines and ended the war between the Crown and the barons. After both sides had sworn to keep the peace, Louis left England.

It was clear that there was no place for Isabella in the English political establishment. She began demanding the dower rights awarded her in 1200 and 1204, in particular, Saintes and the Île d'Oléron, which were supposed to form part of her daughter Joan's dowry. Her demands were rejected, the castles of Exeter and Rockingham were taken from her, and she was denied repayment of a debt of 3,500 marks (£1,715,000), which she insisted—falsely—that John had left her in his will. These were factors in her decision to return to Angoulême. There, she could rule as an independent countess. Her mother had tried to govern her lands on her behalf, but they had been repeatedly attacked by Hugh de Lusignan, who was determined to seize control of them. Angoulême was also under threat from the French, who were bent on conquering all Poitou. It was clear that Isabella was needed in her domain.

In the late summer of 1217, she returned to Angoulême, leaving her children behind; Isabella was only three and Eleanor two. Historians have assumed that she abandoned them seemingly without a qualm, but they had already been removed from her care and there was no question of their being allowed to leave England. It would have become clear to her that she would be playing a very insignificant role in their lives. Even so, the alacrity with which she left to pursue her own interests may have felt like an abandonment to her children, whose future relations with their mother were sometimes strained.

The English council approved Isabella's return to Angoulême, anticipating that she would rule her domain with the interests of her son in mind. On July 24, the guardians of the realm wrote to the men of Niort, asking them to offer all assistance to her as she traveled south. "The Queen passed through Poitou and came to Angoulême, her native town, which was her heritage," and received a civic welcome there. "She took the people's homage and remained thenceforth lady of Angoumois,"[2] proving an active ruler. She regained control of Cognac, which her forebears had lost in the 1180s when Richard I gave it to his bastard son. It was a prosperous port on the Charente, grown rich because of the salt trade.

Around June 2019, she wrote an imperious letter, now badly defaced, to the Papal legate, Pandulf Verraccio, Bishop of Norwich, who was notorious for interfering in every aspect of government. She had become involved in a bitter dispute with Bartholomew de Le Puy, her seneschal in Angoulême, whose estates she had seized, and whose sons she had taken hostage. But the English council supported Bartholomew. Angrily, Isabella wrote to Pandulf:

> You will know that we have offered to restore to Bartholomew de Puy, at the entreaty of our son, the King of England, and of his Council, all his land, his possessions and the rents he received, and also all his hostages, save for his two sons, whom we desire to hold in fair and fitting custody until we are without fear that he will seek to do us wrong, as he once sought to wrong the other barons of the land, to our despite. If he refused this offer of ours, we offered him the sure judgement of our court, but he totally rejected this. We are very surprised that our son's council have instructed Sir Hugh de Lusignan and Sir Geoffrey de Neville, Seneschal of Poitou, to support Bartholemew against us. We know many who will trouble us on Bartholemew's behalf, and our son's council should be aware lest it issues any instructions as a consequence of which we are driven away from our son's council and affairs. It will be very serious if we are to be removed from our son's council.[3]

It may have been in consequence of this dispute, or her demand for Saintes and Oléron, that, on March 17, 1219, the Bishop of Saintes excommunicated Isabella. This came at a bad time, as her mother, the Countess Alice, had died on February 12, and Hugh de Lusignan's wife, her cousin Matilda, was still pressing her claim to Angoulême. But Isabella had remedies at hand. The previous July, the Pope had given her permission to have mass celebrated privately, even during a general interdict. In March, he extended his protection to her on account of her devotion to the Holy See, declaring that she could not be excommunicated, or her lands placed under an interdict, without Papal sanction. It seems that the interdict was soon lifted.

* * *

Her sister-in-law was not so lucky. Berengaria's financial situation should have improved after the signing of Magna Carta, which guaranteed that a widow should receive her dower within forty days of her husband's death, but John had ignored that provision entirely. On June 8, 1216, he had written to Berengaria to tell her once again that he could not afford to pay her allowance:

> Beloved sister, once queen of England, due to the disruption of our kingdom by the behaviour of our barons, whom the enemy of the human race has incited against us, and, moreover, by the coming of Louis, who fears neither God nor Church in his efforts to seize our realm, we have already spent most of our money, and every day we spend more and more. Having complete faith in your affection at this time of adversity, we earnestly seek your patience and acceptance of the delay in payment of the money we owe you, until such time as, by God's will, the clouds disappear and this land rejoices in peace once more. Then the pecuniary debt owed to our dear sister shall be paid joyfully and thankfully.

This letter may have prompted Berengaria to appeal again to the new Pope. The kindly Honorius III took her case to heart, complaining to the Archbishop of Tours of John's "frequent acts of injury and theft" in respect of her dower, and ordering him to pay it.

Berengaria was issued more safe-conducts to visit England in 1215 and 1216; John had given her permission to travel wherever she pleased, and she and her servants were granted exemption from all the usual customs at the ports. Yet it is unlikely that she did go to England, for it would not have been safe to journey around a land at war. She was in Le Mans on August 23, 2016, when she presided as judge over a trial by combat, in which two champions engaged over the honor of a young lady.

That year, a new bishop called Maurice was elected to the see of Le Mans. He was stern and zealous, and determined to defend the chapter's rights. He clashed almost immediately with Berengaria when he tried to exact dues from parts of the city just beyond the cathedral's jurisdiction. The Queen, already irritated by clerics trying to avoid paying taxes to her by claiming benefit of clergy, was angered. When Maurice appealed to King Philip to defend his rights, the King set up a commission, which found in favor of the Queen.

In 1216-17, Berengaria once again came into conflict with Bishop Maurice when her bailiff exacted taxes on animals sold in an area controlled by the cathedral chapter, which promptly demanded the money back. "Several canons, acting on the authority and instruction of the chapter, strongly warned Queen Berengaria to see that the money was returned." It was only a trifling amount, but there was a principle involved. Berengaria "replied that she would not return the money because this customary right was hers." The canons "told her that the chapter was ready to grant a hearing to her representatives and pass judgement. She replied that she would have none of it, and, after she had been warned several times about this by the chapter, and still refused to do anything about it, the chapter placed the church and the city under [an] interdict." The bailiff was excommunicated.[4]

Once again the churches were shut, and the bells stayed silent. The dead lay unburied in the cemeteries, the streets and even in the branches of trees. "Because of the interdict, Queen Berengaria left Le Mans and moved to Thorée."[5] In 1216, she had made a gift in perpetuity of her house there to the Knights Hospitallers for the soul of Richard I; now she called in the favor by asking for it to be loaned back to her. That she was prepared to hold out indefinitely over the payment of such a small sum of money when her people were being deprived of the sacraments of the Church bears testimony to her resolve and tenacity—and possibly her stubbornness and pride. But Pope Honorius was of the opinion that the chapter were "moved more by hostility than by concern for what is right."

John's death had been a setback to Berengaria's hopes of receiving the arrears of money owed to her by the English Crown. In December 1216, Honorius had written to the Archbishop of Tours, reminding him that he had a sacred duty to succor widows, notably "our dearest daughter in Christ, the former Queen of the English, who has had to endure frequent acts of injury and theft, both by clerics and laymen."

Early in Henry III's reign, Berengaria claimed back the modest sum of £4,040 (about £3,000,000). When she appealed once more to the Pope for help, he ordered the Knights Templar in England to come to her aid.

They acted as her agents, intervened on her behalf, demanded guarantees for payment and tried to save her from penury and further financial losses. Still the arrears kept mounting up, and Berengaria was obliged to send more messengers to England to beg for them to be paid.

Her quarrel with the cathedral chapter was finally settled when the clergy of her chapel persuaded the Bishop to lift the interdict, on the assurance that she would pay the money the chapter insisted she owed them. She appealed to a Papal legate, but he ruled that she must repay the money, which she finally did in 1220. In 1218, the Queen returned in procession to Le Mans and was received with honor by the cathedral clergy and great rejoicing by the people.

Twice that year, Honorius assured her of his special protection, but, by now, she was in despair at not having received any money from England. This may have been the reason why she decided to contact her brother, King Sancho. On March 12, 1219, the Seneschal of Poitou and Gascony was informed that Henry III had issued a safe-conduct permitting Berengaria or her envoys to travel through those regions, should she wish to visit Navarre. It is clear that she did send envoys, and that they did not fare well on the journey, for, in 1220, the safe-conduct was reissued with orders that restitution be made to them for the injuries done them. Whatever the Queen's business, it did not have a positive impact on her situation.

William the Marshal, that great statesman, died on May 14, 1219, and was buried in the Templars' church in London, having been received into their order on his deathbed. "Look there," wrote the author of *L'Histoire de Guillaume le Maréchal*, "and see the best knight to be found in the world in our times." The government of England was now placed in the hands of the Papal legate, Pandulf Verraccio, Peter des Roches, and the Justiciar, Hubert de Burgh, a triumvirate that ruled wisely and well on behalf of the young King, acting according to the principles of Magna Carta. In September or October 1217, Hubert had married Isabel of Gloucester, King John's former wife, but she had died soon after the wedding and been buried in Canterbury Cathedral.

Angoulême's situation was becoming increasingly precarious. It was

vulnerable to attacks by the Lusignans and the French. In vain did Isabella appeal to the English council for support, but already there was
tension between her and the regents because it was becoming clear that
she was determined to rule Angoulême independently, and not just for
the benefit of her son. Around 1218–19, she wrote in hectoring tones to
the young King:

> To her dearest son, Henry, by the grace of God, the illustrious King
> of England, I, Isabella, by the same grace of God his humble mother,
> Queen of England, always pray for your safety and good fortune.
>
> Your Grace knows how often we have begged you that you should
> give us help and advice in our affairs, but so far you have done nothing.
> Therefore, we attentively ask you again to despatch your advice quickly
> to us, but do not just gratify us with words. You can see that, without
> your help and advice, we cannot rule over or defend our land. And, if
> the truces made with the King of France were to be broken, this part of
> the country has much to fear. Even if we had nothing to fear from the
> King himself, we do indeed have such neighbours who are as much to
> be feared. So, without delay, you must formulate such a plan which will
> benefit this part of the country which is yours and ours. It is necessary
> that you do this to ensure that neither you nor we should lose our land
> through your failure to give any advice or help. We even beg you to act
> on our behalf, that we can have for the time being some part of those
> lands which our husband, your father, bequeathed to us. You know
> truly how much we owe him, but, even if our husband had bequeathed
> nothing to us, you ought, by right, to give us aid from your resources so
> that we can defend our land. On this, your honour and advantage de-
> pend.[6]

Of course, John had left no bequests or lands to Isabella in his will.[7]

On November 5, 1219, Hugh IX de Lusignan died of wounds he received at the siege of Damietta in Egypt during the Fifth Crusade. The
following year, his son, Hugh X, returned home. He was then thirty-
seven, Isabella thirty-three. Hugh was ruthless, volatile and impulsive,
but he had his attractions. Marrying him was the most effective way of
neutralizing the threat posed by the Lusignans to Angoulême. In the

spring of 1220, Isabella had her daughter's betrothal to Hugh broken and married him herself, "without leave of her son, the King, or his council."[8] Her actions echoed the circumstances of her betrothal to John, twenty years earlier, and gave rise to "much talk."[9] Joan was only ten, too young to be badly affected by the loss of her betrothed, but Isabella was determined to gain possession of Saintes and Oléron, while Hugh seized this opportunity to create the great unified lordship his father had fought for, and sire an heir to it; he did not want to wait for Joan to grow up.

Marriage to Isabella made Hugh count of Angoulême, increased his wealth and consolidated the couple's domains into a great feudal power. It seems to have been more of an equal partnership than Isabella's marriage to John; if anything, she was the dominant partner. She was aware of her superior rank, styling herself queen of England and duchess of Aquitaine and continuing to use the empty titles of duchess of Normandy and countess of Anjou. She had coins issued in Angoulême showing her as queen, rather than countess. She and Hugh ruled firmly together, jointly issuing numerous charters, and extended their borders, forcing Poitevin lords who had hitherto enjoyed virtual independence to accept them as overlords.

But the uniting of Lusignan, La Marche and Angoulême was exactly what John had married Isabella to avoid, so she could hardly have expected her son and his advisers to be pleased about her marriage, which was, in any case, a gross dereliction of duty on the part of both her and Hugh, for Henry III was their overlord and had a vested interest in their marriages, and that of his sister.

Early in May, Isabella wrote to Henry, justifying her actions, again coming across as imperious and high-handed:

> We hereby signify to you that, when the counts of La Marche and Eu [Hugh's uncle Raoul] departed this life, the Lord Hugh de Lusignan remained alone and without heirs in Poitou, and his friends would not permit that our daughter should be united to him in marriage because her age is so tender, but counselled him to take a wife from whom he might speedily hope for an heir; and it was proposed that he should take a wife in France, which, if he had done, all your land

in Poitou and Gascony would be lost. We, therefore, seeing the great peril that might accrue if that marriage should take place, when our counsellors could give us no better advice, ourself married the said Hugh, Count of La Marche. Let Heaven witness, we did this rather for your benefit than for our own.

Lest Henry and his advisers should be in any doubt, she gave tacit warning of the consequences if they did not accept her marriage and give Hugh his rights as her husband:

> Wherefore, we entreat you, as our dear son, that this thing may be pleasing to you, seeing it conduces greatly to the profit of you and yours, and we earnestly pray you that you will restore to him his lawful right [i.e. her dower], that is Niort, the castles of Exeter and Rockingham and 3,500 marks [£1,715,000], which your father bequeathed to us. And so, if it please you, deal with him, who is so powerful, that he may not remain against you, since he can serve you well, for he is well-disposed to serve you faithfully with all his power. And we are certain, and undertake, that he shall serve you well if you will restore to him his rights, and therefore we advise that you take opportune counsel on these matters. And when it shall please you, you may send for our daughter, your sister, by a trusty messenger and your letters patent, and we will send her to you.[10]

The King and his councilors were incensed, concluding that Isabella had married Hugh as a means of bolstering her own power in the south. "As the Queen took this step without asking the consent of anyone in England, the council of regency withheld her dower from her, to the indignation of her husband."[11] They also refused to send her the money she was still insisting had been bequeathed to her by King John, and petitioned the Pope, in the King's name, to have the couple excommunicated. Hugh and Isabella retaliated by threatening to go over to the French. They refused to surrender Saintes and Oléron and began stirring up discontent among Henry's subjects in Poitou. Isabella kept Joan with her as a hostage until her dower rights were restored, obliging the child to write to the King, assuring him of Hugh's loyalty. "My messenger will know that I am safe and unharmed," wrote the ten-year-old girl, probably at her mother's dictation. "I strongly beseech you not to credit what unfaithful persons say to you against our lord, Hugh de Lusignan."[12]

On May 17, 1220, Henry III, now twelve, was crowned again, at Westminster Abbey. The crown used, which had survived King John's final journey, was believed to be that of St. Edward the Confessor, England's royal Saxon saint, for whom Henry had a great devotion. He would bequeath it to his successors so that they too could be hallowed with the aura of St. Edward's sanctity.

Henry III needed Hugh de Lusignan, his most powerful southern vassal, to keep Poitou loyal. It was important that there was no rift. On May 22, he summoned Hugh to England to discuss their affairs and commanded him to send Joan to La Rochelle, to be delivered to the King's officers. Henry wanted his sister back promptly because Alexander II of Scots wanted to marry her. When his orders were ignored, the King complained to Pope Honorius of Hugh and Isabella's conduct and, on September 25, 1220, Honorius threatened them with excommunication.

"Cease to molest your son!" he thundered. "Restore the sister of the King of England." He also asked Henry to reinstate his mother's rights and dues in England and Gascony. His exhortations bore fruit. In October, all parties agreed to comply by the Pope's terms and Henry paid Isabella the arrears of dower she claimed were owing to her.

In November, Hugh escorted Joan to Oléron, whence she returned to England. In June 1221, she would be married to Alexander II at York.

That year, Isabella bore an heir, the future Hugh XI. A second son, called Aymer de Valence, after his birthplace in Charente, arrived the following year. There would be seven more children, making Isabella a mother at least twelve times over. It was widely thought that she favored her second family more than her first.

Despite demands from the English council, Hugh had repeatedly refused to pay homage to Henry III for his lands in Poitou until he and Isabella received her English dower lands. In September 1221, the council retaliated by confiscating those lands until Hugh swore allegiance. Amid fears that Isabella and Hugh would ally themselves with France against England, the Papal legate, Pandulf, stepped in to mediate. By April 1222, the Queen's dower had been restored.

* * *

When, in 1220, Henry had issued Berengaria a safe-conduct to visit England, she accepted. On July 7, she had been among the vast throng gathered in Canterbury Cathedral with the twelve-year-old King to witness the translation of Becket's bones to a new shrine in the choir loft of the Trinity Chapel, and attended the mass celebrated by the Archbishop of Rheims.

Further arrears of her dower payments had accumulated, and the guardians of the realm had finally agreed to double the annual payments and grant her the revenues of the tin mines of Devon and Cornwall in respect of the arrears owed her. Again, the Templars acted as her agents and guarantors.

On November 24, 1220, Berengaria sent her chaplain, Gautier, a Cistercian friar, to Peter des Roches, Bishop of Winchester, "beseeching you humbly and devotedly, with all the humility that we can, that you will cause us to be satisfied about the money due to us according to the composition of our dower."[13] Gautier obtained 1,000 marks (£490,000) of Berengaria's dower and insisted that future payments be paid more frequently.

In 1222, Berengaria's sister, Blanche, Countess of Champagne, retired to the Cistercian convent of Argensolles, which she had founded the year before. She had ruled as regent for twenty-one turbulent years and successfully fought a war to ensure her son's succession. But she did not enjoy her peace for long. In 1224, her brother, Sancho VII, became ill and retired from public life, and she was called upon to rule Navarre until her death in 1229.

In 1222, the cathedral chapter of Le Mans had again disputed Berengaria's right to impose a tax on them, leading to more ill feeling between them and her clergy at Saint-Pierre-la-Cour. She had already remonstrated with members of the cathedral clergy who kept wives when they were supposed to be maintaining their vows of chastity. It had reached the point where, as the Pope related, "certain individuals [were] caught in a brawl."

On Palm Sunday, it was customary for the Dean and chapter to walk in procession to the cathedral, carrying the relics of St. Scholastica. This year, Berengaria, "accompanied by a large crowd, led the procession," but "the Bishop and chapter refused to admit them and shut the doors of the church in their faces, to their utter confusion, creating scandal and dismay among the onlookers."[14]

Each side demanded that the other be censured. The quarrel led to the Bishop placing Le Mans under another interdict, which was only lifted when Pope Honorius demanded that the chapter concede the right of "his beloved daughter in Christ Berengaria" to levy a tax on them. He stridently condemned the Bishop, accusing him of issuing interdicts, not in the cause of justice, but out of a desire to injure Berengaria. But the cathedral chapter remained obdurate. When the Queen complained, the canons pointed out that their tonsure exempted them from secular interference and civil punishment. On April 4, "surprised and grieved," Honorius authorized Berengaria to deal with them as citizens. Tensions between her and the cathedral kept surfacing until 1223, after which better relations appear to have prevailed.

Despite all this, Berengaria had become greatly loved in Le Mans for her good works and charity toward the disadvantaged. She supported the hospital of Hôtel-Dieu de Coëffort, founded by Henry II in 1180 to succor the poor, the sick, orphans and pilgrims, and was a benefactress of the abbey of Notre-Dame de la Couture. People now called her "the white Queen," probably because she wore white robes in emulation of the Cistercians, whom she revered.

When, in March 1227, Berengaria's good friend Pope Honorius died, she found in his successor, Gregory IX, another champion. That year, his conscience prodded by Gregory, Henry III at last formalized Berengaria's dower rights. Twenty-eight years after her husband's death, she finally, at the age of about sixty-two, received what was due to her. It gave her more security and freed her from penury. No longer did she have to defray the cost of sending envoys to England, which had been the biggest outlay in her modest expenditure.

Relations between Isabella and the English council remained fraught. In 1224, her dower properties in England were again confiscated, to her fury. When, in April that year, Louis VIII, the new King of France, determined upon conquering Poitou and Gascony, sought the support of Hugh and other lords, he promised him not only Saintes and Oléron, but also Bordeaux, as inducements. In June, Hugh and Isabella defected to the French and Hugh swore fealty to Louis. Louis offered Isabella a handsome annuity in return for her surrender of her disputed dower rights in England. The English council promptly countered by offering her Niort, the money she insisted John had left her and greater compensation for the loss of her land in France, but she refused them all.

Louis now invaded English-held Poitou, leaving Hugh to reduce and occupy Gascony. Early in 1225, Henry III's brother Richard led an army into Gascony and halted Hugh's progress. When the English government cunningly assigned Isabella a larger pension in lieu of her dower lands, Hugh made peace. In May, Richard was rewarded with the earldom of Cornwall. It was the foundation of the enormous wealth he would amass.

6

"The White Queen"

✠

Hugh and Isabella clearly felt no loyalty to Henry III or the English council; Isabella invariably prioritized her own interests above her son's. Although Henry, now nearly nineteen, had been hoping to meet with his mother in France in the early summer of 1226, Hugh made it very clear whose side he and Isabella were on by renewing his homage to Louis in May. Again, the council confiscated Isabella's dower, giving her lands to her son, Richard of Cornwall, who had recently been named count of Poitou. Richard was now seventeen. While they were young men, there was rivalry between him and his brother the King, and Richard, the stronger character of the two, was to oppose Henry on three occasions, wresting large financial rewards as the price of making peace. Thereafter, however, he would be loyal. In 1226, Richard again invaded his mother's domains, in a vain attempt to establish his suzerainty.

On November 8 that year, Louis VIII died and was succeeded by his son, twelve-year-old Louis IX. He was to become one of France's greatest kings and would be canonized for his saintliness. He was also a just, fair and bountiful ruler with a social conscience, and a great warrior who strove to keep his realm at peace. His mother, Blanche of Castile, had brought him up to be virtuous and devout. "I love you, my dear son, as much as a mother can love her child," she told him, "but I would rather see you dead at my feet than that you should ever commit a mortal sin." She was to rule efficiently and intelligently as regent until 1234, when Louis attained his majority.

Hugh and Isabella soon found that their power in Poitou was being gradually undermined by the French. Realizing that they had made a bad decision, and feeling resentful, they did not acknowledge an invitation to Louis IX's coronation.

In January 1227, at nineteen, Henry III was declared of age and took control of the government of England. According to Matthew Paris, King John had "bred no worthy children, but only such as took after their father." Henry did not have John's worse vices; "he always afforded strict justice to everyone, and never allowed it to be subverted by bribery."[1] But, setting the pattern for much of his reign, he "acted imprudently and without advice of his nobles."[2] As a king, he was feeble; as a man, he was self-willed, tactless, naïve and sometimes foolish, with a capacity for deception. He had "a heart of wax,"[3] being malleable and inconstant. He acted impulsively without considering the consequences.

He had been reared to kingship in a tradition that dated back to the time of the Normans, when the King had made all the executive decisions. But he lacked the competence and vigor of his Norman predecessors, and the world was changing. Henry's great ambition was to recover the French lands lost by his father, but he had no talent for warfare. His reign would witness baronial intrigues, factional conflict and the emergence of a party dedicated to establishing good government in accordance with Magna Carta. By 1234, thanks to his dismissal of Peter des Roches and his having imported many Poitevins as government officials and advisers, he had alienated his barons.

Henry did have notable qualities. He was charitable, kind, virtuous and pious, and attended mass thrice daily, which even the saintly Louis IX deemed immoderate. He had a profound devotion to St. Edward the Confessor. It has been pointed out that both Henry and his favorite saint had been abandoned by their mothers, and that Emma of Normandy, the mother of St. Edward, never featured in Henry's devotional projects, perhaps reflecting Henry's ambivalent attitude to his own mother. All his life, he would treat Isabella with reverence, even when she betrayed his trust and sorely tested his patience. He showed great generosity to her and his stepfather, but the actions of Isabella and Hugh were governed by self-interest, and Isabella's loyalty did not always favor her eldest son.

Henry was a great patron of the Church and the new orders of preach-

ing friars, the Franciscans and the Dominicans. He was a civilized, cultivated man who took a great interest in art and architecture, and a great
builder. In his palaces, he loved vivid color and elaborate decor. He spent
lavishly, lived in luxury and established a rich court culture. His reign
saw the rebuilding, in the early English Gothic style he so admired, of
several great cathedrals, notably Wells, Lincoln, Peterborough and Salisbury. His patronage—and his extravagance—enhanced the splendor and
dignity of the English monarchy.

It now suited Isabella to seek England's friendship. She had sent several
letters to Henry asking for aid against an anticipated French invasion,
but to no effect. It was probably at this time that she wrote to him on
behalf of herself and "our husband, your father," warning that, if the
French invaded, she would be unable to defend Angoulême: "I have often
asked your help without success. I desire to be fed with words no longer.
If the truce with France should be broken, there would be great danger,
both to your lands and to mine."

Frustrated, Isabella and Hugh were driven to reach an accord with the
Regent, Queen Blanche. On March 16, 1227, new treaties were agreed at
Vendôme. Under their terms, Hugh and Isabella became vassals of King
Louis and secured their future prosperity—as they thought. At Tours,
Queen Blanche paid them compensation for the loss of Isabella's dower,
as well as confirming their right to Saintes and Oléron. Their son Hugh
was to be betrothed to Blanche's three-year-old daughter, Isabelle, and
their eldest daughter, Isabella, to Isabelle's brother, six-year-old Alphonse.
Isabella was to have Saintes and Oléron as her dowry.

In 1228, Henry III petitioned the Pope to annul Isabella's marriage to
Hugh. The couple were endlessly troublesome, and Isabella never scru-
pled to exploit her alliance with the French to force Henry to give her
more money. The Pope refused to interfere because there were no canonical grounds for an annulment, but this did not stop Henry trying
again ten years later, with a similar lack of success.

In 1228, Hugh and Isabella began building a new castle at Angoulême.
The city was defended on its north and west sides by a mountainous es-
carpment, and on the east by the old Châtelet, but it was accessible from
the south, where it had no other defense than an old Roman wall. The

new castle, which was built to the southeast, would not be finished for many decades. Hugh and Isabella extended the Châtelet itself, although the polygonal keep known as the Tour Lusignan and the great hall, both of which they envisaged, were not added until the late thirteenth century.

In 1228, Queen Blanche and the fourteen-year-old King Louis visited Berengaria at Le Mans. The two queens had much in common and struck up a friendship. Louis liked Berengaria too and, in official documents, was to refer to her, with unusual warmth, as "our dear, beloved and faithful kinswoman."

Berengaria had long wanted to establish a religious foundation, a wish perhaps inspired by her sister, who had founded the Cistercian abbey of Argensolles, and by Adam, Abbot of Perseigne, although he did not live to see the Queen's dream become reality. His successor, Gautier, would support her in realizing it.

Queen Blanche was a deeply pious woman. She and Louis were also interested in seeing Berengaria's proposed foundation come to fruition and, during their visit, they gave her money toward the founding of an abbey. In August 1228, Louis granted his "very dear kinswoman, Queen Berengaria" forty-six acres of woodland, seven acres of meadows and two acres of gardens bordering the River L'Huisne at L'Epau, lying between the city of Le Mans and the forest to the east. In September, Berengaria herself bought adjoining lands from the hospital of Coëffort and six neighboring properties from private individuals.

On March 25, 1229, she formally founded the abbey of L'Epau. That very day, she asked the monks of Cîteaux Abbey to begin constructing the church and conventual buildings. In 1230, she purchased from Alix of Blois, Abbess of Fontevraud, a vineyard that adjoined the land on which L'Epau was being raised. In May, King Louis and his mother came to the abbey to confirm their gifts to their "dearest relative and kinswoman" and see how the building work was progressing.

That month, as soon as the monastery was habitable (it would not be fully completed until 1365), the first abbot and his monks arrived. In June, Berengaria purchased two water mills on the banks of the L'Huisne. An unsubstantiated old tale relates that she was advised to do so after the monks complained of the noise made by the mills. She was told that the sound would make them think of the money they would earn from them and cease grumbling.

Berengaria did not live to receive the bull of Pope Gregory IX confirming her foundation, which was issued in January 1231, or to witness the abbey's consecration by Geoffroi de Laval, Bishop of Le Mans, at Candlemas, February 2. It was probably in her palace of Le Mans that "she came to a most happy death."[4] She is last mentioned in contemporary records on November 12, 1230, when Henry III ordered payment of her dower. Several necrologies of Maine record that she died in 1230, while her obit was celebrated annually in Le Mans Cathedral on December 20, which was probably the date of her death.

She died beloved of the poor for her goodness and generosity and was buried in her abbey, probably in the chapter house. Significantly, she chose to lie at L'Epau rather than at Fontevraud with Richard. The latter probably had too many associations with the Plantagenets, her unhappy marriage and her formidable mother-in-law.

Her coffin was carried to L'Epau by Cistercian monks, and her funeral was attended by the canons of Saint-Pierre-la-Cour, representatives of the cathedral chapter and a great throng of grieving citizens. "It was a sight wondrous to behold and many wept as they prayed." Afterward, the monks set up a Latin epitaph in the sanctuary of the church at L'Epau, by the high altar. It stated that "the frail body of our rightful lady was buried in here this temple," the word "frail" suggesting that Berengaria had been ailing for some time before her death.

Her tomb was not built until the late thirteenth century. Her graceful effigy shows her crowned and veiled, wearing a tight-sleeved, flowing gown clasped at the throat with an *agrafe*; her mantle is fastened with a cord across the breast. At her waist is a belt from which hangs an almoner, a purse containing coins for alms. She holds a book opened to show an image of her lying either on the ground or on a bier, with lit candles on each side. It may portray her deathbed or her tomb. The sculptor had perhaps seen the effigy of Queen Eleanor, which also holds a book. Berengaria's feet rest on a dog, for fidelity, and a lion, which may represent King Richard. The effigy was once painted in bright colors.

Fire swept the abbey complex in 1365, and the tomb of Berengaria was probably damaged. In 1602, it was brought into the church and, in 1672, it was repaired and moved to the choir, in front of the high altar. A new epitaph was placed on it, which read: "The mausoleum of the most serene Berengaria, Queen of the English, distinguished founder of this monastery, was restored and placed in this more majestic spot, and in it were placed the bones taken from the former tomb." In 1679, a new tomb chest was sculpted with quatrefoils. Inside was laid an oak box containing the bones found in the old tomb with scraps of linen and pieces of gold-embroidered fabric.

During the French Revolution, the abbey was suppressed. When Charles Stothard, the English painter and engraver, visited in 1816, the church was being used as a barn and he found parts of the tomb chest lying on the floor and Berengaria's effigy buried under a heap of wheat. It was in good condition, although part of one arm had been broken off (it was later reattached). Near the effigy lay what Stothard thought to be the Queen's bones. He was told that there had been nothing inside the chest but the small box put there in 1679. He insisted that the tomb and remains be treated with respect. When he returned a year later, the effigy was standing up in a wall niche.

In 1821, the tomb was placed in the north transept of Le Mans Cathedral. A nineteenth-century photograph shows that the effigy was almost broken in two around the hips. The contents of the oak box were examined in 1920. They comprised several long bones wrapped in linen: two matching femurs, part of a left tibia, and a fragment of a femur belonging to a female aged between fifteen and sixteen. Clearly, these could not all have been Berengaria's bones.

In 1960, a vault containing the remains of a woman was found beneath the chapter house. The bones were examined in 1963 by experts at the University of Caen, who found that they had belonged to a female aged between sixty and sixty-five, who had been about five foot six inches tall and had suffered a dislocated hip. She had had a narrow face, a broad forehead, a pointed nose and arched brows. Traces of brass around the skull were conjectured to have come from a crown placed on the body at its original burial, but stolen at some time in the past; a post-mortem trauma to the skull probably resulted from its forced removal. The identification with Berengaria was controversial, but is now accepted by many historians. However, there is a strong line of provenance for the bones in the wooden box, which were taken from the original tomb and mixed with others at some stage, so the remains found in the chapter house may not be Berengaria's.

In 1988, the Queen's effigy was returned to the chapter house at L'Epau and laid on a new tomb chest placed on the site of the vault containing the remains found in 1960. It is inscribed: "Berengaria, most humble former Queen of the English."

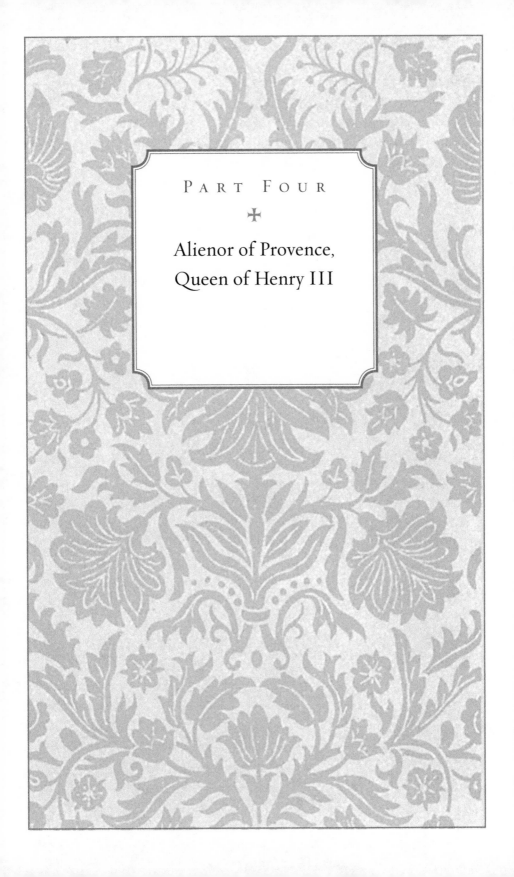

PART FOUR

✠

Alienor of Provence,
Queen of Henry III

I

"The Younger Virgin of
This Most Lovely Race"

✝

ONE OF QUEEN BLANCHE'S OPPONENTS WAS PETER MAU-
clerk, Count of Brittany, who wanted to expand his own territory.
In August 1229, he had urged Henry III to invade France and reclaim his
lost lands, promising him that the lords of Brittany and Normandy
would declare for him, and that his mother and Hugh de Lusignan would
rise in his support. For the King, now twenty-two, the proposal was irresistible. It took him several months to convince his barons, but, finally, in
May 1230, he sailed for France. In return for Hugh's support in recovering Normandy, he had agreed to invade Poitou and quell opposition to
the Lusignans, who were resented by their vassals for allying with the
French.

On May 3, Henry's ship put in at Saint-Malo in Brittany, where he,
Richard and their sister Eleanor were reunited with their mother, Queen
Isabella, whom they had not seen in thirteen years. She accompanied
them to Dinan, where it was agreed that they would all travel to Nantes
for a meeting with Hugh de Lusignan.

Henry needed Hugh as an ally. Earlier that month, he had sent the
Seneschal of Gascony on a private mission to Hugh and Isabella and
granted his mother an increased pension as an inducement. But the
meeting at Nantes did not go well, possibly because Isabella demanded
more money from the King. Queen Blanche had made generous over-

tures to Hugh and Isabella, aiming to wean them away from Henry, offering them an even larger pension. The couple came away from Nantes ready to renew their treaty with the Regent.

On June 8, the King's steward informed the English council of the Lusignans' defection. There was nothing Henry could do about it. Hugh and Isabella were now in an outwardly strong position, having consolidated their lands into a formidable power bloc and centralized their administration. Henry's only consolation was that some of their vassals remained loyal to him.

Queen Blanche wanted to press ahead with the nuptial alliance between her daughter, Isabelle of France, and Isabella's son Hugh. In June 1230, the marriage contract was signed, but Isabelle, just five years old, repudiated it, protesting that she did not wish the wedding to go ahead since she was determined to remain a virgin. That appealed to her pious mother and brother, who respected her wish, but it scuppered the betrothal, freeing Isabelle for a life of piety, in which she would earn a reputation as a saint.

By 1234, Henry III had failed in several attempts to find a suitable bride, negotiations for marriage alliances with Scotland, Austria, Brittany and Bohemia having all fallen through. He was now in his late twenties and his councilors were pressing him to wed. Secretly, he entered into negotiations to marry Joan, the fourteen-year-old heiress of Simon de Dammartin, Count of Ponthieu and Montreuil, a vassal of the King of France. Already famed for her beauty, she was the granddaughter of Alys of France, who had been rejected by Richard I. Simon held his titles in right of his wife, Marie, the heiress to Ponthieu and Montreuil, and Henry envisaged them passing to himself on the death of his putative mother-in-law, giving him a foothold in northern France.

On April 8, 1235, the proxy wedding of Henry III and Joan of Ponthieu went ahead. Afterward, Henry dispatched proctors to Rome to obtain a dispensation because he and Joan were related within the forbidden degrees, and asked for his bride to be sent to England. He began planning her coronation, which was to take place on the feast of Pentecost. But King Louis, influenced by his mother, withheld his consent to the marriage for fear of the English King gaining territory next to the Norman border, which would give him a base from which to recover Normandy. His agents in Rome effectively blocked the dispensation, whereupon Henry instructed his envoys to press the Pope to recognize his union with Joan.

By late June, Amadeus, Count of Savoy, and his brother, William, Bishop-elect of Valence, had begun urging Henry to cement an existing alliance with the Holy Roman Emperor that would counterbalance the influence of the French, suggesting that he consider a marriage with the daughter of one of the Emperor's vassals, namely their own niece, Alienor of Provence, sister of the Queen of France. On May 27, 1234, at Sens Cathedral, Louis IX had married Marguerite of Provence, the eldest daughter of Ramon Berenger IV, Count of Provence, and Beatrice of Savoy.

William of Savoy was "a brilliant and handsome man."[1] He had held benefices in England since 1220, was influential in diplomacy on an international scale, and had been instrumental in bringing about Marguerite's illustrious marriage. In suggesting an alliance between Alienor and Henry, he was looking to further advance his own family and extend its power into England.

Henry himself had European ambitions. Provence and Savoy were fiefs of the Empire, and their rulers controlled communications between northern Europe and Gascony and the western Alpine passes into Italy, which would be useful to him. They had close links to the Papacy and many European princes, whose support in his quest to regain his lost empire Henry meant to win in return for large financial inducements. He lost interest in Joan, believing that an alliance with Provence would be as advantageous to him as it was to Louis, and would bind him more tightly to the Emperor, as William of Savoy had pointed out.

There was actually no need for Henry to reinforce his alliance with the Empire; his sister Isabella was about to marry the Emperor Frederick II. But what Louis IX had, Henry III wanted. He foresaw—as did his approving councilors—that marriage to the sister of the Queen of France would bring England and France closer together. The Pope and King Louis were to endorse the match for the same reason, and because it would strengthen Provence against the aggression of its territorial rival, neighboring Toulouse. Raymond VII was Henry's first cousin and ally and could hardly attack Provence if its count was allied to Henry by marriage. What Henry failed to appreciate was that the Emperor supported Raymond VII in his ongoing border warfare with Ramon Berenger and was not likely to look kindly on the marriage.

Henry quickly made up his mind to pursue the alliance with Provence. "It was the younger virgin of this most lovely race whom the King of England sought as his wife through [his] ambassadors." On June 22, 1235, he sent "most solemn and prudent men into Provence on a discreet mission to Count Ramon with letters expressing his most heartfelt desire to contract marriage with the Count's daughter, Alienor."[2] The solemn and prudent men were led by Robert Grosseteste, Bishop of Lincoln.

That same day, Henry wrote to Alienor's Savoyard uncles, Count Amadeus and Bishop William, assuring them that he was interested in cementing their friendship by marrying their niece, and asking for their help in bringing about the match. He informed them that, although he had married another lady, he had discovered that there was an impediment to that union. William now deployed his diplomatic skills to bring about as prestigious a match for Alienor—who had been present at her sister's wedding and coronation—as Marguerite's had been.

"Count [Ramon] was a famous man and a vigorous warrior." He had even climbed the Alps. But, "because he was constantly fighting, nearly all his treasure had flown to the winds."[3] He had been caught up in the Albigensian Crusade, a Papal initiative against Provençal Cathar heretics, which led to the founding of the Inquisition. Defending his lands had left Ramon impoverished. Yet "a wise and courteous lord was he, and of noble state and virtuous, and in his time did honourable deeds."[4]

Ramon had been born in 1205, making him only seventeen at the time of Alienor's birth. He had become count of Provence on the death of his father in 1209. In 1219, at fourteen, he was married to twelve-year-old Beatrice, daughter of Thomas, Count of Savoy, "a lady of remarkable beauty, gracious mien, wise and affable." Beatrice bore twin boys, who died at birth in 1220, and four daughters. The two younger girls were Sanchia (born 1228) and Beatrice (born 1229/31), who was her father's favorite because she showed him the greatest affection. All inherited Beatrice's looks. "There was no mother in all the world, in all the female sex, who had such a fruitful womb and could boast such beautiful daughters."[5] Through their marriages, these "four daughters, each one of them a queen,"[6] were to establish a pattern of political and cultural kinship that stretched across Europe from England to Sicily.

In June 1235, according to Matthew Paris, Alienor was "already twelve" years of age. Paris also stated that she had scarcely completed her fourteenth year when she married Henry in January 1236, which suggests a birthdate late in 1222. Her name is usually given as Eleanor, but Alienor is the Provençal version that appears in some charters and official documents and has been used here to differentiate her from her future daughter-in-law, Eleanor of Castile.

The county of Provence lay between Savoy and the Mediterranean. It was a golden land of sun-drenched summers, fortified hilltop villages, Romanesque churches, fields of flowers, lavender and olive trees, rocky outcrops and mountains. Aix-en-Provence, Avignon and Arles were its chief cities. Count Ramon's principal seat was Tarascon on the River Rhône; he wintered in Aix-en-Provence and spent his summers at the palace of Brignoles, which he gave to his wife on their marriage. He also owned the castle at Les Baux, which stood on a high crag south of Avignon.

Alienor's native tongue was Occitan. She was "very fair to behold"[7] and was called "la Belle." She grew up in a court famous for its courtly literature, music, poetry and tournaments. In Provence, the legends of King Arthur were popular. It was said that another hero, Charlemagne, had bequeathed the county to the poets, and troubadours were welcomed like lords by Ramon Berenger, whose grandfather, Alfonso II of Aragon, had himself been a great poet. Ramon and Beatrice were also poets, a talent they shared with Romeo de Villeneuve, a poor man who had been received into the Count's household and shown himself trustworthy and able. The poet Dante Alighieri referred to "the shining light of Romeo," whom Ramon appointed tutor to Alienor to teach literacy skills and verse.

Alienor was influenced not only by the vibrant Provençal culture, but by religious mentors who inspired her and her sisters, fostering their piety and shaping them into generous benefactresses of the Church. It was clearly a happy childhood, given her closeness to her family in later life.

* * *

Henry's envoys "were welcomed by Count Ramon with the utmost honour and courtesy,"[8] and negotiations for the alliance proceeded.

Referring to the sisters' marriages, Dante stated that "this grandeur all by poor Romeo had accomplished been." Romeo de Villeneuve was now head of the Count's household and a key figure in the negotiations. A letter of Queen Marguerite's implies that she too had been instrumental in bringing about Alienor's marriage, although she may have overstated her role, since she was very much in the shadow of her mother-in-law, Queen Blanche, and would remain so until the latter's death in 1252. But no one had to use much persuasion. Ramon willingly agreed to the King's proposal. Henry's returning envoys assured him that Alienor was of handsome appearance. At that, he made up his mind. On July 16, he recalled his ambassadors from Rome, instructing them that they were no longer to press for a dispensation for his union with Joan of Ponthieu. There was uncertainty as to how the French would react, but when William of Savoy asked King Louis for a safe-conduct for Alienor to travel to England through France, it was granted. Evidently Queen Blanche saw this alliance as a lesser threat than that with Joan of Ponthieu. Three years later, she would arrange for her kinsman, Ferdinand III, King of Castile, to marry Joan.

Henry appointed proctors and instructed them to secure as large a dowry as possible. When they departed on October 6, they carried with them six different letters asking for amounts descending from 20,000 marks (£9,800,000)—twice Marguerite's dowry—to 3,000 marks (£147,000). Ramon balked at the sum of 20,000 marks; he had so far been able to pay only one fifth of Marguerite's dowry. He also expressed concern about the inadequate dower Henry proposed to settle on Alienor during the lifetimes of Queen Berengaria and Queen Isabella, whose dowers he also had to fund. The King had promised to dower Alienor with "the cities and holdings which were usually delivered by my predecessors, the kings of England, to the queens of England."[9] These, however, were in Queen Isabella's hands.

The King's envoys lowered his demand, in turn, to 15,000 marks, 10,000 marks, 7,000 marks, 5,000 marks and, finally, 3,000 marks. In fact, Henry was so keen to marry Alienor that, on October 19, he instructed his envoys "to conclude the marriage forthwith, either with money or without, but, at all events, to secure the lady for him and conduct her safely to England without delay." In the end, Ramon agreed to pay a dowry of 10,000 marks (£4,900,000), the same sum Louis IX had received with Marguerite.

Because of this haggling over the dowry, the marriage contract was not signed until November 23. The proxy wedding went ahead that same day at the castle of Tarascon. In December, Alienor left Arles. Her father and William of Savoy headed her escort of "more than 300 horsemen [and] a large number of attendant followers,"[10] including several cousins and relations, all looking to profit from her marriage. Among those in her personal train were the Lady Guillelma (or Willelma) de Attelis, who had looked after her since her childhood and would continue to serve her in England.

The bride's party traveled north overland, with crowds following in great numbers. On December 15, they reached Vienne, where William of Savoy, as dean of the cathedral, confirmed the terms of the marriage contract.

Henry "celebrated Christmas joyfully at Winchester, awaiting with burning anticipation the arrival of his envoys"[11] with news of the coming of his bride. In January 1236, he sent the bishops of Ely and Hereford and the Master of the Temple across the English Channel to convey Alienor to England.

She and her retinue were feasted for several days by Theobald IV "the Troubadour," Count of Champagne and King of Navarre, who "went out joyfully to meet them and accompanied them as a guide through his dominions, during a journey of five days and more. He also, being generous by nature, bore their expenses in horses and men."[12] At the end of their visit, Count Ramon bade farewell to Alienor and rode back to Provence, leaving her in the care of William of Savoy.

Theobald escorted Alienor and her retinue to the French border, where King Louis, Queen Marguerite and Queen Blanche were waiting to receive them. They learned that "their passage was not only free, but honourable," for the royal party escorted them to the coast and entertained them. Alienor may have noticed that Queen Blanche, jealous of the younger Queen, kept Marguerite strictly supervised, and that Marguerite resented this. She and Louis were clearly happy together, but Blanche kept them apart as much as she could. Alienor was doubtless relieved that *her* future mother-in-law was miles away in Poitou.

Alienor and her train "embarked at the port of Wissant, hastened across the sea with rapid course and reached the port of Dover sooner than was expected. They landed safely around 10 January, and proceeded to Canterbury, where, four days later, the King hastened to them and rushed to embrace his returning ambassadors."[13]

Thirteen-year-old Alienor found her twenty-eight-year-old future husband to be a stocky man of about five foot six with a narrow forehead and a drooping eyelid. He was gentle in manner, kind, affectionate and generous. Only occasionally did he have flashes of the famous Plantagenet temper, as when he ripped the clothes off one jester and tipped another into the Thames.

Henry was delighted with his beautiful dark-haired bride. Many portraits or images of him, Alienor and other royal persons in stone, glass or metal were commissioned in the thirteenth century. Sadly, most are lost. Alienor's stone head surmounts a roof boss by the entrance to the Chapter House of Westminster Abbey, with a companion head of Henry III on the other side; there are roses of Provence in the moldings. Other heads said to represent Alienor can be seen in Ditchling Church, Sussex, the north porch of Bridlington Priory (perhaps inspired by a royal visit to York in 1251), the church of the Holy Cross at Sherston, Wiltshire, and Much Wenlock Church, Shropshire, where Henry and Alienor were guests on several occasions. The queen with a hawk on her wrist who appears in the thirteenth-century floor tiles of the Chapter House in Westminster Abbey may also represent Alienor.

"Having seen the damsel and welcomed her and accepted her for himself," Henry gave gifts of gold to Alienor and her train. The wedding in Canterbury Cathedral immediately followed, the ceremony being performed by Edmund Rich, Archbishop of Canterbury, "assisted by the bishops who had arrived with the damsel, in the presence of many magnates, nobles and prelates."[14] A drawing of the couple survives in Matthew Paris's *Historia Anglorum*, showing a diminutive Alienor next to a much taller Henry. The gap of more than three years between the wedding and the birth of their first child suggests that the marriage was not consummated immediately. Alienor later held strong views on marriages being consummated too soon, urging that her granddaughter was too young at thirteen to be wed.

Henry had spared no expense on Alienor's coronation because he wanted to underline the importance of this marriage alliance. On January 19, the King and Queen made a state entry into London. Thanks to Matthew Paris, who was present, we have the first detailed description of the coronation of an English queen.

> There were assembled at the King's nuptial festivities such a host of nobles of both sexes, such number of religious men, such crowds of the populace and such a variety of actors that London, with its capacious bosom, could scarcely contain them. The whole city was ornamented with silks and banners, chaplets and hangings, lights and torches, with wonderful devices and extraordinary representations, and all the roads were cleansed from mud and dirt and everything offensive. The citizens went out to meet the King and Queen, dressed out in their ornaments.

There were "many pageants" and "in the night, the city was [lit] with lamps, cressets and other lights without number."

Henry escorted Alienor to the Palace of Westminster, where her chamber, which overlooked the River Thames, had just been redecorated and adorned with historical paintings.

For her coronation, he gave her a great golden crown set with gems, costing £1,500 (£1,100,000), a rich mantle lined with ermine, nine garlands or chaplets for her hair, all of gold filigree and precious stones, and jeweled girdles of gold; in total, he spent £30,000 (£14,7000,000). Queen Marguerite had sent her sister a perfume bottle in the form of a silver peacock with a tail set with precious stones and sapphires.

On Sunday, January 20, the chief citizens of London proceeded to Westminster "dressed in silk garments with mantles worked in gold, mounted on valuable horses to the number of 360, gallantly trapped with new bits and saddles and riding in troops arranged in order, every man bearing a cup of gold or silver in his hand. The King's trumpeters led the way, with horns sounding," which "struck all who beheld it with astonishment."

Beneath a purple silk canopy borne by sixteen barons of the Cinque Ports, the King walked to Westminster Abbey along a carpet of blue ray (a striped fabric), wearing his crown and his coronation robes. "The nobles performed the duties which, by ancient right and custom, pertained to them at the coronations of kings. John the Scot, Earl of Chester, carried the sword of St. Edward, which was called Curtana, before the King, [and] kept the people away with a wand when they pressed forward in a disorderly way." Gilbert, the Earl Marshal, holding his wand of office, preceded the King into the abbey.

Alienor came next, beneath her own canopy of estate, and was supported on either side by two bishops. At the door to the abbey, she paused while prayers were offered up to the Virgin Mary that she might be fruitful, then proceeded up the nave. In "a ceremony of unparalleled splendour," she was anointed on the head with holy oil and crowned queen "with incomparable solemnity" by the Archbishop of Canterbury. The prayers he recited reminded her of her duty to emulate not only the Virgin Mary, but also the Biblical women Rebecca and Rachel, who had borne sons to carry on the line of King David. Henry, watching the ritual, "sat on his throne and glittered very gloriously" in his robe of gold tissue.

Afterward, the King and Queen walked along a carpet of striped English burel (felt)—the longest ever yet seen in England—to Westminster Hall. The Earl Marshal had arranged the banquet. Guests were amazed at "the dainties of the table, the overflowing richness of many wines, the profusion of meats and dishes, the abundance of game, the variety of fish, the joyous sounds of the gleemen, the gaiety of the jugglers, the comeliness of the attendants."[15] At the high table, William de Warenne, Earl of Surrey, acting as butler and cupbearer, tasted the wine in the royal goblets before offering it to the King and Queen. When he gave Alienor hers, she rose and bowed to the company, at which everyone stood, clinked cups and cheered three times for the royal couple.

As soon as Henry and Alienor had returned to the palace, there was a scuffle between the doorkeepers and scullions for the golden cloth that had hung behind the high table, which ended up torn in pieces. The doorkeepers then fought the cooks for the leftover food.

On her coronation day, in emulation of the Virgin enthroned next to Christ, Alienor interceded with the King for a felon who had infringed the forest laws, and secured a pardon for him. The ceremony may have been stage-managed, but, over the long years ahead, she would make many such successful intercessions, even for those who had committed murder. A queen's plea for mercy demonstrated her influence; it showed the gentler face of monarchy and was likened to the light of dawn that scatters the errors of discord. It also provided the King with a pretext for showing clemency when it would otherwise have looked weak to do so. Possibly it was already customary for a Queen to make intercessions on her coronation day, as it was traditional for her to receive petitioners after she had given birth.

In the eight days that followed, "royal solemnities and goodly jousts" were held in Tothill Fields by Westminster. Henry had emptied his treasury to pay for the wedding and the coronation. The people of London and the barons had "amply supplied funds" for his marriage, but, when he asked the lords to approve a tax on all his subjects' property to make up the shortfall, they refused, saying that, as he had wasted the money on unnecessary extravagances, he should defray the expenses of his wedding as best he could.

2

"Our Dearest Love"

✠

TORRENTIAL RAINS MARKED ALIENOR'S FIRST WEEKS AS QUEEN. The Thames burst its banks at Westminster and the palace was flooded, obliging the King to take her to Winchester. It was a far cry from sunny Provence. Yet there were compensations. This was a royal marriage in which love quickly flowered. Henry was a true, devoted, even uxorious husband, happy in his domestic life—a family man in every sense; and Alienor, who had a strong sense of family loyalty, was to prove a loving and fiercely supportive wife. He adored her; even in the dry language of the official records, she is frequently referred to as his "dearest love" or "beloved love."

Intelligent, kindly, courteous and self-controlled, Alienor had a strong, forceful character, much courage and "liberality of heart."[1] She was tenacious and resolute in standing up for her rights and those close to her. She could also be grasping, extravagant and frivolous. She and Henry outlaid money on a vast scale on their palaces, their families, their clothes, their jewels, their court, their charities and their patronage of the arts. Henry lavished gifts on her, such as a silver plate embellished with shields of gold, an enameled gold goblet, rings, jeweled girdles and brooches.

She exercised considerable influence over him, while he placed great trust in her and relied heavily on her advice. Because of this, she was able to wield more power and influence than any queen consort since Eleanor of Aquitaine. Her decisive political importance was attested to in the letters of the influential Adam Marsh, a Franciscan friar and Oxford theologian who was "one of the greatest clerks of the world," "knew everybody" and was in her confidence. He was a great mentor to her, spiritually and in other ways. Alienor demanded much of Marsh, employing him on delicate diplomatic tasks and insisting he support her in practical ways. It is clear from his letters that this was at times burdensome to him.

On January 21, the King issued a charter granting Alienor, "by way of dower, for her life, £10,000 yearly of land in England": the towns already promised her, plus the cities of Worcester and Bath and "a third part of all the lands which the King [has] in Ireland, Gascony and elsewhere beyond the seas."[2] The settlement was never sufficient to fund her extravagance, and she would always be short of money and looking to the King and others to supply more. William de Tarrant, the keeper of her dower lands, was universally hated and feared by her tenants because of his ruthless exactions.

Over the years, Alienor would use her influence to extend the types of fines that attracted queen-gold, although the Exchequer Rolls show that she often pardoned or discharged debts of it. As patron of the Jews, she was entitled to receive "her gold of the Jewry."[3] Like previous queens, she also had the right to dues on goods landed at Queenhithe in London. The King ordered that all cargoes of corn and wool had to be unloaded there, and Alienor made it her business to ensure that as many ships as possible did so, which made her unpopular with the Londoners. Her support of Henry's heavy taxation only added to her notoriety.

Another increasingly lucrative source of funding for the Queen was the acquisition of the wardships of noble heirs, which the King could grant her without financial loss to the Crown. Until a ward came of age, their guardian was entitled to use the money from their estates, ostensibly for their own good, although many guardians made a profit out of it. They could also make money through brokering marriages for their wards. Alienor was granted many wardships, lands and the right to marry off heirs, and might earn an average of £750 (£547,000) annually. On top of that, she condoned, and profited by, her officials' ruthless exploitation of wards in her care. Wardships were never a constant income because, once wards came of age or married, their guardian had to return their lands to them. Nevertheless, from around 1250, Alienor received several valuable escheats—estates that had reverted to the Crown after the death, without heirs, of their owners—which provided her with another source of revenue, although it was never enough. She often borrowed money from foreign merchants, loans she could not always repay.

She was not unremittingly rapacious. Her charities were extensive, and Adam Marsh wrote of her inexhaustible liberality. She was generous to religious foundations and a great patron and benefactor of the Franciscans and, to a lesser extent, the Dominicans, the Augustinian Friars of the Sack and Cistercian nuns. In 1259, she established a Dominican friary at Dunstable.

She is the first English queen for whom detailed financial records survive. They show that, in 1236, she had a modest income from grants paid into the Queen's wardrobe, a household department established for her that year, and was subordinate to her husband in regard to all decisions about her finances. Her wardrobe was not just a large storage facility for clothes, but a chamber where her clothes, jewels and other personal belongings were kept. Her personal expenditure is not documented because it was incorporated into the King's accounts.

By the end of Henry's reign, Alienor was in complete control of her income, and it had been established that the queen consort could operate as a *femme sole* during the King's lifetime, with the right to issue writs, acquire or grant land and bequeath her personal possessions.

The official records are full of financial transactions involving Alienor, mostly in respect of grants made to her. She clearly had a finger in many pies and was punctilious in safeguarding her rights. She proved to be highly effective—indeed, rigorous—at managing and keeping track of her household accounts, estates and finances and ensuring that she received what was due to her. She had her own treasurer, who accounted to the Exchequer, and her own council, which exercised jurisdiction over her officials and was the ultimate arbiter in disputes, since her tenants could not sue her in law; she could only be tried in the King's court. All her acts, of course, were subject to the King's approval.

Alienor introduced into England the rich court culture of the south. She brought with her the Provençal taste for music, poetry and chivalric romances, and introduced fitted baths, glass windows, tiled floors, wainscoting (wood paneling) on walls, painted hangings, carpets from Spain, curtains, cushions and table forks—a southern European item that found little favor in England. When she rode abroad on her palfrey, she sat on a saddle studded with gold and decorated with orphreys (embroidered borders).

She introduced the rose into the English royal insignia. She used the golden rose of Provence as her personal badge, as did her eldest son, Edward I, whose great seal would feature his mother's rose emblem. Her second son, Edmund, Earl of Lancaster, had a red rose badge, which was the origin of the red rose of Lancaster. Her arms were the red and yellow pallets of Provence; they can be seen in the medieval stained-glass windows of St. Edmund's Chapel in Westminster Abbey.

Reading was one of Alienor's pleasures. She obtained books from Paris and Oxford and sometimes exchanged them with noble ladies. She purchased romances of Arthur, Charlemagne, Alexander the Great and William the Conqueror. In 1255, Marguerite sent her an illustrated "Bible moralisée," now in the Pierpont Morgan Library. Around 1273/4, her chaplain, the Franciscan friar John of Howden, dedicated his devotional poem "Li Rossignos" ("The Nightingale") to her, describing her as "pious and pure."[4] No fewer than twenty-three manuscripts have been associated with her; they were either owned by her or commissioned for (or by) her. They include the beautiful Trinity Apocalypse, executed around 1250–5 and now in Trinity College, Cambridge. It is of rich workmanship lavishly embellished with gold leaf and contains many references to chivalry and romance. Internal evidence suggests that this may have been commissioned by, or for, Alienor.

The Queen loved clothes and instituted a new fashion—the wearing of chaplets, or garlands, of gold set with jewels, filigree work or artificial flowers in gold and silver, studded with jewels. The Pipe Rolls record that her "necessary expenses" covered gowns of russet, green and blue fastened with long strings of pearl buttons and edged with gold or silver thread, fur-trimmed hoods and cloaks, capes to wear in wet weather, caps and hose of wool or linen, wimples, veils, chemises, kerchiefs, shoes, slippers and goatskin boots. Her gowns were designed by Colin and Richard, her tailors. She ordered headdresses and trimmings from Paris, rich fabrics from Florence and frieze, a woollen plain-weave cloth, from Ireland. The King, the Queen and their servants and courtiers had new clothes for the great feasts of the Church. Alienor's jewels were looked after by her treasurer. In a single year, 1252–3, she spent £200 (£146,000) on 61 rings, 91 brooches and 33 belts.

Gardens were one of Alienor's chief passions. Henry created them for her at Clarendon and at Odiham Castle, Rutland. The latter was enclosed by a 2,000-foot-long hedge and a boarded fence with five doors; inside were turfed seats and even a garderobe behind a hedge. He also gave her a "house of fir, running on six wheels [and] roofed with lead"—which sounds like an early form of van. In 1245, another garden was laid outside her chapel at Woodstock. At Westminster, she could stroll along paved walks past lawns, cherry and pear trees and vines. At Windsor, her windows overlooked a courtyard in which a Provençal gardener called Fulk made an herb garden, and she had other herb gardens at Kempton Palace and Winchester. The latter was re-created in the 1980s inside the walls of Winchester Castle, outside the Great Hall; it is laid out as a garden of the period with turf seats, bay hedges, a pleached alley, a water channel, an arbor with a chamomile lawn and borders of flowers and herbs that would have been grown in the thirteenth century.

Henry III's extensive building works in the royal castles and palaces provided for the first time for a separate establishment of apartments for the queen consort and her household. Alienor's were often referred to as the Queen's Hall and the Queen's Chapel. Thanks to the wealth of records of works that survive, we have detailed descriptions of the apartments of an English queen. Henry and Alienor lavished money on these lodgings. Their apartments would become known as the "privy palace."

Westminster was Henry's foremost and favorite palace and he outlaid a fortune on it. The vast twelfth-century Painted Chamber was believed to stand on the site of the room in which Edward the Confessor had died in 1066, and it did service as Henry's principal apartment, his bedchamber and audience chamber. He had the walls covered with Old Testament scenes and the ceiling painted with figures in lozenges or roundels. When the murals were uncovered in 1819, after being boarded over for centuries, they were found to be "diversified with colours, emblazoned with silver and gold and enriched with stucco patterns in a superb and elegant manner." A painting of the coronation of Edward the Confessor adorned the wall behind the King's bed.

In most of the royal residences, Henry and Alienor had separate chapels or oratories; Henry built ten new chapels for Alienor and eight for himself. They were designed in the collegiate form in which the Sainte-Chapelle in Paris had been built, as at Kennington Palace, south of London, where, in 1237, Alienor's new chapel had an upper gallery for her use, while her household worshipped in the nave below; similar chapels were built for her at Windsor and Winchester. At Westminster, her chapel had eight lancet windows, "superbly gilt and coloured," and a marble altar and font.

In 1237, when Alienor's great chamber at Windsor was being rebuilt, a window depicting the Tree of Jesse was installed, the family tree of Christ symbolizing the Queen's duty to provide male heirs. The same year, paintings of the four Evangelists were commissioned for the walls of her new chamber at Westminster. In 1240, the figure of Winter was added above the mantelpiece, "with such sad countenance and other miserable attitudes of the body that he may be truly likened to winter."[5] Drawings of the Queen's chamber and chapel were made by William Capon in 1823 before those rooms were lost in the fire that consumed most of the Palace of Westminster in 1834. The medieval decor had then been replaced by much later schemes, but Alienor's chapel had largely survived intact, and Capon's drawings show walls and moldings that had once been painted in vivid primary colors and gilded. Columns with capitals supporting arches flanking the windows and doors can be seen. Between the capitals were two stone crowned heads, probably representing Henry and Alienor.

Hygiene had improved since King John had provoked astonished reactions when he had as many as eight baths in six months. Cleanliness had become the mark of gentle birth, and the upper classes washed regularly on rising in the morning and before meals; the King's chamberlain would be waiting with a basin of water and a towel. Henry took more baths than his predecessors had done, so we may assume that Alienor did too. Royal baths were made of wood, lined with sponges and linen, surmounted by a canopy and filled with herbs and rose water. At Westminster, Henry installed a bath house with hot and cold running water, which was piped from tanks and cauldrons heated in a furnace. Water was also piped from cisterns into the chambers of the King and Queen. Henry had a separate room in which his hair was washed.

He was fussy about sanitation. He complained when his privies smelled and constantly demanded that they be improved or replaced, at whatever cost, as his constable valued his life and liberty. A grille was inserted under the vent of the King's privy at Westminster to prevent assassins from climbing up the shaft and stabbing him. The windows of the royal privies were also barred and had glass painted white for privacy and to exclude drafts.

Henry provided Alienor with a great household, independent of his and headed by a chamberlain, who commanded a hundred servants, and a steward, who was in charge of the Queen's service household. Alienor had several chaplains, who were "constantly performing divine service for the Queen."[6] She employed various physicians, including Nicholas of Farnham, later Bishop of Durham, who was also her mentor in her early years as queen. She had a treasurer, a marshal, a sergeant, a lawyer, clerks and ushers of her chapel and chamber, clerks who dealt with correspondence and administrative matters, valets, messengers, porters, a carter of the Queen's chariot (who checked the state of the roads before she traveled), cooks, saucers, bakers, yeomen, a laundress and a host of others who served on her estates.

The Queen's wardrobe had an office staffed by a keeper and clerks who kept records of her purchases and possessions. Payments were made to the keeper of the wardrobe for the expenses of her household. In 1265, the clerk of the wardrobe rendered accounts for her expenses for the past eight years, which afford a fascinating insight into the expenditure and lifestyle of a thirteenth-century queen. Payments had been made for the linen department, butlery, kitchen, scullery and hall; for servants' liveries; horses, the shoeing of them, farriery, saddles and reins; oblations for holy days, daily alms, private alms and tending the poor; eleven jeweled garlands with emeralds, pearls, sapphires and garnets, bought for the Queen's use; robes and shoes for the Queen's family; silk mantles, upper garments and linen hose for the Queen's ladies; jellies, spices, apples, pears, other fruits and almonds; wax and various wardrobe expenses;

gifts to knights, clerks and messengers coming to the Queen; and "secret gifts." The expenditure totalled £21,960 3s. 7½d. (over £16,000,000). In that period, Alienor spent £10,446 3s. 3d. (£7,624,000) above her income.

The number of cooks who worked for her is testimony to her love of rich food, which she shared with the King. She had a sweet tooth and enjoyed fruit, figs, dates and almonds. At Lent 1236, Henry ordered that "since, after lampreys, all fish seem insipid to both the King and the Queen, the Sheriff [of Gloucester] shall procure as many lampreys as possible, place them in bread and jelly and send them to the King."[7] In 1258, a merchant of Bordeaux supplied twenty casks of wine for Alienor's use.[8]

The Queen was surrounded by noble ladies and damsels. Guillelma de Attelis headed this female household; she is described as *majorissa* (literally, mayoress) of the Queen's chamber. She earned more than any other female attendant and was the recipient of several royal grants. In 1258, the King bestowed an annuity of £48 (£35,000) on Guillelma, "who, from the childhood of the Queen, has served her, and now, wearied in the service and worn out by old age and sickness, does not wish to follow the Queen, but proposes for her better quiet to dwell in the abbey of Lacock."[9] When Guillelma died in 1262, her daughter Isabel took her place.

Emma and Margaret Bisset were damsels. In 1237, when Emma lay sick at Worcester, the King ordered that two horses be found to bring her to London, if she was well enough to travel. If not, a cart was to be procured to convey her. She seems to have left Alienor's service soon afterward, having gone blind. In 1238, the King granted Emma Bisset, "sometime damsel of the Queen," £11 1s. (£8,000) a year for life.[10] In 1242, at the instance of Queen Alienor, the King granted the same pension to Margaret Bisset, who may also have resigned on account of ill health, as she died soon afterward. Some ladies served the Queen well into her—and their—old age. If any damsel misbehaved, the Earl Marshal was authorized to beat her.

3

"The Eagles of Savoy"

✠

Along with some of her Provençal servants, the new Queen's relations had stayed on at court, possibly at her request, for she was very young and in a strange land, and had a passionate loyalty to her family, which was to dominate her actions throughout her life. Richard of Cornwall complained that the King was giving too many gifts to these foreigners and suggested that it would be politic to send Alienor's Provençal attendants home, as King Louis had dispatched her sister's, but Henry did not take this wise advice. His intention was to court the support of his wife's family and, through them, forge links with other continental princes and further his ambitions in Europe.

Alienor's maternal grandfather, Thomas, Count of Savoy, who died in 1233, had had eight sons, the "eagles of Savoy," who "carried the fame of their house across Europe"—and, being forever out of funds, squabbled over their inheritance while exercising smooth diplomacy in a political field that stretched from England to Italy. At the root of all this lay a burning desire for self-advancement and the successful pursuit of their dynastic claims in Europe.

Alienor was close to her uncles, who, finding no prospects at the court of France, saw her marriage as a stepping stone to their advancement in England. From 1236, they and many other Savoyards were welcomed by Henry and Alienor, who, demonstrating a lack of judgment and foresight, showered them with generous grants of lands, money, wardships, offices, titles, bishoprics and privileges, and encouraged the English nobility to intermarry with them. It has been estimated that more than 170 high-ranking Savoyards came to England during the period of Alienor's queenship, and that between 70 and 85 of them stayed, forming a powerful political faction at court, of which Alienor became the leader, emerging as the epitome of the great lady who exercised influence through manipulating her network of family connections and countrymen. She was in touch with her Savoyard affinity almost to the exclusion of English courtiers and nobles. They exercised great influence over her and were highly instrumental in forging her political role. Matthew Paris blamed her for spurring the King to favor them, and Henry for "being under the influence of his wife" and letting her get away with it. This was the common view, and Alienor's popularity suffered accordingly.

Some who were favored had talent and ability; they were not mere parasites. Some assimilated themselves smoothly into the English political establishment. Others were not so meritorious. But there was general resentment against them all, for they were regarded as undeserving interlopers who were usurping the rightful privileges of the indigenous nobility. It was said that Henry had been a good king as long as he had remained a single man.[1]

However, "the King thought he could never do enough to justify his love for the Queen and her family."[2] He readily allowed them a share in the government. From the first, Alienor's uncle, the clever diplomat William of Savoy, exercised a powerful influence over Henry and became his "chief counsellor,"[3] receiving lavish gifts. In April 1236, the King's Council was reconstituted under William's guidance and unpopular policies were approved. Henry told the Pope how heavily he relied on William. However, his attempt to make him bishop of Winchester to satisfy the Queen was blocked by the cathedral clergy, who refused to elect him. In retaliation, the King kept the see vacant. By then, the barons were beginning to feel excluded from the government. "It was a cause of astonishment to many that the King followed the advice of the Bishop more than he ought, despising, as it appeared to them, his own natural subjects" and counselors. "Highly indignant," they were wondering why Bishop William "did not betake himself to France to manage the affairs of the French kingdom, like he does here, by reason of his niece, the Queen of that country."[4] Matthew Paris loathed William, whom he accused of pulling the kingdom to pieces, and this hatred colored all his later accounts of Alienor's Savoyard relations.

Among others who received favor was Peter of Aigueblanche, a Provençal clerk who had come to England in Alienor's train and was described in 1236 as a knave. Matthew Paris wrote of his "fox-like cunning" and the "sulphurous stench" of his existence. Yet Peter would be made bishop of Hereford, where he proved a vigorous shepherd to his flock and built the north transept of the cathedral.

Henry failed to comprehend the distrust with which these foreigners were viewed. His continual openhandedness toward them exposed the unsatisfactory relations he had with his own barons and would cause increasing resentment and jealousy, not just at court, but throughout England. It proved impossible to stem the King's generosity. The interlopers squeezed money from him and used it to gain preferment elsewhere. Hoping for rewards, they even hectored the Pope to demand more taxes from the English people. They never ceased urging Henry to recover Normandy and other French territories lost by his father, and encouraged him to make expensive invasion plans.

In the summer of 1236, Henry took Alienor to Glastonbury to see the supposed tomb of Arthur and Guinevere. They were at Westminster on October 13 for the feast day of Edward the Confessor, when, to win the saint's favor for his bride, Henry offered rich cloths of damask at his shrine and a golden image of Alienor. On January 1, 1237, as an act of piety, he commanded his treasurer to distribute food to 6,000 poor people at Westminster for the health of the souls of himself, Queen Alienor and any children they might have.

That Christmas, the barons had demanded—in vain—that the Queen's relatives be removed from the counsels of the King. By January 1237, Henry was deeply in debt, provoking anger and popular outrage when he enforced a tax to meet the costs of his marriage. In February, William of Savoy, who had other interests abroad, left England for a short while because he was so unpopular.

The complaints escalated; it was said that Henry was becoming uxorious and suffering his realm to be ruled by strangers. Again, there were calls for them to be removed, but to no avail.

* * *

In February 1236, Henry had made a new truce with King Louis, in which he undertook "not to implead or vex Hugh, Count of La Marche, and Isabella his wife, the King's mother, at any time during the truce."[5] The following year, Louis IX's brother Alphonse, now seventeen, angered Isabella when he broke his contract to marry her daughter and espoused Joan of Toulouse instead, at the behest of Queen Blanche.

On September 22, 1237, Henry and Alienor met Alexander II of Scots and Queen Joan in York for a peace conference. Joan, now "an adult of comely beauty,"[6] returned south with Alienor. The two of them went on a pilgrimage to Canterbury, possibly to pray that they might be blessed with children. "Although often summoned back by her husband," Joan "refused to return" to Scotland[7] and remained with Alienor through the winter of 1237–8.

Henry and Joan's sister Eleanor was at court for the Christmas festivities. In 1224, at the age of nine, she had been married to the Marshal's son, William, 2nd Earl of Pembroke, at Westminster. After he died in 1231, she had taken a vow of chastity in the presence of the Archbishop of Canterbury, swearing to forsake men in order to become closer to God. Now, aged twenty-three, beautiful and elegant, she had come under the spell of Henry's friend Simon de Montfort, who was rapidly becoming one of the King's chief advisers and favorites.

Simon had arrived in England in 1229. His father, also Simon, had a fearsome reputation for having ruthlessly ravaged Provence and the Languedoc during the ferocious and bloody Albigensian Crusade. The younger Simon was acquisitive and self-seeking, hot-headed and combative, but also a serious-minded, thoughtful man who acted on principle, a natural, intelligent and charismatic leader and forward-thinking politician, so pious that he wore a hair shirt next to his skin. For all that, he seduced Eleanor, leaving the King no alternative but to permit them to wed. Henry was outraged by Simon's conduct and angry that he had made Eleanor break her vow of chastity, a greater offense to the Church, which had her under its protection as a vowess, than it was to the King, provoking angry complaints from the Archbishop of Canterbury and other clergymen.

The marriage took place in secret on January 7, 1238, at Westminster. The King himself gave the bride away. The marriage brought Simon power and rich honors. Breaking her vow did not incur any severe punishment for Eleanor, but Simon later went to Rome to obtain the Pope's dispensation releasing her from it.

Richard of Cornwall and the barons were scandalized by the marriage, which had taken place in secret without their being consulted, as was their right. They rose in arms and confronted the King at Stratford-atte-Bow, east of London. Henry fled to the Tower while William of Savoy bought off Earl Richard before leaving England for good.

Late in January, Queen Joan was preparing to return to Scotland when she was taken ill in London. Her brothers were sufficiently reconciled to be with her on March 4, when she died in their arms at the royal manor of Havering, Essex. She was buried, at her own request, in the Cistercian abbey of Tarrant in Dorset, of which Queen Alienor was patron. Tradition has it that her coffin was made of gold.

On September 9, 1238, Henry and Alienor were at Woodstock when a deranged man presented himself before the King and demanded that he resign the realm to him, for "he had the mark of royalty on his shoulder." As Henry's servants seized the interloper, the King enjoined them, "Let him alone in his folly." They obeyed, but, "in the middle of the night, the madman climbed by the window into the King's bedchamber with a naked knife in his hand and came to the King's bed. By God's providence, the King was with the Queen," a telling detail revealing that their marriage had now been consummated. Margaret Bisset was on duty. A devout, learned woman, she was reciting her psalter by the light of a candle. "When she saw the madman searching every corner so that he could kill the King, shouting wildly, she was astounded and began to scream. The servants were awakened and came running in haste. They broke down the door which the burglar had barred, overbore his resistance, seized him, bound him with chains and put him to the torture." He revealed that he had been sent to kill the King by Sir William de Marisco, an outlawed murderer who had taken refuge on Lundy Island.

On September 20, Henry ordered his bailiffs at the ports to look out for and apprehend Marisco for the attempt on his life, "as we know for certain through a certain ribald whom he sent to kill us and our Queen."[8] Marisco was not caught until 1242, when he was dragged to the scaffold at Coventry, hanged until he was dead, then disemboweled and quartered. This was probably the first time that the punishment of hanging, drawing and quartering was used in England.

At Westminster, on the night of June 16–17, 1239, Alienor gave birth to her first child, a healthy son with silver-blond hair. There was great joy, for "it was feared the Queen was barren," and an exultant Henry rewarded the messenger who brought him the news with £10 (£7,300). "At the King's wish, [the infant] was called Edward,"[9] after the Confessor. In celebration, *Christus Vincit* was sung in the royal chapel. Sybil, the wife of Hugh Gifford, one of the King's justices, was granted £10 a year, "in consideration of her good service to the Queen at the time of her first childbearing."[10]

"At this event, all the nobles of the kingdom offered their congratulations, and especially the citizens of London, for the child was born in London; and they assembled bands of dancers with drums and tambourines and, at night, illuminated the streets with large lanterns. A great many messengers were sent to make known this event, who returned loaded with costly presents." Unfortunately, Henry "deeply clouded his magnificence as a king, for, as the messengers returned, [he] required of each what he had received, and those who had received least, although they brought valuable presents with them, he ordered [them] to send them back with contempt; nor was his anger appeased till each person had given satisfactory presents." This was tantamount to extortion, and one baron remarked, "God gave us this child, but the King sells him to us."[11]

The infant Lord Edward, as he would be known in his father's lifetime, was baptized in Westminster Abbey by Otto, the Papal legate, and confirmed by Archbishop Edmund Rich. His uncles, Richard of Cornwall and Simon de Montfort, and the Earl of Hereford, were godfathers. After the christening, the court moved to Windsor. In August, Edward's nursery was established there, at the west end of the royal apartments, near the Queen's lodgings. It had a wainscoted chamber and a privy chamber, both with barred windows, and a chapel. The baby was placed in the care of Hugh and Sybil Gifford and two wet nurses, and the King appointed a chaplain whose sole duty was to pray for the health and estate of his precious son. The little prince was dressed in robes of silk, scarlet and cloth of gold, some lined with fur. All Henry III's children would be well dressed, conspicuous display being considered essential to maintain the majesty of royalty.

Henry and Alienor would prove to be exemplary, loving parents. The Queen was fiercely protective of her children's interests, and ambitious for them. She spent a lot of time with them when they were young and would often interrupt her travels with the King for extended sojourns at Windsor, where they were brought up, sometimes staying for more than thirty weeks in a year. She bought clothes for them and took responsibility for their education, which had to befit them for kingship and potential queenship.

The Lord Edward grew up to be a sturdy boy, "devoted from his earliest years to the practice of arms"[12] and able to speak English. Until the age of seven, he remained mostly at Windsor, where he was brought up with other high-born boys, including his cousin, Henry of Cornwall, who was four years his senior. The young Edward became "famed for enjoying the enduring protection of the Lord of Heaven. As a boy, he was once in the middle of a game of chess with one of the knights in a vaulted room when, suddenly, for no apparent reason, he got up and walked away. Seconds later, a massive stone, which would have crushed anyone who happened to be underneath it, fell from the roof on to the very spot where he had been sitting."[13] Edward attributed his escape to Our Lady of Walsingham, whose shrine in Norfolk he visited a dozen times.

The King summoned all the great ladies of the land to attend the Queen's churching on August 9 at Westminster Abbey, and Simon de Montfort brought his wife, Eleanor. Another of the Queen's uncles, Thomas of Savoy, Count of Flanders, had recently arrived in England. The King had ordered that the streets of London be swept and that the citizens put on their finest attire for his visitor. Now, he was incandescent, having discovered that Simon had secured a loan of 2,000 marks (£980,000) from the Count, naming Henry as guarantor without asking him first. This had the King working himself up into a fury at having been forced to give his sister to Simon in the first place.

As Alienor was preparing to leave the palace to go in procession to Westminster Abbey, Henry exploded, raging at his brother-in-law, "You wickedly and secretly defiled my sister and, when I discovered this, I gave her to you, against my will, to avoid scandal." He accused Simon of bribing the Pope to secure the dispensation releasing Eleanor from her vow of chastity, and hit a tender spot, because there is ample evidence that Simon's conscience plagued him over the breaking of that vow. Henry also castigated Simon for naming him as a guarantor without his permission and ordered him and Eleanor not to enter the abbey. The couple remonstrated and pleaded, but in vain. At length, they returned to the palace of the bishops of Winchester at Southwark, which the King had lent them.

The altercation cast a shadow over the lavish churching ceremony. The abbey was ablaze with the 500 tapers that had been lit around St. Edward's shrine for the occasion, and echoed to the sound of the "*Laudes Regiae*," which dated from the coronation of the Emperor Charlemagne in 800 and had first been sung in England at the crowning of the Conqueror's Queen, Matilda of Flanders, in 1068. Alms were distributed and a great feast was held in celebration, with musicians playing.

The rift between Henry and Simon did not heal. Henry sent his officers to force Simon and Eleanor to vacate the Bishop's palace and banned them from the court. Simon vowed vengeance on the Queen, whom he believed had poisoned Henry's mind against him. Henry ordered Simon's arrest and would have sent him to the Tower if Richard of Cornwall had not intervened. It was enough to make Simon and Eleanor flee England for France.

In November 1239, Henry was so distressed to learn that William of Savoy had died—possibly from poison—in Italy that he ripped off his clothes and threw them in the fire. In 1240, therefore, he was pleased to welcome again to England Alienor's uncle, Thomas, Count of Savoy, and his brother, Boniface, Bishop of Belley in Burgundy, a man "of lofty stature and handsome figure." During their short visits, they were lavishly entertained, the King having made the Jews foot the bill. Missing the counsel of the late Bishop William, Henry wanted Thomas to stay as his replacement, but Thomas had obligations abroad. When he went back to Savoy, he carried with him an open invitation from the King to his kinsmen, urging them to come to England.

On September 29, 1240, Queen Alienor gave birth to a daughter at Windsor Castle. The infant was baptized Margaret for St. Margaret, whose aid the Queen had invoked during her labor. Henry was so overjoyed that he gave gold to his wife and their new baby. At Alienor's churching, the *"Laudes Regiae"* was again sung and the King donated a candlestick to Westminster Abbey,[14] in which Alienor placed the large candle she had carried at the ceremony.

Margaret was sent to join her brother Edward at Windsor, where Henry now extended the nursery range; in time, it would occupy three sides of the courtyard containing Alienor's herb garden. The state apartments now stand on the site of the thirteenth-century nurseries and the grand staircase rises on the site of the herb garden. By 1265, the children's household probably numbered thirty people, including their keeper, four ladies, a chaplain, a clerk, six yeomen, a cook and a laundress.

The King continued to honor Alienor's family. In April 1240, at her request, he had granted her uncle, Peter of Savoy, the honor, or lands, of the earldom of Richmond, Yorkshire, and invited him to come to England. He was not given the title of earl, although he was often called "Earl of Richmond." In December, Peter arrived—and stayed, "as he perceived that it was such a profitable country."[15] He was possibly Alienor's favorite uncle, and one of the ablest. He was then thirty-eight, and had once nearly entered the Church, having been appointed a canon at Valence and Lausanne; but, being more of a soldier than a priest, and being greedy for territory, he had resigned and married an heiress.

Peter was a prudent and proud man, "discreet and circumspect,"[16] and brave as a lion. Skilled in war and diplomacy, and a fine administrator, he would inherit the mantle of William of Savoy, becoming one of Henry and Alienor's most loyal and trusted advisers and the leader of the Savoyard faction at court. In January 1241, the King knighted him in Westminster Abbey and hosted a lavish banquet in his honor.

Peter was aware that the English barons resented the favor the King showed him; they called him "Little Charlemagne" because of his perceived empire-building. He persuaded Henry to let him leave England, but Henry lured him back by appointing him warden of the Cinque Ports and granting him the castle and honor of Pevensey and custody of the late Earl of Surrey's lands.

Working with the Queen to increase her influence and political power as mother of the heir, Peter and his brothers encouraged her to surround the Lord Edward with Savoyards and use her maternal role to advantage. Bernard of Savoy, who was probably the bastard son of the Queen's grandfather, Thomas, Count of Savoy, would be appointed constable of Windsor Castle in 1244, and his nephew, Stephen de Satenay, was put in command of the Windsor garrison. Alienor also appointed a Savoyard clerk to control access to her son.

At Christmas 1240, the King gave Alienor, "our dearly beloved Queen," a "cup of pure gold." It was a last-minute purchase, made on December 19, suggesting a typical lack of forethought on the part of an otherwise thoughtful husband. A total of 500 bulls, 80 pigs, 58 boars (then being hunted to extinction), 40 roe deer, 1,500 lambs, 200 kids, 1,000 hares, 500 rabbits, 7,000 hens, 1,100 partridges, 100 peacocks, 20 swans, 20 herons and bitterns and over 50 cranes were slaughtered for the Yuletide feast that year.

On the death of Edmund Rich, Archbishop of Canterbury, the previous November. Alienor had taken it "upon herself, for no other reason than his relationship to her," to write to the Pope recommending as his replacement her uncle, Boniface of Savoy, whom Matthew Paris thought "notable for his birth rather than his brains" and who, "in learning, manners and years," was "an unsuitable candidate." The Pope, "when he had read the letter, thought it proper to name this man, who had been chosen by a woman; and it was commonly said that he was chosen by female intrigue."[17] On February 1, 1241, Henry III formally nominated the absent Boniface to the see of Canterbury and, that same day, the clergy chose him "as shepherd of their souls."[18]

4

"Most Impious Jezebel"

✠

Lthough the French held part of Poitou, the English were still claiming the whole county as theirs by right. In his will, Louis VIII had asked that his son Alphonse be named count of Poitou, yet Isabella was determined that the title should go to her own son, Richard of Cornwall, who was then away on crusade. However, in June 1241, when Alphonse came of age, Louis IX formally invested him with the county of Poitou in a splendid ceremony at Saumur. In July, he summoned the Poitevin nobility to Poitiers to pay homage to their new count. Hugh had to attend as count of Angoulême and a resentful Isabella went with him, simmering because she believed her son had been slighted. Unknown to either Hugh or Isabella, Queen Blanche, mistrusting their loyalty, had appointed a spy, a burgher of La Rochelle whom they knew well, to keep an eye on them. His report survives in the Archives Nationales in Paris, in dense handwriting on a small piece of parchment, and gives detailed insights into the events of that summer.[1]

Hugh had become increasingly uneasy about the expansion of French power in the south, while Isabella was furious about the cool reception she received from King Louis and the Regent, who kept her waiting for three days in Poitiers before they would see her. Even then they did not rise to receive her, or speak to her, according precedence instead to Alphonse's wife and the Abbess of Fontevraud, offering them seats while Isabella was left standing. Enraged at the slight, she was pointedly absent when Hugh reluctantly paid homage to Alphonse for his lands in Poitou and when he invited King Louis, his mother and Count Alphonse to Lusignan. After they had left, she stormed into the castle of Lusignan and ordered it to be stripped bare of everything they had used during their stay: hangings, chests, stools, blankets, mattresses, altar cloths, cauldrons, ladles, ornaments and even a statue of the Virgin from the chapel. Furious with Hugh for paying homage and consorting with those who had wronged her son, she ranted that "she was a queen and she disdained to be the wife of a man who had to kneel before another."

Hugh observed that, if she had ransacked Lusignan to furnish the castle of Angoulême, she might have spared herself the pains, for he would gladly have bought her as much and more.

"Get out of my sight, wretch!" she hissed. "You are a base knave and a disgrace to your people!"

The French spy recounted how she had everything loaded on to carts and taken to Angoulême, where she had the gates barred against her husband. Hugh arrived two days later to find himself locked out and was obliged to spend three nights at a nearby hostel run by the Knights Templar. Repeatedly, he sent messages and gifts to Isabella, begging to be admitted to the castle, but she continued to rage against him. In the end, she relented, but when they came face to face, she burst into tears of rage.

"Wretch!" she stormed. "Did you not see at Poitiers how they kept me waiting for three days, to the delight of the King and Queen? How, when I was at last received by them in the chamber where the King sat, he did not call me to his side, did not bid me sit next to him? It was done by spite, to disgrace me before our own people! There I was, kept standing like a kitchen wench! They rose for me neither when I came nor when I departed. I forbear to say more—the shame and despair are stifling me, even more than their forwardness in stealing my lands! I shall die of it— of rage—if God does not make them suffer for it! They shall lose their lands, or else I shall lose all I have and die of it, to boot!"

Hugh was "distracted." He knew there were only two options: either they swallowed their pride and welcomed the French—or they rebelled.

"Command me, lady!" he muttered. "I will do all in my power, you know it well."

"If you do not, you will never lie by my side again!" Isabella ranted. "I will not suffer you in my sight." Nor would she leave the castle until Hugh had sworn to ask Henry to join him in a push to drive the French out of Poitou. Hugh gave way and assembled his forces.

This quarrel, of course, was reported to Queen Blanche by her spy. Matthew Paris's account corroborates that report and makes it clear that it was Isabella who incited Hugh to rebel against King Louis.

That summer saw Isabella pursuing her vendetta against the French King. To win them to her side, she did the Poitevin lords "great honour, more than was her wont, for she loved them not." Many declared for Hugh, and secret meetings were held at Parthenay, but Isabella feared that a large convention of barons might attract attention, so she summoned them to the castle of Angoulême, unaware that the spy in her household was reporting all her moves to his masters. There, the lords swore to rise against the French at the first opportunity. Hugh and Isabella had been thorough in raising support: backing them were the Emperor Frederick II, James I, King of Aragon, the Duke of Brittany and Raymond VII of Toulouse. Another secret conclave took place at Pons, where the lords and chief officers of Gascony joined the rebels, which they would not have done without Henry III's sanction.

On December 11, 1241, Henry's treasurer delivered to Hugh and Isabella "certain writings of covenants between the King and them."[2] By the middle of December, Isabella and the Seneschal of Gascony had persuaded Henry openly to ally with her and Hugh, and aid them in conquering French Poitou, on the pretext that, in creating Alphonse count of Poitou, Louis had broken his alliance with England. Eager to recover his lost domain, Henry agreed, ignoring his barons' disapproval, for Hugh had assured him that the Poitevin and Gascon lords, the Count of Toulouse and the King of Navarre would support the invasion.

Hugh decided to besiege La Rochelle and block the road from Niort, to prevent supplies from reaching the French. Attempts by King Louis and Queen Blanche to settle the Lusignans' grievances by diplomatic means foundered. At Alphonse's Christmas court at Poitiers, Hugh and Isabella announced that they were withdrawing their allegiance because they considered him to be a usurper. Hugh told Alphonse, "I declare and swear to you that I will never make nor observe any bond of allegiance to you, injurious man that you are, who have shamelessly taken away his county from my son-in-law [sic] Richard while he was faithfully fighting for God in the Holy Land." Alphonse's crossbowmen angrily raised their weapons, but Hugh "boldly burst through the midst of them," with Isabella following. The couple set fire to the lodging that had been assigned them and, accompanied by their men-at-arms, rode through the night toward Lusignan.

Since 1237, meetings of the Great Council had been known as parliaments, from the French *parler*, meaning "to talk." In January 1242, the first real English Parliament—effectively a Great Council of magnates—was summoned, and the King proposed an invasion of France, but the barons would not support it, castigating the Lusignans and telling him, "You have, to your peril, put too much faith in, and have promised your presence in person to those notorious nobles [who] ought not to be trusted, as they are noted for manifold treachery." In a bullish mood, they granted Henry a pittance in taxes, forcing him to practice economies.

For the rest of Henry's long reign, parliaments would usually be held at least once a year. They would not incorporate a wider representation of the people for some years, but the consultative nature of them was increasingly emphasized.

The King now had to summon his feudal levies by imposing fines and taxing the Jews, and managed to raise a formidable army. At Easter, Louis summoned his barons for war.

On April 5, Henry issued a charter providing for Alienor to receive a reasonable dower if he died fighting the French. On April 14, he purchased gold to make a zone, or girdle, for "our beloved Queen," and paid for the redemption of a clasp, an alb and a stole, which had been offered in Westminster Abbey "for the oblations of our Queen."[3]

Like the barons, Alienor objected to Henry going to war, but for a different reason. She feared that, if he was killed, Richard of Cornwall, who had rebelled against Henry three times, might try to seize the crown, so she enlisted the support and protection of her uncles for her son. Henry himself was determined to secure the Lord Edward's smooth succession and commanded that, if he himself died during the campaign, the strategic castles on the Welsh marches were to be delivered to the Queen for the use of their son. In April, the custodians of the castles of Dover and Kenilworth were ordered to surrender them "to no one but the King and, in the case of the King's death, to no one but Alienor the Queen and, if Alienor cannot come personally to receive it, then to no one but one of her uncles."[4] Thanks to Alienor's maneuvering, Richard was not to be regent or guardian of the prince; she herself would head the regency.

Richard was angered at being ousted, but Henry and Alienor had found a way to mollify him. His first wife, Isabella, the daughter of William the Marshal, having died in 1240, he had been smitten with the beauty of Alienor's sister Sanchia when visiting Provence on his return from the Holy Land. Henry and Alienor were aware of this and confident that, if Richard married Sanchia, his interests would naturally become linked to those of the Queen's party. He would be bound to support Henry's policies. Alienor pushed for the match, envisaging not only the neutralizing of her perceived enemy, but also having the company of her sister in England. Henry proposed the marriage to Richard, who was keen, but demanded a large dowry, which Alienor persuaded Henry to pay.

In the spring, Peter of Savoy and Peter of Aigueblanche were sent to Provence to broker the marriage. The contract would be signed on July 17, when the proxy wedding took place at Tarascon, but the war with France would render it too dangerous for Sanchia to journey to England.

Henry had now completed his preparations for the invasion of Poitou. On May 9, accompanied by a heavily pregnant Alienor, Richard of Cornwall and a large retinue, he sailed from Portsmouth, arriving at Royan in Gascony eleven days later. Isabella, now fifty-three, was waiting at the quayside and kissed Henry "very sweetly" as he disembarked.

"Fair son," she said, "you have a great heart, who come to send succour to your mother, whom the sons of Spanish Blanche would vilely trample beneath their feet. But now, please God, it shall not be as they intend." Hugh stepped forward and gave Henry what the King later described as "the kiss of Judas."[5]

Henry sent Alienor to the safety of La Réole, thirty-seven miles southeast of Bordeaux, to bear her child while he fought the French. Hugh had promised to bring as many soldiers as Henry could wish for, counting on the support of his Poitevin allies, who were "all eager to face the King of France."[6] But Henry was appalled to discover that their combined forces numbered only about 30,000. Louis had raised 50,000 men and had already quelled the rebellion in Poitou.

Henry did not lack courage, but he had no great ability for war, as events would prove. In May, when Louis and Alphonse invaded La Marche, he advanced into French Poitou, but then hastened south to be with Alienor, who had fallen ill and, fearing capture by Gascon rebels, had had to flee La Réole and seek the greater safety of Bordeaux, where her welcome was no less chilly. As Simon de Montfort later recalled in a letter to Henry, the Gascons "did not have mercy on the Queen in her pregnancy, when she was lying ill at La Réole, and when she was delivered at Bordeaux." Henry's presence calmed the situation. The Queen's child, who was born on June 25, was baptized Beatrice. Her father called her "Beautiful B."

The King's extravagant celebrations to mark the birth of his daughter delayed his departure for Poitou, which proved disastrous, as town after town was falling to Louis. Finally, on July 21, the armies met at Taillebourg, where Louis set a trap and Henry and Hugh rushed headlong into a crushing defeat. Henry was only narrowly saved from capture by the heroism of his brother Richard, who dressed up as a pilgrim, crossed the French lines and negotiated with Louis a one-day truce that gave Henry time to retreat to Saintes. But Louis came after him and took Saintonge, obliging him once more to flee ignominiously, as his Poitevin supporters fell away. Simon de Montfort was appalled. "You should be taken and locked up!" he raged at the King.

Inevitably, there were further recriminations. The Poitevins abandoned Henry, Henry's angry barons went home, full of contempt for his poor military showing, and Louis never forgave the Lusignans for their treachery. "There was La Marche's folly most rife, who madly dashed his forces against the King; thus did he so he might beguile his wife, whose rashness never willed a rasher thing."[7] Hugh castigated Henry for running away, whereupon Henry complained that Hugh had not brought as large a force as he had promised. Matthew Paris reported a conversation that took place between them in July, when Henry asked Hugh, "What of your promise? Did you not send us impassioned pleas, begging me to come here? Were you not to bring us as many soldiers as we could wish for, all eager to face the King of France?"

"I never said that," Hugh declared.

"I have your writing to that effect here with my chamberlain," Henry said.

"I neither wrote nor signed it," Hugh insisted.

"What's this?" Henry flared. "Did you not send me messengers and letters till I was weary of them, all beseeching me to return hither and chiding me for my delay? Where are these men you promised?"

"I never did any such thing," Hugh replied. "God's body, blame my wife, your mother! By the threat of God, I am guiltless of her machinations!"

With that, they fell out, Henry fled to Bordeaux and Alienor, "who honoured him"[8] despite his defeat, while Hugh and Isabella speedily switched their allegiance back to Louis, deeming it the safest course, and sued for peace. They sent their eldest son, Hugh, ahead to Poitiers as a hostage to their good intentions, then followed with their other children. On July 26, the whole family knelt before Louis and "cried him mercy with many sighs and tears. The King, seeing the Count, his wife and children, on their knees before him, so humbly crying him mercy, forgave him all,"[9] on condition that they did homage to Alphonse for Lusignan, La Marche and Angoulême. Nevertheless, he withdrew their pensions, installed French garrisons in those castles, and insisted they give up their claim to Saintes and join forces with him to do battle with Henry.

Louis's pardon left Hugh and Isabella much the poorer, and their domains more vulnerable to French expansion. Isabella's reputation was in the dust. She was vilified by the French for inciting the rebellion, and blamed by the Poitevins and the English for its collapse.

In gratitude to Richard for rescuing him at Taillebourg, Henry promised him the lieutenancy of Gascony, but Alienor had long wanted it for the Lord Edward and persuaded Henry to rescind the grant and bestow the revenues of Gascony on their son. When Henry demanded that Richard renounce all claim to Gascony in exchange for estates worth £500 (£365,000) yearly, there was a heated quarrel, during which he threatened his brother with imprisonment. Tempers cooled, but Richard remained resentful and, in September, sailed back to England.

That month, having failed in another bid to reconquer French Poitou, Henry made a five-year truce with Louis—who laid down moderate terms on account of their wives being sisters—and embarked on a month of entertainments in Bordeaux, where he and Alienor remained for the next year, earning the criticism of Matthew Paris for dallying abroad when they were needed in England. But Henry was deploying his time usefully, doing his best to suppress unrest and win the loyalty of his Gascon barons. The most powerful of them, Gaston de Béarn, was Alienor's cousin. It was she who persuaded him to swear fealty to Henry.

Hugh and Isabella were seething at their defeat and humiliation. It was now clear that Henry III would never recover French Poitou, and that it might yet be overrun by Louis. The couple resolved on a preemptive strike and began to plot treason.

Late in 1242, a French knight accused Hugh of having paid two serfs to assassinate King Louis and Count Alphonse, promising them riches in return. The serfs managed to infiltrate themselves into the royal kitchens, where they were seen "throwing venom into the King's meats" and instantly apprehended. Apparently, they had also considered stabbing the royal brothers with a poniard. The attempt had very nearly succeeded.

Under interrogation, one of the would-be assassins confessed that he had tried to kill the King at Isabella's instigation, and that she personally had given him the poison to put in Louis's dish or cup. Louis had the two serfs executed and decided to proceed against the Lusignans. A congress—a court of investigation—was set up on the borders of Poitou, and the King laid before local magistrates proofs of the treason of Hugh and Isabella, believing that Hugh was the mastermind behind the attempt.

"The tidings came to the Countess [Isabella] that the two knaves had been seized in their wicked act and hanged. She was so wroth that she took up a knife and would have struck herself, but that her people took it from her. And when she saw that she could not have her will, she rent her wimple and her hair, and was so downcast that she took to her bed and remained long uncomforted."[10]

Isabella was praying that her queenly rank would protect her from receiving common justice, so when she was summoned to appear before the court, she showed herself highly affronted. She went, nevertheless, taking a large retinue, but was not allowed to enter the building because evidence was being laid. Furious, she remained seated on her horse outside the door, refusing to budge until the sight of one of the witnesses who had betrayed her, coming to give testimony, struck fear into her, and with good reason. Attempted regicide was regarded as the most heinous of crimes, since it attacked the monarch's divine right. In France, those found guilty of it were tortured, then torn apart by four horses. That had been the penalty meted out to Brunhilde, a seventh-century Frankish queen accused of regicide; it would be imposed again in the sixteenth century, and in 1610, when Henry IV was assassinated. Fearing that she was doomed, Isabella galloped away in fear.

She was still at liberty early in 1243, but living in terror of being dragged off to the court. Concerned for her children's future security, she urged Henry to renounce to her and Hugh all his claims on Angoulême, to which he agreed. Thereupon, in March 1243, Isabella and Hugh divided their lands among their children.

It was not long before Isabella's fear of arrest forced her to abandon her husband and her second family. "Bethinking herself of her many misdeeds, she fled to the sanctuary of the abbey of Fontevraud." There, "she did conceal herself in a secret cell, clad in the religious habit, finding herself even there in scant safety, for many of the French and, indeed, the Poitevins, pursued her with implacable hatred, asserting that she should be called not Isabelle, but most impious Jezebel, for having sowed the seeds of many crimes, considering her as the origin of the disastrous war with France."[11] The secret cell was in the guest house and was used for sick or impenitent visitors, but it was within the grounds of the abbey, which offered sanctuary to those in need of it. Here, Isabella "lived at her ease."

"The whole brunt of this disgraceful business fell upon her unfortunate husband and son. They were seized and about to be tried on this accusation of poisoning, when the Count of La Marche offered to prove in combat with his accuser, Alphonse, that his wife was belied."[12] In other words, the allegations against Isabella had been false. This was in the summer of 1243. Hugh's son offered to fight Alphonse instead, but Alphonse refused to engage with either of them because of the infamy of the Lusignans. "Evil tidings hasten fast," and the matter "reached the ears of Isabella in the secret chamber of Fontevraud."[13] It was at this point that she took the veil and "eked out her existence as a nun."[14]

It is hard to imagine that she was driven to do so by piety; her dark, feisty, dictatorial character was ill-suited to the obedience of the cloister. It seems that keeping herself safe was her imperative, more important to her than husband, children, wealth or status.

She remained immured in her hidden chamber for three years, dying there on June 4, 1246. Wishing to make atonement for her sins, she gave orders that her body be buried in the common grave of the nuns, a site now occupied by the Salle Capitulaire, or Chapter House. In her will, she left £1,000 (£730,000) to the abbey, of which £100 (£73,000) was to fund a chantry priest to say masses for her soul and the mending of the nuns' clothes. She left Queenhithe to Richard of Cornwall, who gave it to the citizens of London, although Queen Alienor continued to collect taxes on goods loaded there.

On June 2, 1246, Isabella had written to Louis IX, asking him to permit her sons by Hugh to take possession of her domains. She was succeeded as countess of Angoulême by the eldest, Hugh. Her husband outlived her, dying in 1249. Their son, Hugh XI, would be killed in 1250, fighting in Egypt during the Seventh Crusade, and was to be succeeded by his son, Hugh XII.

Isabella had been the unwitting catalyst for the loss of Normandy and a constant thorn in the side of the English Crown for the best part of three decades. Her defection to the French had caused untold trouble for her eldest son. Yet Henry III dutifully ordered his court into mourning for several weeks and founded chantries for his mother at Westminster, Malmesbury and St. Thomas's Hospital, Marlborough. He ordered the friars of Oxford to perform obsequies for her and funded a feast for them and the poor scholars of Oxford and Cambridge. In 1250 and 1251, he requested all the abbots and priors throughout Normandy "to inscribe the day of the death of the King's mother in their martyrology and cause Masses to be celebrated and prayers to be made for her soul, especially on her anniversary."[15]

Under the terms of the humiliating truce Henry had made with Louis in April 1243, the French were to have all Poitou and some towns in Gascony. It was now safe for Alienor's sister Sanchia to set out for England, and it was decided that their mother, their sister Beatrice and their uncle, Philip of Savoy, would accompany her. When the bridal party reached Bordeaux, they met up with the King and Queen, and spent the summer there with them. Alienor was unwell in the early autumn, so Henry returned to England ahead of her on September 25 to order preparations for Richard and Sanchia's wedding. At his command, every house between St. Paul's Cathedral and Westminster Abbey was hung with tapestry, red cloth and cloth of gold for his reception, even though he was not exactly returning in glory.

On November 14, 1243, the ship carrying Alienor, Sanchia, Beatrice and the Countess of Provence docked at Dover, where Richard was waiting to greet them. During her visit, the Countess Beatrice brought about a reconciliation between the King and Simon de Montfort, for which Henry increased her annual pension and also gave her a costly gold eagle, the emblem of the House of Savoy.

On November 23, 1243, Richard and Sanchia were married at Westminster Abbey. Henry, Alienor, the Countess of Provence and her daughter Beatrice attended and were present afterward at the gargantuan banquet in the "house of Almayne," which Richard of Cornwall had built in the northern area of the palace precinct. "Worldly pomp, and every kind of vanity and glory, was displayed in the gleemen [minstrels], the variety of their garments, the number of dishes and the multitude of feasters."[16] Thirty thousand dishes are said to have been served. Thomas of Savoy, Count of Flanders, had come to England for the wedding, bringing with him a bolt of luxury fabric for his sister and her daughters, from which gowns trimmed with squirrel were made up at the King's expense.

After the wedding, Henry confirmed Richard in the earldom of Cornwall and granted him the honors of Wallingford and Eye. In return, Richard renounced all claim on Gascony.

Not familiar with the name Sanchia, the people of England called the new Countess of Provence "Cynthia." Matthew Paris wrote of her "pleasant looks." As Alienor had hoped, Richard's marriage bound him even more closely to the court party, but, predictably, it was not popular. "The whole community in England, taking it ill, began to fear that the whole business of the kingdom would be disposed of at the will of the Queen and her sister, who would be, as it were, a second queen."[17] But Sanchia, who was shy and reticent, did not have the temperament to push herself forward.

The King and Queen spent Christmas at Richard's castle of Wallingford, where they were feasted by the newly married couple. Alienor's mother and her sister Beatrice were present too. Early in 1244, the Countess departed for Provence. She took with her a loan of 4,000 marks (about £1,960,000) from Henry, which would enable Ramon to fight his wars;

against this, she had pledged as security Tarascon and four other Provençal castles, which would be reserved for the use of the King and Queen of England. Matthew Paris described how "the King and a large number of the magnates of the realm accompanied [Beatrice] to the coast. But, before the Countess could board her ships at Dover, messengers reached her with the dreadful news of the illness unto death of her husband, Count Ramon. When the King heard this, he grieved inconsolably." Alienor must have been equally distressed to hear of her father's illness. He was only thirty-nine.

She may have received some comfort when, in February 1244, Boniface of Savoy, Archbishop of Canterbury, made his second visit to England to receive the temporalities of his see. He would be consecrated on January 15, 1245, but he was in England only infrequently until 1256, preferring to carry out his duties as commander of the Papal guard in Rome, and would not be enthroned at Canterbury until 1249.

That February, Boniface passed over the King's candidate, Robert Passelewe, for the vacant bishopric of Chichester, approving the election of a more holy and scholarly clergyman, Richard Wych. Henry was outraged and forbade Wych to carry out his episcopal duties. Alienor took a diplomatic approach, writing to her husband:

> Most excellent, most revered King Henry, by the grace of God, the illustrious King of England [etc.], his own consort, the most humble and devoted Alienor, by the same grace of God Queen of England, greetings and obedient duty with all reverence.
>
> We inform your lordship that, by the grace of God, we and our children are safe and well, which we lovingly hope you are also, with all our heart and soul. We also inform your royal Majesty that, a day past, the Archbishop of Canterbury informed us by letter that he had learned by the reports of some people that we were angry with him because of what he had done in the matter of the diocese of Chichester. He begged that we would not be upset over this matter, nor be turned against him. We, in turn, informed him that it was not surprising if we were turned against him, since he offended you in this matter, and he could in no way have our good wishes while he incurred your wrath.
>
> Having heard and learned this, he came to us in person, signifying to us that, in the aforementioned and all other matters, he would fulfil

your wishes to the best of his powers. We advised him that, if he wanted
to assuage our indignation, then he would fulfil your wishes. For while
you and he remained in discord, there was no way we would forego our
own anger and indignation. Therefore, we beseech your most excellent
lordship, with all possible affection, that you will deign to inform us
often, if you so wish, of your state (pray God it be well and happy) and
of what pleases your will. May your Excellency prosper forever in the
name of the Lord.[18]

Alienor also told Henry that Passelewe knew nothing of theology and
that it was felt that his severity in enforcing the forest laws rendered him
unsuitable for promotion to a bishopric. His talents would better serve
the King in his present capacity. Henry allowed himself to be persuaded.

Boniface was later to be called the most hated man in England. Matthew Paris reviled him for his foreign interests and neglect of his flock.
When Boniface traveled to make visitations or collect his dues, he did so
wearing chain mail under his episcopal vestments and took with him an
intimidating band of ruffians. Even Alienor thought him too quarrelsome. Against all expectations, however, and in spite of his overbearing
manner, he proved to be a capable, reforming primate of England.

In August 1244, the Lady Margaret, aged four, was betrothed to Alexander, the three-year-old heir of the King of Scots. The marriage was arranged to bring about a peace between England and Scotland, who had
been at bitter odds for so long. To celebrate the betrothal, Henry instructed his servants that, "upon Friday next after the Epiphany, they
should cause to be fed in the great hall at Westminster, at a good fire, all
the poor and needy children that could be found; and, the King's children being weighed and measured, their weight and measure to be distributed for their good estate" in coins of silver. On another occasion, he
had the combined weight of his children given in silver to the needy people of Windsor.

When Joan, Countess of Flanders, the wife of Thomas of Savoy, died
in December 1244, Thomas could no longer claim to be count of Flanders and took up permanent residence in England, hoping for rich
bounty from his niece's husband, who obligingly granted him and his
brother Amadeus pensions.

Alienor was then in the late stage of her fourth pregnancy. Henry was desperate for another boy and had a thousand candles lit at the shrines of St. Thomas and St. Augustine in Canterbury for her safe delivery. He also promised the Abbot of St. Edmundsbury that, if God sent him a son, he would name him after the martyr St. Edmund, England's then patron saint, to whom he had a deep devotion.

The Abbot of Westminster lent Alienor one of his abbey's most sacred relics, the girdle of the Virgin, which was believed to ease the pains of childbirth. On January 16, 1245, as Henry afterward related to the Abbot of St. Edmundsbury, "when our beloved consort, Alienor, our Queen, was labouring in the pains of childbirth, we had the antiphon of St. Edmund chanted for her. When the following prayer was not yet finished, the bearer of our present letter, our valet, Stephen de Salines, came to tell us the news that our Queen had borne us a son. So that you may have the greater joy of this news, we have arranged for it to be told you by Stephen himself."[19] At the baptism, when "the King, in his joy, bestowed the name Edmund" on his son, he offered an embroidered chasuble at the high altar of Westminster Abbey; another was made from the christening robe. Alienor was churched to the familiar strains of the "Laudes Regiae."

That year, Henry began rebuilding Westminster Abbey, a project most dear to his heart. It was already established as the coronation church of English sovereigns, and his intent was to build a beautiful new shrine for the relics of Edward the Confessor in a magnificent Gothic setting that reflected the glory of God and the best that medieval craftsmen could produce. Around that time, Queen Alienor was presented with a manuscript, La Estoire de Seint Aedward le Rei (The Story of St. Edward the King), written by Matthew Paris and dedicated to her. It was a somewhat embellished account in Norman French of the Confessor's life, epitomizing the cult of the royal saint as observed at court.

In the 1230s, Henry and Alienor had separately voiced a wish to be buried in the Temple Church in London, but, in October 1246, due to his increasing devotion to St. Edward, the King expressed his intention to be buried in Westminster Abbey, which he confirmed in his will of 1253. His plan was to establish Westminster as a royal mausoleum, where he and his descendants could lie for eternity in close proximity to the sainted Edward. Alienor made known her wish to be buried with him.

* * *

On August 19, 1245, Alienor's father, Count Ramon, died. Henry, who was campaigning in Wales when the news reached him, attended a requiem mass, "at the same time strictly forbidding everyone from announcing this event to the Queen, his wife, lest she be overcome with grief."[20] He felt that he should be the one to break the news to her on his return.

Grief may have been superseded by anger for, in his will of 1238, Ramon had left Marguerite and Alienor their dowries of 10,000 marks (£4,900,000) each, while Sanchia and Beatrice were each to receive half that amount—and Beatrice, Ramon's favorite child, got Provence. "Daughter," he had written in a last letter to her, "you have always been the most loving of all your sisters to me. I know that, by God's will, all my daughters save only you have been married nobly and been exalted in the eyes of all Christendom. To you, therefore, I give and leave in my will all my lands, treasures, castles and possessions. For your sisters are not poor and I have made provision for them elsewhere."[21] On his death, Beatrice became countess of Provence.

Henry and Alienor were naturally unhappy about the settlement, for co-heiresses normally received equal shares of an inheritance. In this case, the three eldest sisters did not receive the money bequeathed to them. Furthermore, five of the castles that had been left to Beatrice were in fact Henry's, loaned as security for the debt Ramon had not repaid, but "the King did not meet with compassion or condolence from anyone on account of this loss or disgrace."[22] Marguerite was the most unhappy because, as the eldest sister, she regarded Provence as hers by right, if anyone was having priority. King Louis backed her, being determined to secure Provence for France. In December, he successfully intrigued with Beatrice of Savoy, Archbishop Boniface, Philip of Savoy and even Pope Innocent IV to marry Beatrice to his younger brother, Charles, Count of Anjou. It appears that Henry and Alienor knew nothing of this scheme, or of Boniface's collusion. It was agreed that if Beatrice died, Sanchia would inherit Provence, bypassing Marguerite and Alienor. When he found out, Henry III protested to the Pope, but in vain. Marguerite, Alienor and Sanchia, aggrieved though they were, had no choice but to agree and settle for money paid by Charles in lieu of their rights to the succession of Provence.

On January 31, 1246, Beatrice's marriage took place at Aix-en-Provence and Charles assumed the title of count of Provence in right of his wife, taking over the rule of Provence and establishing a French court there. Alienor, Marguerite and their mother, who quickly regretted sanctioning the alliance, never liked or trusted Charles and collaborated in various fruitless schemes to unseat him. Henry was put out because his mother-in-law had given the French sixteen castles he had been maintaining at great cost. When word of his displeasure reached the Countess Beatrice, she retorted that her only regret was to have handed over her daughters to the English.

Around this time, at the Queen's petition, Henry gave land on the Strand to Peter of Savoy. Peter built a house on the site, which came to be known as the Savoy Palace. It is his golden statue that graces the present-day Savoy Hotel, which stands on the site.

5

"The Scum of Foreigners"

✠

HENRY REASSIGNED ISABELLA'S DOWER LANDS TO ALIENOR, who was at last in full possession of her dower. She handed much of her newfound wealth to her relatives, lavishing large sums on her mother. Even the King was annoyed at that, especially when it was discovered that money paid to the Countess Beatrice over the past five years had been diverted to Charles, Count of Anjou. When word of this seeped out, Alienor became even more unpopular.

On June 17, 1246, Henry, Alienor, the Lord Edward and Richard of Cornwall witnessed the dedication of Beaulieu Abbey, Hampshire, where Richard's first wife, Isabella Marshal, was buried. Afterward, Edward became very ill and lay sick at the abbey for three weeks. A distraught Alienor sent for three doctors, paid for medicines, and refused to leave her son, remaining a constant presence by his bed until he was better. This shocked the Cistercian monks, for it contravened their rule to have a woman in their infirmary nursing a patient; they felt so strongly that they deposed the Prior and the cellarer for allowing it.

In 1246, the French finally conquered English-held Poitou, which left the Lusignans dispossessed. In 1247, at Hugh's behest, Henry invited his half-siblings, Aymer de Valence, Guy, seigneur of Cognac, Geoffrey, seigneur of Jarnac, William de Valence and Alice to his court "to enrich themselves as plentifully as possible with the delights and wealth of England." "The lord King went to meet these brothers and his sister with great joy. With a fatherly embrace, he promised them handsome gifts and ample possessions, and this he fulfilled even more abundantly than he had promised,"[1] showering them with favors, high offices, estates, pensions and honors, just as he had done for the Savoyards, although his affection for his half-siblings went deeper.

The Lusignans were proud, grasping, combative and lawless. "No Englishman could get his right or obtain a writ against them." Aymer was illiterate and worldly, but Henry secured for him a prebend in London. He gave the rapacious William de Valence a rich heiress in marriage, making him lord (later earl) of Pembroke. In August 1247, Henry married Alice de Lusignan to John de Warenne, Earl of Surrey, a match that aroused the resentment of the English nobility, especially since Alice looked down on the English, whose language none of the Lusignans spoke.

Within a short time of their arrival in England, the Lusignans, especially William, had established themselves as rivals to the Savoyard party. Alienor and Peter of Savoy bitterly resented them as rivals for the King's bounty and did their utmost to have them expelled. Alienor was greedy for wardships and other benefits for herself and her Savoyards and was jealous when Henry gave them to his half-brothers. For their part, the Lusignans were resentful of the Queen because she controlled public moneys and had allied the Savoyards with the Lord Edward, rendering them almost invincible. She continued zealously to advance, enrich and favor the Savoyards, determined to counteract the threat from Henry's half-siblings.

Henry's favoritism toward the Lusignans aroused the disgust of his barons, who were already aggrieved about the advancement of the Queen's kinsmen and resented his preferment of foreigners above his own nobility. They regarded the Lusignans as rapacious parasites.

In May 1247, Henry and Alienor received Peter of Savoy at Woodstock. Peter had been abroad since the previous year, when he had persuaded his brother, Amadeus, Count of Savoy, to acknowledge Henry III as his overlord. When he arrived at Woodstock, he brought with him, to the barons' disgust, "some unknown ladies for the purpose of giving them in marriage to the nobles of England."[2] One was the Queen's cousin,

Alasia of Saluzzo, who was married that May, at Woodstock, to Edmund de Lacy, son of the Earl of Lincoln; another, Alice, was wed to Richard de Burgh, son of the lord of Connaught.

In the next decade or so, Alienor would procure aristocratic English marriages for four more of her kinsfolk. The King saw them as a means of securing the loyalty of the barons, but they "were evidently annoying and unpleasant to many of the nobles of England, who considered that they were despised,"[3] for they wanted to secure noble heirs for their own daughters. Matthew Paris castigated the King for intermingling "the noble blood of Englishmen with the scum of foreigners." Much of the blame was heaped on the Queen.

The early months of 1248 found King Louis preparing for a crusade, for the Ayyubid Muslims had seized Jerusalem. Hearing that Louis was raising a great army to recapture it, Henry III was eager to join him, and take Alienor with him, since Marguerite was going with Louis. But Gascony was seething in turmoil and strife. Anarchy prevailed, as Gaston de Béarn rebelled repeatedly against English rule. In May 1248, Simon de Montfort was appointed the King's lieutenant in Gascony, demanding seven years, men and money to quell the broiling unrest in the duchy. But his rule proved to be harsh, and alienated many more Gascon lords, forcing him to employ bands of armed mercenaries to keep order.

In December 1248, Stephen de Charron, Prior of Thetford, "a Savoyard by birth, who declared himself to be a relation or kinsman of the Queen and had assumed airs of pride from that circumstance, invited his brothers to come to his house at Thetford." There, during a night of carousing, he quarreled with a monk, who stabbed him "without the least hesitation at perpetrating such a crime within the precincts of a church." As the Prior lay dying, "the monk again rushed upon him, and with heavy blows buried the knife up to the handle in his lifeless body." Alienor was outraged at the murder of her kinsman, and "the King, worried by the continual complaints of the Queen, ordered the murderer to be chained and, after being deprived of his eyes, to be thrown into the lowest dungeon in the castle of Norwich."[4]

* * *

Impoverished by his extravagance, Henry and Alienor could not afford the usual lavish court festivities, so they kept the Christmas of 1248 in the City of London, extorting gifts worth 2,000 marks (£980,000) from the citizens. In 1249, Henry arranged for the Queen and the Lord Edward to dine with the merchants of London, making the merchants pay for the honor. Alienor even took her relatives along. There was much resentment at this, and anger that the King had repeatedly circumvented Magna Carta, but there was no effective opposition, for the barons and clergy were too busy quarreling among themselves.

On April 17, Henry issued a charter providing that, in the event of his death, Queen Alienor was to be "guardian of the King's heir and land during his minority."[5] That year, Peter of Savoy was given the keepership of the Lord Edward's lands. In September, as Alienor had wished, Henry bestowed the duchy of Gascony on his son, who was now ten. Real authority in Gascony lay in the hands of Simon de Montfort, but he was still struggling to control the persistent unrest there.

Around October 1249, the King petitioned Pope Innocent IV to confirm the validity of his marriage to Alienor. It seems that he was concerned that, because of his uncanonical union with Joan of Ponthieu, the legitimacy of his children might be queried when he negotiated marriages for them. The Pope agreed to an inquiry "for the honour of the King and his children so that nothing can be imputed against them on this score in the future."[6] In March 1252, he issued a Papal bull confirming the marriage.

In 1250, still desperate for money, the King and Queen began to practice economies. They ceased making grants and donations, coerced visitors to court to extract loans from them, reduced their servants' remuneration, ceased wearing their royal robes and daily invited themselves and the Lord Edward to dinner with barons or rich Londoners. Henry's frugality did not extend to his building works. In 1250, he ordered that a new range of state lodgings be built in the Lower Ward at Windsor for himself and Alienor, at a cost of £10,000 (£7,300,000). A lawn was created between these apartments and the splendid new chapel Henry built. Both ranges were ruined in a fire in 1296, but part, and the lawn, survives in the Dean's Cloister, as does a splendid scarlet gesso door adorned with gilded ironwork at the east end of St. George's Chapel; it once led to Henry's chapel.

Henry III did not persecute the Jews. It was his mission to convert them, while milking them for money. But, needing cash, "the King extorted from the most unfortunate Jews a heavy ransom in gold and silver, becoming, from a king, a new kind of tax gatherer."[7] Alienor, whose father had respected and employed Jews, seems to have had an ambivalent attitude toward them that hardened into anti-Semitism as she grew older. She did take at least one Jewish family under her protection, and granted them privileges, but she was also accused of extorting money from Jews, above the queen-gold she received from the punitive fines Henry imposed on them. In 1251, for example, the King took "inestimable sums of money from all rich men, namely of Aaron, a Jew, born at York, 14,000 marks [over £6,860,000] for himself and 10,000 marks [£4,900,000] for the Queen."[8]

In March 1250, Henry took the cross from Archbishop Boniface. As he began preparing for the crusade, enthusiasm for the venture swept through the court. In May, the King instructed the Master of the Temple to lend Alienor a copy of the Chanson d'Antioche, a French history of the crusades, which so captivated her that she had Rosamund's old chamber at Winchester painted with the story of Antioch and Richard I fighting Saladin. Similar Antioch murals were executed in her chambers at Westminster and at Clarendon.

Henry II's former hunting lodge at Clarendon had become one of the more important royal residences. Alienor's chapel there contained stained-glass windows portraying "Mary with her Child, and a queen at [her] feet, with clasped hands holding a label, Ave Maria." In 1251, stone reliefs of the twelve months of the year were installed in Alienor's hall above the fireplace. An almost intact tiled floor from her chamber was uncovered during excavations on the site and is now in the British Museum.

Zeal for the crusade faltered when Louis's army was annihilated in battle and he was taken prisoner. He was soon ransomed, and spent the rest of his time in the Holy Land establishing Acre as the Christian capital.

* * *

On November 4, 1250, thanks to heavy pressure from the King, Aymer de Valence was made bishop-elect of Winchester. Henry hoped he would "illuminate this church, like the sun, with rays of his regal generosity, which distinguished him on his mother's side."[9] In this, Aymer singularly failed. He was the most unpopular of the foreign favorites, and he and his brother William soon fell out with their rival, Archbishop Boniface.

Early in 1251, having received bitter complaints from Gascony about the rule of Simon de Montfort, the King sent royal commissioners to the duchy to resolve the ongoing disputes between Simon and Gaston de Béarn. Alienor had urged Henry to support Simon, but the King heeded the complaints of the local seigneurs and called for an inquiry into his brother-in-law's rule.

Soon after midnight on St. Dunstan's Day (May 19) 1251, Alienor was in her apartments at Windsor when "all the world, as it seemed, became black, and thunder was heard as if a long way off, with flashes going before. And, about the first hour, the thunder coming nearer, with the lightnings, one stroke, more dreadful than the rest, as if the Heaven were hurling itself upon the Earth, transformed with fear the ears and hearts of those hearing it with its sudden crash upon the bedchamber of the Queen, where she was then abiding with the children and her household, and crumbled the chimney to powder, cast it to the ground and shook the whole house. And, in the adjoining forest of Windsor, it overthrew, or tore asunder, thirty-five oak trees."[10] Alienor and her children had had a miraculous escape, after what must have been a terrifying experience. Her lodging was rebuilt in 1256–61, with marble pillars and a wainscot painted green with gold stars.

At Christmas 1251, the King and Queen kept great state at York with ten-year-old Alexander III, King of Scots, who had succeeded his father in 1249. Henry spent £65 18s. 4d. (over £48,000) on jewels alone for the occasion. On Christmas Day, he knighted Alexander in York Minster. On December 26 Alexander and the Lady Margaret, aged eleven, were married. Because there had been fighting in the streets between English and

Scots, the King ordered that the wedding take place early in the morning while few people were abroad.

Henry had invited the Archbishop of York to officiate. To his dismay, the Archbishop found that he was also expected to contribute to the cost of the feast that followed, for which he, the citizens of York and local lords provided 200 deer, 300 does, 200 bucks, 300 boars and 60 fat oxen, while the King's fishermen brought 230 fish. Henry and Alienor wore robes of samite embroidered in gold and ermine cloaks, and Alienor sported a veil of silk called a *cointoise*, which trailed before and behind her. The following day, she and her ladies wore even more costly robes of a new pattern, leading Matthew Paris to liken them to "magpies and peacocks who delight in feathers of various colours." This latest fashion, imported from the Continent, was the cyclas, a rectangle of rich material that had an opening for the head and hung full-length over the gown in the front, with a train at the back.

The wedding was marred by a very public row between the King and Simon de Montfort, who had come to England to demand that Henry reimburse him for the upkeep of the royal castles in Gascony. Relations between the two men were already fraught because of Henry having ordered the inquiry into Simon's rule. He refused Simon's demand but, in January 1252, after he had threatened to transfer ownership of the castles, Alienor persuaded him to pay Simon what he owed him.

At that time, Henry's commissioners returned from Gascony. Their report acquitted Simon of malpractice, but the duchy was in revolt against his rule and the King refused to let him return to quell it. He continued to question Simon's financial dealings and demanded that he defend himself before the royal council at Westminster. Simon complied, only to have Henry publicly censure him.

"Who can believe that you are a Christian?" Simon raged at him. Had Alienor not interceded, backed by Peter of Savoy, the King would have punished him harshly.

On February 25, at Reading, she summoned Adam Marsh, who was friends with the Montforts, to join discussions "concerning the business of the lord King and his heirs."[11] Marsh saw Simon and his wife at Odiham Castle and Bromhall, after which Simon, accompanied by Peter of Savoy, visited the Queen at Windsor. By March, thanks to Marsh's good offices, Henry and Simon had reached an agreement of sorts over the

Gascon finances, and a truce had been concluded with the seigneurs, but Simon felt angry and humiliated. He resigned his office to the Lord Edward and went to France, leaving his pregnant wife behind. Alienor sent Adam Marsh to mollify Richard of Cornwall over the appointment of her son as lieutenant of Gascony, an office he had evidently hoped to occupy himself.

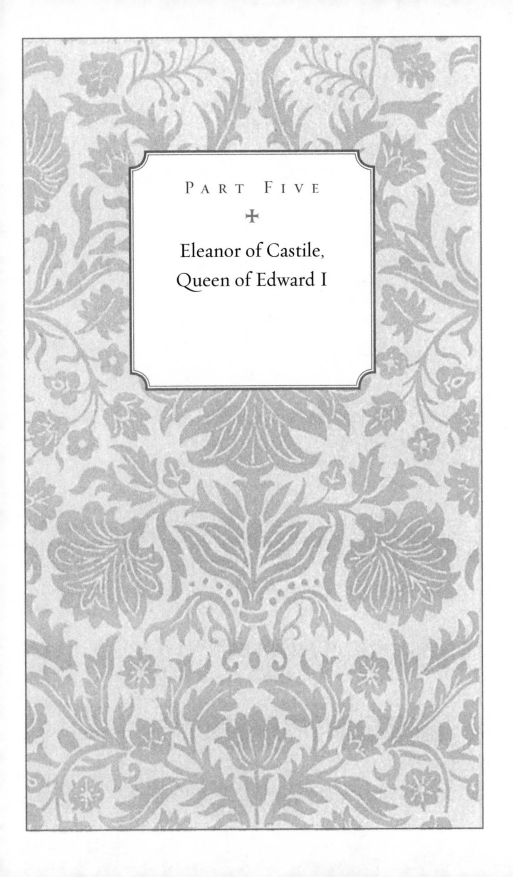

PART FIVE

✠

Eleanor of Castile,
Queen of Edward I

"Prudence and Beauty"

✠

FOR A YEAR FROM JULY 1252, ALIENOR SPENT MOST OF HER TIME at Windsor with her growing family. Edward was now thirteen, Beatrice ten and Edmund seven. She bought shoes for them all, gowns for Beatrice, tunics for the boys and a silk tabard for Edward, as well as hawking gloves for herself and Beatrice. Hawks were essential symbols of rank, and royal children were taught falconry from the age of eight. In 1253, Alienor gave Edward and Beatrice brooches to present to their nurses and to Edmund of Cornwall, Richard and Sanchia's four-year-old son. When Edmund was ill at Windsor that year, three of the Queen's doctors attended him and his mother bought him penides, sticks of boiled sugar used to treat colds and other ailments.

Alienor had become close to her sister-in-law, Eleanor de Montfort. Evidently the tensions between their husbands did not impinge too greatly on their friendship, probably because the bond between them was far from political. One Easter, Adam Marsh suggested that the two women meet "to treat earnestly of the salvation of souls."[1] In September 1252, when Eleanor was pregnant, the Queen sent a messenger to find out if she was keeping well. When, at Michaelmas, Eleanor bore a daughter, Alienor rewarded the messenger with 40s. (£1,460) and sent one of her own children's nurses to attend her sister-in-law at Kenilworth and take her a gift of a jewel. The baby was baptized Eleanor. In November, from Winchester, Alienor sent another messenger to Kenilworth, and the two women stayed in touch well into the new year. In December, the Queen sent the Countess another jewel. She also sent gifts of jewelry to

Eleanor's damsel, knights and ladies who were closely associated with the Montforts.

Henry and Alienor had had their differences, but, in 1252, they had a serious falling-out. Ten years earlier, the Queen had been granted the wardship of the lands of Roger de Tosny, lord of Flamstead, but not his privilege to present candidates to church livings on his estates. In 1251, however, "confident in her right,"[2] Alienor had installed her chaplain, William de London, in the church of Flamstead, a benefice in Tosny's gift, whereupon the King dismissed William, replacing him in December 1251 with a trusted royal clerk. In March 1252, discovering that William de London was still in the post, a furious Henry ordered the Sheriff of Hertford to remove him, and dismissed him from the Queen's household. "Glowing with anger," the King chastised the Queen, asking, "How high does the arrogance of woman rise if it is not restrained?"[3] Alienor was indignant, and her friend, Robert Grosseteste, Bishop of Lincoln, backed her, excommunicating the King's clerk and placing the church at Flamstead under an interdict.

The case went to court the following August. It was startling for the King's subjects to see him and the Queen battling it out in public. Henry marshaled twenty-one lawyers to defend his rights, but Alienor won, and William de London was restored to his benefice, which led to a coldness between the royal couple. Adam Marsh's letters reveal that both Alienor and Eleanor de Montfort made efforts toward a reconciliation.

That autumn, Archbishop Boniface quarreled with the King's half-brother, Bishop Aymer, over which of them had the right to appoint a new prior to the hospital of St. Thomas at Southwark. Aymer had ensured the election of his own candidate when Boniface went overseas, but the Archbishop's officer, Eustace de Lenn, excommunicated the new Prior on the grounds that Boniface had not confirmed the appointment, and imprisoned him in the Archbishop's palace at Maidstone. Not to be bested, Aymer's brother, William de Valence, sent men-at-arms to release him. They sacked and burned the palace, took Eustace captive, roughed him up and abandoned him in the countryside.

The quarrel highlighted the rivalry between the factions. Alienor and Peter of Savoy were furious with Aymer, but Henry needed both the Lusignans and the Savoyards to counter the growing hostility of Simon de Montfort and the barons, and was resolved to deal with each side equitably. On November 4, when Alienor took Boniface's part, the King reacted angrily, depriving her of control of her lands and her right to queen-gold, and sending her away to Guildford, and thence to Winchester, ahead of the court moving there for Christmas.

On his return later that month, Archbishop Boniface was so enraged at what had happened that, with his Provençal clergy in train, he forced his way into St. Thomas's hospital and assaulted the hapless sub-prior, calling him a traitor, which sparked an unholy brawl between the Archbishop's Savoyard attendants and the monks. But, when the latter complained to the King, Henry refused to take action against Boniface. Boniface excommunicated Bishop Aymer, who promptly had the ban declared null. Henry asked Peter of Savoy to intervene, but he refused and was expelled briefly from court. It looked as if the friends of the King and the Queen would soon come out in open conflict.

Alienor's banishment lasted fifteen days, during which she was obliged twice to ask Henry for money. She stayed in touch with Boniface and Peter, and sent a message of support to Eustace de Lenn. By November 18, in the interests of making peace between the warring factions, Henry had summoned her to join him at Clarendon; he restored her queen-gold ten days later, and they spent Christmas together at Winchester.

As Henry had wished, Alienor worked to reconcile Archbishop Boniface to Bishop Aymer and smooth relations between the rival factions. At New Year, when she distributed gifts, she gave decorated belts to William de Valence and Geoffrey de Lusignan, and herself received gold plate from Aymer. Her gift to the King was a crystal goblet; he gave her a jeweled girdle. By January 1253, when he took her to Westminster for the feast of St. Edward and afterward to Windsor, good relations had been restored.

Around late February or early March, Alienor conceived a child. It has been suggested that this marked a reconciliation between her and Henry after a long estrangement, inferred from the assumption that they had had no children for eight years. Yet it is often stated that, between 1247 and 1260, Alienor bore Henry four sons, Richard, John, William and Henry. All were said to have been buried in Westminster Abbey, save Henry, who was interred in the Temple Church in London. Their names,

dates and places of burial are listed in early-fourteenth-century insertions in the *Flores Historiarum*, a chronicle that covers the period from the
Creation up to 1326. These insertions were made by a monk of Westminster, which lends them some authenticity, for he would surely have
known who was buried there and whose obits were being commemorated.

Yet the existence of these sons has been questioned by modern historians for, whereas the births, lives and deaths of Henry and Alienor's
other children were extensively documented, there is no mention of these
four boys in any contemporary source apart from the *Flores*. Around the
times they were said to have died, Henry and Alienor displayed no signs
of grief or mourning. Furthermore, in three of his works, Matthew Paris
lists Henry's children as Edward, Edmund, Margaret, Beatrice and Katherine. He does not mention any others. In the "Genealogical Chronicle
Roll of the English Kings" (Royal MS. 14 B VI), drawn up in the early
1270s and now in the British Library, Katherine is shown posthumously
with Edward, Edmund, Margaret and Beatrice. Yet her supposed brothers, who would surely have merited greater prominence because they
were male, are absent.

Documentation for the births and deaths of short-lived royal children
is often missing from the records. It could be that Richard, John, William
and Henry died at birth or too young to merit a mention. After bearing
four children in six years, it would make sense that Alienor bore four
more in the eight years between 1245 and 1253. If, however, the four
younger sons are spurious, we might wonder why there was a gap of eight
years between children. Although it has been conjectured that there was
a long estrangement between the royal couple, sparked by Alienor's opposition to the Lusignans, during those eight years they fell out on just
four occasions, which does not suggest a prolonged breach serious
enough to stop them sleeping together. If Alienor did not bear those four
sons, she may have suffered unrecorded miscarriages or stillbirths.

Given the specific information in the *Flores Historiarum*, it is possible
that Richard, John, William and Henry were short-lived sons who escaped mention by the chroniclers. The staff of the royal nursery had increased to thirty by 1265, long after Henry's older children had left it,
and when only one royal infant (a daughter of the Lord Edward) occu-

pied it, which suggests that more staff had been engaged in the 1250s to look after Henry's younger sons.

Some years earlier, when a fire at Westminster Palace destroyed the original copy of Magna Carta, Alienor had foolishly supposed it was null and void. On May 13, 1253, needing the cooperation of his magnates in raising taxes, Henry was forced to renew the charter when the barons and bishops gathered around him in Westminster Hall, each holding a lighted taper, and Archbishop Boniface called down the wrath of heaven on anyone who did not uphold its provisions. Then the lords raised their hands and cast their tapers to the floor, plunging the hall into darkness, that the souls of those who flouted Magna Carta "thus be extinguished and stink and smoke in hell." Thoroughly intimidated, Henry readily swore to uphold the charter as "a man, as a Christian, a knight and a king crowned and anointed."

By 1253, Gascony was in a state of anarchy. The previous year, after Simon de Montfort retired to France, some Gascon lords had asked Alfonso X of Castile to press his claim to the duchy, with a view to ousting Simon—and Alfonso decided to take advantage of the situation. Late in 1252, to Henry's alarm, he had laid claim to Gascony, on legally dubious grounds, and taken homage from Gaston and other Gascon seigneurs. In fact, Alfonso's claim dated from 1204, when his grandfather, Alfonso VIII, had invaded Gascony on the highly unlikely pretext that Henry II had pledged it to him on his marriage to his daughter Leonor. But there was no mention of this in her marriage treaty.

Henry III considered declaring war, but opted instead for a peaceful solution, possibly on the advice of his trusted secretary, John Maunsel, who may have suggested pursuing a match between the Lord Edward, who was approaching fourteen, and Alfonso's sister Eleanor, which offered a means of preventing the loss of Gascony. Convinced of the wisdom of this, Henry acted swiftly.

Eleanor was the only daughter among the six children of the saintly Ferdinand III, a great-grandson of Eleanor of Aquitaine, by his second wife,

Joan, Countess of Ponthieu and Montreuil—that same Joan whose hand Henry III had tried to win in 1235. We know that Eleanor had been born in 1241 because, on the first anniversary of her death, forty-nine candle-bearers walked in the obit procession, one for each year of her life. Her parents were apart for the thirteen months prior to Ferdinand's return from a campaign in Andalucia in February 1241, so Eleanor must have been born late that year, in November or December.

At the time of her birth, King Ferdinand established his seat of government in Andalucia in southern Spain. She grew up in a court renowned for its literary excellence and was probably tutored by Dominican friars, for whose order she had a special reverence, for St. Dominic had been born in Castile in 1170; he was canonized in 1234. Under the friars' guidance, Eleanor learned literacy skills, read histories and classical works and imbibed ideals of charity and personal devotion to Christ.

On August 5, 1250, at King Ferdinand's behest, Pope Innocent IV issued a dispensation permitting Eleanor to be married to anyone related to her within the fourth degree of consanguinity. In May 1252, aged just ten, she was present when her father died at Seville and her half-brother, Alfonso X, succeeded. Now thirty-one, he was the oldest of Ferdinand's ten children by his first wife, Elisabeth of Hohenstaufen. Like Sancho of Navarre, he became known as "the Wise" and presided over a court of rich cultural diversity. He was interested in science, astrology, music and poetry, and was a great legislator.

Immediately after Alfonso's accession, Henry III proposed a marriage between the thirteen-year-old Lord Edward and Eleanor, who had remained at Seville with her mother. In May 1252, he sent John Maunsel and the Bishop of Bath to Castile to negotiate the marriage and an advantageous peace treaty. Alfonso was amenable, but insisted that Henry give Edward lands worth a hefty £10,000 (£7,300,000) annually and that Eleanor be handsomely dowered, although he offered no dowry with her; instead, he agreed that, if the marriage went ahead, he would cease to press his claim to Gascony, which would save the English Crown the vast outlay needed to defend it. Henry accepted these terms.

With the situation in Gascony still critical and Gaston de Béarn still in revolt, the King had resolved to go there himself and rule from Bordeaux. On June 1, he made his will, demonstrating the trust he placed in Alienor: "I commit the guardianship of Edward, my eldest son and heir, and of my other children, and of my kingdom of England and all my other lands, to my illustrious Queen, Alienor, until they arrive at full age." He again instructed that he was to be buried in Westminster Abbey.

On June 2, 1253, the King asked the Scottish guardians of the realm if Queen Margaret might visit her mother and stay with her until Alienor's child was born, since she would need "some grain of consolation" when he had gone overseas, but the guardians refused. Since her arrival in Scotland in 1252, the young Queen Margaret had been virtually their prisoner, isolated from her husband and swept up in the quarrels that blighted his minority. Alienor had sent go-betweens to Scotland to report on Margaret's welfare, and rewarded them handsomely for their services, but she and Henry had been unable to ameliorate their daughter's situation. The problem would have to be shelved for now.

On June 22, Henry entrusted his Great Seal to Alienor's keeping, warning that decrees issued under any other seal would be null and void. On July 3, "the King committed the governance of the realm of England and the lands of Wales and Ireland to Queen Alienor, with the counsel of his brother, Richard, Earl of Cornwall, until his return from Gascony."[4] There was no love lost between them: Richard was still resentful about being deprived of the lieutenancy of Gascony, and Alienor was bent on thwarting his acquisitive demands for land.

That same day, a mandate was issued to all justices, sheriffs, constables and bailiffs "to be intendant to Queen Alienor during the King's absence in Gascony, and, if the lot of humanity falls to the King in Gascony, to deliver the castles, lands etc. to the Queen for her to keep to the use of Edward, the King's son."[5] Henry made arrangements for her to receive land worth £200 (£146,000) yearly "for the maintenance of her chamber"[6] and 60 tuns of wine and venison from the Great Park at Windsor, where Eleanor de Montfort visited her that summer. On July 7, the King formally appointed Alienor regent.

On July 8, 1253, Theobald I of Navarre died and was succeeded by his fourteen-year-old son, Theobald II. Immediately, Alfonso of Castile claimed suzerainty over Navarre, which would leave him ideally placed to overrun Gascony, and pressed Theobald to wed his sister, seeing this as a far more advantageous alliance than one with England. But the Queen of

Navarre declared that her son would never marry Eleanor of Castile and turned to Aragon for support against Alfonso's ambitions.

On August 6, 1253, Henry sailed from Portsmouth. "The young Edward, after his father had many times embraced and kissed him, stood crying and sobbing on the shore."[7] Apart from not wishing to be separated from the King, Edward must have felt frustrated at not being permitted to go with him and share in the rule of his own duchy.

In Henry's absence, the Queen delegated much of the routine administration of government to the Chancellor, reserving the more important business to herself. She was no figurehead. She sat as judge in the King's court. Pleas were held before her in council and in the court of the Exchequer. Letters patent were issued in her name or jointly with Richard. She received embassies. She controlled the royal finances with the aid of the barons. She paid a bribe from her own revenues to keep the French out of the war. To finance Henry's campaign, she zealously exacted queengold on all moneys paid to him and imposed heavy taxes and fines on the citizens of London. She borrowed from Florentine bankers and Jews and tried to wrest funds from the barons. From Gascony, Henry ordered all those English lords who had failed to raise their feudal levies to account for themselves before the Queen. In short, Alienor functioned highly effectively as a regent, ruling England for nine months with Richard as her adviser and a council to assist her.

On October 13, at the King's behest, she observed the feast of St. Edward at Westminster, with great ceremony. On November 25, she bore her child at Westminster. The King afterward rewarded her yeoman, William de Valers, with an annuity of £15 (£11,000) "for the happy report he brought to Gascony of the birth of a fair daughter called Katherine"[8] because she was born on St. Katherine's Day. The name was new to the Plantagenet family, but widely favored at that time, for the virgin martyr St. Katherine of Alexandria was a popular saint, revered for her purity and learning. Like the royal chapels at Ludgershall and Nottingham, Alienor's chapels at Clarendon and Guildford were dedicated to St. Katherine, suggesting that she had a particular devotion to the saint. On the day of her birth, Katherine was christened with great pomp by Archbishop Boniface.

Alienor rose "safely from childbed."[9] Government did not stop for childbirth, and she was attending to business from the day her daughter arrived.

Throughout the autumn of 1253, Henry had been enmeshed in difficulties with Gaston de Béarn, who was encouraging King Alfonso in his territorial ambitions, while Alfonso was still threatening Gascony and undermining its stability. Another embassy to Castile to negotiate a peace and a marriage had failed to achieve any success. In December, the King sent a request for aid against Alfonso to Alienor and Richard, ordering them to raise troops and money to aid his war in Gascony, and to appeal to the King of Scots. At the end of December, in the King's name, they pressed Alexander III's guardians to summon his magnates and bishops to Edinburgh Castle to hear the King's messenger plead for aid and counsel. Predictably, the Scots refused, but they did acknowledge the rightness of the King's cause.

On December 27, Alienor and Richard summoned Parliament, and two knights from each shire were called to Westminster to act on behalf of those they represented. Thus, Alienor deserves the credit for making one of the earliest moves toward democracy in England. Parliament met in January, but, because the King's emissaries were delayed, it had to be adjourned. Before it rose, the Queen managed to obtain pledges for aid from the barons.

She had sent Henry some troops, but raising the money he needed was proving difficult, so she forwarded 500 marks (£245,000) from her private coffers as a New Year gift. Finding that the queen-gold she had demanded on fines imposed on the citizens of London by the King had not been paid, she had two of the sheriffs committed to the Marshalsea prison. It was pointed out that she had no right to claim the tax, since queen-gold was payable only on voluntary fines. The sheriffs were released, but were again imprisoned later that year, along with the Mayor, for failing to pay the increased taxes levied in support of the King. Alienor also ordered that all ships docking in the port of London were to use her dock and pay handsomely for the privilege. These exactions made her even more unpopular with the citizens of London.

She was planning to join Henry in Bordeaux. On January 30, 1254, at

Westminster, she issued a royal writ to the barons of the Cinque Ports: "The King is in great need of his magnates of England and is therefore sending to arrest all ships ready for the crossing of the Queen, Edward, the King's son, and Richard, Earl of Cornwall" for their "coming to him in Gascony."[10]

On February 6, she went to her churching at Westminster, after which she presided over a lavish feast, which she had arranged herself. On April 2, Henry would command his treasurer to acquire "five handsome swaddling bands" of cloth of gold "and have them sewn together, and a handsome border fastened around them, with shields of the King's arms, so that the King may find them ready the next time he comes to London. They are to be offered at Westminster for Katherine, the King's daughter, in the manner in which he has formerly been accustomed to offer for each of his children."[11]

On February 11, 1254, Alienor and Richard summoned another Parliament, which was to meet after Easter in London. Two days later, they wrote to the King from Windsor:

> We had been treating with your prelates and the magnates of your kingdom of England about your subsidy, and the archbishops and bishops answered us that, if the King of Castile should come against you in Gascony, each of them will assist you [with money raised] from his own property, so that you will be under perpetual obligations to them; but, with regard to granting you an aid from their clergy, they could do nothing without the assent of the clergy; nor do they believe that that clergy can be induced to give you any help, unless the tenth of clerical goods granted to you for the first year of the crusade might be relaxed at once by your letters patent; and they will treat with the clergy to induce them to assist you with a tenth of their benefices, in case the King of Castile should attack you in Gascony. But, at the departure of the bearer of these presents, no subsidy had as yet been granted by the clergy.
>
> Moreover, if the King of Castile should come against you in Gascony, all the earls and barons of your kingdom who are able to cross the sea will come to you in Gascony with all their power. But, from the other laymen who do not sail over to you, we do not think that we can obtain any help for your use, unless you write to your lieutenants in

England firmly to maintain your great charters of liberties, and to let this be publicly proclaimed through each county, since, by this means, they would be more strongly animated cheerfully to grant you aid. For many persons complain that the charters are not kept by your sheriffs and bailiffs as they ought to be kept.

Be it known, therefore, to your lordship, that we shall hold a conference with the clergy and laity at Westminster about the aid, and we supplicate to your lordship that you will write us your good pleasure concerning these affairs with the utmost possible haste. For you will find us prepared and devoted, according to our power, to solicit the aid for your use and to do and procure all other things which can contribute to your convenience and the increase of your honour.

Urged by the King and Queen, Simon de Montfort had joined Henry in Gascony and offered his support. His presence was so intimidating to the rebels that many decided it was prudent to offer their allegiance to the King. By February, Henry had managed to calm the disturbances, and Alfonso had been diverted from his purpose by a rebellion at home, led by his brother Enrique. On February 11, John Maunsel and Peter of Aigueblanche were again sent to Castile, carrying peace proposals that were finally acceptable to Alfonso, although he insisted that, before the marriage of Edward and Eleanor went ahead, Henry must settle on Edward estates worth 15,000 marks (£7,350,000) and furnish Eleanor with a suitable dower. In March, Alienor would arrange for the conveyance of the lands awarded to her son.

On February 14, 1254, "mainly because of the Queen's insistence,"[12] Henry created the Lord Edward duke of Gascony and earl of Chester and granted him large estates in England, Wales, Ireland and Gascony, with the income Alfonso had demanded, a settlement that "mutilated" the King.[13] Henry now sought the advice of Joan of Ponthieu, the widowed Queen of Castile, over arrangements for the marriage of her daughter, while Alienor, anticipating that she would soon be traveling to Castile for her son's marriage, ordered the fitting-out of 300 ships.

Early in 1254, Pope Innocent IV wrote to Henry III offering him the kingdom of Sicily for his ten-year-old son, Edmund, to be held as a Papal fief.

The nominal ruler of Sicily, of whom the Pope was guardian, was an infant, Conradin of Hohenstaufen, grandson of the Emperor Frederick II, but there had long been conflict between the Papacy and the Hohenstaufens, whom the Pope regarded as usurpers in Sicily. Alienor desperately wanted a crown for her younger son, but the price would be a crippling 135,541 marks (£66,415,090), which Innocent needed to pay his debts. Nevertheless, in March, Henry accepted, promising to pay this exorbitant sum. His subjects were horrified, and the barons refused to sanction any grant of taxation to support the "Sicilian business," as they called it, foreseeing that Henry's championing of the Pope against the family of the Holy Roman Emperor would involve him in costly foreign wars that would bring no benefit to England.

Alienor made strenuous efforts behind the scenes, marshaling her countrymen to make the dream of Edmund's kingship become reality. The Papal chaplain who acted as negotiator was a Savoyard associate of Peter of Savoy, and the Queen's uncles, Peter, Philip and Thomas, were among the nine proctors appointed to ensure Edmund's smooth succession, as was Peter of Aigueblanche. Thomas of Savoy was especially active in working with Alienor to secure Sicily for Edmund and, in 1255, she, in return, would impoverish herself, Henry and Archbishop Boniface to support Thomas's ambitions in northern Italy. Her determination only served to unite Henry's opponents and made her even more hated.

On May 14, 1254, the Pope confirmed Edmund as king of Sicily. A week later, Conradin died, and his bastard uncle, Manfred of Hohenstaufen, refused to surrender Sicily to the Papacy and set himself up as regent. Months of conflict followed, but, by December, Manfred had firmly entrenched himself as ruler of Sicily. Alienor's dreams of a crown for Edmund now seemed hopeless, yet she would not relinquish them. She and Innocent's successor, Alexander IV, were bent on war, for different reasons, but the Pope ordered that King Henry fund it out of the crusading tax imposed on the English clergy. Predictably, that was not popular.

When Parliament met after Easter 1254, it refused to grant the King any aid because Simon de Montfort, just back in England, had assured the assembly that there was now no threat from Gascony. Alfonso had realized that he could not win the duchy and that he needed the friendship of England. Even so, Henry believed that Edward's marriage to Eleanor was a necessity, and the only way of protecting Gascony, should Alfonso have second thoughts.

Quelling the unrest in Gascony had left the monarchy impoverished. While Henry pawned some of his treasures to pay his soldiers and his debts, Alienor was forced to raise loans from Richard of Cornwall and foreign merchants.

On April 1, a treaty providing for the marriage of the Lord Edward to Eleanor of Castile was signed at Toledo. Under its terms, Alfonso renounced all claims to Gascony and confirmed Edward's right to inherit Ponthieu and Montreuil from Eleanor's mother. In turn, Henry promised to assist Alfonso in his conflict with Navarre and to ask the Pope to commute his vow to go on crusade to Jerusalem, so that he could join Alfonso on a crusade in Africa. This doubtless raised some eyebrows at Westminster, and few can have believed that Henry really meant to fulfil this obligation. Alfonso demanded that he knight Edward himself so that he could see that he was "worthy in mind and body" of Eleanor, and sent him a safe-conduct to travel to Castile. Edward, for his part, undertook to marry Eleanor and dower her well.

In England, the Castilian marriage was deeply unpopular. After experiencing an influx of the parasitic relations of two queens, the King's subjects had come to detest foreigners and feared that this new royal bride would be no different from her predecessors.

In April 1254, Henry commanded Alienor to bring Edward to him in Bordeaux. After her departure, Richard of Cornwall was to be sole regent of England. When Parliament met at Westminster on May 4 and promised to send aid only in the unlikely event of the King of Castile invading Gascony, Alienor raised money for Henry by pawning the crown jewels to Richard.

On May 17, she was still at Windsor. Her departure was delayed because of a dispute between the rival fleets of Yarmouth and the Cinque Ports that had escalated into violence. The King, hearing of this, sent orders that Alienor was not to travel and threatened the barons of the Cinque Ports that, if they harmed her or interfered with her passage, he would "betake himself to the bodies of them, their wives and children, their lands and tenements, so that they shall forever feel themselves aggrieved." By the time his letter arrived, Alienor, "concealing her annoyance at these circumstances,"[14] had circumvented the dispute by refusing to use any ship from Yarmouth or the Cinque Ports.

Alienor and Richard were jointly attesting patents up until her departure on May 29, when she resigned as regent. That day, as she was about to embark at Portsmouth, the King's messenger arrived with the order forbidding her to sail. Having just addressed Henry's concerns, she ignored it and departed with her two sons, her daughter Beatrice, her sister Sanchia, Archbishop Boniface and forty knights. She took with her some of the King's treasure and the money raised from putting the crown jewels in pawn.

When she arrived in Bordeaux around June 10–11, Henry was so overjoyed to see her that he overlooked her disobedience. That week, they celebrated Edward's fifteenth birthday. On July 18, it was agreed that his marriage would take place five weeks after Michaelmas. Alfonso would knight him on October 13, the feast of St. Edward the Confessor. Before signing the betrothal contract, Edward declared that he had agreed "willingly and spontaneously" to marry Eleanor, "of whose prudence and beauty we have heard by general report."

On July 20, in Edward's name, Henry assigned to Eleanor of Castile a dower of lands, manors and castles in England and Gascony that would bring her an annual income of £1,000 (£730,000); this would increase to £1,500 (over £1,000,000) "when she is raised to be queen."

Early in August, while the King and Queen were in Bordeaux, they received a visit from the mother of the bride, Joan of Ponthieu, Queen Dowager of Castile, who was traveling north, having angered Alfonso by supporting his rebellious brother Enrique. He had banished her to Ponthieu, obliging her to miss her daughter's wedding. Henry and Eleanor were not going either. Their presence was needed to keep Gascony stable.

2

"Like Brothers and Sisters"

✠

TOWARD THE END OF SEPTEMBER, EDWARD SET OFF FOR
Castile later than expected, attended by a modest retinue, with a
journey of 290 miles ahead of him. Astrologers had predicted that the
most auspicious date for him to arrive at Burgos, the capital of Castile,
was October 5, but he did not get there until the eighteenth, too late to
be knighted on St. Edward's feast day. But Alfonso declared himself well
satisfied with his future brother-in-law and introduced him to his bride.
Eleanor was now twelve. She spoke Castilian and some French, so they
could communicate.

Little is recorded of her appearance. She was described as "fair and elegant," but there are no adulatory tributes to her beauty, and we do not
know if she was dark or blonde. Her tomb effigy (made some time after
her death by a craftsman who may never have seen her), the statues of her
on the Eleanor crosses and the one, with Edward, on Lincoln Cathedral
(the heads being Victorian restorations) are formal images of a queen,
not true likenesses; likewise the figures of Eleanor and Edward, with their
arms, on a heraldic clasp now in the Walters Art Museum at Baltimore.
Thirteenth-century corbel heads of a king and queen in the chancel of
St. Mary Magdalene's church, Whatlington, Sussex, probably represent
the couple, but these too are in no sense portraits. The head of a queen
on a fifteenth-century bell in the tower of Sundon Church, Bedfordshire,
is said to represent Eleanor. There is a nineteenth-century statue of her
on All Saints' Church at Harby. Various manuscript illustrations of her

survive, but were probably drawn by monks who had never set eyes on her and were not intending realistic portrayals.

Edward's initial opinion of his bride is not recorded. She may have found him an attractive youth. His hair, which had been silver-blond in childhood, was now much darker. He was handsome and grew to be six-feet-two-inches tall—his skeleton was measured when his tomb was opened in 1774—towering head and shoulders above the average and earning himself the nickname "Longshanks." "His brow was broad and the rest of his face regular, except that his left eyelid drooped, like his father's. His long arms were in proportion to his supple body; it was said that no man was ever endowed with greater muscular strength for wielding a sword. The length of his legs ensured that he was never dislodged from his seat by the galloping and jumping of horses."

Some found Edward intimidating. He had inherited his forceful character from his mother, and was growing up to be autocratic, short-tempered and intolerant. He could also be violent, lawless and cruel. There were tales that he and his aristocratic friends disturbed the peace of religious houses, mugged travelers and stole food from the common people. Yet his "great courage and daring" were also virtues, for he was fearless and energetic and had vision and a gift for leadership, and he was a great exponent of the cult of chivalry, with a passion for the Arthurian legends. He also had a sense of humor. Despite a lisp, he was not lacking in eloquence when persuasive arguments were needed.[1]

His great passion from his youth was for tournaments. He was "the most renowned combatant on steed"[2] and gained a reputation as "the best lance in the world." At Burgos, he excelled himself and won great acclaim at the jousts held in honor of his marriage. After these triumphs, in a splendid ceremony, King Alfonso conferred upon him the accolade of knighthood.

On November 1, 1254, Edward and Eleanor were married at the Cistercian abbey of Las Huelgas, just outside the walls of Burgos, which had been founded by Leonor of England in 1187. On the wedding day, Alfonso formally renounced all claim to Gascony. Great celebrations attended the wedding.

By November 21, the young couple was back in Bordeaux, where Edward was received "with the greatest rejoicings, as though he had been an angel of God." The King and Queen had already left to travel north toward Paris, and he would now reign in Gascony "as prince and lord,"[3] with his own establishment.

Edward and Eleanor spent most of the first year of their married life at Bordeaux. He was evidently pleased with his bride and paid her the compliment of wearing a Castilian gown and biretta when they were relaxing in private. Eleanor's household was relatively small: she had a steward, a keeper of her wardrobe, a knight, several ladies and menial servants. Her marriage brought the desired peace to Gascony, at least to begin with, although Gaston de Béarn would remain an irritant for some time to come. Eleanor's own brother, Alfonso, would threaten to invade the duchy in 1256, breaking the terms of her marriage contract, and only desisted on account of her being Edward's wife.

Henry III "had for some time felt a great longing to visit the kingdom of France and to see his brother-in-law, King Louis, and his wife's sister, Marguerite."[4] He wanted to observe the way the French dressed and behaved, and to visit the churches of the land, especially the King's splendid chapel at Paris, the Sainte-Chapelle, with its unrivaled collection of holy relics, including the crown of thorns Christ had worn on the cross. He sent envoys to Louis, who was keen to forge a rapport with him and not only granted a safe-conduct, but—at Queen Marguerite's request— invited the King and Queen to Paris, whereupon Henry "assembled his household and set off for Orléans with a noble entourage." Louis ordered all his lords and citizens in the places Henry and Alienor would visit "to clear away mud, sticks and all other eyesores and to put out as many flowers, leaves, flags and other adornments as they could, decorating the fronts of their houses and churches with garlands. They must welcome [King Henry] with respect and joy, going out to meet him in their best clothes, with bells pealing, lights and singing."[5]

On November 15, on his way north, Henry visited Fontevraud to pay his respects at the tombs of his forebears and his mother, Queen Isabella. He was appalled to find that she had been buried in a common grave. Although it was explained to him that it had been her wish to be interred there, in expiation of her sins, he had her body exhumed, himself assisting in the task, and helped to carry it to a new burial place in the church, next to the tombs of Henry II, Eleanor of Aquitaine and Richard I. He commissioned a tomb, promising to pay for it presently, "thus fulfilling the Lord's commandment, *Honour thy father and thy mother*."[6] A wooden effigy was made, smaller than the stone royal effigies at Fontevraud, and painted in bright colors. It shows Isabella in death, crowned and lying on a bier, her hands crossed piously on her breast. She wears a blue belted gown with *passements* (decorative trimmings) at the neck and wrists, a red cloak, a wimple and a chin-barbe. The face and costume were clearly inspired by the effigy of Eleanor of Aquitaine.

The Plantagenet tombs had an interesting afterlife. In 1638, they were placed side by side in a new vault in the bay at the western entry to the choir. This "King's vault" was embellished with pediments, urns, stone lions, stained glass and statues, with the kneeling figures of Joanna and Raymond VII at either end. The bones were moved when the vault was broken into in 1744 to make way for the burial of a daughter of Louis XV who died while being educated with her sisters at Fontevraud. They were reburied elsewhere in the abbey. Despite extensive searches, their location remains unknown.

In 1793, during the French Revolution, the abbey of Fontevraud was sacked and the tombs disturbed and vandalized; those of Joanna and Raymond VII were destroyed. In 1806, the abbey was converted into a prison and four remaining tombs were placed in the cellar of an outbuilding. They were still there in 1816, when Charles Stothard made drawings of them and complained that they were subject to continual vandalism by the prisoners, and that Queen Eleanor's left hand and the book it was holding were missing.

In 1846, King Louis-Philippe had the effigies brought to Versailles to be restored and repainted; they were taken back to Fontevraud in 1849. In 1866, after the British government had returned Napoleon Bonaparte's remains to France, the Emperor Napoleon III offered to send the Plantagenet effigies to Westminster Abbey. Queen Victoria initially accepted, then declined in the face of legal opposition in France.

In 1963, the prison closed, and the abbey was restored to something of its former glory, with the four tombs being placed in the south transept of the church. In the 1990s, they were moved to the choir, and remain there today. After more than 800 years, the effigies are remarkably well preserved.

* * *

On November 20, at Marmoutier, Henry and Alienor received news of their son's marriage. Henry hosted a lavish feast in the young couple's honor, which cost him a fortune. His barons were distinctly unimpressed and strongly censured him for his extravagance, but Henry was not listening.

In November, he and Alienor visited Pontigny Abbey and offered at the tomb of Archbishop Edmund Rich, who had officiated at their wedding and had been canonized in 1246. Later that month, they were at Chartres Cathedral, which afforded Henry inspiration for the design of Westminster Abbey. At Chartres, the royal couple met up with King Louis, who gave them a warm welcome. He had arranged a family reunion, bringing his wife, Marguerite, the Countess of Provence and her youngest daughter, Beatrice, Countess of Anjou, "and they all took great pleasure and comfort in greeting and talking to each other."[7] Marguerite gave Henry a basin of mother-of-pearl shaped like a peacock and inlaid with gold, silver and sapphires.

Early in December, the royal party were all together at Saint-Germain-en-Laye, whence they traveled in their own chariots to Paris. The two queens, Eleanor and Marguerite, wore robes trimmed with ermine. Their great procession, which included a thousand richly dressed knights on fine horses, was welcomed on December 9 by church bells and garlanded students singing and dancing. Louis had offered Henry the use of his palace of the Louvre or any other royal residence, but Henry chose the Old Temple, built by the Knights Templar in the twelfth century, because it was large enough to house his retinue, which appeared to the people to resemble an army.

In Paris, the four sisters were reunited when Sanchia, Countess of Cornwall, arrived. That there was rivalry between them is evident from Matthew Paris's description of Sanchia hastening to Paris with "a great and noble retinue, lest her condition should appear inferior to that of her sisters. They joined forces with mutual greetings, familiar conversation, congratulations and consoling each other. Their mother, the Countess Beatrice of Provence, was also present, an older Niobe, but extremely beautiful, gazing with fond pride upon her children. No mother in all womankind had so much reason to be proud and happy in fair and exalted offspring as she in her daughters."[8] Observing the family reunion, Louis said to Henry, "Have we not married two sisters, and our brothers the other two? All that shall be born of them, sons and daughters, shall be like brothers and sisters."[9] Indeed, it was largely thanks to these close family connections that there would be peace between England and France for the next four decades.

Henry and Alienor stayed in Paris for eight days. On the second day, he hosted a meal of meat, fish and wine for the poor people of the city. "Crowds assembled, rushing in masses and vying with one another in their endeavours to see the King of England, and his fame was carried to the skies by the French, on account of his munificent presents, his hospitality during that day, his bountiful almsgiving and select retinue, and because the King of France had married one sister and he, the King of England, another."[10]

On the third night, Henry played host to Louis, Marguerite and numerous other royal and noble guests at what was called "the feast of kings" because so many crowned heads were present. It was held in the great hall of the Old Temple and was said to outrival the feasts of King Arthur and Charlemagne. Henry insisted that Louis sit in the seat of honor at the center of the high table. It was later alleged that Marguerite, Alienor and Sanchia made Beatrice sit on a stool at their feet, a petty revenge for her having inherited Provence.

Affording eight days of talks between the two kings, this visit went a long way toward calming the political tensions between England and France. One of the benefits was the forging of a friendship between Henry and Louis, and also between Henry and Marguerite, which comes across in the letters they sent each other right up until his death. Afterward, Marguerite continued to exchange letters with her nephew, Edward.

During Henry's visit to Paris, Louis took him to see many of the city's churches and the glorious Sainte-Chapelle; according to a poem of the time, Henry so wanted the chapel that he would readily have put it in a cart and carried it away. Instead, it offered further inspiration for the building of Westminster Abbey.

Henry and Alienor's ship docked at Dover on December 27. There was resentment in England at their long sojourn in France, which was seen as an excessively prolonged pleasure trip, and grumbles at the cost of the lavish alms Henry and Alienor had distributed to the poor of Paris. It was Alienor who got most of the blame. The royal couple only made things worse when, after their state entry into London on January 27, 1255, they demanded a gift of £100 (£73,000) from the city fathers. On top of this, they fined the people of London 3,000 marks (£1,470,000) for letting a murderer escape from Newgate, and demanded that they pay 4d. (£12) a day for food for a white bear that Henry kept in the Tower menagerie. These were all measures to satisfy the creditors who were hounding the King and Queen. The cost of the Gascon campaign had been high, and the royal couple had been more than ordinarily extravagant while visiting France.

On, or shortly before, May 29, 1255, at Bordeaux, after just seven months of marriage, thirteen-year-old Eleanor of Castile bore a daughter who was at least two months premature and who died that day. Her existence is known only from an entry in Edward I's wardrobe accounts for May 29, 1287, which records that Eleanor offered a gold cloth to the church of the Dominican friars at Bordeaux to mark the anniversary of the death of her daughter. No other child of hers is known to have died on that date or been buried in Bordeaux. Given her extreme youth, the fact that she did not bear another child for at least five years, and that she thereafter conceived regularly, it is clear that Edward avoided imperiling her and the Castilian alliance by risking another pregnancy while she was still so young.

The hospital of St. Katherine by the Tower had been founded around 1148 by Matilda of Boulogne, the wife of King Stephen. She had placed it in the perpetual custody of the priory of the Holy Trinity in Aldgate, founded by Henry I's consort, Matilda of Scotland. Each succeeding queen, including Alienor, had become a patron of the hospital. In 1253, without informing her, the Prior of Holy Trinity had installed one of his own canons as master to curb the drinking and quarreling among the inmates. They appealed to the Queen, who complained to the Bishop of London. Faced with such formidable opposition, the Prior had conceded defeat, but his canons, asserting that Alienor was the King's "night bird" who exercised undue influence on him in bed, complained to the Pope, who censured her. In 1255, she tried to wrest custody of the hospital from the priory, but the court of the Exchequer ruled that the priory had established its claim.

In 1257, Alienor would again enlist the support of the Bishop of London, who removed the master appointed by the canons and ordered the Prior of Holy Trinity to refrain henceforth from interfering in the affairs of the hospital. The dispute would drag on until 1261, when the Prior made a formal surrender of the hospital to the Queen. In 1273, Alienor refounded the decayed hospital with a new charter of endowment, providing for a master, three brethren to act as chaplains, three sisters, ten poor beadswomen and six poor clerks. Her foundation still survives today, bequeathed to all her queenly successors down to Elizabeth II.

Henry III had enlarged the nearby Tower of London, building a curtain wall with defensive towers. In 1240, he had had the keep painted white, after which it was known as "the White Tower." He improved the Norman royal lodgings and built the aisled King's Hall, and the Wakefield and Lanthorne towers to provide private apartments for himself and Alienor. In 1239, her chamber was wainscoted and painted white with a design of roses of Provence and *trompe l'oeil* pointing imitating decorative stonework.

In the late summer of 1255, Henry and Alienor had concerns about two of their daughters. In August, the infant Katherine was not with her siblings at Windsor, but living at Swallowfield, Berkshire, with the kid she had been given as a pet. It is likely that she was being brought up separately because she needed special care. In 1257, Matthew Paris described her as "speechless and helpless, but very beautiful in appearance," suggesting that she was dumb and disabled in other ways.

It has been credibly suggested that Katherine developed a rare genetic disorder called Rett syndrome, which affects about one in 12,000 girls. She would have grown normally for at least six months before her development slowed down and she began to regress, losing her speech and motor function. In the final stage of the illness, she may have suffered muscle weakness and become unable to walk and totally dependent. The syndrome is caused by a mutant gene and is not inherited or passed down to future generations.

Henry and Alienor were also disturbed by reports that, in Scotland, the young King and Queen were being treated as pawns by the Earl of Menteith and the Justiciar, who were rivals for the regency, and that Menteith was keeping them captive in Edinburgh Castle, subject to the tyrannical guardianship of Robert de Ros.

An anxious Alienor sent the renowned Reginald of Bath, her physician, to Scotland to discover the true situation. He found fifteen-year-old Margaret pale, agitated, full of complaints and anxious at being "forbidden the comfort of mutual embraces" with her husband. It was afterward said that, when Reginald expressed his indignation, he was poisoned, but he was actually dying of tuberculosis. Before he succumbed to it on the way south, he wrote to the King stating that Margaret was being "unfaithfully and inhumanely treated by those unworthy Scots."[11]

Henry did not hesitate. He marched north at the head of an army, taking Alienor with him, condemning what he termed treason and vowing to aid Alexander, whom Alienor "loved like an adoptive son."[12] By the time they reached the castle at Wark-on-Tweed, Northumberland, Alienor was so alarmed for her daughter that she fell ill and there were fears for her life. Henry sent envoys to Edinburgh, who spoke with the young Queen and established that her complaints were genuine, whereupon Ros was dismissed and punished. At Henry's demand, Margaret and Alexander visited him and Alienor at Wark. When they arrived, the King and Queen saw that their daughter had grown into a young woman of great beauty and humility. Amicable talks took place and, a day later, when Alexander was taken to Roxburgh, Margaret was allowed to stay with her parents.

Henry again sent representatives to Scotland to resolve the situation and, at length, Alexander was freed, a new council of regency was established and English influence in Scotland was restored. On September 20, Henry wrote to the young King: "The Queen of Scotland is to remain with the sick Queen, her mother, his beloved consort, at Wark Castle, until the Queen is sufficiently recovered to be capable of travelling southward." Alexander's council agreed that Margaret might accompany

Alienor, on condition that she be returned to him when her mother was better. On Alienor's recovery, Margaret returned to Scotland. The King and Queen visited her and Alexander at Roxburgh, then rode south to London, visiting religious houses on the way and, according to Matthew Paris, fleecing them.

3

"The Disseminator of
All the Discord"

✠

I N THE AUTUMN OF 1255, ELEANOR OF CASTILE TRAVELED TO
England, leaving the Lord Edward in Gascony. "The King of England
gave orders that his eldest son's wife should be received with the utmost
honour and respect, especially in London, with processions, illumina-
tions, bells, singing and every conceivable demonstration of ceremonial
rejoicing."[1] But the welcome the King intended was marred before Eleanor ever set foot in England by the behavior of her half-brother, Sanchez,
Bishop-elect of Toledo, who had preceded her to negotiate a marriage
between one of his brothers and Henry's daughter Beatrice, a plan that
came to nothing. In a land seething against rapacious foreigners, the
haughty and extravagant Sanchez and his party had flung their weight
about and made themselves unpopular. Therefore, when Eleanor landed
at Dover "with great pomp and circumstance" around October 9, bringing with her a huge retinue of Castilians, she was "looked upon with
suspicion by all England."[2] It was variously rumored that these foreigners would be the latest in the procession of royal parasites, that they intended to overrun and seize the realm, or that they would press the King
to support the war to liberate the Spanish kingdoms from the Moors and
drain England dry. According to Matthew Paris, they were all adulterers,
fornicators and murderers.

At Dover, Eleanor was received by Reginald de Cobham, the castellan
of Dover Castle, where she was "lodged with honour." He had been com-

manded by the King to escort her to London, but was dismayed when he saw how badly provided for she was. For all her great retinue, she had barely anything to wear, no decent mount and no money for necessities. He immediately notified the King, who sent 100 marks (£49,000), a gift of jewels and a fine palfrey. By the time these arrived, Eleanor had reached Canterbury, where her offerings at the shrine of Thomas Becket—silken palls, a silver alms dish and two gold brooches—had also been provided by the King, as she had nothing of her own to give. Decked out in her new finery, she visited other shrines on the way to London, Henry having ordered that she be provided with more lengths of cloth of gold and silk as offerings.

He had intended that she should make her state entry into London on the feast of St. Edward, October 13, but this proved impossible because of the delay caused by providing her with a suitable wardrobe. On October 17, "the citizens of London went out to meet her dressed up in their best clothes."[3] Outside the gates of the City, Eleanor was received by King Henry, the princes of church and state, and leading citizens. Riding a new palfrey, she processed through the torchlit streets of the capital, past windows hung with painted cloth, and was greeted by church bells, songs and music. The fountains spouted wine and the windows rained gold coins. As soon as she arrived at Westminster, the King, eager for her to make her acquaintance with his favorite saint, gave her a gold clasp to offer at the Confessor's shrine and a copy of *La Estoire de Seint Aedward le Rei* in English, now owned by the University of Cambridge. She could not read it herself because she never learned English.

She stayed that night at the lodgings of Bishop Sanchez in the Temple, but soon moved into the apartments prepared for her in the Palace of Westminster by the King and Queen, who had consulted Sanchez about Castilian decor, while Alienor had appointed one of her clerks to establish a wardrobe for her daughter-in-law. Henry had expended much money and care on Eleanor's suite of rooms, and no effort had been spared to make her feel at home and well cared for. Her chambers boasted glazed windows, a raised hearth with a chimney and an adjoining oratory. She found them furnished with silken hangings and tapestries, "so that the place looked more like the inside of a church," the floors being "carpeted after the Spanish fashion"—a luxury virtually unheard of in England, where carpets were very rare and used only to cover tables. "The Spaniards had done this, perhaps following the custom of their country, but the excess of luxury caused muttering and jeering among the people,"[4] especially from those who feared an influx of Spaniards or resented the King's extravagance.

It was not a good beginning. Eleanor was unwelcome, alone in a strange and hostile land, and must have felt some trepidation. "Serious-minded folk with an eye to the future sighed inwardly, weighing up in detail the extravagant welcomes King Henry kept lavishing on so many foreigners. Everyone considered the great show put on for the benefit of the Spaniards impressive, even stunning, and no wonder. But the English lamented the fact that, in the eyes of their own King, they themselves appeared to be the least important of all nations."[5] The muttering ceased, however, when it became clear that most of the Spaniards were being sent home.

In October 1255, ten-year-old Edmund, wearing Sicilian dress, was crowned king of Sicily in Westminster Abbey by the Bishop of Bologna, representing the Pope. Then Henry III knelt before the high altar, vowing to wrest Sicily from Manfred. "The King's heart was elated with pride and full of exultation."[6]

In November, Thomas of Savoy was seized while trying to quell an uprising by his subjects and imprisoned in Turin. A ransom was demanded, and the Queen and Peter of Savoy made efforts to raise it, yet most of Alienor's resources had been expended on the Sicilian project and she had little to offer. So she borrowed money from her tailor and other merchants, offering the revenues of five religious houses as security. Henry, for his part, imposed punitive taxes on an already overburdened and simmering populace.

The Lord Edward returned to England to a rapturous welcome. On November 29, he joined Eleanor at Westminster and shortly afterward took her to Windsor, which became her chief residence for the next few years. She led a sheltered life there while her husband completed his military training and took on adult duties. Sources for the period 1255-9 show that she was associated more with the King and Queen than with Edward in these early years of her marriage. There is no record of her accompanying him when he visited Scotland and Wales in 1256.

In February 1256, Henry and Alienor made a state entry into London wearing their crowns and royal robes. That year, John Maunsel "did invite to a stately dinner the kings and queens of England and Scotland, Edward, the King's son, earls, barons and knights, whereby his guests did grow to such a number that his house at Tothill could not receive them, but that he was forced to set up tents and pavilions to receive his guests, whereof there was such a multitude that seven hundred messes of meat did not serve for the first dinner."[7]

The King and Queen were clearly worried about the health of their daughter Katherine. In March 1256, "it was commanded of Edmund of Westminster that he should have a silver image made in the form of a woman for Katherine, the King's daughter, who has recently been ill."[8] Probably this was an image of Katherine's name saint, made to be placed on a saint's shrine for intercessionary prayers. Alienor was with Katherine at this time. When her messenger arrived with the news that the child was better, Henry rewarded him with a robe.[9]

He had still not paid the money he had promised to the Pope for Edmund's crown. That spring, he appealed to Alexander IV, who granted him nine months' grace and urged King Louis to fund an English crusading force that might just find itself detained in Sicily, fighting for the Pope, en route for the Holy Land.

In August 1256, King Alexander and Queen Margaret visited England. At Woodstock, Henry "met them with the greatest rejoicing [and], as they approached, rushed into their embraces and exchanged sweet and familiar converse with them."[10] On August 15, Alexander and Margaret were present at Woodstock when the feast of the Assumption was celebrated with unusual splendor.

In 1257, there was famine in the land, yet Alienor again demanded that the citizens of London pay her queen-gold, and the King made them obey.

On January 13, thanks to his own bribery and the efforts of his Savoyard uncles, Richard of Cornwall was elected king of Almayne (Germany) and king of the Romans, as the anticipated heir to the Holy Roman Empire. Henry and Alienor urged him to be lavish in buying the votes of the electors who decided who should be emperor. It was another grandiose scheme to inflame the anger of the barons.

On January 18, Alienor's mother, the Countess Beatrice, was informed that the King had accepted the peace terms negotiated by the King of France between her and her son-in-law, Charles of Anjou, Count of Provence, "saving the right of Alienor the Queen."[11] As a result of this, Henry and Alienor accepted from Charles repayment of the money Henry had lent Count Ramon in exchange for the five castles pledged to him as security.

In the spring of 1257, Henry made an unsuccessful attempt to conquer Wales, and sent Alienor to the safety of Nottingham Castle. But she had to leave because she could not endure the fumes from the pit coal that was burned in houses in the town, although she certainly intended to return because, in 1258, the Sheriff of Nottingham was commanded to have the Queen's chamber in Nottingham Castle painted with scenes from the history of Alexander the Great. On another occasion, many years later, Alienor had to leave Gillingham, Dorset, because of fumes and smoke in the air. Possibly she suffered from asthma.

Edward had been enjoying only limited independence since his marriage. He could not give grants of land. His officers were chosen for him, or approved, by his parents. One, Sir Geoffrey Langley, had served the Queen well, especially in her dubious dealings with the Jews, and she and the King rewarded him by appointing him Edward's steward in Wales. In 1256, Langley had incited a rebellion there, and the King sent Edward to suppress it, but with insufficient support. In the face of bad weather and fierce resistance, Edward hastened back to court to replenish his meager funds, being obliged to wheedle from Alienor and Peter of Savoy a cash sum in exchange for a rich wardship his father had given him.

Angered at having had to beg from his mother, Edward looked to the Lusignans for aid, a move guaranteed to infuriate her. They encouraged him in his thuggish tactics against the Welsh. One of their allies was Richard de Clare, Earl of Gloucester, whose son was married to Alice de Lusignan. Alienor was determined to wean Gloucester and Edward away from the Lusignans and, in 1257, she accomplished this at a secret meeting at Tutbury Castle.

* * *

On May 3, 1257, Katherine died at Windsor, aged three. "The Queen, her mother, as a result of her anguish, was seized of a grievous illness that neither physician nor human consolation could alleviate." As had happened when she had been distraught over Margaret's plight, she "was so overcome with grief that it brought on a disease, which was thought to be incurable, as she could obtain no relief."[12] Fearing that she might die, she vowed to go on a pilgrimage to the shrine of St. Alban if her life were spared. The King too was immersed in grief and suffered a recurrence of the tertian fever that had visited him intermittently for a while. Despite being prostrated with sorrow and illness, Henry and Alienor rewarded the nurses who had so diligently looked after Katherine at the end with 10 marks (£4,900), and Henry appointed a chaplain at the Charing hermitage to say prayers for the soul of his daughter.

Katherine was interred at Westminster with great ceremony. Hers was the first burial in the uncompleted church there. She was almost certainly buried in St. Edmund's Chapel. In 1258, a temporary tomb chest was erected and covered by a pall. In 1267, Henry ordered Simon of Wells to "make a tomb over the body of Katherine, the King's daughter." By July, Simon was expected to have built a small tomb richly decorated with marbles and mosaics, and "should have made a copper-alloy image," but nothing was finished, so he was dismissed. Henry then commissioned his goldsmith, William de Gloucester, to fashion an effigy of silver gilt. Not until 1272 did William present his account for the wooden effigy, which was "gilded with gold" and studded with 180 pearls and amethysts. This tomb was the earliest recorded monument built for a child in England.

On April 29, 1257, Richard and Sanchia sailed from England to Germany. On May 17, the new King and Queen of Almayne were crowned at Aachen. Edmund was present, representing his father. Henry and Alienor had wanted to attend, but Richard had put them off, fearing that they might upstage him.

In June that year, an army led by Edward was massacred near Carmarthen. In August, Henry and Edward led another army into Wales, but that expedition too ended in ignominious failure. In October, Henry gave up and returned to Westminster. Edward was seething, not against the Welsh, but against his parents: his father, who had been defeated, and his mother, who had put in place his officers in Wales, the very men who had let him down. He now began appointing men of his own choosing, on whom he could rely. This show of independence troubled Alienor, who was determined to remain in control of her son's affairs. In October, she took Eleanor of Castile and a great train of ladies on a pilgrimage to St. Albans Abbey, where she offered a length of baudekyn—silk shot through with gold—at the saint's shrine. Mother- and daughter-in-law got on well; there seems never to have been any jealousy between them.

The year 1258 brought storms. The weather was atrocious, with torrential rain and widespread frost, which ruined the harvest. The mood of the weather was reflected in the deteriorating relations between the King and his barons. The Queen, her Savoyard kinsmen and the royal councilors were becoming more concerned about the influence the Lusignan brothers wielded over Edward, who, needing to raise money, had just mortgaged some of his English manors to them, notwithstanding the fact that they had recently "shamelessly scandalised and defamed" the Queen,[13] while Bishop Aymer had done all in his power to provoke the King against her, and encouraged the disobedience of the Lord Edward.

The royal couple's fears were compounded when, on April 1, 1258, Aymer's armed retainers killed one of the servants of John FitzGeoffrey, a former justiciar of Ireland who was close to the Queen. An angry Fitz-Geoffrey appealed to the King, but Henry ignored his complaint. It was the final straw for the barons, who were alarmed to see the Lusignans riding roughshod over English justice and literally getting away with murder.

Bankrupted by his foolish venture in Sicily—so far, he had managed to pay less than half of what was due to the Pope—Henry summoned Parliament to Westminster, hoping to raise money through a grant of taxation. But the barons were in no mood to be accommodating; they had had enough of the King's misgovernment and were determined to limit his power and extravagance and stop him abusing his position. They were also ready to target Alienor. "The great men of the land were exasperated with the Queen and also with the King's Poitevin brothers and the Queen's Savoyard kinsmen, because, wherever they held sway, they behaved unbearably, like tyrants."[14] Alienor was able with impunity to resist the collecting of taxes from her estates and blithely turned a blind eye to the rapaciousness of her stewards. Her chief priority at this time was not the eradication of abuses within the government of the kingdom, but ridding the realm of what she saw as the pernicious influence of the Lusignans so that her own influence, and that of her faction, could flourish unimpeded.

On April 12, headed by Simon de Montfort, seven magnates, among them Peter of Savoy, John FitzGeoffrey and the Earl of Gloucester, appeared before the King in armor (although they left their swords outside) and demanded that a committee of magnates be established to control his actions, and that the Lusignans be exiled.

The measures they insisted on putting in place were far more stringent than those laid down in Magna Carta. Effectively, it was a curbing of royal power. In return for a grant of the revenue he desperately needed, Henry reluctantly swore to abide by reforms that were to be laid down by a royal commission of twenty-four elected magnates, half of whom were to be chosen by the King, and half by the barons.

Around June 10, 1258, when what became known as the "Mad Parliament" met in Oxford, a series of new reforms was drawn up. The Provisions of Oxford placed the government under the joint direction of the King and a permanent elected baronial council of fifteen, which would advise him on state affairs and control official appointments. On pain of excommunication, all the high officers of the realm were to swear allegiance to the King and the council. Parliament was to meet three times a year to consult on further reforms and ensure that the King kept his promises. A justiciar was appointed (for the first time since 1234) to oversee local administration and hear complaints, and most of the sheriffs were replaced by knights holding land in the shires they administered. All Crown lands that had been alienated were to be restored, and a committee was formed to regulate wardships and queen-gold—a direct attack on Alienor. There was to be a review of the households of the King and Queen, although very little would be done about that.

Soon, though, the barons began quarreling among themselves, and a new party of lesser magnates emerged under the leadership of the implacable Simon de Montfort, who was exasperated with the King and determined to see the reforms implemented.

Alienor, Edward, Archbishop Boniface, Peter of Savoy and even Richard of Cornwall, who was known to support his brother, were obliged to swear allegiance to the King and the council, which was tantamount to swearing to uphold the Provisions. Alienor seems, at first, to have accepted them, but their impact was brought home to her when, in May, she tried to have the estate of the dying Edmund de Lacy, son of the Earl of Lincoln, settled upon his wife Alasia, her cousin. The King supported her, but the council of barons decreed that the inheritance should be split between Alasia and her mother-in-law, who was countess of Lincoln in her own right. Seeing the Provisions being invoked to the detriment of her relatives, Alienor now did her utmost to influence Henry and Edward against them.

In Parliament, the Lusignans, who thought themselves to be above the law anyway, publicly repudiated the Provisions. On July 18, constrained by the barons—and doubtless encouraged by Alienor—Henry banished his half-brothers from the realm. They fled abroad, blaming the Queen's enmity for their banishment. When Aymer asked permission to go to Paris to study there, King Louis refused, "being exasperated by a complaint made against these Poitevins by the Queen of France to the effect that they had shamelessly scandalised and defamed her sister, the Queen of England."[15]

Alienor was glad to see the Lusignans exiled, but her son felt differently. Now nineteen, Edward was bold, athletic and dashing, with the confidence that came from having a loving, stable family background. He took after his uncle, Richard of Cornwall, having none of the weakness of his father, and he also had his mother's strong character. However, his increasingly unpleasant traits of recklessness and disloyalty were becoming more evident. When he offered his support and friendship to the Lusignans, forsaking his mother's Savoyard relations, a quarrel erupted between him and his father. Alienor, it was said, was the cause of all the malice. She must have been devastated.

Constrained by the Provisions, Henry was unable to keep his promises to the Pope in regard to Sicily. Alienor had been hoping that Thomas of Savoy would step in and help. He had recently been freed from captivity, thanks to her efforts and those of his family, but when he arrived in England that year, it was on a stretcher, for his health had been broken in prison. He died the following February.

In January 1259, Richard and Sanchia visited England and were met at

Dover by Henry, Alienor and Archbishop Boniface. Richard's son, Henry of Almayne, had refused to swear to uphold the Provisions until he knew his father's views. Richard was worried that his lands would be confiscated if he opposed them. On January 23, confronted by the massed baronage at Canterbury, he took the oath. He and Sanchia would remain in England until June 1260.

On October 13, the King observed the feast of St. Edward at Westminster with his usual magnificent display. Knowing it would please him, Alienor hurried from St. Albans to be present, even though she was unwell and the weather was foul.

With his barons gaining control, Henry needed more than ever to conclude a peace treaty with France, even though that meant abandoning his dreams of recovering the lost Angevin Empire and formally surrendering to Louis those territories that he and his father had lost. Fortunately, his long-standing kinship with Louis through their wives came into play and helped smooth the protracted negotiations. But Edward opposed the peace terms, fearing they would endanger his interests in Gascony. On October 15, 1259, he allied himself with Simon de Montfort, swearing to do all in his power to aid and counsel him and his supporters. That led to a monumental row with his parents. Alienor could not forget how her son had shunned her relatives and was appalled that he had now apparently abandoned his father. She would henceforth do her best to stir up Henry against Edward and Montfort.

On November 6, Henry and Alienor left Westminster for Dover. Before boarding their ship, Alienor defiantly granted a wardship to one of her stewards, flouting the Provisions and her oath of allegiance to the baronial council. On November 14, she and Henry crossed to Wissant. On November 24, they arrived at Saint-Denis, where they were met by King Louis. They entered Paris the following day and Alienor was reunited with her mother and sisters Marguerite and Beatrice, who had been involved in discussions about the new treaty. The Countess Beatrice had probably brought with her a book she had commissioned in 1256 for herself and her daughters. It was *Le regime du corps*, a health, hygiene and pregnancy manual written by her physician, Aldobrandino of Siena.

The Treaty of Paris was sealed on December 4, 1259. Under its terms, Henry III formally renounced Normandy, Maine, Anjou, Touraine and

Poitou in return for French recognition of his right to Gascony, lands in Cahors, Limoges and the Périgord, financial support for 500 knights for two years and the marriage of his daughter Beatrice to John, the son and heir of John I "the Red," Duke of Brittany, in settlement of the Duke's claim to the earldom of Richmond. Alienor was present when Henry paid homage to Louis for Aquitaine, and formally renounced any rights she had in the domains he had ceded.

Louis now persuaded his sister-in-law Beatrice to give up her rights to Provence in exchange for a large pension. He then transferred them to her husband, Charles. It now looked as if Alienor and Marguerite would never receive the 10,000 marks (£4,900,000) their father had willed each of them, although both were determined not to let the matter rest.

Henry and Alienor kept Christmas in Paris amid disturbing rumors that Edward, who had gone to Gascony for three months, was plotting to overthrow his father, which Henry, to his grief, believed. Aiming to win support against her son and the barons, Alienor gave gifts to Queen Marguerite and many other ladies, and had rings distributed to the knights of Flanders, whom she hoped to charm into doing her service should the need arise.

Because of the death of Louis's heir, a boy of fifteen, Beatrice's wedding took place a week later than planned, on January 22, 1260, at Saint-Denis. Louis, Marguerite, Alfonso X of Castile and Joan of Ponthieu were among the guests. Simon de Montfort had allotted the King and Queen ample supplies for the celebrations, and Alienor may have given her daughter a book of hours as a wedding gift. After Beatrice's marriage, Alienor remained close to her and involved in her affairs. Beatrice would bear six children, one of whom was named after her mother.

After the wedding, Henry and Alienor traveled north and lingered at Saint-Omer for two months, spending Easter there. After another report reached the King that Edward was plotting to depose him, he rejoiced to receive a conciliatory letter from his son, who had now returned to England. Alienor had pawned some jewels to raise money, and she and her friends had begun recruiting a mercenary force against the barons, so she was determined to stop Edward collaborating with them. At her behest, Henry made the mistake of sending the Earl of Gloucester to England. Gloucester and Edward hated each other, and the Earl was determined to force the prince back into his father's camp. In the King's name, he summoned the barons to London to perform the feudal military service they owed Henry.

On April 23, 1260, the King and Queen returned to England with their mercenaries, to find their son begging for a reconciliation. Henry refused to see him, saying that, if he did, he would not be able to prevent himself from embracing him. He made Edward stew for a fortnight before receiving him at a parliament held in St. Paul's Cathedral, which Alienor attended. Edward swore he had meant no disobedience and begged for mercy from his father. He gave his parents the kiss of peace, but Alienor made it clear that her forgiveness was dependent on her being able to choose his friends, which naturally would see off Simon.

Henry attempted to put Simon on trial, but he could not count on much support. When Louis sent the Archbishop of Rouen to England with a watching brief, Henry and Alienor tried to get him on their side, but Simon won him over. The trial collapsed when news came that the Welsh leader Llywelyn ap Gruffydd, who had declared himself prince of Wales in 1258, had captured the royal castle at Builth. Simon now "emerged as the leader of the baronage."[16] Such was his supremacy that he was able to remove Peter of Savoy from the King's council.

4

"The Serpent-Like Fraud and Speech of a Woman"

✣

WHEN THE BISHOP OF DURHAM DIED IN AUGUST 1260, Henry and Alienor wanted to replace him with the trusty John Maunsel. They invited the cathedral chapter to a feast at Westminster hosted by the King, during which, as prearranged, a message arrived from the Queen, who was at Marlborough, praying the King to put Maunsel's name forward. In September, Henry and Alienor wrote separately to the chapter, urging the election of Maunsel. When Edward put forward another candidate, who would be for the "whole people," rather than his mother's choice, the monks promptly elected their own man.

By October, Edward had allied himself to Simon and the Earl of Gloucester, and they dominated the Parliament that met that month. A staggered Henry III was powerless to do anything about it. At the end of the month, Richard and Sanchia arrived in London. Their arrival in Germany in June had been met with hostility and, in the end, they had fled home. The following month, Peter of Savoy would also return to England. On October 30, Alexander III and Queen Margaret came to London, where there was a great family reunion. Margaret was pregnant and Alexander had given in to her wish to bear her first child in England, with her mother for support. In the middle of November, he returned to Scotland, leaving Margaret behind.

A reconciliation of sorts had taken place between the King and his son, but only on condition that Edward leave England for a while. He took himself and Eleanor off to Gascony, where he indulged his love of tournaments and came under the influence of his mother's relatives, who did their best to persuade him that his place was by his father's side. But, while visiting Paris in November, Edward again began to fraternize with the Lusignans, much to the dismay of his parents.

The death of Bishop Aymer on December 4 removed the most unpopular of the Queen's kinsmen. Richard came down from Berkhamsted to spend Christmas with Henry and Alienor because Sanchia was too unwell to visit court. On February 28, 1261, Queen Margaret gave birth to a daughter, another Margaret, at Windsor. There was anger in Scotland that she had chosen to bear her child on English soil.

For months, there had been a tense stand-off between the King and Simon de Montfort. In December, Simon had gone to France. In January 1261, Henry appealed to the Pope to absolve him from his oath to observe the Provisions of Oxford. Alienor was later blamed for this and accused of meddling "with counsel, or with message or with woman's trick."[1]

In February, Henry and Alienor set up their court in the Tower of London, which Henry had fortified the previous autumn, envisaging that, if it came to a showdown with his barons, he might need a secure refuge for himself and his family. He forced every citizen of London over twelve years of age to swear allegiance to him and offered financial inducements to anyone who would fight for him. He admitted to the City only barons he could trust. Those he didn't took to skulking beyond the gates with large bodies of troops.

With the King's position so weak, the Savoyards and the Lusignans were fast realizing that, to ensure their future prosperity, they should unite in support of the King. William de Valence wanted to return to England with Edward, but Henry forbade it, then changed his mind, much to Alienor's disgust, because he needed his half-brothers' support. Alienor could only insist that, before William set foot in England, he must swear an oath before Queen Marguerite that he would not defame her, Alienor, ever again.

Emboldened by the imminent arrival of the Lusignans, Henry left the Tower with Alienor and rode to Dover, where he placed the castle in loyal hands. The King and Queen then moved to Winchester, where, in April, they welcomed Edward, who had returned to England with William de Valence, to whom the King and his son showed much favor. It was clear that the prince's loyalty now lay with his parents. "From that time, Edward, flattered by his mother, held to his father's side and favoured aliens as kinsfolk."

In May, a mercenary force summoned by the King arrived in England. Henry was considering asking Louis, or even Marguerite, to arbitrate in the quarrel between himself and his barons, but there was no need because, in April 1261, the Provisions of Oxford were annulled by Papal bull. Henry's appeal to Rome had persuaded the dying Pope Alexander IV to absolve him and his supporters from his oath to observe the barons' reforms. Henry triumphantly made the bull public on June 12 at Winchester, declaring that he would rule his kingdom as he saw fit.

The barons—and Edward—were appalled. They had had no idea that the King had gone behind their backs and appealed to the Pope. Many who would have stayed loyal to Henry went over to Simon. There were rumblings about an uprising and, on June 22, the King and Queen returned to the Tower. Henry dismissed the council that had been forced on him and resolutely ignored the Provisions, determined not to be cowed by the barons. He accused Simon and Gloucester of usurping his authority and alienating his heir.

In July, fearing that Simon would try to enlist French support, Henry and Alienor traveled to Paris to find that Louis's welcome was as warm as ever. He and Marguerite promised to aid them against Simon, hoping that the King would resolve the quarrel without again having to surrender any of his sovereign rights. In case she needed to pawn them again, Henry had given Alienor the authority to dispose of the crown jewels, which had been redeemed from Earl Richard and which she had brought to France and entrusted to Queen Marguerite for safekeeping in the church of the Templars in Paris.

Edward and Eleanor had also left England in July, for a sojourn in Bordeaux. Meanwhile, Simon was organizing active opposition to the King's rule, undermining the powers of the royal sheriffs and attempting to summon Parliament. Resentment simmered as Henry continued to reassert his authority, importing more foreign mercenaries and removing his opponents. Civil war seemed a real possibility.

In October, thanks in part to the efforts of the Queen and John Maunsel, several barons defected from Simon to the royalist party. Among them was Gloucester, who was accused of desertion on account of "the promises or favours of the Queen."[2]

Declaring that "he preferred to die landless than depart from the truth," Simon fled to France. Without their leader, his followers began squabbling among themselves. In November, Henry and the barons signed a treaty at Kingston, agreeing to submit their disputes to arbitration, with the King having the right of appeal to the Pope.

On November 9, 1261, Sanchia died at Berkhamsted Castle. The King and Queen ordered a requiem mass at Westminster Abbey and funded masses for Sanchia's soul in the chapel of St. John the Evangelist in the Tower of London, where they sought shelter from October 14 to December 9, protected from any menaces of the barons. Because of this, Alienor was unable to attend her sister's funeral at Hailes Abbey, Gloucestershire, which Richard of Cornwall had founded in 1246.

In February 1262, Edward and Eleanor returned from Gascony. Alienor was still determined to break the association between Edward and the Lusignans and see off her son's other undesirable supporters. At Michaelmas, Henry had ordered that Edward's financial affairs be subject to an audit, which showed them to be in much disorder. Late in February, the Queen wrote to warn her son that his steward, Roger Leyburn, had cheated him of funds, and urged him to make Leyburn account for himself. When Leyburn refused, Edward seized his revenues to make good the deficit, and also revoked a grant he had made to him. Leyburn was allowed to remain in his service, but, between May and June, the Queen worked to rid Edward's retinue of those whom she considered to have a bad influence on him. This, in part, had the effect she had anticipated, for Edward began to draw close to his father, and Alienor was able to take charge of his finances; but she had made an enemy of Leyburn and driven him over to the barons' side. In June, she and Henry made Edward exchange many of his estates in England and Wales for payments of money from the Treasury, depriving him of the means to raise his tenantry.

By the summer, there was widespread discontent at the King's inept rule and his abandonment of the barons' program of reform. Alienor and her party were blamed for exercising undue control at this time and became the target of the most vitriolic complaints.

On July 14, 1262, Henry departed for France to meet with Louis and attend meetings of the Paris *parlement*. Alienor, Edward and Eleanor accompanied him. In September, Henry and Edward succumbed to an epidemic and were very ill. Henry wrote to Edmund that he could barely walk around his chamber. He did not recover until September 30, so the talks with Louis had to be postponed.

On October 10, on the advice of Peter of Savoy, Henry supplemented the Queen's dower, originally £1,000 (£730,000), with "£3,000 yearly of land."[3] This increase would ensure that the Savoyards continued to prosper after his death.

The King was now informed that Leyburn and others who had been dismissed from Edward's household had formed a party of disaffected men who were stirring up discontent, particularly against the Queen and her countrymen. But he did not return home. In October, he went on a pilgrimage to Rheims Cathedral that extended into November. He was awestruck by the architecture, which would be reflected in the design of Westminster Abbey.

Back in England for a lightning visit that month, Simon had appeared in Parliament and read out a letter purportedly from the Pope, revoking his rejection of the Provisions. There is no evidence that he had ever received such a letter, still less that the Pope had written it, but the barons believed him, as did many others.

On December 20, Henry finally returned to England, having realized that it would be prudent to make peace with Simon and abide by the Provisions—for now. To this end, he had asked for King Louis's help. On Christmas Eve, he learned that the Welsh, under Llywelyn ap Gruffydd, had united and risen against English border garrisons.

The royal family spent an anxious Christmas at Canterbury before moving to Rochester to celebrate New Year, when William de Valence gave Queen Alienor a peace offering in the form of a ring.

In the new year, the King summoned the Lord Edward home to deal with Llywelyn's encroachments on the Welsh borders. By the end of February 1263, Edward and Eleanor had returned to England with an army that Eleanor had helped to raise, enlisting mercenaries from Ponthieu, her mother's domain. Realizing that the conflict between his father and the barons was coming to a head, Edward hastened from London to the security of Windsor, taking Eleanor with him. He garrisoned the castle with a large force of Flemish mercenaries, who occupied themselves with ravaging the countryside round about. Under an agreement reached the previous year, Windsor, like other royal castles, should have been surrendered to the barons, but Edward was determined to keep it. In April, when he embarked on his Welsh campaign, he left Eleanor there.

In March, Henry had insisted on his lords swearing a general oath of allegiance to Edward, recognizing him as the heir to the throne. But the barons made it conditional upon he himself swearing once more to observe the Provisions of Oxford. Henry refused, whereupon, in late April, Simon returned to England, accused Henry, Alienor and Edward of perjury, and came out in armed rebellion against the King, supported by many barons.

By June 19, with Simon's troops poised to occupy the capital, Henry, Alienor and Richard of Cornwall had barricaded themselves into the Tower of London as armed citizens angrily thronged at the gatehouse. The King had few soldiers, no funds and barely any provisions. No one in London would give him or Alienor "a ha'penny worth of credit,"[4] so Alienor pawned her jewels to the Templars.

Simon now offered the Mayor and citizens of London an ultimatum: would they uphold the Provisions, or oppose them? Prudently, they declared that they were for them. In the Tower, Richard of Cornwall urged the King to seek a rapport with the barons, while Alienor urged him to resist them.

On June 24, a deputation of Londoners waited on the King and handed him a letter from Simon demanding that he implement the Provisions of Oxford inviolably, denounce as mortal enemies all who opposed them, and expel Edward's mercenaries. It was made clear that the barons were willing to compromise on certain points, but Archbishop Boniface took fright and fled at once to France. Hot on his heels went John Maunsel. When the barons sent Henry of Almayne after him, Alienor dispatched her servant, Ingelram de Fiennes, to capture him, ensuring that Boniface and Maunsel got to Paris unharmed.

After receiving reports of the critical situation in London, Edward had abandoned his campaign in Wales and taken up residence at the priory of St. John at Clerkenwell. On June 29, he descended on the Temple with a band of knights and found the gates closed. "When, at his request he was given the keys, he said he wished to see the jewels belonging to the

Queen, his mother. Summoning the keeper, he, by this deceit, entered with his men into the Temple treasury and there, breaking open with iron hammers that they had brought with them certain chests, he carried away a thousand pounds" as well as the jewels, retreating with his booty to Windsor.[5]

Alienor was pleased to hear of her son's daring deed. She was strongly against Henry coming to an agreement with his opponents. But this one rash act of Edward's had a devastating impact on the royalist cause. The people of London were outraged at his brazen ransacking of the Temple. They threw in their lot with the barons and rose in rebellion. The barons were likewise incensed, blaming Henry for his son's outrage. On July 4, a frightened Henry sent envoys to negotiate a peace with them.

Enraged at the capture of Henry of Almayne, the barons demanded that he be freed. On July 10, Henry capitulated and authorized his nephew's release, although Richard of Cornwall advised the Justiciar that the Queen's consent should be sought as well, fearing that the King's order would not be obeyed by Ingelram de Fiennes. He also commanded the Lord Edmund, who had been given charge of Dover Castle, to surrender it to the barons.

That day, a deputation of magnates arrived at the Tower and forced Henry to agree to Simon's demand that the kingdom be ruled only by Englishmen and that all foreigners be banished, "never to return." He had no choice, as the barons were now in control of southeastern England and most of the ports. "The King, fearing that he would be close pressed in the Tower of London by the army of the barons, made peace for a time with them and promised to preserve the Provisions made at Oxford, but the Queen, instigated by woman's malice, did all in her power to prevent his doing so, and opposed the barons as far as she could,"[6] striving "with all her strength" to get Henry to stand up to his enemies.[7] The criticism was justified; she was not just being made a scapegoat, although clearly there was much resentment at a woman, and a foreigner at that, interfering in government.

Alienor was now hated throughout England as the embodiment of all that was wrong with Henry's rule: his extravagance, his promotion of foreign favorites and his repressive taxation. She was castigated for opposing the Provisions. The Melrose chronicler called her "the root, fomentor and disseminator of all the discord between her husband, King

Henry, and the barons of his kingdom." If she had been heedless of the strength of popular feeling before, that hatred was now to be brought home to her. The barons were seizing her castles and estates "because they saw that she had turned openly against the Provisions of Oxford."[8] Leyburn and others were burning her crops and her property. Anyone associated with the reviled Queen was a target. There were violent raids and attacks on the lands of Bishop Boniface, Peter of Savoy and other countrymen of hers in fifteen counties. In June, Peter of Aigueblanche, Bishop of Hereford, was manhandled out of his cathedral and imprisoned. Soon afterward, he fled abroad.

Furious at Henry's capitulation to the barons, with its dire implications for her Savoyards, Alienor decided of her own accord to join Edward at Windsor and rouse him to stop Simon entering London, knowing that Henry was unlikely to resist such an incursion. On St. Mildred's Day (July 13) 1263, she left the Tower by boat. As she neared London Bridge, a mob of "the lower orders of the City" gathered there and "assailed her and her men shamefully with base and foul words," throwing stones and mud in the hope of capsizing the boat. Some pelted Alienor with rotten eggs and sheep's bones, yelling, "Drown the witch!" "She was with difficulty freed by the Mayor of London and was compelled of necessity to return to the Tower. The King did not let her enter"—he was probably angry at what she had taken upon herself—"but she was conducted in safety to St. Paul's by the Mayor and was lodged in the Bishop's house."[9] There she stayed for two days while tempers cooled, before continuing her journey to Windsor. Edward was furious when he heard of this insult to his mother. In time, he would exact a bloody revenge on the Londoners.

On July 15, the barons entered the City. Thoroughly unnerved, Henry hastened to come to terms with them. The next day, he surrendered his royal prerogative and his rule to Simon de Montfort, asking naïvely, "Am I a prisoner?" Peace between the King and the barons was proclaimed. Henry surrendered the Tower to Simon, who now took control of London.

On July 22, the King and Queen returned to Westminster, but Edward refused to submit to the barons and tore off to Bristol, where the townsfolk, resentful of the depredations of his knights, besieged the castle, which he had occupied. Thanks to the intervention of the Bishop of

Worcester, a peace was agreed. Edward, however, was still set on military action; he was not interested in seeking a diplomatic resolution to the conflict, as his father and uncle Richard were. He rode back to Windsor, where Eleanor was in residence, and many marcher knights came flocking there to aid him in his raiding and plundering. The barons now thought Edward as slippery as his father. They marched on Windsor with the King in tow, whereupon, on August 1, Edward had no choice but to surrender the castle. He galloped away in a temper, having bidden farewell to his mother and left her to express gratitude to his knights and distribute rings to them on his behalf.

Support for the King was building on the Continent. Louis and Marguerite were horrified to hear of how the Londoners had insulted Alienor. For the next two years, Archbishop Boniface and Peter of Savoy ensured that Louis was kept abreast of developments in England, and royalist exiles—among them John Maunsel and Peter of Aigueblanche—and Englishmen living in Boulogne, Montreuil and nearby coastal towns were in contact with Louis, Marguerite and the Pope, intriguing against Simon.

The barons seized more of Alienor's lands and castles. They appointed Roger Leyburn a royal steward, much to her fury and the King's. Alienor urged Henry to make war on Simon and his supporters. It was suggested that the quarrel be referred to the arbitration of King Louis, to which the barons grudgingly agreed. On August 16, 1263, Henry informed Louis that he wished to come to France with the Queen and his sons to seek his counsel.

On September 9, at a Parliament held in St. Paul's Cathedral, Henry formally agreed to peace terms imposed by the barons and bound himself once more to observe the Provisions of Oxford—a promise he had no intention of keeping. That month, as Henry's overlord, Louis formally summoned him, Alienor and their sons to France to present their case against the barons. Simon resolved to go too, to give his side of the quarrel, trusting that Louis, with his reputation for fairness, would rule in his favor.

On September 18, Henry left Westminster with Alienor and their sons. The barons had made them swear oaths that they would return in October. Three days later, the royal party sailed to Boulogne, where they were received by Louis, Marguerite, the Countess Beatrice, Archbishop Boniface, Peter of Savoy and many French lords and exiled English royalists.

Simon and some of the barons arrived too, finding themselves isolated in this great gathering of the King's friends.

Henry laid his complaints before Louis, and Alienor's uncles urged the French King to denounce Simon and his adherents, at which Simon protested that he was not bound to answer for his deeds in the court of the King of France. On October 4, Alienor had a private meeting with Louis at Boulogne. She was bent on war, and Marguerite urged her brother-in-law, Alphonse, Count of Poitiers, to assist Alienor by lending her his galleys at La Rochelle to transport mercenaries to England. Alphonse, however, preferred to stay neutral, and Louis felt that the King's complaint would be better dealt with by an English court, so nothing was resolved.

On October 7, keeping his oath to the barons, Henry left for England with Edward. He made Alienor stay behind, in breach of her oath, not only because Edward intended to forge alliances with men she considered traitors and did not want her interfering, but also because she could the more easily aid the royalist cause from France. She remained in Paris with her sister, her son Edmund, Peter of Savoy and Archbishop Boniface, who had just excommunicated those who had risen against King Henry. Soon afterward, with Marguerite's help, Alienor began raising men for an invasion of England. Peter of Savoy, John Maunsel and Peter of Aigueblanche worked indefatigably to assist her and pawned the King's jewels to raise money.

Henry arrived in London on October 12. When Parliament sat again that month, there was a violent clash between the King and Simon. Edward left, offering the thin excuse that he wanted to visit his wife. Instead, he took possession of Windsor Castle, coming out in open opposition to the barons. Henry joined him there, and Henry of Almayne came over to their side.

The King began raising an army, although both parties were reluctant to engage in a civil war. Moderates like Richard of Cornwall were exhorting Henry and Simon to work for a peaceful compromise. Louis had again offered to mediate and, on November 1, after Henry had again sworn always to uphold the Provisions, the barons agreed. In December, the King made an abortive attempt to seize Dover, to give the Queen's army a bridgehead into England. He encouraged Marguerite and the Countess Beatrice to offer her aid.

Louis had informed Pope Urban IV of the King's situation, asking him to intervene. Alienor herself had written to the Pope, urging him to instruct Louis to rule in Henry's favor. In response, Urban issued another bull annulling the Provisions of Oxford. On November 22, he wrote to Henry, Alienor, Edward and Simon, "the chief disturber of the realm," informing them that he had appointed a legate with powers to restore Henry's authority and ordered the barons to obey him. His mission was to bring peace to England. The legate was instructed to absolve Henry of the oaths he had sworn under duress to the barons and absolve Alienor and Edmund of their oaths to return to England. The barons retaliated by forbidding him to set foot in England.

Henry had been lucky to obtain Papal support, for Urban was angry with him for his failure to pay what he owed for Edmund's crown. On December 18, he revoked the kingdom of Sicily, and Edmund was obliged to renounce all claim to it, much to his mother's disappointment. The Pope now offered Sicily to Alienor's brother-in-law, Charles of Anjou, who was better placed to wrest it from the Hohenstaufens. Charles's wife, Beatrice, urged him to accept because she wanted to be a queen, like her sisters.

Early in January 1264, Henry returned to France to appeal to King Louis for justice, taking with him the crown jewels. Simon had to stay in England because he had sustained injuries in a riding accident. Predictably, Louis refused to agree to any attempt to limit royal sovereignty. On January 23, at the Mise (writ of settlement) of Amiens, at which both Henry and Alienor pleaded the King's case, Louis found in Henry's favor in every point, and ruled that, as the Pope had annulled the Provisions of Oxford, they were of no effect. The chronicler William Rishanger—who spoke for many people in England—believed that the French King had been "seduced, deceived and beguiled by the serpent-like fraud and speech of a woman, that is, the Queen of England." Thanks to her, he declared, "the heart of this King [Henry] was changed from good to bad, from bad to worse, and from worse to worst."

Because Alienor was adamant that England was not safe for her, Louis offered her asylum in France and agreed to finance her and Edmund. Subject to Henry's ratification, she was to receive a substantial sum in return for her husband's rights in Limoges, Cahors and Périgueux. Henry agreed to Louis's terms, which gave Alienor the wherewithal to raise more troops for a royalist invasion of England. He instructed her, Peter of Savoy and John Maunsel to receive from Louis the money due to him under the terms of the Treaty of Paris for the upkeep of 500 knights for two years. On February 14, 1264, the King appointed the Queen and Peter of Savoy to receive those funds, in his name. They were also empowered to redeem the King's jewels from the Old Temple in Paris and use them to Henry's advantage, as they saw fit. That day, the King and Edward sailed for England.

In England, the people were suspicious of Alienor's intentions:

> The Queen went beyond sea, the King's brethren also,
> And ever they strove the Charter to undo;
> They purchased that the Pope should assoil, I wis,
> Of the oath and the Charter, the King and all his.
> It was ever the Queen's thought (as much as she could think)
> To break the Charter by some woman's wrench.[10]

Simon refused to accept Louis's ruling. Civil war between the King and the barons was now inevitable. On his return to England, Henry summoned his magnates to muster at Oxford before March 30 for a campaign in Wales; his true purpose, however, was to raise an army against Simon and his supporters. The Second Barons' War had begun.

Alienor continued to raise mercenaries and gather ships. By April 19, Gaston de Béarn had joined her at Saint-Omer. On May 7, she begged Alphonse to place an embargo on English ships in his ports in Poitou and turn them over to her for her fleet, for her husband's treacherous barons were doing their best to disinherit him and their children. But Alphonse refused, saying it would be a violation of French law and would cause great harm and danger. Undaunted, Alienor kept trying to persuade the citizens of Poitou voluntarily to provide her with boats.

In the spring, having enlisted the aid of royalist exiles in Boulogne, Montreuil and other coastal ports in northwest France, she sailed along the coast to Flanders to find mercenaries to fight for Henry. She did everything she could to raise men to support the King's cause, cultivating as many influential people as possible. Louis made no move to support or stop her, but Marguerite did her utmost to muster ships and troops. Alienor was also supported in her efforts by her mother, who traveled to

Savoy to enlist mercenaries. She exploited to the full her family connections.

Early in April, Edward left Windsor with his mercenaries, commanding Eleanor, who was about three months pregnant, not to leave the castle under any circumstances. She was guarded by the constable and a garrison of Gascon mercenaries, and attended by Joan de Munchesni, Countess of Pembroke, the wife of William de Valence, as well as knights, ladies, a steward, a clerk and menial servants. Some time earlier, Eleanor had borne her second child, who was with her at Windsor. This must have been Katherine, whose death is recorded the following September. Her date of birth is unknown, but she had perhaps been born on St. Katherine's Day, November 25, in 1261–3, and named after the saint—or possibly for Katherine, the late daughter of the King and Queen.

Edward joined the King and marched on Northampton, which they took on April 6. Hearing that Rochester Castle was under attack, they moved south to Kent to relieve it, then swung west to Sussex and the little town of Lewes. Here, on May 14, 1264, a great battle was fought between royalist and baronial forces. The King's army outnumbered the barons' by four to one.

The battle saw Edward, now twenty-five, demonstrating for the first time the military expertise and gift for leadership that would win him fame as a war leader. His judgment only failed when he took revenge on the Londoners for insulting his mother the previous year, shouting her name as he pursued them relentlessly and cut many down, then chased them too far and became trapped. When he returned, the royalist forces had been defeated. The King had sought sanctuary in Lewes Priory, where he was taken prisoner. When the barons threatened to execute Richard of Cornwall and other captives, Edward had no choice but to cede victory. He and Henry were taken as prisoners to Wallingford Castle. William de Valence, the Earl of Surrey and others fled to the Queen in France, leaving many casualties dead on the field.

The barons' victory left Simon in control of the King and the government. On May 15, the Mise of Lewes was drawn up, its terms favorable to the barons, and Henry and Edward were made to affix their seals to it. A copy was sent to King Louis so that he could see that Henry had agreed to the peace terms and would hopefully dissuade Alienor from pursuing her invasion plans.

Commissioners were appointed to direct the King's actions, while Edward was to be held as a hostage to ensure his compliance. Henry was now a puppet king. Simon treated him with respect, but constrained him to do his will. Henry sought refuge in continual prayer, invoking the aid of St. Edward to rescue him from his bondage.

Window in Poitiers Cathedral donated by Eleanor of Aquitaine
in commemoration of her wedding to Henry II in 1152.

The Hall of Lost Footsteps in Eleanor's palace at Poitiers.

Henry II, for whom "the world was not enough." (Tomb effigy in Fontevraud Abbey.)

Henry, the Young King. Despite being described as "a little lower than the angels," he was "a prodigy of unfaith." (Tomb effigy in Rouen Cathedral.)

Archbishop Thomas Becket, who changed "from a patron of play actors and a follower of hounds to a shepherd of souls." (Window at Canterbury Cathedral.)

The legends attached to Henry II's mistress, Rosamund de Clifford, inspired John William Waterhouse to portray Eleanor of Aquitaine spying on her rival. (National Museum of Wales.)

Chinon Castle, one of the great strongholds of the Plantagenets.
Henry II died here in 1189.

The mound on which once stood the city, cathedral and castle of Old Sarum.
Eleanor of Aquitaine was held prisoner in this windswept place.

The tomb effigies of
Eleanor of Aquitaine
and her son Richard I
in Fontevraud Abbey.
She called him "the
staff of my old age,
the light of my eyes."

The kitchen Eleanor built
at Fontevraud.

The mural in the church of Sainte-Radegonde at Chinon may depict the Plantagenets, with Eleanor of Aquitaine, crowned, in the center.

The tomb of "the beautiful Navarroise," Berengaria of Navarre, in the abbey of l'Epau, Le Mans.

In this romantic painting, Charles Allston Collins portrays
Berengaria's fears for the safety of her husband, Richard the Lionheart.
(Manchester Art Gallery.)

William the Marshal,
"the best knight
who ever lived," who
served five kings.
(Tomb in the Temple
Church, London.)

King John's effigy in Worcester Cathedral. "He was a very bad man."

Isabella of Angoulême. John was said to have lost Normandy under the quilts of his marriage bed. (Tomb effigy in Fontevraud Abbey.)

The seal of Hugh de Lusignan X, Isabella's second husband. She broke her daughter's betrothal to him and married him herself.

Henry III, King of England. He had "a heart of wax," but was a devoted, uxorious husband—a family man in every sense. (Tomb effigy in Westminster Abbey.)

The abbey of l'Epau, founded by Queen Berengaria in 1229.

The marriage of Henry III
and Alienor of Provence. He was
twenty-eight, she just fourteen.
(From the Historia Anglorum, Chronica
Majora of Matthew Paris, British Library.)

Thirteenth-century heads of
Alienor of Provence in
Westminster Abbey (above)
and Bridlington Priory (below).

Modern statue of Alienor's uncle, Peter of Savoy, above the entrance to the Savoy Hotel, which stands on the site of his palace. The English regarded the Queen's relations as "the scum of foreigners."

Henry III's brother, Richard, Earl of Cornwall, King of Almayne, married Alienor's sister Sanchia. (Statues in Meissen Cathedral.)

Edward I and his wife, Eleanor of Castile. "He loved her above all earthly desires." (Chronica Roffense, British Library.)

The abbey of Las Huelgas at Burgos, Castile, where the couple were married in 1254

Eleanor of Castile. Her aggressive policy of acquiring desirable properties and enforcing her dues caused much resentment, hardship, "outcry and gossip." (Glass in St. Mary Magdalene's Church, Himbleton, Worcestershire.)

Edward I. "Since the time of Adam, there had been no one to surpass him in nobility, splendor, wealth or learning." (Painting above the sedilia in Westminster Abbey.)

Leeds Castle, acquired by Eleanor of Castille, became a dower palace of the queens of England. Her "gloriette" stood on the smaller island.

am meam

This illustration in the Alphonso Psalter, made for Eleanor's son, may depict her with hunting dogs. (The Alphonso Psalter British Library.)

Eleanor of Castile's tomb effigy in Westminster Abbey. No English queen was ever honored with such elaborate obsequies.

Eleanor's statue on the cross at Hardingstone. The Eleanor Crosses were erected at each stopping place where the Queen's body had rested on its journey from Harby to Westminster.

Only three of the twelve crosses survive
those at Geddington (top left),
Hardingstone (top right)
and Waltham (left).
Edward I's chief concern was to
ensure his wife's passage into Heaven.

5

"In Inestimable Peril"

✝

WHEN ESCAPED ROYALISTS BROUGHT NEWS OF THE CATAS-
trophe of Lewes to the Queen in France, she was "grieved to hear
the course events had taken,"[1] realizing that there was now no one to
uphold the royalist cause but herself and those magnates who were with
her. She was so "anguished and wearied with grief"[2] that William de Valence and the Earl of Surrey, who had both been at odds with her in the
past, remained at her side, comforting her by looking ahead to better
times. She gave no thought to coming to terms with Simon, but became
more determined than ever on mounting an invasion of England to rescue Henry and take vengeance on his enemies.

On June 1, the Pope, learning of the disaster at Lewes, sent a legate to
threaten Simon and the barons with excommunication if they did not
return to their obedience to their lawful King.

That day, Alienor was in Paris, where she obtained from Louis the
money due to Henry under the terms of the Treaty of Paris. To raise more
funds, she and Peter of Savoy pawned the crown jewels to Louis. She
pledged her own jewels and took out substantial loans from Florentine
bankers and Enrique of Castile, Eleanor's half-brother, all guaranteed by
Peter of Savoy, who himself borrowed money to support her cause. She
was then able to raise troops of mercenaries from Poitou, Brittany, Savoy,
Spain and Germany. She even enlisted the aid of her former enemies, the
Lusignans. With their help, she recruited men from France and the Low
Countries, but she had the best response in Gascony, where she raised

Edward's feudal levies. She bought horses and distributed gifts to woo those she needed to support her.

Alienor's activities were reported in England, making her even more despised. The barons clearly feared the potential of the Queen and her daughter-in-law to make trouble for them. They knew how formidable and determined Alienor could be, and that she had an army at her back, and they had discovered that Eleanor had sent for mercenary archers from Poitou to defend her at Windsor and could command more forces from abroad if she chose. The barons decided that both women would have to be curbed.

On June 4, the King was compelled to summon Parliament. This time, Simon decreed that four knights be appointed to represent each shire, instead of the two Alienor had sent for in 1254. Parliament required the King to act in accordance with the advice of a council of nine. He was forced to forbid Alienor to raise money for him, and was to have letters sent "to all the shires of England, commanding all the adjacent sea coasts to be guarded by an ample force of armed men against adversaries coming from foreign parts."[3] He was also made to write to King Louis, insisting that no army be sent to relieve him. These strictures had the effect of forcing Alienor into a position where she was acting in contravention of the King's orders.

Eleanor was still at Windsor when she learned that the King and Edward were prisoners of Simon de Montfort. The barons wanted her under their surveillance, suspecting that she was plotting to summon more mercenaries from Castile. On June 17, they insisted that Henry command her to "go out with her daughter, her steward, her ladies, damsels and the rest of her household, and to come to Westminster to stay there, and not to fail, as the King undertakes to excuse her to Edward, her lord," who had ordered her to remain at Windsor.[4] Henry promised that he would "keep her harmless and receive them into his safe-conduct." The Countess of Pembroke was sent to a nunnery.

It seems that Eleanor disobeyed the order, for it was reissued a week later. Reluctantly, she traveled to Westminster, probably aware that she and Katherine were to be held there as hostages for her husband's good behavior. Windsor Castle surrendered to the barons on July 26, and Edward's Gascon mercenaries were sent home.

* * *

In the summer of 1264, Queen Alienor was at Saint-Omer with her invasion force. She had already exhausted the money granted by Louis, yet, while "mourning happier times,"[5] she remained indefatigable, working herself into "a sweat" as she gathered men and commandeered ships. Thanks to her heroic efforts, she had "succeeded in getting together a great army that, if they had once landed in England, would presently have subdued the whole population of the country."[6] By August, she had an enormous force under her command, assembled at the ports of Bruges and Damme on the Flemish coast. Her mercenaries were eager to invade, "thirsting for English blood," as one hostile chronicler put it. Simon regarded the invasion threat as serious, and strengthened England's defenses along the south coast, positioning a large army on Barham Downs in Kent, ready to attack if the Queen's force landed.

And yet this formidable army was never deployed. Persistent stormy weather and adverse winds prevented the invasion fleet from crossing the Channel. By October, Alienor was desperate for funds. The cost of maintaining her forces was high, and she had incurred debts she could never repay. When storms dispersed her ships, she had to appropriate others, among them "certain ships of Southampton, arrested in Bordeaux by order of the Queen."[7] When, at the end of October, she ran out of the money needed to pay her mercenaries, they deserted. The chronicler of St. Edmundsbury opined that, as "the sea and coasts were strongly guarded by an English army, the enemy was afraid to sail."

One might have expected the indefatigable Alienor to rise above her misfortunes and make fresh efforts to launch her invasion, but there was a compelling reason why she abandoned the enterprise. Henry had forbidden it. Fearing the consequences for himself, he had even appealed to Louis to prevent it, reminding him that he, Edward and Henry of Almayne were hostages for the Queen's good behavior and confiding his fears that her actions were placing them "in inestimable peril." In the face of that, Alienor could do nothing. It must have been galling, after all the time, effort and money she had spent on raising her army. Yet it was said that it must always stand to her praise and honor that, for the sake of her husband and son, she had made such valiant and vigorous efforts on their behalf.[8]

* * *

On September 5, Eleanor of Castile's infant daughter Katherine died at Westminster. The loss of her only child while her husband was in prison and she herself was held in captivity by the barons must have been a dreadful blow, not just for her, but for the King, who had been moved in August to Canterbury, where he had the date of his granddaughter's death entered in the necrology of Christ Church. It is possible that Eleanor had not even been with her daughter when she died, but had been made to accompany the King to Canterbury. Before October 3, Katherine had been buried in Westminster Abbey. Golden palls embroidered with Katherine wheels were provided for the funeral. Eleanor was now virtually destitute and had to borrow money for living expenses from the Justiciar.

The barons feared that the Queen would transfer more of the King's continental lands and rights to revive her enterprise. On November 18, 1264, they made Henry write to her from Windsor:

> The King to the Queen, health and sincerely affectionate love. Blessed be God that we have a well-grounded hope of having a firm and good peace in our kingdom, on which account be cheerful. Moreover, we have heard that certain persons at this time propose to make a sale or alienation of our lands and of the prerogative of ourself and our son in those parts, to the disinheritance of us and our heirs, against our will, which you ought by no means either to wish or permit, wherefore we send to command you that you suffer nothing to be done or attempted in such matters.

He assured her of his continued affection for her and their children.

With other recourses barred to her, Alienor, ever resourceful, now tried to engineer Edward's escape. In November, she managed to contact some of his household knights who were under siege at Bristol. In December, she sent word to them "that Wallingford was but feebly guarded and that her son might be released if he and the Bristol garrison would attack it by surprise."[9] The knights made the attempt, but had to back down when the defenders threatened to catapult Edward from the battlements on a mangonel, a siege engine that fired heavy stones from a bucket. At Edward's plea, the attackers were forced to withdraw. The barons promptly transferred Henry and Edward to the greater security of Kenilworth Castle.

In October, Alienor had asked Louis and Marguerite to urge the Pope to excommunicate the English barons who had risen against their King and were now acting unlawfully in his name, but Urban IV died before he could respond. Late in 1264, Alienor and Marguerite wrote to his successor, Clement IV, reminding him of Henry's zeal for the Church and urging him to support the King by sending a legate to England to deal with the barons. In return, Clement issued bulls in Henry's favor and appointed a legate, Cardinal Ottobuono Fieschi, Alienor's uncle by marriage, ordering him not to make peace with the barons until Simon de Montfort, "that pestilent man, with all his progeny, be plucked out of the realm of England."

On December 14, Simon compelled the King to summon Parliament. But he was becoming high-handed in his rule. On December 24, he forced Edward to cede the earldom of Chester to him, alienating the marcher lords. Other barons were beginning to resent his despotic approach and compare it unfavorably to their King's weak government, and some began to change sides.

Henry spent Christmas at Woodstock in the company of his heavily pregnant daughter-in-law, Eleanor; on December 7, she and her ladies were provided with new clothes for the feast. The Liberate Rolls refer to her giving birth to a daughter called Joan in December 1264 or January 1265 and to her churching on February 3, for which she wore a robe made of "cloth of murrey." On January 25, the King paid for medicine for Eleanor, which suggests that she was unwell after the birth. By April, she was again short of funds because Simon had seized control of her lands and Edward's, and she was once more obliged to borrow to cover her expenses.

On January 20, when Parliament met, Simon de Montfort ensured that representatives of the people were summoned—two knights from every shire and two burgesses from selected towns, thus incorporating the middle classes into the political establishment for the first time and laying the foundations for parliaments of the future.

In February, Alienor traveled south to Gascony, where she managed to secure the allegiance of the seigneurs to the King and maintain royal authority. Meanwhile, William de Valence had been recruiting knights in Poitou and sending them to Wales to join royalist supporters there.

In England, the fortunes of the monarchy were about to undergo a dramatic reversal. On March 11, Edward was brought to Westminster and publicly entrusted to the custody of the King, a ceremony that might have afforded him a brief reunion with his wife, whom he had not seen for nine months. He remained, nevertheless, a captive of Simon, who immediately removed him and his father from London, leaving Eleanor at Westminster.

Alienor enlisted her friend, Maud de Braose, wife of Roger, Lord Mortimer, a staunch supporter of the King, to plot Edward's escape. Maud covertly conveyed the Queen's instructions to Edward at Hereford. On May 28, 1265, Edward organized a series of horse races or exercises in which he could compete with his attendants. Maud had concealed a mount behind some trees and, in the chaos of the sport, Edward made his escape to the freedom of Roger Mortimer's castle at Wigmore. Immediately, he won over Gilbert de Clare, the new Earl of Gloucester—who was nicknamed "the Red" on account of his red hair and fiery temper— and began to rally men to the royalist cause, determined to overthrow Simon. When Alienor learned that her son had got away, she sold some of her jewels so that she could send him money. Sometime after July 26, she left Bordeaux.

By August, recruiting on the Welsh borders among the disaffected marcher lords, Edward had raised a formidable army, which surprised Simon's forces on August 1 at Kenilworth and cut them to pieces. Simon managed to escape, taking the King with him, but Edward had tasted vengeance and pursued his enemy to Evesham, where, on August 4, he again took the baronial forces by surprise, outnumbering them two to one.

"Such was the murder of Evesham, for battle there was none," wrote the chronicler Robert of Gloucester. It was a massacre, one of the bloodiest battles in English history. The King, who was wounded in the shoulder by those trying to rescue him, wandered around in the melée crying out, "I am Henry, the old King of England. Do not hit me—I am too old to fight!" He was led to safety by Roger Leyburn, who had switched his allegiance back to the royalists.

Henry, Simon's heir, "perished in full view of his father, split by a sword." When the fighting stopped, Simon himself lay dead, killed by Roger Mortimer and chopped to pieces by victorious royalists; his head, with his testicles strung on his nose, was sent as a trophy to Lady Mortimer. Evesham was a resounding victory for Edward. As Montfort and his son were buried in the nearby abbey, the barons had to face the fact that their cause had been crushed.

Henry owed his restoration to his son, who would thereafter be closely associated with him in the government of the realm and, for the rest of the reign, was effectively in charge. The King recuperated at Gloucester and Marlborough, wishing to be reunited with his wife and share his triumph. He wrote to Queen Marguerite, urging her not to delay her sister's return.

As a jubilant Alienor prepared to travel back to England, order was gradually being restored and there was steady reconstruction, but the victory at Evesham was followed by a campaign of revenge on those who had supported Simon. Their lands were confiscated by Parliament and given to royalists, arousing much bitterness. In October, the first of the manors "lately belonging to the King's enemies" was granted to Eleanor of Castile; others were given to Queen Alienor. Gradually, the King was reconciled to his barons, which owed much to Edward's diplomacy and good sense.

Edward and Eleanor were at some point reunited, either at Westminster or Windsor. Their infant daughter Joan died before September 5, 1265, when she was buried in Westminster Abbey. Two days later, the King purchased a length of cloth of gold for a pall. Late in September, he returned at last to Windsor.

On October 8, Queen Marguerite replied in lighthearted vein to Henry's letter asking her to hasten the Queen's return to England.

> We declare to your Excellency that, though we desire not a little to be in her company, and especially in the present happy state which, by the divine guidance, we have brought about, yet because we fear lest you should come into the bonds of some other lady on account of her long delay, we have taken steps to hasten as much as may be her departure. And, as long as we know the Countess of Gloucester is engaged in your affairs, we shall not have good patience till we shall know that our sister is in your society.

Marguerite was joking, for Maud de Lacy, widow of Richard de Clare, Earl of Gloucester, was a miserable, rampantly litigious woman, and the last person Henry would have pursued amorously, even though she was rich.

Maud's daughter-in-law was Alice de Lusignan, Countess of Gloucester, the King's cousin. There were rumors that Edward was enamored of Alice, who was reputedly very beautiful. Although she was his half-aunt, she was just a year or so older than he, and they had been friends for some years. In the spring of 1264, just before Lewes, the King had denounced her husband, the Earl of Gloucester, as a traitor, and Edward had held Alice prisoner in Tonbridge, Kent, after taking the castle there, although he had soon freed her. They were said to have begun an affair at this time.

Discretion was maintained; veiled references to the liaison are few and tantalizing. Edward had grown up with the example of his parents' happy, faithful wedlock before him, and the relationship may have ended when he released Alice from captivity, or when her husband was reconciled to the King in November 1264. Gilbert and Alice were to separate in 1267, and Edward and Gloucester would remain hostile toward each other. In 1269, the Earl refused to attend Parliament because he believed that Edward was plotting to seize his person. He also hinted that he suspected Edward of having committed adultery with his wife. There is no suggestion of any rift between Edward and Eleanor, whose fourth child was conceived around October 1265.

That month, learning that Alienor would soon be returning to England, Henry traveled to Canterbury to await her arrival. There, on October 26, he created their son Edmund earl of Leicester, the title that had been borne by Simon de Montfort, but been forfeited to the Crown. Edward, meanwhile, had gone to Dover to take the castle from Simon's widow. On October 28, after it had been surrendered, Eleanor de Montfort and her children left England, having been forbidden to take anything with them. She and her daughter the older Eleanor became nuns at Montargis, France, where Eleanor was to die in 1275. On May 24, 1267, the King magnanimously ordered, "as it was arranged at another time before the Queen of England," that the Countess should receive, via her proctor, £500 (£365,000) annually in dower.[10] Evidently Alienor still felt some sympathy for the sister-in-law who had once been her friend.

On October 29, a ship carrying the Queen and her son Edmund from France docked at Dover. Accompanying them was Cardinal Ottobuono Fieschi, the Papal legate, whom Alienor had persuaded to accompany her to show that she came in peace—and, if need be, to excommunicate the barons who had opposed the King. Together, sneered a hostile Londoner, Alienor and the legate "made a great cursing." At Dover, Edward and Richard of Cornwall greeted the Queen's party and escorted them to Canterbury, where King Henry was eagerly awaiting them. There, on October 31, Archbishop Boniface, who had returned to England after Evesham, hosted a great feast for the royal party.

In London, the two royal couples were afforded a state reception of great magnificence. The King had not forgotten the insults offered by the citizens to his Queen, and the Mayor and sheriffs had been made to surrender themselves and their property, with the keys to the City, to his mercy, and take down the gates.

Edward and Eleanor gave thanks for their restoration at the priory of the Knights Hospitallers at Smithfield and were entertained at another lavish feast in the priory of St. John at Clerkenwell. Edward installed Eleanor in the Savoy Palace, then rode off to deal with pockets of rebellion in Kent.

A chronicler of Furness wrote that Alienor was restored to her former status and influence. Superficially, it may have seemed so. Given that Edward was now effectively ruling England, she would henceforth not enjoy as much power as before, although she would be consulted at the highest levels of government and remain influential. Peter of Savoy, now count of that province, had gone home to govern his domains, and her other relations would never again have the influence that had been theirs before the war. From now on, she would devote her energies to working for peace and good accord, smoothing the way for her son's accession.

6

"The Way to Heaven"

✛

ELEANOR OF CASTILE NOW CAME INTO HER OWN. SHE WAS twenty-four, and the events of the last two years had matured her. She knew her rights and was vigorous in defending and pursuing them. Having received manors that had belonged to Earl Simon's supporters, she developed a taste for property and was determined to acquire a large landed portfolio, in which she took a detailed interest. She was aware that people were beginning to think of her as avaricious. In 1265, she suggested in a letter to John of London, her agent, that he adopt an acquisitions strategy that "will tend to make us seem less covetous."

Like the Queen, Eleanor had been granted the wardships of several royal wards. She took a great interest in arranging high-status marriages, and was in a unique position to assert her influence in this sphere. In her time, she was to involve herself in negotiations and preparations for no fewer than twenty matches—of relations, courtiers, godchildren and friends—in which she was often the prime mover. One of her aims was probably to establish a network of dependable, loyal clients and friends. Wisely, however, she did not arrange English marriages for her countrymen.

She also contrived to marry damsels in her household to men in the King's household, thus increasing her own sphere of influence at court. Some of the children of these marriages would be brought up with her own. She was amenable to one girl preferring the cloister to the husband she had chosen for her, but angry when, in 1280, Eleanor de Ewell, the daughter of a clerk of the wardrobe, refused to marry the son of the

King's physician; the Queen promptly confiscated money she had put on deposit for the girl with Lombard bankers.

Eleanor had spent a lot of time apart from Edward, but, from now on, she would be preoccupied with bearing children—her next four babies arrived in four successive years. He seems to have regarded her as a supportive wife whose duty it was to give him as many offspring as possible, and he took delight in talking about his large family. The couple was probably growing emotionally closer in this period, especially if Edward's involvement with Alice de Lusignan was in the past. There are no hints that he had other lovers.

The lands confiscated from Alienor were now restored to her. On November 2, 1272, she persuaded Henry to release some Londoners who had been imprisoned on her account, but his mercy did not extend to the leading citizens. Late that year, he compelled them to "submit themselves" to justice for the attack on Queen Alienor in 1263, and the Mayor, aldermen and sheriffs were sent to various prisons. Some were evicted from their houses, and Henry imposed heavy fines on the rest as the price of his forgiveness. On January 10, 1266, the pardon "to the citizens of London of their trespasses against the King and the Queen" would formally be confirmed by charter.[1]

Some of the money raised in fines was given to Alienor, but she had to send every penny to France to pay those who had financed her during her exile. Henry used his share to buy back his rights in Limoges, Cahors and Périgueux, which the Queen had sold to pay her mercenaries.

On December 8, 1265, Henry and Alienor departed from London on a progress. At Christmas, they were at Northampton, where they discussed with the legate ways of dealing with those who were still in opposition to the Crown. There were pockets of baronial resistance, notably at Kenilworth, where some rebels had entrenched themselves. The King and Queen were fearful that war would break out again. Roger Leyburn was dispatched abroad to recruit mercenaries, and Alienor went to Dover to welcome them.

At Windsor, on the night of July 13–14, 1266, Eleanor of Castile presented the Lord Edward with a son, whom they named John, possibly for Edward's dead brother, or for King John. The people of London rejoiced at the birth of a royal heir, dancing in the streets and joining processions to give thanks, and the "delightful news" that the royal succession was assured into the next generation was conveyed to Henry and Edward, who were besieging the rebels at Kenilworth Castle. Henry gave the messenger £20 (£14,600), arranged for alms to be distributed to the poor and sent wine to the royal ladies at Windsor and offerings to the shrine of St. Edward.

Eleanor was churched on August 24. Bearing an heir cemented her position, and several successful intercessions she made with the King on behalf of convicted murderers, and the favor he showed her, bear testimony to her enhanced status. A family man at heart, Henry III rejoiced to see his son enjoying the benefits of what was becoming a happy marriage, and he was delighted with his grandchildren. But all was not well with the infant prince. Matthew Paris stated that evil signs had attended him at birth, and he may not have been expected to survive infancy.

In October, through the good offices of the legate Ottobuono, the Provisions of Oxford were finally annulled by the Dictum of Kenilworth, which provided for the dispossessed barons to buy back their confiscated property—at a price. Eleanor of Castile found that the manors she had acquired since Evesham were being reclaimed, but, in their place, the King made new grants to her. In 1268, she was given the right to claim queen-gold in Ireland, while Alienor would continue to receive it from England.

Kenilworth surrendered to the King in November. Henry and Alienor spent Christmas with Richard of Cornwall at Northampton. There, the younger Simon de Montfort was received into the King's peace on account of having saved Richard's life at Kenilworth, for which Richard now gave him thanks.

On January 4, 1267, Alienor's mother, the Countess Beatrice, died, aged about sixty-nine. She had "shed a halo of light over the whole extent of Christendom,"[2] and her daughters must have grieved deeply for her.

There was anger in some quarters over the Dictum of Kenilworth. A rising in the north was quickly suppressed by the Lord Edward. In the spring, Gloucester rebelled against the King. Alienor was then at Windsor, but, on March 12, she rode to Dover Castle to arrange for the provision of supplies and weapons in case they were needed for a siege, and remained there until July 7.

On April 8, Gloucester launched an assault on London, during which the citizens attacked the Queen's lodgings at Westminster. But thanks to the goodwill Alienor had fostered when building Continental support in 1264–5, Henry was able to enlist a force of mercenaries and, on June 16, Gloucester was defeated by the Lord Edward. Two days later, Henry rode into London in triumph. Shortly afterward, he created Edmund earl of Lancaster, founding the famous House of Lancaster that would one day rule England.

On September 13, the manor, park and house of Havering, Essex, granted to Queen Alienor in 1262, were finally committed into her keeping in exchange for an annual rent. They would remain part of the dower of the queens of England until 1537. The palace, which had been built before 1066 and was surrounded by a park, was extensively reconstructed by Henry for Alienor. In 1268, he installed in her chamber twenty windows emblazoned with heraldic glass, to her specifications. The walls boasted murals of the Four Evangelists, while the chapel had one of the Annunciation, as well as windows fitted with stained glass depicting the arms of Provence, and a small statue of the Virgin and Child.

On September 23, 1267, Alienor's sister Beatrice died, aged about thirty-eight, leaving her widower, Charles of Anjou, as ruler of Provence and Sicily. Alienor and Marguerite now began to take a close interest in the administration of Provence, to which both felt they had a hereditary right.

On November 19, 1267, at a Parliament held at Marlborough, the Statute of Marlborough was drawn up affirming Magna Carta and most of the Provisions of Oxford, apart from those laying constraints upon the King; in this, the hand of Edward can be seen. Parts of the statute are still in force today.

In January 1268, when King Louis called for a new crusade to reclaim Jerusalem from the Muslims, an eager Edward wrote asking Pope Clement IV what he thought of the idea. The Pontiff counseled that it would be unwise for him to leave his aged father so soon after the establishment of peace in England and while men's minds were still bitter, so the matter was shelved for the present.

On May 6, Eleanor gave birth to a second son at Windsor Castle; he was named Henry, in honor of the King. He was given into the care of a nurse called Amicia de Dernford and joined his siblings in the royal nursery at Windsor, while his mother moved into the thirteenth-century palace that had been built in the bailey of Guildford Tower. Its great hall boasted a large mural telling the story of Dives and Lazarus. The Queen's apartments were hung with tapestry and carpeted. In 1258, a garden had been designed for Alienor by the King's painter, William the Florentine, probably in the Italian style; it had a cloister with architectural columns supporting the roof, with a lawn in the center. Guildford was to become one of Eleanor of Castile's favorite residences.

She now had a larger household appropriate to the mother of the heir to the throne. It included a chaplain, a steward, keepers of her wardrobe and chariot, a cook, a laundress, a tailor and three clerks. Among her waiting women was Alice de Luton, Edward's former nurse.

In May 1268, after a long illness, Peter of Savoy died in Savoy. In his will, he bequeathed the honor of Richmond to Queen Alienor and his palace of the Savoy in London to the hospice of the Great St. Bernard in Savoy. Alienor must have been disappointed, because Peter's first will, drawn up in 1255, had left all his property in England to her. But, in 1270, the Provost of Great St. Bernard would grant her the Savoy Palace. She, in turn, would give it to Edmund of Lancaster in 1284. It would remain in the hands of the House of Lancaster until its destruction in 1381.

Alienor had paid £2,000 (£146,000) for the marriage of a wealthy heiress, ten-year-old Aveline de Forz, for Edmund. It was a worthwhile outlay, made with foresight, for this union would bring him the earldoms of Devon and Aumale and make him one of England's premier magnates and a mainstay for his brother Edward. On April 8, 1269, Edmund wed Aveline in Westminster Abbey. His mother paid for the celebrations. The marriage was not consummated until 1273, when Aveline was fourteen.

May 1269 saw another royal wedding, when Henry of Almayne married Alienor's cousin Constance, the daughter of Gaston de Béarn, at

Windsor. The match had first been discussed when the Queen was in Gascony in 1265, and the wedding was the fruit of her careful diplomacy, her intention being to win over Gaston's loyalty to the English Crown.

On June 18, 1269, Eleanor bore a daughter at Windsor, who was named after the Queen and herself, and who will be referred to here as Eleonore (a medieval variant) to distinguish her from her mother. The child was provided with a baby carriage covered in green cloth, lined with silk and suspended between two horses. When she was just four days old, her father began negotiating a marriage for her with the son of the Count of Burgundy, a plan that came to nothing.

In July, John, Edward's elder son, turned three. It appears that he was now thought likely to survive, for the barons acknowledged him as his father's heir in a ceremony in Westminster Hall. Edward and Eleanor looked on as the great lords swore fealty to the handsome little boy.

That summer, Henry was preparing to visit France to meet King Louis, whom the Pope had appointed to lead the new crusade to Jerusalem. He asked his brother-in-law if Alienor might accompany him, "so that we may be cheered by the sight of her and by talking with her."[3] Louis responded by issuing a personal invitation to her, knowing her to be useful in maintaining the accord between England and France.

In August, the royal couple crossed the Channel. Two ships were provided for Alienor and she received a new palfrey. At the meeting with Louis, the King and Queen agreed to set out for the Holy Land in a year's time. If Edward was unable to go then, he would follow as soon as possible. Louis advanced him a substantial loan, for which Edward pledged the revenues of Gascony as security; he also promised to send his son Henry to Louis as a token of his good faith. In the autumn, Henry and Alienor returned to England and preparations were set in train for little Henry, just fifteen months old, to be sent to France in the care of his nurse. The chivalrous Louis either released Edward from the agreement before Henry left, or sent the child back immediately.

By 1269, the east end, transepts and choir of Westminster Abbey had been built, leaving the Norman nave to stand for another century. On October 13, the entire royal family was present when the new church was dedicated to God, and St. Edward the Confessor's bones were reverently moved by the King, his two sons and Richard of Cornwall to a new coffin and translated to a magnificent shrine in a chapel behind the high altar. The golden shrine, which would soon be a great place of pilgrimage, had been built by Italian craftsmen; it had a wooden canopy and was adorned with statues of kings and saints. Its base was decorated with a beautiful mosaic known as Cosmati work, which can also be seen in the pavement of the sanctuary before the high altar. Queen Alienor offered a silver image of the Virgin Mary and jewels of great value at the shrine, which would in time become encircled by the tombs of the Plantagenets, whose desire was to spend eternity as close to the saint as possible, while Henry III reserved St. Edward's old coffin for himself. Since then, every English monarch except Edward V and Edward VIII has been crowned before the high altar, near the royal saint's bones.

From 1270, the King's health began to decline. He had to face the fact that he would not be able to keep his crusader's vow. That spring, Cardinal Ottobuono again preached the crusade, and Parliament granted money for the venture. The legate spoke with such fervor that Edward and Edmund of Lancaster both took the cross, followed by Henry of Almayne, the earls of Gloucester and Surrey, William de Valence and hundreds of others. Eleanor was going too, as was Edward's sister Beatrice, with her husband, John of Brittany. It was now quite acceptable for ladies of rank to accompany their husbands on crusade, and it would have been unthinkable for Eleanor, the daughter of the renowned crusader Ferdinand III, not to do so. She was following precedent, for her mother had accompanied her father. The Tudor historian William Camden—whose source is unknown—stated that, when someone pointed out to Eleanor that she might be placing herself in danger, she replied, "Nothing ought to part those whom God hath joined. The way to Heaven is as near, if not nearer, from Palestine as from England or my native Spain."

Eleanor's insistence on accompanying Edward suggests that her feelings for him, and her zeal for the venture, transcended her concerns about leaving her three young children behind. From now on, she would be Edward's almost constant companion. It was said that Eleanor was "inexpressibly dear to him." "He loved her above all earthly desires," wrote a chronicler. In later years, Edward himself would write: "I loved her tenderly." The love and supportiveness between them would become much talked of by their contemporaries. One historian has called them "the quintessential power couple of the thirteenth century."[4] For Edward, this happy union followed the example of his parents, whose love for each other he had witnessed since infancy.

Preparations for the crusade would continue throughout the summer, with Edward raising money, ships and men. Eleanor and her mother-in-law, the Queen, went on pilgrimage to several English shrines. At that of St. Freomund at the Augustinian priory at Dunstable, a daughterhouse of Holy Trinity, Aldgate, Alienor offered an altar cloth in thanksgiving for the health of her grandchildren, while their mother gave a length of gold brocade for them.

In July 1270, the King gave his formal consent in Parliament to Edward going on crusade. On August 4, Edward and Eleanor bade farewell to him and the Queen. At sixty-two, the ailing Henry III must have been grieved at the prospect of his beloved heir journeying so far from him, and may have feared that they might never meet again.

Edward placed his children in the care of Richard of Cornwall, who was to receive regular payments for their maintenance. They were looked after on a daily basis by their keeper, Mary of Valoynes, and their tutor, Nicholas de Havering. It may seem strange that Edward did not entrust the children to the King and Queen, but he probably wanted to ensure stability in his absence by demonstrating that they would not come under his unpopular mother's influence. Beatrice and John of Brittany did leave their children in the care of Henry and Alienor, and Edmund of Lancaster appointed Alienor to look after his affairs while he was away.

On August 20, Edward and Eleanor sailed from Portsmouth with the crusading army and made for Gascony, intending to press on to Castile for a meeting with King Alfonso. But, on Edward's arrival, he learned that Archbishop Boniface, who had traveled ahead, had died on July 18 in Savoy. Wishing to ensure the election of his chancellor, Robert Burnell, to the see of Canterbury, Edward made a hurried visit back to England, leaving Eleanor at Aigues-Mortes with the army. His journey was in vain, for he failed to secure Burnell's election.

* * *

Shortly before September 10, 1270, Alienor persuaded the King to grant
her "the keeping of the bridge of London."[5] After a year, having been
warned that the bridge was in a precarious condition, she resigned from
her post, but reclaimed it a fortnight later, having decided that the revenues were worth the risk of its collapsing. There would be complaints
that the Queen "taketh all the tolls and careth not how the bridge is
kept,"[6] and some of the arches did collapse in 1281, due to lack of maintenance. Only then did she resign her keepership.

When Edward returned to Aigues-Mortes in late September, he learned
that King Louis and his army had left in July for Tunis. Abandoning their
plan to visit Alfonso, Edward and Eleanor set off for Morocco, stopping
in Sicily, where they visited Palermo Cathedral. In 1268, Eleanor's half-
brother, the volatile Enrique, had led an insurrection against Charles of
Anjou, but had been defeated and imprisoned. Eleanor tried to intercede
for him, but in vain; he would remain in prison for nineteen more years.

The agreed plan was that Edward and Louis would join forces and
overthrow the Egyptian Sultan Baybars, whose forces were encroaching
on the Holy Land. But, on November 9, when Edward and Eleanor arrived at Tunis, they were informed that Louis had died there, of dysentery, on August 25. Charles of Anjou had been chosen as commander in
his stead. Edward was determined to continue with the crusade, but the
other leaders were beginning to waver, and a lot of the French had gone
home.

On November 20, the depleted crusading armies left Tunis, having
been persuaded by Charles to rendezvous in Sicily. When, at Trapani, a
terrible storm sank most of their ships, Edward's vessels miraculously
survived. He tried to persuade his fellow crusaders to press on to the
Holy Land, but they were demoralized and refused to agree. Charles came
to terms with Sultan Baybars, while Philip III, the new King of France,
and Edward's other allies decided to go home, having been paid an inducement by the Sultan. Edward was shocked, seeing the pact as a betrayal of the great cause, but the other leaders were adamant: the treaty
could not be violated. Still, he refused to put his seal to it, and only reluctantly agreed to winter in Sicily as the guest of Charles of Anjou, swear-

ing that he would keep his oath to go to the Holy Land, even if it cost him his life.

The allies went their separate ways, with Edward, his pregnant wife and his army remaining in Sicily. Charles, a generous host, placed two castles in Palermo at the royal couple's disposal. La Zisa had been built in the Moorish style by Arab craftsmen in the twelfth century, and stood in the vast hunting park of Genoarda, which meant "Paradise on Earth." It had flowing water and even an early form of air conditioning. Islamic influence was also evident in the architecture of La Cuba, built in 1180 by William II of Sicily, who had married Joanna Plantagenet.

Eleanor may still have been in Sicily when she gave birth to a daughter—probably called Juliana—who died at Acre on September 5 that year.

In the middle of Lent, Edward left Sicily with Eleanor and his crusading force for the Holy Land. After a brief sojourn in Cyprus to take on provisions, they sailed to Syria, where, in May, they disembarked at Acre, the only remaining crusader fortress on the Syrian coast. The city was still under siege, but the Saracens fell back in the face of Edward's advance and Acre was saved for the Christians. Edward and Eleanor probably established themselves in the vast castle known as the Knights' Halls, where Queen Berengaria had stayed some eighty years earlier.

On March 13, 1271, Simon de Montfort's sons came upon their cousin, Henry of Almayne, at mass in the church of San Silvestro in Viterbo, Italy. They had not forgotten that he had decapitated their father at Evesham and now had their revenge by murdering him during the service, for which sacrilege they were excommunicated by the Pope, at a shocked Edward's behest.

The royal family suffered another bereavement on August 3, when the five-year-old Lord John died at Wallingford Castle. Richard of Cornwall arranged his burial in Westminster Abbey. John's death left Edward's surviving son, three-year-old Henry, as second in line to the throne.

The King and Queen spent the Christmas of 1271 at Eltham, a splendid palace built by Anthony Bek, Bishop of Durham, and later bequeathed to Alienor. The Yuletide season was overshadowed by the news that Richard of Cornwall had been paralyzed by a stroke. The King and

Queen had to take charge of their grandchildren, Eleonore and Henry. Henry III was beginning to descend into senility, so the children stayed at Windsor with Alienor, who spent lavishly on them and gave them roast partridge for dinner as a treat. Eleonore became close to her grandmother, spending a lot of time with her. Ale, wine and milk were provided regularly for the children and their nurses, and Eleonore and Henry had baths on the eves of Christmas, Easter and Whitsunday. They were provided with fur-lined robes with silk cords and silver buttons, hats adorned with peacock feathers, and gloves with the thumbs emblazoned with the arms of England.

On April 2, Richard died at Berkhamsted Castle and was buried in Hailes Abbey beside his wife Sanchia. Their son, Edmund, succeeded him as earl of Cornwall.

When Henry III's health started to fail in February 1272, he urged Edward to come home, but Edward felt that he should not abandon the crusade, and he and Eleanor stayed on in Acre. He won victories at Cahow and Haifa, and took Nazareth, but his forces were too small and too stricken by illness to take any decisive action, and he was chiefly occupied with consolidating his position and carrying out spectacular but inconclusive raids. In the spring of 1272, Eleanor bore another daughter, who became known as Joan of Acre.

On June 17, Edward was roused from sleep to be told that a messenger from the Emir of Jaffa wanted to see him. Accounts differ as to the pretext the man used to gain access to Edward. He may have been a member of the highly secret and fanatical Islamic order of Assassins, or he had perhaps been sent by Sultan Baybars.

When Edward received him, the man raised his dagger and stabbed him in the arm, "making a deep, dangerous wound." Edward retaliated with a sharp kick, floored him with a stool and made a successful grab for the dagger, accidentally cutting his own forehead as he killed his assailant with a thrust to the head.

Either the dagger was poisoned or infection set in. Within a day, Edward's condition became so grave that he made his will. It was brief; he appointed executors and named John, Duke of Brittany, as the guardian of his children. While Eleanor was provided with a substantial dower in the event of his seemingly imminent death, she was not named among the executors and it was clear that she was to have no political role in widowhood.

Everyone thought Edward was dying. Eleanor was distraught. She was with him when an English surgeon arrived, took one look at the wound and declared that "the whole of the darkened flesh" must be cut away, a grim procedure in the days before anesthetics.

A long-established tradition has Eleanor sucking the poison from the wound. No contemporary chronicler refers to this; it is first related in the *Historia Ecclesiastica* written by the respected Italian scholar Bartolomeo (Ptolemy) of Lucca, in or before 1314: "They say that with her tongue she licked his open wounds all the day and sucked out the humour, and thus, by her virtue, drew out all the poisonous matter." Bartolomeo based his tale on hearsay, but it was repeated as fact by Roderigo Sanctius, Bishop of Valencia, who wrote a history of Spain in the late fifteenth century. The Elizabethan historian William Camden came across that history in his researches. A fourteenth-century chronicler, John of Ypres, had the King's Savoyard friend Otto de Grandison sucking out the poison, but it was with Eleanor as its heroine that the story became a celebrated episode in English history, only questioned in recent years.

According to the contemporary account of Walter of Guisborough, Eleanor cried and shrieked when Edward agreed to have the putrefied flesh cut away. The surgeon ordered Edmund of Lancaster and Edward's friend John de Vesci, "Take this lady away and do not let her see her lord again until I say." Turning to Eleanor, he said, "It is better, lady, that you should weep than the whole of England should mourn." In the end, Edmund and John de Vesci had to carry her out, "weeping and wailing." It is possible that attempts to suck out the poison had been made, and that both stories have elements of truth in them.

Edward's recovery was slow. When he did recover, he decided it was time to leave Acre and return to Europe. He had come to recognize Sultan Baybars as a brilliant military strategist and to accept that any hostile action against him would fail. On September 22, 1272, having concluded a ten-year peace treaty with the Sultan, Edward sailed for Sicily with Eleanor and his army. Early in November, after seven weeks at sea, they landed at Trapani, where they were welcomed by King Charles. It was here that news awaited them of the death of their son John, more than a year previously. Edward's grief was not as overt as people expected. He and Eleanor had not seen their children for more than two years and had been in no hurry to get home to them.

Eleanor has attracted criticism from modern historians as a mother who was uninterested in her children. Royal mothers were often separated from their offspring and did not undertake the day-to-day care of them. Their duty was to ensure that their children were properly looked after and educated, and to take an active interest in their marriages. Eleanor of Castile did all these things and more, yet the evidence suggests that she did not bond closely with all her children. She spent four years away from them, from 1270–4, and she would again be absent from their lives from 1286–9.

There are many examples of close relationships between medieval mothers of high rank and their children—witness Alienor of Provence, who, whatever her other failings, was an involved and loving mother. But it is clear that Eleanor's love for her husband always came first. Nevertheless, when she was separated from her children, she wrote often, inquiring about their health, and was stern with those who did not keep her informed. She looked constantly to their interests, their upbringing and their education; she controlled appointments to their households, including those of her cherished Dominican friars, and, when her daughters were older, she kept them with her. Significantly, her contemporaries did not complain about her lack of maternal concern. They would have considered that she had done her duty by her children.

On October 1, Henry III reached sixty-five, a good age for the thirteenth century. But, while visiting the abbey of St. Edmundsbury, he suffered what appears to have been a mild stroke. He recovered after resting at the abbey, only to fall ill at a meeting of the council there, after which he hurried back to Westminster. Alienor was by his side as his condition deteriorated over the next fortnight. She persuaded him to grant her more wardships "towards the full upkeep of her household" when she was residing away from him. Clearly, she was looking ahead to a time when he would no longer be with her.

As Henry lay mortally ill at Westminster, the people of London began to riot in protest about a mayoral election. On November 16, 1272, in his dying moments, he could hear, outside his windows, angry citizens chanting, "We, we are the commune of the City!" He sent for the Earl of Gloucester and commanded him to keep England safe until Edward's return, which Gloucester swore to do. Earthly duty done, Henry "fell asleep in the Lord."[7]

Thus ended a happy royal marriage that had lasted for nearly thirty-seven years. On a personal level, it had been a success; on a political one, far less so. Recognizing in Alienor a woman of great ability, determination and loyalty, Henry had allowed her to exploit her role as queen to its fullest extent, yet he had failed to curb her when her nepotism, acquisitiveness and poor judgment had threatened the stability of the monarchy and even its very survival.

Alienor must have felt bereft after Henry died. Her children and her close relatives were either far away or dead. Yet she did not give in to grief. Her priority was to help ensure a smooth succession. The great seal was delivered to her on the morning after Henry's death by the Chancellor, John de Kirkeby. With her consent, the Knights Templar arranged the late King's magnificent funeral. On November 20, the feast of St. Edmund, his body, clad in a crown and royal robes of red samite embroidered with orphreys and gems, was buried before the high altar of Westminster Abbey in the former coffin and tomb of Edward the Confessor. An effigy was placed on the bier and borne in procession to the church. It was said that the late King "shone with greater splendour and glory when dead than he had ever appeared when living."[8] Henry's interment in the abbey firmly established it as a royal mausoleum like that of the kings of France at the abbey of Saint-Denis.

Henry's will of 1252 had provided for Alienor to be regent while her children were minors, but the new King was an adult, and, at fifty, she may have felt unequal to the task. On the day of the funeral, she summoned a council of peers and prelates to convene at the Temple, where, by her consent and appointment, the Lord Edward was proclaimed king by Gloucester, who was to act as joint guardian of the realm with the Chancellor, Robert Burnell, and others until the King returned. At Gloucester's behest, the barons swore fealty to Edward I.

At Henry's death, Alienor's debts amounted to a staggering £20,000 (about £14,500,000). Her dower at that time was £4,000 (nearly £3,000,000) a year, but it was not granted to her until August 23, 1273. In the interim, she was assigned an allowance of 10 marks (£4,900) daily by the council, the sum King Henry had given her for the expenses of her household. The first patent issued by Edward I was for the "ample assignation of a dower to Alienor, Queen of England, mother of the King."[9] This dower, which was to revert to the Crown on her death, gave Alienor control of substantial wealth and she managed it with great acumen.

7

"The Flower of Christendom"

✝

EDWARD WAS STILL IN SICILY WHEN, IN DECEMBER OR JANU-
ary, a courier brought the news of Henry III's death and his accession to the throne. The new King, who was thirty-three, was plunged into
mourning for the loss of the father he had loved. King Charles expressed
surprise that his grief far exceeded that for his son John, to which Edward replied, "The loss of infants might be repaired by the same God that
gave them. But, when a man has lost a good father, it is not in the course
of Nature for God to send him another."

Edward sent word to the English council that he would hasten home.
But, possibly because of his weakened state, the couple had to make the
journey at leisure. It may be that the King was suffering from what is now
called post-sepsis syndrome, which manifests itself in fatigue and insom-
nia, and can last for months. Yet he was evidently confident that his formidable reputation ensured the safety of his throne in his absence.

In December, Edmund of Lancaster returned from the crusade to a
rousing welcome and traveled with Queen Alienor to Windsor, so that
she could be with her grandchildren. He later revealed that, next to his
father, he felt a great closeness to his mother. Edmund's loyalty to his
brother, and the close bond between the members of the royal family,
owed much to Henry and Alienor's love for each other and their children,
and their parenting skills. Alienor was to spend much time at Windsor
during her widowhood. She stayed less frequently at Clarendon, Guildford, Ludgershall, Marlborough and, occasionally, Westminster. Many of
her servants remained with her; some had served her for decades.

* * *

Immediately after Christmas, Edward and Eleanor left Sicily for the Italian mainland. Pope Gregory X had sent Queen Alienor a pastoral letter of condolence after the death of Henry III, and now wrote to Eleanor, asking her to persuade Edward to visit him. The royal couple reached Rome on February 5, 1273. There, they had an audience with Pope Gregory at the Papal palace at Orvieto, where the Pontiff awarded Edward the accolade of the Golden Rose, which was presented to illustrious persons as a mark of paternal esteem and honor.

While in Rome, Edward was struck down by a lingering illness, which may have been the aftermath of sepsis. He soon recovered, and he and Eleanor made a triumphal progress through Tuscany, then visited Bologna, Padua and Milan. Everywhere, they were feted and cheered by the crowds who flocked to see them. They descended from the Mont-Cenis pass on June 7 to find a deputation of English lords waiting to pay homage to their new King. The couple then traveled north and stayed at Philip of Savoy's castle of Saint-Georges-d'Espéranche, the design of which was to influence those of the castles Edward would later build in Wales.

From Savoy, Edward and Eleanor crossed into Gascony. On the way north through France, Eleanor realized that she was pregnant again, and Edward sent her back to Gascony to bear her child, then went on alone to Paris, where, from July 26 to August 6, he was honorably entertained by Philip III, to whom he paid homage for Gascony.

At Limoges, on July 26, the citizens afforded Eleanor a magnificent reception and laid on a great feast, at which they begged her to persuade the King to assist them against the oppressive regime of their Viscountess, Margaret of Burgundy. Eleanor sent a messenger to Edward, informing him of their plight, and he responded at once, sending a small army that quickly routed Margaret's forces and put an end to her tyranny.

On August 8, Edward left Paris. Instead of pressing on to England, he returned to Gascony to suppress yet another uprising by the incorrigible Gaston de Béarn; protecting his continental possessions had to take precedence over returning to his kingdom. He traveled south to Limoges, where he was reunited with Eleanor, then took her to Saintes, and thence to Bordeaux, arriving on September 8.

* * *

One autumn day, Edward and Eleanor were sitting side by side on a couch in the palace at Bordeaux when a flash of lightning zigzagged through the window, striking dead two barons who had been standing just behind them. By a miracle, the King and Queen escaped unhurt, but Eleanor, who was well advanced in pregnancy, had suffered a severe shock. It must have been a relief when, on November 24, at Bayonne, she safely delivered a healthy son. Her half-brother, King Alfonso, who was visiting at the time, stood sponsor at the baptism and, at Eleanor's request, the baby was named after him. After the christening, the child was given into the care of an English nurse, Felicia de Shortford.

At Bayonne, Alfonso, perhaps prompted by Eleanor, took the opportunity to remind Edward of the terms of his marriage contract, which provided for her annual income to be increased to £1,500 when she became queen.

On November 30, Edward met with Henry the Fat, King of Navarre, and negotiated a marriage between the Lord Henry and Joan, the heiress to Navarre, King Henry's infant daughter. Through this union, Navarre would come under the control of the English Crown, extending Edward's southern dominions.

In April 1274, Edward and Eleanor left Gascony with Joan of Acre and baby Alfonso, who was sent ahead to England with his nurse and installed in his own chambers in a royal manor house in Windsor Forest, which Henry III had had built in 1244–6. On May 8, the King and Queen were received in procession by the people of Limoges, then rode north through France. In Ponthieu, they visited Eleanor's mother, Queen Joan. When they departed for England, two-year-old Joan of Acre was left in the care of her fond and indulgent grandmother, with whom she would stay for the next four years.

On August 2, Edward and Eleanor sailed from France, landing the same day at Dover. Edward had been reigning for the best part of two years, but this was the first time he had set foot in England as king. From Dover, he and Eleanor traveled to Canterbury, where Alienor and their children, Henry, Eleonore and Alfonso, were waiting to greet them. The elder siblings can barely have remembered their parents, who had been away for four years.

Six-year-old Lord Henry now had his own household, supplied with eighty knights. With him lived his sister Eleonore and their cousin John "Brito" of Brittany. In the spring, Henry's health had begun to give cause for concern. On Whitsunday, he had been washed in a gallon of wine residue in the hope that it would do him some good. A man was paid to gather healing herbs for him, which were cooked in earthen pots. Henry was fed larks, partridges and pears to revive his appetite. His physician, the scholarly churchman Hugh of Evesham (who enjoyed the patronage of Queen Alienor), prescribed many confections of sugar and licorice, and Henry and his sister were also given pomegranates, quinces and almonds.

In July 1274, at the age of eighteen months, Joan of Navarre, Henry's betrothed, had succeeded her father as queen of Navarre and countess of Champagne. When Henry married, he would be a king, and English interests in Gascony would be extended and protected.

At Tonbridge Castle, on their way to London, the King and Queen were entertained by the Earl of Gloucester. A few days later, they were guests of John de Warenne, Earl of Surrey, at Reigate Castle.

On Saturday, August 18, Edward finally entered his capital, where he and Eleanor received a magnificent welcome from the citizens "and all the nobles of the realm, clerics and laymen together." The city was "lavishly decorated," the Londoners were decked out in their finery, and the streets were hung with cloth of gold and tapestries, "without thought of the cost, in order to glorify the King."[1] The conduits ran with red and white wine, and, in Cheapside, the royal couple were showered with gold and silver coins by the merchants and burgesses. The Palace of Westminster had been refurbished and enlarged at a cost of more than £1,000 (£730,000), and the royal couple returned there to find the way to Westminster Abbey carpeted with cloths woven at Candlewick (Cannon) Street in readiness for their coronation, which was to take place the next day. It would be the first crowning in the new abbey church of Westminster, and also the first English coronation at which a king and queen would be crowned together. Edward's sisters, Queen Margaret of Scots and Beatrice, Countess of Brittany, had come to London with their husbands for the occasion. The only discordant note was struck by his brother Edmund, who refused to attend the coronation because Edward had denied him the honor of carrying the sword Curtana.

On August 19, Edward, clad in fine silk, and Eleanor, glittering with jewels, passed in separate processions to the abbey, each having a canopy with jingling bells held aloft above their head. Foremost among the throng of guests was the Dowager Queen Alienor; there too were the King's children, Henry and Eleonore, and their cousin, eight-year-old John of Brittany, all resplendent in new robes. Edward and Eleanor were crowned by Robert de Kilwardby, Archbishop of Canterbury. "The King took up the crown and shone in glory before the peers of his realm. The Queen, like the King, shone radiantly, glorious in her regal crown."[2] It was set with emeralds, great pearls, rubies and sapphires from the Orient.

After the ceremony was over, Edward and Eleanor left the abbey wearing their crowns and processed back to the palace for the coronation banquet, at which they presided at the high table, still wearing their crowns and royal robes. The Lord Henry sat nearby, wearing a chaplet of flowers. Beyond Westminster, all London was feasting in the King's honor—and getting riotously drunk on the free wine flowing in the conduits.

During the feast, the King of Scots arrived with a hundred knights on horseback to pay his respects. When the knights dismounted, the horses were allowed to run free, the knights declaring that anyone who laid hold of one could keep it as a gift. Not to be outdone, the earls of Gloucester, Pembroke and Surrey and a hundred English knights gave away their horses as well.

Two weeks of feasts and celebrations followed. Westminster and London were packed with visitors. Wooden huts were built in the precincts of the palace to create extra kitchen space, and forty ovens were installed. The food had been on order since February, when it was thought that the King's return was imminent: 440 cows and oxen, 430 sheep, 450 pigs, 16 fat boars, 278 flitches of bacon and 22,460 capons and other poultry. The clergy were asked to donate as many swans, cranes, peacocks, rabbits and kids as possible. The food was not only served to the court, but distributed daily to all comers.

One notable absentee from the coronation was Llywelyn ap Gruffydd.

In 1267, Henry III had recognized him as prince of Wales, but he had refused to pay homage to the King. Edward had invaded Wales and driven Llywelyn westward into the mountains of Snowdonia, blockading all the passes and coastal routes and effectively placing him under siege. Llywelyn, determined that Wales should remain an independent principality, was still holding out and, in response to Edward's invitation, had sent a message saying that he could not attend because he would not pay homage to him as a vassal.

Edward I was to prove a firm, powerful king. He was resolved to restore and strengthen the authority of the Crown and bring good government, law, order and prosperity to his kingdom through a program of progressive legislation, for which he would become known as "the English Justinian." No longer was he the rash, impetuous young tearaway who had fought the barons, but "the flower of Christendom" who was resolved to curb their power whilst still retaining them on the Great Council. He would pursue the ideals of Simon de Montfort, working to establish representative government and the principle that statutes and grants required popular assent. He was a born leader, determined, industrious and energetic, and showed great shrewdness and wisdom in choosing his advisers.

"He was so handsome and great, so powerful in arms; he had no equal as a knight in armour for vigour and valour. Since the time of Adam, there had been no one to surpass him in nobility, splendour, wealth or learning."[3] He rooted out abuses, restored order in the kingdom and worked indefatigably to establish England as the primary monarchy in the British Isles.

Privately, Alienor of Provence was to wield great influence during the reign of her son, just as her sister did with Philip III. Both queens looked to their sons, especially Edward, to prosecute their rights to Provence, which they claimed in lieu of the dowries they asserted had not been paid.

As a dutiful son, Edward looked after his mother. Besides her dower, he made many further financial provisions for her, both in England and

Gascony. Many of her letters to him survive. She continued to protect Savoyard interests and did not hesitate to advise the King on international affairs. She commended to him Aumary Peche, whose father, Bartholomew, "took care of you when you were a child." She often interceded on behalf of clerics or religious houses. In one letter, she expressed gladness that Edward liked a house at Bindon that she had given him. In another, she thanked him for some fine fat cranes he had sent her, asking whether she preferred the heads without the bodies or the bodies without the heads; it seems to have been a private joke between them.

The King did not reply to his mother's letters as often as she wished, earning himself veiled rebukes, of which this is typical: "Know, dear son, that we are in good health, after our fashion, but we will be much better when we hear good news from you." On another occasion, Alienor reprimanded him: "Know, dear Sire, that we are very badly served by you since we have heard no news of your estate, and of how things have been with you since you left us. We are letting you know that we are in good health, thanks be to God."

8

"The Queen Would Like
Our Lands to Hold"

✠

O UTWARDLY, ELEANOR OF CASTILE FITTED THE MEDIEVAL
ideal of a queen. Of personable appearance, elegant in dress and
manner, she possessed many of the virtues admired by her contemporaries, one of whom called her "a pious, modest and merciful lady, a lover
of all English people and a support for her whole realm." Some saw her
as virtuous, fruitful, wise and meek, "an honour of womanhood." Not all
of this was true.

Eleanor was a devoted and supportive wife and accompanied Edward
on his endless journeying. Her life revolved around travel and repeated
pregnancies. Edward was the dominant partner in the marriage, yet Eleanor probably exerted considerable influence in private. He would not permit her to exercise the kind of political power his mother had enjoyed,
and she was never allowed to act as regent, but her frequent exchanges of
letters with leading magnates suggests that she was active behind the
scenes. The King did involve her in diplomatic relations between England
and Castile and there is ample proof that, in this respect, "strife ever
found a peacemaker in her."

Others learned not to anger Eleanor, for she clearly had a vindictive
side. Her officials adopted a more deferential tone than was customary
when writing to her; one bailiff began his letter: "To the high and very
noble lady, my Lady Eleanor, by the grace of God Queen of England, Lady
of Ireland and Duchess of Aquitaine, her valet, John le Boteler, if it please

her, sends greeting and as much as he can of reverence, service and honour."[1]

In 1279, John Peckham (or Pecham), the forthright and very learned Franciscan Archbishop of Canterbury, advised the Prioress and nuns of Castle Hedingham to admit Agnes, the daughter of Sir Roger Beauchamp, as a nun. When they refused, he wrote them a very stern letter, threatening that, if they did not at once receive her, he would punish them so as to strike terror into other offenders. He added that the Queen was particularly interested in Agnes Beauchamp and, if they were wise, they would be glad to receive her.[2] In 1283, after receiving angry letters from Eleanor, Godfrey Giffard, Bishop of Worcester, advised the Prior of Deerhurst to present the Queen's chaplain to the church of Welford to avoid arousing her anger. That same year, Archbishop Peckham warned Giffard not to oppose the Queen's wish to have her physician installed as rector of All Saints Church, Crondall. In 1290, Eleanor threatened to prosecute Giffard for non-payment of a debt, which he insisted he did not owe her. Robert Burnell, the Chancellor, urged him to pay up anyway if he knew what was good for him, and offered to be present at a meeting with Eleanor, that "this affair will find a happier end when you have had speech with the lady Queen in our presence."[3]

As queen, Eleanor had a great household to support and a ceremonial role to play. This all needed funding, but she was a businesswoman of consummate ability and a tough administrator. She kept strict control over her household accounts and engaged in wide-scale economic activity like no queen before her. Thanks to this, those who came after enjoyed greater autonomy in daily financial matters.

Above all else, Eleanor gained a reputation for being grasping. The chroniclers repeatedly complained of her avarice. Yet her dower of £4,500 (£3,300,000) a year, settled on her in October 1275, may not have been sufficient to support her, and initially it was all she had to live on. Because Queen Alienor still lived and held dower lands that should have been her daughter-in-law's, Eleanor's income needed augmenting. Thus she looked for ways of increasing her wealth, with extraordinary vigor. During her queenship, she acquired lands worth £50,000 (£36,500,000), yielding £2,500 (over £1,800,000) yearly, more than half the value of her dower. She and her clerks kept a close eye on new *inquisitions post mortem* to see which tenants of the Crown had died and whether she could procure any of their lands. "She acquired many manors, and those the best." Most were situated near her dower estates, which she was bent on enlarging. A popular doggerel ran: "The King he wants to get our gold; the Queen would like our lands to hold."[4]

Between 1286 and 1289, Eleanor collected the massive sum of £4,875 (about £3,500,000) in queen-gold, which Queen Alienor had made over to her. In good years, her Exchequer at Westminster recorded an income of about £10,000 (nearly £7,000,000). She died a rich woman. Yet her aggressive policy of acquiring land and desirable properties, and enforcing her dues, caused much resentment, hardship, "outcry and gossip," especially—as often happened—when she foreclosed on estates pledged against their owners' debts.

She was not above breaking or perverting the law when it came to getting what she wanted. She did not hesitate to evict, dispossess or imprison tenants who offended her. At Havering, when local people protested against her rabbit warrens being extended, thus impinging on local hunting rights, the twelve spokesmen were jailed. The tenants of a house seized by her agents were also arrested, falsely charged with imaginary crimes and imprisoned, while their infant was left lying in its cradle in the road. In 1283, the Queen bought a manor and immediately ordered her bailiffs to contest the boundaries, giving her a pretext to seize another hundred acres from her neighbors. On at least two other occasions, she unlawfully appropriated lands beyond the boundary of her own properties.

Her officers were clearly afraid of her, and often inflated the value of the dues she could expect to receive. Many were corrupt and practiced extortion. In some cases, where she had remitted a rent or due because her tenants were too poor to pay, her bailiffs and reeves would still demand it. She did little overall to put an end to these unsavory practices, yet on occasion—especially toward the end of her life—she did step in to right a wrong. In 1285, for example, when her bailiffs had been caught extorting money and injuring some of her poor tenants, she charged her steward, William de St. Claire, to investigate. But her stewards, especially Hugh Cressingham, were sometimes as rapacious as her bailiffs; even the King complained that Cressingham was ignoring royal mandates and conducting his duties in an unprecedented fashion. Given that people were frightened of Eleanor, it is incredible that her officers would have acted without her sanction.

Occasionally, Edward intervened to restrain her, but he did little to redress the complaints of her oppressed and overburdened tenants about harsh practices. In fact, he made no real effort to curb her activities, because the large portfolio of property she was amassing made her independent financially and increased the Crown estate. A list of the manors Eleanor had acquired by 1281 shows that he had helped her to purchase them. Her acquisitions made her a magnate on a grand scale.

In 1283, when Archbishop Peckham wrote asking her to intercede in a quarrel between the King and the Bishop of Winchester, he warned her, in her own interests, that many of her husband's subjects held her responsible for his oppressive rule because of her powerful influence over him:

> My lady, the saints teach us that women are naturally greater in pity and more devout than men are, and Scripture therefore says, "He that has no wife will wander about mourning." And because God has given you greater honour than to others, it is right that your pity should surpass the pity of all men and women in your lordship. Wherefore we ask you, for God's sake and Our Lady's, that you will incline the heart of our lord the King towards our dear brother, the Bishop of Winchester. My lady, we require you, for God's sake, that you will so do in this matter that those who say that you cause the King to use severity may see and know the contrary.

Peckham reminded Eleanor that it was incumbent upon women to set an example of charity and mercy and urged her to mitigate the behavior of her officers. Reparation to her tenants, he told her, must precede absolution. "My lady, for God's sake, let pity overcome you, and Our Lord keep you, body and soul, forever."[5] His letter reflects the popular view of her in her own day.

Eleanor was not interested in curbing the depredations of her officials. Her wardrobe accounts show that she communicated with them often by messenger, and she is known to have visited many of her properties during her frequent travels, so she must have been aware of their activities;

certainly she knew of the complaints against them. That became clear on her deathbed, when she asked that these wrongs be redressed. But, in her lifetime, she did little in response to the grievances. The fact that she dismissed or sued only those officials who had failed to collect satisfactory revenues indicates not only that her officers had been ordered to raise as much money as possible, but also that she was determined that they would do so by whatever means. Many were well rewarded by her with gifts and benefices, some of which she had used aggressive tactics in acquiring.

Edward honored her deathbed request to right the wrongs she had done and ordered an inquest into the administration of her estates, since her tenants had made so many complaints about her officials. "For the sake of the Queen's soul," compensation was paid by her executors to those who had suffered wrongdoing. Among them were people who had been forced to pay unjustly high or inflated rents, wrongly evicted, cheated of their inheritances, ill-treated until they paid money demanded of them, forced to pay tolls and customs for which they were not liable or deprived of pasture or fishing rights. One had had his millstream diverted by the Queen's bailiffs, depriving him of his livelihood. Others had had horses stolen from them. An official had prevented a tenant's will from being proved, pretending the man had died intestate and appropriating his goods to himself. A bailiff had imprisoned a Norwich tenant so that he himself could entertain a prostitute in the man's house. One man had been ejected from his lands and had to pay a stiff sum to get them back. A married couple who been falsely accused of stealing from the Queen were pulled out of bed, beaten, subjected to the hue and cry and imprisoned, despite their neighbors offering bail, until they agreed to give up the tenement they rented from Eleanor. Many received damages.

The fact that some complaints were rejected shows that the hearings were fair and that most pleas were probably genuine. It is clear that certain individuals bore grudges against the Queen's officials or were just trying to get money from the executors. Some of Eleanor's officers escaped lightly. Sir Richard de Weston, a judge who committed prisoners to Nottingham jail, was prosecuted for falsifying jail delivery records, but pardoned "for the salvation of the soul of Eleanor, the late Queen consort." In the fifty years after her death, dispossessed owners made many attempts to recover manors that had been conveyed to her through dubious means.

It was expected that a queen would use her influence to persuade her husband to rule with justice and mercy rather than encouraging him to be harsh, yet recorded instances of Eleanor's intercessions are fewer than those made to Edward by his mother. She interceded with him on just three occasions, in each case asking him to pardon a murderer, and there is no record of favors being granted at her instance. Yet we do find her asking the King's clerks to respond to the requests of petitioners, as a favor to herself, which suggests that Edward had delegated to her the authority to deal with such petitions.

Under Eleanor, the Queen's personal household had evolved. In 1290, it numbered 148 persons, of whom fewer than ten percent were female. Prudently, she chose her ladies and damsels from the ranks of the English gentry. Some were related to her or were married off to her advantage. Her favorites were Margery de Hausted, who was entrusted with her jewels, and Ermentrude de Sackville and her daughter Eleanor, who was probably one of at least eight namesakes to whom the Queen was godmother.

For all her faults, Eleanor seems to have inspired devotion in her servants and been a well-loved mistress. She was kind to those who served her, providing medicines when they were sick, granting them leave even when she needed them, supporting their children, attending weddings, giving away books, and ordering medicines for those who were sick. Many members of her household were rewarded after her death for good service.

Her establishment comprised a chamber, wardrobe, office of the robes, pantry, buttery and kitchen. Her household roll for 1285–6 shows that, besides her chamberlain, steward and other officers, she employed a butler, two cooks, a saucer, a tailor, a hairdresser, a huntsman, a coachman, a messenger, two keepers of hounds and twenty-three valets. Geoffrey de Aspall, the keeper of her wardrobe, who held more benefices than he could hope properly to administer, was a cultivated man who wrote treatises on Aristotle. To transport her belongings between residences, Eleanor had eight carters and twenty-four sumpter men. She often took all her furniture when she traveled, and so many belongings that extra horses and carts had to be hired.

It was important for a queen to be seen to be charitable, dispensing alms in person, as Alienor did. Eleanor was as generous as Edward in her almsgiving: in 1289–90, she provided food on Fridays for a total of 9,306 paupers at 1½d. per head. In the 1280s, she and her daughters participated in the Royal Maundy ceremonies. In the cold winter of 1283–4, she asked the King to give liberally so that the poor could eat. She dispensed alms of 2s. (£73) a day, doing this in person when traveling, although she usually deputed her chaplains and almoners to do it for her. Thus, not being generally visible in her charitable acts, she was not widely looked upon as a generous person.

Eleanor had several favored residences, among them Guildford Tower, Windsor, Langley, Woodstock and Eltham. She kept great state at all the royal palaces and houses and enjoyed a magnificent standard of living. Tapestries and painted hangings from Cologne, carpeted floors, glazed windows and Damascus metalwork were extravagant luxuries she favored. She loved vivid colors; her chambers and chapels were brightly painted and gilded. In 1278 alone, Edward bought her seven carpets. She enjoyed weaving tapestries herself and owned several sets. Her beds were made up with linen sheets and pillows, and counterpanes of velvet. She liked bathing, and installed the first tiled bathrooms at Westminster, Leeds Castle and Langley, where there may have been plumbing for hot water. Her rooms were illuminated by candles with decorative bands of vermilion and green.

Her extensive collection of gold and silver plate, much of it made for her by Adam, the King's goldsmith, included thirty-four pitchers, ten chalices, ten cups of silver gilt and enamel, over a hundred small silver cups (in which to serve the wine she loved), cups of jasper, plates and dishes of silver, gold salt cellars and alms-bowls, silver hanapers (basketwork containers for drinking vessels, or hanaps), benison cups engraved with holy legends, and enameled silver jugs. At the Feast of the Circumcision in 1284, Edward gave her a cup made from 238 gold florins. She also owned forks of crystal and of silver with handles of ebony and ivory, knives with handles of gold and jasper, and enameled knives with silver sheaths. She brought to England lusterware from southern Spain, fragments of which have been found in excavations near the Queen's apartments at Clarendon.

Eleanor possessed many precious jewels and costly pieces made of amber, jet and coral, most of them purchased from merchants in Paris or Florence. As well as her great crown, she had one set with Indian pearls and another with rubies, emeralds and large pearls. One of her gold rings was adorned with a great sapphire said to have been set by St. Dunstan, the tenth-century Archbishop of Canterbury.

Among her other valuables were Venetian glasses and vases, gaily painted bowls from Andalucia, basins of Damascene work, which was popular in Castile, and Moorish majolica "of outlandish colour," which had been brought to England by a Spanish ship that docked at Portsmouth. She owned bejeweled combs of ivory, looking glasses of burnished silver gilt, mirrors of glass in ivory cases, a silver bodkin in a leather case, enameled caskets from Limoges, silver bookmarks, and five serpents' tongues set in a flagpole of silver.

She dressed in robes of gold, or silks from Damascus and Tripoli; her furs and feathers were imported from France, and she wore gilded shoes and purses. Church vestments of very high quality, embroidered with the arms of England and Castile (now in the Musée Historique des Tissus in Lyon, and the Metropolitan Museum of Art, New York), were probably made for her chapel.

In 1286, Edward gave Eleanor a crystal and jasper chess set, which had been presented to him by the Knights Templar. He knew she would appreciate it, for she had grown up in a court where chess and other board games were popular, as is shown in the contemporary royal manuscript *Libro de los Juegos* (*Book of Games*), commissioned by her brother in 1283. Eleanor borrowed a chess manual from Cerne Abbey, and she and Edward played a version called "the game of four kings"; they also enjoyed backgammon, "griasch" (possibly ninepins), dice and charades. Minstrels, jesters, acrobats, pipers and strolling players were welcome at their court. Edward kept harpists, fiddlers, a tabourer, trumpeters and five "minstrel kings." Eleanor employed two fools, Robert and Thomas.

For all his stern reputation and his famous Plantagenet temper, Edward had a sense of humor and enjoyed a spot of fun with his wife's ladies, with whom he was clearly on relaxed terms. Five of them once hoisted him up in a chair and would not put him down until he agreed to pay them 40s. (£1,390) each. Court custom decreed that, if seven of the Queen's damsels caught the King lying in bed on Easter Monday, he had to pay them a ransom. The devout were supposed to abstain from sex during Lent, so this would have been the first opportunity in weeks for Edward to sleep with his wife, and he would have been eager to join her in bed. He had to pay up on at least three occasions before the damsels would let him do so.

Eleanor kept a good stable of fine Spanish horses, and studs at Hampton, Horsington, Woodstock and Eastwood, as well as hawks, greyhounds and bercelet hounds, for hunting on foot, and evidently shared her husband's passion for falconry and chasing stags. An illustration in the Alphonso Psalter, made for her son, shows a lady wearing a gold circlet above her headdress and a blue surcote with trailing skirts; she holds by the leash three hunting dogs. This may be Eleanor. Her children were taught to hunt at an early age and provided with their own dogs.

Eleanor loved birds. At the King's Mews at Charing, near London, she kept an aviary containing nightingales and parrots from Sicily. Another was constructed at Westminster.

Edward was an indulgent, loving and generous husband who genuinely enjoyed pleasing his wife. He ordered that gardens be made for her at various residences, including Langley, a moated house in the Chiltern Hills in Hertfordshire that she leased from Edmund, Earl of Cornwall, in 1279. Eleanor enjoyed the pleasures of horticulture, about which she was very knowledgeable. She may have introduced the hollyhock into England; its old name was Spanish rose. At Langley, she made a garden in which she planted fruit trees and vines. In 1289, she returned from Bordeaux with gardeners from Aragon, who dug wells, probably for ornamental fountains, suggesting that Eleanor planned a water garden, or "paradise garden," like those in her native Castile. They also created an apple orchard.

Langley seems to have been her favorite seat in her later years. It stood on a hillside overlooking the River Gade and was built around three courtyards. Eleanor spent lavishly transforming it into a royal palace, employing the best London masons, carpenters, craftsmen and artists. The hall was decorated with "fifty-four shields and four knights seeking a tournament." Langley had a deer park, water mills, meadows, a paved cloister and two vineyards. In nearby Cain's Field, Eleanor kept a camel and a lion cub. To the north of the palace stood a Dominican priory. The Queen's presence at Langley led to the expansion of the village; by the time of her death, it was holding a weekly market and a Whitsun fair.

Eleanor certainly enjoyed fruit. She ate lots of pears, apples and quinces, and imported pomegranates, oranges, lemons, figs, raisins and dates. In 1280, she obtained grafts of the Blanc Durel apple from France, which were spliced by James Frangipane, her vine keeper. Like Alienor of Provence, she favored Cailloel pears. Dishes served by her cooks were often made with olive oil, onions—she ordered seventeen baskets in 1280—and citrus fruits. She loved fish, and cheeses from Brie and Champagne.

She seems to have been healthy and robust—witness her eighteen pregnancies and her extensive travels. Her zeal for hygiene and fresh-air pursuits and her southern taste in food would have contributed to her well-being.

Eleanor encouraged and supported an expanding circle of artists. She employed musicians for herself and her children. She showed an interest in the universities of Oxford and Cambridge and, in 1290, corresponded about one of her books with an Oxford scholar. Coming from a court with a tradition of learning, she was a great patron of letters, unusually literate for a woman of her time. She kept a library of devotional and illustrated manuscripts, bought or commissioned books for her own use and had a scriptorium, unique in northern Europe, employing an illuminator and two clerks as copyists. Wherever she went, her books and the staff of her scriptorium traveled with her.

It was possibly Eleanor who brought to England a Castilian manuscript of St. Beatus of Liebama's commentary on the apocalypse, written in 776, which may have inspired some of the illustrations in the Trinity Apocalypse owned by her mother-in-law. She discovered a Latin treatise called "Ierarchie" ("Hierarchy") in the house of the Friars Minors at Southampton and commissioned Jean de Pentham, a French friar, to translate it into his native tongue for her. Although she spoke Castilian, she knew French. At Acre, during the crusade, she is said to have had one of her clerks transcribe, as a gift for Edward, Flavius Vegetius Renatus's *De Re Militari* (*The Art of War*), originally dedicated to the Roman Emperor Valentinian in the fourth century. Edward and Eleanor appear on

the title page of the Douce Apocalypse of *c.* 1270, a richly illustrated manuscript now in the Bodleian Library. The banner of the Earl of Gloucester, who was long at odds with Edward, appears among those of Satan's
host, while Simon de Montfort is shown fighting for the Devil. It is clear
that, of the royal couple, Eleanor was the one who sourced and commissioned books.

She owned several romances, all stored in a chest. Around 1280, when
the French writer Girard of Amiens was at the English court, Eleanor
dictated to him an Arthurian romance about a princess of Northumbria
called *Escanor*, which she had composed herself; it ran to nearly 26,000
verses.

She exchanged books with her brother Alfonso, whose tastes may have
influenced hers. She sent him Edward's manuscript of Rustichello de
Pisa's romance *Meliadus* (1273), about the father of Tristan, which inspired the first Arthurian text to be written in Castile. She received from
Alfonso *The Book of Muhammed's Ladder*, describing how Muhammed as-
cended to Heaven and saw all the wonders God had revealed to him. Alfonso may also have sent her a copy of his weighty code of law, the *Sieta
Partidas*.

Like her brother, Eleanor had progressive ideas about the education of
women. She ordered writing tablets for her daughters, which suggests
that she herself had been taught to write as well as to read. Although
forty-seven of her letters survive, none is in her own hand; she would have
dictated them to her clerks. During a visit to Cambridge in 1289, she
bought a psalter and seven books of hours as primers for the princesses.
In 1290, she appointed a scribe from her scriptorium to assist with her
children's correspondence. She enjoyed the more conventional feminine
arts of embroidery and weaving and taught her daughters those skills,
buying silks and spindles. She was also interested in heraldry.

Like other thirteenth-century queens, Eleanor kept her own chapel,
where she observed the obits of her deceased relatives. Its contents filled
two coffers when she went on her travels. She bought primers, books of
hours, paternosters and rosary beads of coral and jet, in keeping with the
observance of the private devotions the mendicant friars encouraged.
Nearly every summer, she made a progress to her favorite shrines, a practice that would be emulated by her daughters.

She was the greatest royal foundress since Matilda of Scotland in the early twelfth century, a devout and bountiful benefactor and patron to churches and religious houses. Her special devotion to the Friars Preachers, especially the Dominicans, has been noted, and she and Edward were benefactors of the new church of the Black Friars in London, where, in time, the hearts of Eleanor and her son Alfonso would be buried. She founded Dominican priories in London and Chichester; to others, she was a generous donor. She chose her confessor and her children's tutors from the Dominicans. In 1280, they admitted the Queen and her young ones to the confraternity of their order and made them beneficiaries of their charity at Oxford.

Having a special devotion to Edward the Confessor, Eleanor was bountiful to Westminster Abbey and endowed it with many manors and holy relics, including the finger of St. Nicholas, the patron saint of children. Many other churches and religious houses benefited from her generosity. She endowed the Royal Hospital of St. Katherine by the Tower and gave vestments from her own chapel to the cathedrals at Bath and Lichfield. She established a hospital dedicated to St. John the Baptist at Gorleston, a church at Macclesfield, an almshouse at Rhuddlan and houses of Grey Friars at Rhuddlan and Chichester. In 1280, the Franciscans made her and her children members of the Third Order of St. Francis—lay men and women who supported the friars and shared in their good works. These are just some examples of Eleanor's religious patronage—the full list is much longer. Yet the chroniclers rarely mention her piety, probably because she also despoiled many religious houses of their lands and rights.

Devout Eleanor may have been, but she was not averse to having financial dealings with the Jews. She had entrusted some of her gold to the keeping of Jews. In 1269, a new statute banned the King's subjects from purchasing debts owed by Jews in order to gain the interest, a practice Eleanor had adopted, but she was still entitled to receive queen-gold whenever the King taxed the Jews, and some of this came in the form of debts transferred to her by Jews. Furthermore, the King could still grant a Jewish debt to anyone he pleased, and several were granted to the Queen, whereby she gained lands that had been pledged to secure the loan.

In 1275, when the Statute of Jewry banned usury and gave the King wider control over the exchange of Jewish debts, he granted Eleanor the right to take over debts owed to the Jews, which gave her greater scope to indulge her acquisitiveness for property and possessions, but was seen as underhanded and reprehensible. After that, although she extended her patronage to some Jews, securing for one the post of chief rabbi of London in 1281, she began expelling Jews from her lands.

In 1283, Archbishop Peckham sent her a strongly worded rebuke for committing the sin of usury, expressing outrage at the scandal her dealings with Jewish usurers was causing, and the profits she was making by foreclosing on lands Christians had pledged against the debts to Jews of which she had relieved them.

> For God's sake, Lady, when you receive land or manor acquired by usury of Jews, take heed that usury is a mortal sin. Therefore, I say to you, my very dear lady, before God and before the court of Heaven, that you cannot retain things thus acquired, if you do not make amends to those who have lost them. You must therefore return the things thus acquired to the Christians who have lost them. My lady, know that I am telling you the lawful truth, and if anyone gives you to understand anything else, he is a heretic. I do not believe that you retain in any other manner things thus acquired, but I would wish to know it, by your letter, so that I can make it known to those who think otherwise.[6]

Eleanor ignored Peckham's censure. Three years later, he again castigated her for continuing to profit from the debts she had taken over, writing to her clerk of the wardrobe:

> A rumour is waxing strong throughout the kingdom of England, and much scandal is thereby generated, because it is said that the illustrious lady Queen of England, whom you serve, is occupying many manors, lands and other possessions of nobles, and has made them her own property—lands which the Jews extorted with usury under the protection of the royal court. It is said that, day by day, the said lady continues to acquire plunder and the possessions of others by this means, with the assistance (though we ourselves do not believe it) of certain clerks who are of the tribe of the devil and not of Christ. There is public outcry and gossip about this in every part of England. Wherefore, as a gain of this sort is illicit and damnable, we beg you, and firmly

command and enjoin you as our clerk that, when you see an opportunity, you will be pleased humbly to beseech the said lady on our behalf
that she bid her people entirely to abstain from the aforesaid practices,
and restore what has been seized in this way or, at any rate, make satisfaction to those Christians who have been wickedly robbed by usury.[7]

The good Archbishop could have spared himself the effort.

9

"Chosen Lambs"

✠

THE FIRST OFFICIAL DOCUMENT ISSUED BY THE KING AFTER arriving in London was an order for the payment of the expenses of his children, whom he left in Queen Alienor's care. Evidently Eleanor was content for this to happen. She sent frequently to ask after their health, and the six-year-old Lord Henry received from her a white palfrey. But, in October 1274, he fell critically ill at Guildford, and Alienor summoned her physicians and sent news to the anxious parents in London. Turning to God and the saints for help, they had wax candles of Henry's height made, which were lit before several shrines, including St. Edward's at Westminster and St. Thomas Becket's at Canterbury. It availed them nothing.

It is often stated that they did not go to their dying son, and it may be that Eleanor, who was four months pregnant, was advised to avoid any contagion, but there exists in the National Archives a letter[1] from a "Queen Eleanor" to Robert Burnell, dated October 14 at Guildford, the year not being given. Eleanor's biographer, Sara Cockerill, has weighed the internal evidence in the letter and concluded that there is a slight possibility that it was written by her, in which case she might have been with Henry when he died on October 16. He was buried in Westminster Abbey on October 20, and his heart was sent in a reliquary to the church at Chilworth. In 1275, Alienor, who had brought him up for most of his short life, and was with him at the end, would found a house of Dominican friars in Guildford in his memory, and his heart would be reinterred there; on each anniversary of his death, it was solemnly exposed to the congregation. Henry's betrothed, the little Queen of Navarre, was to be married to Philip IV of France in 1284. Their daughter Isabella would marry Edward II of England, the son of Edward I and Eleanor of Castile.

Alienor was hoping that her late husband might achieve sainthood for his pious deeds and peacemaking, and that a cult would grow around his tomb in Westminster Abbey. For that to happen, miracles needed to take place, but there were very few pilgrims seeking them. One man claimed that King Henry had restored his sight, but when an excited Alienor recounted this to King Edward, he was dismissive. Angrily, she ordered him to leave the room, and he obeyed. But, as he told a friar, "I knew my father's justice well, and am sure he would have gouged out the eyes of that scoundrel rather than restore his sight to him."[2]

On November 10, 1274, fifteen-year-old Aveline, Countess of Lancaster, died giving birth to short-lived twins. Edmund was left desolate, for he had come to love his young bride. Moreover, because she left no heirs, he could not inherit her lands—his mother's grandiose plans for him had come to nothing. He had Aveline buried in a beautiful tomb in Westminster Abbey.

Alienor had suffered this and other grievous bereavements in the past two years, but Fate was relentless. On February 26, 1275, her elder daughter, Margaret, fell ill and died, aged thirty-four. Less than a month later, on March 24, her younger daughter, Beatrice, died unexpectedly while visiting her mother. Alienor had instilled in her a devotion to the Franciscan order, to which she herself was a staunch friend, and it was at Beatrice's own request that she was interred in Greyfriars' Church, Newgate. In the midst of her terrible grief, Alienor's chief consolation, according to the chronicler Thomas Wykes, was her joy in her grandchildren.

Around March 15, the old Queen received heart-lifting news from Windsor, where Eleanor had borne another daughter, who was named Margaret, probably after Edward's late sister. On April 17, after a short lying-in period, Eleanor was off with Edward on another progress, during which, in fulfilment of a vow they had made in the Holy Land, they visited the shrine at St. Edmundsbury. Making long journeys around the kingdom would henceforth be part of the annual pattern of their lives, and their itineraries were often plotted to afford Eleanor an opportunity to visit some of her many dower properties. This progress lasted eight days and covered 191 miles, so the royal couple must have traveled about 24 miles a day.

On Maundy Thursday, April 18, Queen Alienor visited St. Albans. The powerful abbey had a monopoly on grinding corn and fulling cloth, and the townsfolk were doing their best to break it. Bent on appealing to the Queen Dowager, they lined the main road to await her procession. But Roger de Norton, the wily Abbot, escorted her via "a private way." Some women of St. Albans guessed what had happened and chased after her, crying out against the oppression of the Abbot and asking her to intercede for them with the King, declaring that they placed all their hope in her, just as they trusted in the mercy and pity of the Queen of Heaven.[3]

Alienor stopped her chariot and reprimanded Abbot Roger for keeping the people from her. One of the women was summoned to approach her, but was so in awe of the Queen that she was unable to speak, so the townsfolk's case was explained by others coming up behind her, who presented a petition to the Queen, craving "your help, which you have often given us." It made no difference; even after Alienor's intervention, the dispute was settled in the abbey's favor.[4]

In 1275, Edward began substantially to improve the Tower of London's defenses, building a second curtain wall and a moat. He had a wharf constructed and an impregnable fortified main entrance erected. He built new royal lodgings in St. Thomas's Tower, overlooking the river, and beneath it a great water gate, which later became known as Traitors' Gate. Eleanor's chambers were decorated in green and vermilion, and gardens were laid out for her, with lawns, fruit trees and beds of lilies. In the summer, the King and Queen were at Kempton and Windsor. In August, when they visited Oxford, there were great celebrations. The citizens ran out of the gates to greet them, enthusiastic crowds lined streets festooned with decorations, and the women had all donned their best clothes and were carrying lighted tapers. Everywhere, there were demonstrations of love for Edward and his consort.

In the 1270s and 1280s, persecution of the Jews in England gathered momentum. Alienor may well have influenced the King's policy against them. In January 1275, probably at her behest, he made a grant to her "that no Jew shall dwell or stay in any towns which she holds in dower,"[5] enabling her to expel them from her lands. When one Jacob Cock was ordered to leave Andover, he countered by suing her steward for robbery, prompting an angry letter from Alienor to the King.

In 1276, Queen Eleanor was granted lands in Milk Street, London, which had lately belonged to a dispossessed Jew. Later, she was given houses formerly owned by Jews in the city of York. Numerous grants issued to her in the period 1276 to 1290 show that she benefited from the dispossession of the Jews. In 1283, at Conwy, Edward granted her all the concealed goods of condemned Jews, past and future. It is not surprising that the beleaguered Jews hid their valuables; such goods were often found when houses were ransacked.

Yet there is evidence that Eleanor felt some sympathy for the Jews. In 1281, she secured the appointment of Hagin of London as high priest, "with the assent of the commonalty of the Jews of England." By 1290, Hagin was known as "the Jew of the King's consort," and that year he obtained Eleanor's consent to sell his London houses to Christians. By then, the Jews knew that they would soon be expelled from England— Edward had already banished them from Gascony in 1287—so this was one of the few ways in which the Queen could offer them assistance. Her efforts to mitigate the worst effects of the persecution irritated Edward, who perhaps felt that she should have been showing more Christian zeal against the Jews; in 1287, he accused her of letting her love of money outweigh her love of religion. The fact that Hagin was still under the Queen's protection in 1290 shows that Eleanor followed her conscience and overcame Edward's objections.

Edward had repeatedly pressed Llywelyn ap Gruffydd, Prince of Wales, to swear allegiance to him, but Llywelyn kept offering what the King termed "frivolous excuses." Edward's attempts to impose English laws on Wales and divide it into shires had already met with much opposition and open rebellion. Late in 1275, learning that Llywelyn was planning to marry Eleanor de Montfort, Edward's twenty-three-year-old cousin, the King had her arrested as she traveled to Wales for the wedding. When Llywelyn demanded his bride, Edward refused to send her to him.

In February 1276, Eleanor de Montfort was placed in the care of

Queen Eleanor at Windsor and remained in her household for more than two years, during which time they became friends. Edward had not ruled out the plan to wed Eleanor de Montfort to Llywelyn, but meant to arrange the alliance to his own advantage.

That spring, he opened negotiations for the marriage of his daughter, Joan of Acre, who was still living with her grandmother in Ponthieu. The chosen bridegroom was Hartmann, the talented favorite son of Rudolf of Habsburg, King of Germany, who was acting as Holy Roman Emperor, although never crowned as such. It was agreed that the wedding would take place in the spring of 1278, when Joan was six. Alienor and her sister Marguerite, who had returned to Provence on her widowhood, had pushed for the marriage. Marguerite, who believed that Provence was rightfully hers and never ceased in her efforts to wrest it from Charles of Anjou, wanted it to go to Joan and Hartmann on her death. In 1274, on the grounds that it had reverted, failing male heirs, to the Holy Roman Empire, Marguerite had persuaded Rudolf to invest her with it, even though Charles was still ruling there.

In April 1276, the court was at Kempton Palace, where, on May 1, Eleanor bore another daughter, who was named Berengaria after the Queen's grandmother, who had unified the kingdoms of Castile and León. On June 16, Queen Alienor accompanied King Edward to Chichester Cathedral to witness the translation of the remains of her old friend, Bishop Richard Wych, who had died in 1253 and been canonized in 1262, to a new shrine behind the high altar. In July, the King and Queen went on progress in Sussex, Kent and Essex, returning to London in October for the opening of Parliament. By then, Edward's patience with Llywelyn had run out and he declared war on the Welsh. To begin with, the fighting would be confined to border skirmishes.

Queen Alienor had a special affection for Amesbury Priory, which, according to legend, was where Guinevere sought refuge after her adultery with Lancelot was discovered. Thanks to royal patronage, it had flourished in the century since its re-founding by Henry II as a cell of the abbey of Fontevraud. Under the rule of the Prioress, there were seventy-six nuns, mostly drawn from the upper classes, a prior, six chaplains, a clerk, and sixteen lay brothers. The community had grown prosperous on sheep farming; it owned 4,280 sheep, 200 oxen and 300 pigs. In 1265, Henry III had granted gifts to the nuns of Amesbury, asking them to celebrate the obits of himself and Alienor after their deaths.

Alienor had long been a visitor and patron of the priory. Like many high-born widows, Eleanor of Aquitaine, Berengaria of Navarre and Isabella of Angoulême had all retired to convents during widowhood, and in 1276, following their example, Alienor withdrew to Amesbury. She had perhaps contemplated doing so for some time, possibly since the deaths of her daughters. She wanted to become a nun, but she still needed to pay off her huge debts and could not enter the religious life until the Pope had given her permission to retain her dower. As a boarder at Amesbury, she did not lead an enclosed life, but enjoyed the freedom to travel, continued to take an interest in royal affairs, and had works done to improve the conventual buildings.

Determined to subdue the Welsh, Edward stepped up his campaign and began building an intimidating "iron ring" of strong, impregnable castles in strategic sites encircling Wales. They were designed by his Savoyard master mason, James of St. George. The cost of building them was prodigious. Work on Flint Castle, one of the first, began in the summer of 1277, when Edward and Eleanor were staying at the nearby Cistercian abbey of Basingwerk.

On August 16, the royal couple were at Vale Royal in Cheshire for the founding of the Cistercian abbey they were building as a thanks-offering for Edward's deliverance from a rough sea crossing in the winter of 1263-4. They envisaged Vale Royal becoming one of the greatest monasteries in the realm. Each laid a foundation stone, and Eleanor laid another for Alfonso.

A week later, Edward's armies marched into Wales. In September, the King and Queen followed, staying at Deganwy and Rhuddlan, where James of St. George had already begun work on another great castle. Edward's policy was to starve Llywelyn into submission and, to this end, when the harvest was due in, he seized Anglesey, "the granary of Wales." As winter drew in and food became scarce, Llywelyn sought a truce. Edward was merciful. In December, he summoned the Welsh ruler to a parliament at Westminster, where Llywelyn finally paid homage for Wales as a vassal prince. Only then did Edward agree to allow his marriage to Eleanor de Montfort to take place.

In December, the Queen bore a daughter who is called Isabella in some sources, but who lived only until January 1278, when she was buried in Westminster Abbey with her siblings, John, Henry, Joan, and Berengaria, who had died sometime after June 7, 1277. Eleanor lay in for nearly a month, while Edward attended to business in Kent, whence he sent her venison.

In March, the court stayed at Quenington and Down Ampney in Gloucestershire, a tradition Edward and Eleanor had established in 1276 and would follow for at least the next six years, always visiting in February or March, probably for the hunting. At Quenington, they lodged in the twelfth-century preceptory of the Knights Hospitallers. At Down Ampney, they stayed in the new manor house, which was rebuilt around 1500. Before Easter, they moved on to Eleanor's manor of Queen Camel, which lay near the ancient ringed hill fort known as Cadbury Castle, which some believed to be the site of King Arthur's Camelot.

On April 17, Edward kept the Easter court at Glastonbury, another site associated with King Arthur. Like his forebears, he was fascinated by the Arthurian legends; he identified himself with Arthur and was determined to put paid, once and for all, to the cherished hope of the Welsh that the legendary King would one day rise and aid them against the English. To this end, on April 19, he staged an elaborate ceremony, summoning the entire court, with the Abbot and convent, to assemble at sunset in the abbey church by the tomb believed to contain the remains of Arthur and Guinevere. At the King's command, it was opened, revealing two caskets adorned with paintings of the legendary couple. Inside were bones "of marvellous beauty," which were left on display until the next day, when King Edward wrapped the remains of Arthur in a silken shroud and laid them back in their casket, and Queen Eleanor followed suit with those of Guinevere. The caskets were sealed with lead to deter thieves, and the King and Queen commanded that a new black marble tomb be built before the high altar and that the skulls be displayed "for the veneration of the people."[6] At the Reformation, the tomb, with its sculpted lions and effigy of Arthur, was destroyed and the bones dispersed. The site of the reburial is still marked in the abbey ruins.

In May, at Westminster, Edward ratified the treaty providing for the marriage of Joan of Acre and Hartmann of Habsburg. In June, he dispatched Sir Stephen de Pencaster and his wife Margaret to fetch Joan from Ponthieu.

Eleanor attended a tournament at Windsor on July 9, wearing a mantle of Parisian furs. In August and September, she and Edward made a leisurely progress through the Welsh Marches. Eleanor de Montfort accompanied them, and the Queen escorted her to Worcester for her wedding to Llywelyn on October 13, the feast of St. Edward the Confessor. Edmund of Lancaster gave the bride away and Eleanor supported her at the altar and presented her with a costly head veil, the mark of a married woman. The wedding, which was funded by King Edward and attended by the King of Scots, was the occasion of great festivities, but Llywelyn was resentful at having been forced to acknowledge Edward as overlord of Wales. After the wedding, he and his bride traveled to Westminster with the Queen.

In the middle of November, the court left London for East Anglia. Norwich Cathedral had been partially destroyed by fire in 1272, when there had been riots in the city, and on Advent Sunday, November 26, the King, the Queen and the nobility were present at the re-consecration of the restored cathedral and the enthronement, that same day, of a new bishop. Then it was back to Windsor for Christmas.

In March 1279, at Woodstock, Eleanor bore another daughter, Mary. She was barely out of childbed when news arrived that her mother, Queen Joan, had died on March 16 at Abbeville. Eleanor was now countess of Ponthieu and Montreuil in her own right. These fiefs were held of the King of France, to whom she now owed homage. Edward had been expecting Hartmann of Habsburg to come to England and marry Joan of Acre, but when, in April, word came that Hartmann had to postpone his visit, Edward decided to go to France so that Eleanor could formally take possession of her inheritance.

On May 11, the King and Queen sailed from Dover and journeyed to Amiens, where, on May 23, Eleanor did homage to Philip III for her domains. She and Edward stayed for a week in Abbeville, where they set her affairs in order. She would now receive revenues from Ponthieu and Montreuil to augment her generous dower. In 1280–81, to give legitimacy to her new role as countess, she commissioned *The Romaunt of Isembart* (now lost), based on the life of a heroic mythical ancestor, which she had illuminated in Paris. In reality, her role in Ponthieu was confined to acting within the diplomatic sphere and overseeing administration. It was Edward who ruled in her name, and she was never styled countess in England.

In 1279, having heard alarming rumors that Charles of Anjou and King Rudolf were planning a marriage between their children, on whom they intended to settle Provence as the newly restored kingdom of Arles, Alienor wrote to the King:

> Sweet son, if this alliance is made, we may well be disturbed in the right that we have to the fourth part of Provence, which thing would be great damage to us, and this damage would be both ours and yours. Wherefore, we pray and require you that you will specially write to the King [Charles] that, since Provence is held from the Empire and his dignity demands that he should have right done to us, he will regard the right that we have and cause us to hold it. Of this thing we especially require you, and commend you to God.[7]

On April 3, Edward wrote to Rudolf, saying that he shared Alienor's concerns, for he wanted Provence for his own daughter, Joan of Acre, and surely Rudolf wanted it for his son Hartmann. Alienor need not have worried; in the end, the marriage alliance between the children of Charles and Rudolf never took place.

In 1280, Alienor asked Edward if two of her granddaughters could keep her company at Amesbury. He sent his one-year-old daughter Mary and her cousin, Eleanor of Brittany, to live with the old Queen, and granted Alienor the right to dispose of Mary in marriage or religion. Eleanor was deeply dismayed when a bishop, primed by her mother-in-law, proposed that Mary be dedicated to God as a nun. When she adamantly refused, the Bishop rebuked her for "withholding from Heaven a chosen lamb from her numerous flock." Eleanor may have reflected that God had already taken to Himself eight of her lambs.

As soon as they were considered old enough, the royal children were allowed to accompany their parents on their travels. On October 6, 1280, Alfonso, Eleonore, Joan, Margaret and Mary were present with the King and Queen in Lincoln Cathedral amid a throng of magnates and prelates for the consecration of the new east end of the Angel Choir and the translation of the body of St. Hugh of Lincoln to its new shrine behind the high altar. It is possible that the statues of Edward and Eleanor on the south front of the cathedral were erected in commemoration of this occasion. That autumn, the royal couple traveled north to Cumbria, where they stayed for several days at Lanercost Priory near Hadrian's Wall. After visiting Newcastle and Durham, they returned south in October.

That month, Alienor traveled to Mâcon in Burgundy to meet Marguerite, who was still intriguing against Charles of Anjou. They and their Savoyard relatives formed the League of Mâcon with the objective of enforcing their claims to Provence by armed might. The two queens agreed to assemble their forces at Lyon the following May. At Marguerite's request, Edward had promised them troops, which they now asked him to dispatch, declaring that they had "special confidence" in him to right the wrong done them. In November, Edward informed Marguerite that he would appeal to Charles of Anjou and, if that failed, threaten war.

Early in 1282, Edward and Eleanor received the grievous news that their daughter Joan's betrothed, Hartmann of Habsburg, had drowned on December 20 when his boat capsized on the River Rhine. That put paid to one of Edward's plans for a foreign alliance. But, in 1275, Pedro III, King of Aragon, had proposed marriages between his heir, the Infante Alfonso, and Edward's daughter Eleonore, and between his daughter, the Infanta Isabella, and the Lord Alfonso. After years of discussions, Edward finally approved of the plan and, early in 1282, he and Pedro appointed proctors to conclude the marriages. In February, the two queens were at Guildford, where the twelve-year-old Lady Eleonore consented in writing to her marriage to Alfonso of Aragon, attaching the seals of her mother and grandmother in token of their approval.

Constance of Sicily, Pedro's Queen, insisted that Eleonore be sent to Aragon immediately, but Edward replied that his wife and his mother were against her going at such a tender age—she turned thirteen on June 18—and that Eleanor wanted to wait at least eighteen months from Michaelmas next, and preferably two years. Both queens were doubtless drawing on their own experience, having been married at about the same age, while Eleanor had lost her first child when she was thirteen. Pedro agreed. Eleonore's proxy marriage ceremony took place on August 15. She was to remain with her parents until she was fifteen. Edward took his womenfolk's advice and kept all his daughters unwed until they had passed that age.

Trouble had been brewing in Castile since the death of the King's heir, Ferdinand de la Cerda. Alfonso's second son, Sancho, claimed to be his rightful successor, notwithstanding the fact that Ferdinand had left two sons of his own. Alfonso supported the claims of his grandsons to succeed him, but Sancho had the support of the nobility. Civil war broke out and, in the spring of 1282, Eleanor learned that Alfonso had been forced to acknowledge Sancho as his heir. Thereafter, she kept regularly in touch with him, learning—much to her dismay—that his efforts to reassert his authority were proving futile.

In Sicily, that Easter, there was another revolt, against the harsh rule of Charles of Anjou. It began with a riot outside a church in Palermo while vespers was being sung, and the rising became known as the Sicilian vespers. Two thousand Frenchmen were massacred, and the war that ensued would drag on until 1302, when James II, King of Aragon, secured the Sicilian throne. In 1284, Charles would be driven from the island. It was left to Marguerite's son Philip to persuade her to accept revenues from Anjou in settlement of her claim to Provence.

10

"Undaunted in Battle"

✠

IN MARCH 1282, AFTER EDWARD AND ELEANOR HAD PAID THEIR
annual visit to Down Ampney, they learned that Llywelyn's brother
Dafydd had risen in rebellion, which boosted Welsh resolve to remain
independent. At Devizes, over Easter, the King began planning an offensive. Eleanor was to support him throughout. For the next two years, her
forays into the property market virtually ceased.

In May, Edward summoned his feudal levies to Worcester, determined
on conquering Wales. He planned a three-pronged attack, with himself
leading a force into north Wales, while Roger Mortimer led the offensive
in the center and the Earl of Gloucester attacked the south. There would
be gains and losses on both sides, but, for months, Llywelyn managed to
evade the encroaching English forces.

Edward and Eleanor spent much of June in Chester. By then, Alfonso
of Castile had again been overwhelmed by civil war and appealed to Edward for aid, urging him to give full credence to matters Eleanor would
reveal to him. But Edward's time was increasingly occupied with the conflict with Llywelyn, and he had not the resources to help Alfonso.

In July, the King and Queen moved to Rhuddlan Castle, where Edward
had summoned his forces. With them were their daughters Eleonore and
Joan, the younger children having been left at Windsor. Rhuddlan Castle
was still under construction, but Edward did everything possible to make
Eleanor comfortable during her stay. Knowing how fond she was of gardens, he had a fenced courtyard built for her, with a fishpond, benches
and a lawn laid with 6,000 slabs of turf. Fishermen were paid daily to

provide food for her table. Edward even built a house for the goldsmith Eleanor had brought with her. In return, she lent him money to have the building works completed. Messengers were deployed to bring her news of the King while he was out campaigning. One such messenger was fortunate enough to bring news of the taking of Dolwyddelan Castle, for which the Queen rewarded him with £5 (£3,470).

On August 7, at Rhuddlan, Eleanor gave birth to a daughter, who was baptized Elizabeth and became known as "the Welshwoman." Eleanor paid minstrels to perform at her churching and provided a basin, tankards, a chest and a bucket for the nursery. She kept this child with her for most of the first two and a half years of her life.

In October, Edward was still at Rhuddlan, raising more troops after the tide of war seemed to be veering in favor of the Welsh. But, on December 11, 1282, Llywelyn was attacked and killed in an ambush at Aberedw, Radnorshire. The "warlike Prince" of the bards had "stayed undaunted in battle against a foreign nation" and paid the price. When his head was brought to Edward, the King was jubilant.

Llywelyn's wife, Eleanor de Montfort, had died in June after giving birth to a daughter, Gwenllian. Dafydd, who now succeeded his brother as prince of Wales, took charge of the infant and sought peace terms, but Edward demanded his surrender. Dafydd promptly disappeared.

Eleanor was still at Rhuddlan in February 1283, when Edward gave her Daffyd's castle of Caergwrle, or Queen's Hope. In August, Eleanor and Edward were staying there when fire gutted the fortress. They escaped unhurt, but the castle was never rebuilt. In June 1283, Edward granted Eleanor the right to hold a weekly market in the town he was planning to build below Rhuddlan Castle.

The King and Queen were still unhappy about their daughter Mary becoming a nun. As a royal princess, she was a valuable political asset in the marriage market. They probably objected to her entering religion at so tender an age, and because they knew that she was not suited or inclined to the life of the cloister, which proved to be the case. The King had been corresponding with Isabeau Davoir, Abbess of Fontevraud, on the matter for some months, and when, in March 1283, she asked when she could receive Mary into the order, he replied tersely that the disposal of the child lay with his mother, Queen Alienor. At Alienor's instance, the Abbess wrote to "the most excellent mother," Queen Eleanor, reminding her of the "great honour" she and the King would accrue by giving their daughter to God, and that Mary's prayers could win them favor in heaven. Still Eleanor would not give her consent.

Dafydd continued to evade Edward. In March, the King invaded Gwynedd, lodging with Eleanor in Llywelyn's hall at Conwy, which he would soon tear down to build Conwy Castle. There, he sent for hangings for Eleanor's chamber and created another garden for her pleasure. On April 25, Castell y Bere, Dafydd's last bastion of resistance, fell to Edward. The war was all but won, and all that remained was to capture Dafydd himself. The King dispatched no fewer than 7,000 men to find him.

In May, during the construction of Caernarfon Castle on the southern shores of the Menai Strait, a sarcophagus containing what was thought to be the body of the fourth-century Roman Emperor Magnus Maximus was discovered. The Emperor had actually died in Italy, but the King and Queen were present when his supposed remains were reburied near Dolwyddelan Castle, where they were staying. Edward had chosen to exploit a Welsh legend from the twelfth-century romance *The Mabinogion*, in which Magnus Maximus dreamed that he visited a great city and castle on the site of Caernarfon. Edward's castle would be built to resemble the walls of Constantinople, emphasizing its Imperial connection. He ordered that a town be built around the castle, which was to be his chief administrative center for governing Wales.

By June 20, Edward, Eleanor and their daughters had arrived at Rhuddlan, where Edward proposed to celebrate his birthday. The next day, Dafydd ap Gruffydd was captured and brought to him there, bringing the war to an end. Edward had him imprisoned and his daughters and his niece Gwenllian immured in nunneries in Lincolnshire, ensuring that they would never bear children to inherit the royal Welsh bloodline.

The King now consolidated his conquest of Wales. For much of the time, Eleanor remained with him. They were at Conwy until July 12, 1283, when they moved to the as yet unfinished castle at Caernarfon, where they lodged for a month in a temporary timber-framed eight-room palace. Edward had sent Eleanor's chamberlain ahead to see that her chamber was hung with tapestries in readiness for her arrival. He had ordered the building of new royal apartments with views of the gardens and the hills and caused turf to be laid outside Eleanor's chambers, providing a squire to water it in the evenings. The Queen's Tower and Queen's Gate at Caernarfon would be named after her.

On October 3, having been tried and convicted of treason, Dafydd became the first person of rank to suffer the new penalty for treason. He was dragged through the streets of Shrewsbury on a hurdle tied to a horse's tail, hanged by the neck, then cut down alive and disemboweled, his entrails being burned before him for "his sacrilege in committing his crimes in the week of Christ's passion." Then his body was chopped into quarters "for plotting the King's death." His rotting head was displayed next to his brother Llywelyn's at the Tower of London. Edward granted Eleanor several Welsh estates confiscated from Dafydd and others. Immediately, her officials raised rents and rode roughshod over her tenants' rights.

The King and Queen made a triumphal progress along the Welsh Marches and spent Christmas together at Rhuddlan, where they hosted a feast for 500 poor people. Afterward, they traveled to York, where, on January 8, 1284, they witnessed the translation of the relics of St. William Fitzherbert, Archbishop of York, to a new shrine. Then they returned to Wales, the Queen to Rhuddlan Castle and the King to Caernarfon.

Early in 1284, when Edward announced that he and Eleanor intended to go on another crusade, Alienor finally got him to agree that Mary, who was not yet six, could be dedicated to God. Both of them overruled Eleanor's objections. Eleanor of Brittany, who was four years older than Mary, was to be dedicated with her.

In 1284, the King abandoned his plan to marry Alfonso to Isabella of Castile in favor of a new alliance with Floris V, Count of Holland, whereby Alfonso would wed the Count's daughter, Margaret, and Edward's two-year-old daughter, Elizabeth, would marry Floris's newborn son, John. That year, Elizabeth's sister Margaret was betrothed to another John, the heir to the duchy of Brabant. Edward allowed Eleanor a prominent role in the negotiations.

It was probably for Alfonso's coming marriage that Eleanor or Edward commissioned for him two beautiful psalters. One, now in the British Library, is called the Alphonso Psalter. It bears the arms of the prince and Margaret of Holland and may have been made by Dominican friars in London. An illustration of an eager boy riding a white horse may represent Alfonso. The other manuscript, known as "The Bird Psalter" after its illustrations, which reflect Eleanor's love of birds, may have been made at Winchcombe Abbey and is now in the Fitzwilliam Museum, Cambridge.

In March, the Statute of Rhuddlan was enacted, bringing Wales formally under English rule and creating a new principality vested in the English Crown. Eleanor was pregnant again, and Edward wanted their child to be born at Caernarfon with its ancient imperial connections. That March, he sent for her and their daughters, Eleonore, Margaret, Joan and Elizabeth, to join him there, commanding her, for safety, to take a roundabout route inland instead of traveling around the coast as usual. To further protect her, he declared it an offense in Wales for anyone to strike the Queen or snatch anything out of her hand.

At the end of March, Eleanor arrived at Caernarfon, where she lodged in the same temporary apartments as before, in the middle of a building site. That spring, Edward installed nine glass windows in the royal chambers overlooking the lawn laid down for the Queen in 1282. On April 16, the couple celebrated Easter in great state, Edward having sent to London for their coronation robes. Soon afterward, he returned to Rhuddlan, forty miles away.

The last days of Eleanor's pregnancy were overshadowed by news that her brother, King Alfonso, had been overthrown by his son, Sancho. Distraught, she begged Edward to intercede with Sancho for Alfonso's restoration, but Alfonso died on April 4. Sancho IV kept his hold on the Castilian throne by executing 4,400 of Alfonso's supporters.

On April 25, 1284, the feast of St. Mark the Evangelist, Queen Eleanor gave birth to another son. Tradition has it that he was born in a small, ill-lit room in the magnificent Eagle Tower. The room measured eight feet by twelve and had no fireplace, but had reportedly been hung with tapestries. However, it is unlikely that the tower had been completed by 1284, so the birth probably took place in the timber palace, which would be dismantled soon afterward.

At Rhuddlan, Edward was given the news by a Welsh messenger, Griffin Lloyd. The jubilant father knighted Lloyd on the spot and made him a grant of land. Then he hastened off to Caernarfon to greet his new son, who was baptized Edward, after his father and Edward the Confessor, on May 1. "At his birth, many rejoiced."[1] After the loss of two or three other boys, this child was especially precious, for the succession was now doubly assured. Even in far-off London, there were celebrations. In an ebullient mood, Edward conferred a charter of privileges on Caernarfon and distributed money to feed 100 paupers.

A later tradition has it that, because the Welsh had told Edward that they would only accept a ruler who had been born in Wales and could speak neither French nor English, the King laid his newborn son on his shield and presented him to the Welsh people, saying, "He who has been born among them shall be their Prince." The story was first written down in 1584 and based on an oral tradition, but it is probably spurious, since young Edward was not created prince of Wales until 1301.

A local Welshwoman, Mary Maunsel, was appointed his nurse, and he was given other Welsh attendants. A carved oak cradle reputed to have been slept in by him was on display at Caernarfon Castle in the nineteenth century; it was three feet long, on rockers, and wooden birds stood sentinel on posts at each end. Its whereabouts today is unknown.

Alienor's letters show that she took an interest in the welfare of her grandson from the time of his birth. Her Gascon steward, Sir Guy de Ferre, would be appointed the prince's tutor.

In 1284, Edward designated ten-year-old Alfonso earl of Chester, in readiness for his marriage to Margaret of Holland. Alfonso was "a comfort to his father" and the King was indulgent to him. The royal accounts record numerous purchases made for the boy: a toy cart, a gaily painted crossbow, a wooden model of a castle, a little boat, items of clothing, hawks, hounds, and chaplets of flowers to wear on ceremonial occasions. In the early summer, demonstrating his father's gratitude for his victory over the Welsh, Alfonso offered Llywelyn's golden torque at the shrine of Edward the Confessor.

The King and Queen left Caernarfon in June, after Edward had finally announced to Pope Martin IV his intention of going on another crusade. In July, in Nefyn, the King held a round table to celebrate his victory over the Welsh, and there were tournaments and dancing. The reputed crown of King Arthur was presented to the King with a relic of the True Cross and jewels.

Eleanor took her new son and his entourage to Conwy Castle and thence to Rhuddlan. There, Edward's nurse fell ill and was replaced by English-born Alice Leygrave, who would later receive rewards for good service to her charge. He seems to have become closer to her than he ever was to Eleanor, and later referred to her as "our mother, who suckled us in our infancy."

II

"Medicinal Waters"

✜

IN 1284, ELEANOR'S HEALTH BEGAN TO GIVE CAUSE FOR CONcern, as evidenced by payments for medicines for her use over the coming months. This may have been a consequence of Edward's birth. Sixteen pregnancies in rapid succession could have led to iron-deficiency anemia, the symptoms of which are fatigue, breathlessness, palpitations and pallor. Yet all the evidence points to her having contracted malaria. From now on, she would suffer periodical recurrences of fever, which manifested itself in chills and sweating.

Tragedy struck on August 19, 1284, when ten-year-old Alfonso, "the hope of knighthood," caught a fever after drinking contaminated water and died at Windsor. The King and Queen heard the tragic news at Conwy, as they were preparing to go on a triumphal tour through Wales to visit various shrines. Archbishop Peckham wrote a letter of condolence to the King, lamenting the "terrible accident which resulted in the death of the child who was the hope of us all."[1] Everyone must have been concerned that the royal succession was now vested in one tiny infant.

Edward and Eleanor carried on with their journey, having sent the Lord Edward and his sisters to Acton Burnell in Shropshire. The grieving parents were not present when Alfonso was buried beside the Confessor's shrine in Westminster Abbey, or when his heart was interred in the church of the Black Friars in London. There is no record of them ordering any masses for his soul—or, indeed, for any of the children they had lost, as the almonry accounts reveal. Yet, in time, Eleanor would have her heart buried with that of her dead son.

In September, the King and Queen visited Chester and Vale Royal Abbey, where Edward gave the monks a silver chalice made from the melted-down seals of Llywelyn, Dafydd and Eleanor de Montfort. They went on to Overton, where a thousand Welsh minstrels played for them. In October, they traveled to Conwy, Caernarfon and Harlech to see how work on Edward's new castles was progressing, and he granted free boroughs in various places, to bring prosperity to Wales. On November 26, the royal couple visited St. David's, the Welsh capital, as guests of Bishop Thomas Bek, and attended a service in the cathedral. Then it was on to Cardiff, Caldicot and Chepstow. On December 21, the King and Queen traveled to Bristol for a Christmas reunion with their children.

The following April, they made a triumphant entry into London to mark Edward's conquest of Wales and received a rousing reception. On May 4, led by the Archbishop of Canterbury holding aloft the captured sacred Cross of Neith, which was believed to enshrine a piece of the True Cross, they walked in solemn procession, with all the barons and fourteen bishops, from the Tower to Westminster Abbey, where the cross was offered at the high altar.

On July 1, Edward, Eleanor, the Lord Edward and the five princesses spent six days sailing down the Thames, then traveled overland to Canterbury on a pilgrimage to Becket's shrine, which Edward enriched with bejeweled gold statues, while Eleanor offered gold. The family stayed at Canterbury for a fortnight, then visited Dover and spent a week at Leeds Castle, which Eleanor had acquired in 1278 from William, the son of Roger Leyburn. She had purchased a large debt he owed to a Jew and accepted the castle as security, giving Leyburn little in compensation.

Set on two islands in a lake, Leeds was to pass from Eleanor to succeeding queens of England, and is today regarded as one of the most beautiful castles in the world. Eleanor carried out extensive building works there. On the smaller island, she reconstructed the keep, or gloriette—the word meant a "little room" or pavilion in a sumptuous residence or park. She built a great hall on the ground floor of the gloriette, and a chapel and chambers on two floors. Running water was fed into the castle via a conduit. The King's chambers were in the tower across the barbican bridge connecting the two islands, which were linked to the shore by another bridge protected by a barbican and gatehouse. The surrounding park, where Eleanor hunted, contained gardens, fishponds, a mill and vines. She grew black grapes at Leeds, from which she had wine made in 1290.

That summer, Edward and Eleanor rode to Amesbury to visit Queen Alienor, who was unwell. Eleanor of Brittany had been admitted to the convent in March (she would become abbess of Fontevraud in 1304), and Alienor had persuaded Edward that it was now time for Mary to enter the community. Her strong will prevailed even upon Eleanor, who assented only "with difficulty" and not without protest, for her daughter was just six. On August 15, 1285, the feast of the Assumption, Mary and thirteen other girls of noble birth, all robed in white, were dedicated to God in the presence of the King and Queen, Queen Alienor and all the royal children. Edward gave each girl a sapphire ring. Eleanor seems to have felt the loss of this daughter keenly, and was resentful. She would allow her officers to despoil Amesbury of its forest rights, as she had despoiled other religious houses of lands and entitlements.

Edward settled £100 (£74,000) a year and a dress allowance on Mary. He provided her with firewood, wine and even jewels. She was given her own apartment in the priory, where her father was to visit her several times. She begged him, for the ease of her heart, to send her news of him by every messenger.

For now, Mary would complete her education under the guidance of the nuns. She would not take her final vows until December 1291, when she was twelve, the youngest age at which a religious could be professed. She grew up to be a very worldly nun who clearly had no vocation, loved gambling and often left her cloister to visit the court and her family. When Edward and Eleanor moved on to Winchester after her dedication, and the King met with his barons and held a tournament and a round table, Mary joined them.

Eleanor and Edward kept Christmas at Exeter with their daughters Eleonore, Joan and Margaret. At New Year 1286, Edward gave Eleanor a gold cup and a gold pitcher decorated with enamel and precious stones. It was by far the most expensive purchase of goldsmith's work that he made that year.

On January 23, 1286, on their way back to London, the family visited Alienor and Mary at Amesbury. Mary may have looked on enviously at her sisters' silk gowns and silver buttons, the kind of finery that was forbidden her now. During the visit, Edward promised his mother that, if she herself entered any religious order, she could retain all her possessions in England and Gascony until Michaelmas 1287 and have for life various castles, lands and tenements.

Edward now turned his attention to the affairs of Gascony. It was seven years since he had visited the duchy, having been occupied with the Welsh war. Now Philip IV, the new King of France, was urging him to do so, in the interests of maintaining peace. Judging that England and Wales were in a sufficiently settled state, Edward resolved to base himself in Gascony for a time and rule from there. Eleanor was to accompany him, but their children would be left behind, the Lord Edward in his own household and his sisters in the care of Eustache Hatch, who served both the King and Queen.

Eleanor was again unwell that winter, when medicines were purchased for her. In February, she and Edward visited their children at Langley before returning to London. Later that month, she was still poorly. In March, she sent a wax candle of her own height to be burned at a saint's shrine, in the hope that holy intercessions would restore her to health.

After the spring sojourn at Quenington, Edward visited Amesbury in March. When he left, he took Mary with him and she stayed with the court at Winchester for a month. Possibly she was finding it hard to adjust to her new life for, in May, she spent another month with her family, this time journeying to Dover. When it was time for her to return to Amesbury, her mother arranged for her to have 50 marks (about £24,500) annually to supplement her income.

The King and Queen returned to Westminster, where Edmund of Cornwall was invested as regent. Eleanor, now forty-four, was pregnant again when, on May 13, with a great train, she and Edward embarked at Dover. Alienor had planned to cross the sea with them and visit her relatives in Savoy before taking the veil, but there is no record of her doing so, although she had come with her granddaughters to bid the King and Queen farewell.

The royal fleet docked at Wissant. At the end of May, the very handsome Philip IV welcomed them at Amiens, where Edward paid homage for Gascony. Philip escorted the couple to Paris, where they stayed for two months at the abbey of Saint-Germain-des-Prés. The kings feasted each other, and Eleanor bought jewelry for her daughters and sent it home to them with a crown and other gifts she had received in France. In July, she was again unwell, which may have delayed her and Edward's departure for Gascony.

On July 7, 1286, "that generous and religious virago, Alienor, Queen of England, mother of the King, took the veil and religious habit at Amesbury on the day of the translation of St. Thomas, Archbishop of Canterbury."[2] "She deposed the diadem from her head and the precious purple from her shoulders, and with them all worldly ambition."[3] She took vows of poverty, chastity and obedience, although her vow of poverty would not be too onerous, for she had asked the Pope "for a special dispensation to free her from the duty of embracing poverty" and "obtained leave of [him] to keep possession of her dower in perpetuity, according to her wish."[4] This attracted some criticism from monastic chroniclers, but Alienor still had enormous debts. Edward would continue to pay her dower until her death. From now on, she would write to him and others as "Alienor, humble nun of the Order of Fontevraud."

Her conduct in the religious life was exemplary. "She filled her hands with good works. She spent her whole time in orisons, vigils and works of piety. She was a mother to the neighbouring poor, especially to orphans, widows and monks, and her praise ought to resound above that of all other women. Besides other large charities, she distributed every Friday £5 [£3,470] in silver to the neighbouring poor."[5] Yet she continued to interest herself in worldly affairs and would remain a fervent persecutor of the Jews, urging the King to take harsh measures against them.

Alienor proved useful to her order. She wrote once to Edward:

> Sweetest son, our Abbess of Fontevraud has prayed us that we would entreat the King of Sicily to guard and preserve the franchises of her house, which some people wish to damage; and, because we know well that he will do much more for your prayer than for ours, for you have better deserved it, we pray you, good son, that, for love of us, you will request and especially require this thing from him, that he would command that the things which the Abbess holds in his lordship may be in his protection and guard, and that neither she nor hers

may be molested or grieved. Good son, we wish you health in the sweet Jesus, to Whom we commend you.[6]

Early in August, the King and Queen left Paris and began a leisurely progress south to Gascony, probably because Eleanor was convalescent. Their route took them to the abbey of Fontevraud, where they saw the tombs of the early Plantagenets. In September and October, they sojourned in Saintonge. There, Eleanor gave birth to a short-lived child called Beatrice. When she and Edward resumed their journey, she was ill again, and was bought medicines and syrups, which were then used to treat a wide variety of ailments.

The King and Queen followed the course of the Dordogne toward the Agenais. Late in October, they were at the bastide of Libourne, built by Roger Leyburn in 1270. On November 15, they were in Agen, where they remained for almost a month, because Eleanor was still unwell. Not until the middle of December did they reach Gascony, where there were further purchases of medication.

They spent the Christmas of 1286 in the priory of Saint-Macaire, not far from Bordeaux. The court feasted in a hall brilliant with candles, to the strains of 125 minstrels. Gaston de Béarn was among the guests and presented Edward with a noble charger. Edmund of Lancaster brought Brie cheese.

In January, the court finally reached Bordeaux. February found Edward touring the Médoc and hunting wolves. In March, he and Eleanor visited Langon and Bazas, where they made offerings in the cathedral, in which was venerated the handkerchief of St. Veronica, used to wipe Christ's sweat as He staggered under the weight of His cross.

In March 1287, Edward himself fell ill at the royal fortress of Blanquefort on the Gironde, a residence much favored by him and Eleanor. There were fears for his life, but his strong constitution aided his recovery, and he was back in Bordeaux on April 2 to celebrate Easter, when he and Eleanor were entertained by a little boy who played the bagpipes and a damsel who danced for them. But, on Easter Sunday, the King was nearly killed when the floor of a tower room crumbled beneath him and sent him and his lords crashing eighty feet to the ground. He was lucky to escape with just a broken collarbone.

In June, Edward returned to Blanquefort and again took the cross, intending to go on another crusade sometime in the future. For the next sixteen months, he and Eleanor remained in Gascony, residing chiefly at Bordeaux or Blanquefort. From there, Edward governed his distant kingdom and his duchy, and life was relatively peaceful. That they missed their children is evident from the many gifts they sent home, especially to their daughter Eleonore, whose coming marriage was much on their minds. On May 29, Eleanor observed the obit of her first child in the church of the Friars Preachers in Bordeaux.

On June 22, the King and Queen set out by boat for Oléron to meet with Eleonore's betrothed, Alfonso III, now King of Aragon. Edward had arranged ten days of feasting and entertainments in honor of his future son-in-law. The marriage had been forbidden by the Pope, with whom Alfonso was at odds, but Edward promised to press for a dispensation. Even though Eleanor was unwell, and vigils were kept for her at the chapel of St. Thomas in Bordeaux, she was involved in preparations for the meeting and buying gifts. Plans were made for the wedding, which was to take place in England the following summer.

On August 5, Alfonso accompanied Edward and Eleanor to Mauléon, where the Queen had a herb garden. There were jousts and feasts in his honor. In September, the royal party moved on to the great Romanesque abbey of Saint-Sever in Les Landes, where Eleanor asked her knight, Richard de Bures, to make a pilgrimage on her behalf to the shrine of St. James at Compostela, a journey of more than 500 miles, which she was not well enough to undertake herself. It is clear that she was hoping for a cure for her illness.

On November 21, Edward and Eleanor returned to Blanquefort, where they spent Christmas. That December, Eleanor was unwell again with "a double quartan fever," a type of malaria that struck for two days then offered a day's respite before flaring up again.

The spring of 1288 found them camping by a building site at the confluence of the Garonne and Dordogne rivers, where Edward was building a new bastide, begun in January and named Burgus Reginae (Queenburgh)—another statement of his love for Eleanor. The dearth of written evidence on Burgos Reginae indicates that the project was abandoned early on, and today it is impossible to locate its actual site.

In July, Edward and Eleanor began a leisurely journey south for another meeting with King Alfonso. In August, in the foothills of the Pyrenees, Eleanor became sick again and her physician, Peter of Portugal, who was traveling with her, had to obtain medicines and syrups from Bayonne, 73 miles away. In September, Edward was obliged to go on ahead, crossing the Pyrenees to Jaca, where he and Alfonso negotiated a new settlement. On October 28, at Canfran, they concluded a treaty.

On Edward's return, he and Eleanor retired to the fortified bastide of Bonnegarde, where they kept Christmas. When Edward crossed the Pyrenees to meet again with Alfonso, Eleanor traveled to Oloron-Sainte-Marie to receive the corpse of Edward's friend, John de Vesci, who had died on February 10 at Montpellier. The Queen must have been instrumental in arranging for his body to be sent back to England and for masses to be said for his soul. She and Edward kept in touch by letter and he sent her preserved ginger, which was regarded as a sovereign remedy for many ailments. Edward's loyal knight, Otto de Grandison, sent Eleanor gifts of a lion and a lynx, which were dispatched with their keeper to the menagerie in the Tower of London.

In March, Edward joined Eleanor and they returned to Bordeaux. They remained in Gascony from April to July 1289, by which time the King had been away from England for more than three years. It had "seemed too long to both him and his," observed the scholarly Dominican William of Hotham, who was in Edward's household. It probably seemed long to Eleanor, who apparently suffered a recurrence of fever in April, when Peter of Portugal was provided with a silver vessel for her syrups, which she was clearly taking regularly.

On March 19, 1286, Alexander III, King of Scots, had been killed when his horse fell from a cliff during a storm. His sons having died, his sole heir was his three-year-old granddaughter Margaret, "the Maid of Norway," the only child of his daughter Margaret, who had married Erik II, King of Norway. The crown of Scotland was immediately claimed by Robert le Brus and John Balliol, who were both descended from the royal line, but the guardians of Scotland rejected them.

In May 1289, Edward proposed that the Lord Edward marry the Maid of Norway. Such a marriage would unite England and Scotland and bring Scotland under English rule, which couldn't have suited Edward better. Because the two children were close cousins, the King applied to the Pope for a dispensation. He urged that Margaret cross to England to be brought up in Queen Eleanor's court; he would return her to Scotland when she was older and the country was in a more stable state.

In July, the King and Queen set off on a slow progress back to England that took them through France, where they visited shrines, made offerings for their children and perhaps prayed for a cure for Eleanor. They spent a fortnight at Abbeville and the abbey of La Gard in Ponthieu.

On August 12, their flotilla sailed from Wissant and made land at Dover the same day. There on the quayside stood the five-year-old Lord Edward and his sisters, Eleonore, Joan, Margaret, Elizabeth and Mary. Edward would barely have remembered his parents; he had been two when they went to Gascony. He had been summoned from the royal manor of Langley, now called King's Langley, where he had spent much of his short life. The princesses had been staying at the Palace of Westminster in chambers called "the Maiden Hall." Elizabeth, who had inherited her mother's love of books, was only seven and she too must have regarded her parents as near strangers. From now on, Eleonore, Joan, and Margaret, the three eldest princesses, all lively and headstrong, would live mainly at court.

From Dover, the King traveled with his family to Canterbury and Leeds Castle, staying there for over a week. He left Eleanor there while he went hunting in Essex, but they were together again for a progress through East Anglia, during which they made a pilgrimage to the shrine of Our Lady of Walsingham. Many went there hoping for miraculous cures, and Eleanor may have been seeking the Virgin's intercession for her restoration to health. It is possible that she was pregnant once again, or recovering from a confinement; she bore her last child, the short-lived Blanche, in 1289 or 1290. This birth may have finally wrecked her health, undermining her immunity from malaria. She was in her late forties and had had eighteen children, more than any other English queen.

On October 12, the royal party returned to the Palace of Westminster. Three days later, they were at Amesbury, visiting Alienor and Mary, and stayed for two weeks. At Salisbury, Edward met the ambassadors of the King of Norway and concluded the marriage alliance between his son Edward and the little Queen of Scots. The wedding was to take place within the next year. In March 1290, when the Scots ratified the treaty, it was agreed that the young couple would be married as soon as Margaret arrived in England, and that the Lord Edward would become king of Scots in her right. Edward promised that Scotland would "remain free in itself, and without subjection from the kingdom of England."

After Eleanor had paid a visit to Dorset to cheer her sick lady, Ermentrude de Sackville, in early December, she and Edward returned to Westminster on December 22 to keep Christmas in great state. Her New Year's gifts included seventy-two gold paternosters. In January 1290, she sent a gift of cheese to her mother-in-law at Amesbury.

In February, the King and Queen moved to Windsor. That month, Eleanor was very ill, and paid a court goldsmith, William de Farendon, to make "images of the Queen's likeness when she fell sick," presumably as offerings at shrines. Clearly fearing that she might be dying, she gave money to religious houses, storing up treasure in heaven, and outlaid funds so that a chapel in the monastery of the Black Friars in London could be made ready for the burial of her heart near to Alfonso's. There is no record of any hunting expenses for her after February, indicating that she was no longer well enough to follow the chase.

But she rallied and, on February 20, she and Edward left Windsor for the manor of Langley Marish, Berkshire, where, as it was Lent, they dined on herrings, salt cod, conger eels, oysters and whelks. Their progress then took them to Abingdon, Quenington and Woodstock, where they kept Easter on April 2 in the company of all their children. Edward noticed Eleanor's laundress, Matilda of Waltham, watching him preparing for a hunt and bet her that she could not ride with him and be in at the kill. She proved him wrong and won. The Queen's accounts show that, at this time, Eleonore, Joan and Margaret usually traveled with her. Edward was indulgent to his daughters, buying them covered wagons, jewels and new gowns to replace those they had outgrown or torn.

On April 17, the royal couple were back at Amesbury for a conference attended by Queen Alienor, the Archbishop of Canterbury, five bishops and William de Valence, at which the King discussed his plan to go on another crusade and put his affairs in order, which suggests that, at this stage, he did not consider Eleanor's bouts of malaria to be too serious. It was essential that he make plans for the succession in the event of his dying overseas. After consulting those present, he issued an ordinance settling the succession to the throne on Edward; if Edward died without heirs, the throne would go to each of his sisters in turn. The King also discussed with his mother the marriages he was proposing for Margaret and Joan with, respectively, John of Brabant and the Earl of Gloucester, who was present and was required to swear to uphold the arrangements made for the succession. On Alienor's advice, Edward resolved to ask the tenants of the Crown for aid toward these marriages.

In emulation of King Arthur, Edward held another splendid round table at Winchester. On April 30, he and Eleanor attended the wedding of eighteen-year-old Joan of Acre to Gloucester, who was forty-seven, which took place in Westminster Abbey. All the royal children, including Mary, attended, and the King and Queen gave their daughter a French headdress and a golden belt encrusted with emeralds and rubies as wedding presents. The feisty Joan had refused to go ahead with the nuptials until she was provided with the same number of attendants in her train as her sisters, obliging a testy Edward to hire more. To ensure that she and her future children were handsomely provided for, Edward made Gloucester renounce his estates and re-granted them jointly to him and Joan. Eleanor was lucky in that the first of her daughters to marry was not going to some distant land, never to return, but Edward was angry with Gloucester for taking Joan away from court so soon after her marriage.

On June 24, Edward was again in a bad mood and refused to attend Roger Bigod's wedding at Havering. Eleanor went, but made sure that Edward was entertained—and mollified—by musicians she herself had hired.

On July 8, the royal family gathered again at Westminster for Margaret's wedding to John of Brabant. Joan of Acre, being difficult again, declared that she wasn't going, due to some imagined slight. Her parents, who had ordered seven gowns for her, made their displeasure clear by giving them to Margaret for her trousseau. The wedding was celebrated with high pageantry, although the bride seems to have been reluctant, Edward having perhaps coerced her into submission. The abbey was thronged with guests and the King and Queen walked in solemn procession with the bride and groom from the Palace of Westminster to the church and back again afterward for the wedding feast. As 426 minstrels played, a "subtlety"—a castle modeled in sugar by the Lord Edward's master cook—was set before the Queen. When a squire displeased the King at the feast, the famous Plantagenet temper flared, and he received a blow from the royal fist. Despite this unpleasantness, many of the guests, including Joan and her husband, seized upon the occasion to take the cross, vowing to go on crusade to the Holy Land.

In 1287, Edward had seized all the property of the Jews and transferred their debts to himself. On July 18, 1290, he issued a decree expelling all Jews who refused to convert to Christianity from England, on the grounds that they had violated the Statute of Jewry and continued to practice usury. They were to leave by All Saints' Day, November 1. It was one of the cruelest acts of his reign, yet it was a popular move, for the Jews were widely resented.

The expulsion was enforced ruthlessly—it has been estimated that between two and three thousand Jews left the realm; most went to France or Germany. Only a few converted. One chronicler believed that the King had acted on his mother's advice, but that is unlikely, because the exodus deprived Alienor of an important source of funding. Edward made up for the shortfall in Jewish revenue by increased taxation, which his grateful subjects were happy to pay.

That July, "medicinal waters" were obtained for Eleanor from the Lord Edward's household, but she was well enough to go on her usual summer progress to various shrines, before returning to Westminster for her daughter Eleonore's wedding to Alfonso III, King of Aragon, on August 15. Again, the ceremony was held at Westminster Abbey, but this time the bridegroom was represented by a proxy. Before the wedding, the King quarreled violently with his daughter and, in another fit of Plantagenet temper, threw her coronet into the fire. Fortunately, relations between them had improved by the time they arrived at the abbey. Edward's outbursts may have been born of anxiety about the health of his beloved wife.

The new Queen of Aragon was destined never to consummate her marriage. Her father had determined to keep her in England until she was fifteen, by which time her husband had died.

12

"The Impiety of Death"

✠

I N AUGUST, EDWARD, ELEANOR AND THEIR DAUGHTERS, ELEO-
nore and Margaret, set out on a summer progress. They sojourned for
a week at Langley, then traveled around Northamptonshire, Leicester-
shire and Nottinghamshire. On September 20, they arrived at Clipstone,
where Joan of Acre joined the party, and Eleanor received a deputation of
men from Overton, come to complain of her bailiff's exorbitant demands. On September 23, the royal party set out on a journey that took
them to Dronfield, Tidswell, Chapel-en-le-Frith, Macclesfield, Ashford,
Chesterfield and Langwith. That day, the Queen summoned Peter of Portugal, either because she was feeling unwell or because she wanted him to
accompany her in case she became ill. Entries in the wardrobe book of
Edward I indicate that, although her illness was troubling, there was still
no cause for concern. Had there been, she surely would not have embarked on the journey.

The seven-year-old Maid of Norway had already sailed for Scotland.
Edward had sent Anthony Bek, Bishop of Durham, north with gifts to
welcome her, and the lords of Scotland were gathering at Scone Abbey
for her coronation. But rough winds blew her ship to Orkney, where she
died on September 26, probably of food poisoning, or possibly of dehy-
dration from severe seasickness. This tragedy not only deprived the
young Lord Edward of a bride and a kingdom, but led to a succession
crisis. There was no clear heir to the Scottish throne—and thirteen claim-
ants would come forward.

Edward abandoned all thoughts of going on crusade and determined to march north to the Scottish border. In September, his mother wrote to him saying she had heard that he intended taking young Edward with him, and urging that he leave the boy behind in England, because "when we were there [in the north], we could not avoid being ill, on account of the bad climate. We pray you, therefore, deign to provide some place in the south where they can have a good and temperate climate and dwell there while you visit the north."

On October 11, Edward returned to Clipstone, where he had summoned Parliament to meet on October 27 to discuss the news from Scotland. His concern about Eleanor's failing health is perhaps reflected in his summoning his younger children, Edward and Elizabeth, to join the court there.

Two more physicians were now in attendance on the Queen: her own doctor, Master Leopardo, and another sent by her son-in-law, the King of Aragon. On October 18, these physicians sent a sergeant of the household to an apothecary in Lincoln for syrups and medicines. The Queen seems to have been pleased with the services of Master Leopardo, for she gave him a silver goblet and left him a legacy in the will she made at this time; there was also a smaller legacy for the Aragonese doctor.

Edward sat in Parliament until it rose on November 13. When he and Eleanor left Clipstone for Lincoln that day, they got as far as Laxton, eleven miles to the east, where the Queen had to rest for four days. On November 14, the Lord Edward and Elizabeth were sent south to Langley, in accordance with Queen Alienor's wishes, which suggests that Eleanor's condition was not considered critical and that Edward was still planning to go north. Joan of Acre also headed south, toward London.

When Eleanor was able, the royal train traveled on seven miles to Marnham, where they lodged for two days. On November 20, the King and Queen arrived in the little village of Harby in Lincolnshire, where Eleanor "was stricken by a grave illness"[1] and could go no farther. Her malady was described as "a low fever,"[2] or an autumnal or double-quartan fever, the type of malaria that had troubled her for three years. Without treatment, the disease can recur, although with lessening severity, and the patient can develop an immunity, although pregnancy can wipe that out, and Eleanor had not long since borne a child. It was known that malaria could be deadly; today, untreated, it kills nearly half a million people a year. In Eleanor's case, it was said that her mild fever was the beginning of her wasting away.

Sir Richard de Weston, a knight of the Queen's household, placed his manor house at Harby at her disposal. It stood to the west of the church of All Saints, but there is no trace of it now apart from a small stretch of the moat, which probably surrounded both manor and church, and overgrown foundations.

Eleanor remained at Harby with Eleonore, Joan and Margaret, passing her time weaving, using instruments obtained in Aylsham, Norfolk, "for the Queen's use." Daily nursing seems to have fallen to two of her damsels, who were each rewarded with great dowries in her will. Also in attendance were William, her tailor, and her daughter's cook, who did his best to revive the Queen's failing appetite. Both were also left legacies. Eleanor bequeathed to her daughter Elizabeth a crown adorned with rubies, emeralds and pearls. She also left bequests to many religious houses, the University of Oxford and poor scholars.

She had been planning to establish a community of Dominican nuns at the royal manor of Langley, but her project never came to fruition. She had also conceived the idea of founding another at Dartford, Kent, but it would be left to her son, Edward II, to carry out her wish. She left a bequest to Vale Royal Abbey, but the King, for reasons that are obscure, made it clear that he wanted nothing more to do with that foundation and, again, Edward II had to fulfil his mother's request.

On November 23, Eleanor's servants bought parchment for her in Lincoln so that she could write letters. According to the wardrobe records, she had "at that time become infirm." The next day, four urinals were bought for her so that she would not have to leave her bed to visit the privy.

Priests were summoned, including William de Kelm, the parish priest at Harby. Eleanor's countryman, Garcia de Ispania, brought a crucifix for her. Believing that she would soon be facing divine judgment, she suffered remorse for her wrongdoings. "After she devoutly received the sacrament of the dying, she earnestly prayed her lord the King, who was listening to her requests, that everything unjustly taken from anyone by her or her ministers should be restored, and any damages satisfied."[3] As has been described, ample proof of those wrongs would be found when the council looked into her affairs, and redress made.

Until November 28, when more medicines were sent for, Edward attended to official business at Harby, issuing a stream of writs. Then he suddenly ceased all political activity, for Eleanor died between 6 p.m. and midnight that night. The King was present, with Oliver Sutton, Bishop of Lincoln, and William de Kelm offering spiritual comfort.

To Edward, it must have seemed unbelievable that he had lost his beloved companion of thirty-six years. They had so rarely been parted. Eleanor had been "inexpressibly dear to him" and, without her, "he waxed heavy as lead," being cast into a deep depression. For five days, he did not attend to any business. On the evening of the Queen's death, he wrote to John Romanus, Archbishop of York, and desired him to solicit the prayers of the faithful for the soul of Queen Eleanor, "our wife from our childhood." The Archbishop granted forty days of indulgence to those who answered the call to prayer. A full peal of bells tolled in York Minster, announcing the sad tidings, and the mourning began. No English queen was ever honored with such elaborate obsequies. They would serve as a focus for national unity and as a statement of royal authority and majesty.

Eleanor's body was taken to the Gilbertine priory of St. Katherine at Lincoln, where the nuns embalmed it. Having removed the heart and viscera and stuffed the cavities with eight gallons of barley and a pound of incense, they wrapped the corpse in six ells of linen, then laid it in a coffin full of spices. A wooden effigy of the Queen, in royal robes, crown and scepter, was laid on the horse-drawn bier, the earliest such effigy recorded in England. The coffin was borne to Lincoln Cathedral, where the viscera were deposited, pending the King's instructions. It was then common for hearts and entrails to be buried in different tombs, although the practice was condemned by the Pope in 1299 and fell out of use in England in the fourteenth century.

Eleanor's body lay in state at Lincoln until December 4, when the funeral cortège assembled for the long journey south to Westminster Abbey, where, in accordance with her wish, Edward had directed that the Queen be interred beside the shrine of St. Edward the Confessor. "In extreme grief,"[4] he followed the bier all the way to St. Albans, keeping a distance of nine miles. The cortège did not take the usual route south via Huntingdon, Royston and Cheshunt, but traveled through more populated areas, enabling the mourners to lodge overnight at important religious houses, where Eleanor's bier could lie in state while prayers were said for her soul, and affording more people a chance to see the procession and pay their respects.

At Grantham, it is likely that the mourners stayed at the inn of the Knights Templar (now the Angel and Royal), which stood near St. Wulfram's Church, where the Queen's body rested, or at the priory of the Grey Friars. Then they rode on, probably lodging at the house of the Black Friars at Stamford, the royal manor of Geddington, Delapré Abbey at Hardingstone, Stony Stratford, Woburn Abbey, Dunstable Priory, St. Albans Abbey and Waltham Abbey in Essex.

Before the journey had even commenced, Edward "gave orders that, in every place where her bier had rested, a cross of the finest workmanship should be erected in her memory, so that passers-by might pray for her soul."[5] This reflected his desire to speed his beloved Eleanor's passage into heaven—and his determination to immortalize her legend in idealized images of her. Each evening, at every stopping place, the Chancellor and other lords earmarked suitable sites for the crosses. On December 15, masses were said for Eleanor's soul in various churches across the land, including that of the Grey Friars in Newgate, London.

Edward left the procession at St. Albans or Waltham Abbey and rode ahead to London. As the cortège neared the capital, a deputation of citizens clad in black cloaks and hoods went to meet it and provided an escort into the City. On December 14, the coffin was at last borne into London through Cheapside, where "the King was waiting with all the leading nobles and churchmen of the realm."[6] It rested that night in the priory of Holy Trinity in Aldgate and then, on successive days, lay in state in the Franciscan friary at Newgate and the Dominican friary at Blackfriars, before being carried via Charing to Westminster Abbey.

Eleanor's funeral took place there on December 17, with great solemnity and "all due respect and honour."[7] It was conducted by Oliver Sutton, Bishop of Lincoln, because Archbishop Peckham and the Abbot of Westminster had fallen out and were not speaking to each other. "Never was woman buried with such magnificence in our time," wrote the Barnwell annalist. Eleanor went to her grave in royal vestments, complete with a crown and scepter (or copper-gilt substitutes, such as were found in Edward I's tomb in 1774); shavings of gold leaf had been strewn over her forehead and breast. A document was laid in the coffin, probably an indulgence granted by her Dominican chaplain for the remission of her sins, and a penitential candle was placed on the grave.

Eleanor's magnificent tomb in Westminster Abbey was positioned at the feet of that of Henry III. Work on it began a week before Christmas, but it would not be completed for three years. It was of gray Purbeck marble, and is the earliest surviving royal heraldic tomb chest in England, with two rows of shields adorning each side: in the lower row appear the towers of Castile, the purple lions of León and the bendlets of Ponthieu. It may have been commissioned by Eleanor herself, given her interest in heraldry. New floor tiles were laid around the tomb, depicting Eleanor with St. Edward and St. Thomas, emphasizing her devotion to them.

In 1291, Edward gave permission for the viscera of the Queen to be buried beneath the altar of the Lady Chapel at the east end of the Angel Choir in Lincoln Cathedral. In 1293, a tomb chest of Purbeck marble would be erected in that chapel. It was the King's intention that identical crowned effigies of Eleanor be made for both tombs, and he commissioned William Torel, a citizen and goldsmith of London, to make metal images like the ones to be seen on the French royal tombs at Saint-Denis. Torel was also ordered to make a similar effigy of Henry III. He was paid £1,700 (£1,250,000) by the King for the three effigies and a tomb canopy.

Early in 1291, he set up his workshop in a house on the cloister garth of Westminster Abbey. He spent two years making the life-sized figures, using the innovative *cire perdue* (lost wax) process of metal casting. The Lincoln effigy was cast in copper gilt. A drawing of it made by William Dugdale in the seventeenth century shows that it was almost identical to the Westminster effigy. The Lincoln tomb and effigy were destroyed in 1644, during the Civil War; in 1891, they were replaced by a replica made of stone and gilded bronze.

The Westminster effigy was made by Torel to an extremely high standard, cast in bronze, then gilded with 476 gold florins of Lucca. It was set with jewels of paste or enamel, long since lost (only the sockets remain), as is the scepter placed in one hand and the carcanet around the Queen's neck; her other hand holds the cord of her mantle, after the style of French royal effigies. Torel is thought to have based the effigy on Eleanor's seal. It may represent the Queen on the day of her coronation, wearing her hair loose beneath her crown, dressed in simple flowing robes and holding a scepter. It is an idealized image, not one of a forty-nine-year-old woman who had borne eighteen children. It was placed on Eleanor's tomb before the spring of 1293 and rested on a gilded bed diapered with the castles and lions of Castile and England.

A rich wooden canopy of tabernacle work was erected over the tomb. In the fifteenth century, this was replaced by a plain one of oak in the Perpendicular style. An artist, Walter de Durham, painted panels to adorn the canopy and the base of the tomb chest, although only traces remain today. Beneath the Queen's feet, it is still possible to see a painting of Sir Otto de Grandison, her champion, kneeling before the Virgin and Child. The Westminster tomb was finished with a Latin epitaph; translated, it reads: "Here lies Eleanor, sometime Queen of England, wife of King Edward, son of King Henry, and daughter of the King of Spain [sic] and the Countess of Ponthieu, on whose soul God, in His mercy, have pity. Amen." Around the tomb, on the ambulatory side, was erected an iron grille made by Thomas of Leighton in 1293–4 to protect it from fortune hunters.

On December 24, 1290, Edward left Westminster and went into retreat at the college of canons at Ashridge Abbey, Hertfordshire, founded by Edmund, Earl of Cornwall, to house a precious relic believed to be Christ's Blood. Here, he mourned his Queen. "His solace was all reft [cut off] sith [since] she was gone. On fell things he thought, and waxed heavy as lead, for sadness overmastered him since Eleanor was dead."[8] "For the rest of his days, he mourned her and offered unceasing prayers on her behalf to our gracious Lord Jesus."[9] In a letter to Yves, Abbot of Cluny, written on January 4, 1291, to request prayers for Eleanor's soul, Edward wrote: "The impiety of death, which spares no man, has stricken our heart with vehement sorrow and turned the harp of our house into mourning. Our Queen of good memory, whom in life we dearly cherished, and whom, in death, we cannot cease to love, has been prayed for constantly." He sent Sir Otto de Grandison to the Holy Land to offer prayers for Eleanor. Sir Otto had a terrible journey and was away for five years.

The tombs of the Queen were paid for by her executors, out of her own funds, which also financed the building of what became known as the "Eleanor crosses," which were an innovation in England. Work on them commenced early in 1291. The royal account rolls for this period survive, so the project is well documented.

There were twelve memorials, all different, though each was surmounted by a crucifix, which is why they were called crosses. Spire-shaped and made of Caen stone, with three storeys, they were inspired by the Montjoie crosses erected between Aigues-Mortes and Saint-Denis to mark the funeral procession of Louis IX. There are images of two such crosses in the fifteenth-century manuscript called *Les Très Riches Heures du Duc de Berri*; one bears a striking resemblance to the Eleanor crosses. There is a drawing of one of the latter in the fourteenth-century Luttrell Psalter in the British Library.

Edward had originally "arranged that the Queen's portrait should be painted on each cross,"[10] but the finished crosses had niches containing statues of her and panels on the lower storeys depicting heraldic shields bearing the arms of England, Castile, León and Ponthieu; all were painted and gilded. Sculpturally, they drew a parallel between the Queen and the Virgin Mary. The statues all have flowing hair (veiled at Geddington) and elaborately draped gowns. Each cross once bore the carved legend *Orate pro anima*, exhorting people to pray for the Queen's soul.

The crosses were erected at each stopping place where Eleanor's body had rested on its journey from Harby to Westminster. Only three survive: those at Geddington, Hardingstone and Waltham. Nine—at Lincoln, Grantham, Stony Stratford, Woburn, Dunstable, St. Albans, Cheapside and Charing—were destroyed during the Civil War of the 1640s. The cross at Stamford was ruinous by 1659 and was demolished. A few marble fragments of the Cheapside cross survive today in the Guildhall Museum; they were found in 1838 in a sewer.

As they were set up in prominent places by the roadside, the crosses were consecrated. They reflect the very latest style of English decorated architecture so favored by forward-thinking London masons. The ornamental work was carried out to a very high standard. Edward agreed on a price of £2,000 (£1,471,000) for the crosses, but the final figure was far higher, since the two London crosses alone cost £1,000 (£735,500). These were the most splendid, for they were made by the foremost master masons, and the Charing cross was the largest of them all. The name Charing is of Saxon origin and meant "a turning"; there is no basis to the romantic myth that the village was named after King Edward's *chère reine* (dear Queen), of which Charing was supposed to be a corruption.

The Geddington cross, the best-preserved of the three that still stand today, is triangular in shape. The stone lacework suggests that a Spanish architect may have worked on it. It was restored in 1800, 1840 and 1890, and is somewhat weather-worn. There are three statues of Eleanor above the second story; her bowed head has given rise to the local nickname "the weeping Queen."

The Hardingstone cross, on the London Road near Northampton, is octangular and stands on a base of nine steps (there were originally twelve). The statues of Eleanor are six-feet-six high. In 1460, it was noted that the upper stage had gone. Restorations were carried out in 1713, 1884, 1984 and 1989. Far from the willowy figures on the Geddington cross, the statues on the one at Hardingstone show a queen with a more matronly figure.

The Waltham cross, just off the old North Road in Cheshunt, has also been much restored over the centuries. Richly decorated, it is hexagonal in design. It is evident from a drawing of 1812 that the nineteenth-century restoration altered this cross considerably. In the 1950s, its statues were replaced with replicas and are now on loan to the Victoria and Albert Museum.

In 1856, the Chatham and Dover Railway Company, then building Charing Cross station, decided to fund the building of a new seventy-foot-high cross to commemorate Queen Eleanor, to be placed in front of the station. This was sculpted in 1863–5 by E. M. Barry, but it was not designed to resemble the original.

There was a thirteenth cross, but it was not one of the series commissioned by King Edward. Beaumond Cross in Newark is thought to have been built in Eleanor's memory by Oliver Sutton, Bishop of Lincoln. It is a tall column set on steps and was restored and decorated in 1778. There is a reproduction of an Eleanor cross at Sledmere, Yorkshire, which was built in 1895 by Sir Tatton Sykes. It is now a war memorial.

In erecting the crosses, Edward I's chief concern was to ensure his wife's passage into heaven, where he trusted he would be reunited with her. His efforts in that direction were stupendous. He granted numerous petitions "for the good of the late Queen's soul." He endowed generous grants of alms and celebrations of mass for her throughout his realm. The Archbishop of York would inform the King that, in the six months after her death, 47,000 masses had been said for her. Indulgences were given to those who offered up prayers for the late Queen.

Edward founded several chantries for Eleanor, notably at Westminster, the Black Friars in London, Leeds Castle and Harby, where there is a small Victorian statue of her over the east door and a plaque on the chancel floor commemorating her death. The list of other chantries founded for her is long, stretching into the reign of Edward II, but nowhere was she more earnestly prayed for than in Westminster Abbey, where Edward ordered that thirty candles be placed around her tomb, two to be kept burning daily, and all to be lit on feast days, a custom observed until the Reformation. His gifts of twelve manors, lordships and hamlets to Westminster yielded a massive £200–£300 (£1,471,000–£2,206,500) a year to fund her annual obit, when 100 wax candles were lit around her tomb, bells tolled in her memory, the office was sung hourly for twenty-four hours and substantial alms were given as "dole" to up to 20,000 poor people who attended the service, many of whom must have traveled from far and wide. Along with mementoes of St. Edward, pilgrims visiting Westminster could buy souvenirs of Eleanor, lead badges stamped with the arms of Castile and León.

The wooden effigy of the Queen, which had lain on her bier as her body was brought to London, was kept at Westminster Abbey. It was seen, with those of Edward I and later royal and notable persons, by John Dryden in the seventeenth century but, in the eighteenth century, some of these effigies were "sadly mangled,"[11] broken and stripped of their clothing; Horace Walpole called them "the ragged regiment." Today, the wooden effigies of Eleanor and Edward are long lost.

Epilogue

✠

E DWARD WAS IN THE NORTH WHEN, ON JUNE 25, 1291, ALIENOR
of Provence died at Amesbury Priory. "The fleeting state of worldly
glory is shown by the fact that the same year carried off two English
queens, wife and mother of the King, both inexpressibly dear to him."

Nuns were usually buried in their convents, wearing the habit of their
order. Being professed, Alienor could not be buried beside Henry III in
Westminster Abbey, as she had planned, and to her son Edmund's dismay; yet she was still to be interred with the honors due to a queen. "The
nuns of Amesbury, not being able to sepulchre the Queen Mother with
sufficient magnificence, had her body embalmed so that no corruption
ensued and, in a retired place, reverentially deposited it till Edward returned from his Scottish campaign. On the King's return, he summoned
all his clergy and barons to Amesbury, where he solemnly completed the
entombing of his mother, appropriately on the day of the Nativity of the
Blessed Mary [September 8], in her conventual church, where her obsequies were reverentially celebrated" with great state.[1] She was buried before the high altar. The King had summoned the Abbot of Glastonbury
to participate.

Edward founded a chantry for his mother at Amesbury and ordered
an annual obit in her memory, promising the convent an endowment of
£100 (£73,550) a year. But, although Alienor's obit was celebrated for
thirty-six years after her death, he never kept his promise, and the nuns
were still petitioning his grandson, Edward III, for the endowment in
1329.

Edward settled his mother's debts and built a tomb for her at Ames-bury. Walter of Hereford, the chief mason at Caernarfon Castle, was working on it in 1291. That year, Edward erected two crosses in the style of those built for his late wife: one was for his mother, the other for his sister Beatrice. Neither survives.

Edward had brought back from Lincoln an urn containing his beloved Eleanor's heart. On November 21, 1291, he went to Amesbury to receive his mother's heart, which he "carried with him to London—indeed, he brought there the hearts of both the queens."

On November 28, 1291, the first anniversary of Queen Eleanor's death was observed with great solemnity at Westminster by the King and many nobles. On Sunday, December 6, "before a vast multitude," the hearts of the two queens were "honourably interred, the maternal heart in the church of the friars minors [at Newgate],"[2] where Alienor's daughter Bea-trice was buried, and a tomb was built to house it. In the sixteenth cen-tury, the monument was recorded as standing south of the presbytery, with Beatrice's sepulchre to the north. In 1547, during the Reformation, the royal tombs at Greyfriars were dismantled and their materials sold.

Queen Eleanor's heart was also buried that day, near the heart of Alonso; in the church of the Black Friars in London, where her body had rested before burial. In 1290, she had paid the Friars Preachers to build a chapel in which her heart was to be interred. She is the only queen of England to have had three tombs. The third was erected in the friars' chapel, and on it was placed a golden statue of an angel holding a heart, made by Adam the goldsmith. Three enameled gilt images adorned the tomb and a painted cloth depicting Eleanor hung over it. Her heart tomb was lost when Henry VIII dissolved the Dominican friary in the sixteenth century.

In 1292, William Torel's gilt-bronze effigy of Henry III was laid on the King's tomb near St. Edward's shrine in Westminster Abbey. In 1871, when the tomb was opened, a small engraving was found on the under-side of the lid, depicting a crowned and veiled queen and a young nun praying to a larger, unfinished figure; it was probably meant to represent Alienor and her granddaughter Mary adoring the Virgin Mary.

After the Dissolution of the Monasteries, Amesbury Priory was ac-quired by Edward Seymour, Earl of Hertford. When he pulled down the church, which was falling into decay, Alienor of Provence's tomb was destroyed. The location of her remains is now unknown. In the early seventeenth century, Inigo Jones reported that a stone coffin containing a corpse, richly appareled, was found built into a wall in the former prioress's house, which had been incorporated into Abbey Mansion, erected by Hertford on the site of the priory; the coffin was still visible in 1662.

Alienor of Provence had won respect in her old age. Her undoubted abilities, her cunning, determination, inner strength, tenacity and intelligence—and her husband's indulgence—had enabled her to exercise the kind of power the Norman queens had enjoyed. She had been one of the chief causes of the struggle between Henry III and his barons, yet she was instrumental in bringing it to an end.

Arguably, Eleanor of Castile brought out the best in Edward. His rule became harsher after her death.

Edward may have felt some comfort in knowing that his adored wife's memory was to be honored as no English queen's had ever been before with those three magnificent tombs and twelve beautiful crosses. They would bear in perpetuity the idealized image of the Queen he wanted his subjects to remember: the embodiment of gracious, submissive queenship in the image of the Virgin Mary, which the statues of her closely resemble; certainly, they had an enduring impact on people's perceptions of Eleanor, transforming her from an avaricious, intimidating woman into a near saint.

This change was first apparent twenty years after her death, when a monk of St. Albans praised her piety in a work probably presented to her son, Edward II: "As the dawn scatters the shadows of the waning night with its rays of light, so, by the promotion of this most holy woman and Queen throughout England, the night of faithlessness was expelled." She "surpassed all women of that time in wisdom, prudence and beauty; indeed, except that it would appear to be flattery, I would say that she was not unequal to a Sybil in wisdom." He added that she was "tearfully mourned by not a few," which seems unlikely.

Within a century of Eleanor's death, her legend had become firmly entrenched in the public consciousness and she had come to embody the ideal queen. According to the late-fourteenth-century chronicler Thomas Walsingham: "To our nation, she was a loving mother, the column and pillar of the whole realm. She was a godly, modest and merciful princess. The English nation in her time was not harassed by foreigners, nor the country peopled by the purveyors of the Crown. The sorrow-stricken she consoled, as became her dignity, and she made them friends that were at discord."

These descriptions of the devout, gentle and merciful Queen underpinned the popular perception of Eleanor of Castile that has come down over the centuries and only recently been overturned by modern scholarship. Yet no one could contest that Eleanor was an exemplary model of wifely devotion, and it is upon this, along with the tale of her sucking the poison from Edward's wound, and those beautiful crosses he raised to her memory, that her legend largely rests.

Select Bibliography

✠

Primary Sources

Adam of Domerham: *Historia de rebus gestis Glastoniensibus* (2 vols., ed. T. Hearne, Oxford, 1727)

Adam of Eynsham: *Magna Vita Sancti Hugonis Episcopi Lincolniensis (The Life of St. Hugh, Bishop of Lincoln)* (ed. Decima L. Douie and David Hugh Farmer, 2 vols., London, 1961, reprinted Oxford, 1985)

Additional MSS (The British Library)

Aelred of Rievaulx: "Relatio de Standardo" (in *Chronicles of the Reigns of Stephen, Henry II and Richard I*)

Alighieri, Dante: *Paradiso* (Digital Dante, https://digitaldante.columbia.edu)

Aliscans (ed. Claude Régnier, Paris, 1990)

Ambrose: *L'Estoire de la guerre sainte* (ed. G. Paris, Paris, 1897; in *Three Old French Chronicles*; trans. M. J. Hubert and J. La Monte as *The Crusade of Richard Lionheart*, New York, 1941)

Ancient Charters, Royal and Private, prior to A.D. 1200 (ed. John Horace Round, London, 1888)

Andreas Capellanus (Andrew the Chaplain): *De Amore: The Art of Courtly Love* (trans. and ed. John Jay Parry, New York, 1941)

Anecdotes historiques d'Etienne de Bourbon (ed. A. Lecoy de la Marche, Paris, 1877)

Anglo-Latin Satirical Poets and Epigrammists of the Twelfth Century, Vol. 1 (ed. Thomas Wright, Cambridge, 1872)

The Anglo-Saxon Chronicle (trans. and ed. G. N. Garmonsway, London, 1954)

Annales Angevines et Vendômoises (ed. L. Halphen, Paris, 1903)

"Annales Londonienses" (in *Chronicles of the Reigns of Edward I and Edward II*)

Annales Monastici (5 vols., ed. H. R. Luard, London, 1864–9)

"Annals of Bermondsey" (in *Annales Monastici*)

The Annals of Dunstable Priory (trans. David Preest, ed. Harriet R. Webster, Woodbridge, 2018)

Annals of the Kingdom of Ireland by the Four Masters (ed. J. O'Donovan, Dublin, 1851)

"Annals of Margam" (in *Annales Monastici*)

Annals of Osney, Cotton Tiberius MS A.ix fols. 2–102 (The British Library)

"Annals of Tewkesbury Abbey" (in *Annales Monastici*)

"Annals of Waverley" (in *Annales Monastici*)

Annals of Winchester (British Library Cotton Domitian MS. A.xiii. T)

Anthology of the Provençal Troubadours (ed. R. T. Hill and T. G. Bergin, Yale, 1941; reprinted 1973)

Archaeologia, or Miscellaneous Tracts Relating to Antiquity (102 vols., various editors, The Society of Antiquaries of London, 1773–1969)

Archives historiques de Poitou (Poitiers, 1872)

Archives municipales de Bordeaux (ed. H. Barckhausen, Bordeaux, 1890)

Arnulf of Lisieux: *The Letters of Arnulf of Lisieux* (ed. Frank Barlow, London, 1939)

Baker, Sir Richard: *A Chronicle of the Kings of England* (London, 1643)

"The Barnwell Annals" (in Walter of Coventry: *Memoriale*)

Bartholomeo (Ptolemy) of Lucca: *The Life and Works of Tolomeo Fiadoni (Ptolemy of Lucca)* (ed. J. M. Blythe, Turnhout, 2009)

Benoît de Sainte-Maure: *Chronique des ducs de Normandie* (ed. F. Michel, Paris, 1938)

——*Le roman de Troie* (ed. Leopold Constans, Paris, 1904–12)

Bernard of Clairvaux: "Epistolae: S. Bernardi, Opera Omnia" (ed. J. Mabillon, in *Patrologiae Latinae*, Vol. 182, ed. J. P. Migne, Paris, 1844–64)

——*The Letters of St. Bernard of Clairvaux* (trans. and ed. Bruno Scott James, Chicago, 1953)

——*Oeuvres complètes de Saint Bernard* (Paris, 1873)

Bernard de Ventadour: *Bernard von Ventadour, seine Lieder* (ed. Carl Appel, Halle, 1915)

Bertran de Born: *The Poems of the Troubadour Bertran de Born* (ed. William D. Paden Jr., Tilde Sankovitch and Patricia H. Stablein, University of California, 1986)

——*Poésies complètes de Bertran de Born* (ed. A. Thomas, Toulouse, 1888)

Bibliothèque des Croisades: History of the Crusades (4 vols., ed. Joseph Michaud, Paris, 1829; trans. W. Robson, 3 vols., London, 1852)

Bibliothèque Nationale Paris, Latin MS. 5452

Bohaddin: "The Crusade of Richard I, 1189–1192" (in *English History from Contemporary Writers*)

Bouchet, Jean: *Les annales d'Aquitaine* (Poitiers, 1644)

Brompton, John: *Chronicon Johannis Brompton, Abbatis Jorvalensis, ab anno quo S. Augustinus venit in Angliam usque mortem Regis Ricardi Primi* (London, 1652)

Brooke, Ralph: *Catalogue and Succession of the Kings, Princes, Dukes, Marquesses, Earls and Viscounts of this Realm of England since the Norman Conquest* (London, 1619)

The Brut, or the Chronicles of England (2 vols., ed. F.W.D. Brie, London, 1906–8)

Calendar of Charter Rolls preserved in the Public Record Office (6 vols., London, 1903)

Calendar of Close Rolls (The National Archives)

Calendar of Documents preserved in France illustrative of the History of Great Britain and Ireland, Vol. I, 918–1206 (ed. John Horace Round, London, 1899)

Calendar of Documents relating to Scotland (5 vols., ed. Joseph Bain, Edinburgh, 1881–8)

Calendar of Entries in the Papal Registers relating to Great Britain and Ireland (ed. W. H. Bliss, 1893; London, 1960)

Calendar of the Liberate Rolls (3 vols., London, 1916–64)

Calendar of Patent Rolls preserved in the Public Record Office (London, 1906)

Calendars of Patent Rolls (The National Archives)

Cambridge Corpus Christi College MS. 471

Cambridge University Library MS. Ii.vi.24, fol. 98r

Camden, William: *Britannia* (London, 1586)

——*Remains of a Greater Work Concerning Britain* (London, 1605)

Capgrave, John (1393–1464): *The Book of the Illustrious Henries* (ed. and tr. F. C. Hingeston, London, 1858)

Carmina Burana (ed. A. Hilka and O. Schumann, Heidelberg, 1930–70)

Cartulaire de l'Eglise du Mans: Livre Blanc du Chapitre (MS. 259, Archives départmentale de la Sarthe)

"Cartulaire du Chapitre Royale de St. Pierre de la Cour" (ed. Menjot d'Elbenne and L. Denis, in *Archives historique du Maine*, Vols. 4, 1907, and 10, 1910)

Catalogue des actes de Philippe Auguste (ed. Léopold Delisle, Paris, 1856)

Catalogue of Romances in the Department of Manuscripts in the British Museum (ed. J. A. Herbert, London, 1883–1910)

Les chansons de croisade avec leurs mélodies (ed. Joseph Bédier and Pierre Aubry, Paris, 1909; reprinted Geneva, 1974)

Charter Rolls: Rotuli Chartorum (ed. T. D. Hardy, London, 1837)

Choix des poésies originales des troubadours (ed. F.J.M. Raynouard, Paris, 1816–21)

Chrétien de Troyes: *Arthurian Romances* (trans. D.D.R. Owen, London, 1987)

——*Philomena, conte raconte d'après Ovid par Chrétien de Troyes* (ed. Charles de Boer, Paris, 1909)

The Chronicle of Ernoul and Bernard the Treasurer (ed. L. de Mas Latrie, Paris, 1871)

The Chronicle of Ernoul and the Continuations of William of Tyre (ed. M. R. Morgan, Oxford, 1973)

Chronicle of Gloucester Abbey (ed. W. H. Hart, London, 1863)

The Chronicle of Lanercost (ed. Joseph Stevenson, Edinburgh, 1839)

Chronicle of London, 1089–1483 (ed. Sir Harris Nicolas, London, 1827)

The Chronicle of Meaux (3 vols., ed. E. A. Bond, London, 1866–8)

The Chronicle of Melrose Abbey (ed. D. Broun and J. Harrison, Woodbridge, 2007)

The Chronicle Roll of the Kings and Queens of England (Broxbourne MS. 112:3, Bodleian Library)

The Chronicle of Tewkesbury Abbey, 1066–1262 (Bodleian Library MS Lat. misc. b. 2 (R))

Chronicles of London (ed. C. L. Kingsford, Oxford, 1905)

Chronicles and Memorials of the Reign of Richard I (2 vols., ed. William Stubbs, London, 1864–5)

Chronicles of the Reigns of Edward I and Edward II (ed. W. Stubbs, London, 1882)

Chronicles of the Reigns of Stephen, Henry II and Richard I (4 vols., ed. Richard Howlett, London, 1884–90)

The Chronicon of Battle Abbey (ed. J. S. Brewer, London, 1846)

Chronicon Monasterii de Abingdon (2 vols., ed. Joseph Stevenson, Cambridge, 1858)

"Chronicon Turonensis Magnum" (in *Receuil des Chroniques de Touraine*)

Chronique de Londres (ed. G. J. Aungier, London, 1844)

La Chronique de Marigny (ed. Léon Mirot, Paris, 1912)

"Chronique de Saint-Denis" (in *Receuil des historiens des Gaules et de la France*)

Chroniques des comtes d'Anjou et des seigneurs d'Amboise (ed. L. Halphen and R. Poupardin, Paris, 1913)

Chroniques des églises d'Anjou (ed. P. Marchegay and E. Mabille, Paris, 1869)

Chroniques de Normandie (ed. Francisque Michel, Rouen, 1839)

Chroniques de St. Martial de Limoges (ed. H. Duples-Agier, Paris, 1874)

Collection des mémoires relatifs à l'histoire de France depuis la fondation de la monarchie français jusqu'au 13e siècle (32 vols., ed. F.P.G. Guizot, Paris, 1823–36)

A Collection of all the Wills of the Kings and Queens of England (ed. John Nicholls, London, 1780)

Cotton, Bartholomew de: Historia Anglicana, known as The Norwich Chronicle (ed. H. R. Luard, London, 1859)

Cotton MSS (The British Library)

Court, Household and Itinerary of King Henry II, instancing also the Chief Agents and Adversaries of the King in his Government, Diplomacy and Strategy (ed. Robert W. Eyton, London, 1878; reprinted New York, 1974)

Curia Regis Rolls: Rotuli Curia Regis (ed. F. Palgrave, London, 1835)

Drayton, Michael (*see* More, Sir Thomas, et al.)

Dudo of Saint-Quentin: *De Moribus et Actis Primorum Normanniae Ducum* (ed. Jules Lair, Caen and Oxford, 1865)

"The Early Charters of the Augustinian Canons of Waltham Abbey, Essex 1062–1230" (in *Studies in the History of Medieval Religion*, ed. Rosalind Ransford, Woodbridge, 1989)

English Historical Documents, 1042–1189 (trans. and ed. D. C. Douglas and George W. Greenaway, London, 1953)

English History from Contemporary Writers (ed. D. Nutt, London, 1888)

"Epistolae Cantuariensis" (in *Chronicles and Memorials of the Reign of Richard I*)

Epistolae: Medieval Women's Latin Letters (https://epistolae.ctl.columbia.edu)

Excerpta Historica (ed. S. Bentley and Sir Harris Nicolas, London, 1831)

Fantosme, Jordan: "Metrical Chronicle: Chronique de la guerre entre les Anglais et les Ecossais en 1173 et 1174 (Chronicle of the War between the English and the Scots in 1173 and 1174)" (in *Chronicles of the Reigns of Stephen, Henry II and Richard I*)

FitzNigel, Richard: *Dialogus de Scaccario: Dialogue concerning the Exchequer* (trans. Charles Johnson, London, 1950; reprinted 1963)

FitzStephen, William: *A Description of London* (trans. H. E. Butler with "A Map of London under Henry II" by Marjorie B. Honeybourne, Historical Association Pamphlets, Nos. 93 and 94, 1934)

——*Materials for a History of Becket* (ed. J. C. Robertson, London, 1875–85; trans. W. H. Hutton: "St. Thomas from the Contemporary Biographies," in *English History from Contemporary Writers*)

——"Vita Sancti Thomae: The Life of Thomas Becket" (trans. and ed. G. W. Greenaway, in *The Life and Death of Thomas Becket, Chancellor of England and Archbishop of Canterbury*, London, 1961)

Florence of Worcester: *Florenti Wigorniensis Monachi Chronicon ex Chronicis: The Chronicle of Florence of Worcester* (2 vols., ed. B. Thorne, London, 1848–9; trans. and ed. Thomas Forester, London, 1854)

Flores Historiarum, MS. 6712 (Chetham's Library, Manchester)

Florilege des troubadours (trans. and ed. André Berry, Paris, 1930)

Foedera, Conventiones, Litterae et cujuscunque generis Acta Publica (20 vols., ed.

Thomas Rymer et al., London, 1704–35; ed. A. Clarke and F. Holbrooke, 7 vols., London, 1816–69)

Foliot, Gilbert: *The Letters and Charters of Gilbert Foliot* (ed. A. Morey and C.N.L. Brooke, Cambridge, 1967)

"A French Chronicle of London" (in *Chroniques de Londres*)

Geoffrey of Monmouth: *Historia Regum Britaniae: The History of the Kings of Britain* (trans. and ed. A. Griscom and R. E. Jones, New York, 1929; ed. J. Hammer, Cambridge, Massachusetts, 1951; trans. Lewis Thorpe, London, 1966)

Geoffrey de Vigeois: "Chronica Gaufredi Coenobitae Monasterii S. Martialis" (ed. Philippe Labbé, in *Nova Nibliotheca Manuscriptorum Librorum*, Vol. 2, Paris, 1657; in *Receuil des historiens des Gaules et de la France*)

Geoffrey de Vinsauf: *Poetria nova* (trans. Margaret Nims, ed. Martin Camargo, Toronto, 2010)

Gervase of Canterbury, *Opera Historica: The Historical Works of Gervase of Canterbury* (2 vols., ed. William Stubbs, London, 1879–80)

Gesta Abbatum Monasterii Sancti Albani: Chronici Monasterii S. Albani (Vol. 1, ed. H. T. Riley, London, 1867)

"Gesta Edwardi de Carnarvon" (in *Chronicles of the Reigns of Edward I and Edward II*)

Gesta Francorum et Aliorum Hierosolimitanorum: The Deeds of the Franks and the Other Pilgrims to Jerusalem (ed. Rosalind Hill, London, 1962)

"Gesta Henrici Secundi: The Deeds of Henry II" (in *English Historical Documents 1042–1189*)

The Gesta Normannorum Ducum (2 vols., ed. Elizabeth M. C. Van Houts, Oxford, 1995)

Gesta Regis Ricardi: The Deeds of King Richard (2 vols., ed. William Stubbs, London, 1864)

Gesta Stephani: The Deeds of Stephen (trans. and ed. K. R. Potter, London, 1955)

Giraldus Cambrensis: *The Autobiography of Giraldus Cambrensis* (trans. and ed. H. E. Butler, London, 1937)

——*Opera* (8 vols., ed. J. S. Brewer, J. F. Dimmock and George F. Warner, London, 1861–91)

Gislebert de Mons: *La Chronique de Gislebert de Mons* (ed. L. Vanderkindere, Brussels, 1904)

Godfrey Giffard's Register (Worcester and Hereford Record Office, MS. 713)

Gottfried von Strasburg: *Tristan, with the Surviving Fragments of the Tristan of Thomas* (ed. A. T. Hatto, London, 1960)

La Gran Conquista de Ultramar (4 vols., ed. Louis Cooper, Bogota, 1979)

Grandes Chroniques de France, Royal MS. 20 E i–v (The British Library)

The Great Rolls of the Pipe for the First Year of the Reign of King Henry II (in *The Red Book of the Exchequer*) (ed. H. Hall, 3 vols., London, 1896)

The Great Rolls of the Pipe for the Second, Third and Fourth Years of the Reign of King Henry II, 1155–1158 (ed. Joseph Hunter, London, 1844)

The Great Rolls of the Pipe of the Reign of Henry the Second, 5th to 34th Years (30 vols., London, 1884–1925)

The Great Rolls of the Pipe for the Thirty-Third Year of the Reign of King Henry the Second, A.D. 1186–7 (ed. John Horace Round, London, 1915)

The Great Rolls of the Pipe for the First Year of the Reign of Richard I, 1189–90 (ed. J. Hunter, London, 1844)

The Great Rolls of the Pipe for the Reign of Richard I (ed. D. M. Stenton, London, 1925–33)

Guiart, Guillaume: *Branches des royaux lignages* (ed. J. A. Buchon, Paris, 1920)

Guillaume le Breton: *Gesta Philippe Augusti: Philippide* (2 vols., ed. H. F. Delaborde, Paris, 1882–5)

Guillaume de Nangis: "Chronique" (in *Collection des mémoires relatifs à l'histoire de France*)

Helinant de Froidmont: "Chronicon" (ed. J. P. Migne, in *Patrologia Latinae*, Vol. 212, Paris, 1855)

Henry of Huntingdon: *The Chronicle of Henry of Huntingdon* (trans. and ed. Thomas Forester, London, 1853)

——*Historiae Anglorum: The History of the English* (ed. T. Arnold, London, 1879)

Herbert of Bosham: *Materials for the History of Thomas Becket* (ed. J. C. Robertson, London, 1875–85)

Heriger of Lobbes: "Epistola ad quemdam Hugonem monachum" (*Patrologia Latinae*, 139, http://patristica.net/latina/)

Higden, Ranulf: *Polychronicon* (9 vols., ed. Joseph Rawson Lumby, London, 1882)

Histoire des ducs de Normandie et des rois d'Angleterre (ed. Francisque Michel, Paris, 1840)

L'Histoire de Guillaume le Maréchal, Comte de Striguil et de Pembroke (3 vols., trans. and ed. Paul Meyer, Paris, 1891–1901)

The Icelandic Life of Becket: Thomas Saga Erkibyskups (trans. and ed. Eirikr Magnusson, London, 1875–83)

Illustrations of Ancient State and Chivalry from Manuscripts Preserved in the Ashmolean Museum (ed. W. H. Black, Roxburgh Club, London, 1840)

Issue Rolls and Registers (Exchequer of Receipt) (The National Archives)

Issues of the Exchequer, from King Henry III to King Henry VI (ed. F. Devon, London, 1837)

Jocelin of Brakelond: *Chronica Jocelini de Brakelonde: De Rebus Gestis Samsonis, Abbatis Monasteri Sancti Edmundi* (trans. and ed. H. E. Butler, Oxford, 1949)

Joffroi de Poitiers: *Roman d'aventures du XIIIe siècle* (ed. Perceval B. Fay and John L. Grigsby, Geneva and Paris, 1972)

John of Hexham (*c*.1160–1209): *Historia Regum* (ed. T. Arnold, London, 1882–5)

John the Long: "Johannis Longi Chronica S. Bertini" (in *Monumenta Germaniae Historica Scriptores*)

John of Marmoutier: "The Chronicles of the Counts of Anjou and Historia Gaufredi Ducis Normannorum et Comitis Andegavorum: The History of Geoffrey, Duke of Normandy and Count of Anjou" (in *Chroniques des Comtes d'Anjou*)

John of Salisbury: *Ioannis Saresberiensis Historia Pontificalis: John of Salisbury's Memoirs of the Papal Court* (trans. and ed. Marjorie Chibnall, London, 1956; reprinted Oxford, 1986)

——*The Letters of John of Salisbury* (ed. W. J. Millor and H. E. Butler, London, 1955; revised C.N.L. Brooke, 2 vols., London, 1965)

——*Materials for the History of Thomas Becket* (ed. J. C. Robertson, London, 1875–85)

——*Policraticus: The Statesman's Book* (trans. John Dickinson, New York, 1927)

John of Ypres: "Chronicon Sythiense S. Bertini" (in *Thesaurus Novus Anecdorum*, Vol. 3, ed. Edward Martene and Ursin Durande, Paris, 1717)

Lambert of Wattrelos: "Annales Cameracenses" (in *Monumenta Germaniae Historica Scriptores*)

Langtoft, Piers: *The Chronicle of Pierre de Langtoft, in French Verse from the Earliest Period to the Death of Edward I* (2 vols., ed. T. Wright, London, 1866–8)

Layamon (*see* Wace, Robert and Layamon)

Letters of the Kings of England, Vol. 1 (ed. James O. Halliwell-Phillipps, London, 1848)

Letters of Medieval Women (ed. Anne Crawford, Stroud, 2002)

Letters of the Queens of England, 1100–1547 (ed. Anne Crawford, Stroud, 1994)

Letters of Royal and Illustrious Ladies of Great Britain, Vol. 1 (ed. Mary Anne Everett Wood, London, 1846)

Liberate Rolls (The National Archives)

The Life and Death of Thomas Becket, Chancellor of England and Archbishop of Canterbury (trans. and ed. G. W. Greenaway, London, 1961)

Le Livere de Reis de Brittanie e le Livere de Reis de Engleterre (ed. John Glover, London, 1865)

The Lyfe of Saynt Radegunde (ed. Henry Bradshaw, Cambridge, 1926)

Lyrics of the Troubadours and Trouvères (ed. Frederick Goldin, New York, 1973)

Manners and Household Expenses of the 13th and 15th Centuries (ed. Beriah Botfield and Thomas Hudson Turner, London, 1841)

Map, Walter: *De Nugis Curialium: Courtiers' Trifles* (ed. T. Wright, 1850; trans. and ed. M. R. James, Oxford, 1914; revised C.N.L. Brooke and R. B. Mynors, Oxford, 1983)

Marie de France: *Lais* (ed. A. Ewart, Oxford, 1944)

Marsh, Adam: *The Letters of Adam Marsh* (2 vols., ed. C. H. Lawrence, Oxford, 2006, 2010)

Materials for the History of Thomas Becket, Archbishop of Canterbury (various accounts, ed. J. C. Robertson, Vols. 1-6, and J. B. Sheppard, Vol. 7, London, 1875-85)

Medieval Age: Specimens of European Poetry from the 9th to the 15th Century (ed. Angel Flores, New York, 1963)

Memoranda Rolls (The National Archives)

Memorials of St. Edmund's Abbey (3 vols., ed. T. Arnold, London, 1890-6)

Milles, Thomas: *The Catalogue of Honour or Treasury of True Nobility* (London, 1610)

Minstrel of Rheims: *Récits d'un ménestrel de Reims au treizième siècle, or, The Chronicle of Rheims* (ed. Natalis de Wailly, Paris, 1876; in *Three Old French Chronicles*)

Miscellanea Genealogica et Heraldica (ed. W. Bruce Bannerman, London, 1912)

"Der mittelenglische Versroman über Richard Löwenherz: The Middle English Romance of Richard the Lionheart" (trans. and ed. Karl Brunner, in *Wiener Beiträge zur Englischen Philologie Vol. 42*, Vienna and Leipzig, 1913)

Monumenta Germaniae Historica Scriptores (Berlin, 1826–present)

More, Sir Thomas; Drayton, Michael; Hearne, Thomas, and others: *The Unfortunate Royal Mistresses, including Rosamund Clifford and Jane Shore, Concubines to King Henry the Second and Edward the Fourth, with Historical and Metrical Memoirs of those Celebrated Persons* (London, 1825)

Mouskes, Philippe: *Chronique rimée* (ed. Frédéric-Auguste-Ferdinand-Thomas, Baron de Reiffenberg, Brussels, 1838)

The National Archives, Special Collections

Neve, John le: *Fasti Ecclesiae Anglicanae, 1066–1300* (9 vols., ed. Diana E. Greenaway, London, 1968–present)

Niketas Choniates: "Die Krone de Komnenen: die Regierungszeit der Kaiser Joannes und Manuel Komnenos (1118-1180) aus dem Geschichtswerk des Niketas Choniates" (trans. Franz Grabler, *Byzantine Geschichtzschreiber VII*, Graz-Vienna-Cologne, 1958)

——*Nicetae Choniatae Historia: Corpus Scriptorum Historiae Byzantinae* (ed. Emmanuel Bekker, Bonn, 1835)

Niño, Pedro: "Sumario de los Reyes de España" (in *Colección del Las Crónicas y Memórias de los Reyes de Castilla*, Madrid, 1782)

Norgate, Kate, and Carr, A. D.: "Joan (Lady of Wales)" (*Oxford Dictionary of National Biography*, Oxford, 2004)

The Northamptonshire Geld Roll (12th C.–13th C.) (2 vols., trans. Abraham Farley, London, 1783)

Nouvelle anthologie des Troubadours (ed. J. Audiau, Paris, 1928)

Odo de Deuil: *De Ludovici VII Francorum Regis, Profectione in Orientem* (trans. and ed. Virginia D. Berry, New York, 1948; ed. H. Waquet, Paris, 1949)

Oeuvres de Rigord et de Guillaume le Breton, historiens de Philippe Auguste (2 vols., ed. H. F. Delaborde, Paris, 1882–5)

Paris, Matthew: *Chronica Major* (7 vols., ed. H. R. Luard, London, 1872–3)

——*Historia Anglorum, sive, ut vulgo dicitur, Historia Minor* (3 vols., ed. Frederick H. Madden, London, 1866–9)

Patrologiae Latinae, Cursus Completus a Tertullian ad Innocentium III, Series Latinae (221 vols., ed. J. P. Migne, Paris, 1844–64)

Peter of Blois: *Petri Blensis Archidiaconi Opera Omnia* (4 vols., ed. J. A. Giles, Oxford, 1846–7)

The Peterborough Chronicle: Chronicon Angliae Petriburgense, 1070–1154 (ed. J. A. Giles, London, 1945; ed. Cecily Clark, Oxford, 1970)

The Pipe Roll of the Bishopric of Winchester, 1208–9 (ed. H. Hall, London, 1903)

The Pipe Roll of the Bishopric of Winchester, 1210–1211 (ed. N. R. Holt, Manchester, 1964)

Pipe Rolls (The National Archives)

Political Songs of England from the Reign of John to That of Edward II (ed. T. Wright, London, 1839)

Powell, David: *The History of Cambria, Now Called Wales* (London, 1584)

"The Progeny of the Monarchs of the Englishmen," Harley MS. 1416 (The British Library)

Psalter of Eleanor of Aquitaine (ca. 1185) (https://www.kb.nl/en/themes/medieval-manuscripts/psalter-of-eleanor-of-aquitaine-ca-1185)

Ptolemy of Lucca (*see* Bartholomeo [Ptolemy] of Lucca)

Rada, Rodrigo Jiminez de, Archbishop of Toledo: "De Rebus Hispaniae" (in *Historia de los hechos de España*, ed. Juan Fernández Valverde, Madrid, 1989)

Ralph of Coggeshall: *Radulphi de Coggeshall Chronicon Anglicanum: The English Chronicle* (ed. Joseph Stevenson, London, 1875)

Ralph of Diceto: *Radulfi de Diceto Decani Londoniensis Opera Historica: The Historical Works of Master Ralph of Diceto, Deacon of London* (2 vols., ed. William Stubbs, London, 1876)

Ralph Niger: *Radulphi Nigri Chronica* (ed. Robert Anstruther, London, 1851)

Raoul de Cambrai (ed. Sarah Kay, Oxford, 1992)

Reading Abbey Cartularies (2 vols., ed. Brian R. Kemp, London, 1986-7)

The Receipt Roll of the Exchequer for Michaelmas Term 1185 (ed. Hubert Hall, London, 1899)

Receuil des actes de Henri II, roi d'Angleterre et duc de Normandie, concernant les provinces françaises et les affaires de France (4 vols., ed. Léopold Delisle and Elie Berger, Paris, 1906-27)

Receuil des actes de Philippe Auguste, roi de France (3 vols., ed. H. F. Delaborde et al., Paris, 1916-66)

Receuil d'annales Angevins et Vendômoises (ed. L. Halphen, Paris, 1903)

Receuil des chroniques de Touraine (ed. A. Salmon, Tours, 1854)

Receuil des historiens des croisades: Auteurs occidentaux et orientaux (5 vols., Paris, 1872-1906)

Receuil des historiens des Gaules et de la France: Rerum Gallicarum et Francicarum Scriptores (24 vols., ed. Léopold Delisle, M. Bouquet et al., Paris, 1738-1904)

The Red Book of the Exchequer (3 vols., ed. H. Hall, London, 1896)

Les registres de Gregoire X et Jean XXI (ed. J. Guiraud and L. Cadier, Paris, 1892-1906)

Registrum Epistolarum Fratris Johannis Peckham, Archiepiscopi Cantuariensis (3 vols., ed. C. T. Martin, London, 1882-6)

Richard of Devizes: *Chronicon Richardi Divisensis de tempore Regis Richardi Primi: Richard of Devizes: Chronicle of the Times of King Richard the First* (trans. and ed. John T. Appleby, London, 1963)

Richard le Poitevin: "Ex Chronico" (in *Receuil des historiens des Gaules et de la France*)

Rigord: "Gesta Philippi Augusti: The Deeds of Philip Augustus" (in *Oeuvres de Rigord et de Guillaume le Breton*)

Rishanger, William: *Chronica* (ed. H. T. Riley, London, 1865)

Robert of Gloucester: *The Metrical Chronicle of Robert of Gloucester* (ed. William Aldis Wright, London, 1857)

Robert of Torigni: "Chronica Roberti de Torigneio, Abbatis Monasterii Sancti Michaelis in Periculo Maris" (in *Chronicles of the Reigns of Stephen, Henry II and Richard I*)

——*The Chronography of Robert of Torigni* (ed. Thomas N. Bisson, Oxford, 2019)

Roger of Howden: *Annals* (2 vols., trans. and ed. Henry T. Riley, London, 1853)

——*Chronica Magistri Rogeri de Houedene* (4 vols., ed. William Stubbs, London, 1868–71)

——*Gesta Regis Henrici Secundi et Gesta Ricardi I: The Deeds of King Henry the Second and the Deeds of Richard I, A.D. 1169–1192, Known Commonly under the Name of Benedict of Peterborough* (2 vols., ed. William Stubbs, London, 1867)

Roger of Pontigny: *Materials for the History of Thomas Becket* (ed. J. C. Robertson, London, 1875–85)

Roger of Wendover: *Chronica Rogeri de Wendover liber qui dictus Flores Historiarum: Flowers of History* (formerly ascribed to Matthew Paris) (ed. H. O. Coxe, London, 1841–4; trans. J. A. Giles, 2 vols., London, 1849; ed. H. J. Hewlett, London, 1886–9; 3 vols., ed. H. R. Luard, London, 1890)

Le Roman de Mélusine ou Histoire de Lusignan par Coudrette (ed. Eleanor Roach, Paris, 1982)

Le roman de Renart (2 vols., trans. and ed. Jean Dufournet, Paris, 1985)

"Rotuli Hundredorum temp. Hen. III & Edw. I." (in *Turr' Lond' et in Curia Receptae Scaccarij Westm. Asservati* (2 vols., ed. William Illingworth, London, 1812, 1818)

Rotuli Litterarum Patentium in Turri Londonensi Asservati (ed. T. D. Hardy, London, 1835)

Rotuli Normanniae in Turri Londonensi Asservati (ed. T. Duffus Hardy, London, 1835)

Rotuli Parliamentorum (The Rolls of Parliament) (7 vols., ed. J. Strachey, London, 1767–1832)

Rotulus nunciorum Reginae Eleanorae (Records of the Queen's Remembrancer, The National Archives)

Royal and Historical Letters illustrative of the Reign of Henry II (2 vols., ed. W. Shirley, London, 1862, 1866)

Royal Wardrobe Records (The National Archives)

Royal Writs in England from the Conquest to Glanville (ed. R. C. van Caenegem, London, 1959)

Rymer, Thomas: *Foedera* (London, 1704–35; ed. T. Hardy and others, London, 1816–69)

Sanctius, Roderigo: "Historiae Hispaniae" (in *Hispania Illustrata*, Frankfurt, 1579)

Scottish Annals from English Chroniclers, A.D. 500 to 1286 (ed. Allan Orr Anderson, Toronto, 1908)

Select Cases of the Court of King's Bench under Edward I (ed. G. O. Sayles, London, 1939)

Shakespeare, William: *King John* (ed. E.A.J. Honigmann, London, 1954)

Simeon of Durham: *Historical Works* (2 vols., ed. T. Arnold, London, 1882–5)

The Song of Roland (trans. D.D.R. Owen, London, 1972)

Speed, John: *The History of Great Britain* (London, 1611)

Statutes of the Realm, 1101–1713 (11 vols., London, 1810–28)

Stow, John: *The Annals of England* (London, 1580)

——*A Survey of London* (London, 1598, 1603)

Suger: *Oeuvres de Suger* (ed. A. Lecoy de la Marche, Paris, 1867)

——*Vie de Louis VI le Gros par Suger, suivie de l'histoire du roi Louis VII: Historia Ludovici VII* (ed. Auguste Molinier, Paris, 1887; ed. Henri Waquet, Paris, 1929)

Templo, Richard de: "Itinerarium et Peregrinorum et Gesta Regis Ricardi" (in *Chronicles and Memorials of the Reign of Richard I*)

——*The Itinerary of King Richard I* (ed. Lionel Landon, London, 1935)

Thomas of Britain: *Les fragments du roman de Tristan, poème du XIIe siècle* (ed. Bartina H. Wind, Geneva and Paris, 1960)

——*The Romance of Tristram and Ysolt by Thomas of Britain* (trans. Roger Sherman Loomis, New York, 1931)

Thomas Agnellus: "De Morte et Sepultura Henrici Regis Junioris" (in Ralph of Coggeshall: *Radulphi de Coggeshall Chronicon Anglicanum*)

Three Old French Chronicles (trans. Edward Noble Stone, Seattle, 1939)

Treaty Rolls preserved in the Public Record Office (ed. Pierre Chaplais, London, 1955)

Trevet, Nicholas: *Sex Regum Angliae (Annals of Six Kings of England)* (ed. Thomas Hog, London, 1845)

Uc de Saint-Circ: *Bernartz de Ventadorn* (trans. Todd Tarantino, The Cantos Project, http://thecantosproject.ed.ac.uk)

Vidal, Pierre: *Poésie* (ed. D. S. Avalle, Milan, 1960)

Villani, Giovanni: Nuova Cronica (Vatican Library BAV Chigiano L VIII 296)

Wace, Robert: *The "Arthurian" Portion of the Roman de Brut* (tr. Eugene Mason, Cambridge, Ontario, 1999)

——*Le roman de Brut* (2 vols., ed. J. Arnold, Paris, 1938–40; ed. and tr. Judith Weiss, Exeter, 2002)

——*Le roman de Rou* (ed. A. J. Holden, Paris, 1970)

——*Roman de Rou et des Ducs de Normandie* (trans. Alexander Malet, London, 1860)

Wace, Robert, and Layamon: *Arthurian Chronicles* (trans. Eugène Mason, London 1912, 1962)

Walter of Coventry: *Memoriale Walteri de Coventria: The Historical Collections of Walter of Coventry* (ed. William Stubbs, London, 1872-3)

Walter of Guisborough: *The Chronicle of Walter of Guisborough* (ed. H. Rothwell, London, 1957)

Wardrobe and Household Accounts (The National Archives)

Weever, John: *Ancient Funeral Monuments within the United Monarchies of Great Britain, Northern Ireland and the Islands Adjacent* (London, 1631)

William IX, Duke of Aquitaine: *Les chansons de Guillaume IX* (ed. Alfred Jeanroy, Paris, 1927)

William of Newburgh: *Historia Rerum Anglicarum: The History of English Affairs* (3 vols., ed. Thomas Hearne, Oxford, 1719; in *Chronicles of the Reigns of Stephen, Henry II and Richard I*; in *English Historical Documents, 1042-1189*; trans. and ed. P. G. Walsh and M. J. Kennedy, Warminster, 1988)

William of Tyre: *The Chronicle of Ernoul and the Continuations of William of Tyre* (ed. M. R. Morgan, Oxford, 1973)

——*La Continuation de Guillaume de Tyr* (ed. M. R. Morgan, Paris, 1982)

——*Guillaume de Tyr et ses continuateurs* (2 vols., ed. M. Paulin, Paris, 1879-80)

——*A History of Deeds Done beyond the Sea* (2 vols., trans. and ed. E. A. Babcock and A. C. Krey, New York, 1943; reprinted 1976)

Wykes, Thomas: "Chronicon vulgo dictum Chronicon Thomæ Wykes. AD 1066-1289" (in *Annales Monastici*)

Secondary Sources

Abel, F. M.: *L'Etat de la cité de Jérusalem au XII siècle* (Jerusalem, 1920-2)

Adair, John: *The Royal Palaces of Britain* (London, 1981)

Alienor d'Aquitaine (ed. Philippe Chevreul, Nantes, 2004)

Amatxi, Amuma, Amona: Writings in Honor of Basque Women (ed. Linda White and Cameron Watson, Reno, 2003)

Anglo-Saxon England, Vol. 19 (ed. Michael Lapidge, Malcolm Godden and Simon Keynes, Cambridge, 2007)

Appel, C.: *Bertrand van Born* (Halle, 1931)

——*Provenzalische Chrestomathie* (Leipzig, 1912)

Appleby, John T.: *England Without Richard, 1189-1199* (London, 1965)

——*Henry II: The Vanquished King* (London, 1962)

——*John, King of England* (London, 1959)

Arbellot, F.: *Vérité sur la mort de Richard Coeur de Lion* (Paris, 1878)

d'Arbois de Jubainville, M. H.: *L'histoire des ducs et des comtes de Champagne* (Paris, 1860)

The Art of Needlework from the Earliest Ages (ed. Mary Stanley, Countess of Wilton, London, 1841)

Asbridge, Thomas: *The Greatest Knight: The remarkable life of William Marshal, the power behind five English thrones* (London, 2015)

Ashdown, Dulcie M.: *Ladies in Waiting* (London, 1976)

Ashe, Geoffrey: *The Quest for Arthur's Britain* (London, 1968)

Ashley, Maurice: *The Life and Times of King John* (London, 1972)

Aurell, Martin: *Alienor d'Aquitaine et l'essor de Fontevraud* (Fontevraud, 2013)

Badham, Sally F., and Oosterwijk, Sophie: "The Tomb Monument of Katherine, Daughter of Henry III and Eleanor of Provence" (in *The Antiquaries Journal*, 92, 2012)

Baker, Darren: *Henry III: The Great King England Never Knew It Had* (Stroud, 2017)

——*The Two Eleanors of Henry III: The Lives of Eleanor of Provence and Eleanor de Montfort* (Barnsley, 2019)

——*With All for All: The Life of Simon de Montfort* (Stroud, 2015)

Barber, Richard: *The Devil's Crown: Henry II, Richard I, John* (London, 1978)

——*Henry Plantagenet: A Biography of Henry II of England* (London, 1964; reprinted 1972)

Bard, Rachel: "Berengaria of Navarre: Medieval Role Model" (in *Amatxi, Amuma, Amona: Writings in Honor of Basque Women*)

Barker, J.R.V.: *The Tournament in England, 1100–1400* (Woodbridge, 1986)

Barlow, Frank: *The Feudal Kingdom of England, 1042–1216* (London, 1955)

Barratt, Nick: *The Restless Kings: Henry II, His Sons and the Wars for the Plantagenet Crown* (London, 2008)

Bartlett, W. B.: *Richard the Lionheart, The Crusader King of England* (Stroud, 2018)

Baxter, Ron: *The Royal Abbey of Reading* (Woodbridge, 2016)

Bayley, J.: *The History and Antiquities of the Tower of London* (London, 1830)

Beamish, Tufton: *Battle Royal* (London, 1965)

Beaumont, Marion: "A Parade of Distinguished Ladies" (in *Notre Histoire: Fontevraud*, June 1991)

Beaumont James, Tom, and Gerrard, Christopher: *Clarendon: Landscape of Kings* (Bollington, 2007)

Beech, G. T.: *A Rural Society in Mediaeval France: The Gatine of Poitou in the Eleventh and Twelfth Centuries* (Baltimore, 1964)

Bennett-Connolly, Sharon: *Heroines of the Medieval World* (Stroud, 2017)

Benton, John F.: "The Court of Champagne as a Literary Centre" (*Speculum*, 36, 1961)

Benz St. John, Lisa: *Three Medieval Queens: Queenship and the Crown in Fourteenth-Century England* (New York, 2012)

Bernard, C.: "Notice Historique de Littéraire sur les Filles de Raymond Berenger" (*Annales des Basses-Alpes*, Vol. 15)

Bezzola, R. R.: *Les origines et la formation de la littéraire courtoise en occident, 500–1200* (5 vols., Paris, 1944–63)

Bienvenu, Jean-Marc: "Aliénor d'Aquitaine et Fontevraud" (*Cahiers de Civilisation Médiévale*, 29, 1986)

Biles, Martha: "The Indomitable Belle: Eleanor of Provence" (in *Seven Studies in Medieval English History and Other Historical Essays presented to Harold S. Snellgrove*, ed. R. H. Bowers, Michigan, 1983)

Bingham, Caroline: *The Crowned Lions: The Early Plantagenet Kings* (Newton Abbot, 1978)

——*The Life and Times of Edward II* (London, 1973)

Black, Edward L.: *Royal Brides: Queens of England of the Middle Ages* (Lewes, 1987)

Bloch, M.: *Les rois thaumaturges* (Strasburg, 1924)

Boase, T.S.R.: "Fontevrault and the Plantagenets" (*Journal of the British Archaeological Association*, 34, 1971)

Boissonade, Prosper: "L'ascension, le déclin et la chute d'un grand état féodal du Centre-ouest: les Taillefer et les Lusignans, comtes de la Marche et d'Angoulême et leurs relations avec les Capétiens et les Plantagenêts, 1137–1314" (*Bulletins et Mémoires de la Société archéologiques de la Charente*, 1935)

——"Les comtes d'Angoulême—les ligues féodales contre Richard Coeur de Lion et les poésies de Bertran de Born, 1176–1194" (*Annales du Midi*, 7, 1895)

——*Histoire de Poitou* (Paris, 1926)

Boussard, Jacques: *Le comté d'Anjou sous Henri Plantagenet et ses fils, 1151–1204* (Paris, 1938)

——*Le gouvernement d'Henri II Plantagenet* (Paris, 1956)

Boutan, Andre: "La reine Bérengère perdue et retrouvée" (*Bulletin de la Société d'Agriculture, Sciences et Arts de Sarthe*, 8, 1969)

Boutière, Jean, and Schutz, A. H.: *Biographies des troubadours: textes provençaux des XIIIe et XIVe siècles* (Paris, 1964)

Bouton, Etienne, Kervella, Gilles, and Niaussat, Michel: *L'Epau, l'Abbaye d'une Reine* (Le Mans, 1999)

Boyd, Douglas: *Eleanor, April Queen of Aquitaine* (Stroud, 2004)

Bregy, Katherine: *From Dante to Jeanne d'Arc: Adventures in Mediaeval Life and Letters* (New York, 1964)

Brewer, Clifford: *The Death of Kings: A Medical History of the Kings and Queens of England* (London, 2000)

Bridge, Anthony: *Richard the Lionheart* (London, 1989)

Brindle, Steven, and Kerr, Brian: *Windsor Revealed: New light on the history of the castle* (London, 1997)

Bromilow, John K.: *Berengaria of Navarre, Queen of Richard the Lionheart* (www .churchmonumentssociety.org)

Brooke, Christopher: *From Alfred to Henry III* (Edinburgh, 1961)

——*The Twelfth-Century Renaissance* (London, 1969)

Brooke, Christopher, and Keir, Gillian: *The History of London: London 800–1216: The Shaping of a City* (London, 1975)

Brooke, C.N.L.: "The Marriage of Henry II and Eleanor of Aquitaine" (*The Historian*, 20, 1988)

Brooke, Z. N., and Brooke, C.N.L.: "Henry II, Duke of Normandy and Aquitaine" (*English Historical Review*, 61, 1946)

Brooke-Little, J. P.: *Boutell's Heraldry* (London, 1973)

Broughton, Bradford B.: *The Legends of King Richard I, Coeur de Lion* (The Hague, 1966)

Brown, Cornelius: *A History of Nottinghamshire* (London, 1896)

Brown, E.A.R.: *The Monarchy of Capetian France and Royal Ceremonial* (Aldershot, 1991)

Brown, Geoff: *The Ends of Kings: An Illustrated Guide to the Death and Burial Places of English Monarchs* (Stroud, 2008)

Bruce, J. C.: *The Evolution of Arthurian Romance from the Beginnings down to the Year 1300* (2 vols., Baltimore, 1928)

Brundage, James A.: *Richard Lionheart* (New York, 1973)

Bryant, Arthur: *The Age of Chivalry* (London, 1963)

——*Makers of the Realm* (London, 1953)

Burke, John and John Bernard: *The Royal Families of England, Scotland, and Wales, with their Descendants etc.* (2 vols., London, 1848 and 1851)

Burke's Guide to the Royal Family (Burke's Peerage, 1973)

Burrell, M. A.: "The classification of Blandin de Cornouailles: the romance within and without" (*Florilegium*, 2001)

Burtt, Joseph: "Queen Eleanor of Castile: Some new facts illustrative of her life and times" (*The Archaeological Journal*, June 1853)

Cannon, John, and Hargreaves, Anne: *The Kings and Queens of Britain* (Oxford, 2001)

Carducci, Giosuè: "Un poeta d'amore nel secolo XII" (in *Opere*, Vol. III, Bologna, 1893)

Castor, Helen: *She Wolves: The Women Who Ruled England Before Elizabeth* (London, 2010)

Castries, Duc de: *The Lives of the Kings and Queens of France* (New York, 1979)

Cazel, F. A., and Painter, S.: "The Marriage of Isabella of Angouleme" (*English Historical Review*, 62, 1948, and 67, 1952)

Chamberlin, E. R.: *Guildford: A Biography* (London, 1970)

Chambers, F. W.: "Some Legends Concerning Eleanor of Aquitaine" (*Speculum*, 16, 1941)

Chapman, Robert L.: "Notes on the Demon Queen Eleanor" (*Modern Language Notes*, June 1955)

Chardon, Henri: "Histoire de la Reine Bérengère, femme de Richard Coeur de Lion et Dame Douarière du Mans" (*Bulletin de la Société d'Agriculture, Sciences et Arts de Sarthe*, 10, 1865-6)

Chauou, Amaury: *Sue les pas de Alienor d'Aquitaine* (Rennes, 2005)

Chayter, H. J.: *The Troubadours* (Cambridge, 1912)

Cheney, C. R.: *Hubert Walter* (London, 1967)

Chibnall, Marjorie: *The Empress Matilda* (Oxford, 1991)

Chronicles of the Age of Chivalry (ed. Elizabeth Hallam, London, 1987)

Church, Stephen: *King John: England, Magna Carta and the Making of a Tyrant* (London, 1215)

Churchill, Sir Winston: *A History of the English-Speaking Peoples* (London, 1956)

Clédat, Léon: *Du rôle historique de Bertrand de Born (1175-1200)* (Paris, 1879)

Cockerill, Sara: *Eleanor of Aquitaine* (Stroud, 2019)

——*Eleanor of Castile: The Shadow Queen* (Stroud, 2014)

Coldstream, Nicola: "The Commissioning and Design of the Eleanor Crosses" (in *Eleanor of Castile, 1290–1990: Essays to Celebrate the 700th Anniversary of her Death*)

Colombet, François, and Bruant, Nicholas: *Fontevraud: Royal Abbey between Chinon and Saumur* (Paris, 1999)

The Complete Peerage (13 vols., ed. V. Gibbs, H. A. Doubleday, D. Warrand, Thomas, Lord Howard de Walden and G. H. White, 1910-59)

Cooke, Robert: *The Palace of Westminster* (London, 1987)

Corvi, Steven J.: *Plantagenet Queens and Consorts: Family, Duty and Power* (Stroud, 2018)

Costain, T. B.: *Magnificent Century* (London, 1951)

——*The Three Edwards* (London, 1958)

Coulton, G. G.: *Life in the Middle Ages* (4 vols., London and New York, 1930)

The Court and Household of Eleanor of Castile in 1290 (ed. John Carmi Parsons, Toronto, 1977)

Crouch, David: *William Marshal: Court, Career and Chivalry in the Angevin Empire 1147–1219* (London, 1990)

Crusading and Masculinities (ed. Natasha R. Hodgson, Katherine J. Lewis and Matthew M. Mesley, London, 2019)

The Cultural Patronage of Medieval Women (ed. J. H. McCash, Georgia, 1996)

Cunnington, Phyllis, and Lucas, Catherine: *Costume for Births, Marriages and Deaths* (London, 1972)

Dart, John: *The History and Antiquities of the Abbey Church of Westminster* (2 vols., London, 1723)

Davenport, Mila: *The Book of Costume* (New York, 1948)

Davis, H.W.C.: *England under the Normans and Angevins, 1066–1272* (London, 1905)

Davis, John Paul: *The Gothic King: A Biography of Henry III* (London, 2013)

De-la-Noy, Michael: *Windsor Castle, Past and Present* (London, 1990)

Delisle, Leopold.: "Mémoire sur une lettre inédite adressée à la Reine Blanche par un habitant de La Rochelle" (*Bibliothèque de l'École des Chartes*, 17, 1856)

Demimuid, Maurizio: *Jean de Salisbury* (Paris, 1873)

Denholm-Young, N.: *Richard of Cornwall* (Oxford, 1947)

The Dictionary of National Biography (ed. Leslie Stephen and Sidney Lee, 63 vols., Oxford, 1885–1900; Oxford, 1998 edition)

Diehl, Charles: *La Société Byzantine à l'Époque des Comnènes* (Paris, 1929)

Diener, Bertha: *Imperial Byzantium* (trans. Eden Paul and Cedar Paul, Boston, 1938)

Djordjevic, Igor: "King John (Mis)Remembered: The Dunmow Chronicle, the Lord Admiral's Men, and the Formation of Cultural Memory" (*The Review of English Studies*, Western Michigan University, Vol. 67, September 2016)

Dodson, Aidan: *The Royal Tombs of Great Britain* (London, 2004)

Doran, J.: *The History and Antiquities of the Town of Reading in Berkshire* (London, 1836)

Dougherty, Martin J.: *Medieval Kings and Queens* (London, 2018)

Douie, D. L.: *Archbishop Geoffrey Plantagenet* (York, 1960)

Dronke, Peter: *Mediaeval Latin and the Rise of the European Love Lyric* (2 vols., Oxford, 1965–6)

Duby, Georges: *Women of the Twelfth Century: Eleanor of Aquitaine and Six Others* (Cambridge and Oxford, 1997)

Duffy, Mark: *Royal Tombs of Medieval England* (Stroud, 2003)

Dufour, J. M.: *De l'ancien Poitou et de sa capitale* (Poitiers, 1826)

Dugdale, Thomas, and Burnett, William: *Curiosities of Great Britain, England and Wales Delineated* (9 vols., London, 1854–60)

Duggan, Alfred: *Devil's Brood: The Angevin Family* (London, 1957)

Dusseau, Joelle: *Alienor aux deux royaumes* (Pamplona, 2004)

Earenfight, Theresa: *Queenship in Medieval Europe* (New York, 2013)

Edwards, Cyril: "The Magnanimous Sex Object: Richard the Lionheart in the Mediaeval German Lyric" (in *Courtly Literature: Culture and Context*, ed. Keith Busby and Erik Cooper, Amsterdam and Philadelphia, 1990)

Edwards, J. G.: "Edward I's Castle Building in Wales" (*Proceedings of the British Academy*, 32, 1946)

Eleanor of Aquitaine, Lord and Lady (ed. Bonnie Wheeler and John Carmi Parsons, New York, 2002)

Eleanor of Aquitaine: Patron and Politician (ed. W. W. Kibler, Austin, Texas, 1976)

Eleanor of Castile, 1290–1990: Essays to Celebrate the 700th Anniversary of Her Death (ed. D. Parsons, Grantham, 1991)

L'Empire des Plantagenets: d'Alienor à Richard Coeur de Lion (various contributors, l'Histoire Editions, 2013)

Enjoubert, Hilaire: *Les Quatres Soeurs qui furent Reines* (Paris, 1952)

Evans, Michael: *The Death of Kings: Royal Deaths in Medieval England* (London, 2003)

Eyton, E. W.: *The Court, Household and Itinerary of Henry II* (London, 1878)

Facinger, Marion: "A Study in Mediaeval Queenship: Capetian France, 987–1237" (in *Studies in Mediaeval and Renaissance History*, Vol. 5, Nebraska, 1968)

Farcinet, C.: *Hughes IX de Lusignan et les comtes de la Marche* (Vannes, 1896)

Fawtier, Robert: *The Capetian Kings of France* (trans. L. Butler and J. Adam, London, 1960)

Field, John: *Kingdom, Power and Glory: A Historical Guide to Westminster Abbey* (London, 1996)

Foreville, R.: *L'Eglise et La Royauté en Angleterre sous Henri II Plantagenet* (Paris, 1943)

Forgotten Queens in Medieval and Early Modern Europe (ed. Valerie Schutte and Estelle Paranque, Abingdon, 2019)

Fougère, Sophie: *Isabelle d'Angoulême, Reine d'Angleterre* (Payre, 1998)

Fowler, G.: "Henry FitzHenry at Woodstock" (*English Historical Review*, 49, 1924)

Gee, Loveday Lewis: *Women, Art and Patronage, from Henry III to Edward III: 1216–1377* (Woodbridge, 2002)

A Genealogical History of the Royal Families of England from William the Conqueror to the Present Royal Grandchildren (London, 1753)

Gervaise, F. A.: *Histoire de Suger* (3 vols., Nevers, 1721)

Gillingham, John: *Conquests, Catastrophe and Recovery: Britain and Ireland, 1066–1485* (London, 2014)

——*The Life and Times of Richard I* (London, 1973)

——"Richard I and Berengaria of Navarre" (*Bulletin of the Institute of Historical Research*, 53, 1980)

——*Richard I* (Yale, 1999)

——*Richard the Lionheart* (London, 1978)

Gillingham, John, and Danziger, Danny: *1215: The Year of Magna Carta* (New York, 1204)

Giraud-Labalte, C., and Giraud, P.: *Fontevraud* (Rennes, 1996)

Given-Wilson, Chris, and Curteis, Alice: *The Royal Bastards of Mediaeval England* (London, 1984)

Gold, Claudia: *King of the North Wind: The Life of Henry II in Five Acts* (London, 2018)

Goldstone, Nancy: *Four Queens: The Provençal Sisters Who Ruled Europe* (New York, 2007)

Goodall, John: *The English Castle* (Yale, 2011)

Gough, Henry: *The Itinerary of Edward I* (2 vols., Paisley, 1900)

Gough, R.: *Sepulchral Monuments in Great Britain* (2 vols., London, 1786-96)

Grant, Lindy: "Eleanor of Aquitaine" (in *Medieval Kings and Queens*, BBC History, Bristol, 2017)

Green, Mary Anne Everett: *Lives of the Princesses of England from the Norman Conquest* (6 vols., London, 1849-55)

Grousset, René: *Histoire des croisades et du royaume franc de Jérusalem* (3 vols., Paris, 1934-6)

Hall, Hubert: *Court Life under the Plantagenets* (London, 1890)

Hallam, E. M.: "The Eleanor Crosses and Royal Burial Customs" (in *Eleanor of Castile, 1290-1990: Essays to Celebrate the 700th Anniversary of her Death*)

——"Royal Burial and the Cult of Kingship in France and England, 1060-1330" (*Journal of Medieval History*, 8, 1982)

Hamilton, J. S.: *The Plantagenets: History of a Dynasty* (London, 2010)

Hammond, Peter: *Her Majesty's Royal Fortress of the Tower of London* (HMSO, London, 1987)

Hampden, J.: *Crusader King* (London, 1956)

The Handbook of British Chronology (ed. Sir F. Maurice Powicke and E. B. Fryde, Royal Historical Society, 1961)

Harvey, B.: *Westminster Abbey and its Estates in the Middle Ages* (Oxford, 1977)

Harvey, John: *The Plantagenets* (London, 1948)

Harvey, Ruth E.: *The Troubadour Marcabru and Love* (London, 1989)

Haskell, Daniel C.: *Provençal Literature and Language, Including the Local History of Southern France* (New York, 1925)

Haskins, Charles Homer: *The Renaissance in the Twelfth Century* (Cambridge and Harvard, 1927; reprinted New York, 1957)

Hassall, W. O.: *They Saw It Happen, 55 B.C.–A.D. 1485* (Oxford, 1957)

——*Who's Who in History, Vol. I, 55 B.C.–1485* (Oxford, 1960)

Hearsey, John E. N.: *Bridge, Church and Palace in Old London* (London, 1961)

Hedley, Olwen: *Royal Palaces* (London, 1972)

Heltzel, Virgil B.: *Fair Rosamund: A Study of the Development of a Literary Theme* (Evanston, Illinois, 1947)

Henderson, Philip: *Richard Coeur de Lion* (New York, 1959)

Henry II: New Interpretations (ed. Christopher Harper-Bill and Nicholas Vincent, Woodbridge, 2007)

Heslin, Anne: "The Coronation of the Young King in 1170" (in *Studies in Church History*, Vol. 2, ed. G. J. Cunning, London, 1968)

Hibbert, Christopher: *The Court at Windsor* (London, 1964)

——*The Tower of London* (London, 1971)

Hichens, Mark: *Wives of the Kings of England, from Normans to Stuarts* (Brighton, 2008)

Hilliam, David: *Crown, Orb and Sceptre* (Stroud, 2001)

——*Kings, Queens, Bones and Bastards* (Stroud, 1998)

Hilton, Lisa: "Medieval Queens" (in *Royal Women*, BBC History Magazine, Bristol, 2015)

——*Queens Consort: England's Medieval Queens* (London, 2008)

Hindley, Geoffrey: *The Book of Magna Carta* (London, 1990)

The History of the City and County of Norwich (ed. R. Browne, Norwich, 1768)

The History of the King's Works, Volumes I and II: The Middle Ages (ed. H. M. Colvin, R. Allen Brown and A. J. Taylor, London, 1963)

Hodgson, C. E.: *Jung Heinrich, König von England, Sohn König Heinrichs II, 1155–83* (Jena, 1906)

Holt, J. C.: *King John* (Cambridge, 1963)

Hope, W. H. St. J.: "On the Funeral Effigies of the Kings and Queens of England" (*Archaeologia*, 60, 1907)

Hopkins, Andrea: *Most Wise and Valiant Ladies* (London, 1997)

Howard, Philip: *The Royal Palaces* (Boston, 1970)

Howell, Margaret: "The Children of King Henry III and Eleanor of Provence" (in *Thirteenth-Century England, Vol. 4*)

——*Eleanor of Provence: Queenship in Thirteenth-Century England* (Oxford, 1998)

Howitt, M.: *Biographical Sketches of the Queens of England* (London, 1866)

Hunter, Joseph: "On the Death of Eleanor of Castile, Consort of King Edward the First, and the Honours Paid to her Memory" (*Archaeologia*, March 1841)

Huscroft, Richard: *Tales from the Long Twelfth Century* (Yale, 2016)

Hutchison, Harold F.: *Edward II: The Pliant King* (London, 1971)

Imbert, Hughes: *Notice sur les vicomtes de Thouars* (Thouars, 1864)
Impney, Edward, and Parnell, Geoffrey: *The Tower of London: The Official Illustrated History* (London, 2000)

James, François-Charles: "The Abbey and the Plantagenets: A Family Business" (in *Notre Histoire: Fontevraud*, June 1991)
Jenner, Heather: *Royal Wives* (London, 1967)
Joliffe, J.E.A.: *Angevin Kingship* (London, 1955)
Jones, Christopher: *The Great Palace: The Story of Parliament* (London, 1983)
Jordan, William Chester: "Isabelle d'Angoulême, by the grace of God, Queen" (*Revue Belge de Philologie et l'Histoire*, 1991)

Keepe, Henry: *Monumenta Westmonasteriensia* (London, 1683)
Keevill, Graham D.: *Medieval Palaces: An Archaeology* (Stroud, 2000)
Kelly, Amy: "Eleanor of Aquitaine and her Courts of Love" (*Speculum*, 12, 1937)
——*Eleanor of Aquitaine and the Four Kings* (Harvard and London, 1950)
Kenaan-Kedar, Nurith: "The Enigmatic Sepulchral Monument of Berengaria (ca. 1170-1230), Queen of England (1191-1199)" (*Studies in Art History*, Vol. 12, Tel Aviv University, 2007)
Kiessman, Rudolph: *Untersuchen über die Bedeutung Eleanorens von Poitou für die Litterature ihrer Zeit* (Bernberg, 1901)
King, Edmund: *Medieval England* (London, 1988)
King John: New Interpretations (ed. S. D. Church, Woodbridge, 1999)
The Kings and Queens of England (ed. W. M. Ormrod, Stroud, 2001)
Kirchhoff, Elisabeth: *Rois et reines de France* (Paris, 1996)
Knowles, Dom. D.: *The Episcopal Colleagues of Thomas Becket* (Cambridge, 1961)
——*Thomas Becket* (London, 1971)
Kostick, Conor: "Eleanor of Aquitaine and the Women of the Second Crusade" (in *Medieval and Early Modern Women: Essays in Honour of Christina Meek*, Dublin, 2010)

Labande, Edmond-René: "Les filles d'Aliénor d'Aquitaine: étude comparative" (*Cahiers de Civilisation Médiévale*, 29, 1986)
——"Pour une image véridique d'Aliénor d'Aquitaine" (*Bulletin de la Société des Antiquaires de l'Ouest*, 4th Series, 2, Poitiers, 1952)
Labarge, Margaret Wade: *Mistress, Maids and Men: Baronial Life in the Thirteenth Century* (London, 1965)
——*Simon de Montfort* (London, 1962)
——*Women in Medieval Life* (London, 1986)

Lane, Henry Murray: *The Royal Daughters of England* (2 vols., London, 1910)

Larrey, Isaac de: *Histoire d'Éléonor de Guyenne* (Rotterdam, 1691; London, 1788)

Lees, Beatrice A.: "The Letters of Queen Eleanor of Aquitaine to Pope Celestine III" (*English Historical Review*, 21, 1906)

Legg, L.G.W.: *English Coronation Records* (Westminster, 1901)

Lehman, H. Eugene: *Lives of England's Reigning and Consort Queens* (Bloomington, 2011)

Lejeune, R.: "The Literary Role of Eleanor of Aquitaine" (*Cultura Neolatina*, 14, 1954)

——"Rôle littéraire de la famille d'Aliénor d'Aquitaine" (*Cahiers de Civilisation Médiévale*, 1, 1958)

Lewis, Matthew: *Henry III: The Son of Magna Carta* (Stroud, 2016)

Leyseer, Henrietta: *Medieval Women: A Social History of Women in England 450–1500* (London, 1995)

Licence, Amy: *Royal Babies: A History, 1066–2013* (Stroud, 2013)

Lindley, Philip: "Romanticising Reality: The Sculptural Memorials of Queen Eleanor and their Context" (in *Eleanor of Castile, 1290–1990: Essays to Celebrate the 700th Anniversary of her Death*)

The Lives of the Kings and Queens of England (ed. Antonia Fraser, London, 1977)

Lloyd, Alan: *King John* (Newton Abbot, 1973)

Loades, David: *The Kings and Queens of England: The Biography* (Stroud, 2013)

Lofts, Norah: *Queens of Britain* (London, 1977)

Loomis, Roger Sherman: "Edward I, Arthurian Enthusiast" (*Speculum*, 28, 1953)

——*Arthurian Literature in the Middle Ages: A Collaborative History* (Oxford, 1959)

——"Tristram and the House of Anjou" (*Modern Language Review*, 17, 1922)

Louda, J., and Maclagan, M.: *Lines of Succession: Heraldry of the Royal Families of Europe* (London, 1981)

Lyttelton, Lord George: *The History of the Life of King Henry the Second* (4 vols., London, 1767–71)

Macheco, Comtesse de: *Histoire d'Eleonore de Guyenne, Duchesse d'Aquitaine* (2 vols., 1822)

The Magna Carta Project (http://magnacarta.cmp.uea.ac.uk/)

Magne, Felix: *La Reine Alienor, Duchesse d'Aquitaine* (Pau, 1999)

Markale, Jean: *Eleanor of Aquitaine: Queen of the Troubadours* (Paris, 1979; Rochester, Vermont, 2007)

Marlow, Joyce: *Kings and Queens of Britain* (London, 1977)

Marshal, E.: *The Early History of Woodstock Manor* (Oxford, 1873)

Marshall, Rosalind K.: *Scottish Queens, 1034–1714* (East Linton, 2003)

Martindale, Jane: "Eleanor of Aquitaine: The Last Years" (in *King John: New Interpretations*)

Marvaud, F.: "Isabella d'Angoulême ou la Comtesse-Reine" (*Bulletin de la Société Archeologique et Historique de la Charente*, 1, 1856)

McAuliffe, Mary: *Clash of Crowns* (Plymouth, 2012)

McCann, Nick: *Leeds Castle* (Derby, 2000)

McKendrick, Scott, Lowden, John, and Doyle, Kathleen: *Royal Manuscripts: The Genius of Illumination* (The British Library, London, 2011)

McLynn, Frank: *Lionheart and Lackland: Richard I, King John and the Wars of Conquest* (London, 2006)

McNamara, JoAnn, and Wemple, Suzanne: "The Power of Women through the Family in Medieval Europe, 500–1100" (in *Women and Power in the Middle Ages*)

Meade, Marion: *Eleanor of Aquitaine: A Biography* (London, 1977)

Medieval Monarchs (ed. Elizabeth Hallam, London, 1990)

Medieval Mothering (ed. John Carmi Parsons and B. Wheeler, New York, 1996)

Medieval Queenship (ed. John Carmi Parsons, Stroud, 1994)

Michaud, Joseph: *A History of the Crusades* (3 vols., trans. W. Robson, New York, 1881)

Mitchell, Mairin: *Berengaria, Enigmatic Queen of England* (Burwash, 1986)

La Monte, J. L.: *Feudal Monarchy in the Latin Kingdom of Jerusalem, 1100–1291* (Cambridge, Massachusetts, 1932)

Moore, Olin H.: "The Young King, Henry Plantagenet (1155–1183)" (in *History, Literature and Tradition, Ohio State University: University Studies*, Vol. 2, No. 12, 1924)

Morris, David: *The Honour of Richmond* (York, 2000)

Morris, Marc: *A Great and Terrible King: Edward I and the Forging of Britain* (London, 2008)

——*The Bigod Earls of Norfolk in the Thirteenth Century* (Woodbridge, 2005)

——*King John: Treachery, Tyranny and the Road to Magna Carta* (London, 2015)

——"Was King John Really That Bad?" (in *Medieval Kings and Queens*, BBC History, Bristol, 2017)

Munro, D. C.: *The Kingdom of the Crusaders* (New York, 1935)

Neal, David S.: "Excavations at the Palace and Priory of King's Langley" (offprint from *Hertfordshire Archaeology*, undated)

Neve, John le: *Fasti Ecclesiæ Anglicanæ* (3 vols., ed Thomas Duffus Hardy, Oxford, 1854)

Nicolin, Roland: *Richard Coeur de Lion, le roi-chevalier du XIIe siècle* (Chambray, 1999)

——*L'épopée des Plantagenets face aux Capetiens* (Chambray, 1995)

Nitze, W. A.: "The Exhumation of King Arthur at Glastonbury" (*Speculum*, 9, 1934)

Norgate, Kate: *England under the Angevin Kings* (2 vols., London, 1887)

——*John Lackland* (London, 1902)

——*Richard the Lion Heart* (London, 1924)

Norris, Herbert: *Costume and Fashion, Volume Two: Senlac to Bosworth, 1066–1485* (London, 1927)

Norton, Elizabeth: *England's Queens: The Biography* (Stroud, 2011)

——*She Wolves: The Notorious Queens of England* (Stroud, 2008)

Ormond, Richard: *The Face of Monarchy* (Oxford, 1977)

Owen, D.D.R.: *Eleanor of Aquitaine, Queen and Legend* (Oxford, 1993)

The Oxford Dictionary of English Etymology (Oxford, various editions from 1966)

Pacaut, Marcel: *Louis VII et son royaume* (Paris, 1964)

Pain, Nesta: *The King and Becket* (New York, 1967)

Painter, Sidney: "The Houses of Lusignan and Châtellerault, 1150–1250" (*Speculum*, 30, 3, July 1955)

——"The Lords of Lusignan in the Eleventh and Twelfth Centuries" (*Speculum*, 32, 1957)

——*The Reign of King John* (Baltimore, 1949)

——*William Marshal, Knight-Errant, Baron and Regent of England* (Baltimore, 1933; reprinted Toronto, 1982)

Palmer, Alan and Veronica: *Royal England: A Historical Gazetteer* (London, 1983)

Panton, Kenneth J.: *Historical Dictionary of the British Monarchy* (Lanham, 2011)

Parrott, Kate: *Shakespeare's Queens of England* (Victoria, 2007)

Parsons, John Carmi: "Eleanor of Castile: Legend and Reality through Seven Centuries" (in *Eleanor of Castile, 1290–1990: Essays to Celebrate the 700th Anniversary of her Death*)

——*Eleanor of Castile: Queen and Society in Thirteenth-Century England* (New York, 1995)

——"Mothers, Daughters, Marriage, Power: Some Plantagenet Evidence, 1150–1500" (in *Medieval Queenship*)

——"'Never was a body buried in England with such solemnity and honour': The Burials and Posthumous Commemorations of English Queens to 1500" (in *Queens and Queenship in Medieval Europe*)

——"Piety, Power and the Reputations of Two Thirteenth-Century English Queens" (in *Women of Power 1: Queens, Regents and Potentates*)

——"Ritual and Symbol in English Medieval Queenship to 1500" (in *Women and Sovereignty*)

Pernoud, Régine: *Blanche of Castile* (London, 1975)

——*Eleanor of Aquitaine* (Paris, 1965; London, 1967)

Petit-Dutaillis, Charles E.: *Le déshéritement de Jean sans Terre et le meutre d'Arthur de Bretagne* (Paris, 1925)

——*Feudal Monarchy in France and England from the Tenth to the Thirteenth Century* (trans. E. D. Hunt, New York, 1964)

The Plantagenet Chronicles (ed. Elizabeth Hallam, London, 1986)

The Plantagenet Encyclopaedia (ed. Elizabeth Hallam, London, 1996)

Plumb, J. H.: *Royal Heritage* (London, 1977)

Pohu, Abbé, Curé de Fontevraud: *The Royal Abbey of Fontevraud* (Lyon, undated)

Poole, Austin Lane: *From Domesday Book to Magna Carta, 1087–1216* (Oxford, 1951)

Poole, R. L.: "Henry Plantagenet's Early Visits to England" (*English Historical Review*, 47, 1932)

Powicke, Sir F. Maurice: *King Henry III and the Lord Edward* (2 vols., Oxford, 1947; reprinted in one volume Oxford, 1950)

——*The Loss of Normandy, 1189–1203* (Manchester, 1913; reprinted 1961)

——*The Thirteenth Century, 1216–1307* (Oxford, 1962)

Powrie, Jean: *Eleanor of Castile* (Studley, 1990)

Prestwich, Michael: *Edward I* (London, 1988)

——*The Three Edwards: War and State in England 1272–1377* (London, 1980)

Priestland, Pamela and Neal: *In Memory of Eleanor: The Story of the Eleanor Crosses* (Radcliffe-on-Trent, 1990)

Prigent, Daniel: "If Walls Could Talk" (in *Notre Histoire: Fontevraud*, June 1991)

Queens and Queenship in Medieval Europe (ed. Anne Duggan, Woodbridge, 1997)

The Quest for Arthur's Britain (ed. Geoffrey Ashe, London, 1968)

Raby, F.J.E.: *A History of Christian-Latin Poetry from the Beginnings to the Close of the Middle Ages* (Oxford, 1953)

Ramsay, Sir J. H.: *The Angevin Empire, or the Three Reigns of Henry II, Richard I and John, 1154–1216* (Oxford, 1903)

Reese, M. M.: *The Royal Office of Master of the Horse* (London, 1976)

Richard, Alfred: *Histoire des ducs et des comtes de Poitou, 778–1204* (2 vols., Paris, 1903)

Richardson, Helen G.: "King John and Isabelle of Angoulême" (*English Historical Review*, 1946, 1950)

——"The Letters and Charters of Eleanor of Aquitaine" (*English Historical Review*, 74, 1959)

———"The Marriage and Coronation of Isabella of Angoulême" (*English Historical Review*, 61, 1946)

Robinson, J. A.: "Peter of Blois" (in *Somerset Historical Essays*, London, 1921)

Roche, T.W.E.: *The King of Almayne* (London, 1966)

Rose, Alexander: *Kings in the North: The House of Percy in British History* (London, 2002)

Rosenberg, Melrich V.: *Eleanor of Aquitaine, Queen of the Troubadours and of the Courts of Love* (Boston and New York, 1937)

Round, John Horace: *Feudal England* (London, 1895; reprinted London, 1964)

Saaler, Mary: *Edward II* (London, 1997)

Salvini, J.: "Aliénor d'Aquitaine" (in *Dictionnaire de biographie française*, Paris, 1933–67)

Salzman, L. F.: *Edward I* (London, 1968)

Sandford, Francis: *A Genealogical History of the Kings and Queens of England and Monarchs of Great Britain, from the Conquest, anno 1066, to the year 1707* (London, 1707)

Saul, Nigel: *The Three Richards: Richard I, Richard II and Richard III* (London, 2005)

Scarisbrick, Diana: *Jewellery in Britain, 1066–1837* (Norwich, 1994)

Schlight, John: *Henry II Plantagenet* (New York, 1973)

Schramm, P. E.: *A History of the English Coronation* (trans. G. Wickham-Legg, Oxford, 1937)

Seeley, R. B.: *The Life and Reign of Edward I* (London, 1860)

Seven Studies in Medieval English History and Other Historical Essays presented to Harold S. Snellgrove (ed. R. H. Bowers, Michigan, 1983)

Seward, Desmond: *The Demon's Brood: The Plantagenet Dynasty that Forged the English Nation* (London, 2014)

———*Eleanor of Aquitaine: The Mother Queen* (London, 1978)

Siete Partidas (ed. Gregorio López de Tovar, Salamanca, 1555)

Smith, C. E.: *Papal Reinforcement of some Mediaeval Marriage Laws* (Louisiana, 1940)

Smith, Emily Tennyson (Bradley), and Micklethwaite, J. T.: *Annals of Westminster Abbey* (London, 1898)

Snellgrove, H. S.: *The Lusignans in England* (Albuquerque, 1950)

Somerset, Anne: *Ladies in Waiting* (London, 1984)

Souden, David: *The Royal Palaces of London* (London, 2008)

Spinks, Stephen: *Edward II, the Man: A Doomed Inheritance* (Stroud, 2017)

Starkey, David: *Crown and Country* (London, 2010)

Steane, John: *The Archaeology of the Medieval English Monarchy* (London, 1993)

Stenton, Frank M.: *Norman London* (Historical Association Pamphlet, London, 1934)

Stimming, Albert: *Bertran van Born* (Halle, 1892)

Stones, E.L.G.: *Edward I* (London, 1968)

Storey, Gabrielle: "Berengaria of Navarre and Joanna of Sicily as crusading queens: Manipulation, Reputation and Agency" (in *Forgotten Queens in Medieval and Early Modern Europe*)

Stothard, C. A.: *The Monumental Effigies of Great Britain* (ed. J. Hewitt, London, 1876)

Strickland, Agnes: *Lives of the Queens of England* (8 vols., London, 1852; reprinted Bath, 1974)

Strickland, Matthew: *Henry the Young King, 1155–1183* (Yale, 2016)

Strong, Roy: *Coronation* (London, 2005)

Struthers, Jane: *Royal Britain: Historic Palaces, Castles and Houses* (London, 2011)

Stubbs, William: *The Early Plantagenets* (London, 1903)

Swabey, Ffiona: *Eleanor of Aquitaine, Courtly Love and the Troubadours* (Westport, 2004)

Térouanne, Pierre: "A la quête d'une tombe sans nom" (*Bulletin de la Société d'Agriculture, Sciences et Arts de Sarthe*, 8, 1969)

Thirteenth-Century England, Vol. 4 (ed. P. R. Coss and S. D. Lloyd, Woodbridge, 1992)

Thomas, Antoine: *Bertran van Born, poésies complètes* (Toulouse, 1888)

Thompson, Kathleen Hapgood: The Counts of the Perche *c*.1066–1217 (unpublished D.Phil. thesis, University of Sheffield, 1995)

Tolley, T.: "Eleanor of Castile and the 'Spanish' Style in England" (in *Harlaxton Medieval Studies 1: England in the Thirteenth Century*, ed. W. M. Ormerod, Stamford, 1991)

Trabut-Cussac, J. P.: *L'Administration Anglaise en Gascogne sous Henri III et Edouard I de 1254 à 1307* (Geneva, 1972)

Treece, Henry: *The Crusades* (New York, 1964)

Trindade, Ann: *Berengaria: In Search of Richard the Lionheart's Queen* (Dublin, 1999)

Trowles, Tony: *Treasures of Westminster Abbey* (London, 2008)

Turner, Ralph V.: *Eleanor of Aquitaine* (Yale, 2009)

——"Eleanor of Aquitaine and Her Children: An Inquiry into Mediaeval Family Attachment" (*Journal of Medieval History*, 14, 1988)

——*King John: England's Evil King?* (Stroud, 2005)

Tyerman, Christopher: *Who's Who in Early Medieval England, 1066–1272* (London, 1996)

Vaissete, Joseph: *Abrégé de l'histoire générale de Languedoc* (5 vols., Paris, 1799)

Vale, Malcolm: *The Princely Court: Medieval Courts and Culture in North-West Europe* (Oxford, 2001)

Verity, Brad: *Katherine Plantagenet (1261/2–1264), Firstborn Child of Edward I* (www.royaldescentblogspot.com)

——*The Marriage of Edward I and Eleanor of Castile in 1254* (www.royaldescent blogspot.com)

Villepreux, L. de: *Eléonore de Guyenne* (Paris, 1862)

Vincent, Nicholas: "Isabella of Angoulême: John's Jezebel" (in *King John: New Interpretations*)

Walker, Curtis Howe: *Eleanor of Aquitaine* (Richmond, Virginia, 1950)

Ward, Jennifer: *Women in England in the Middle Ages* (London, 2006)

Ward, P. L.: "The Coronation Ceremony in Mediaeval England" (*Speculum*, 14, 1939)

Warren, W. L.: *Henry II* (London, 1973)

——*King John* (London, 1961)

Weir, Alison: *Eleanor of Aquitaine, By the Wrath of God, Queen of England* (London, 1999)

Wilkinson, Louise J.: *Eleanor de Montfort: A Rebel Countess in Medieval England* (London, 2012)

Wilson, Derek: *The Plantagenets: The Kings that made Britain* (London, 2011)

——*The Tower of London: A Thousand Years* (London, 1998)

Wilson-Lee, Kelcey: *Daughters of Chivalry: The Forgotten Children of Edward I* (London, 2019)

Windsor Castle: A Thousand Years of a Royal Palace (ed. Steven Brindle, London, 2018)

Winston, Richard: *Becket* (London, 1967)

Women and Power in the Middle Ages (ed. M. Erler and M. Kowaleski, Athens, Georgia, 1988)

Women of Power 1: Queens, Regents and Potentates (ed. Theresa M. Vann, Dallas, 1993)

Women and Sovereignty (ed. Louise Olga Fradenburg, Edinburgh, 1992)

Woodstock and the Royal Park: Nine hundred years of history (ed. John Banbury, Robert Edwards, Elizabeth Poskitt and Tim Nutt, Oxford, 2010)

Woolgar, C. M.: *The Great Household in Late Medieval England* (Yale, 1999)

The World of Eleanor of Aquitaine (ed. Marcus Bull and Catherine Leglu, Woodbridge, 2005)

Sources of Quotes in the Text

✠

PART ONE:
ELEANOR OF AQUITAINE, QUEEN OF HENRY II
1 "An Exceedingly Shrewd and Clever Woman"

1 Heriger of Lobbes
2 Gervase of Canterbury
3 Giraldus Cambrensis
4 Bibliothèque Nationale Paris, Latin MS 5452; "Fragmentum Genealogicum ducum Normanniae et Angliae Regum," in *Receuil des historiens des Gaules et de la France*, 18
5 *L'Histoire de Guillaume le Maréchal*
6 Richard le Poitevin

2 "Mutual Anger"

1 John of Salisbury
2 William of Tyre
3 Ibid.
4 Cited by Harvey: *The Troubadour Marcabru and Love*
5 John of Salisbury
6 Ibid.
7 Ibid.
8 William of Newburgh

3 "My Very Noble Lord Henry"

1 Giraldus Cambrensis
2 *Chroniques des comtes d'Anjou*
3 Arnulf of Lisieux
4 Giraldus Cambrensis
5 *The Anglo-Saxon Chronicle*

6   Walter Map

7   Giraldus Cambrensis

8   Ibid.

9   Ibid.

10   Walter Map

11   Henry of Huntingdon

12   Giraldus Cambrensis

13   Ibid.

14   Henry of Huntingdon

15   Peter of Blois

16   Giraldus Cambrensis

17   Gervase of Canterbury

18   William of Newburgh

19   Ibid.

20   Gervase of Canterbury

21   Ibid.

22   William of Newburgh

23   Cited by Alfred Richard

24   Walter Map

4 "Behold, the Lord the Ruler Cometh"

1   Henry of Huntingdon

2   Robert of Torigni

3   Giraldus Cambrensis

4   Ralph of Diceto

5   *Choix des poésies originales des troubadours; Bernard von Ventadour, seine Lieder;* Uc de Saint-Circ

6   Henry of Huntingdon

7   Ibid.

8   Robert of Torigni

9   Ibid.

10   Henry of Huntingdon

11   Ibid.

12   Ibid.

13   *The Anglo-Saxon Chronicle*

14   Henry of Huntingdon

15   *The Chronicon of Battle Abbey*

16   Henry of Huntingdon

17   Ibid.

18   Ibid.

19   William of Newburgh

5 "High-Born Lady, Excellent and Valiant"

1 *The Anglo-Saxon Chronicle*
2 William of Newburgh
3 Ibid.
4 Richard FitzNigel
5 Ralph of Diceto
6 Translation by Owen in *Eleanor of Aquitaine*
7 John of Salisbury
8 Cited by John le Neve
9 *Charter Rolls*
10 Memoranda Rolls

6 "Rich Lady of the Wealthy King"

1 Jocelin of Brakelond
2 John of Salisbury
3 Peter of Blois
4 Walter Map
5 Giraldus Cambrensis

7 "All Things Were Entrusted to Thomas"

1 William FitzStephen
2 Ibid.
3 Roger of Howden
4 John of Salisbury
5 Geoffrey of Monmouth
6 Roger of Howden
7 *Receuil des historiens des Gaules et de la France*
8 Pipe Rolls

8 "The King Has Wrought a Miracle"

1 Ralph of Diceto
2 Roger of Howden
3 Robert of Torigni
4 Gervase of Canterbury
5 *Patrologiae Latinae*
6 Matthew Paris
7 Herbert of Bosham
8 Pipe Rolls
9 Ralph of Diceto
10 Herbert of Bosham

11   William FitzStephen
12   Herbert of Bosham
13   *Materials for the History of Thomas Becket*
14   Ibid.
15   William of Newburgh
16   *Materials for the History of Thomas Becket*

9 "The Wench Rosamund"

1   John Brompton

10 "A Whirlwind of Clouds"

1   Richard of Devizes
2   *L'Histoire de Guillaume le Maréchal*
3   *Epistolae: Medieval Women's Latin Letters*

11 "We Are from the Devil"

1   *L'Histoire de Guillaume le Maréchal*
2   Gislebert de Mons
3   *L'Histoire de Guillaume le Maréchal*
4   Geoffrey de Vigeois
5   Walter Map
6   Giraldus Cambrensis
7   Walter Map
8   William of Newburgh
9   *L'Histoire de Guillaume le Maréchal*
10   Giraldus Cambrensis
11   Ibid.
12   William FitzStephen
13   Roger of Howden
14   William FitzStephen
15   William of Newburgh
16   There are two other versions of the King's speech in *Materials for the History of Thomas Becket*, this being an amalgamation of all three.
17   *Materials for the History of Thomas Becket*
18   *English Historical Documents*
19   Roger of Howden
20   William of Newburgh
21   Ralph of Diceto
22   *Materials for the History of Thomas Becket*

12 "Beware of Your Wife and Sons"

1 "Chronicon Turonensis Magnum"
2 Ralph of Diceto
3 Roger of Howden
4 Richard de Templo: *The Itinerary of King Richard*
5 *Charter Rolls*, Charter of Eleanor to the abbey of Fontevraud, 1199
6 Richard de Templo: *The Itinerary of King Richard*
7 "Gesta Henrici Secundi: The Deeds of Henry II"
8 Giraldus Cambrensis
9 Cited by Kelly: *Eleanor of Aquitaine and the Four Kings*
10 Geoffrey de Vigeois
11 Jordan Fantosme
12 Giraldus Cambrensis
13 Ralph of Diceto
14 Roger of Howden
15 Matthew Paris
16 *The Chronicle of Melrose Abbey*
17 William of Newburg
18 Ibid.
19 Ibid.
20 Ralph of Diceto
21 Giraldus Cambrensis
22 Ralph of Diceto
23 Gervase of Canterbury
24 Ralph of Diceto
25 *Receuil des historiens des Gaules at de la France*
26 Gervase of Canterbury
27 Richard le Poitevin
28 Gervase of Canterbury

13 "The Eagle of the Broken Covenant"

1 Roger of Howden
2 Ralph of Diceto
3 Ibid.
4 Roger of Wendover
5 Ralph of Diceto
6 William of Newburgh
7 Ralph of Diceto
8 Giraldus Cambrensis
9 Geoffrey de Vigeois

10 Gervase of Canterbury
11 "Rotuli Hundredorum"
12 Roger of Howden
13 Ranulf Higden
14 Ibid.
15 Ralph of Diceto
16 Ibid.
17 Ibid.
18 Walter Map
19 Roger of Howden
20 Ralph of Coggeshall

14 "Freed from Prison"

1 Ralph of Coggeshall
2 Richard of Devizes
3 Matthew Paris
4 Roger of Wendover
5 Matthew Paris
6 Giraldus Cambrensis
7 Roger of Howden
8 Gervase of Canterbury
9 Roger of Howden
10 "Gesta Henrici Secundi: The Deeds of Henry II"
11 Ralph of Diceto
12 William of Newburgh
13 Ralph of Diceto

15 "His Heart's Desire"

1 *Gesta Regis Ricardi*
2 *The Chronicle of Meaux*
3 Roger of Howden
4 *L'Histoire de Guillaume le Maréchal*
5 Giraldus Cambrensis
6 Ibid.
7 Ibid.

16 "Her Third Nesting"

1 *L'Histoire de Guillaume le Maréchal*
2 William of Newburgh
3 Ibid.
4 Ralph of Diceto

5   *Gesta Regis Ricardi*
6   *L'Histoire de Guillaume le Maréchal*
7   Ibid.
8   Ralph of Diceto
9   *Gesta Regis Ricardi*
10 Roger of Howden
11 Roger of Wendover
12 Roger of Howden
13 Ibid.
14 Ralph of Diceto
15 Ibid.
16 *L'Histoire de Guillaume le Maréchal*
17 Matthew Paris
18 Ralph of Diceto
19 Ibid.
20 Richard de Templo: *The Itinerary of King Richard*
21 Ibid.
22 Roger of Wendover
23 Ralph of Diceto
24 Ibid.
25 *Gesta Regis Ricardi*
26 Richard of Devizes
27 Jocelin of Brakelond
28 *The Chronicle of Ernoul and Bernard the Treasurer*
29 William of Newburgh
30 *La Gran Conquista de Ultramar*
31 Rodrigo Jiminez de Rada
32 *La Gran Conquista de Ultramar*
33 William of Newburgh
34 Ambrose

PART TWO:
BERENGARIA OF NAVARRE, QUEEN OF RICHARD I
1 "The Beautiful Navarroise"

1   William of Newburgh
2   Roger of Howden
3   Richard de Templo: *The Itinerary of King Richard*
4   Richard of Devizes
5   Ambrose
6   Ralph of Diceto

7 Roger of Howden
8 Ibid.
9 Richard de Templo: *The Itinerary of King Richard*
10 Roger of Howden
11 Richard de Templo: *The Itinerary of King Richard*
12 Ambrose
13 Annals of Winchester
14 Piers Langtoft
15 *The Chronicle of Ernoul and Bernard the Treasurer*
16 Ambrose
17 *The Chronicle of Ernoul and Bernard the Treasurer*
18 Richard de Templo: *The Itinerary of King Richard*
19 *Gesta Regis Ricardi*
20 *The Chronicle of Ernoul and Bernard the Treasurer*
21 *Gesta Regis Ricardi*
22 Ibid.
23 Richard de Templo: *The Itinerary of King Richard*
24 Geoffrey de Vinsauf
25 Ibid.
26 Ambrose
27 Richard de Templo: *The Itinerary of King Richard*
28 Ambrose
29 Ibid.

2 "The Disturber of Your Kingdom"

1 Ambrose
2 Piers Langtoft
3 *The Chronicle of Ernoul and Bernard the Treasurer*
4 *L'Histoire de Guillaume le Maréchal*
5 Richard of Devizes
6 Ibid.
7 Ibid.
8 *Charter Rolls*
9 Richard of Devizes
10 Ibid.
11 Ibid.

3 "The Devil Is Loosed!"

1 Roger of Howden
2 Ibid.
3 Ibid.

4 Ralph of Diceto
5 Ibid.
6 Gervase of Canterbury
7 *Foedera*, Vol. 1
8 *L'Histoire de Guillaume le Maréchal*
9 Gervase of Canterbury
10 Roger of Howden
11 *Foedera*, Vol. 1
12 Ralph of Diceto
13 Ibid.
14 Ibid.
15 Ralph of Coggeshall
16 William of Newburgh
17 Ralph of Diceto
18 Ibid.
19 Roger of Howden
20 Ralph of Diceto

4 "An Incurable Wound"

1 William of Newburgh
2 Roger of Howden
3 Ralph of Diceto
4 Roger of Howden
5 Ralph of Diceto
6 *L'Histoire de Guillaume le Maréchal*
7 *Charter Rolls*
8 Roger of Howden
9 *The Oxford Dictionary of English Etymology*
10 Roger of Howden
11 Ibid.
12 Adam of Eynsham
13 Roger of Howden
14 Matthew Paris
15 Ralph of Coggeshall
16 Ibid.

5 "Motherly Solicitude"

1 Adam of Eynsham
2 Ibid.
3 *Charter Rolls*
4 Ralph of Coggeshall

5 *Charter Rolls*

6 Ibid.

7 Ibid.

8 Ibid.

9 Gervase of Canterbury

10 Richard of Devizes

11 *Charter Rolls*

12 Matthew Paris

13 Roger of Howden

PART THREE:
ISABELLA OF ANGOULÊME, QUEEN OF KING JOHN

1 "A Splendid Animal"

1 Roger of Howden

2 Ibid.

3 *L'Histoire de Guillaume le Maréchal*

4 *Histoire des ducs de Normandie*

5 Ralph of Diceto

6 Roger of Wendover

7 Matthew Paris

8 Adam of Eynsham

2 "An Incomparable Woman"

1 *L'Histoire de Guillaume le Maréchal*

2 *Foedera*

3 *Charter Rolls*

4 Ralph of Coggeshall

5 Roger of Wendover

6 Ralph of Coggeshall

7 *Histoire des ducs de Normandie*

8 Ralph of Coggeshall

9 Ibid.

10 Roger of Wendover

11 Ibid.

12 *L'Histoire de Guillaume le Maréchal*

13 *Histoire des ducs de Normandie*

14 Roger of Wendover

15 Ibid.

16 Ibid.

17 Ibid.
18 *L'Histoire de Guillaume le Maréchal*
19 "Annals of Waverley"
20 Cited by Bienvenu in "Aliénor d'Aquitaine et Fontevraud"

3 "I Have Lost the Best Knight in the World for You"

1 *Annales Angevines et Vendômoises*
2 Rodrigo Jiminez de Rada
3 Cartulaire de l'Eglise du Mans
4 Roger of Wendover
5 *Histoire des ducs de Normandie*
6 *The Chronicle of Meaux*
7 Matthew Paris
8 Roger of Wendover
9 *Rotuli Litterarum*
10 Ibid.

4 "Clouds That Have Overcast Our Serenity"

1 *Rotuli Litterarum*
2 *Calendar of Patent Rolls*
3 Ibid.
4 *Rotuli Litterarum*
5 *Annals of the Kingdom of Ireland*
6 Stow: *A Survey of London*
7 Matthew Paris
8 Ibid.
9 Ibid.; Ralph of Coggeshall
10 Ibid.
11 Matthew Paris

5 "Cease to Molest Your Son!"

1 *Histoire des ducs de Normandie*
2 Ibid.
3 The National Archives, Special Collections 1/3/181
4 Cartulaire de l'Eglise du Mans
5 Ibid.
6 The National Archives, Special Collections 1/2/5
7 *Calendar of Patent Rolls*
8 Matthew Paris
9 *Histoire des ducs de Normandie*

10   The National Archives, Special Collections 1/3/182
11   Matthew Paris
12   The National Archives, Special Collections 1/3/187
13   The National Archives, Special Collections 1/1/23
14   "Cartulaire du Chapitre Royale de St. Pierre de la Cour"

6 "The White Queen"

1   Roger of Wendover
2   Matthew Paris
3   Ibid.
4   Rodrigo Jiminez de Rada

PART FOUR:
ALIENOR OF PROVENCE, QUEEN OF HENRY III
1 "The Younger Virgin of This Most Lovely Race"

1   Matthew Paris
2   Ibid.
3   Ibid.
4   Giovanni Villani
5   Matthew Paris
6   Dante Alighieri
7   Matthew Paris
8   Ibid.
9   Ibid.
10   *Treaty Rolls preserved in the Public Record Office*
11   Roger of Wendover
12   Matthew Paris
13   Ibid.
14   Ibid.
15   Ibid.

2 "Our Dearest Love"

1   Adam Marsh
2   *Charter Rolls; Calendar of Patent Rolls*
3   *Charter Rolls*
4   Cambridge Corpus Christi College MS 471
5   Liberate Rolls
6   Calendar of Close Rolls
7   Ibid.

8 Issue Rolls and Registers
9 *Charter Rolls*
10 Ibid.

3 "The Eagles of Savoy"

1 William Rishanger
2 Matthew Paris
3 *The Annals of Dunstable Priory*
4 Matthew Paris
5 *Calendar of Patent Rolls*
6 *The Chronicle of Lanercost*
7 Matthew Paris
8 Ibid.
9 Ibid.
10 *Charter Rolls*
11 Matthew Paris
12 Nicholas Trevet
13 William Rishanger
14 Liberate Rolls
15 Matthew Paris
16 Ibid.
17 Ibid.
18 Ibid.

4 "Most Impious Jezebel"

1 Leopold Delisle
2 *Calendar of Patent Rolls*
3 Liberate Rolls
4 *Charter Rolls*
5 *Receuil des historiens des Gaules et de la France*
6 Matthew Paris
7 Philippe Mouskes
8 Matthew Paris
9 Grandes Chroniques de France
10 Ibid.; see also Guillaume de Nangis, and the "Chronique de Saint-Denis"
11 Matthew Paris
12 Ibid.
13 Guillaume de Nangis
14 Matthew Paris

15 Ibid.
16 Ibid.
17 Ibid.
18 *Letters of the Queens of England, 1100–1547*
19 *Memorials of St. Edmund's Abbey*
20 *Memorials of St. Edmund's Abbey*
21 Matthew Paris
22 Ibid.

5 "The Scum of Foreigners"

1   Matthew Paris
2   Ibid.
3   Ibid.
4   Ibid.
5   *Charter Rolls*
6   *Foedera*
7   Matthew Paris
8   *Charter Rolls*
9   Matthew Paris
10 Ibid.
11 Adam Marsh

PART FIVE:
ELEANOR OF CASTILE, QUEEN OF EDWARD I

1 "Prudence and Beauty"

1   *Epistolae: Medieval Women's Latin Letters*
2   Matthew Paris
3   Ibid.
4   *Charter Rolls*
5   Ibid.
6   Ibid.
7   Matthew Paris
8   *Charter Rolls; Calendar of Patent Rolls*
9   Matthew Paris
10 *Calendar of Patent Rolls*
11 Calendar of Close Rolls
12 Matthew Paris
13 Ibid.
14 Ibid.

2 "Like Brothers and Sisters"

1 William Rishanger
2 Piers Langtoft
3 *Charter Rolls*
4 Matthew Paris
5 Ibid.
6 Ibid.
7 Ibid.
8 Ibid.
9 Ibid.
10 Ibid.
11 *Scottish annals from English chroniclers*
12 Matthew Paris

3 "The Disseminator of All the Discord"

1 Matthew Paris
2 Ibid.
3 Ibid.
4 Ibid.
5 Ibid.
6 Ibid.
7 Stow: *A Survey of London*
8 Calendar of Close Rolls
9 Ibid.
10 Matthew Paris
11 *Charter Rolls*
12 Matthew Paris
13 Ibid.
14 *Memorials of St. Edmund's Abbey*
15 Matthew Paris
16 *Memorials of St. Edmund's Abbey*

4 "The Serpent-Like Fraud and Speech of a Woman"

1 Robert of Gloucester
2 *The Chronicon of Battle Abbey*
3 *Calendar of Patent Rolls*
4 *The Annals of Dunstable Priory*
5 Ibid.
6 Matthew Paris
7 Flores Historiarum

8   Thomas Wykes
9   *The Annals of Dunstable Priory*; Matthew Paris
10   Robert of Gloucester

5 "In Inestimable Peril"

1   *Memorials of St. Edmund's Abbey*
2   *The Annals of Dunstable Priory*
3   Ibid.
4   *Calendar of Patent Rolls*
5   Thomas Wykes
6   Matthew Paris
7   *Calendar of Patent Rolls*
8   Flores Historiarum
9   Robert of Gloucester
10   *Calendar of Patent Rolls*

6 "The Way to Heaven"

1   *Charter Rolls*
2   Matthew Paris
3   Calendar of Close Rolls
4   Theresa Earenfight
5   *Calendar of Patent Rolls*
6   Stow: *A Survey of London*
7   John Capgrave
8   Thomas Wykes
9   *Calendar of Patent Rolls*

7 "The Flower of Christendom"

1   Thomas Wykes
2   Ibid.
3   Piers Langtoft

8 "The Queen Would Like Our Lands to Hold"

1   The National Archives, Special Collections 1/11/11
2   *Registrum Epistolarum Fratris Johannis Peckham*
3   Godfrey Giffard's Register
4   Walter of Guisborough
5   *Registrum Epistolarum Fratris Johannis Peckham*
6   Ibid.
7   Ibid.

9 "Chosen Lambs"

1 The National Archives, Special Collections 1/22/29
2 Nicholas Trevet
3 William Rishanger
4 *Gesta Abbatum Monasterii Sancti Albani*
5 *Calendar of Patent Rolls*
6 Adam of Domerham
7 The National Archives, Special Collections 1/6/180

10 "Undaunted in Battle"

1 Flores Historiarum

11 "Medicinal Waters"

1 *Registrum Epistolarum Fratris Johannis Peckham*
2 Flores Historiarum
3 Thomas Wykes
4 Flores Historiarum
5 *The Chronicle of Lanercost*
6 The National Archives, Special Collections 1/16/156

12 "The Impiety of Death"

1 William Rishanger
2 Annals of Osney
3 Flores Historiarum
4 William Rishanger
5 Ibid.
6 Ibid.
7 Ibid.
8 Piers Langtoft
9 William Rishanger
10 Ibid.
11 John Dart

Epilogue

1 Thomas Wykes
2 Ibid.

Index

✠

About the Author

ALISON WEIR is the *New York Times* bestselling author of a series of biographies on England's medieval queens, beginning with *Queens of the Conquest*, as well as numerous historical biographies, including *The Lost Tudor Princess, Elizabeth of York, Mary Boleyn, The Lady in the Tower, Mistress of the Monarchy, Henry VIII, Eleanor of Aquitaine, The Life of Elizabeth I,* and *The Six Wives of Henry VIII.* She is also the author of historical novels including most recently the Six Tudor Queens series about the wives of Henry VIII, which includes *Katharine Parr: The Sixth Wife; Katheryn Howard, The Scandalous Queen; Anna of Kleve, The Princess in the Portrait; Jane Seymour, The Haunted Queen; Anne Boleyn, A King's Obsession;* and *Katherine of Aragon, The True Queen.* She lives in Surrey, England, with her husband.

alisonweir.org.uk
alisonweirtours.com
Twitter: @AlisonWeirBooks